Horatio F. Brown

The Venetian printing press

An historical study based upon documents for the most part hitherto unpublished

Horatio F. Brown

The Venetian printing press
An historical study based upon documents for the most part hitherto unpublished

ISBN/EAN: 9783742837622

Manufactured in Europe, USA, Canada, Australia, Japa

Cover: Foto ©Thomas Meinert / pixelio.de

Manufactured and distributed by brebook publishing software
(www.brebook.com)

Horatio F. Brown

The Venetian printing press

THE

VENETIAN PRINTING PRESS.

AN

HISTORICAL STUDY

BASED UPON DOCUMENTS FOR THE MOST PART

HITHERTO UNPUBLISHED.

BY

HORATIO F. BROWN.

WITH TWENTY-TWO FACSIMILES OF EARLY PRINTING.

LONDON:

JOHN C. NIMMO,

14, KING WILLIAM STREET, STRAND.

MDCCCXCI.

TO

MY FRIEND

JOHN ADDINGTON SYMONDS.

PREFACE.

THIS book consists of two parts. First, an historical study of the Venetian Printing Press from its origin down to the fall of the Republic, based, in a large degree, upon the documents which form the second part of the book.

In this study I trace the history of the Venetian press from its introduction, through the sixteenth century—noting especially how press legislation grew up, preceded by custom and practice, and then formulated in law; how the government dealt with such questions as copyright, protection, and censorship; how the Guild of Printers and Booksellers was founded and governed; how the book trade came under the influence of the Index and the Inquisitorial censorship, and how the Republic endeavoured to protect the trade, thereby involving itself in a long struggle with the Church of Rome—till we reach the slow decline of the Venetian press through the seventeenth and eighteenth centuries, in spite of the legislation which was designed to preserve it.

I have called the work a study, rather than a history of the Venetian press, because I feel that a true history of that press would require far more bibliographical knowledge than I possess. This book will have fulfilled its purpose if it serves as a pioneer along a line of research which has never been adequately explored, except at its beginning, and then almost entirely from a bibliographical, not from an historical or legal point of view.

The second part of the book contains the documents which served as a basis for the study. By far the larger part are published now for the first time. In some cases I have reprinted documents which have already seen the light, because I know that they are difficult of access to English students. These documents fall into several groups.

1. The laws of the Republic on the subject of the printing press and the book trade. Though many of these laws were printed on loose sheets at the time of their issue, for use among the officials and the book trade, and

still exist here and there as curiosities, yet I believe they are now collected and published together for the first time.

2. A table showing the number of monopolies, copyrights, *imprimaturs*, and patents granted by the College, the Senate, or the Council of Ten, from the year 1469 to 1596. The late Professor Rinaldo Fulin published in the *Archivio Veneto* (tom. xxiii. parte 1) an abstract of these documents down to the year 1526. From that year onwards I transcribed the originals in full, and have referred to them in the course of my Introduction. But in the process of printing the present volume it was found impossible to include them, owing to their bulk. I hope to offer them as a supplement, should the reception of this book justify the belief that the public desires to possess them.

3. The *Mariegole*, or matriculation book of the Guild of Printers and Booksellers, containing the first bye-laws of the corporation, is transcribed from the unpublished original now at the Museo Civico di Venezia.

4. A selection of documents from the unpublished minute-book of the Guild of Printers and Booksellers, bound up with the Mariegole.

5. Documents illustrating the relations between the Curia and the Republic on the question of the book trade. They are all of the nature of *Consulte*, or official memorials presented, on the invitation of the government, by its own officers or experts.

6. The list of Venetian printers and booksellers is based on Emmanuele Cicogna's unpublished MS. list, now at the Museo Civico. But I have been able to add a considerable number of names from other sources, though the list is, no doubt, incomplete.

7. The analysis of press prosecutions before the Holy Office in Venice has been compiled directly from the documents of the Venetian Inquisition now at the Frari.

8. The entries in the Bookseller's Journal of 1484 have been transcribed from the MS. at the Marciana Library in Venice (Cl. xi. Cod. xlv.). Sig. B. Calore, of the State Archives, has called my attention to a similar day-book now at the Frari, but as yet uncatalogued. It is marked on the outside "1596, *Baratti*, A." The first entry is dated 1596, and the last 1603.

Mr. T. W. Allen has given me most valuable help and advice while reading the proofs of the earlier chapters. My thanks are due to Sig. Giovanni Saccardo for his constant helpfulness, especially in indicating such useful sources of information as Morelli's *Zibaldoni* and the Valuation Rolls (*Estimo*) of the Republic; also to Com. Castellani, the Prefect of the Marciana, for his courtesy in allowing me to make facsimiles of several specimens of early Venetian printing. Sig. Castellani's interesting work,

La Stampa in Venezia, appeared when these sheets had already gone to the printers; but I have been able to avail myself of the information it contained, acknowledging my debts in their proper place. Mr. Blades' valuable monograph on Signatures appeared after the sheets were passed for press; so, too, did Sig. Bernoni's *Dei Torresani, Blado e Ragazoni,* Milano, Hœpli. I further wish to express my gratitude to Sig. Camillo nobile Soranzo of the Marciana, to the Abbate Nicoletti of the Museo Civico, and to Sig. Giomo of the Archivio di Stato for their unfailing help and courtesy. The late Director of the Archivio, Com. Cecchetti, is now beyond the reach of thanks. His death is an irreparable loss, and to him above all I feel myself indebted.

Horatio F. Brown.

CONTENTS.

CHAPTER I.

[1461.] 1469—1470.

THE FIRST BOOKS AND THEIR PRINTERS.

CHAPTER II.

1469—1481.

JOHN OF SPEYER AND NICOLAS JENSON.

CHAPTER III.

1469—1481.

HOW THEY PRINTED.

CHAPTER IV.

1470—1515.

FROM JENSON TO ALDUS.

CHAPTER V.

1484—1485.

A BOOKSELLER OF 1484.

CHAPTER VI.

1490—1515.

THE EPOCH OF ALDUS.

CHAPTER VII.

1469—1517.

BOOKS BEFORE LEGISLATION.

CHAPTER VIII.

1469—1528.

BOOKS BEFORE LEGISLATION.

CHAPTER IX.

1517—1549.

EARLIEST LEGISLATION.

CHAPTER X.

1549—1595.

THE GUILD OF PRINTERS AND BOOKSELLERS.

CHAPTER XI.

1549—1596.

THE GOVERNMENT AND THE GUILD.

CHAPTER XII.

1500—1600.

THE VENETIAN PRESS IN THE SIXTEENTH CENTURY.

CHAPTER XIII.

1548—1593.

THE INQUISITION.

CHAPTER XIV.

1548—1593.

THE INDEX AND THE BOOK TRADE.

CHAPTER XIX.

1600—1699.

PRESS LEGISLATION DURING THE SEVENTEENTH CENTURY.

CHAPTER XX.

1604—1699.

THE GUILD DURING THE SEVENTEENTH CENTURY.

CHAPTER XXI.

1700—1796.

PRESS LEGISLATION AND THE GUILD DURING THE EIGHTEENTH CENTURY.

CHAPTER XXII.

1765—1796.

LAST WORDS WITH ROME.

DOCUMENTS.

LIST OF ILLUSTRATIONS.

LIST OF THE MORE IMPORTANT WORKS REFERRED TO IN THIS BOOK.

1. Hain, *Repertorium Bibliographicum.* Stuttgartiæ. Sumptibus Cottæ. 1838. 4 vols.
2. Panzer, *Annales Typographici.* Norimbergæ. 1793-1803. 11 vols.
3. Holtrop, *Catalogus librorum sæculo xv impressorum.* Hagæ Comitum. 1856.
4. Paitoni, *Venezia la prima città fuori della Germania ove si esercitò la stampa.* Venezia. 1756.
5. Sardini, *Esame sui principii della Francese ed Italiana tipografia, ovvero storia critica di Nicolas Jenson.* Lucca. 1796. 2 vols.
6. Renouard, *Annales de l'imprimerie des Aldes.* Paris. 1803. 3 vols.
7. Didot, *Alde Manuce.* Paris. 1875.
8. Fulin, *Documenti per servire alla storia della tipografia Veneziana.* Venezia. Visentini. 1882.
9. Berlan, *La introduzione della stampa in Milano.* Venezia. 1884.
10. Reusch, *Der Index der Verbotenen Bücher.* Bonn. Cohen. 1883, 1885. 2 vols.
11. Cecchetti, *La Republica di Venezia e la Corte di Roma.* Venezia. Naratovich. 1874. 2 vols.
12. Romanin, *Storia documentata di Venezia.* Venezia. Naratovich. 1853-1861. 10 vols.
13. Sarpi, *Opere.* Helmstat. 1761. 8 vols.
14. Zaccaria, *Storia Polemica delle proibizione de' Libri.* Roma. 1777.
15. Legrand, *Bibliographie Hellénique.* Paris. Le Roux. 1885. 2 vols.
16. Omont, *Spécimens de caractères Hébreux, Grecs, Latins, et de musique gravés à Venise et à Paris par Guillaume le Bé.* Paris. 1889.
17. Passano, *I novellieri italiani.* Torino. 1878. 2 vols.
18. Cicogna, *Iscrizioni Veneziane.* Venezia. 1824-1853. 6 vols.
19. Cicogna, *Bibliografia Veneziana.* Venezia. 1847.
20. Soranzo, *Bibliografia Veneziana.* Venezia. 1885.
21. Sanuto, *Diarii.* Venezia. 1879. In course of publication.
22. Paruta, *La Legazione di Roma.* Deputazione Veneta di Storia Patria. Serie IV. Miscellanea. Vol. VII. Venezia. 3 vols.
23. Fisher, *Introduction to a Catalogue of Early Italian Prints.* London. 1888.
24. Archivio Veneto.
25. Morelli, Zibaldoni MSS. at the Museo Civico di Venezia.
26. Rossi, *Costumi.* MSS. at the Marciana.
27. Meermann, *Origines Typographicæ.* Hagæ Comitum. 1765. 2 vols.
28. Maittaire, *Annales Typographici.* Hagæ Comitum. 1719. 9 vols.
29. Ferrario, *Storia ed analizi degli antichi Romanzi di Cavalleria.* Milano. 1828. 5 vols.
30. Castellani, *La stampa in Venezia dalla sua origine alla morte di Aldo Manuzio seniore.* Venezia. Ongania. 1889.
31. Castellani, *I privilegi di Stampa e la proprietà letteraria in Venezia.* Venezia. Visentini. 1888.

THE VENETIAN PRINTING PRESS.

CHAPTER I.

[1461.] 1469—1470.

THE FIRST BOOKS AND THEIR PRINTERS.

The *Decor Puellarum* and the date 1461—The date attacked—Arguments in favour of the date, (1) the date itself, (2) contemporary evidence, Italian and foreign, (3) popular tradition, (4) official tradition—Arguments against the date, (1) decree of the Cabinet, (2) colophon of the *Epistolæ Familiares*, (3) Jenson's silence from 1461 to 1470, (4) identity of the *Decor Puellarum* with the editions of 1471.

OWEVER large may be the share which Italy took in the application and development of typography, she can lay no claim to the invention of the art of printing with moveable type. Even if we take the earliest date which can be assigned to a book printed in Italy, it is certain that Germany had preceded her by several years. German printers brought the new art, already matured, across the Alps; and whatever may be the subsequent glories of the Italian press, however honourable her position as foster-mother to typography, she cannot wear the laurels of invention on her brow.

At the very outset of our study we are met by a difficulty upon this question, What is the earliest date which may be assigned to a book printed in Italy? This question is closely connected with the special subject of this treatise—the Printing Press of Venice—and introduces us immediately to the origins of that Press.

The year 1465 is now almost universally assigned as the date of the first type issue from any Italian press.[1] That year is the date which appears in the *Lactantius*, printed at Subiaco by Sweynheym and Pannartz.[2] There is, however, another book in existence, which, by the date it bears, contests the priority of the Subiaco *Lactantius*. This book is the famous *Decor Puellarum*,[3] printed, as the colophon declares, by Nicolas Jenson in the year 1461.

The *Decor Puellarum* is a book of instruction to young girls how best to rule their lives. It was composed, most probably, by a Carthusian monk, Giovanni Corner, known, under his conventual name of Giovanni di Dio, as the author of several other similar works of devotion. The writer speaks of *noi altri Certosini*; and there is sufficient proof from internal evidence[4] that the book was written by a Venetian for Venetian girls. The book is not very rare; but before its date was impeached, it commanded large prices as the earliest monument of Italian typography. The *Decor Puellarum* is a small quarto volume, intended for the pocket; it contains 118 leaves unnumbered; it has twenty-two and twenty-three lines to the page, and thirty-three words to the line. The type is Roman; the height of composition 126 mm., and its width 75 mm. There are no signatures nor catchwords. There is no title-page, but the title is given in majuscule at the head of the first page. The colophon is printed in the same type as the title. No place of printing is named.[5]

The date 1461 has been attacked. It is said that MCCCCLXI. was

[1] From papers in the archive of the Barbarigo family it appears that, in 1447-8, a certain *Zuan de Biaxio bidelo e miniador da Bologna* possessed *forme*, *i.e.* wood blocks, *da stampar donadi et salterj*. *Archivio Veneto*, tom. xxix. p. 88. The exemption of books from customs dues is recorded in 1433. *Ibid.* p. 89.

[2] Hain, *9,806. The *Lactantius* is the first book with a date printed at Subiaco. But on the authority of Sweynheym and Pannartz themselves, a *Donatus*, now lost, preceded the *Lactantius*. In their appeal to Pope Sixtus IV., dated 1472, they speak of *Donatus pro puerulis, unde imprimendi initium sumpsimus*.

[3] Hain, 6,069.

[4] *e.g.*, leaf ix. verso, line 15, *goze* for *ghioccie*; leaf x. recto, l. 1, *quindexe* for *quindice*; leaf xliii. recto, l. 19, *zudese* for *giudice*, and this phrase, *andando couerte secūdo lusanza de Venexia*.

[5] The Marcian Library contains two copies of the *Decor Puellarum*, press-marked ZZ, 4, 41392, and ZZ, 4, 41393 respectively, which we shall call *Decor* A and *Decor* B. In examining these two copies it became apparent that down to leaf xxi they belonged to different editions; from leaf xxii to the end they are identical. The measurements of the title-lines vary, and on almost every leaf down to the bottom of leaf xxi verso there are variations. The collation of *Decor* A is as follows: gathers, 4, 4, 2, 3, 6, 4, 7, 1, 7, 2, 8, 2, 7, 1, 1; prickings and ruling on the right-hand margin of the recto of each leaf down to leaf xxi are visible. The collation of *Decor* B is: gathers, 4, 6, 3, 6, 4, 6, 3, 5, 4, 6, 4, 5, 3. The British Museum, the Bodleian, and the Bibliothèque Nationale copies agree with *Decor* B. *Decor* B is printed throughout in Jenson's well-known character. *Decor* A, down to leaf xxi, is in a different character. These leaves were possibly printed for someone who had lost the earlier leaves of the original copy.

QVI COMENZA LO SECVNDO CAPITVLO DEL SECVNDO VE-STIMENTO NVPTIALE DE ZE-TANINO CREMESINO.

DRIEDO ALA SANCTA con-feſſione cariſſime ſeguita lo ſecundo ueſtimento de la uera oratione ornata ſolamente de do ſorte de recami:zoe dargẽto:e doro.lo recão

JENSON. *Decor Puellarum.* A. 1461 [1471].

QVI COMENZA LO SECVNDO CAPITVLO DEL SECVNDO VE-STIMENTO NVPTIALE DE ZE-TANINO CREMESINO.

DRIEDO ALA SANCTA con-feſſione cariſſime ſeguita lo ſecundo ueſtimento de la uera oratione ornata ſolamente de do ſorte de recami:zoe dargẽto:e doro.lo recão

JENSON. *Decor Puellarum.* B. 1461 [1471].

ſopponendoui ad ogni ſpirituale & temporale correctione de qualunque diuotiſſima perſona di zaſchaduno perito maeſtro & ſapientiſſio doctore de la uoſtra ſãctiſſima madre ecclesia catholica di roma.

ANNO A CHRISTI INCARNA-TIONE. MCCCCLXI. PER MAGI-STRVM NICOLAVM IENSON HOC OPVS QVOD PVELLA-RVM DECOR DICITVR FELICI-TER IMPRESSVM EST.

LAVS DEO.

JENSON. *Decor Puellarum.* Colophon. 1461 [1471].

printed for MCCCCLXXI. by an error which arose through the omission of the Roman numeral X.

This attack upon the date of the *Decor Puellarum* has raised the following questions, in which national and civic pride have been deeply engaged. For if 1461 be not the correct date, then Subiaco takes the place of Venice as the first home of Italian printing; and Jenson, the Frenchman, has to yield his position of prototypographer in Italy to the Germans Sweynheym and Pannartz. Venice is obliged to fall back upon the *Epistolæ Familiares*,[1] printed by John of Speyer in 1469, and therefore gives precedence not only to Subiaco, but also to Rome (1467), and stands on a level with Milan, where the *Miracoli della Gloriosa Verzine Maria*[2] was printed in 1469, by or for Lavagna.

It is not surprising, therefore, that a warm controversy should have taken place round the date of the *Decor Puellarum*. The details of this controversy are so well known, however, that it is hardly necessary to give more than a brief summary of the strongest arguments for and against the correctness of the date as printed in the book itself, and adverse or favourable to Jenson's position as prototypographer of Venice.

The first argument in support of the date 1461 is the presence of that date in the book itself. It would require strong evidence to upset a printed date against which no protest was raised at the time, though much honour and fame depended upon its accuracy. Would the friends of John of Speyer have allowed 1461 to stand unimpeached when it overshadowed his 1469, and robbed his *Epistolæ Familiares* of much of its glory? On the other hand, misprinted dates are by no means uncommon in these early books;[3] and if the date of Jenson's book were notoriously inaccurate, that very notoriety might have prevented the friends of John from protesting when the *Epistolæ Familiares*, the Pliny, and other issues from John of Speyer's press, were before the world to confute any claim which Jenson might venture to found upon a false date. We must remember, too, that the *Decor Puellarum* was a work of small moment and probably of narrow circulation as compared with the *Epistolæ Familiares*, in which John of Speyer asserts his own priority uncontradicted by Jenson.

[1] Hain, 5,164.

[2] Hain, 11,227. The authenticity of the date of this edition has been severely attacked, and as warmly defended by Professor F. Berlan in his opuscule, *La Introduzione della Stampa in Milano*, &c., *Venezia*, 1884. See *Archivio Ven.*, xxix. 209.

[3] Hain, 1,310; *e.g.*, we find *Appianus, latine, Petro Candido interprete. Peregrinus de Pasqualibus. MCCCCLCXV.* for *MCCCCXCV.*, and Erhard Ratdolt's edition of Mataratius, dated 1468, but really 1478. Hain, *10,889. Holtrop, *Cat. B. R. H.*, Pars II., No. 435. Serna, *Dic. Bibliog.*, t. i. p. 172.

The supporters of Jenson rely much upon the evidence of his contemporaries. We have no proof that Jenson ever explicitly claimed the priority for himself; and, although there is abundant testimony to his excellence as a printer, it is doubtful whether any of his contemporaries, save one, actually asserted for him the priority in his art. Ognibene da Lonigo's (Leonicenus) introduction to Jenson's edition of Quintilian,[1] published in 1471, contains the following passage, in which he describes Jenson as *librariæ artis mirabilis inventor, non ut scribantur calamo libri, sed veluti gemma imprimantur ac prope sigillo.* Ognibene was Jenson's reader and corrector; in this passage he seems to claim for the printer the invention of his art, which is, of course, claiming far too much. For this exaggeration Ognibene is corrected by the Cologne Chronicle[2] of 1499. But, upon the authority of Ulrich Zell, the Chronicle gives the cities in which the art of printing first appeared in the following order: Mainz, Köln, Strasburg, Venice. This would, by implication, make in favour of the earlier date of the *Decor Puellarum*—unless there be some other work, now lost, to which the Cologne chronicler was referring—for if the *Decor Puellarum* belong not to 1461, then Subiaco and Rome take the precedence of Venice.

The colophon of *Phalaridis, Epistolæ* (Oxford, 1485[3]) is a further testimony in Jenson's favour. It runs thus—

Hoc Theodoricus Rood quem Collonia misit
Sanguine Germanus nobile pressit opus
Anteque sibi socius Thomas fuit Anglicus Hunte
Dii dent ut Venetos exsuperare queant
Quam Jenson Venetos docuit vir Gallicus artem
Ingenio didicit terra Britania suo
Caelatos Veneti nobis transmittere libros
Cedite nos aliis vendimus o Veneti.

These verses prove that public opinion abroad assigned the priority of printing in Venice to Jenson.

The chronicle of Jacopo Foresti, of Bergamo,[4] shows that men's minds were confused on the question, who invented printing with moveable type? but, like Ognibene, Foresti claims too much for Jenson when he writes, *ars imprimendi libros . . . quam alii repertam asseverant a Guttenburgo, alii a quodam alio nomine Fausto, alii a Nicolao Jenson prædicant.* The passage shows, however, what a high position Jenson held among printers; and it is remarkable that there should be no mention of those equally able workmen, John of Speyer and Windelin his brother, especially if the world generally recognized their position as the earliest printers in Venice.

[1] Hain, *13,647. [2] Fol. 311. See Castellani, *L'origine ted. e l'origine oland.*, &c., p. 19.
[3] Hain, 12,886.
[4] *Supplementum Chronicarum. Venetiis. Bernardinus de Benaliis.* 1483. Hain, *2,805.

The testimony of Polydorus Vergilius and of Marc' Antonio Sabellico is, perhaps, rather to Jenson's excellence than to his priority in Venice. Vergilius says, *artem quidam nomine Conradus, Romam primo in Italiam attulit, quam dein Nicolaus Jenson Gallus primus mirum in modum illustravit;* and Sabellico's witness is even more explicitly to Jenson's ability as a printer, *sed omnium maxime opibus et eleganti litterarum forma multum cæteros antecelluerunt Nicolaus Jenson et Joannes Colloniensis, ambo Theutonici.* Writing, in his *Enneades*, of Doge Malipiero's reign (1457-1462), Sabellico says, *per idem tempus libraria impressio apud Italos vulgari cœpta est.* This would agree with the date 1461, but not with 1465. Sabellico, in his History of Venice, repeats the statement that printing in Italy began in the reign of Malipiero; he was a contemporary, and is a good witness. Neither Vergilius nor Sabellico make any reference to the brothers from Speyer.

By far the strongest testimony to Jenson's priority is that borne by one of his most distinguished and most accurate contemporaries, Marino Sanuto. In the *Cronica Sanuda*,[1] under the reign of Malipiero, and in the year 1461, Sanuto says, *et in tempo di questo Doxe Venexia stette in paxe et in quiette, et in questa terra poi per tutta l'Italia fò principià larte del stampar di libri, qual havè principio da alcuni Todeschi, trai quali uno chiamado Nicolo Jenson Todesco, fò il primo che in Venecia facesse stampar libri, et vadagnò assaissimi denari sicchè vene richissimo.* It is true that, under the year 1469, 18th Sept., the date of the monopoly granted to John of Speyer, Sanuto wrote, *fo presso, attento l'arte del stampar sia venuta a luce, chel sia conscesso a Zuane de Spira stampa l'Epistole di tullio et plinio per 5 anni altri non stampino.* This is in perfect agreement with the tenor of the official minute reciting the concession to John of Speyer, and is valuable as interpreting the meaning of that minute. Sanuto merely declares that the art of printing has come to light; he does not say that John was the agent; whereas in the previous passage he positively affirms that Jenson was the first to print in Venice. Sanuto was born in 1466, so that he was quite a child at the date of Jenson's death in 1480; but he is usually so accurately informed—for example, in this very case of John's monopoly—and so painstaking in his record, that his evidence must be reckoned of the highest value. Sanuto clearly is of opinion that Jenson was the first printer in Venice; and this testimony, whether it be the result of positive knowledge, or merely the expression of current belief, is very important.

Popular Venetian opinion assigned the origin of printing in Venice to

[1] MS. alla Marciana, cl. vii., cod. cxxv., a MS. written in the last century, but based upon the original *Cronica Sanuda*, as is proved by confronting this codex with Muratori's edit. *Rer. It. Scrip.*, xxii. Muratori followed perhaps the original, more likely a copy in the library at Modena.

the year 1461, as is proved by Giovanni Palazzi's designs for playing cards,[1] bound up in the little volume, *La virtù in giuoco*, 1681, where, on the back of the *Cavallo di Spade*, there is a woodcut of a printing press at work, and underneath it this inscription, *arte della stampa introdotta in Venetia dalla Dandola Dogaressa Malipiera.*

And, lastly, official opinion, down to the fall of the Republic, was undoubtedly in favour of Jenson, and of the date 1461. The report upon Printing and the Book Trade, presented to the Senate by the Rifformatori dello Studio di Padova, opens with these words, *L'arte della stampa, dalla Germania passata in Venezia verso il* 1461,[2] &c.

So far, then, Italian contemporary evidence, except that of Sanuto, either asks too much for Jenson, or else confines itself to lauding him as a skilled and excellent workman. But Sabellico and Sanuto both place the introduction of printing in the reign of Malipiero, and this makes in favour of 1461, as against 1469. Foreign opinion, as expressed in the Cologne Chronicle and the Oxford colophon, are in Jenson's favour. Sanuto, a valuable witness, is decidedly in support of Jenson's priority in Venice, and so, too, are popular and official Venetian opinion down to the fall of the Republic.

To come now to the arguments in support of John of Speyer's priority, and of the *Epistolæ Familiares* against the *Decor Puellarum* as the first book printed in Venice. In the year 1793 the Abbate Jacopo Morelli, Prefect of the Marcian Library, published[3] the earliest official document relating to the Printing Press in Venice. That document is an order of the Collegio,[4] or Cabinet, of Venice, dated 18th September, 1469. The order was moved for by the Doge's councillors, and grants to John of Speyer the monopoly of printing in Venice and its district for five years to come, and protects him from foreign competition by the importation of books printed elsewhere. The document will be found *in extenso* in the Appendices.[5] It is sufficient, for the present purpose, to quote the preamble, upon which a large part of the attack on Jenson's priority is based. It runs thus: *Inducta est in hanc nostram inclytam ciuitatem Ars imprimendi libros: Indiesque magis celebrior ac frequentior fiet! per operam studium et ingenium magistri Joannis De Spira. Qui*

[1] Museo Civico di Venezia.

[2] See Appendices.

[3] Jacopo Morelli, *Operette*, ii. 408, 410. *Venezia, Alvisopoli*, 1820.

[4] The Collegio was composed of the Doge, his six Councillors, the Chiefs of the Quarantia and the various Savii. Its function was to prepare all legislation to be submitted to the Senate or the Ten. See Brown, *Venetian Studies*, p. 187.

[5] It has frequently been published; among others by Professor Rinaldo Fulin, *Documenti per servire alla storia della Tipografia Veneziana. Venezia, Visentini*, 1882; recently, and more accurately, by Sig. Castellani, *La Stampa in Venezia*, p. 69; but in no case with a sufficient regard for the signs of punctuation. For that reason, and because of its great importance, it is reprinted in this book.

ceteris aliis vrbibus hanc nostram prȩelegit! vbi cum coniuge liberis et familia tota sua inhabitaret exerceretque dictam artem librorum imprimendorum: Jamque summa omnium comendatione impressit epistolas Ciceronis! Et nobile opus plinij De naturali historia In maximo numero! et pulcherrima litterarum forma! pergitque quottidie alia preclara volumina imprimere! adeo ut industria et virtute huius hominis! multis prȩclarisque voluminibus! et quidem peruili precio locupletabitur. The question turns upon the way in which this passage is to be read. Are there two propositions, or only one? Does the clause *per operam studium*, &c., belong equally to the two preceding clauses, *inducta est* and *indiesque*, or only to the latter, the *indiesque* clause? Does the sense run that the art has been introduced by Master John, and will grow more celebrated through Master John? or that the art has been introduced—first clause—and will grow more celebrated, thanks to Master John—second clause? The supporters of John wish to read the sentence as one proposition, and to couple his name with the clause *inducta est*; the friends of Jenson, and of the date 1461—if there be any left—take the opposite view. The answer depends very much upon the stopping. As Sig. Castellani prints the passage, with a comma after *libros* and none after *fiet*, the name of John appears to be separated from the clause *inducta est*, and to be connected only with the *indiesque* clause. But the stopping is not accurately rendered; the sign after *fiet* is ignored. If there is a comma after *libros* and a comma after *fiet*, all three clauses would be taken as forming one single proposition; and the *per operam . . . Magistri Joannis* would refer both to *inducta est* and to *indiesque celebrior fiet*. Morelli and Fulin both print commas after *libros* and *fiet*. Professor Berlan, on the other hand, declares that there is no such stop as the comma after *fiet* to be found in the manuscript. As transcribed above, the passage stands punctuated in the original with two dots after *libros*, and a dot and a stroke after *fiet*. Morelli and Fulin treat these two different signs as both of them equal to commas. It is more likely that the two dots are really a colon, and possess the value of a colon, that is to say, they merely mark a pause in the rhetorical construction of the sentence, but do not break the sentence into various distinct propositions—the meaning of the sentence runs on continuously over the clause marked off by the colon; in which case we shall have to admit that the Cabinet intended to affirm that the art of printing was introduced by John of Speyer; though the nighest contemporary interpretation of their meaning, that given by Sanuto, will not bear out such a reading.

The second point urged in support of John of Speyer's priority is the colophon to the *Epistolæ Familiares* of 1469. It runs thus—

Primus in Adriaca formis impressit aenis
Urbe libros Spira genitus de Stirpe Joannes

In reliquis sit quanta vides spes lector habenda
Quom labor hic primus calami superaverit artem.

Here John of Speyer makes a distinct claim to priority—a claim which was never disputed. But we must remember that if John's claim was not disputed, no more was Jenson's date.

If the date 1461 on the *Decor Puellarum* be correct, we have to account for a blank space of nine years between the appearance of that volume and the Eusebius, *De Evangelica Præparatione*[1] of 1470, which is generally recognized as Jenson's next claimed and dated work. During this period Jenson produced nothing—an inactivity which contrasts strangely with the rapid production of his press from the year 1470 onwards. Maittaire,[2] who is in favour of the date 1461, attempts to surmount this objection by suggesting that Jenson probably did print during these nine years, but that his works are either lost, or lie buried in libraries. Such an argument, however, inventing, to suit a theory, books of whose existence we know nothing, can hardly be admitted. Professor Berlan meets the difficulty by citing other instances of a like silence.[3] This argument of silence is not, of course, an absolute proof that Jenson did not print during the years from 1461 to 1470; but, nevertheless, it must be allowed some weight in considering the accuracy of the date of the *Decor Puellarum.*

Perhaps the strongest argument against the date 1461 is the identity of type and format between the *Decor Puellarum* and the other books printed by Jenson in 1471, the *Palma Virtutum*,[4] the *Gloria Mulierum*,[5] the *Parole devote*.[6] On leaf 59 of the *Decor Puellarum* the author recommends these works to the young girls for whom he is writing. From this recommendation it has been argued that these books were already in print, which would make the *Decor Puellarum* subsequent to them, and therefore not earlier than 1471. Though the argument is not clear to demonstration, yet it must be allowed to have some force in guiding us to an opinion on the date of the *Decor Puellarum.*

Such are the main arguments on one side and on the other of this controversy over the date of the first book printed in Venice. The question will always be open to discussion; but the consensus of modern criticism at present tends, wrongly we think, to consider the dispute as settled in favour of John of Speyer and his edition of the *Epistolæ Familiares* of 1469.

[1] Hain, 6,699.
[2] *Annales Typographici.* Hagæ, 1719, i. p. 38.
[3] *Op. cit.*, p. 67.
[4] Hain, 12,283. Serna, 1043.
[5] Hain, 7,783. Serna, 652.
[6] Hain, 12,422.

CHAPTER II.

1469—1481.

JOHN OF SPEYER AND NICOLAS JENSON.

Death of John of Speyer—His works—Number of copies he printed—Nicolas Jenson, his birthplace and early life—He settles in Venice—His first books—Amount of work he produced—His fame—Made Count Palatine—His wealth—His home and family—Reported sale of his character—His partnerships—His death—The firm of John of Cologne, Nicolas Jenson, and associates.

HE material available for the early lives of John of Speyer and of Nicolas Jenson is extremely scanty. Very little is known about either of them before they came to Venice. About John and Windelin, his brother, we have no information beyond the fact that they were natives of Speyer,[1] in Rhenish Bavaria. It is not known where they learned their art, nor from whom; nor yet how long they had been settled in Venice before they began to print. The order of the College granting a monopoly of printing to John, shows that they were well received, and that a prosperous career was opened to them. But John's life in Venice was a very brief one. He died in 1470, the year after the appearance of the *Epistolæ Familiares*, and while he was engaged upon his edition of Saint Augustine's *De Civitate Dei*.[2] The edition was completed by Windelin, who records the event in the colophon to the work:

subita sed morte peremptus
Non potuit coeptum Venetis finire volumen.
Vindelinus adest ejusdem frater et arte
Non minor: Adriacaque morabitur urbe.

[1] Windelin calls himself *e spira natus* in the colophon to the *Somnium Scipionis*, 1470. Hain, 5,257. And Raphael Zovenzoni addresses the city of Speyer thus: *Spyra tuum nomen toto celebrabitur orbe | Quę Vindellini diceris esse parens. Ciceronis, De Divinatione*, 1471. Hain, *5,334.

[2] Hain, *2,048.

And, in confirmation of the fact, the famous monopoly of 1469 bears on its margin these words: *nullius est vigoris quia obiit magister et auctor.*

But in the short space of time between 1469, when the *Epistolæ Familiares* appeared, and 1470, when he died, John produced the following works:

Plinii, *De Naturali Historia.*[1]
Livii, *Historiarum Romanarum Decades.* Vol. I.[2]
Ciceronis, *Epistolæ ad Familiares.* Second Edition.[3]
S. Aurelii Augustini, *De Civitate Dei.*[4]

John was engaged upon this work when he died. From the colophons of these works we are able to gather the number of copies in each edition (except the one volume of Livy and the unfinished St. Augustine), and the time he took to print them.

Of the first edition of the *Epistolæ Familiares* John printed one hundred copies; and of the *De Naturali Historia* the same number. He took nearly three months over the work:

Qui docuit Venetos exscribi posse Joannes
Mense fere trino centena volumina plini
Et totidem magni Ciceronis Spira libellos.[5]

The colophon to the second edition of the *Epistolæ Familiares* contains this statement:

quarto nam mense peregit
Hoc tercentenum bis Ciceronis opus.

From which it seems that the second edition of the *Epistolæ* consisted of six hundred copies, published in two issues of three hundred each; and that the whole six hundred took four months to print. So that in seven months John of Speyer had printed eight hundred volumes at least, besides the

[1] Hain, 13,087.

[2] Two other volumes were completed by Windelin, and published under his name in 1470. Hain, 10,130.

[3] Hain, 5,165. The following differences between the first and second editions are noticeable. 1st edition: height of comp., 226 mm.; width, 148 mm.; leaves, 125; fin. verso; lines, 41 to full page. 2nd edition: height of comp., 226 mm.; width, 136 mm.; leaves, 137; fin. recto; stitched in gathers of 6, 6, 2, 6, 4, 6, 4, 6, 4, 6, 4, 6, 4, 5, minus last leaf. These differences seem to show that, after printing off his first edition, John probably distributed the type; otherwise he would not have been at the labour of recomposing it. Possibly he did not expect such a large sale. He profited by his experiences, and kept up the type of his second edition, making a second issue of three hundred copies when the first issue was exhausted.

[4] Hain, *2,048.

[5] Colophon to the St. Augustine. Windelin is referring to the first edition of Cicero's Letters.

NOs cõtra rationẽ deprędendẽdi falsas demõstabimus q̃do etiã luxuriã aduersus fraudes miũi dec& pręter illa quę ĩ prĩcipalibus qbusq; generibus priuatĩ dixiũs trãslucentẽ matutio ꝓbari cẽsent: aut si necesse ẽ ĩ q̃rta horã postea uetãt. Experimẽta pluribus mõis cõstãt: primũ põ lere si grauiores sẽtiũt: post hęc corpe fictitiis pustulę ĩ ꝓfũdo apparẽt scabritia ĩ cute ĩ capillamẽto frigoris icõstãtia prius q̃ ad oculos ꝑueniat desinens nitor.

¶ Quem modo tam rarum cupiens uix lector haber&:
Quiq; etiam fractus pene legendus eram:
Restituit Venetis me nuper Spira Ioannes:
Exscripsitq; libros ęre notante meos.
Fessa manus quondam moneo: Calamusq; quiescat.
Nanq; labor studio cessit: & ingenio.

.M.CCCC.LXVIIII.

JOHN OF SPEYER. PLINY, *De Naturali Historia.* 1469.

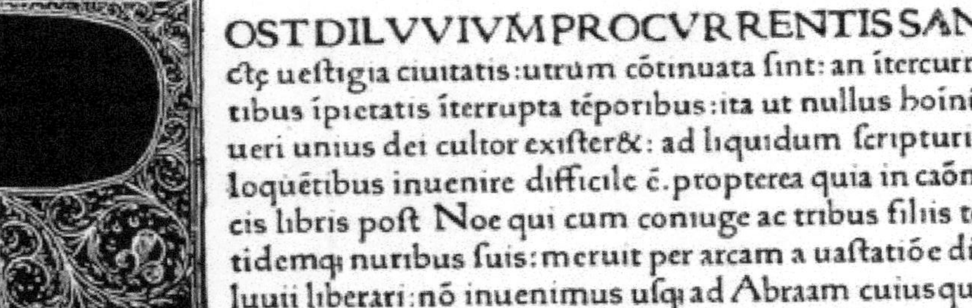

OST DILVVIVM PROCVRRENTIS SAN
ctę uestigia ciuitatis: utrum cõtinuata sint: an itercurré
tibus ipietatis iterrupta téporibus: ita ut nullus hoinũ
ueri unius dei cultor exister&: ad liquidum scripturis
loquẽtibus inuenire difficile ẽ. propterea quia in caõni
cis libris post Noe qui cum coniuge ac tribus filiis to
tidemq; nuribus suis: meruit per arcam a uastatiõe di/
luuii liberari: nõ inuenimus usq; ad Abraam cuiusquã
pietatem euidenti diuino eloquio prędicatam: nisi q Noe duos filios suos
Sem & Iaph& prophetica benedictione commẽdat: intuẽs & pręuidẽs quod
longe fuerat post futurum. Vnde factum est etiam illud: ut filiũ suũ mediũ
hoc est primogenito minorem ultimoq; maiorem: qui peccauerat in patrem:
non in ipso sed in filio eius suo nepote maledicer& his uerbis. Maledictus

John and Windelin of Speyer. S. Augustine, *De Civitate Dei.* 1470.

edition of the first volume of the Livy, whose number is not stated, and a certain portion of the edition of St. Augustine.

About Nicolas Jenson our information is considerably fuller. He was a Frenchman, son of Jacob Jenson of Sommevoire,[1] near Bar-sur-Aube, in the department of Aube, in the diocese of Troyes, and the district of Champagne. He had a brother, named Albert, whom he left his heir general. Jenson does not state how old he was when he made his Will, and we are not able to fix the date of his birth; but his biographer Sardini[2] places it somewhere about 1420. Jenson served his apprenticeship in the Paris mint, and was promoted to be master of the mint at Tours. When the rumoured discovery of the new art of printing reached France, Jenson was sent to Mainz, in 1458, by Charles VII. to learn the secrets of the invention, and to bring them back to France with a view to opening a printing press in that country.[3] Jenson fulfilled his commission, and reached France again in the year 1461, when Louis XI. had just ascended the throne. We do not know why he did not remain in France, nor whether he printed in that country; but the next certain information we possess about him is the publication of his books in Venice.

There were many reasons to influence Jenson in his choice of Venice as the scene of his operations. In the first place, the tide of printers was flowing steadily towards Italy. Apprentices who had acquired the new art in Germany[4] set out to seek their fortunes by the exercise of their skill. It was natural that they should turn to Italy, where the nobles were rich, where learning had its home, where manuscripts were stored in abundance for printing to reproduce, where there was a public, both lay and ecclesiastic, ready to pay for these reproductions. The Republic offered special attractions in the security afforded by its government, and in the protection and liberty she promised to all who settled in her dominions. Venice was, moreover, the best mart for the distribution of goods; and the trade in paper was facilitated by the ease and cheapness of sea carriage.

Jenson settled in Venice, and began issuing books—if we abandon the date of the *Decor Puellarum*—in 1470; that is, nine years after we last

[1] *Archivio Veneto*, tom. 33, p. 457. Jenson's Will, dated 7 Sept., 1480. Among the *Atti Notarili* of Girolamo Bonicardi, Jenson signs himself. *ego Nicolaus Jenson quondam Ser Jacobi de Sommavera, trecen. dioceseos.* Jenson's Will has been published *in extenso* by Sig. Castellani, *La Stampa in Venezia*, p. 85.

[2] Sardini, *Esame sui principii della Francese ea Italiana tipografia ;. ovvero storia critica di Nicolao Jenson.* Lucca, 1796-98.

[3] This information is based upon a MS. note in the Library of the Arsenal, Paris. See Castellani, *L'origine tedesca e l'origine Olandese dell' invenzione della Stampa*, p. 30.

[4] By far the larger number of early Italian printers are German: Sweynheym and Pannartz, of Subiaco and Rome; Ulrich Han, of Rome; Gensberg, of Rome; John of Speyer and Christofer Valdarfer, of Venice; Numeister, of Foligno, &c.

heard of him just returned to France from Mainz. Whether Jenson brought his type with him to Venice, or whether he cut[1] it there, is not known. When he did begin work he produced continuously every year, from 1470 till his death in 1480. His activity was very great. During these ten years Sardini counts one hundred and fifty-five editions, known to be by him or attributed to him as issuing from his press. And this number must be augmented by several works unknown to Sardini, but catalogued by Holtrop.[2]

There is some uncertainty as to which was the first book published by Jenson in the year 1470. There is no precise date, no indication of the day or month, in any of the four undoubted issues from his press in this year; it is difficult, therefore, to determine the priority among them. Panzer,[3] and Hain following him, however, claims another book for Jenson—Guarini, *Regulæ Grammaticæ*[4]—and on the strength of its colophon, which runs thus:

FINIS
MCCCCLXX DIE QVINTO
MENSIS IANVARII.

he assigns it to the year 1470. If Panzer were right in ascribing this edition to Jenson, and assigning it to the year 1470, we should probably have here the first book printed in Venice by that master. But both the ascription and the assignation are very doubtful. In the first place, the Venetian printers dated their work *more Veneto*;[5] and in that case the book can only belong to the year 1471[6] of our reckoning. In the second place, an examination of the type of the Guarini raises doubts as to whether the book be printed by Jenson at all.[7] And if we reject the Guarini, that leaves us with the four undoubted Jensons of 1470: the Eusebius, *De Evangelica Præparatione*; Justinus, *Epitomata*;[8] Cicero, *Epistolæ ad Atticum*;[9] and Cicero, *Rhetorica* and *De Inventione*.[10] General opinion places the *De Evangelica Præparatione* at the head of the list.

[1] Many of these early printers were either die-sinkers or goldsmiths. See Panizzi, *Chi era Francesco da Bologna?* Londra, Pickering, 1873, p. 16.

[2] *Catalogus B. R. H.*, p. 392 *et seq.*

[3] Panzer, iii. 20, *videtur primum Nicolai Jenson tentamen Venetiis.*

[4] Hain, 8,108.

[5] Didot, *Alde Manuce*, Paris, 1875, p. 62, note 1; Fulin, *op. cit.*, No. 4; *Archivio Veneto*, 1, 161; *e.g.*, see Hain, *9,924, where the two parts of Lascaris' *Erotemata* are dated respectively 1494 *ultimo Februarii* and 1495 *octavo Martii.* See Castellani, *La Stampa in Venezia*, p. 40.

[6] The Venetian year began on March 1.

[7] There are certain notes of Jenson's type which do not appear in the Guarini, *e.g.*, the *i*'s are dotted straight above the letter instead of to the right hand; the contractions are not those used by Jenson; the *h*'s are more Gothic in form than those used by Jenson.

[8] Hain, 9,647.

[9] Hain, *5,214.

[10] Hain, *5,057.

VM primum Romã ueni: fuitq; cui recte ad te lĩas datem: nil prius mihi faciendum putaui q̄ ut tibi absenti de reditu nostro gratularer: cognoui enĩ ut uere scribã te in cõsiliis mihi dãdis fortiorem: prudẽtiorẽ q̄ me ipsum: etiam propter meam in te obseruantiã nimium in custodia salutis meæ diligentem: eundẽq; te qui primis temporibus erroris nostri: aut totius furoris particeps et falsi rumoris sotius fuisses: acerbissĩe dissidiũ nostꝝ tulisse plurimũq; operæ studii diligentiæ laboris ad conficiendũ reditum meũ cõtulisse. Itaq; hoc tibi uere affirmo ĩ maxĩa lætitia & exoptatissima gratulatiõe unum ad cumulandum gaudium conspectum: aut potius cõplexum mihi tuum defuisse: quem semel nactus nunq̄ dimisero: ac nisi etiam prætermissos fructus tuos tuæ suauitatis præteriti tẽporis oẽs exegero ꝓfecto hac restitutione fortunæ me ipse nõ satis dignũ iudicabo. Nos adhuc in nr̃o statu: quod difficillime recuperari posse arbitrati sumus

JENSON. CICERO, *Epistolæ ad Atticum.* 1470.

In estimating the amount of work executed by Jenson, much depends upon being able to state the size of the editions issued by him. But, unlike the brothers John and Windelin, Jenson never, so far as we are aware, mentions the number of copies of any book printed by him. There is one consideration, however, which would point to the belief that Jenson's editions were large ones. Second editions of Jenson's issues, if not unknown, are certainly very rare.[1] When we remember the extent of his reputation and the vogue he had, this can only be explained by supposing that his original editions were large.

To Jenson's fame as a printer there is abundant testimony to be found among his contemporaries. We have already quoted the witness of Sabellico, Polydorus Vergilius, and Marino Sanuto. One of Jenson's own publications, the *Gregorii Papæ IX., Decretales*, of 1475,[2] furnishes a yet more eloquent demonstration of the extent to which his fame had spread beyond Venice, and of the esteem in which he was held. Jenson had been summoned to Rome, where the Pope, Sixtus IV., had conferred on him the title of Count Palatine, and other rewards and honours. This we gather from a letter written by Pietro Treci to Francesco Colucia, one of Jenson's readers, and printed at the end of this volume of the Decretals. The passage runs: *Quod Nicolaum ipsum ex urbe roma istuc salvum adventasse scribis gratulor, et eo magis quod et comitem palatinum a summo pontifice factum et aliis quam pluribus privilegiis in sue virtutis prerogativam eum donatum decoratumque audio . . . quis enim pro meritis digna ipsi premia conferre possit cum tam brevi temporis curriculo non modo gentilium scriptorum preclara opera jam pene extincta sua prudentia, impendio ac liberalitate elegantissime instauraverit, verum et sacrorum impressione seu potius reparatione librorum divino ingenio ac mirifica arte totam ecclesiam illustraverit, et decoraverit adeo ut deo propitio in omnem terram exiverit nomen ejus et in fines orbis terre opera ejus.* In the phrase *verum et sacrorum impressione* we probably see the reason why he was thus honoured by the Papal Court—to reward him for the publication of the devotional and canonical works which issued from his press in the years 1473 and 1474, and to encourage other printers to follow the same lines.

Not fame alone but wealth also had come to Jenson during these five years of active work in Venice. The words *impendio ac liberalitate*, in the passage already quoted, seem to show that he had the means to spend, and was willing to spend on his editions. But beyond this conjecture we have the explicit statement of Sanuto that *vadagnò assaissimi denari sicchè vene richissimo*; and if Sanuto calls him *richissimo* in Venice of the fifteenth century,

[1] A second edition of the *De Evangelica Præparatione* is quoted by Hain, 6,701, in the year 1476. Sardini records it as doubtful. Panzer, iii. *225.

[2] Hain, *8,002.

that must have meant a really large fortune. The terms of Jenson's Will furnish considerable information as to the amount of his fortune. We know that he devised about four thousand golden ducats, bequeathing the sum of 465 ducats in legacies, besides providing a dower of 600 ducats for each of his three daughters' marriage portions, and 400 ducats for his son Nicolò when he reached the age of twenty-five years. The rest of his fortune he left to his brother Albert; but we do not know what proportion the legacies bore to the residue. On the whole, these legacies do not seem to be very large, if we compare them with the dowries of one hundred thousand ducats apiece bestowed by another Venetian printer, Thomaso Giunta, upon his two daughters.[1]

At the time when his Will was drawn up, Jenson was living in the parish of San Canciano.[2] His place of business appears to have been at San Salvador; in the Matriculation roll of the Confraternity of San Gerolamo[3] he is entered as *Nicolò Xanson di San Salvador*. There is no evidence that he was ever married, but in his Will he makes provision for Zanetta, the mother of his three daughters, Giovanna, Caterina, and Barbara, and of his son Nicolò, who, at the time of his father's death, was in London.

In the year 1479, Jenson is said to have sold his type to Andrea de' Torresani de Asola, the father-in-law of Aldus Manutius. It is possible that he may have sold a set of matrices punched by his punches. Such a practice was not unknown among printers,[4] and Andrea de' Torresani, in 1482-3, published the *Lectura super primo Decretalium*,[5] which he declares to have been printed *inclytis famosisque characteribus optimi quondam in hac arte magistri Nicolai Jenson Gallici, quo nihil praestantius nihil melius*. But that was two years after Jenson's death, and the type may have come into Andrea de' Torresani's hands by other means. It is certain, from the terms of his Will, that Jenson was in possession of his punches at the time of his death in 1480; and he opened the work of his press that year with a series of devotional publications, the *Nosce te*,[6] the *Corona senum*,[7] the *De immensa charitate Dei*,[8] the *De humilitate interiora*,[9] and the *Flos vitæ*,[10] all printed in his familiar Roman type.

[1] Castellani, *I privilegi di Stampa*, p. 16.

[2] In his Will he is described as, *habitator Venetiarum in confinio sancti Canciani*.

[3] Cicogna, *Inscrizioni Veneziane*, vi. 954, 955.

[4] Guillaume Le Bé, in 1546, says, *Je vendis une frappe à Florence à M. Lorenzo Turentin, imprimeur du Duc*. H. Omont, *Specimens de Caractères Hebreux, etc.* Paris, M.DCCC.LXXXIX, p. 14.

[5] Hain, *12,313. [6] Hain, 9,388. [7] Hain, 9,390.

[8] Not in Hain. Brit. Mus. C., 11. a. 14.

[9] Not in Hain. Brit. Mus. C., 11. a. 14.

[10] Not in Hain. Brit. Mus. C., 11. a. 14. Sardini ascribes all three to John the Carthusian.

This series of devotional works is very inferior in careful workmanship to the similar series published in 1471; but it is interesting as being the last work produced by Jenson alone. This year Jenson entered into partnership with John of Cologne, who had been printing in Venice from the year 1471, partly alone, but partly also, after 1473, in partnership with John Manthen. John was a member of the Confraternity of S. Gerolamo, along with Jenson; his name appears on the Matriculation roll as *Zuan da Cologna stampador de S. Paternian,*[1] in which parish he and many other printers lived. The terms of the contract between Jenson and John of Cologne are not known; but Jenson supplied the type.[2] Whether John of Cologne supplied the money to work the partnership we are unable to state positively; but we may notice that his name always precedes that of Jenson in the signature of the firm, seeming to indicate that he was chief partner in the business.

Jenson's personal participation in the business was very soon terminated. On Sept. 7, 1480, he was seriously ill, and caused his Will to be drawn up. He desired to be buried at the Church of S. Maria delle Grazie,[3] and that his executors shall there erect to his memory *unum monumentum simplex et absque pompa.* His brother Albert, his executor and residuary legatee, is to pay for the masses to be said for the testator's soul, when he has realized Jenson's share in the firm *Zuan da Cologna et Nicolo Jenson.* His share in the plant of this firm is to be valued, and offered to the firm. His brother shall keep 500 ducats of the proceeds, and the remainder is to be placed against his debit account with the firm of Nicolas Jenson and Co. He leaves the following legacies: to his *compare* Jacotino de Rubeis, 100 ducats; to his *comare* Jacotino's wife, 200 ducats, both of gold; 50 ducats to the Church of *S. Pietro di Sommavera, in partibus suis gallie ubi sepultus est quondam Ser Jacobus ipsius testatoris pater;* 50 ducats to the Rainaldo, husband and wife; 50 ducats to his cousin Giovanna; 15 ducats to Pietro Benzon, the shopman in the warehouse of the company, and other bequests. From the sale of the plant he excepts his punches, which he bequeaths to his *compare* Peter Ugelleymer—*non intelligantur nec comprehendantur ponzoni cum quibus stampantur matres cum quibus matribus fiunt litteræ et projiciuntur, sed omnino ipse testator ipsos ponzones exceptuavit et exceptuat ac eos voluit et vult dominum Petrum Ugelleymer compatrem suum*

[1] Cicogna, *Inscr. Ven.*, vi. 954, 955.

[2] Jenson at the time of his death was a member of two firms, as appears from various passages in his Will; one was styled Nicolas Jenson and Co., *societate Nicolai Jenson et sociorum,* the other, formed later, John of Cologne and Nicolas Jenson, *sui heredes habuerint denarios ab ipsius testatoris societate nuncupata zan da Cologna et Nicolaus Jenson, aut a prima societate, Nicolaus Jenson et socii intitulata.*

[3] A small island of the Lagoon, between S. Giorgio Maggiore and S. Clemente; church destroyed.

dilectissimum habere debere et ipsos eidem domino Petro legavit et dimisit. Nicolò, his son, on reaching the age of twenty-five, is to receive the sum of 400 ducats, and Albert, his brother, is to supply Zanetta, the mother of Jenson's children, with food, clothes, and 12 ducats a year.

From this illness Jenson never recovered. He died in the same month of September, though we do not know the exact day. A contemporary, Felino Sandei, records his death in a note written in Sandei's own copy of Leonardo Aretino; it runs thus: *Venetiis obiit Nicolaus Jenson anno* 1480. *mense septembris, cum toto pene orbem libros sua arte atque suo ingenio impressos seminasset.*[1]

The firm of John of Cologne and Nicolas Jenson continued to work after Jenson's death, and a considerable number of books appear with Jenson's name still recorded as a partner in the firm. None of these, however, was issued during Jenson's life. The first of these publications with the imprint of the firm is Baldus, *Lectura super sexto Codicis*, dated *pridie Kalendas Decembris*, 1480,[2] rather more than two months after Jenson's death. The next year, 1481, gives us a continuation of this edition of Baldus in six volumes; also *Thomæ de Aquino, opus super quarto libro Sententiarum.*[3] But by the month of April, 1481, it appears that the provisions of Jenson's Will as regards his punches had been executed, and that the firm no longer possessed them. The *Apparatus Decretalium, Innocentii Papæ IV.*,[4] is dated *Olympiadibus dominicis Anno vero millesimo. cccclxxxi. tertias nonas Apriles;* at the end we find this statement: *exactum insigne hoc atque præclarum opus ductu auspitiis optimorum Joannis de Colonia Nicolai Jenson sociorumve Qui non tamen summam curam adhibuere ut sint hec et sua queque sine vicio et menda verum etiam ut bene sint elaborata atque jucundissimo litterarum caractere confecta ut unicuique prodesse possint et oblectare . . . . Huiusce autem operis artifex extitit summus in hac arte magister Joannes de Selgenstat alemanus qui sua solertia ac vigiliis divoque imprimendi caractere facile supereminet.* The Jenson type, his punches, had been withdrawn from the firm, and John of Cologne called upon Master John of Selgenstat to cut a new set. The Gothic type produced by John of Selgenstat is far inferior to the type employed by Jenson.

Jenson's name continued to appear in the imprint of the firm down to the end of the year 1481. His heirs had, under his Will, a pecuniary interest in the works which bear his name. After the year 1481 the name of Nicolas Jenson disappears from the annals of the Venetian Press.

[1] Sardini, *op. cit.*, lib. ii. p. 117.
[2] Hain, *2,297.
[3] Hain, *1,484. Holtrop, *Cat. B. R. H.*, 418.
[4] Marciana, cix. 3, 40,054.

CHAPTER III.

1469—1481.

HOW THEY PRINTED.

Roman, Gothic, and Greek character—Double columns—Signatures—Catchwords—Registers—Numeration—Imprints—Format—Capitals and initials—Colophons and prefaces—Paper—Ink—Cost of an edition—Partnerships.

THE three earliest Venetian printers, John and Windelin of Speyer and Nicolas Jenson, employed three kinds of character in their presses—Roman, Gothic, and Greek. Neither John of Speyer nor Nicolas Jenson used more than one fount of Roman minuscule type; that is to say, they used only one set of punches. John of Speyer's punches passed at his death to his brother Windelin, and were in use by John of Cologne in 1479.[1] Of Jenson's Roman type Sardini asserts that *niun bibliografo ha mai scoperto differenza alcuna nella qualità dei caratteri rotondi dello Jenson per tutto il corso che tenne aperto il suo negozio in Venezia*; and again, *ci siam dunque potuto avedere che uno solo sia il carattere rotondo minuscolo di Jenson.* This is true. The characteristics of the Jenson type[2] are maintained all through his work; and if we note a marked difference in the freshness and sharpness of the print of one year as compared with that of another, this is

[1] Dibdin, *Bib. Spenc.*, iii. 462, speaking of Platina's *Vitæ Pontificum*, 1479.

[2] 1. Jenson dots his *i*'s to the right hand of the letter; John of Speyer straight above the letter.

2. Jenson places his signs of contraction slightly to the right of the letter; John of Speyer straight above the letter.

3. Jenson prints *æ*; John of Speyer prints *ę*. Jenson's *h* is formed so; John of Speyer's is formed so, *h*.

4. Jenson uses ꝛ for *et* at the end and sometimes in the middle of words; I do not find John of Speyer doing so.

5. The stroke of Jenson's *d* is slightly prolonged below the loop.

6. The lower loop of Jenson's *g* slopes upwards from left to right.

7. The tail of Jenson's *q* is both shorter and thicker than John of Speyer's *q*.

8. Jenson has four ligatures, *ff*, *fi*, *ſſ*, and *ſt*; five signs of punctuation; five signs of contraction.

to be attributed to the fact that the more brilliant print is the result of a fresh casting from the old matrices, or possibly even from fresh matrices newly stamped from the original punches.[1]

Neither John of Speyer nor Nicolas Jenson debased or altered their Roman type; but this example was not followed by all their contemporaries in the art of printing. As the art spread and brought with it a demand for cheap books, the question of economy in space made itself felt as offering one of the principal means by which the price of books might be lowered. Roman type accordingly suffered changes. Under stress of this demand for economy in space, it underwent two modifications disastrous to its beauty; first, the loops of the letters were made oval instead of round; and, secondly, the strokes of the looped letters were allowed to encroach on a portion of the loop.

The early masters of printing in Venice began by using Roman character.[2] Renouard asserts that the return to Gothic character was forced upon the printers of Italy by the demands of the reading public for inexpensive books. There certainly was a large economy in space, and therefore in cost, secured by the use of Gothic type.[3] John of Speyer printed the few books he issued in Roman type; but his brother early began the use of Gothic. Windelin of Speyer and not Jenson[4] appears to have been the first printer in Italy to make use of Gothic character. In the year 1473 he issued Roberto di Litio's *Quadragesimale* in Gothic; and he continued occasionally to use that character; for example, in his edition of Dante,[5] 1477. St. Augustine's *De Civitate Dei* of 1475[6] is usually given as the earliest instance of Jenson's use of Gothic character. But Hain and Holtrop both cite *Gratiani Codex*,

[1] The way in which the type was produced was as follows: the artist first of all cut upon a punch of hard metal a raised form of each letter. The excellence of his fount depended on the skill with which he executed this part of his business; his whole artistic resources were expended to render the form on the punch as perfect as possible. Impressions were taken from these punches in soft metal, and these were called the matrices (matres) or moulds, from which the actual type was founded. The type, by use, might become blunt; the moulds, by use, might lose their clearness of line; but as long as the hard-metal punches retained their form intact, the typographer could always renew his fount. Punches lasted a long time. Jenson employed his one set during his eleven years of copious work, and they were worth bequeathing to his compare Ugelleymer in 1480. And the punches for the type from which Aldus printed Bembo's *Aetna*, in 1495, lasted sixty years from that date.

[2] The first book printed at Speyer, the *Postilla Scholastica*, 1471, is in Roman character. Castellani, *La Stampa, &c.*, p. 11. Serna, 1,141.

[3] Sardini, *op. cit.*, proves how great that saving is. He calculates that the *Mamotrectus* of Jenson (1479), if printed in its equivalent Roman character, would occupy double and four per cent. more space than it does in Gothic.

[4] Audifredi makes it a reproach to Jenson that he introduced Gothic character to the Italian press. Sardini cites as proof to the contrary the Litio of 1472, ascribing it to Windelin of Speyer. The Litio of 1472 is by Franz Renner of Hailbrun, and is in Roman character. The Litio in Gothic by Windelin is dated 1473. Neither in Hain.

[5] Hain, 5,942.

[6] Hain, *2,051.

En hic ille est de illis maxime: qui irridere: atq; obiurgare me solitus est: quod me non tecum (præsertim cum abs te honorificentissime inuitarer) cõiungererẽ. ἀλλ' ἐμὸν οὔποτε θυμὸν ἐνὶ στήθεσσιν ἔπειθεν audiebã enĩ pceres clamitãtis. Sed tamẽ idem me cõsolatur etiam hominẽ perustum: & inanem: gloria uolunt incendere atq; ita loquuntur.

Sed me minus iam mouent ut uides. Itaq; ab Homeri magni eloquentia cõfero me ad uera præcepta εὐριπίδου. μισῶ σοφιστὴν ὅστις οὐχ αὑτῷ σοφός quem uersum senex Præcilius laudat egregie: & ait posse eundem: & ἅμα πρόσσω καὶ ὀπίσσω uidere: & tamen nihilominus αἰὲν ἀριστεύειν καὶ ὑπείροχον ἔμμεναι ἄλλων

JENSON. CICERO, *Epistolæ Familiares.* 1471.

1474,[1] as printed by Jenson in Gothic, and we take this work to be the first example of his use of that character. The *De Civitate* is a beautiful book, and we understand the abundant testimony to the excellence of Jenson's Gothic character which is borne by his contemporary Felino Sandei in a note appended to his own copy of the Decretals. The note is dated October 18th, 1502, and runs thus: *Permutavi cum fratribus Sanctæ Mariæ Novæ de Urbe, quorum erat hoc Decretum, dedique eis aliud Decretum, novissime impressum Venetiis a Tortis in forma solemni et ligatum tectumque pulcre, dono etiam dedi eis Decretales sextum et Clementinas in bona forma et ligatas, hæc ideo quoniam caracteres litterarum Nicolai Jensonis, quibus hoc Decretum impressum est, aptiores clarioresque et senilibus occulis commodiores expertus sum.* From the year 1474 onwards Jenson reserved his Roman type chiefly for the classics, and constantly uses Gothic character for the production of sacred books and for works on Canon Law—the publications which most probably acquired for him his reputation in Rome and his honours from the Papal Court. The majority of these publications are splendid specimens of printing, but it cannot be denied that occasionally some of Jenson's Gothic printing, notably in the *Mamotrectus* of 1479,[2] is not worthy of his high repute.

As regards the use of Greek by these earliest Venetian printers. John of Speyer did not cut any Greek character. The Greek passages in his *Epistolæ Familiares* of 1469 are left blank, to be filled in by hand. Jenson was the first to introduce Greek character to the Venetian printing press.[3] The earliest instance of Greek printing which issued from Jenson's press is to be found in his edition of the *Epistolæ Familiares* of 1471. The character has been copied from no particular hand.[4] Neither in the *Vallæ Elegantiæ*,[5] nor in the *Suetonii Vitæ*,[6] both of this year, is there any Greek printing; blank spaces are left for the Greek passages. Greek character appears, however, in the *Tortellii Orthographia* of 1471[7]; in the Aulus Gellius of 1472,[8] and in the Macrobius[9] of the same year; in the Diogenes Laertius of 1475[10]; and in the Nonius Marcellus of 1476.[11] Throughout all these works the Greek fount remains unaltered, and it is probable that Jenson never had more than one set of Greek punches. But though he possessed a fount of Greek type, Jenson never essayed to print a Greek book. Indeed, the instances of Greek books in Italy before the date of Aldus are very rare. Milan leads the way with Lascaris' Greek Grammar in 1476; and

[1] *Catalogus B. R. H.*, 404. Hain, *7,886. [2] Hain, *10,559.

[3] The *Lactantius*, printed at Subiaco by Sweynheym and Pannartz in 1465, is said to contain the first Greek character printed in Italy.

[4] The Greek alphabet is complete. There are two forms of pi (π and ϖ). The breathings and accents have been cut with the letters, and there are three ligatures, σσ, σr, σθ.

[5] Hain, 15,802. [6] Hain, *15,117. [7] Hain, *15,564.

[8] Hain, 7,519. [9] Hain, 10,426. [10] Hain, *6,199. [11] Hain, 11,901.

Venice follows in 1484-5, 5 Feb., with Pellegrino da Bologna's edition of Chrysoloras' *Erotemata* in Greek and Latin.[1]

With Jenson the practice of printing in double columns began when he made his first publication in Gothic character, Gratian's *Codex*, in 1474. From that date onwards it is his custom when using Gothic to print in double columns. Only one instance is cited where Jenson printed in double columns and in Roman character, that is, Jacopo da Voragine's *Le legende di tutti li sancti et le sancte*.[2]

The earliest books very rarely have either signatures, catchwords, registers, or numeration of leaf or of page. This is the more remarkable as in the fifteenth century it was not unusual for copyists to employ both signatures, catchwords, and numeration in their manuscripts.[3] In the earliest printed books, however, they are very rare; though instances are cited of signatures in manuscript[4]—whether by a contemporary hand or not, is not stated. The Varro, *De Lingua Latina*,[5] ascribed to John of Cologne, and to the year 1474, is an instance of the early use of signatures. It is not till the year 1476 that we find Jenson using signatures. That year gives us the following issues from his press with signed gathers: *Nova Compilatio Decretalium*[6]; *Clementis Papæ V. Constitutiones*[7] (these two in Gothic character); and, in Roman character, *Nonius Marcellus, De proprietate sermonum*.[8] From the year 1476 onwards Jenson uses signatures in every publication by him that we have seen.

The first book printed with catchwords in Venice is the first book issued by Windelin of Speyer alone, without the concurrence of his brother John.[9] It is the *editio princeps* of Tacitus' *Annales*,[10] undated, but assigned to the year 1470. It is said to be the first book printed with catchwords in Italy. In no instance that we can quote does Jenson use catchwords in his books printed in Gothic or in Roman character.

Two kinds of register were in use among the early Venetian printers. We find registers of the signatures of the sheets, stating whether they are *ternions, quaternions, quinions*, &c. Or we find a register composed of the signature of the sheet and the first word on the recto of each leaf[11] in each gather up to the middle of the gather; thereby indicating whether the gather

[1] Didot, *op. cit.* Legrand, *Bibliographie Hellénique*, Paris, 1885, vol. i., No. 2, cites an edition s. l. a. et typ., but assigns it to Florence and the year 1484.

[2] Sardini, iii. p. 37. Not in Hain. Marciana, 40,407.

[3] *e.g.*, Marciana, *Lat. Cod.* ccccxiv.

[4] See Quaritch, *Mon. Typographica*, ii., No. 36,464.

[5] Hain, 15,858.

[6] Holtrop, *Cat. B. R. H.*, 407.

[7] Holtrop, *Cat. B. R. H.*, 408.

[8] Hain, 11,901.

[9] The colophon describes it as *artis gloria prima sue.*

[10] Hain, *15,218, wrongly ascribed to John of Speyer.

[11] Which would be the catchword of the leaf if catchwords were used.

is a *ternion*, *quaternion*, or *quinion*, &c. The register is the printer's instruction to the binder how he is to bind up the sheets; whether they are in gathers of four, five, or six, &c. In the case of Jenson we find signatures before we find registers. The earliest instance of a register issuing from his press is in the Plutarch of 1478.[1] It is a register of the second kind—a register by the first words of the recto of each leaf, not a register of the signatures of the sheets; and in no case does he seem to have used any other kind of register.

The practice of numbering the leaf or the page comes later than the use of signatures or catchwords. It may have been introduced to suit the convenience of scholars, when they began to discover that, by the aid of printing, they could discuss disputed passages with other scholars at a distance through the simple method of reference to page and line of identical editions. We are not able to quote any instances in which Jenson numbered his leaves. In the year 1480 the leaves of the Thomas Aquinas, *De Veritate*, are unnumbered, but the numeration of the books is given, *Liber Primus*, *Liber Secundus*, &c. We find earlier instances of this numeration of books in the *De Civitate Dei*, by Jenson, in 1475. But it is certain that Jenson very rarely, if ever, used numeration of leaves or pages, and that it was quite a late development of the printers' habit and custom.

It was certainly the usual practice of these early Venetian printers to place their own name and the place of printing in their books. All four[2] works in which John of Speyer had a share, show his name, the place of printing, and the year. Jenson's editions almost all bear his name, the place, and the year, either in a separate imprint or in a colophon. The *Decor Puellarum*, as already observed, is an exception to the rule; it has Jenson's name, but not the place of printing. The devotional series of 1471, the *Decor Puellarum*, the *Parole Devote*, the *Palma Virtutum*, and the *Gloria Mulierum*, do not give the place of printing, and the last does not give the printer's name. In the year 1471, Jenson, for the first time, adopts more accurate dating than by the year only. In the *Æmilii Probi*, (Cornelius Nepos) *De Vita excellentium*[3] he gives year, month, and day. So, too, in the Quintilian and in the *Parole Devote* of the same year; in the Decretals of 1475 and the St. Augustine of the same year; in the Plutarch of 1478-9. But it cannot be said that the printer had any rule on the subject; his tendency is to use the full date more frequently as time goes on. But, although it was the custom for printers to name themselves, the place, and the date, the exceptions to the rule are numerous. Both Jenson and Windelin of Speyer sometimes omit one or other or all of these notes; and other printers frequently do so. Indeed, the number of unclaimed books, whose parent and whose birthplace it

[1] Hain, *13,127. Sardini, iii. p. 50.

[2] Omitting the one volume of the Livy.

[3] Hain, *5,733.

is difficult to determine, is very large—surprisingly large when we remember the high esteem in which printers were held, and the large claims they make upon the gratitude of their own age, and upon immortality in the future.

It is with a view to the proper assignment of these *editiones ancipites* that the late Mr. Bradshaw's method is so valuable. Until all the distinguishing characteristics of each known typographer are collected and displayed in precisely the same way as the characteristics of a genus in natural history are collected and displayed, the ascription of unclaimed books must always remain a matter more or less of conjecture.

The format of the earliest books printed in Venice was usually folio or quarto. The instances of octavo before Aldus are very rare.[1] The size, however, both of folio and of quarto varies very considerably, according to the size of the original sheet before it was folded. This variation in size induced printers and booksellers to modify the terms folio and quarto, and to talk of *folio grande*, *folio piccolo*, and so with the term quarto, in the hope of giving a more accurate idea of the real size of the volume. But these terms are too vague; the variations are too numerous to be classed under so few headings, and the only satisfactory method by which the size of a volume can be described is by giving the height and the width of the composition.[2] John of Speyer adopted folio form for the few works which he lived to print, and he was followed in this practice, almost without an exception, by his brother Windelin; though we have the undated Martial, in quarto, ascribed to Windelin and to the year 1471. Jenson's earliest editions are also in folio; but in 1471 he began to print the series of small devotional works in quarto, and continued to issue quartos and folios till the close of his career.

It was the custom to print these early books without capitals at the beginnings of the paragraphs or chapters. A large space was left in which the letter might be hand-painted in colours, and frequently as an indication to the illuminator, that he might not mistake the letter he had to paint, the letter in minuscule was printed in the blank space to be occupied by the illuminated capital, and the second letter of the first word of the chapter or paragraph was printed in majuscule, probably to modify the too great disparity in size between the illuminated capital and the minuscules which composed

[1] As an example we have the *Pisanello*, printed by Paganino de Paganini in 1485. Hain, *2,166.

[2] These are the measurements of six folios by Jenson in the years 1470 and 1471:

Eusebius	h. 223 mm. w. 135 „	Aretino	h. 180 mm. w. 106 „
Justinus	h. 170 „ w. 101 „	Valla	h. 222 „ w. 117 „
Cicero	h. 220 „ w. 175 „	Tortelli	h. 267 „ w. 110 „

the rest of the word. Many of the illuminated capitals in these early Venetian books are worked in gold and colours, with beautiful designs of interlacing ribbon, in the same style as the capitals which adorn the MSS. of Cardinal Bessarion, and other MSS. of the fifteenth century. Sometimes the initial letters of the chapter or paragraph were not illuminated, but merely rubricated by hand. Neither illumination nor rubrication by hand, however, belong to the subject of early Venetian printing. Later on we shall have to call attention to the printed rubrics, and to the floriated, foliated, and storied initials in use among subsequent masters, but neither of the prototypographers of Venice employed them.

No parts of a book are more useful to the bibliographical student than the prefaces and the colophons. It is in these that the printer usually inserts as much of the history of the book as he desires to communicate to the reader. Among the early Venetian printers the colophon frequently consists of verses in honour of the typographer and his art, and sometimes lays claim to the honours of a first edition [1] or refers to a first edition printed elsewhere.[2] The colophons frequently contain extravagant laudation of the printer. Jenson's colophons are, as a rule, more modest than those of Windelin of Speyer. It is only towards the close of Jenson's career, in the dedication of the St. Thomas Aquinas of 1480, that we find such lavish encomiums as the following: *Nicolaus Jenson gallicus vir imprimis catholicus : erga omnes gratus : beneficus : liberalis : verax : constans : pulcritudine : magnitudine : fidelitateque impremendi : in toto terrarum orbe : pace omnium dixerim : primus.*

In the headings and the colophons of these early books the influence of the manuscript makes itself felt in such phrases as *incipit ; feliciter finit ; explicit ; Deo gratias ;* ἐγράφη, of the Aldine Musæus. But there is an immense difference in the sense of labour expressed by the scribe and the ease and rapidity claimed by the printer. Compare such phrases as, *Quia qui nescit scribere putat hoc esse nullum laborem. O quam gravis est scriptura : oculos gravat, renes frangit, simul et omnia membra contristat. Tria digita scribunt, totus corpus laborat,*[3] with—

Fessa manus quondam, moneo, calamusque quiescat :
Namque labor studio cessit et ingenio.[4]

A great variety of terms is used to express the different parts taken by

[1] Windelin of Speyer's Quintus Curtius, s. a., but ascribed to 1470. Hain, *5,878.

[2] Cf. Cicero's Epistles. Jenson, 1470. *Attice, nunc totus Veneta diffunderis urbe, Cum quondam fuerit copia rara tui*, referring, perhaps, to the Roman edition of the same year. And Windelin's Lactantius, 1472, refers to the Roman edition of 1468, in these lines: *Presserat hunc primo mundi caput inclyta Roma ; Post regina premit nempe colenda maris.*

[3] From the Westgoth Rechtsbuch ap. Wattenbach, *Schriftwesen im Mittelalter*, Leipzig, 1875, p. 235.

[4] John of Speyer's Pliny, 1469.

the various members of a printing house in the production of a book. We find such words as *impensis; sumptibus; opera; cura; studio; manu; digitis; labore; per; confectus ab; compositus per.* It is not easy to distinguish the exact meaning of all these words as regards the art of printing, and it is possible that they were used in no very close and rigid sense by the printers themselves. Yet, generally speaking, *impensis* and *sumptibus* refer to the capital furnished (like the Greek δαπάνῃ of Aldus and the ἀναλώμασι of the Greek editions by Vlastos and Caliergi[1]); *manu, labore,* and *digitis* refer to the actual mechanical part of the work, the pressing, &c. (like the πόνῳ καὶ δεξιότητι of Vlastos and Caliergi[2]); *cura* and *studio* perhaps refer to the correction and revision of the text (like the διορθώσει και ἐπιμελείᾳ of many later Greek editions[3]); *confectus ab* and *compositus per* indicate the composition or setting up of the type in the forme (like the συνθηκῄ of Aldus[4]). As an example we quote the colophon of the edition of Æsop's Fables, printed at Modena in 1481[5]: *Mutinæ. Impressus impensa et opera Dominici Rhochociola per Thomam septem castrensem et Joannem Franciscum socios, compositus per me Nicolaum Jenson,* which seems to mean that the book was printed at Modena through the initiative and at the charges of Rhochociola, by Thomas of the seven castles and John Francis in company, from type set up by Nicolas Jenson.[6]

One of the reasons which induced so many foreign printers to settle in Venice was the excellence of the paper and the ease and cheapness with which it could be obtained. The first rag paper was made somewhere about the year 1300; and the trade of paper making soon took root in Italy.[7] At Parma, Bologna, Pescia, Lucca, and Fabriano, famous manufactories were established. At Padua a paper mill was at work as early as the year 1366; and in 1373 the Senate forbade the exportation of rags from the Venetian dominions. The account book of the Ripoli printing press (1474) has preserved to us the prices which were paid for some of these papers.[8] For example, Bologna, large folio, was the most expensive; it cost 6 lire 8 soldi the ream; Bologna, medium, cost 3 lire 10 soldi; Bologna, inferior, cost 3 lire. Fabriano, with the mark of the catapult, cost 3 lire

[1] Legrand, *op. cit.*, i. cxxv.

[2] Legrand, *loc. cit.*

[3] *e.g.*, Legrand, *op. cit.*, ii., No. 270, 272, 282.

[4] Didot, *op. cit.*, p. 37, where the Latin equivalent of συνθηκῄ is *compositio.*

[5] Panzer, ii. p. 147. Hain, 294.

[6] Panzer and Apostolo Zeno have determined that this Jenson is not our Nicolas Jenson. Their arguments are not convincing. They have to suppose the existence of another Nicolas Jenson, printer, of whom we know nothing else. See Morelli, *Codices Naniani*, p. 153.

[7] Symonds, *Renaissance in Italy*, ii. 371. We find one Collo da Colle, in 1377, renting a fall of water in the Val d'Elsa, near Florence, to drive his mill.

[8] Fineschi, *Notizie storiche sopra la Stamperia di Ripoli.* Firenze, 1781, p. 48.

the ream; and with the mark of the Maltese cross, cost 2 lire 6 soldi. Paper from Colle cost the same. Prato paper cost 2 lire 10 soldi; and paper from Pescia, with the mark of the eye-glasses, 2 lire 18 soldi, and with the mark of the gloves, 2 lire 8 soldi.[1] Each of these paper manufactories had its distinguishing water-mark. Sardini has made a catalogue of these water-marks and the date of their first appearance[2] in Jenson's publications. An examination of his work proves that he by no means confined himself to paper of one manufactory. His earliest works show the marks of the balances, the catapult, and the cross arrows more frequently than any other.

Besides paper, vellum was used by the early Venetian printers for the production of a few *exemplaires de luxe*; for example, the *De Civitate Dei* of 1475, by Jenson; the *editio princeps* of Plautus, by John of Cologne and Windelin of Speyer, published in 1472; and Jenson's Breviary of 1478; the Virgil of 1470, by Windelin, and the same printer's Petrarch of the same year.

In the accounts of the Ripoli Press, already quoted, we find a bill for the materials required to make ink. These materials are linseed oil, turpentine, greek pitch, black pitch, marcassite, cinnabar, rosin, solid and liquid varnish, gall, vitriol, and lac. Receipts for the manufacture of ink are to be found in the various pamphlets on caligraphy published in Venice during the sixteenth century.[3] The Venetian writers recommend the use of wine for dissolving the gall. Wattenbach[4] quotes a receipt for ink from a Codex of the year 1412, in which small beer is recommended. The receipt is German: *Ad faciendum bonum incaustum*, it runs, *Recipe gallas et contere minute in pulverem; funde desuper aquam pluvialem vel cerevisiam tenuem, et impone de vitalo quantum sufficit juxta existimationem tuam et permitte sic stare per aliquot dies et tunc colla per pannum et erit incaustus bonus. Et si vis* (*scl. scribere*) *tunc impone modicum de gummi arabico, et calefac modicum circa ignem ut solus incaustus tepidus fiat, et erit incaustus bonus, et indelibilis, super quocunque cum eo scribis.*

The business of printing was costly, but at the outset the heaviest charges fell, not for the actual printing materials, but for the purchase, the collation, and the correction of manuscripts. In this respect the classics, in which the question of the text was much in dispute, and the ingenuity of scholars alive, must have been the most expensive. As an instance of how much an edition of the Bible cost at this period, and as a good example of a

[1] Sardini, *op. cit.*, ii. p. 147. But prices had risen by the year 1548, see Paul Manutius' Price List. Didot, *op. cit.*, p. 116.

[2] For the Fabriano water-marks, see Aurelio Zonghi, *Marche di carta di Fabriano dal* 1293 *al* 1599, Fabriano, 1881.

[3] Marcian Library, Miscellanea, 2,061, *Calligrafia*.

[4] *Op. cit.*, p. 197.

contract between a publisher and a printer, we may take the notarial agreement concluded on March 14th, 1478, between *Leonardus quondam Ser Girardi de la Ymania de Rassani*, printer, dwelling in the parish of San Benedetto, and *Nicolaus quondam domini Arigini de Franchaforte theotonicus.* Master Leonard shall print well and diligently, in good faith and without fraud, nine hundred and thirty Bibles on common paper, for Nicolaus. The expenses shall be borne by Master Leonard; and he must deliver the Bibles within next June; nor during this period, nor for nine months after, may he print nor cause to be printed any other Bibles. Nicolaus shall pay Master Leonard four hundred and thirty golden ducats, and shall furnish all the paper required. Payment shall be made in this way: upon the consignment of every quinternion of all the copies, Nicolaus shall pay five ducats. Of the nine hundred and thirty copies, Master Leonard shall have twenty for himself. Nicolaus shall furnish as much paper as Master Leonard may demand, and Master Leonard shall be bound to reprint any copies which are not to the satisfaction of Nicolaus.

The Bible in question is possibly the Bible cited by Le Long[1] as *impressa Venetiis per Leonardum de Wild de Ratisbona expensis Nicolai de Franckofordia. M.CCCC.LXXVIII.* If so, the contract was executed. From the petition of Paganino de Paganini,[2] if he spoke the truth, we learn that the current price of a Bible with the ordinary glossary was, in the year 1492, twelve ducats, and Nicolo de Lyra's commentary cost five ducats. Paganino intended to spend four thousand ducats on printing the Bible, Glossary, and Commentary[3] all together, and promises not to charge more than six ducats for the whole, but he does not say how many copies he intended to print. But if Paganino could recoup himself for an outlay of four thousand (silver?) ducats by selling at six ducats, it is clear that Nicolaus of Frankfort must have made a large profit by selling his Bible at twelve ducats. The price of Bibles varied very much, however, for we find such widely differing entries in the Bookseller's day-book of 1484,[4] as *Bibia con Nicolo de Lira, lire* 3, and *Bibia con Nicolo de lira, ligata, ducati* 5.[5] It is difficult to translate these various figures into terms of our currency; but supposing we take the golden ducat to be worth a little over one pound sterling, this would make the cost of an edition of the Bible, of nearly one thousand copies, in 1478, about five hundred pounds of our money, not counting paper.[6]

[1] *Bibliotheca Sacra*, contin. ab A. G. Masch, iii. p. 125. Cf. Fulin, *op. cit.*, p. 21.

[2] Fulin, *op. cit.*, pp. 24, 25.

[3] See Le Long, iv. 378. Hain, 3,174.

[4] See below, chap. v.

[5] See extracts from day-book in Appendix.

[6] See Gallicciolli, *Memorie Venete*, Venezia, 1795, i. 484, where the value of the golden ducat in 1450 is given as lire 6, soldi 4. But Renouard, *op. cit.*, iii. 248, gives the value of the golden ducat in modern equivalent at a far lower figure. He there takes the ducat at about ten shillings of our coinage.

The production of books being costly, it is not surprising to find that these early printers frequently entered into partnerships for the purposes of their business. For instance, John of Cologne and Windelin of Speyer were associated, in 1472, for the production of the *editio princeps* of Plautus;[1] from 1473 to 1480 John of Cologne is associated with Manthen de Gheretzem, *qui una Veneciis fidelitur vivunt*, they say of themselves; Bernard Pictor, Erhard Ratdolt, and Peter Loslein were in partnership from 1476 to 1478. If we may judge from the analogy of a similar association in Milan, these partnerships were drawn up in due legal form. The Milanese contract[2] is dated 10th of May, 1472, and the contracting parties are Antonio Zarotto of Parma, Pietro Gabriele, Maestro Cola, Pedro Antonio de Burgo and Gabriel Pavero de Fontana. Zarotto of Parma is to cut the type and prepare the ink; the four other members of the company are to supply the funds for carrying on the business. The rent of the premises is to be borne by all five equally. Of the profits, one third is to go to Zarotto, the remaining two thirds to be divided equally among the four other members. The association is to last for three years, and no one of the members may withdraw before the expiry of that term. Gabriel Pavero is elected treasurer and rector of the company; he is to be responsible for its books, utensils, manuscripts, &c. His pay for this service shall be one copy of every work which issues from the presses of the company. The consent of all the partners is necessary to the undertaking of any business transaction. Payment to the reader, copier, and corrector is to be made in books which issue from the press. The copies given to the members of the company, in payment of special services, are not to be put upon the market at a price lower than the company's selling price. The members are not to have any connection with other printing houses, and are bound to secrecy about the business operations of their company. After the expiry of three years no member is obliged to remain in the company. If the company is broken up, the plant shall belong to Antonio Zarotto, after he shall have satisfied the claims of his companions. The company opens with three presses.

It is Antonio Zarotto, the typefounder and master printer, who is the chief person in the company, and to him falls the largest share of the gains; Gabriel Pavero, the editor, ranks only equally with the other members of the firm. It is remarkable that the typefounder should be by far the most important person in a society of printers and publishers.

[1] Hain, 13,074.

[2] Sardini, iii. p. 85.

CHAPTER IV.

1470—1515.

FROM JENSON TO ALDUS.

The spread of the art—German printers—Christopher Valdarfer—Clemente da Padova—Philippus Venetus—Erhard Ratdolt, Bernard Pictor, and Peter Loslein—The brothers de Gregoriis, Matheo de Co de ca—Benalius de Benaliis—Andrea de Torresani—Ottaviano Scotto—Alessandro Paganino—The book-buying public and the book-market—Extension of the market, and decline in the quality of books.

HE brothers John and Windelin of Speyer and Nicolas Jenson, though they were the first to open presses in Venice, were by no means alone in their trade. Almost contemporaneously with these masters we find other printers flocking into Venice from Germany and other parts of Italy. The rapid expansion of the new art, and the large proportions it assumed immediately after its first appearance, are very striking, and gave promise that Venice would soon become the most important centre of printing in Europe. In the decade between the years 1470 and 1480, we find the names of no fewer than fifty typographers, many of them masters of first-rate importance, who were at work in Venice. Very many of these were Germans. A variety of reasons contributed to draw these Germans to the capital of the Republic. Her geographical position—her proximity to one of the great passes, the Brenner, which led right into the heart of Germany—and as a consequence of this geographical position, the large and powerful colony of German merchants who frequented the city; the presence of the great German change, the Fondaco dei Tedeschi,[1] where every German had an opportunity for meeting his fellow-countrymen, for hearing and sending news, for despatching and receiving goods—all these advantages tended to draw German printers to Venice upon their first arrival in Italy. At the first appearance of the

[1] Cf. Simonsfeld, *Der Fondaco dei Tedeschi in Venedig.* Stuttgart, 1887, ii. p. 287.

PIANGENDO. NOua
mente de christiani le cala-
mitade e lacerbissima pdita
di negroponte : da parte toa mi fono
presetate littere : ne le quale hauendo
lecto quel che de lanimo de la maiesta
de del Re e feruore grandissimo a difendere la Christiana fede scriueui :
ricolsi un pocho la mente : e pigliai
fiato : e cominciai a pregar dio che ne
lefecto dimostrasse quel che cũ parole
lui hauer promesso tu afferme : Ma
sciagurati nui : chio temo che per li
peccati nostri dal inmortai dio abon-
donati non sostegniamo ancora piu
crudeli e piu graui dãni : e finalmẽte
tardãdo e luno a laltro risguardãdo :
la colpa ne gli altri ributãdo : a lultia
dissatione nõ cadamo : O miseri chri
stiani : o ciechi italiani : Afreciamosse
O Bessarione : o che di questo mondo
cum uoler di Dio ne la sempiterna
uita passiamo : o ĩ qualche altro paese

VALDARFER. BESSARION, *Oratio*. 1471.

di tutti del tuō uulgare parlare ti sia
ssisa il riceuuto comandamento chel
tuo principio palesa . Serua adũque
i porti mandati e de beni del tuo pa-
tre non essere ditratore uiui & di me
tuo factore sempre nella mente il no
me porta la chui uita nele mani dela
tua donna amorosa conserua .

Il libro del philocolo di mesere iohã
ne boccatio da certaldo poeta illustre
qui finiscie. Impresso p maestro Gabriele di piero: & del cõpagno maestro Philipot in lalma patria Venetia
nelli ãni del signore. M.cccc.l xxii.
a giorni. xx. di nouembre : Nicolo
throno duce felicissimo imperante .

GABRIELE DI PIERO AND MÆSTRO PHILIPO
BOCCACCIO, *Philocolo*. 1472.

art, printing society in Venice must have been largely German in character. We know that Jenson, for example, had two *compatres* (godfathers to his children, or to whose children he had stood sponsor), both of them German—Johann Rauchfas (Rocfas), who calls Jenson *mio compare*,[1] and Peter Ugelleymer, whom Jenson calls *compater meus dilectissimus*.[2]

It would be beyond the scope of this study, which is chiefly historical, to follow all these early presses throughout their separate careers. It must suffice here to call attention to one or two of the more remarkable among them, with a view to noting the development of the new art by the introduction of features unknown to its earliest exponents.

Almost contemporaneously with the first masters other printers opened their presses in Venice. Even as early as the year 1470, the year in which Jenson began to print, Christopher Valdarfer of Regensburg set up his press and issued the *De Oratore* of Cicero[3]; the *editio princeps*, unless Sweynheym's Roman edition of the same year has priority, of Cicero's Orations[4] appeared in 1471, and also the earliest edition of the Decameron,[5] the edition which is said to have been destroyed at the burning of the Vanities at Florence by Savonarola's followers in the year 1497.[6] The productions of Valdarfer's Venetian press are rare and very few. By 1473 he was in Milan,[7] and he continued to print there till 1488.

In June of the year 1471, we find the first record of an Italian typographer printing in Venice. In that year Clemente of Padua (*Clemens sacerdos*) published the medical work of Mesue, *De Medicinis universalibus*. The work is preceded by a letter of the Venetian Doctor Nicolò Gupalatino, in the course of which the writer praises Clement: *omnium quos novi in Dædaleo præsertim et manuali opere ingeniosissimus . . . Italorum primus libros hac arte formavit*.[8] The following year, 1472, saw the issue of the first book printed by a Venetian; it is Boccaccio's *Philocolo*,[9] the work of Filippo, son of Piero (*Philippus Petri*, as he styles himself, and later, in 1478, after Peter's death, *Philippus quondam Petri*).

The adoption of floriated and foliated borders and initials, in the place of the illuminated or rubricated initials produced by hand in the case of the earliest Venetian printers, is one of the most important advances achieved by subsequent printers. The first example of a book printed in Italy with ornamentation of this sort is said to be Cardinal Torquemada's *Meditationes*,

[1] *Archivio Veneto*, xxxiii. 457. [2] Jenson's Will, *ut sup.* Simonsfeld, ii. 69, 284.
[3] Hain, *5,100. [4] Hain, 5,122.
[5] Hain, 3,272. [6] Pasquale Villari, *La Storia di Savonarola*, i. 506.
[7] Sardini, *op. cit.*, iii. p. 88, who gives a contract, signed at Milan, to which Valdarfer is a party.
[8] Sardini, iii. p. 96. Hain, 11,107, *s. l. et typ. n.* Castellani, *La Stampa*, &c., p. 28.
[9] Hain, 3,296.

published in Rome by Ulrich Han in 1467.[1] In North Italy the earliest specimen of illustration is the *Valturii De re militari*, Verona, 1472,[2] with eighty-two designs of military engines by Matteo Pasti. This was for long supposed to be the first book printed with designs in North Italy. But recently the Vicomte Delaborde[3] has called attention to the Valerius Maximus, printed at Venice by Windelin of Speyer in the year 1471,[4] which possesses a large ornamented capital on the recto of the third leaf.

Though it is possible to cite these early instances of illustration, the practice did not become common in Venice till it was introduced by the famous association of Erhard Ratdolt, Bernard Pictor, and Peter Loslein of Langenzenn, who printed in company from 1476 to 1478. This famous press, as remarkable for the beauty of its type as for its illustrations, produced in its first year Johann Müller's [Monteregionis] *Calendarium*,[5] with a flowered border round the title-page, at the foot of which the following words appear in rubric :

Bernardus pictor de Augusta
Petrus loslein de Langencen
Erhardus ratdolt de Augusta

The page contains a sonnet with a *coda*, beginning—

Questa opra da ogni parte e un libro doro.

The volume contains the five following illustrations—

Tables of the eclipses of the moon.
Lo instrumento de le hore inequale.
Lo instrumento del vero moto de la luna.
El quadrante del Horologio horizontale.
El quadrato generale de le hore.

We also find the *Sphera mundi*[6] of *Magister Jo. de Sacroboscho* (John Holywood) ascribed to this year and this press; and the following year (1477), *Coriolani Cepionis, Petri Mocenici Imperatoris gestorum libri III.*,[7] with flowered initials, and the recto of first leaf within a flowered border, at the bottom of which appear two shields crossed. The colophon runs—

Impressum est hoc opusculum Venetiis per
Bernardum pictorem et Erhard ratdolt
de Augusta, una cum Petro loslein de
Langencen correctore ac socio Laus Deo.
MCCCCLXXVII.

[1] Fisher, p. 306. Hain, 15,722. Woodcuts. Delaborde, *La graveur en Italie*, Paris, 1883, cap. v.

[2] Hain, *15,847. Fisher, p. 314.

[3] *Op. cit.*, p. 252. Fisher, p. 315.

[4] Hain, 15,775.

[5] Hain, 13,789.

[6] Not in Hain.

[7] Hain, *4,849. 4to.; Roman character; leaves 54, not numbered; no catchwords; signatures a, b, c, d, e, f, in 4, g, a 3; no register.

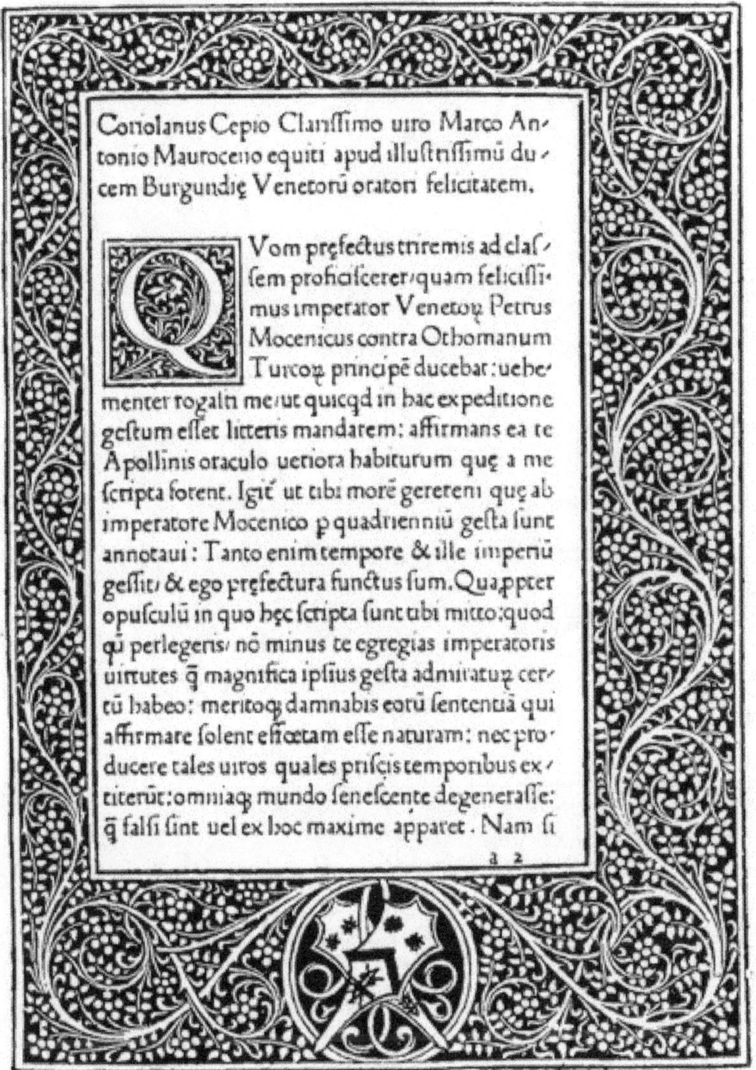

Coriolanus Cepio Clarissimo uiro Marco Antonio Mauroceno equiti apud illustrissimū ducem Burgundię Venetorū oratori felicitatem.

QVom pręfectus triremis ad classem proficiscerer/quam felicissimus imperator Venetorꝫ Petrus Mocenicus contra Othomanum Turcorꝫ principē ducebat: uehementer rogasti me/ut quicqd in hac expeditione gestum esset litteris mandarem: affirmans ea te Apollinis oraculo ueriora habiturum quę a me scripta forent. Igit̄ ut tibi morē gererem quę ab imperatore Mocenico ꝑ quadrienniū gesta sunt annotaui: Tanto enim tempore & ille imperiū gessit/ & ego pręfectura functus sum. Quaꝑpter opusculū in quo hęc scripta sunt tibi mitto: quod qū perlegeris/ nō minus te egregias imperatoris uirtutes q̄ magnifica ipsius gesta admiraturꝫ certū habeo: meritoqꝫ damnabis eorū sententiā qui affirmare solent effœtam esse naturam: nec producere tales uiros quales priscis temporibus extiterūt: omniaqꝫ mundo senescente degenerasse: q̄ falsi sint uel ex hoc maxime apparet. Nam si

a 2

RATDOLT. CORIOLANUS CEPIO, *Mocenici Gesta*. 1477.

Venetiarũ ciuitas incly-
ta condit̃: aut pot⁹ amplia-
circa hec tpa: ãno. 450. non
a pastorib⁹ sicut Roma: sz
a potentiorib⁹ et ditioribus
puinciarũ aduenis: illic ꝑ
psecutiões attile ꝯfugiẽtib⁹
Mirũ ē et sũmo extollendũ
laudis preconio: potuisse a
tot tãq3 diuersis vrbiũ et op
pidorũ ꝑlis ꝯditã ciuitate:
p ãnos mille cũ tali incre-
mẽto ac glie splẽdore: vna-
nimiq3 sagacitate ꝯfuare.

RATDOLT. *Fasciculus temporum.* 1480.

This also is a beautiful book, possessing the usual characteristics of Ratdolt's type.[1] In the same year (1477) the company issued the Dionysius, *De situ orbis*,[2] with flowered capitals and a flowered border, and the earliest specimen of the Greek character of this press. The colophon is precisely the same as that of the Cepio, only that Loslein is called *eorum correctore ac socio*. When the association of these three artists came to an end in the year 1478, Ratdolt continued to work alone, and produced many illustrated volumes. In the year 1480 he published *Chronica, seu Fasciculus Temporum*,[3] with flowered capitals and border, and on leaf 3 verso, a picture of Noah's ark, and on leaf 37 verso, a view of Venice, with the ducal palace. Monteregionis' (Johann Müller) *Ephemerides*[4] followed next year; and in 1482 Euclid's *Elementa*,[5] with a dedication to the Doge: *Erhardus ratdolt Augustensis impressor serenissimo alme urbis venete Principi Joanni Mocenigo S.* This volume has the title in rubrics, within a flowered and painted border.

This year (1482) gives us also the *Hyginii Astronomicon*,[6] with the title in rubrics, and numerous woodcuts of the constellations and planets, and the abundant use of an excellent Greek type, which Ratdolt adopted for the first time in this year.

Five pages of woodcuts appear also in the *Publicii Ars memorię*[7] of this same year. In 1483 the *Tabulæ* of Alfonso,[8] King of Castile; and in 1485, Albohazen Haly's *Liber in judiciis stellarum*,[9] and Durandi, *Rationale Divinorum Officiorum*.[10] This work is printed in double columns, and the dedication shows it to be the third edition:

> *bis nostra*
> *memoria eneo caractere, carthis impressus dinoscitur,*
> *quique vel librariorum culpa vel illorum quos*
> *vulgus stampatores nominantur erroribus plenus*
> *dicebatur et erat.*

[1] The *e*'s very much sloped; the *i*'s dotted high above the letter; the loops of *a* and *e* thin and meagre; no z, but zeta instead, ζ; the *b* and *d* and *p* and *q* formed by an *o* and a stroke which has not invaded the *o* at all. This book contains some instances of a poor Greek type.

[2] Hain, *6,226. 4to.; Roman; leaves 42, not numbered; lines 25 and 26 to a full page; no catchwords; signatures a, b, c, d, in fours, e a 5, last leaf blank; no register.

[3] Hain, *6,926. Fol.; Gothic; 68 leaves, numbered; beginning after table of contents; no catchwords; no signatures.

[4] Not in Hain. 4to.; Gothic; 364 leaves, not numbered; no catchwords; signatures, a 2 a 2, a a 5, followed by 25 unsigned gathers of 7.

[5] Hain, *6,693. Gothic; leaves 138, unnumbered; no catchwords; signatures, a a 5; b to r in 4; two kinds of type used; no register.

[6] Hain, *9,062. Gothic; leaves 58; no catchwords; signatures a to f in 4 [a 3 signed b 3], and [d 3 signed c 3], g, a 5.

[7] Hain, *13,545. [8] Hain, *868. [9] Hain, *8,349. [10] Hain, *6,490.

After the disruption of the society Ratdolt almost invariably uses Gothic character for his works. The Eusebius, *Chronicon*,[1] of 1483, is a partial exception. The chronicle itself is in Gothic character, but the commentary is in Roman.

Another member of the firm, Peter Loslein, also continued to print on his own account after the disruption of the society. From his press we have *Isidori Hispalensis, De summo bono*, 1483,[2] in Gothic character, which has a strong resemblance to that employed by Ratdolt.

Round the identity of the third member of this famous firm, Bernard Pictor, a long controversy has been waged. The colophons of the works published by the association leave us in no doubt as to his nationality—he is Bernard of Augsburg, a compatriot of his partner Ratdolt. It is usually taken for granted that *pictor* describes Bernard's profession, and that this epithet designates him the draughtsman employed to ornament the books which Loslein edited and Ratdolt printed. But as the surname, almost invariably in the case of the books issued by this firm,[3] is printed with a small initial, the Christian name alone having a capital, it does not follow that *pictor* describes Bernard's profession; it may have been a Latin translation of his surname. Whoever *Bernardus pictor* was, to him are ascribed the many designs which bear as their mark the minuscule b—even those which illustrate the *Hypnerotomachia*.[4]

Besides the press of Ratdolt, which continued to work till 1485, the three firms, the Brothers de Gregoriis of Forli, Matheo di Co de ca[5] or Capcasa of Parma, and Benalius de Benaliis, all distinguished themselves in this particular branch of the trade. If we wish to appreciate the immense advance the art of illustration had made between 1476 and 1500, we have only to compare any of the woodcuts in Ratdolt's books with such splendid productions as the Petrarch of 1497, by Bartolomio de Zani da Portesio,[6] with its magnificent engravings of the Trionfi, or the illustrations to the more famous *Hypnerotomachia* of 1499.[7]

[1] Hain, *6,717. [2] Hain, *9,279.

[3] This is a very general custom. We find it continuing through the sixteenth century. In Greek books it also appears. Cf. Legrand, *op. cit.*, Nos. 124, 178, 214, but it is not an absolute rule. Cf. No. 177.

[4] Fisher, p. 316. Hain, *5,501.

[5] See *Archiv. Ven.*, xxx. 172. Co de ca's shop was at San Giuliano. From his Will, dated 12th August, 1491, we know that he worked in company with his brother Giovanni.

[6] Fisher, *op. cit.*, pp. 319, 329. Hain, *12,776. *Biblioteca Canal, Crispani, nunc exitans*, Bassani Pozzato, 1885. The engravings have the sign of the scallop shell.

[7] It is probable that the majority of these illustrations and ornaments were printed from metal plates. Mr. Fisher argues in favour of metal, basing his view on an examination of

PROEMIO DI MESSER POGIO BRACCIOLINI FIORENTI- NO NELA HISTORIA DI XE NOPHONTE DELLA VI- TA DI CYRO RE DE PERSI AL SERENIS- SIMO RE ALPHON SO DA RA- GONIA.

b

AVENDO MOLTI *i questa nostra era cõseguitato nõ piccola gloria della industria et ingegno loro, in hauere tradot- to qualche opera di Greco in la- tino, io anchora ho determinato di prouare se potessi i simile gra do di exercitatione acquistarmi & dignita & honore, ilperche di Greca ho fatta Latina la hystoria di Xeno phonte della vita di Cyro superiore Re de Persi, opera certamente egregia & degna di assai extimatione, & che oltre alla cognitione della hystoria che è preclarissi- ma, cõtiene in se, & ci dimostra quale debba essere vno principe iusto sino da teneri anni, laquale fatica sanza dubbio ho presa volentieri per dare notitia à latini di quello libro che è necessario à Chi reggie, & da gli anti chi nostri excellentissimi sommamente è suo commendato, in tanto che Cicerone scriue hauerlo tutto consumato per lassiduita de leggierlo, & Scipione Aphricano ha-*

ALESSANDRO PAGANINO. XENOPHON, *Vita di Cyro.* 1527.

Among the many names of distinguished printers that we meet with during this period, none is more famous than that of Andrea de Torresani of Asola. We have already seen that by the year 1482-3 he announced his edition of Nicolao Panormitano's *Lecturæ*, to be printed in Jenson's type, *inclytis famosisque characteribus optimi quondam in hac arte magistri Nicolai Jenson gallici.* Andrea de Torresani continued to print, either alone or in company, down to the year 1499, when his daughter Maria married Aldus Manutius. After the death of Aldus, Andrea continued to direct the Aldine Press during the minority of his grandson Paulo, the heir to Aldus' business. Andrea's own sons followed the calling of their father, and their name occurs in the history of the book trade, both in Venice and in Paris.[1]

Another great printer, Ottaviano Scotto, citizen of Modena, also opened his press in Venice in 1480. Scotto founded one of the largest printing and publishing houses in that city, and employed such distinguished workmen as Simon de Luere, Bonetto Locatello, and Alberto Rossi. After his death his heirs continued the business, trading under the name of *Hæredes Scotti.*

One other name—that of Alessandro Paganino—calls for special notice, on account of his peculiar upright italic type. Paganino set up his press first of all at Toscolano, on the Lake of Garda, but subsequently removed to Venice, and printed there down to the year 1531.

The most noticeable feature about the period from the beginning of printing down to the appearance of Aldus on the scene, is the rapidity with which the art of printing extended, and the number of presses which were opened, thus pouring out upon the market a continuous stream of books. There is an interesting testimony as to the avidity with which some of these early publications were bought up by scholars. In a copy of Petrarch's *Canzoniere*, with an autograph commentary in a contemporary hand, probably by Antonio da Canal—written about the year 1516, when Canal was already eighty years of age—the following notice of the Petrarch printed by Windelin of Speyer in the year 1470, occurs: *non se ne catta piu alcuno, che subito fu venduto, e a pagarlo cento ducati non lo troveria.*[2] Windelin's Petrarch was bought up at once, and did not come into the market again as a secondhand book; so that Antonio da Canal was unable to find a copy at any price.

The public received the new art gladly. But at the outset it must have been a comparatively limited public, hardly more extended than the public

the impressions of the first and of the second editions of the *Hypnerotomachia.* A period of forty-six years elapsed between the appearance of these two editions, "yet no symptom of breakage is visible, which must have been the case had wood blocks been used to print from."

[1] See *Catharina da Siena. Epistole* appresso Federico de Torresani, 1548.

[2] Morelli, *Zibaldoni*, tom. primo, 605. Cod. Cicogna, 3,205.

to whom the calligraphers appealed. For these earliest books must have cost large sums to purchase. In the history of the early Venetian Press nothing is more remarkable than the extreme beauty of the first books which were issued by the prototypographers, and the rapidity with which deterioration sets in. The earliest printers had manuscripts before them as their models, and, to some extent, their rivals. The invention of printing from type was little more than the discovery of a new method in the practice of an art which had been for long in existence, the art of copying. There is a perfect continuity of aim and of method between the copyist and the printer; only the means differ. Printers are constantly insisting that their printed character is either undistinguishable from manuscript, or superior to it.[1] The copyists soon recognized the danger to their art, and, as early as the year 1474, we find them petitioning the Senate of Genoa to expel the printers.[2] In Venice, however, the new art met with no overt opposition. The support of the government was conceded at once and in the most public manner. It was only at the outset of printing, however, that typographers and copyists could come into collision. The printer and the copyist really appealed to different publics—their markets were not identical. But the printers had to create their market, to reach and to waken their public, and that could only be done by drawing attention to their new art through an attack on the market of the copyists. That market was pre-eminently aristocratic and exclusive. None but princes and great ecclesiastical establishments could afford a library. It was more than aristocratic, it was fastidious; the beauty of the manuscript was as highly prized as its accuracy.[3] Printers at the outset ran the risk of being rejected by such patrons if they permitted themselves a rapid, careless, or cheap style of production; yet this was the market by which they had to make their name, by which they had to live, till they could touch that wider market, which they helped to create and upon which they subsequently subsisted. Printers dared not appeal directly to the poorer book-buying public—it hardly existed in sufficient number to form a paying public. They could not afford to appear in the aristocratic market with books less beautiful than the manuscripts which they sought to supplant, for the failure to please these aristocratic patrons might have given the victory to their rivals the copyists, might have induced the book-buying world to condemn, as mean and ugly, the productions of the new art; and the printers

[1] In Paris the first printed books which reached that city are said to have been passed off as MSS. Sardini, iii. p. 78, n. 3. Cf. the phrases, *manum mentiens*, *impressos digitis Vindelinis*, *stampirà molto meglio in grecho de quello che se scrive a penna*.

[2] Sardini, *op. cit.*, i. pp. 42, 43. See, too, Don Filippo de Strata's invectives against printers. Berlan, *op. cit.*, p. 13. Sardini, iii. p. 80, on the copyists at Paris.

[3] Wattenbach, *op. cit.*, p. 265.

might, for a time at least, have been driven from the field by neglect, before they could reach the greater market which was being prepared for them by the Renaissance. That such a result was not impossible is proved by the reappearance of the copyist's art in the sixteenth century. The quality of books had fallen low, and there was a kind of æsthetic revival—the lovers of beautiful books returned to the old method of production.[1] The earliest works which issued from the press were of that great beauty which we know because they were produced for fastidious purchasers. But a change soon came over the market to which printers appealed. The revival of learning created another public, different in character from the princely collectors—a public eager for knowledge, no longer fastidious as to the garb in which it presented itself, and by the very facts of the case debarred from the selfish pleasure of unique proprietorship. The demand now was for cheap books, and books in abundance. This movement towards the cheapening and universal diffusion of books manifested itself quite early in the history of the art in Venice. The decline in the quality of the workmanship was extraordinarily rapid; and by the year 1480, books infinitely inferior to anything produced in 1470 were not only common, but the rule, although the great printers still continued to publish *éditions de luxe* for the use of their more wealthy patrons.

[1] Cf. Legrand, *op. cit.*, No. 103, when speaking of Nicander (Andronicus) Nucius of Corfu. The result of the printing press was to lower the pay of the copyist, already poorly remunerated. Nucius talks of himself as *πενίᾳ συζῶν*, and Michel Apostolios gives himself the title of *βασιλεὺς τῶν τῇδε πενήτων*. Among the well-known employers of copyists are Alberto Pio of Carpi (circ. 1510) and Alfonso d'Este (circ. 1552). Don Diego de Hurtado de Mendoza, Spanish ambassador in Venice, also employed calligraphers. See Mr. T. W. Allen's article in the *Classical Review*, Feb., 1889, p. 12.

CHAPTER V.

1484—1485.

A BOOKSELLER OF 1484.

A bookseller's journal—What he sold—His prices—The books in greatest demand—His stock-in-trade—His gains.

HE Marcian Library possesses a document of great value as throwing light upon the book trade of Venice in the years 1484 and 1485. This document is the *Zornale*,[1] or day-book of a Venetian bookseller. It is an oblong ledger, bound in parchment, and tied with thongs. Its leaves are of paper, and number one hundred and fourteen. The bookseller's name does not appear; but on the outside of the parchment wrapper there is a sign with initials. The register professes to cover from May 17, 1484, to January 19, 1487-8. In reality the entries stop in the month of October, 1485; so that the document affords us a survey of this bookseller's operations for one year and a half. The ledger or day-book records the movement of the shop from day to day; the sales that were effected, the names of the books sold, the prices paid, and in some few cases the names of the purchasers. The bookseller dealt in a large variety of works. We find upon his lists the classics, bibles, missals, works on canon law, breviaries, romances, school-books, poetry. At the end of the journal he has entered the various replenishments of his stock which he found himself obliged to make from time to time, and in this way we are able to judge what books were in greatest demand. The books were probably sold as a rule unbound, for in many cases we find it specially stated that such and such a book is bound; and also certain occasional disbursements to the binder are noted now and

[1] Biblioteca Marciana, *Ital. Cl.* xi., cod. xlv.

again. Several of the entries throw light on the way in which a bookseller of the fifteenth century conducted his business. He bought the books from the printer-publishers for cash, and he sold them for cash to the general public; but in many cases, for the other needs of his business, he was able to pay in kind. Such entries as the following are not uncommon: Chronicle given in exchange for oil; Life and Miracles of the Madonna given to Lazarus the binder; the Hundred Novels given to Master Pezin the binder; the Hundred Novels and the Fifty Novels given to the book-binder; a small Bible, Mamotrectus, and Legendary, given to Peter the proof-reader; the Practice of Raynoldo given to Dionisio, on account for wine; Cicero's Orations in exchange for wine; Virgil with Servius' Commentary, bound, exchanged for two quarts of Schiavonian (Dalmatian) wine and thirty soldi in cash; an Abacus to the miniaturist; a large assortment of books to Ser Ostathio and Ser Filippo for flour. In some cases books were given away as presents, chiefly to priests and monks; while, from another entry, Given to a brother of the Minorites on credit, it seems that customers were allowed to run accounts, though no indications of bad debts appear in the day-book.

Large extracts from the Journal will be found in the Appendix. Where the name of a book is important or interesting, the price paid for it has been recorded. *Facetiæ*, poetry, and romances brought very low prices. For example, Poggio's *Facetiæ* sells for nine soldi; the *Inamoramento d'Orlando* for one lira; Cecho d'Ascoli, sixteen soldi; the *Morgante*, one lira, ten soldi; *Cinquanta Novelle*, one lira; the *Arte di Ciromantia* and the *Laudi della Madonna* for ten soldi each; Altobello, fifteen soldi, and the cookery book by Platina, *De honesta voluptate*, for fourteen soldi. On the other hand, Dante with a commentary sold for one ducat. Petrarch with a commentary fetches three lire; Pietro d'Abano's *Conciliator*, one ducat, six soldi; the *Digestum Vetus*, one ducat, five lire, six soldi; Plutarch's Lives, two ducats; Strabo, four lire; Lucretius, one of the most popular classics, fifteen soldi; Thucydides, one lira, nine soldi. Plato, Dante, Petrarch, and Diogenes Laertius, all together, bring two ducats, one lira. The *Dialogo de Santa Caterina de Siena*, published with its beautiful engravings, by Matheo de Co de ca in 1483, sells for two lira, bound up with the *Libro della Beata Caterina da Bologna.* Ptolemy, with figures, fetches three ducats, four lire, eighteen soldi. A little Suetonius cost only four soldi, and a little Martial fifteen soldi.

Both from the number of copies sold and from the prices obtained we find that certain printers and publishers were in special repute. For example, the *Bibia del Grisolare*[1] sells for one ducat, one lira, ten soldi; whereas a Bible with no specified printer fetches only three lire. Again, the Decades of Livy,

[1] Possibly Jacopo Grasolario, the publisher of Cyprian's *Epistolæ*, 1483. Hain, *5,898.

stampa del Grisolare, cost the same price as the *Bibia del Grisolare.* When the work on sale is from any distinguished press, the fact is usually specified. Among the printers' names recorded in this way we come across Ottaviano Scotto, Piero Veronese, Bressan, la Compagnia,[1] Magistro Silvestro, Pagani, Magistro Francesco, Zuan Andrea (Valvassore?).

At the end of the ledger the owner has made an entry. It is headed: *y. h. s.* 1484 *a di* 17 *mazo. Qui si fara ricordo de libri intrarano in bottega et prima.* It is a list of the books with which he opened, and the number of copies of each which he had on stock. His stock-in-trade on the 17th of May, 1484, consisted of one thousand, three hundred, and thirty-seven volumes. Some of the more popular works figure in many copies; for example, Juvenal, ten copies; *Erotemata greco,* ten copies; Michel Scott, ten copies; Isidore's *Etymologiarum,* once ten copies, and again eighty copies; Donatus, ten copies; *Peregrinatio ad Jerusalem,* thirteen copies. On the 31st of May, the bookseller had to take in a new supply of books, and the names and number of copies of each of these are entered in the ledger. From this fresh list we gather that books of devotion were running out of stock. So, too, school-books like the Donatus and Pisanella; though on May 17th he had sixteen copies of the latter, yet he finds it advisable on the 31st to purchase ten more. Juvenal, too, was sold out, and the Letters of Pope Pius. By June the 9th his supply of Itineraries to Jerusalem had run out, and he purchased thirty-two more copies. So he goes on, refreshing his stock from month to month. The catalogue of his original stock-in-trade and of his additions will be found *in extenso* in the Appendix.

The ledger closes with a summary of the takings in the shop from 7th Sept., 1484, to 1st Oct., 1485. The summary begins by stating that on the 7th Sept., 1484, there was in hand (*in bottega per avanti*) two hundred and fifteen ducats, three soldi. This sum perhaps represents the takings from the 17th of May, when the register opens, down to the 7th September. The four following months, September, October, November, and December, brought in three hundred and eighteen ducats. The smallest takings are during the warm months, July, August, and September; but the journal does not extend over a sufficient period to allow us to determine whether this was permanently the case. The bookseller's practice was to balance his accounts once a week, though he began balancing eight times a month.

The shop was probably situated either at Rialto or near St. Mark's, as the following note inscribed in the ledger seems to indicate; it is a list of the days on which the shop was to be shut or half shut:

[1] The company is probably that of John of Cologne, Nicolas Jenson, and companions. The Bible referred to is probably their edition of 1481, 4 vols. fol. Le Long, *op. cit.*, i. 252.

"*Qui si notarano le feste ne le quale si tene serate le botege a rialto et piaza* (?) *et quelle harano signata la * se tene aperto a mezo et non si mete fora robe in la balcone.*

"*Sancto Vito a di 15 Zugno.*
* *Sancto Marco a di 26 Zugno.*
Sancto Marsiliano a di primo luglio.
Sancta Maria Elisabet a di 2 luglio.
Sancta Croce a di 14 Settembre.
* *San Magno a di 6 Ottobre.*
* *San Marco a di 8 Ottobre.*
* *San Sebastiano a di 20 Zenaro.*
* *San Marcho a di primo Febraro.*"

CHAPTER VI.

1490—1515.

THE EPOCH OF ALDUS.

Early publications of novels, music, geography, Eastern languages—The advent of Aldus—Two aspects of his work: (1) as scholar, as Hellenist and Humanist; (2) as typographer—His Greek press—Aldus at Sant' Agostino—Rival Greek presses: Gabriel da Brisighella and Zaccharia Caliergi—The Aldine or Neacademia—Aldus as editor—Use of ancient codices as copy—Latin press—Aldus as printer—Greek character—Roman character—Italic character—Consequences of the adoption of this character—Forgeries—Aldus at San Paternian—His first will—His death and funeral.

THE last decade of the fifteenth century is remarkable in the history of the Venetian Printing Press for several reasons. We find in it the beginnings of the great business of romance and novel printing, which Venice retained till quite late in her history. It also witnessed the opening of the musical and of the geographical press in Venice; and we find traces of a press for Arabic and other Eastern languages. But above all, this decade saw the foundation of the Greek press by Aldus, Vlastos, and Caliergi; it is the epoch of Aldus, that is to say, the period in the history of the Venetian Press which has received more attention than any other.

There were several reasons why the *novelieri* should be published so frequently in Venice. At that time the Republic was the freest state in Italy; there was small chance of the books being suppressed on the score of immorality. The social atmosphere was gay, and such books as the *novelieri* produced were likely to find a ready public in Venetian society. The large number of presses in Venice, and the consequent competition, lowered the cost of production, and books of this nature, intended to reach a widespreading market, could not afford to be expensive. Finally, the vast trade of Venice gave facilities for the circulation of these books all over Europe.

In the year 1492 the brothers de Gregoriis published the edition of the Decameron,[1] with vignettes; and in the same year they issued the *Novellino*[2] of Massuccio. The lists of the bookseller of 1484 have already shown us how great a demand there was for such collections as the *Cento Novelle* and the *Cinquanta Novelle*.[3]

The earliest monument of the musical press in Venice is the concession of a monopoly for all printing of figured song and *intaboladure d'organo et de liuto* to Ottaviano de' Petrucci da Fossombrone. The monopoly was granted by the College on 25th May, 1498, and extended to twenty years. Ottaviano in his petition affirms that *ha trovado quello che molti non solo in Italia, ma etiamdio de fuora de Italia za longamente indarno hanno investigato, che è stampar commodissimamente canto figurado, et per consequens molto più facilmente canto fermo*.[4] The first known work by Petrucci appeared two years later, in 1500. It is the *Harmonicæ Musices Odhecaton*, of which an imperfect copy exists at Bologna, and a perfect copy at Treviso.[5] This is the beginning of that large business which, as we shall see, was carried on throughout the next century by Marcolini, by Antonio Gardano, and others. In the year following the concession to Petrucci, 21st January, 1498-9, the College grant to Andrea Corbo a patent for his large letters for choir-books, *quod ipse solus facere possit stampare litteras ejusdem formæ et grossitiei ac magnitudinis*.[6]

Of the earliest geographical press in Venice we find traces in the petition of Girolamo Biondo, 5 April, 1498. Biondo refers to a plan of Venice *prout jacet et situata est*,[7] which, with great pains and diligence, he has caused to be designed and engraved (*designari et intercidi*). It is not certain that this plan of Venice, though the author talks of it as ready, was ever published. It was a precursor of the much more famous plan of the city, published by Antonio Kolb, under date 1500, to which we shall have to refer later on.

In the year 1498 a certain Democrito Terracina, Venetian citizen and dweller in Venice, applied to the College for a monopoly, for twenty-five years, of all books printed in Arabic, Moorish, Syrian, Armenian, Indian, and Barbary. His petition was granted; but he died before May, 1513, without having published any works in these languages, though he had spent much

[1] Fisher, 329. Hain, 3,277.
[2] Hain, 10,888.
[3] See Biagi, *Le Novelle Antiche*, Firenze, 1880, capp. I, II. The bookseller's list corroborates Padre Fineschi's assertion that there was an edition of the *Cento Novelle* published in 1482.
[4] Vernarecci, *Ottaviano de' Petrucci da Fossombrone*, p. 36. Fulin, *op. cit.*, p. 53.
[5] Sig. Castellani announces the discovery in *La Stampa in Venezia*, p. 65.
[6] Fulin, *op. cit.*, p. 56.
[7] Fulin, *op. cit.*, p. 52.

on his preparations. His nephews Lelio and Paulo, sons of Maximi, Democrito's brother, petitioned for a continuance of the privilege for twenty-five years, which was granted to them. Panzer, however, does not record either uncle or nephews, and no publications of the Terracina's press are known to be in existence.[1]

But above all other reasons the period of which we are speaking is made famous by the opening of the Aldine Press in Venice. It would be superfluous, after the exhaustive works of Renouard, Didot, Baschet, and others, to dwell at length on the life and labours of the great scholar and printer Aldus Manutius. Nevertheless, it is desirable briefly to determine the position which Aldus occupies in the general history of the Venetian Press. His wide reputation rests upon two grounds—his work as a scholar, as a Hellenist, and his work as a typographer. These two aspects of Aldus' work are, of course, intimately connected one with the other, but it is possible to separate them and to consider them apart from each other.

Aldus Manutius was born at Bassiano in the duchy of Sermoneta in 1450,[2] so that he was in his forty-fifth year when he began his career as a printer in Venice in 1494. He came to Venice, in 1489, from Carpi, where he had enjoyed the favour of the reigning prince. It was at Carpi that he conceived his great scheme for the publication of the Greek classics. The masterpieces of Latinity had, for the most part, been exhausted by his predecessors. It was natural that some great scholar and printer should turn his attention to the wide field offered by the Greek classics. But as yet no one had seriously attacked the task. In four cities only had Greek books been issued: at Milan in 1476; at Vicenza in 1483; at Venice in 1484-5, and at Florence in 1488. When Aldus began to print, only four Greek classics had been published in the original—Æsop, Theocritus, Homer, and Isocrates. Although printers like Sweynheym and Pannartz, Jenson and Ratdolt, had made essays in Greek character, no one of them had attempted to print a book completely in Greek. The only presses seriously at work upon the production of Greek books were those of the Nerli and Francesco Alopa at Florence. There was, therefore, abundant field for Aldus to occupy. But to carry out his scheme he required ready access to manuscripts. And this need for manuscripts was probably the main consideration which induced Aldus to settle in Venice. Cardinal Bessarion had died in 1474, and left his rich collection of Greek and Latin MSS. to the Republic. In Venice also Aldus knew that he would find a large colony of Greeks,[3] some of them scholars, capable of assisting him in

[1] Fulin, *op. cit.*, pp. 53, 98.

[2] Castellani, *La Stampa*, &c., p. 36, note 1. Amoretti, *Lettera sull' anno natalizio di Aldo Manuzio*, Roma, 1804.

[3] See Legrand, *op. cit.*, biographical notices, *passim*.

his enterprise. The first essays of Aldus' press are the *Galeomyomachia* and the Musæus, *De Herone et Leandro*, both of the year 1494. They were printed under no protection from the government, and possibly Aldus put them out merely as an earnest of what he intended to do. He did not apply to the government for any rights in his Greek character till early in the year 1496 (25 Feb., 1495). He then declares that he has cut *lettere greche in summa bellezza de ogni sorte*; in doing this he has consumed a large part of his fortune; and now he has discovered two new methods by means of which *stampirà si ben et molto meglio in grecho de quello che se scrive a penna.* He accordingly petitions for, and obtains, a copyright for twenty years in all Greek books or translations from the Greek that he may print, and also a patent for his particular method of printing. But before Aldus had secured this protection from the government he had already put out a part of the edition of Aristotle, the work with which he inaugurated his great series of the Greek classics. The Aristotle is in five volumes, and is dedicated to Aldus' old patron, Alberto Pio, the Count of Carpi. From the appearance of the Aristotle down to the year 1500, Aldus continued to issue Greek books under his own name alone from his press. In many cases he had the assistance of Marcus Musurus; for example, in the translation of the Musæus;[1] but the famous Aldine Academy was not founded till the year 1500.[2] In the year 1499 Aldus married the daughter of Andrea de Torresani; and at this time he was probably living at St. Agostino, not in the house which at present bears the tablet recording his residence there, but in one of the small houses in the Calle del Pistor, which opens on to the Campo St. Agostino, as we must conclude from the addresses of two letters written to Gregoropoulos by Zaccharia Caliergi and Musurus, while Gregoropoulos was living with Aldus as his corrector.[3]

Very soon after Aldus began to print in Greek, we find a rival press opened by *Gabriele da Brasichella et compagni*, who *hanno constituto cum summa cura et diligentia stampare in greco et latino . . . cum bellissima et nova inventione.*[4] They petition, in 1498, that no one may be allowed to use this invention nor to print the four following Greek works—the Epistles of Phalaris and Brutus, Pollux, Philostratus, and Æsop's Fables. And in fact the company, which consisted of Bartholomew of Capo d'Istria, Gabriel Braccio of Brisighella, John Bissoli, and Benedict Magno of Carpi, did publish in this year the Epistles of Phalaris[5] and Æsop's Fables.[6] This press, however, hardly proved a serious rival to Aldus, and Braccio subsequently became a member of the Aldine Academy. In the following year, 1499, a much greater

[1] Legrand, *op. cit.*, No. 10.
[2] Didot, p. 519. Castellani, p. 55.
[3] Castellani says 1502. *La Stampa*, p. 51, note 1.
[4] Fulin, *op. cit.*, p. 51.
[5] Hain, *12,871.
[6] Hain, 267.

Greek typographer appeared upon the scene, Zaccharia Caliergi of Rhethymno in Crete.[1] He did not, at first, print alone in Venice. The colophon of Suidas' *Etymologicum magnum*,[2] which appeared in this year, explains his relations to his partner, Nicolas Vlastos, and to his patroness, Anne Notaras, daughter of Lucas Notaras, Duke of Constantinople. Nicolas Vlastos furnished the funds for the press, which was founded on the initiative of Anne Notaras, and Zaccharia Caliergi was the typographer of the association. The editions issued by Vlastos and Caliergi are, in many cases, magnificent; but there seems to have been no jealousy between Aldus and Caliergi, for we find Aldus selling Caliergi's editions along with his own.[3] Caliergi continued to print with Vlastos, and then alone,[4] till 1509 at least. He moved to Rome after the disturbances caused by the wars of Cambrai, and he issued his Pindar there in the year 1515.

In the year 1500, and in company with Gregoropoulos and Carteromachos, Aldus founded the academy with which his name is so intimately associated. The Academy was formed especially for the study of Greek, and for the publication of the Greek classics. All the members were bound, under penalty of a fine, to speak Greek among themselves; but there was no fine for solecisms. The fines were collected in a box, and whenever the sum was sufficiently large, Aldus was bound to furnish a banquet—"not a printer's banquet, but a real New Academicians' feast."[5] The members of the Academy were divided into classes; there were the president, the readers, the correctors, the nobles, the priests, and the doctors. The first list of members numbered thirty-three, among whom we find Linacre of Canterbury. The Greek works published by Aldus after the foundation of the Academy bear various imprints, such as, *in* or *ex ædibus Aldi Romani; apud Aldum Romanum; in Aldi Romani Academia; in Aldi Neacademia.* In the production of this vast amount of work Aldus was assisted by the Greek scholars who were members of his Academy. In his letter to Chalcondylas, in the Euripides of 1503, Aldus says that he is producing at the rate of a thousand and more volumes a month—*quandoquidem mille et amplius boni alicujus auctoris volumina singulo quoque mense emittimus ex Academia nostra.*[6] The work was carried on with almost feverish activity; the readers and correctors preparing the copy in one room while the press was throwing off proofs in another. But this feverish hurry had its drawbacks. In some cases the

[1] Legrand, *op. cit.*, i. cxxv., and No. 23. Caliergi claimed an imperial descent, and for that reason he displays the double eagle as his printer's mark.

[2] Not in Hain. [3] Renouard, *op. cit.*, iii. p. 253. [4] Legrand, *op. cit.*, No. 34.

[5] Renouard, p. 499. Castellani, p. 100.

[6] Caliergi took from the 7th September to the 5th October to set up, print, and publish the 117 leaves of his Galen of 1500. Cf. Legrand, *op. cit.*, No. 29.

editors were so pressed for time that they did not make a working copy of the MS. to be set up, but used the actual original manuscript upon which to make their corrections, emendations, and conjectural readings, and passed the manuscript on to the press-room. This is undoubtedly the case with the manuscript of Hesychius;[1] as Villoison observed, the manuscript is disfigured by ink stains from the compositor's hands, by indications for the catchwords and for the beginnings of the pages. *C'était un mauvais usage de ces temps-là qui nous a fait perdre beaucoup des manuscrits.*[2] It is to be feared that this is true, and that the custom was not uncommon among these early printers. We know, for example, that the Codex Ravennas served not only for the text of the Lysistrata and the Thesmophoriazusæ, which were published in 1516 as a supplement to the Giunta edition of Aristophanes[3] (1515), but actually was in the press-room as the working copy.

To return to the manuscript of the Hesychius; it shows us how the editors of the Academy sometimes worked. The editor in this case is Marcus Musurus, and we see that he erased by pen the contractions and ligatures which might have embarrassed the compositors, and rewrote the words in the margin. He added a mass of corrections, changes, transpositions, and additions, and gave no indication in his edition of the liberties he took with his manuscript. The printers follow Musurus and never the manuscript,[4] only making use of the Aldine ligatures and contractions as they found them in the fount, though the word may have been written out by Musurus in full. It is admitted, as though by way of apology, that Musurus worked in haste, *cursim*, and *quantum per occupationes licuit;* but it would almost seem as though the art of printing, the sense of the multiplication and permanence of books, had induced these editors to treat the manuscript with far less regard than we should consider necessary now. The Aldine editor may have believed that his edition would supersede the manuscript for posterity, and that the fate of the manuscript mattered little. But under these circumstances we can hardly wonder that the possessors of fine manuscripts were chary of entrusting them to Aldus. His complaint against these βιβλιοτάφοι[5] is very bitter; but after all the manuscripts were safest in their tombs.

This feverish haste, this impatience which characterizes the Aldine Society, is, however, part of that very quality which has secured to Aldus his fame and the gratitude of posterity. Aldus and his fellow-workmen were consumed with a desire to extend and popularize learning. The press gave him the means of doing so. The list of his publications is sufficient to prove

[1] Marciana. Zanetti. Cod. DCXXII.

[2] Legrand, *op. cit.*, i. cxvii.

[3] Martin, *Les Scolies du Manuscrit d'Aristophane à Ravenne*, p. v. Von Velsen, *Ueber den Codex Urbinas*, &c., Halle, 1871.

[4] Legrand, *op. cit.*, i. cxvii.

[5] Didot, *op. cit.*, p. 221.

how thoroughly he carried out his intention. When he began to print, only one great Greek classic, Homer, had been issued from the press. When he left off Aristotle, Plato, Thucydides, Aristophanes, Euripides, Sophocles, Homer, Demosthenes, Æsop, Plutarch, Pindar, had been given to the world, most of them for the first time. It would be impossible to overrate the debt which Greek scholarship owes to Aldus as editor and publisher.

The achievements of Aldus' Latin press are naturally not so distinguished as those of his Greek press. He had many forerunners in the field of Latin editorship, and the majority of the great Latin classics had already been printed. But the press which issued such beautiful works as Bembo's *Aetna* (1495), the *Hypnerotomachia* (1499), the Vergil (1501), added considerably to the reputation of Venice as a printing centre. Aldus' Roman character is certainly very beautiful, and bears a strong family likeness to Jenson's Roman; indeed, it is not improbable that Aldus caused his punches to be cut on the model of Jenson's, which, as we know, belonged to his father-in-law, Andrea de Torresani of Asola. Of Aldus' famous italic character we shall have to speak presently, when we come to deal with Aldus as a printer.

The largest claims have been made on behalf of the elder Manutius as a printer. His name has eclipsed the glory of his predecessors, at least in the popular estimation. It is hardly too much to say that common opinion assigns to Aldus the position of earliest, or, if not earliest, at any rate of greatest printer in Venice. Both these claims are wide of the truth. The Venetian Press had been at work a quarter of a century before Aldus began to print. It had passed through its period of early excellence, and had begun to deteriorate when Aldus appeared and restored it to its high position again.

As regards the quality of Aldus' Greek character; when he applied for a monopoly in the year 1495-6, we see that he laid great stress on the *summa bellezza* of his Greek. If we compare this type with that employed by Jenson or by Ratdolt, it is evident that there is a radical difference in the aims of these masters—two distinct tendencies are at work. Aldus' Greek character was copied, as everyone knows, from the handwriting of his friend Marcus Musurus; that is to say, he took as his model a current hand full of ligatures and contractions. He prided himself on the ingenuity displayed in cutting the punches with these ligatures, contractions, and combinations of accent and letter. The beauty of these pleased Aldus, and he wrote an opuscule on the *Abbreviationes, quibus frequentissime græci utuntur*,[1] in which he calls them *perpulchræ*. But it is a question whether this *luxe des ligatures*, as Didot calls it, did not detract from the efficiency and the real beauty of the Aldine Greek type.

[1] *Institutiones Grammaticæ. Venetiis: apud Aldum*, MDVIII.

Jenson, on the other hand, was eclectic in his choice of models. He cut each letter separately in the form which he considered beautiful, and in all probability the accents and breathings were cut on separate punches. The consequence is, that Jenson's Greek printing bears no resemblance to Greek writing; it is essentially printing. Though minuscule in form, it has no radical connection with minuscule manuscript. It is a new departure in the formation of Greek character, or if, in its distinguishing feature of disjoined letters, it has relation to anything in antiquity, it is to the majuscule MSS. of far earlier times. Aldus' Greek printing, on the contrary, is intended to resemble handwriting, and is simply, as far as form is concerned, a continuation of contemporary practice. It is remarkable that, although the Aldine scheme of Greek printing has held the field for so many centuries, we are now returning to the Jensonian idea; we no longer find lists of ligatures and abbreviations at the beginning of our grammars.

The year 1501 brings us to the real innovations which Aldus effected in the art of typography and in the book trade. In that year he obtained from the College a copyright of ten years' duration for all works printed in the *lettere corsive et cancellaresche de summa bellezza non mai più facta.*[1] This type of which he speaks is his famous italic character. Alexander Paganino, as we have seen, had been in the habit of using a kind of italic as early as the year 1491; but his type has nothing in common with that of Aldus, which may be considered as an innovation in the art of printing. Aldus' italic type is a close copy of the handwriting of Petrarch. It was cut for the printer by Francesco da Bologna, who has been plausibly identified with Francesco Raibolini, Francia the painter.[2] As in the case of his Greek character, so with his Latin; Aldus deliberately chooses as his model a current hand. This italic shows the breaks and also the ligatures of a current hand, and Aldus himself speaks with pride and satisfaction of this type as *manum mentiens.*

The first example of this famous italic type which issued from the Aldine Press is the Vergil of 1501. In the title to the Vergil Aldus fully and amply recognizes the claim of the type-cutter, Francesco, to the honours of his type, in the three lines entitled—

In grammatoglyptæ laudem.

Qui Graiis dedit Aldus, en Latinis
Dat nunc grammata scalpta daedaleis
Francisci manibus Bononiensis.

It is quite clear that Aldus here says his Latin type was engraved by Francesco of Bologna, and it is difficult to find any solid justification

[1] Fulin, *op. cit.*, p. 64. [2] Panizzi, *op. cit.* Didot, *op. cit.*, p. 157.

for the complaint that Aldus robbed Francesco of his due honour and renown.[1]

Possibly the adoption of this cursive type brought with it a modification in the manner of producing books, partly called for by the quality of the type itself, partly suggested by the desire for economy. This fine italic character, so like handwriting, was ill suited to the large page of the folio or the quarto volume. Aldus accordingly began to make up his sheets for the most part in octavos[2]—a size that could easily be held in the hand and readily carried in the pocket. The fineness and closeness of his new type allowed him to compress into this format as much matter as the purchaser could buy in a large quarto, or even in a folio, printed with the sumptuous largeness of Jenson's or John of Speyer's Roman character. The public welcomed the new type and size. The College granted Aldus a monopoly for ten years for all books printed in this manner. The price of books was lowered at once. Didot[3] calculates that an octavo of Aldus cost, on an average, two francs and a half, whereas a folio probably cost about twenty francs.

These two innovations on type and on format constituted a veritable revolution in the printing press and in the book trade, which now began to reach a far more extensive market than it had ever touched before. With this wide diffusion of books came the popularization of knowledge at which Aldus aimed. Scholarship began to lose its exclusive and aristocratic character when the classics were placed within the reach of any student who chose to study, meditate, and interpret them for himself. And to Aldus belongs the credit of having, through his new type and size, opened the way to the democratization of learning.

The fame of the Aldine italic must have spread over Europe with extraordinary rapidity, for in the same year (1501) that Aldus issued his Vergil, a forgery of this Vergil was published in Lyons. And Aldus complained bitterly of the constant forgeries to which his works were subjected; *libros nostros et mendose excuderent*, he says of the Lyons forgers, *et sub meo nomine publicarent, in quibus nec artificis nomen, nec locum ubinam impressi fuerint, esse voluerunt.*[4] By a public advertisement he warned his customers how they may distinguish the Lyons forgeries of Vergil, Horace, Juvenal and Persius, Martial, Lucan, Catullus and Tibullus, Propertius, Terence, from the genuine Venetian editions. The Lyons editions are all without notes; they have not the dolphin and anchor; the type has a certain Gallicity

[1] Didot, *op. cit.*, p. 161.

[2] I do not mean to say that 8vo. had never been used before. Paganino de' Paganini and Giorgio Arrivabene had published, in 1485, the *Pisanella* in 8vo.; and Paganino, in 1494, proposed to publish the texts of canon and civil law in this form. Fulin, *op. cit.*, p. 37. See Renouard, *op. cit.*, ii. p. 343. The instances of books in 16mo. are very rare.

[3] Didot, *op. cit.*, p. 165.

[4] Renouard, *op. cit.*, ii. 326.

about it; the majuscules are ugly; there are no ligatures in the Lyons type. To guard himself still more effectually, he applied to the government for protection, which was afforded him by the Ducal decree of 14 November, 1502.

In the year 1506 the wars of the League were disturbing the mainland, and Aldus' property suffered. He was obliged to leave Venice. But before doing so he drew up a Will, dated 27th March. From this Will we learn that he had removed from Sant' Agostino to San Paternian, *in studio domus quam habito, in Vico Divi Paterniani.* From this we may conclude, that not only Aldus' dwelling-house, but probably his printing press, had been removed to San Paternian.[1] This Will of 1506 was cancelled by the Will of 15th January, 1515, drawn up three weeks before Aldus' death. He died on the 6th February, in his house at San Paternian, sixty-five years of age. Musurus, writing to Jean Grolier,[2] laments the pain, *sævæ illius ac damnosæ mortis quæ nobis Aldum benevolum parentem benignumque fautorem eripuit.* In his Will Aldus expressed a wish to be buried at Carpi; but we do not know that his desire was ever fulfilled. A funeral service was celebrated for him at San Paternian, where his body lay in state, surrounded by copies of his many editions. The passage from Sanuto's Diaries which gives this information is so interesting that, although it has been frequently quoted, we reproduce it here: 1514, 8 *Febbraio. in questa matina essendo morto za do zorni qui Domino Aldo Manutio Romano optimo humanista et greco, qual era zenero di Andrea di Axola stampador, il quale ha fatto imprimere molte opere latine et greche ben corrette, et fatte le epistole davanti intitolate a molti, tra le quali assai operette a mi Marin Sanudo dedicò et compose una grammatica molto excellente. Hor è morto stato molti zorni ammalato: et per esser sta precepto de' Signori di Carpi, et fo de la caxa di Pii, ordinò el suo corpo fusse portato a seppellir a Carpi; et la moglie et figliuoli andassero ad habitar ivi, dove quelli signori li dettero certe possessioni. Et il corpo in chiesa di San Paternian posto con libri attorno ivi fu fatto le exequie et una oration in sua laude per Raphael Regio letor publico in questa città in Humanità; et il corpo in un deposito fino si mandi via.*

Sanuto, whether he did so intentionally or not, seems to be right in placing Aldus' fame as a scholar—as a Hellenist and Humanist—before his reputation as a printer. A great printer he certainly was, but not greater than some of his predecessors. His title to the high place of honour which he holds in the history of the Press, is due to his eager desire to popularize learning, and to the success which he achieved in this direction, by the introduction of his italic type and by his octavo volumes of the Latin classics and his *editiones principes* of the Greeks.

[1] The building, which is now the Cassa di Risparmio in Campo Manin, bears a tablet to record Aldus' residence, but it is not certain that it is rightly placed there. See Castellani, *La Stampa*, &c., p. 56.

[2] Legrand, *op. cit.*, No. 48.

CHAPTER VII.

1469—1517.

BOOKS BEFORE LEGISLATION.

The importance of the Venetian Press—The government and the book trade: protection of the art and protection against the art—Various kinds of privileges: (1) Monopolies; (2) copyright to author; (3) copyright to editor; (4) patents; (5) protection, (α) of individual, (β) of art—Petitions for privileges—Certificates in support of petitions—Conditions attached to privileges, (α) as regards the quality of the work, (β) as regards the speed of production, (γ) as regards the rights of others—Duration of privileges—Enforcement of privileges.

E have followed the art of printing from its foundation in Venice down to the opening of the sixteenth century, noting its various developments. In few of these developments was Venice original; her printers do not lead the way. Subiaco probably preceded her in the production of books, Rome certainly in the illustration of books, Milan in printing Greek. Yet it is remarkable how each expansion of the art was taken up at Venice, and received its highest development there. No other city approaches Venice in the number of fifteenth century typographers. Hain gives their number as two hundred and seven; from various other sources the number mounts to two hundred and sixty-eight. If we turn to the other cities of Italy we find that Rome is credited with forty-one typographers, Milan with sixty-three, Naples with twenty-seven, and Florence with thirty-seven.[1] And as no other city approaches Venice in the number of its presses, so no other printers rivalled those of Venice in the richness and the beauty of the volumes which they produced. We have seen, too, that this art sprang almost at once to its highest point of perfection; that subsequent masters did little to improve it; that the art showed a tendency to deteriorate rather than to advance. And

[1] Hain, *op. cit.*, tom. iv. p. 540.

this deterioration is intimately connected with the expansion of the art. As its market grew wider, printing tended to become less of an art and more of a trade, and began to feel the result of those considerations which especially affect trade, the questions of cheap production, profits, large markets, low prices. Commercial greed for gain was followed by its inevitable companion, speed; and speed meant inferior workmanship.[1] The book trade of Venice soon became an important item in the commerce of the city. The government was gradually compelled to devote its attention to so rich a source of wealth, and it is the relations of the government to the book trade that we have now to consider.

The action of the Venetian government as regards the printing press and the book trade of the city falls into two well-defined periods. The first is that which must occupy us during this and the following chapter, the period from the opening of the press in 1469 down to the year 1515—the period before any legislation on the subject of the press or the book trade had taken place. And the action of the government upon this subject presents itself under two aspects: first, the steps it took to protect and encourage the art, and those connected with the art; and, secondly, the steps it took to protect the State from certain dangers which the press brought with it.

Under the first heading we have to deal with monopolies, copyrights, patents, and protection from foreign competition; under the second, we have to observe the action of the government on the question of censorship, religious, moral, and literary.

Monopolies, copyrights, patents, and all other special concessions from the government on the subject of books and of printing are known under the generic name of privileges (*privilegii*). From the year 1469 down to the year 1517 these privileges were usually granted by the College, or Cabinet of Venice, and it is in the *Notatorii del Collegio*, or minutes of the Cabinet, that they are chiefly to be sought for during this period. But occasionally the Senate itself conferred the privilege.[2] Sometimes the chiefs of the Council of Ten are the authority which issues the concession.[3] But as a rule the College was the governmental department to which authors, editors, and printers applied for privileges, down to the year 1517.

It was natural, in the infancy of the art of printing, that those who brought the new art with them to Venice should desire to protect themselves against competition, and to secure, as far as might be, a monopoly, in order to realize the highest profits from their industry. The government, on the other hand, could not foresee the wide dimensions which this new art

[1] Compare the carelessness of Jenson's devotional series of 1480, with the care bestowed on his series of 1471.

[2] Fulin, *op. cit.*, Nos. 9, 14, 126.

[3] Fulin, *op. cit.*, Nos. 166, 178.

would assume, and it was willing to reward the enterprise of the new-comers. It therefore freely granted privileges to those who applied for them, but it did not make the application for a privilege obligatory.

Under this generic name of privilege we must distinguish the various kinds. The first kind of privilege was a monopoly, by which the government conceded to a certain person the sole right to print or sell a whole class of books during a definite period. This was the widest kind of privilege which could be granted. The very outset of the Venetian Press furnishes us with an instance of a monopoly. The order of the Senate which conferred this privilege on John of Speyer[1] is dated 18th Sept., 1469. It is the famous document upon which John's claim to be the prototypographer of Venice so largely rests. On the motion of the Ducal Councillors, and in reply to John's request (*ad humilem et devotam supplicationem predicti magistri Joannis*), the Senate granted him the absolute monopoly of printing in Venice for five years to come, and made the press of John of Speyer the sole medium by which books could be put upon the market. The provisions of this order were to be enforced by a fine, and by the confiscation of the contraband goods and of the material employed in producing them.

The results of such a close monopoly as this would have been most disastrous. We have only to consider the actual production of the next five years, to see how great would have been the loss to literature and to art had the privilege been enforced. What would have become of Nicolas Jenson, of John of Cologne, of Valdarfer, of Renner of Hailbrun, of Nicolas of Frankfort, and of many others? We must remember, too, that several of these masters were already in Venice, preparing their type, perfecting their presses, making ready to take their part in the history of printing. If this privilege were ever really intended to be fully operative, we see how near the Venetian government came to ruining, at the very outset, one of the greatest artistic and commercial glories of their city. For it is not to be supposed that the master printers already in Venice would have patiently waited the expiry of the privilege; they would certainly have carried their skill, their fortunes, and their vigour elsewhere.

It is difficult, however, to believe that the monopoly granted to John of Speyer was intended to be really and stringently binding. It is more probable that the privilege was conferred, as a sort of diploma of merit, by a grateful government upon the prototypographer of their city. In all likeli-

[1] Jenson does not appear to have ever applied for a privilege. After this first privilege to John of Speyer, either the documents have disappeared or the custom of applying fell into disuse. The next instance of a privilege does not occur till seventeen years later, and again between 1487 and 1492 there is a gap in which no privileges are to be found. After 1492 they become more regular and frequent.

hood the government did not fully grasp the importance of the new method of producing books. They may have thought that printing would not prove to be so rapid a process as it did; that the typographer's art would, at most, serve merely to supplement the art of the copyist, and would give to a few wealthy collectors reproductions of codices at present inaccessible. It is to be observed, however, that the phrases of the privilege, *in maximo numero* and *pervili pretio*, hardly bear out this conjecture; and even if they are copied from John's petition without much consideration of their import, as is probably the case, we cannot acquit the government of haste and precipitancy in their first dealing with the art of printing.

Whether the monopoly was designed to be operative or not, John of Speyer solved every difficulty by his death, and the marginal note in the minutes of the College, *nullius est vigoris quia obiit magister et auctor*, relieved his contemporaries from the burden of what might have proved a tyrannous restraint, and allowed the art of printing to embark freely upon its career in Venice.

The second kind of privilege granted by the Venetian government, was a copyright conceded to the author of a work, securing to him his proprietorship in his own production. The second instance of a privilege recorded in the minutes of the College furnishes us with an example of this sort of copyright. On Sept. 1st, 1486, the College bestowed upon Marc' Antonio Sabellico, historiographer to the Republic, the sole right to authorize the publication of his *Decades rerum Venetarum*,[1] under penalty of a fine of five hundred ducats. This is the earliest instance in which the government recognized an author's literary proprietorship in his own work. In this case the property is secured to Sabellico by the phrase, *quod opus prefatum per Marcum Antonium prefatum dari possit alicui diligenti impressori qui opus illud imprimat suis sumptibus et edat et nemini præter eum liceat opus illud imprimi facere*.[2] Although the privilege does not explicitly confer on Sabellico the property in his book, yet this clause, forbidding anyone to print it save the man he may select, was intended to secure full rights to the author.

In the year 1493 the College formally and explicitly recognized the doctrine of literary proprietorship, in the privilege which they granted to Daniele Barbaro—a copyright for ten years in his brother Hermolao Barbaro's *Castigationes Plinii*. The College state their grounds, which are, *arbitrantes quod qui onus et impensiam habuerunt, consequantur etiam utilitatem et commodum, non autem alii illud ab eis auferant*. Hermolao's property in his *Castigationes* is held to have passed to his heir, his brother Daniele.

[1] Hain, *14,053. Printed by Andrea de Torresani in 1487.

[2] Cf. Castellani, *I privilegi di stampa e la proprietà letteraria in Venezia*. Venezia, 1888, p. 6.

From the copyright granted to Petrus Franciscus de Ravenna in the year 1491-2, 3rd January, it seems that the formula in use for conceding literary proprietorship to an author, was the formula used in the case of Sabellico. In this case no one is to print the work called *Fœnix*,[1] *excepto dumtaxat illo impressore, quem prefatus doctor* (*i.e.*, Petrus Franciscus, the author) *preelegerit.*

There are abundant instances of this second kind of privilege, copyright to the author. But they are not so numerous as the examples of the third kind, copyright to editor or publisher for works not their own, or only partially so. The first example of a copyright to an editor, which is recorded in the minutes of the College, is that granted to Joannes Dominicus Nigro for his edition of *Haliabas*[2] and of Xantis de Pisauro, *De Venenis.*[3] The formula is still the same as in the case of copyright to author, no one may print the editions *excepto dumtaxat illo impressore quem prefatus dominus Joannes Dominicus duxerit eligendum.* The same year (1492, 17th August) furnishes us with an example of a copyright granted to a printer-publisher, Bernardinus de Benaliis, *imprimendorum voluminum ingeniosus artifex et magister*, for Bernardo Justiniani's *De origine urbis Venetiarum.*[4] And from this date onwards such copyrights constantly occur.

It was the abuse of this kind of copyright which led to the first legislation on the subject of the press in Venice. By no means all the works for which privileges were demanded, issued from the press. For when the custom of asking for privileges took firm hold on the printing and publishing trade, there was a rush of printer-publishers to secure copyrights in a great number of books which they had small prospect of ever setting up in type, and this block in the printing trade led up to the legislation of the year 1517.

The fourth kind of privilege conceded by the College for the encouragement of the new art was a patent for improvements in the method of the art, or for fresh departures inside the region of the art. A patent for the sole use of any invention naturally carried with it a monopoly in the works produced by that invention. For example, the monopoly in all Greek books which he shall print, granted to Aldus in 1495-6, is conveyed in the same privilege as bestowed on him a patent for his two new methods of printing, which he calls his secrets. And a similar privilege was conceded to Gabriele Braccio da Brisighella and Company for his *bellissima et nova inventione* for

[1] Hain, *13,697. Published by Bernardinus de Choris, x Ianuarii, M.ccccxci.

[2] Not in Hain. Published by the printer, Bernardino Rizzo da Novara, 1492. Cf. Fulin, *op. cit.*, p. 23.

[3] Not in Hain. Published by Rizzo da Novara, 1492.

[4] Hain, *9,638.

printing in Greek; and in 1498 to Ottaviano de' Petrucci da Fossombrone for his invention for printing figured song. Again, in the same year, we find a patent granted to Nicolò Vlasto of Crete, for his *sorte di bellettissime lettere grece, unide cum i suo' accenti, cossa che non fu mai più facta nè si bona ne cussi bella*. In 1500-1 Aldus received a patent for his *lettere corsive et cancellaresche*, and the Chiefs of the Ten undertook to see that his rights were respected. And throughout the whole of the sixteenth century we find patents granted by the government for improvements in the art of printing.

These four kinds of privileges which we have just enumerated were granted as protection from competition inside the state. There is a fifth and last kind of privilege, which was designed to encourage the art in the city, and to guard it against foreign rivals—the sort of privilege known as protection. The government of the Republic was protectionist. It sheltered its industries from external competition. And in the case of printing it declared at once that it would follow its usual practice (*quemadmodum in aliis exercitiis sustinendis et multo quidem inferioribus fieri solitum est*). It therefore provided that John of Speyer's monopoly should be protected from foreign as well as from internal attack, by forbidding the importation or sale of books printed elsewhere. And this protective clause appears, almost invariably, in the privileges subsequently granted by the government.

But besides the protection of the individual author, editor, or printer-publisher, the government also took steps to foster and protect the art generally. It encouraged foreigners to apply for Venetian copyrights, but it soon began to add the proviso that works for which copyright is obtained must be printed in Venice.[1]

The printer-publishers were in the habit of adducing various reasons in support of their petition for a privilege. In the year 1496 Bernardino Rasma[2] approaches the College with a supplication which shows how keen the competition among book merchants was, and the lengths to which they would go in their desire to overreach one another. Bernardino informs the College that "a pernicious and hurtful corruption has crept into the midst of the merchant printers of this glorious city, whereby not only in times past but now-a-days many of them are undone. For when one of them shall have set himself to produce a book of rare beauty—which entails the absorption of all his capital in it—should his brother merchants come to hear of it, they use every cunning device to steal the proofs of the new work

[1] *e.g.* 1519, 15th April, a copyright granted to Manenti, doctor to the Duke of Urbino, *hac tamen conditione, quod antedictus magister Manens obligatus sit hic Venetiis facere imprimi opera prædicta*. And so with Lucantonio Giunta in 1522.

[2] *i.e.* Bernardinus Herasmius Novocomensis. Fulin, *op. cit.*, p. 41.

from the hands of the pressmen, and set to, with many men and many presses, to print the book before the original designer of the book can finish his edition, which, when it is ready for issue, finds the market spoiled by the pirated edition." Against such fraudulent and ruinous competition the printer-publishers sought protection from the government.

Or, again, they plead in support of their appeal, the bad workmanship of their brother printers and the excellence of their own. For example, Braccio of Brisighella and Company set forth how, "by the culpable negligence and ignorance of printers the texts of editions become every day more corrupt, which thing is a dishonour and a public injury to this glorious city. But Braccio and Company, ever solicitous for the honour and welfare of this thrice glorious Republic, are resolved by means of a new and beautiful invention, to print both in Greek and Latin with every care and diligence. In this useful and laudable undertaking they have spent much money, even more than they could afford, but they have done so in the hope of being favourably regarded by your most benignant and clement serenity;" and they accordingly present their petition for a patent and a copyright.

Or, finally, printers sometimes appeal for a privilege on the ground of their misfortunes or distress. They have large families to support, or, like Filippo Pincio—to whom befell the *miserabil caso che brusò la casa cum libri et ogni sua facultade*—they have met with some accident. That printers should apply for a privilege on the grounds of poverty, would seem to show that they believed that there was some pecuniary advantage to be gained from the possession of such a grant.

In the year 1494 we find the first instance of a printer-publisher supporting his application for a privilege by a certificate from competent authorities as to the value of the work which he proposed to publish. No such certificate was at that time required by the government, but the applicant no doubt hoped in this way to facilitate the concession of the grant he sought. The example is that of Bernardino de Benaliis, who petitioned for a copyright in the works of the Beato [1] (at that time not yet Saint) Lorenzo Giustiniani, and of Alessandro Tartagni da Imola,[2] and put in attestations as to the importance of Tartagni's works from the Rector of the Faculty of Jurists, and from many doctors in law at the University of Padua.[3] Foreigners frequently sought the support of the ambassador of some prince in presenting their petition. For example, in the year 1494, Girolamo Biondo of Florence

[1] Hain, 9,477. [2] Hn, * 15,254.

[3] *Visis attestationibus rectoris juristorum et complurium doctorum legentium in florentissimo gymnasio patavino affirmantium opera ipsa futura fore valde proficua et utilia universo orbi.* So, too, in the case of Hieronymus Durante, 1492. Fulin, *op. cit.*, pp. 23, 30.

enlists the support of Antonio di Cauchorio, ambassador of Rimini, to obtain for him a copyright in Joannes Ferrariensis, *De cælesti Vita*, and in the letters of Marsilio Ficino; Richard Pace, ambassador of England, applies for a copyright on behalf of Nicolaus Thomæus[1] for his translation of Aristotle's *Parva Naturalia*, with a commentary; and Bernardino da Landriano is assisted by Taddeo Vimercati, ambassador of the Duke of Milan.[2]

The College did not always grant the petition as it was presented; they occasionally imposed conditions upon the fulfilment of which the validity of the privilege depended. These conditions are mainly of three kinds, affecting the quality of the work to be produced, the speed of production, and other people's rights. As examples of the first kind of proviso, we have the privilege to Bernardino de Benaliis of 1493-4, by which he is bound not to publish the works of Tartagni without those of Giustiniani, nor *vice versâ*, but he must publish both together at one and the same time, and he is obliged to print on *cartha optima charactereque perfecto et quod sint correctissima* (*i.e.*, *opera*). Matheo de Co de ca's privilege of 1494 is limited by the condition that he shall sell *dicte opere pretio honestissimo, si in grosso come menudo*. In 1496, Bernardino da Landriano is bound not to abuse his privilege by forcing up the price.

Conditions as regards speed were occasionally added; as, for example, that the works must have appeared within a year from the date of the petition, or must be printed at a certain rate *per diem*.

The third kind of proviso which the College attached to a privilege was designed to protect other printer-publishers' antecedent privileges, and the College itself from the consequences of granting a copyright in a work which some other publisher had already begun to print. We have an example of such a saving clause in the privilege granted to Alessandro Calcedonio in the year 1493, which closes thus, *declarato, quod hæc gratia intelligatur casu quo opera ipsa sint nova* (that is, new to the press) *et aliquis alius jam non cœperit illa imprimere, vel sibi promissum fuerit.*[3] This proviso is constantly repeated in various forms, for example, *quod non comprehendantur illi qui forte jam initiassent similia opera* (in 1494), and *dummodo prius dicta volumina non fuerint impressa* (in 1502). The College made its intention upon this point so clearly understood, that the executors of Hermann Liechtenstein, when applying in 1494 for a copyright in Vincent de Beauvais' *Speculum*, themselves insert the proviso in their petition, *non derogando tamen ob hoc juribus eorum qui ante presentem diem imprimissent aut imprimi facere cœpissent.*

[1] Calendar of State Papers, Venetian, vol. iii., Nos. 696, 698, from which it appears that Thomæus had been Pace's tutor.

[2] Other instances will be found in my Analysis of privileges, among the Documents.

[3] In this case the works in question had been published in 1492 by Ottaviano Scotto.

All the same, this proviso does not always appear, nor when it did appear was it always sufficient protection for the original holder of a copyright; for we find Lazzaro di Soardi prospectively protecting himself by the proviso that all subsequent copyrights granted for the works named in his petition shall, *ipso facto*, be held as surreptitious and invalid. We must remember that as yet the relations of the government to the book trade were purely tentative and experimental. It was anxious to encourage the trade in every way, but it prepared no machinery for the proper regulation of that trade; it kept no register of the privileges it granted other than the entry in the minutes of the College or of the Senate—and to these petitioners could not have access—and so printers and publishers had no means of knowing whether they were infringing a previous copyright or no.

As to the average duration of privileges in Venice, we find that during the first century of printing the average is about ten years. After the middle of the sixteenth century the average duration has a tendency to rise, till we find it touching twenty years in 1569, in 1587, and in 1593, and reaching twenty-four years and over in 1596. We find, however, wide differences between particular cases; we have instances of copyrights for one year, for five years, for fifteen years, for twenty and for twenty-five years. Occasionally slight concessions in favour of the publisher are made by the clause that the copyright shall run from the date of the issue of the book, and not from the date of the copyright.[1] Or, again, the government grant a prolongation of copyright upon sufficient cause shown why the original copyright period has not been available to recoup the publisher. An interesting example of such a prolongation of copyright is the concession made in 1508-9 to Leonardo Crasso, who eight years previously had published and obtained a copyright in *Polifilo*[2] *vulgar, opera molto utile et fructuosa et de grandissima elegantia*, but had drawn no profit from it, nor had been able to sell it owing to the wars.

It is very doubtful whether these early privileges were at all strictly enforced. The College granted them quite readily, but took no means for registering them for public reference; and it left the petitioners to protect their own interests. Yet, as far as we know, there is no instance of one printer suing another for infringement of his rights. Infringement of copyright did take place, as we know from the complaints presented to the College in 1494-5 by Daniele Barbaro against those who had infringed his copyright in Hermolao Barbaro's *Castigationes Plinii*. And, again, the Chiefs of the Ten in 1499 issue an order to publishers to respect the copyrights granted to Antonio Moretto of Brescia. In 1494-5, Girolamo Biondo and Giambattista, *suo socio*, secure a copyright for ten years in the

[1] For examples, see Analysis of privileges.

[2] *i.e.*, the *Hypnerotomachia*, published by Aldus in 1499.

Letters of Saint Catherine of Siena. These letters were first published by Aldus, however, in the year 1500, and this seems to afford a further proof that these privileges were not strictly observed; otherwise Aldus could not have published a work for which a privilege was still running with five years unexpired. Again Aldus, by the publication of Pollux's Lexicon in 1502, was infringing Gabriele Braccio's copyright in that work, which Braccio and Company had obtained in 1498, while that copyright, again, clashed with the more extensive privilege granted to Aldus in 1495-6; and as a result of this confusion we find the Letters of Phalaris published in 1498 [1] by Gabriele Braccio and Company, and in 1499 [2] by Aldus, without any suit of one against the other, or any determination where the copyright lay.

The whole question of privileges was in confusion. Nor did the penalties attaching to infringement appear to act as deterrents. The court before which cases of contravention of copyright could be tried, is sometimes specified in the privilege itself. Occasionally it is declared that any magistrate of the Republic may try the case; for example, the petition of Soardi in 1503 provides that *ogni magistrato possi ministrar justicia per questa presente gratia.* Sometimes it is the Signori di Notte [3] who are to form the court, but more commonly the Avogadori di Comun.[4] The penalties likewise are specified in the privilege. For the most part they consist in confiscation of the contraband goods, a fine varying from as low as twenty soldi (in 1500) for each copy, to as high as one thousand ducats in the case of Ariosto's copyright in the year 1515. The destination of the fine was also prescribed. As a rule it was divided into three parts, of which the court had one part, the accuser one, and some charity in the city one. Very rarely do we find, as in the year 1500, when two months' confinement is added to the fine, the punishment of prison for infringement of a privilege. Still rarer is suspension from the exercise of the art as a penalty for violating a privilege.

In dealing with the relations between the government and the book trade and printing press upon the question of privileges, in this period before legislation, we have endeavoured to treat the subject of monopolies, copyrights, patents, and protection in an orderly manner. But the action of the government itself was based upon no general principles; it had formulated no fixed rules of conduct. The habit of the printers and publishers and authors, however, was gradually building up a series of precedents, which regulated the conduct of the government when the time for legislation on the matter of the printing press arrived.

[1] Hain, *12,871.

[2] Renouard, *op. cit.*, i. p. 42.

[3] The police magistrates of Venice.

[4] The procurators fiscal of the Republic.

CHAPTER VIII.

1469—1528.

BOOKS BEFORE LEGISLATION.

Protection against the art—Censorship of three kinds: (1) religious, *testamurs* and *imprimaturs*; (2) literary, Marcus Musurus and Andrea Navagero; (3) moral, subdivided into (α) public or political morality, and (β) private morality—The case of Alvise Cinthio degli Fabritii—Resumé.

E have seen how the government, during this first period of its relations to the press, the period before legislation, undertook, though in a vague and indefinite manner, to protect authors, editors, and publishers from piracy at home and from foreign competition. Such protection was afforded by *privileges* of various kinds. In the same vague and indefinite way the government was gradually compelled by circumstances to undertake the protection of the State against certain dangers incidental to the printing press, and this it did by the creation of a censorship—informal at first, but subsequently codified—whose operation is marked by the presence of *imprimaturs*, just as the operation of monopolies, copyrights, and patents is marked by the presence of *privilegii*. As yet, however, there were no laws on the subject of books, and consequently there is no definiteness about this early censorship, no commission to specified officers. The government merely took action upon each case as it arose.

As the College or the Senate granted privileges, so the Council of Ten granted *imprimaturs*. It was inevitable that this censorial duty should fall to the Council of Ten in virtue of its special functions in the State as guardian of morals and committee of public safety. The censorship of the press in Venice offers three aspects, religious, literary, and moral; and moral censorship may be subdivided into censorship of public or political morals, and censorship of private morals.

We have seen that applicants for a privilege sometimes fortified their petition by a certificate, approbation, or *testamur*[1] from competent authorities as to the value of the work for which they demanded a privilege. The earliest example of an ecclesiastical *testamur* printed in a book published in Venice, is that which appears at the beginning of the *Nosce te*, issued by Jenson in the year 1480. It is signed, *Philippus rota juris utriusque doctor; Joannes gusmaci, archipresbyter montis Silicis, ac plebanus Sanctæ Marie nove de Venetiis; Petrus frigerius artium et theologie doctor, archiepiscopus Corphiensis; Mapheus girardo, Patriarcha Venetiarum, Dalmatieque primas; Gabriel brunus, ordinis minorum theologorum, Inquisitor.* As the *Nosce te* was a devotional work, written by a cleric, the Carthusian Giovanni di Dio, he may have been required by his superiors to obtain and even to print the *testamurs* of the above-named theologians, among them being his Patriarch and his Inquisitor. This *testamur* certainly proves an act of ecclesiastical censorship, but over an ecclesiastic; and it is possible that it may have been regarded ecclesiastically as equivalent to an *imprimatur*. No reference to the *Nosce te* occurs in the documents of the College or of the Senate, and we cannot tell whether a privilege was ever granted for the work, and if so, whether any reference was made to this ecclesiastical *testamur*.[2] But it is certain that no such *testamur* was at that time required by the secular government, nor would the government have ever admitted that such a document was equivalent to an *imprimatur*, had those been in use in 1480, which was not the case.

No other instance of such a clerical *testamur* occurs till the beginning of the next century. In the year 1505, 26th Nov., Jacomo di Penzi of Lecco, printer, in his petition to the College for a privilege, states that he has an *imprimatur* from the Chiefs of the Council of Ten, and a *testamur* from the Patriarch as to the quality of one of the works, the *Tre famosissime Questioni*, by Zane, Archbishop of Spalato. There is nothing to show whether the Chiefs had ordered Jacomo to produce this ecclesiastical *testamur*, or whether he had done so of his own accord. In the next year we have a case which resembles that of the *Nosce te*. Silvestro da Prierio, a Dominican, applied to the College for a privilege, and put in the *testamur* of a brother Dominican, who had been appointed by the general of the order to examine Prierio's work. Here the censorship and the censor are both ecclesiastical, but the ecclesiastical *testamur* is presented as an inducement to the secular government to grant a privilege.

[1] All such documents I shall call *testamurs*, as distinguished from privileges and *imprimaturs*.

[2] In the year 1695 the Inquisitor, by endeavouring to substitute a true *imprimatur* for a *testamur*, brought down on himself the anger of the government.

In none of these cases did the secular government order or require the presence of an ecclesiastical *testamur*; the petitioners put in their *testamurs*, believing that these would assist them in obtaining their privilege. But in the year 1508 the Council of Ten, when petitioned for an *imprimatur*, appointed a censor to examine the work from a theological point of view. This was in the case of Gregorius de Gregoriis, who obtained his *imprimatur* for Christoforo Marcello's *Universalis animæ traditionis liber quintus*, because Doctor Vicenzo Querini, who had been appointed to examine the work, declared that it contained nothing opposed to Catholic verity (*quod Doctor Vicenzo Querini cui per capita opus ipsum datum fuit revidendum et bene examinandum, affirmavit nihil in ipso opere esse quod repugnet vel alioquin contrarium sit catholicæ veritati*). This is the first instance of a religious censorship exercised by the secular government. In this case the Council of Ten appoint their own censor to examine the work on the score of Catholic theology, and they grant their *imprimatur* upon the strength of his report. Whether they would have withheld the *imprimatur* had the report been hostile—in other words, whether they gave their censor a deliberative, and not merely a consultive faculty—is not certain, but in all probability the Ten would have felt itself bound by the finding of its censor. How far the action of the secular government in this matter was prompted by the Church it is difficult to say. But it is important to bear in mind that, in this earliest case of obligatory censorship, whether prompted by the Church or moved of its own accord, it is the secular government which initiates the religious censorship and delegates to the censor his authority. The Venetian government never at any time disputed the right of the Church to be protected by censorship from the attack of books subversive of the faith. But it maintained that the State was the proper weapon of defence through which that protection should be secured. In this case of Marcello's book it recognized the need for such a religious censorship. By its order to Querini it virtually said, "Let us hear what may be alleged by the Church as regards the tendency of the work before we grant an *imprimatur*." Venice desired in theological matters to have the opinion of the Church, but only as a guide, the best guide, to its own conduct in granting or refusing its permission to print. The religious censor in Venice acted merely through powers delegated to him by the secular government. The situation was not formulated, nor was it likely to be till divergence of opinion between secular and ecclesiastical authorities arose. But the position was implied in the conduct of the Ten towards Christoforo Marcello's book.

In the year 1512 we have the instance of Bernardino da Venezia, which shows that the habit of seeking the *imprimatur* of the Council of Ten, though not yet obligatory by law, was growing up in custom.

Bernardino applied to the Senate for a privilege in two theological works, and put in the *testamur* of the Patriarch and the *imprimatur* of the Council of Ten.

Three years later the Chiefs of the Council of Ten, in answer to Lazzaro di Soardi's request for an *imprimatur* for various theological works, declare that since Soardi has obtained the *testamurs* of the Patriarch and the Inquisitor, they, *quoad se*, have no objections to offer, and *permittunt fieri quantum præfati Reverendissimus et Inquisitor concessere*. The phrase *quoad se*, which occurs again in an *imprimatur* of the year 1516, is a remarkable expression. It seems to indicate that the Council of Ten had tacitly resigned its direct control over the religious censorship—that they accepted the Patriarch and the Inquisitor as the proper persons to deal with this matter. They no longer, as in 1508, name the censor; if the Patriarch and the Inquisitor are satisfied upon the subject, then the Ten also are satisfied. This result was inevitable; it was the logical consequence of the situation. Granted a religious censorship, it was clear that the Patriarch and the Inquisitor were the proper persons to exercise it; they were experts in the subject, and, as long as the relations between the Church and the Republic remained friendly, the government was perfectly content to accept their decisions on the point. But the fundamental position of the government is not altered. It is the secular authority, not the ecclesiastical, which grants the *imprimatur;* and the use of the word permit (*permittunt fieri*) implied that their permit was necessary, and that they could also forbid. The *imprimatur* to Soardi is of great importance, because it shows that the government had, in practice, delegated the religious censorship to the ecclesiastical authorities, and this custom subsequently became embodied in the law creating the censorial body.

In the same year, 1515, we find the first indications of another question which subsequently became one of keen dispute between the Church and the Republic—the right of the Holy See to grant copyrights, monopolies, *imprimaturs*, &c., in States other than those of the Church, and to support these concessions by the threat of spiritual punishments. Fra Felice of Prato, a converted Jew, had translated certain Hebrew books, and desired to print his translations, along with other Hebrew works, in Venice, at the famous Hebrew press of Daniele Bomberg, whose master printer was Hermann Liechtenstein. Fra Felice had applied to the Pope for a copyright, and this was granted to him both for Rome and the States of the Church under pain of temporal as well as of spiritual punishments, and for the rest of the world under pain of the spiritual punishment of excommunication. Fra Felice did not think the Papal privilege sufficient, and applied to the College for a copyright for ten years. This was granted to him, and the College made no observation upon the Papal brief conferring the privilege on Fra Felice.

But we shall see that later on the Venetian government raised vigorous protests against similar concessions from Rome.

As a final example of the exercise of religious censorship during this period, we have the privilege granted to Bernardino Cinzio, *frate minore*, and supported by *testamurs* from the Apostolic Legate, the Patriarch, and the Inquisitor. No *imprimatur* from the Council of Ten is mentioned. It may have been granted, but as there was no legislation on the question of censorship then in force, such an *imprimatur* was not necessary to the acquisition of a privilege.

As regards the question of religious censorship during this first period in the relations between the Venetian press and the Venetian government, we see that the secular government retained to itself the right of granting an *imprimatur* after revision of the books; it would not, had the question arisen, have allowed that any other authority could grant such an *imprimatur*. On the other hand, the Church authorities had tacitly come to be acknowledged as the proper persons to conduct the religious censorship; and their revision of books from the religious point of view was accepted as final by the government.

The second kind of censorship, the literary censorship, grew up in the same fortuitous way as the religious censorship. The need for something of the kind may have been suggested to the government by the petitions of the printer-publishers themselves, revealing, in many cases, their own defects,[1] for in them we find references to the scandalously inaccurate manner in which certain works have been produced, and promises on the part of the petitioners that every care shall be bestowed upon their edition. The earliest instance of a literary censorship imposed by the government is in the year 1503, when the Senate conferred on Marcus Musurus the office of censor of all Greek books,[2] a post Musurus was still holding thirteen years later. Again, in the year 1509, the Chiefs of the Ten granted to Pietro Cirneo an *imprimatur* for his History of Corsica, after having entrusted it to the examination of Bernardo Bembo,[3] and hearing his opinion that it deserved an *imprimatur*.

Literary censorship in the Humanities took definite form somewhat later than in the case of Hellenistic scholarship, when the Council of Ten issued its

[1] *e.g.*, Fulin, *op. cit.*, No. 16. "*Opus scilicet emendatum, ... tamen multis in locis inemendata et depravata habet.*"

[2] Legrand, *op. cit.*, vol. i., cxii, p. 140. Preface to Gregory of Nazianzen's Orations, 1516. *Jampridem a me cautum est ut e publica græcarum litterarum officina, cui liberalitate beneficioque Veneti senatus tredecim jam annis præsidemus, prodeant non qui sapientiam insipientem insolentes ostendent.* But I cannot find the appointment in the registers of the Senate.

[3] Father of Cardinal Bembo. See *Biog. Univ.* and Soranzo, *Bibliografia Veneziana*, No. 3,850. I am aware that Sig. Fulin considers this as an instance, not of literary, but of political censorship; and he may be right, seeing that the censor is the Ten.

general order of Jan. 30th, 1515-16,[1] which runs thus : "In all parts of the world, and in the famous cities not only of Italy but also of barbarous countries, that the honour of the nation may be preserved, it is not allowed to publish works until they shall have been examined by the most learned persons available. But in this our city, so famous and so worthy, no thought has yet been bestowed on this matter. Hence it comes to pass that the most incorrect editions which appear before the world are those issued in Venice,[2] to the dishonour of the city. Be it, therefore, charged upon our Noble Andrea Navagero to examine all works in humanity which, for the future, may be printed ; and without his signature in the volumes they shall not be printed, under pain of being confiscated and burned, and a fine of three hundred ducats for him who disobeys this order." The Council of Ten intimated their order to the printers of Venice on July 31st of the same year, enjoining upon all printer-publishers not to print *Libro alcuno in humanità se prima el non sera recognito et approbato per correcto, cum subscription de man propria nel exemplare dal Nobel homo Andrea Navajer.* This decree of 1516 shows that the government was, by this time, aware of the commercial importance of the book trade which had grown up in Venice, and of the necessity for placing it under proper control if it was to maintain its reputation and its value. This is the first example of a general or preventive censorship, applied to a whole class of works, namely, all works in Humanity, and not to individual books, as had been the case hitherto.

The third kind of censorship, the moral censorship, divides itself into a censorship of political morals—of the individual's attitude towards his State, and of private morals—of the individual's attitude towards the code of decency and of good conduct. As might be expected, such a close and secret government as that of Venice was extremely jealous of its State documents, and very sensitive to any reflections adverse to itself which might issue from the press. It endeavoured to protect itself from hostile criticism by the use of political censorship. Perhaps the earliest instance of such a censorship is the *imprimatur* granted in the year 1507, 16th July, to Lucantonio Giunta, to print the speech addressed to the Doge by Joannes Rebler, ambassador from Maximilian. In the case of political censorship, no more than in the case of religious and literary censorship, was there as yet any legislation on the subject, and the printer was not bound to apply for an *imprimatur*. But

[1] Consig. X. Misti., xxxix., c. 39to. Fulin. *op. cit.*, p. 15.

[2] It is curious to find the Venetian government itself anticipating Gaspar Scioppius' fierce condemnation of Venetian editors and printers : *Ciceronis Venetæ editiones flammis aboleri debeant ; cruces vero figi typographis ut documento sint aliis, ne tam improbo furto emptores argento emungere et depeculari audeant ; Senatui Veneto curæ esse oportet ne istæ typographorum fraudes tam deformem Veneto nomini maculam inferant.*

no doubt the delicate nature of the publication counselled him to obtain leave first, before going to press, and probably anyone who published matter offensive to the State would have been punished whether there was a law on the subject or not. Again, in the year 1510, the College granted a privilege to Bartholomio de Cori for his *La Obsidione de Padua.*[1] De Cori in his petition asserts that Marco Antonio Lauredan, one of the Chiefs of the Ten, had himself examined the work.[2] The delicate point in both these cases was, no doubt, the conduct of the Republic towards the Emperor Maximilian and during the wars of the League of Cambrai.

On the 20th August, 1515, we find another remarkable example of the application of political censorship as a safeguard against unfavourable opinions on the conduct of the State. Marino Sanuto was engaged upon his history of the advent of Charles VIII. in Italy, and desired to have free access to the papers of the Chancellary with a view to his special subject.[3] The necessary permission was granted him by the Council of Ten for the examination of all State papers two years old and upwards, but only upon condition that, when the work was finished, Sanuto should neither show it to anyone nor publish it till it had been submitted to the Chiefs of the Ten, and their pleasure made known. The following year Sanuto was elected one of the Senate (*nunc est de consiliis secretis, videlicet de Consilio rogatorum*), and *ex officio* he became informed of the current State secrets; that being so, the Chiefs of the Ten removed the prohibition upon the State papers of the last two years, and granted Sanuto power to inspect any papers he might desire to see.[4] Sanuto did not publish this, nor indeed any other of his works, and it was therefore not subjected to examination; but in this document we see that provision is made for protecting the reputation of the Republic by means of a political censorship.

A case nearly identical with that of Marino Sanuto occurred in the same year, 1515. The Chiefs of the Ten granted permission to Andrea Mocenigo to examine State papers older than three years, with a view to assisting him in the history of the League of Cambrai on which he was engaged, and in order that he may know the truth, which *in hystoriis est pars potissima*—a phrase they had already used in granting a similar permission to Sanuto. The same year Mocenigo became a senator, and the chiefs granted to him, as to Sanuto, leave to see all papers *usque in præsens*; but Mocenigo was warned neither to show his work to anyone nor to publish it until he had submitted it to the Chiefs of the Ten. Mocenigo completed his history, and presented it to the chiefs, who ordered the Grand

[1] Cicogna, *Bibliog. Venez.*, No. 1,910.
[2] Fulin, *op. cit.*, p. 16, note, No. 180.
[3] Sanuto, *Diarii*, vii. 109.
[4] Rawdon Brown, *Ragguagli sulla Vita di Marin Sanuto*, Venezia, 1837, iii. 322.

Chancellor, Giampietro Stella, to report upon it. The chancellor declared *dictum opus esse præclarum et dignum maxima commendatione*,[1] and Mocenigo obtained his *imprimatur*. In this case, as Mocenigo desired to publish his work, the examination by the political censor was actually carried out, and the Ten named as censor the Grand Chancellor of Venice, the man under whose care all the State papers of the Republic were placed.

During this period before legislation, we see that as the Church gradually established, in practice, a religious censorship of the press, so the State established a political censorship. If the Church would not allow the publication of matter hostile to its dogma, neither would the State allow the publication of matter hostile to its reputation and its glory. The government, no doubt, argued that this political censorship was in the interests of truth, which *in hystoriis est pars potissima*. But all truths are not convenient; and the State would probably have suppressed hostile truths as well as hostile falsehoods. We must not forget that in 1658 the Senate refused to allow the sale of Pallavicini's History of the Council of Trent, because Pallavicini there maintained that *Pietro Soave Polano* and Paolo Sarpi Veneto were one and the same person. When we reach the opening of the next century —the period of Fra Paolo Sarpi—we shall see how that great statesman formulated the position of the government as regards religious and political censorship.

The need for a censorship of morals, for a guardianship of the purity of the press, was sure to arise sooner or later in Venice. The invention of printing conduced to the spread of knowledge, but it also brought with it immense facilities for the spread of corruption. It is possible, however, that the Venetian government would have taken little or no notice of the licence of the press, had its attention not been forcibly called to the question; it certainly, later on, permitted the publication of scandalous works,[2] and did not hesitate to declare *degne di stampa* books with such suggestive titles as *Il Ritratto della Rufiana*, *Vittima delle Donne*.[3] The event which brought about the censorship of the press upon scandalous publications occurred in 1526, when Alvise Cynthio degli Fabritii published, under copyright for ten years, granted by the Senate, his book *Della origine delli volgari proverbii*. The episode is succinctly recounted in Sanuto's Diaries[4] as follows: " 1526-(7), 29 January. In the Council of Ten. . . . Further

[1] Fulin, *op. cit.*, No. 219. Cicogna, *Bib. Ven.*, No. 792. Foscarini, *Letteratura Veneziana* (Ven., 1854), p. 288. The book was published by Vitali in 1525.

[2] *Certo non posso vedere senza dispiacere qualche libro di rime oscene, dove nelli mandati d'un magistrato tanto sublime si dica che sono degne di stampa.*—Sarpi, *Consulta* ap. *Cecchetti*, *La Rep. di Venezia e la Corte di Roma*, ii. 235.

[3] Archivio degli Esecutori contro la Bestemmia, 1621.

[4] Sanuto, *Diarii*, xliii. 448.

they passed a motion forbidding the printing of any new book in this city unless it has been examined by the Chiefs of the Ten and has received their *imprimatur;* the Chiefs of the Ten shall appoint two persons to examine books. . . . And observe, all this has come about because of a book written by a doctor Domino Alvitio Cynthio, Venetian, dedicated to the Pope, and called *Origine delli proverbii*, in which the author speaks very ill of the monks of San Francesco under the title, 'We all draw the water to our own mill.'[1] The monks complained of this to the Chiefs of the Ten, who sent to seize all the copies of the book; and two noblemen were commissioned to examine the work and to report."[2] On the 30th January, Lorenzo Priuli and Gasparo Contarini were appointed for this duty. Sanuto is perfectly in accord with the official documents, from which we gather the following details. On the last day of September, 1526, Cynthio published his book on the Origin of Vulgar Proverbs. On the 5th October he obtained from the Senate a copyright for ten years, providing that no one might print nor sell the book unless he added as many new proverbs as there were proverbs in the original book.[3] The work is composed in *terza rima*, and is written in the poorest style. It is a dull, uninteresting book, which would have been forgotten long ago but for the famous action to which it gave rise. The first page of the book has this inscription:

ADY
TVM IGNA
VIS
PROCVL
HINC
ABESTE
PROFANI.

This is followed by a sonnet to the reader. Page the third bears the preface and dedication to the Pope, Clement VII.:

Præfatione del libro della origine
Delli volgari proverbi di Aloyse
Cynthio de gli Fabritii della
Poderosa et inclyta città
Di Vinegia cittadino delle
Arti et medicina Dottore
Ad Clemente VII. degli Illustrissimi
Signori de Medici
Imperatore Maximo.

[1] *Ciascun tira l' acqua al suo molin.*
[2] Sanuto, *Diarii*, xliii. 451.
[3] Fulin, *op. cit.*, No. 253.

The seventh page has a sonnet to the reader, setting forth the author's excuse; another sonnet against the author's detractors, *alli Blatteratori et sgridatori del libro et dello autore morditori*, and a sestett addressed to the Pope, whom the author apostrophizes as *O tramontana del mio picchol legno!* Page eight has the following inscription:

IN
ANIMI
DOTES
IVS
FORTVNA NON HA
BET
NEC IN
AMICORVM
DONIS
IMPERIVM.

and another sonnet to the Pope. The colophon, on leaf 194, runs thus: *Con la gratia del sommo Pontefice et della Illustrissima Signoria di Vinegia per diece Anni che nessuno non lo possa stampare ne far stampar et cætera sotto le Censure et pene che nelle dette gratie si legono. A tutti quelli che contrafaranno a quelle. Stampata in Vinegia per maestro Bernardino et maestro Matheo de i Vitali Fratelli Venetiani Adi ultimo Septembrio* MCCCCCXXVI. *in Vinegia.* The book contains forty-five proverbs, and under the proverb *Ciascun tira l'acqua al suo molin*, Cynthio declares that he will display the true character of those who say that they follow the rule of St. Francis. In doing so he gave deep offence to the Franciscans, notably, I suppose, in the lines:

Che dove non toccavan pria quatrino
Hor hanno piene d' oro le gran tasche
Contra il Precetto del suo Serafino.

It would seem that Cynthio had a grudge against the monks of San Francesco della Vigna on account of some merchandise, which he had shipped in the same bottom as carried property of the brotherhood. During a storm, the monks on board had induced the captain to sacrifice Cynthio's goods rather than those of the order, and Cynthio never forgot or forgave the loss he suffered. The privilege cited in the colophon was granted on the 5th October; it forbade anyone to print the book for the next ten years, unless as many new proverbs were added as the original work contained. The penalties for infringement were: loss of all contraband copies, half of which were to go to the accuser, and half to the author; a fine of one golden ducat for each contraband copy, this fine to be applied to the building fund of the

Scuola di San Rocco, of which Cynthio was a member; also a fine of four hundred ducats, two hundred to go to the arsenal, one hundred to the accuser, whose name was to be kept secret, and one hundred to the court which tried the case. The book probably had a wide circulation. Later on Cynthio was ordered by his censors to present a list of those to whom he had sent copies. This list contains thirty names, among others those of the Pope's Legate and the Grand Chancellor of Venice.[1] The monks of St. Francis soon became aware that they had been attacked in the new publication, and on examination of the book they resolved to complain of it on the grounds of heresy and of indecency.[2] I cannot find a copy of their complaint presented to the Chiefs of the Ten, but the result of their action was the publication of a general order on January 29th, 1526-7.[3] The preamble of this order recites that, owing to the freedom which everyone enjoys in Venice, it sometimes happens that obscene and corrupt works issue from the press. To abate this scandal be it decreed that, for the future, no one may publish any new work without having obtained the *imprimatur* of the Chiefs of the Ten, which *imprimatur* shall be granted only after the work has been examined by two censors, who shall send in their report signed and sworn to. On the 30th of January the Chiefs of the Ten sent for Cynthio and severely admonished him, and conferred upon their censors Priuli and Contarini power to compel the author to remove at his own cost anything which they may judge unfit for publication. The censors proceeded leisurely with the examination of the book, for it is not till March 18, 1527, that we hear anything more on the subject. On that date the censors state that they have not understood whether their commission gave them power to compel Cynthio to expurgate; the answer was in the affirmative. When the censors did report, it seems that they had already told Cynthio that he must cancel the obnoxious passages. But in the meantime the monks of St. Francis, apparently on the authority of the Chiefs of the Ten (*mandamento excellentissimorum Dominorum capitum*), had carried off all the copies of the book from the printer's shop. In January of next year Cynthio represented to the chiefs that he had printed the book on an *imprimatur* from them, and a copyright from the Senate, but that the monks had carried off all the volumes, whereby he had suffered a ruinous loss. On this petition the chiefs ordered that all the books shall be recovered from the monks of St. Francis and restored to the author. Part of this order was executed, but before Cynthio could obtain possession of the copies, his printers, by leave of the Ten, laid an embargo on all the copies until the writer should have satisfied them in their dues. On

[1] Cicogna, *Iscriz. Ven.*, vi. 872.
[2] Archivio di Stato, Capi X., Notatorio 7, c. iii.
[3] Archivio di Stato, Cons. X., Parti Comuni, Filza 4. See Documents, p. 196.

the 14th February, 1527-8, the Ten ordered Giovanni Badoer, in whose hands the volumes were, to restore them to the printer's shop in the same number and condition as they were in before the Franciscans seized them, *ut hoc modo nemini jus tollatur.* And here, as far as the documents are concerned, the matter ends. The extreme rarity of the book has led certain authors to declare that it was condemned to be burned.[1] That is not the case, but it is probable that while in the hands of the monks a considerable portion of the edition disappeared. We do not know what became of Cynthio. Cicogna[2] suggests that he died a violent death many years later; he bases his conjecture on a mysterious note, appended to a manuscript copy of a new proverb, in Cynthio's own handwriting, *nota questa satyra essere di propria mano del autore e non vi essere altera copia; et pochi giorni drieto morse, in qual modo non lo dico.* However that may be, the name of Cynthio degli Fabritii will always be associated with the first decided act of moral censorship of the press on the part of the Venetian government. The general order of 1526-7 on the subject of censorship belongs to the period of legislation, and will be dealt with when we come to discuss the legislative action of the government in relation to the press.

So far we have followed the action of the Venetian government in its earliest relations towards the new art and industry which had taken up its chief abode in Venice. As yet there was nothing approaching a regular code of press laws drawn up on general principles; indeed, we could not expect to meet with any such code. In no department of the government, neither in sanitary nor commercial administration, do we find that the legislature acted on fixed principles. Legislation was seldom preventive—it was almost always introduced to meet the occasion; it was either remedial or repressive, called into existence by the requirements of the moment to suit a specific case. And in this way custom and precedent gradually moulded the lines upon which the Venetian press code was constructed. When a law for the regulation of the press was passed, it was usually the embodiment of some custom which had obtained for some time previous; and hence the importance of noting carefully the earliest action of the government on this point. We see, then, that so far as there was any regular practice at all, it was customary to apply to the Chiefs of the Ten for an *imprimatur*, and in the first censorial law that was passed that custom was made obligatory. It was customary for the College, and then for the Senate, to grant privileges, either monopolies or copyrights, and the Senate continued to perform that function till quite late in the history of the trade.

[1] Peignot, *Dictionnaire des principaux livres condamnés au feu*, tom. i. p. 131. *Esprit des Journaux*, 1780, tom. ix.

[2] *Iscriz. Ven.*, v. 587.

The Ten having the duty of granting *imprimaturs*, the leave to print, it was natural that censorship of books, when it became necessary, should also fall to them. We have seen how the Ten allowed to the Church its full weight in the matter of religious censorship, and eventually abandoned that department entirely to ecclesiastics, accepting the verdict of the ecclesiastical examiner as sufficient guide in the question whether it should grant or withhold an *imprimatur*; how it retained in its own hands the censorship of political opinion; how it turned its attention to literary censorship with a view to maintaining the quality of the Venetian book trade; and how it was compelled to establish a censorship over the morality of the press. The next chapter will show us how Venetian press legislation developed upon the lines already indicated.

CHAPTER IX.

1517—1549.

EARLIEST LEGISLATION.

Objects: (1) formulation of custom and precedent; (2) protection and encouragement of the trade; (3) protection of the consumer against bad workmanship; (4) definition of literary proprietorship; (5) creation of a censorial board—Copyright, 1517—Censorship, 1526—Copyright and workmanship, 1533 and 1537—Decline of the art and reasons for this—Censorial board, 1544—Literary property, 1544-5—Foreign imprints, 1547—Appearance of the index of prohibited books—Creation of the guild of printers and booksellers.

HE period with which we have now to deal is the period of active legislation, when the Republic first began to frame its laws for the regulation of the press, and seriously undertook the government of this important industry. During this period the legislation of the Republic was chiefly directed to five points: first, the formulation of custom and the embodiment of precedents in laws; second, the protection of the trade and the attempt to preserve the excellence of the Venetian press; third, the protection of the consumer against bad material and exorbitant charges; fourth, the protection of the author's rights; fifth, the selection of a governmental department to administer the press laws and to regulate the industry. The way in which the legislature endeavoured to carry out these five objects is made clear as we follow the various laws passed upon the matter from time to time.[1]

During the earliest period of the history of the press in Venice, there was no executive department especially charged with the guardianship of the press. The legislative bodies were the Senate and the Council of Ten; and from them issue the laws we have now to examine. Unless we are to count as a law the general order of the Ten establishing a literary censorship in all works in Humanity, the earliest legislation on press affairs is the law of

[1] See Doc. No. 1, p. 195, *et seq.*

the Senate passed August 1st, 1517. The object of this law was to abate the inconveniences and disorders which arose from the existing system of privileges. It has already been observed, when discussing the question of privileges, that they were likely to prove mischievous to the trade, and were open to serious abuse, for a printer-publisher was able to apply for many more privileges than he could use, and thus block the way for other publishers, and check the issue of many valuable books; and this abuse grew common. The trade was throttled. The printer-publishers themselves complain quite early of the *perfida rabia de la concorrentia consueta fra questa miserabel arte.*[1] The preamble of the law of 1517 sets forth that there used to be in Venice printers in great number, from whom the city drew no small revenue, public as well as private; to say nothing of the convenience offered to scholars who could buy their books more readily where they were printed. But for some time past the custom of obtaining privileges has prevailed. These privileges close the road for all but the holder; and the number of privileges has increased to such an extent that many Venetian printers, finding no road open to their industry, have been obliged to migrate, to the damage of public and private interests, and to the general inconvenience. To remedy this evil the Senate now recalled every privilege granted heretofore—anyone is at liberty to print any of the works named in these cancelled privileges. In future no privilege shall be granted except for works which are new, or which have never been printed before (*solum pro libris et operibus novis, numquam antea impressis et non pro aliis*), and such privileges require the support of two-thirds of the Senate.

This was intended to be a radical law, sweeping away a mass of abusive obstruction, and rendering the press free again. It abolished all copyright, except the legitimate copyright in new works. But we shall see presently how the phrase *libri et opera nova* afforded an opening for abuse, and how the printer-publishers availed themselves of it.

The next law, the censorial law of 1526, was published by the Council of Ten as guardians of morals. As we have seen, the law was brought on by a special case, the complaint of the monks of San Francesco della Vigna against Cynthio degli Fabritii's book on the Origin of Vulgar Proverbs. The work received a copyright from the Senate without any question of its scandalous nature being raised. This would seem to show, either that the government had not examined the book at all before licensing it—and this is the more probable, as the copyright was obtained after the book was already printed[2]—or that it was indifferent as to the moral character of the book, or, possibly, that the book did not strike the Senate as being so

[1] Fulin, *op. cit.*, No. 77.

[2] The colophon is dated 30th September. The copyright was granted on 5th October.

offensive as the monks of San Francesco found it. It is most probable that the publication of Cynthio's book would not have called for this censorial law had it not been for the action of the monks. Under any circumstances the question of the moral censorship required to be vividly brought before the government to induce them to pay it serious attention. The case of Cynthio's book was sufficient to do this. The Republic was not spiritually anxious upon the score of indecent literature; but it was fully determined to permit no public scandal, nor the embarrassments which might arise therefrom, for such an inadequate and trivial reason as the publication of obscene literature. The preamble of the law declares that the freedom enjoyed by the press in Venice gives opportunity for the occasional publication of licentious and vicious books. To remedy this scandal for the future, no book may be printed until it has obtained an *imprimatur* from the Chiefs of the Ten. This *imprimatur* is to be granted only after the book has been examined by two censors appointed by the Chiefs, and these censors shall present their sworn report in writing. Books printed out of Venice may not be sold without a similar licence from the Chiefs of the Ten.

This law embodied the existing practice that the Chiefs of the Ten should grant the *imprimaturs;* but such *imprimaturs* were now made obligatory. The law, however, still left vague and uncertain the delegation of the censorial powers of the Ten. The censors are to be any two persons whom the Chiefs may appoint. It was not till some years later that the censorial board was definitely and finally established.

The two laws which come next, the law of January 3, 1533-4, and the law of June 4, 1537, both emanate from the Senate, and deal with the question of copyright, which belonged to the senatorial department. They show us the government seriously alarmed at the decline of the book trade in Venice, and the increasing importation of books printed elsewhere.[1] The Senate attributed this decline to two causes: first, to the faulty construction of the copyright law of 1517, and, secondly, to the carelessness and inferior workmanship of the printers themselves. The law of 1517 was badly framed and worked badly. There was still room for the abuse of copyright; for the law stated no period within which the copyright should become invalid through non-user. The term *pro libris et operibus novis, nunquam antea impressis*, was wide enough to cover a large number of important works still unpublished, and it was sufficient to make some very slight additions or alterations in a work already published in order to declare it a new work under the meaning of the act; there was no definition in the act of how much alteration was

[1] *Vedendosi chiaramente come l' arte della stampa, che soleva esser grandissima in questa nostra città, è andata talmente in ruina che non s' adopera quasi altri libri se non quelli che vengono stampati da Terre aliene.* Doc. No. 1, p. 196.

required to constitute an *opus novum.* An editor had only to apply for a copyright in works which came under either of these classes, in order to prevent any other publisher from issuing an edition of those works. The congested state of the trade became nearly as serious as it had been before 1517.

To correct these evils, the Senate now decreed that all printer-publishers who at present hold copyrights shall be obliged within one year from the date of this act, to have printed in their entirety all the works for which they hold copyrights on pain of forfeiting that copyright. This provision was to apply to all future copyrights. Should a work, however, be so large that it could not reasonably be printed within the year, it is to be held that the law has been satisfied if the printer cast off the work at the rate of one folio a day. No work for which a copyright is obtained may be printed out of Venice under pain of forfeiting the copyright. No printer-publisher may petition twice for a copyright in the same book. Finally, there was another abuse which the Senate desired to remedy, the excessive prices which publishers put upon their issues. For the future all publishers are to submit a copy of each publication to the Proveditori di Comun,[1] who should cause its value to be assessed by experts, and at that price and at no other shall the books be placed upon the market.

Here we find the government dealing first with the congested state of the trade, endeavouring to clear away abuses to give it breathing room, by compelling copyright holders to act *bona fide*, and at the same time protecting its interests, and endeavouring to feed it, by insisting that all copyright books must be printed in Venice; then turning its attention to the regulation of the book market, and protecting the interests of the consumer by establishing an official price; and, lastly, placing this department of the book trade for the first time under an executive branch of government, the Proveditori di Comun.

The second law of this group, the law of 1537, was directed to the same points, the interests of the trade and the interests of the consumer. The preamble attacks the ruinous and disgraceful practices of the Venetian printers, who used to be the best in all the world. But now, for the sake of gain, they use such vile paper that it will not hold the ink, and blots when one desires to make marginal notes in the book. And this is all the more disgraceful because foreign books come to Venice printed on excellent paper. Accordingly, all who obtain copyrights are to use paper that will not blot, under pain of being fined one hundred ducats, of forfeiting copyright, and losing the books, which shall be publicly burned in the Piazza di San Marco. This penalty shall be incurred if of any edition five copies blot, and a copy shall be held to blot if any five leaves in it blot. Pamphlets and

[1] The executive department which had charge of all the arts and industries of the city.

books up to the value of ten *soldi* do not come under the provisions of this law. Furthermore, since the law of 1517 against the conferment of copyright in books which have already been published is frequently evaded, on the plea that a few corrections, alterations, or additions constitute a new work, the law of 1517 is reaffirmed in its literal sense, that new books are those which have never been published before; and should the Senate by chance grant a copyright for a book which has already been published, that copyright is invalid. The Avogadori di Comun[1] are entrusted with the execution of this law.

The law of 1537 is interesting as showing how necessary a registration of copyright—a Stationers' Hall—had become, if the government could admit that it was liable to grant illegitimate copyright. But though urgently required, both on behalf of the government and of the trade, the registration of copyright was not organized till many years later. This law was not wanting in vigour; its terms were strong and its penalties severe. But, as so frequently happened with the laws of the Republic,[2] we cannot be sure that the act was properly enforced. The government entrusted the execution of the law to the law officers, the Avogadori di Comun, but these had no adequate police at their disposal to compel respect for the law. No instance is recorded of a book printed on inferior paper being publicly burned in the Piazza; yet it is not to be supposed that the promulgation of this act was sufficient to correct instantly, once and for all, a long-standing abuse. The conclusion to which we are led, in the face of the continued complaints of the government, is that the press laws were only partially respected. Indeed, one of the most remarkable points brought out by the preambles of the various laws is the steady decline of the Venetian press, over which the government lament in vain. Printing in Venice, in the city where it reached its highest perfection, was not seventy years old, and yet we find the government declaring that the Venetian book trade is almost beaten from the market, and that the art has sunk to a level which renders it a disgrace and not an honour to the city. The Venetian printers themselves are largely to blame for this decline of their art, and the public for which they catered must bear the rest. It was useless for the government to legislate on the subject when producer and consumer were working together to lower the standard. Economy, competition, greed, and cheap workmanship were only counterparts of a larger influence which was affecting the whole literary world of Italy. It is probable that the public for which the Venetian press worked had altered very much in character since the opening of the press. Its own activity must partially have satisfied the demand for worthy editions of great

[1] See Doc. No. 1, p. 197.

[2] There is an old Venetian proverb which says, *Lege Veneziana dura 'na settimana.*

authors, but partly, also, the demand had decreased. The intellectual ferment of the Renaissance was cooling down. Italy was sinking into the torpor which followed the settlement of the country by Charles V. There was no longer the keen demand for the sources of the new learning. Aldus had inaugurated an epoch of cheap literature, but it was literature of a high quality. He was a scholar, and printed for scholars; his cheap books were produced for the market of poor students. There was no fear that, while men like Aldus were printing the classics which they worshipped, the books, whether cheaply printed and cheaply published or not, would be produced in an unworthy form. But now, though cheap literature was still the order of the day, the quality of the literature had changed. The opening of the sixteenth century saw a great influx of light literature—of romances, novels, works of dubious morality—works meant to be lightly read and lightly laid aside, and therefore not calling for fine and careful workmanship. Not only had the quality of the literature and of the reading public changed, but it had in all probability decreased in quantity, so that the book-buying *clientèle* was no longer large enough to compensate a heavy expenditure in the production of books.

Whether this conjecture as to one of the principal causes for the decline of the Venetian press be valid or not, it receives some colour of support from the law issued by the Council of Ten in the year 1542-3. In the preamble the Council call attention to the fact that their *imprimatur* was not always sought, as demanded by the censorial law of 1526. Printers and booksellers venture to print and to sell books which offend the honour of God, are repugnant to the Christian faith, and are many of them most licentious. The Ten accordingly order that, in addition to the penalties already decreed, the printers of all unlicensed books shall be fined fifty ducats; the sellers of such books fined twenty-five ducats; those who hawk them in the streets shall be flogged from San Marco to Rialto, and shall then be imprisoned for six months. A publisher using a false imprint shall be imprisoned for one year, and then banished from Venice in perpetuity, with a price on his head if he return. The enforcement of this law is entrusted to the Esecutori contro la Bestemmia.[1]

Matters must have reached a serious pass. The decree of the Ten displays a large amount of irritation, a desire once for all, by the threat of extreme penalties, to compel obedience from the printing trade. And if any power in Venice could have compelled obedience, it was the dread of the Ten and of their formidable commission, the three Esecutori contro la Bestemmia. The law was to all intents and purposes a re-enforcement of the censorial law of 1526, requiring that all books should be submitted to

[1] A delegation of the Council of Ten, consisting of three members, entrusted especially with the supervision of morals.

the revision of the Ten and licensed by them, with a view to controlling licentious and scandalous publications. But, in spite of the terrible nature of the penalties, and despite the dread of the Council of Ten, it seems that this law was no more respected than the law which it was designed to re-enforce. The attempt to extort obedience by the threat of violent penalties defeated its own object. The punishment being far in excess of the offence, public opinion was against the law, not in favour of it.

An important reform in the administration of the press was initiated the following year (1544) by the Council of Ten. As regards the censorial revision of books upon which the *imprimaturs* of the Ten were based, the custom hitherto had been for the Ten to name its revisers. The council found this vague and indefinite delegation of its powers inconvenient, and resolved now to determine, once and for all, who should be its commissaries in this matter, who should be the permanent censors of the Venetian press on behalf of the secular government. The choice most naturally fell upon the three Rifformatori dello Studio di Padova, or University Commissioners, who were now charged with the examination of all books submitted to the Ten for an *imprimatur;* and that meant all books not clandestinely printed or sold in Venice. The Ten thus formally delegated its powers to the Rifformatori, and this was a first step towards the complete organization of the censorship in Venice. But there were still certain points left undetermined by law; for example, it is not to be supposed that the Ten included the religious censorship in this delegation to the Rifformatori, for it accepted the customary censorship of ecclesiastics on this subject. The final codification of all the various branches of the censorship was not completed till twenty years later.

The next serious abuse with which the Council of Ten was called upon to deal was the infringement of literary proprietorship. It had not been made clear by the terms of any law hitherto passed, whether literary property existed, *ipso facto*, in a work for the author of that work, or whether it was created by the process of obtaining a copyright, as we have seen was the custom in the period before legislation on press matters. Venetian printer-publishers were in the habit of ignoring literary proprietorship altogether, and were accustomed to print any work they pleased, even in direct opposition to the wishes of the author.[1] A law to protect authors became necessary. Accordingly, in the year 1544-5, a decree was issued forbidding anyone to print or to sell any work without having first presented to the Rifformatori dello Studio documentary proof of the consent of the author or of his nearest heirs. All books printed without this consent shall be confiscated and

[1] *Che si fanno lecito d' imprimer senza alcuna loro scienza, anzi contra ogni loro voler.* Doc. No. 1, p. 199.

immediately burned; the printer shall be fined one ducat for each book and each author injured, and imprisoned for one month.

We have already stated that the censorial law of 1543 was evaded as its predecessor of 1526 had been evaded. And the proof is found in the new law of 1547, by which the Ten again endeavour to check the sale of blasphemous, scandalous, and obscene books.[1] The law was evaded by the ostensible importation of such works, bearing a foreign imprint, into Venice. There is some reason, however, to suppose that the majority of these books were printed in Venice itself, and the foreign imprint forged. Such a practice has always been common to the press. Among famous examples are the Pierre Marteau[2] publications with the date Cologne, and in more recent times the imprints *Cosmopoli*, *Londra*, *Lugano*, are well known. It is probable that the government was face to face with the clandestine press which subsequently gave it so much trouble. The Council of Ten now declare that anyone who imports books of this nature shall forfeit the books and pay a fine of fifty ducats. The Esecutori contro la Bestemmia are charged, as usual, with the execution of the decree, and with them are associated the three Savii sopra l' heresia,[3] for the surveillance of the press upon the matter of religion. If the Ten really believed that the works they were endeavouring to suppress reached Venice from abroad, it is rather surprising that they should not at once have ordered an examination at the custom house, as the government was subsequently compelled to do.

The presence of the three Savii sopra l' heresia upon the commission of the Ten for the execution of this law introduces a new element in the history of the Venetian press. We have reached the point at which the Inquisition *hæreticæ pravitatis* began to make itself strongly felt in the history of the book trade. The Lutheran heresy was spreading through the medium of the press, and the first catalogue of prohibited books was shortly to appear in Venice. How far the Venetian government was acting under the influence of the Church in adding the Commissioners on Heresy to the ordinary executive for the enforcement of this law, it is impossible to say; but it is far from improbable that the presence of the three lay assessors to the Inquisition upon the executive board, was due to a compromise with the Church, the result of a desire to assist the Church in the suppression of heresy, while retaining for the government its claim to be the sole source of authority in the dominions of the Republic.

The importance of this period from the ecclesiastical point of view will be considered later on; at present it is necessary to deal with the action of the

[1] Doc. No. 1, p. 199.

[2] Janmart de Brouillant, *Histoire de Pierre du Marteau*, Paris, Quantin, 1888.

[3] The three Venetian noblemen who sat as lay assessors to the Holy Office.

secular government only in relation to the press. This same epoch, which is so important in the ecclesiastical government of the Venetian press, is also of the greatest moment in the general history of that press and book trade. For the year 1548-9 saw the printers and booksellers of Venice created a corporate body, a guild, by the decree of the Council of Ten published on January 18th. The decree sets forth that this art is one of the most important in the city, and yet is almost the only one which has not been erected into a guild. It is necessary that this should now be done, in order that the government may be the better able to lay their hands upon abuses, and to watch over and regulate the course of so valuable an industry. Therefore all those who print or sell books are to be formed into a guild, and the Proveditori di Comun shall draw up the bye-laws for its government. Among the special reasons recited for the constitution of the guild is the difficulty which the Savii sopra l' heresia find in discovering and punishing the publishers of heretical works; there is no one whom they can make responsible for the observance of their regulations on this matter. It seems therefore that, as the initiation of the moral censorship in the press was largely due to the action of the clerics, so too the formation of the guild by an official act of the government is to be attributed to the requirements of the same party. But we must observe that whatever pressure may have been put upon the secular government to induce it to take active measures for the suppression of heretical and scandalous works, the Republic never allowed the Church to appear as governing immediately and without the assistance and consent of the secular power. Neither in the case of this law which created the guild, nor in the proclamation of search for blasphemous and heretical works, is there any mention of the Patriarch, the Nuncio, or the Inquisitor, but only of the three Savii sopra l' heresia, the three representatives of the secular government on the tribunal of the Holy Office. The Republic acknowledged the Church's rights in such matters, but it took care to preserve intact its own position as ostensible ruler and real agent.

The creation of the Guild of Printers and Booksellers marks the epoch of consolidation in the history of the Venetian Press. In the year 1549, the industry took its place as an acknowledged element in the commercial economy of Venice. During this early period of legislation the government had directed its attention to the codification of custom upon the questions of copyright, of censorship and *imprimaturs*, of literary proprietorship, the protection and encouragement of the trade, the interests of the consumer, and the constitution of a proper executive in matters regarding the press. The legislation was not yet complete, and the government found it necessary from time to time to pass new laws on the subject or to amend old ones. But, on the whole, the legislation between the years 1517 and 1549, which we have just been reviewing, and its final outcome in the creation of the Guild of Printers and Booksellers, forms the most important epoch in the internal history of the press in Venice. In the next chapter we shall examine the construction of that guild, and how the government dealt with the new corporation.

CHAPTER X.

1549—1595.

THE GUILD OF PRINTERS AND BOOKSELLERS.

Mariegole of the guild—Bye-laws of the guild—Delays in the formation of the guild—Minute-book of the guild—Legislation by the guild—Taxation—Disorders in the guild—Jurisdiction of the guild.

T the Museo Civico di Venezia there is a manuscript copy of the bye-laws of the Guild, or University, of Printers and Booksellers, *approbati, laudati et confirmati* by the Proveditori di Comun in execution of the decree passed by the Council of Ten in the year 1548-9.[1] This promulgation of the bye-laws is signed by the three Proveditori, Francesco Donato, Paulo Contarini, and Jacomo Marcello, and is dated 14 May, 1567. No notice had been taken of the decree of 1549, and no attempt made to give it effect, until seventeen years later, in 1566, the Ten once more called upon the Proveditori to proceed to the execution of its orders. Thereupon the Proveditori summoned the presidents of the trade to a meeting, at which they were asked to formulate their views, and, after consultation with the presidents and other members of the trade, the Proveditori published the following bye-laws, and enjoined their observance on all members of the Guild of Printers and Booksellers.

"May the glorious and almighty God grant grace to us printers and booksellers who own shops and workrooms in this our fostering city, that we may be able to do that which is for His service, and for the glory and honour of this serene Republic in ordering and ruling the goings of our art; that so, for time to come, our art may guide its actions to the praise of the Divine

[1] Cod. Cicogna, 3,044. These bye-laws of the Venetian guilds are called *Mariegole*, said to be for *Matricule*, the matriculation books.

Majesty and to the general weal, under the protection of the glorious Virgin, Mother of our Lord Jesus Christ, and of this thrice happy and right well-established Republic."

After this dedicatory prayer, commending the guild to its patroness, come the rules of the university:

I. First; be there created a college of our art of printing and bookselling. All the members of this college shall meet in the church of SS. Giovanni e Paolo, in the chapel of the Rosary, and there shall they cause mass to be said by the reverend fathers, at the altar of the Virgin Mary, our advocate and patroness, and on that day a suitable donation shall be made, as the presidents shall think best. On that same day, and in the chapel of the Rosary, all the members of the college shall meet to elect a prior, two councillors, and six assessors, in the way hereinafter prescribed. On that day every master printer or master bookseller shall pay the sum of one lira, four soldi, and that annually. The prior, councillors, and assessors, with all the college, shall attend mass. The prior, councillors, and assessors who are elected at this meeting shall remain in office till the end of February next.

II. Every year on the Feast of St. John the Evangelist the whole college of printers and booksellers shall elect, by box and ballot, a prior, two councillors, and six assessors, from among the best fitted to the needs and the conduct of the art. They shall not be under thirty years of age. The elections are to be conducted as directed below; and the six assessors are to sit with the prior and councillors.

III. Not less than two-thirds of all the members are required to make a quorum. When a quorum has been formed, the syndics shall administer to each member an oath to elect truly and honestly those most fitted to hold office. After which each member present is at liberty to name his candidate. The names of all the candidates shall be put in a box and drawn out by chance; as they are drawn, they shall be ballotted for one by one, till the names of all the candidates shall have been put to ballot. The nine who have obtained most votes—provided always that the votes exceed two-thirds of those present—are elected officers of the guild, and the two who come nearest to the first nine—provided that they have received more than two-thirds of the votes—shall be officers in reserve to take the place of any who cannot attend a meeting. All the officials hold office from the first of March to the last of February.

IV. In the same way the chapter shall elect two syndics, whose duty it is to administer the oath of office to the prior, the councillors, and other officials; also to administer the election oath previous to ballot. No election shall be valid without the presence of at least one syndic. The syndics may also review and censure the action of the officials on any point where they consider that the rules have been violated, and may summon a chapter to approve their revision. They are to have the same authority as that possessed by the syndics of the Grand Guilds[1] (Scuole Grandi).

V. No member may decline either nomination or election, under pain of a fine of ten ducats.

VI. By the usual process the chapter shall elect a secretary, whose duty it is to enter in a book all the laws relating to the press, and the minutes of the guild chapter.

VII. So too a beadle shall be elected at a suitable salary. It shall be his duty to convoke the chapter when ordered to do so, and this he shall do either personally, or by notice left at the shop or house of each member, stating the day and hour and place of meeting; he must also inform the secretary of the citations, so that those who fail to attend may be punished. The prior is not re-eligible till after three years, the councillors and assessors after one year; the assessors in reserve may be re-elected at once.

VIII. The prior shall keep the accounts of the guild in due form and order, income and expenditure properly specified under their various headings, that the funds of the guild may be preserved and may increase. And upon the strong-box of the corporation shall be three different locks, and of the three keys the prior shall have one, and each of the councillors one

IX. Eight days before the expiry of their office, the prior and councillors shall render an account of their administration to their successors, and shall consign to them the strong-box with all the money it contains, and also with all the money it should contain; and if the out-going prior and councillors have given credit to any, that shall remain to their private credit, not as a debt due to the guild. They shall also consign the minute-book and all documents relating to the guild, and such consignment shall be registered in a book kept especially for the purpose. The penalty for failing to make these consignments is ten ducats, half of which shall go to charities and half to the funds of the guild, and so with all fines hereinafter named. No member in debt to the guild may sit in chapter, nor elect, nor be elected, and the officers of the guild shall be bound to prosecute the debtor for his debt.

X. Every motion requires at least two-thirds of the votes before it is carried.

XI. The prior, councillors, and assessors shall represent the guild on all occasions.

XII. When the prior cannot act, his place is to be taken by the senior

[1] The Grand Guilds or Scuole Grandi of Venice were the Scuole di San Marco, di San Teodoro, della Carità, di San Rocco, di San Giovanni Evangelista and della Misericordia. See Sansovino, *Venetia Città nob.*, &c., Venetia, 1663, p. 281.

assessor, and when an assessor cannot act, an assessor in reserve shall take his place.

XIII. Should it seem to the prior, councillors, and assessors desirable to have the assistance of the assessors in reserve, they may summon them to attend the meeting, and should the assessors in reserve refuse without good cause they shall be fined one ducat.

XIV. Should a vacancy occur in any of the offices of the guild, the chapter shall proceed at once to fill the vacancy.

XV. The prior, councillors, and assessors shall be obliged to obey the summons of the beadle, under penalty of a fine of one ducat, unless good cause be shown.

XVI. Absence from a meeting of the chapter shall be punished by a fine of four soldi grossi[1] for the first time; twelve for the second; one ducat for the third, with deprivation of vote for a year.

XVII. When the chapter is in sitting, if the prior or one of the councillors move a resolution and speak to it, no one else may speak or interrupt him under pain of a fine of two ducats. And no member of the guild may dare to reply or to move a resolution till he has obtained leave, and while he is speaking no one may interrupt him under penalty of a fine of one ducat.

XVIII. Every member of the guild is bound to respect and reverence our prior, councillors, and assessors in every place; nor let any dare by word or deed to insult them or assault them, under pain of loss of rights for two years and a fine of three ducats. And likewise the said officers are not to abuse any member of our guild, either in chapter or out of it, under pain of being deprived of office and a fine of six ducats; likewise ordinary members may not insult one another under pain of a fine of six ducats.

XIX. No one may move the chapter except the prior, the councillors, or the syndics in their own department.

XX. No member of the guild can hold office unless for five years previously he has kept a book-shop or sold books at his own house, or printed. Nor may those who are not carrying on trade as booksellers or printers vote, nor hold office.

Such was the primary constitution of the Guild of Printers and Booksellers in Venice—the instrument which the government devised in order to protect and govern the trade. The institution survived the government which created it; it lived through the fall of the Republic and the period of the French Revolution, and only disappeared in the first decade of this century.

[1] A soldo grosso was worth about threepence of our money. It was the fortieth part of a zecchino. See Gallicciolli, *op. cit.*, i. 475.

Although the erection of the guild was ordered in 1548-9, seventeen years elapsed before the bye-laws were formulated and the corporation fairly established. Two phrases, however, in the documents just quoted raise a doubt as to whether some sort of organization of the printers and booksellers did not exist previous to 1567, possibly the undeveloped result of the decree of 1548-9. These phrases are (1) *li Presidenti dell' Arte*, whom the Proveditori di Comun say that they consulted in formulating the bye-laws, and (2) *luogo solito alle nostre congregazioni.*[1] How come the printers and the magistrates to talk of the presidents of the art and of the usual meeting-place, unless some sort of organization of the trade were already established? Whether such an organization existed or not, however, it is clear that the year 1567 saw the real establishment of the guild, recognized by the government, and with bye-laws which were binding on its members.

The sixth clause in the *Mariegole* provided for the election of a secretary to keep the minute-book of the chapters of the guild. That minute-book exists; it is preserved at the Museo Civico among the Cicogna MSS., together with the *mariegole* of the guild. The first document in the minute-book comes four years after the establishment of the guild, and is dated 1571. It modifies the eleventh clause of the original *mariegole* by appointing a board of five members as proctors for the guild, whose function was to represent the guild before all courts of justice, and generally to protect the interests of the corporation. The document is signed by Hieronimo Scotto, prior, Gabriel Giolitto, and Zuan de Varisco, councillors, Giovanni Griffo and Pietro d'Affine, syndics, and Gasparo Bindoni, secretary. Of these names four at least were famous in the annals of Venetian printing, the names of Scotto, Giolitto, Varisco, and Bindoni. The duty of these five delegates, who are to serve *gratis et amore*, was to watch over the rights of the guild, and to see that those rights were not infringed by printers or booksellers who were not enrolled. For we must bear in mind that at its outset membership in this guild, though intended by the government to be obligatory on all printers and booksellers in Venice, was not rigidly enforced. The government had invited the master printers and booksellers to form themselves into a corporation, but had provided no machinery for compelling them to come in. Simultaneously with the nomination of the five delegates, the guild provides for a defence fund, to be raised by a tax imposed upon the members of the guild. Approbation and confirmation by the Proveditori di Comun was necessary before any resolution passed by the chapter of the guild became binding upon its members, and accordingly we find this proposal to levy a tax submitted to the Proveditori and confirmed in August, 1572. This same year, but under the priorship of Francesco Rampazzetto, it appears

[1] *i.e., il luogo de' Genovesi*, at SS. Giovanni e Paolo.

that the five proctors of the guild had been engaged in lawsuits, had spent the money raised for the purpose, and that the suits of the guild were at a stand for want of funds; the chapter, accordingly, vote further supplies.

The priorate of Rampazzetto witnessed other provisions for the good government of the guild. Many of those who open printing presses, but are not matriculated in the guild, are utterly ignorant of the art of printing (*i quali grossamente credendo che l' esercitio della stamparia sia cosa di poca intelligentia si fanno lecito entrar al maneggio di essa per poca cognitione et manco esperienza che ne habbiano*); this brings discredit upon Venice, and ruin and disgrace upon the art. The chapter therefore decree that no one who is not a member of the guild may set up a printing press nor open a book-shop, nor exercise any of the functions of bookseller or printer unless he has served five years' apprenticeship in Venice, articled at the Justitia Vecchia, and afterwards served as workman for three years in this city; he shall then be examined by experts named by the prior and officers of the guild, and, if found able, he shall, on the payment of five ducats, receive matriculation. And similarly, foreigners who desire to exercise the art in Venice must first serve five years in some shop in Venice, be examined and approved, and pay ten ducats before they receive matriculation. These sums are to go to the treasury of the guild. Sons and heirs of those who have been matriculated shall be exempt from payment. The penalty for infringement of the above is fifty ducats. The resolution was carried by fifty-one votes to three; but Jerolamo Torresan, one of the minority, appealed to the Proveditori to refuse their sanction, upon what grounds does not appear. So far from acceding to his request, however, the Proveditori confirmed the resolution, and ordered it to be inscribed in the minute-book. This is by far the most important piece of guild legislation which the corporation had passed as yet. In the first place, it virtually asserts the right of the corporation to regulate all matters relating to printing in Venice, and to jurisdiction over printers and booksellers who were not members of the guild. Although the government had never explicitly bestowed this right to jurisdiction, yet implicitly, by the confirmation of the Proveditori di Comun, it recognized and endorsed it. Again, if matriculation here means enrolment in the guild, as I think it does, then the result of this resolution was to compel all master booksellers and printers in Venice to become members of the guild, or to forfeit all right to exercise their calling. This, no doubt, was simply carrying out the intention of the government when it created the guild, and asserting a right which the government had neglected to grant explicitly. The effect of these resolutions must have been good; matriculation now became a matter of some difficulty and therefore of some honour, and the prestige of the guild was considerably raised.

It was not long before the question of finances and taxation presented itself seriously to the Corporation of Printers and Booksellers. The guilds of Venice—and therefore, of course, this new Guild of Printers and Booksellers—were subject to a tax for the maintenance of the armament. The tax seems to have weighed heavily on the corporations, if we may judge by the difficulty the Collegio della Militia da Mar[1] found in exacting it. All through the minute-book of the Guild of Printers and Booksellers we meet with documents relating to this question of the armament tax—orders to pay, complaints of evasion from the government office, assertions of inability from the prior. We have seen that the five delegates appointed to protect the interests of the guild had spent considerable sums in legal proceedings. Part of this money was money collected to pay the armament tax (*delli scossi che avanzassero dal presente armar*); so that when the tax fell due the sum was not forthcoming. In acting thus the Corporation of Printers and Booksellers seems to have been following a custom common among the guilds; for on the 1st April, 1574, the presidents of the Collegio della Militia da Mar issued a circular to all the heads of guilds, complaining that the tax-money has been spent on lawsuits and other objects, and ordering the money to be kept for the future in a box with three keys—one key to be held by the chief officer of the guild, and the other two by the two senior members.

The long series of acts by which the presidents of the Collegio della Militia da Mar endeavoured to secure the punctual payment of this tax may be followed in the original documents; it would be tedious and unprofitable to dwell longer upon them here.

Nothing is more remarkable in the history of the Venetian printing press than the rapidity with which its practice and its institutions deteriorate. We have seen how sudden and how deep was the fall from the early excellence of the prototypographers; and now, in the case of the guild, the same decline is visible. That instrument, devised by the government for the resuscitation of the art, after barely fourteen years' existence we find corrupt, and therefore ineffectual. The government thought that the blame lay with a faulty code of bye-laws. The Senate expressed that opinion in the year 1577-8, when it commissioned the Cinque Savii sopra le Arti to revise the Matriculation of the guild.[2] No results seem to have followed this order.

[1] The Naval Paymaster's department.

[2] Archiv. d. Stato, Senato Terra. Reg. 52, c. 36.

1577, 11 Jan. "*Essendo l' arte di stampadori tanto utile et importante cosi al publico come al priuato quanto è benissimo noto a cadauno di questo Conseglio, è conueniente ponervi ogni pensiero perche essa sia mantenuta et aumentata quanto più sia possibile. Laonde intendendosi che molti di tali artifici abbandonano questa città portando uia con loro Torcoli et Altri Instrumenti con molto maleficio di detta arte per non esser matricolata come le altre, non si deve mancar di far tale provisione che più non segui di tali disordeni et inconueniente pero;*

We do not know if the Cinque Savii took any steps at all. The exodus of printers and printing material continued, as we learn from the laws of the next century. The abuses in the guild remained. By the year 1581 malversation of funds had already crept into the Guild of Printers and Booksellers, chiefly owing to the carelessness of the auditors and to neglect of the rules providing for a proper consignment of books and accounts at the end of each year. The scandal was so grave that the Proveditori di Comun felt compelled to interfere. They did so in their general order of 12th November, 1581, addressed to the officers of all the guilds of Venice, but with special reference to the Guild of Printers and Booksellers (*precipue nella Confraternità de Librari et Stampatori*).[1] The Proveditori order the outgoing officers to consign all accounts, properly dated, and duly arranged under the heads of income and expenditure, with the names of those to whom money has been paid, and the reason why, within fifteen days after the expiry of their term of office. The new officials shall at once balance the books, and within one month the auditors must have examined the books and declared whether the guild is in debt. If it be in debt, the auditors are to report to the Proveditori, who will proceed against the late officers.

It is not easy to point to the source of this deterioration of the guild. It may be ascribed in part, no doubt, to the general indifference and *laissez-aller* of the Venetian character; partly, no doubt, to occupation with their own private affairs, which prevented the officers of the guild from giving sufficient attention to the management of their corporation, especially when we remember that they were called on to serve *gratis et amore*; partly, perhaps, to the defective character of some of the bye-laws. Some support is given to this last conjecture by the minutes of a chapter held on 4th September, 1586. By the original rules of the guild two-thirds of the members were necessary to form a quorum, and every motion required the support of two-thirds of those present before it could pass.[2] It appears that the need

"*L' andera parte che per autorità di questo Conseglio sia concesso alli cinque Nobeli Nostri eletti dal Consiglio nostro di Dieci sopra le arti di questa città che debbino regolar et matricolar questa delle stampe di quel modo che giudicheranno piu espediente alla conseruatione et augumento suo. Et sia lor data auttorità di proceder contra quei tali che hauessero ardimento di contrauenire alle deliberationi loro, et di desuiare simili Artefici con quelle pene pecuniarie over di Galea o di pregione che ricercheranno li demeriti de contrafattori. Et siano medesimamente tenuti far publicare sotto l' istesse pene, che niuno possi sotto qualsivoglia preteste estrazer di questa città torcoli, fumi, ne altri instrumenti, pertinenti alla stampa.*

+ 155.
— 1.
— 1."

[1] It is possible that this was a formula added in the case of each guild, in order to prevent the guild from thinking that it was not especially aimed at by the general order.

[2] Mariegole, Capitoli III., X.

for a majority of two-thirds hampered the action of the chapter, and made it difficult to pass important measures if they met with even a moderate opposition. It was accordingly moved, that for the future half the members on the books might form a quorum, and that a bare majority of those present should be sufficient to pass a vote. This was put to the chapter, and had 44 ayes and 20 noes; and, according to the existing rule, it could not be carried. But it shows that a large majority of the chapter were convinced of need for reform on this point.

The Corporation of Printers and Booksellers, though it had done much to restore the commercial importance of the trade in books, was not during this early period of its history a very powerful body. It is probable, to judge from the wording of the dedicatory prayer and of the bye-laws, that only master printers and master booksellers (*patroni di stampa et di bottega*) were enrolled in the guild. If we look at the numbers recorded in the votes of the chapter, we see that the highest number is sixty-six, the lowest fifty-one. If we take this as the lowest number that could form a quorum—that is, as one more than two-thirds of the members—we see that the guild could not have numbered more than seventy-five, or less than sixty-six members, the highest number recorded as voting.

The guild included the owners of presses and bookshops only, not their apprentices and journeymen. But even so, the number seventy-five between master printers and booksellers is very low for so famous a centre of the book trade as Venice was. It is improbable that this number represented all the printers and booksellers of the city. The report of the Rifformatori on the history of the book trade in Venice assures us that at the close of this century there were one hundred and twenty-five presses at work in Venice; and we know that it was necessary to print one hundred and fifty copies of the Concordat of 1596, in order to distribute them among the booksellers of the city. These figures would lead us to suppose that the masters printers and booksellers must have exceeded seventy-five in all, and we suspect that there were many who did not belong to the corporation.

The guild claimed jurisdiction over all printers and booksellers in Venice; it forbade them to exercise their calling without having obtained a certificate of competence from the guild, after passing an examination by experts appointed by the guild officers. But we do not know that the guild had any power at its back to enable it to impose its authority; indeed, its claims remained a dead letter until the year 1604, when the Proveditori di Comun conferred powers which made the claims of the corporation a reality.

CHAPTER XI.

1549—1596.

THE GOVERNMENT AND THE GUILD.

Excessive legislation—The clandestine press.

O return to the legislation on the part of the government, which we abandoned at the date of the foundation of the guild. We find that censorial and repressive legislation still continues; the government is still struggling with obscene and scandalous literature, though it ceases to deal with the questions of copyright, protection, and encouragement of the art.

The question of censorship still presented great difficulties. The law had never been sufficiently explicit upon the subject. It required a censorship, but had not designated the censor. On one branch of the question the Ten had delegated its powers to the Rifformatori dello Studio di Padova. But though the University Commission was the proper office to control the literary and political censorship, it did not follow that the commissioners themselves were either the fit persons, or sufficiently leisured to conduct the censorship in person. The whole question required still further definition. In the year 1562, the Rifformatori refer to a custom which has sprung up among printer-publishers of submitting the books they desire to print to any person they may choose, and, on obtaining a *testamur* that the work contains nothing contrary to the law, they receive a certificate from the office of the Rifformatori, and upon that the Ten grant their *imprimatur*.

The result of this abuse is that many scandals arise, and the Rifformatori order their secretary for the future not to grant a certificate for any printing whatsoever (*per stampar qual si voglia cosa*) until the work has been examined by (1) the Inquisitor, or one of his vicars, or some person appointed by the tribunal of the Inquisition; (2) by the noble Marc' Antonio Mocenigo, reader in philosophy, or by some other public reader; (3) by a ducal secretary; so that there shall be in all three persons who examine the work, one ecclesiastic, one reader, and one secretary.[1] The petitioner for a certificate shall bring a *testamur* signed by each of these, declaring that there is nothing in the book contrary to religion, nothing hostile to princes, nothing against morals, and that it is worthy to see the light. The *testamurs* also shall state the number of leaves in the book, and shall quote the first and the last lines. Each of the three persons who read the work shall have as recompense one bezzo[2] for each leaf, which sum shall be paid by the petitioner. And the printer shall bring a copy of the work when printed to the office of the Rifformatori, before it is issued to the public, to ensure that after obtaining his *imprimatur* he has not added anything to the book, or altered it in any way—a thing he may not do without a fresh licence. Together with this law of the Rifformatori dello Studio di Padova we will take the following, passed by the Council of Ten, 17th September, 1566. Seeing that the duty of punishing those who print or sell books without a licence, and books prohibited by our laws (*prohibite dalle Leggi Nostre*), and books printed in Venice with a false place of printing, lies with the Esecutori contro la Bestemmia, but that they cannot perform their duties because they have no notice of the licences which are granted, or because printers forge the words *con licentia*, it is decreed that all those who obtain licences from the Chiefs of the Ten and from the Senate shall, before they print the work, take those licences to the office of the Esecutori contro la Bestemmia, and there they shall be registered in a special volume, free of charge.

The importance of these two laws is obvious. The law of 1562 is a general law, couched in the widest terms, and covering the whole question of censorship. By it the Rifformatori provide for censorship in all four kinds—ecclesiastical, literary, political, and moral—and all this at the expense of the editor! This law rounds off and finishes up the action of the government on the subject of censorship; if they could enforce the law, nothing more remained to be done. It is the law which fully expresses the intention of the government on the subject, and to this law they constantly refer. Again, the law of the Ten, if it could be enforced, opened at the office of the Esecutori contro la Bestemmia what was virtually a Stationers' Hall. The register kept there ought to have represented the whole movement of the

[1] These various certificates are to be found in the Archivio di Stato, Rifformatori dello Studio di Padova, *Licenze per Stampa.*

[2] The bezzo was the same as the quattrino bianco. See Padovan, *Le Monete dei Veneziani*, Venezia, 1881, p. 26. It was worth one quarter of a soldo grosso, which was worth one-fortieth of a ducat. See p. 26, n. 6. Gallicciolli, *op. cit.*, lib. i., Nos. 556, 592.

Venetian press, and to have given us the name of every book published in Venice. Of course it did not do so. The law was evaded.

The Venetian government professed to have the interests of the book trade at heart; yet what a law they had just passed! It was hardly possible to have invented a more irritating and cumbersome process, or to have devised a longer road between an author and the printing press. No wonder that the open press of Venice struggled along with difficulty, or showed signs of decline when hampered by such ponderous restrictions as these. It is most important, in view of the subsequent collision between the Church of Rome and the Republic, to distinguish carefully between the various documents required by the law of 1562, and to bear in mind their proper titles, and the differences implied by them. First then the Inquisitor, the Ducal Secretary, and the Public Reader granted what were called *fede*, that is, affidavits or *testamurs* as to the presence or absence of certain specific qualities—heresy, immorality, disloyalty, or bad literature—in the work they examined. The *testamur* as a statement of fact contained no injunction to expurgate and no permission to print. The secretary to the Rifformatori granted a certificate attesting the existence of the *testamurs;* the Chiefs of the Ten alone granted an *imprimatur*, a right to print. The Senate granted copyright or monopoly, specifying its duration and the punishment for infringement, and the Esecutori contro la Bestemmia granted a certificate of registration.

It is impossible to suppose that the government was not aware of the ruinous nature of their legislation. There is only one explanation which can adequately account for their action—they were fighting the clandestine press. The preambles to these laws are full of expressions such as *quelli che senza licentia stampano et vendono Libri et Historie. Molti dicono Con Licentia ancor che non habbiano havuta licenza. Se alcuno stampasse opera in questa città et facesse parer che fusse stampata altrove*, and so on, in wearisome iteration. The government itself did not like this clandestine press, and no doubt the Church was always ready to point out the scandal and the danger, and to insist on repressive measures. The government thought that by multiplying the machinery and increasing the penalties they could cope with the difficulty; but their action only tended to augment it. Such laws as this of 1562, which they had just passed, could only serve to check the progress of the open press, and to drive the printing activity into clandestine channels. It was natural that the secular government should desire to keep a control over the new industry, whose power and importance they now understood. It was a power they could not afford to neglect—this power which could multiply one man and one utterance a thousand-fold! It was most natural that ecclesiastics, now that Luther had come among them having great wrath, should desire to keep control over the new industry which could re-echo one heretical utterance and reverberate one schismatical cry. But how was it to be done? It was of no use for the government to pass laws which were not observed, and the government of Venice lacked the means to make its laws respected. In fact, Venice had no police at all adequate to its needs, and there was nothing approaching public opinion to take the place of police. Compared with the police of the State, the police of the Church were infinitely more active and more capable; every priest, every friar, was a policeman for his creed, and what is more important still, a policeman by conviction. And so ecclesiastical censorship became a real and living fact; State censorship remained, for the most part, an empty letter, a vain effort to retain control by futile threats unbacked by deeds.

How real the ecclesiastical censorship was, we shall see presently, when we come to the question of the Index and the Concordat, at whose epoch (1595) we have just arrived. But before embarking on this subject, I wish to take a survey of the Venetian Press, its movement and activity during the whole of the sixteenth century, in order thoroughly to understand the condition of that press when Venice and the Church of Rome came into collision upon the subject of the Index. This survey is based upon the copyrights granted by the Senate during this period of which we speak.

CHAPTER XII.

1500—1600.

THE VENETIAN PRESS IN THE SIXTEENTH CENTURY.

Copyright—Duration of copyright—Penalties for infringement of copyright—Average number of copyrights per annum—Refusal of copyright—Cost of printing in Venice—Decline in the Venetian press—The centres of the book trade and of the printing presses—Signs—Distinguished names—Romances—Maps—Travels—Tariffs—Engraving—Greek—Hebrew—Oriental languages—Music.

IT is certain that the *imprimaturs* granted by the Council of Ten, and the copyrights granted by the Senate, do not nearly represent the whole activity of the Venetian Press. The government is constantly declaring the fact in its endeavours to punish those who ignored the press laws and neglected to secure the necessary *imprimatur*. The number of copyrights granted will at once convince us that these could not represent the total amount of printing done in Venice during the sixteenth century. Yet, imperfect as these copyrights are if taken as an index to the whole produce of the press, they are full of interest and curiosity as far as they go, and they serve as a sort of indication of the quality of the work which occupied the Venetian Press during the sixteenth century.

If we examine the average length of time for which a copyright was granted during the sixteenth century, we find that the tendency to prolong the duration of copyright, which was noticed at the close of the previous century, is continued throughout this. But from the year 1560 onwards we find a much higher average of copyright duration than the usual ten years. The average mounts to about nineteen years. If we come to individual cases, however, we find very great variations. The government did not always grant a petitioner copyright for the full term demanded ; sometimes for reasons which we cannot now explain, it appeared to deal hardly with a petitioner. For example, in the year 1509, Doctor Pietro de Mainardi received a copyright in his treatise, *Remedia præservativa ab epidemia*, for one year only, though the government professed itself moved *bonitate operis et justitia hujus modi petitionis*. At the other extreme, we find copyrights granted for terms as long as thirty years.

As regards the penalties which protected copyright during this century, they are the same as those in use in the previous century—confiscation of the contraband volumes, which were given either to the author, or, more rarely, burned ; and a fine, the amount of which varied considerably. The fine as a rule was divided into three parts, and shared between some three of the following—the accuser, the court, the author, the arsenal, or one of the three asylums, the Pietà, the Mendicanti, the Incurabili. It was occasionally divided into two, four, six, and even twelve parts, and apportioned to twelve recipients. There is only one instance in which deprivation of the right to exercise his calling was threatened against a pirate printer ; that is the case of the copyright granted on November 29th, 1559, to Pappa Alesio of Corfu, wherein, besides a fine of two hundred ducats, and of ten ducats for each copy, the printer culprit is to be debarred from the exercise of his profession for ten years.

The number of works for which copyright was demanded in any given year varies greatly, ranging from none in certain years to eighty-two in 1544, eighty-eight in 1549, touching one hundred in 1550, and one hundred and seventeen in 1561.[1] There are naturally periods of activity and periods of depression, usually produced by some external cause. From 1469 to 1498 there is a steady increase, followed by a decline, till we touch bottom in 1511 with one application for copyright in eight works. This decline was due of course to the wars of the League of Cambrai, the unsettled state of the country, the closing of the passes, and the disturbance of trade generally. This period of depression is followed by the first epoch of legislation, which reduced the number of books for which a copyright could be obtained ; and the consequence is that the applications are few, and the works specified not numerous, till the year 1530, when there is a recovery in the trade, which continues till the year 1576. Then the Great Plague began, causing a sudden drop in the activity of the press, from which it did not recover till 1582 ; but it never reached the high point it had gained between 1530 and 1570. In 1596, the year of the publication of the Clementine Index, the Rules, and the Concordat, there were twenty-four applications for copyright in fifty-three works. In the following year there were only seven

[1] See my Analysis of Copyrights in Appendix.

applications; in 1598 eight applications; in 1599 seven applications, and in 1600 ten applications, and these figures corroborate the unanimous testimony of the Venetians as to the ruinous effects of the Clementine Index upon their printing and publishing industry.

Besides copyrights for books, the College and Senate also granted patents for inventions, chiefly improvements in the mechanism of printing. For example, in 1513 the College conceded a patent to Jacomo Ungaro,[1] for fifteen years, for his method of printing *canto figurato*, with the proviso, however, *hoc ne præjudicetur concessionibus, si quæ forte factæ fuissent antehac*, as indeed was the case; for Ottaviano de' Petrucci had already obtained a patent for the same invention in 1498. Again, in 1515, to Daniele Bomberg, for his Hebrew type, *letere cuneate si in rame come in stagno o in altra materia improntate.* Again, in 1516, to Ugo da Carpi, the true inventor of printing in chiaroscuro,[2] *cosa nova et mai più non fatta;*[3] or, again, to Roccho Bonicello, for his improvement in the press.[4] Bonicello in his petition sets forth that at great cost and trouble he has discovered, through the Divine assistance, *tal modo novo di stampar cum la mita mancho della spesa et faticha di quello che al presente si stampa per tutto cio e per quante risme di carta stampano quatro homeni in quatro giorni maxime de libri che vanno stampati rossi et negri,*[5] *et libri di canto, tante io ge ne volio far stampar cum quelli medemi homeni in doy giorni soli di quella istessa beleza et bonta.* In 1551 the same Roccho Bonicello had made a further improvement in the printing frames (*il novo modo di Tellaro*), which he also patented. In 1568 Andrea Brugone patented an invention *di stampare il Rosso et negro in una volta senza levar la carta del timpano.* The government usually granted these patents on the condition that the invention was really new, and that it was practicable, and they required the opinion of experts on this point; though it would seem that they were easily satisfied, for they granted Brugone's petition upon the report of the Proveditori di Comun who, although they had seen no model of the patent, thought that if the petitioner could do all he promised, the patent might be conceded to him.[6]

I know of only two instances in which the Senate refused to grant a petition, though they did not always grant it in the form in which it was presented to them. In 1523, Sigismondo Macasola applied for a copyright in various publications, among them the works of Bortolo Socino; the Senate,

[1] It is probable that Jacomo Ungaro is the same person as *Jacomo todesco gettator de lettere*, mentioned in Aldus' Will. Cf. Fulin, *op. cit.*, p. 80.

[2] Zani, *Enciclop. Metod.*, i. xiv. 338.

[3] Fulin, *op. cit.*, p. 109.

[4] Archiv. d. Stato, S. T., Filza.

[5] *i.e.* devotional works.

[6] *Qualmente non habbiamo veduto edifitio ne modello alcuno in questa materia, ma facendo ditto supplicante quanto si ha offerto, sia concesso, etc.*

while granting his request for the others, refused it for Socino. Whatever may have been the reason for the refusal of a copyright to Macasola, there is less doubt as to the reason in the second case. In 1563, the Senate, by 110 against 80 votes, refused to grant a copyright to Francesco Sansovino for Alvise Pasqualigo's *Lettere Amorose*, although the motion in favour was made by the Ducal councillors, and Sansovino had obtained the *imprimatur* of the Chiefs of the Ten, after the usual *testamurs* from the Inquisitor, the Public Reader, and the Ducal Secretary. The dubious title of the book gave the Senate the opportunity of mortifying Sansovino, with whom they were on bad terms about the payment of a contract for sculpture executed by his father. I do not believe that the Venetian government was very rigid as to the moral qualities of books submitted to it for copyright. It readily granted licences for the works of such dubious writers as Straparolla,[1] La Casa, Doni, Aretino.[1] Upon this point, it no doubt considered that the free censorship exercised by the Church was a sufficient safeguard, and restricted its own censorship to matters which affected the honour or the authority of the State.

The sixteenth century was not a period of great excellence in the history of the Venetian printing press; it was not a century of splendid books. We find convincing testimony to the steady decline in the warning sent by Paolo Paruta from Rome, that unless the Venetian printers used greater care than is their wont of late, Venetian publications will be prohibited by themselves, owing to their great inaccuracy and general badness.[2] A further indication of this decline in the quality of the Venetian press may perhaps be found in the fact that the art of the calligrapher and copyist revived during this century. M. Legrand points out that the profession of copyist was quite common in the middle of the sixteenth century.[3] This leads us to suppose that, owing to the inferiority of workmanship in the press, the few great collectors were returning once more to manuscript volumes as being more beautiful; that there was a kind of artistic revival of calligraphy brought about by the bad work produced from the printing press. As already observed,[4] we find Diego de Hurtado de Mendoza employing Andronicus Nucius, and the French ambassador is frequently in correspondence with Paris on the subject of copyists, who were to be met with more readily in Venice than elsewhere.

But though the quality of Venetian books declined, the Venetian press

[1] Until they were placed on the Index. See Reusch, *Der Index der verbotenen Bücher*, Bonn, 1883, i. 394.

[2] Dep. Ven. di Storia Patria. Series iv. vol. vii. Paolo Paruta, *La Legazione di Roma*. No. 360, 11 March, 1595. *Che se non si usa maggiore diligenza di cio che si fa da qualche tempo in qua . . . . resteranno finalmente proibite da se stesso per le grandissime incorrezioni, etc.*

[3] Legrand, *op. cit.*, No. 103.

[4] See p. 35, note 1.

had the reputation of being very cheap. Cardinal Baronius desired to print his *Annales* in Venice, as there they would cost him one third less than in Rome.[1] Nor, though its general excellence cannot be considered remarkable, was the Venetian press wholly without illustrious names; Lucantonio Giunta, Giolito, Marcolini, the Zanetti, Gardano, the Aldine family, still maintained the reputation of the press. The decline in the art of printing was probably general throughout Italy, and Venice suffered with other cities. But she did not lose her supremacy in such special departments of the art as those of Greek and musical printing. Pope Paul III. and Cardinal Marcello Cervini, when they desired to open a Greek press at Rome, found it necessary to send the apostolic printer, Antonio Blado, to Venice to find the fount of type. And no school of musical printing was more active or more famous than that of Venice.

But however low the quality of the Venetian press declined, there was no falling off in activity. The quantity of work produced was very great. The chief centres of the book trade were at the Rialto, San Salvadore, and along the Merceria to San Marco, in the Frezzeria and at San Moisè. Many of the booksellers adopted some distinctive sign, which may have been hung up outside their shops, and was not unfrequently printed on the frontispiece of books issued by them. We find, for example, *Matthio Pagan in Frezaria al segno della Fede; nella bottega d'Erasmo di Vicenzo Valgrisi; appresso San Moyse al segno dell' Angelo Raffaello per Francesco di Alessandro Bindoni et Mapheo Pasini compagni.* The sign of the Salamander was at the foot of the Rialto on the San Bartolomeo side,[2] and we find such other signs as the Pozzo, Fenice, Speranza, Stella, and very many others whose names will be found in my catalogue of booksellers and printers. Some of the more famous of these book-shops seem to have become the rendezvous of people of culture. When Regnault, one of the parties to the Spanish conspiracy, desired to find Sir Henry Wotton, the English ambassador, it was to a bookseller's shop that he went. We have proof that the Merceria continued to be the chief home of the book trade down to the eighteenth century. Gradenigo, in his *Costumi*,[3] records that *oggi la Merceria sembra un' accademico Liceo, perchè viene in gran parte occupata da Librai a trattenimento de Letterati.*

The printers lived, for the most part, in the parish of San Paternian. Aldus removed to San Paternian from the house he first occupied at Sant'

[1] Paruta, *op. cit.*, vol. ii. p. 111. *Costando le stampe di Venezia un terzo meno di queste.*

[2] Senato Terra, Reg. 61, c. 10. When it became necessary to widen the approaches to the bridge, the government had to buy the shops from the Patriarch, among them the Salamander.

[3] MSS. sæc. xviii. al Museo Civico. I owe this reference to the courtesy of Sig. Giovanni Saccardo.

Agostino, and the *Estimo* or assessment rolls of the various parishes gives us, under San Paternian, a variety of printers' names. In the *Estimo* of 1514 we find Andrea da Axolla in this parish, living in a house belonging to the Doge Nicolò Tron, for which he paid sixty ducats a year. From the same source we learn that Lazzaro de Soardi *stampador et compagni* also rented a house in San Paternian, the property of Alvise Ruzier, for which they paid thirty-one ducats a year. But though San Paternian was the great centre of the printers, we find them scattered all over the town, at Sant' Angelo, at San Stin, at SS. Apostoli, at San Lio, at San Giacomo dall' Orio, and very many in the parish of Santa Maria Formosa.

To turn now briefly to the work done by the Venetian press during the sixteenth century, as far as it is recorded by the copyrights. We have already called attention to the considerable trade in romances and books of chivalry which had sprung up at the close of the last century. The journal of the bookseller of 1484 showed that the demand for such books was large. In 1520 Nicolò degli Agostini applied to the Senate for a copyright in the *Inamoramento di Tristano et Isotha*, the *Inamoramento di Lancilotto et di Ginevra*, and the *Reali di Francia*;[1] and throughout the century the applications for copyrights in such works continually occur. In this particular branch of the trade Nicolo Zoppino de Aristotile of Ferrara (1508-1536), the Da Sabbio brothers, Giovanantonio and Stefano (1516-1560), and especially Michele Tramezzin, took an active part. Tramezzin was a most prolific printer; besides works on theology, history, veterinary surgery, and duelling, he produced a large number of romances, many of them translated from the Spanish.

The copyrights granted to men of literary fame are not unfrequent. The privilege conferred upon Ariosto for his *Orlando*, for instance, bears the date 1515, 25 October, the year before the first edition appeared at Ferrara. The property in his poem is to continue throughout the poet's lifetime, and the penalty for infringement is a fine of one thousand ducats. In the year 1528 the Senate confirmed to Ariosto his copyright of 1515; and in 1535, after his death, his heirs obtained a privilege for his *Comedie*, *Elegie*, *Epigramme*, *Capitoli*, *Sonetti et Stanze*. In 1544 Francesco d'Asola secured a privilege for the poet's posthumous works in prose and verse, and in the same year Paulo Manutio established a property in four hundred *Stanze nove* by Ariosto. In 1531 Francesco Berni applied for a copyright in his *rifacciamento* of Boiardo's *Orlando*; and in the same year Bernardo Tasso secured a similar privilege for his *Amori*, and later again, in 1560, for his *Amadigi*. Besides these, we find copyrights to Aretino, to Cinthio Giraldi (1543), to Jacopo Gigli for the

[1] Fulin, *op. cit.*, No. 223, and see Ferrario, *Storia degli Romanzi di Cavalleria*, Milano, 1828, vol. iv.

poems of Gaspara Stampa (1555), the year after her death; for various works on the duel in the years 1550, 1551, 1553, and 1554; for Trissino's *Italia Liberata;* for Straparolla's *Piacevoli Notte* and Parabosco's *Diporti*.

Maps and charts also occupy a considerable space in the copyrights. It was the age of navigation and discovery, and the demand for geographical works created an important branch of the printing trade. In the year 1529 Zuan Piero de Marin *ha fatto uno mappamondo con tutte le isole, loci et navigatione de novo trovate, opera non mai fatta da altri ma da lui solo.* In 1530 Matteo da Bardolino, on the Lake of Garda, *ha composto uno instrumento astrologico nominato planispherio o sia cœlum planum figurato de conveniente figure delli pianeti et segni del zodaico cum altri circoli necessarii.* In 1536 Francesco d'Asola desires to publish under copyright Orontio Delfinate's maps of France, *loco per loco con le misure et miglia particolar.* In 1546 Domenico dalli Greci petitions the Senate, declaring that he has *superato un lungo et difficile peregrinazo per essermi condutto fino alla città di hierusalem*, and on his return he made a map of the Holy Land, which he desired to publish.

In 1550 Maestro Giacomo (de Gastaldi), *piamontese*, and Michiel Membrè desire to publish their map of Asia;[1] they declare that they intend to begin *dal mare mediteraraneo* (sic) *et andando dritto per levante dove è tutta la Natolia, Soria, et persia, cum il paese dil Sophi, et da poi verso griego tramontana, dov' è il paese dil Catazio, verso mezo dì dove è lindia et isola delle speciarie.* In 1554 we have Gerardo Rupelimontano's map of Europe dedicated to the Bishop of Arras. Two years later we have Floriano da Udine's *Mapamondo*, and in 1561 Matteo Pagano's *Mapamondo in fogli dodeci;* and there are besides many copyrights granted to Giacomo de Gastaldi, *Piamontese*, for maps.

The publication of voyages forms an interesting and also voluminous section of the copyrights. In 1533 we find the heirs of Lucantonio Giunta issuing a series of travels, and from that date onwards travels and voyages occur frequently, under such distinguished and well-known names as Pigafetta, Oviedo, Lopez, Gaztelu. Of Pigafetta, we read in Sanuto[2] that on the 7th November, 1523, "there came before the College a gentleman of Vicenza called the Knight Errant, who has been three years in the Indies to see what was to be seen. And he by word of mouth recounted all those matters, and all the College gave great attention in listening to him. And he got through half his journey. And after dinner he was with the Doge, and spoke for long upon these matters, so that his Serenity, and all who heard him, were astonished at the things which are in India." On July 28, 1524, the Ducal councillors move to grant Pigafetta a copyright in

[1] Senat. Ter., Filza 11. See Marinelli, *Saggio di Cartografia*, Venezia, 1881.

[2] Fulin, *op. cit.*, 122. Sanuto, *Diarii*, xxxv. 97 *verso*.

the history of his voyages which he has written, and on August 5 he petitions the Senate for the concession of this copyright.

In 1536 an edition of Antonio Pigafetta's[1] voyage appeared in Venice, which is, according to Fulin, a mere translation of Fabre's extract in French. From the copyright[2] for this edition we learn that the editor was Antonio Francini, probably a foreigner, for the copyright is granted on condition that he should print in Venice, and that he should issue *la prima parte dell' hystoria general delle Indie fatta per Oviedo, et il summario del viaggio di Antonio Pigafetta atorno il mondo.* Fulin says that the first edition of Pigafetta printed from Italian MS. is that by Amoretti, Milan, 1800. In 1530, Bartolomio Navager and his brothers had applied for a copyright in this work of Oviedo, translated into Italian by their brother Andrea Navager,[3] and it appeared in 1534 as the second book of the *Summario della historia delle Indie Occidentali*, probably printed by Nicolo Zoppino.[4]

There is one other class of books for which copyrights frequently occur; a class which, if any copies still exist, must prove of infinite value to the historian, as throwing light on the economic and commercial conditions of the age. I mean such works as tariffs of customs dues, tables of exchange values, and notably Rizzo Gentillino's *Tavole del valor della terra* (1564) and Agostino Gallo's *Dalla Vera agricoltura* (1564).[5]

Another department in which Venetian printers showed their activity was the art of engraving. In 1516 Ugo da Carpi obtained a patent for his invention *di stampare chiaro et scuro, cosa nova et mai più non fatta.*[6] Hugo, son of Count Astolfo of Panico, as he signs himself, appears to have been the inventor of wood-cutting in chiaroscuro.[7] There were others following the same calling of wood-engraving, notably Benedetto Bordone of Padua, who preceded Ugo da Carpi with his Triumph of Julius Cæsar,[8] his *Mapamondo*, and his *Isolario*,[9] and the engraver of the great plan of Venice, published by Antonio Kolb in 1500. In 1521 Moysè del Castelazzo, a Jew, obtained a copyright in all the illustrations for the Pentateuch which he has already engraved, and for the illustrations which he intends to execute for the rest of the Old Testament. In 1528 Sebastian Serli and Agostino di Mussi wished to publish their copperplates of Venetian architecture, *et accio meglio si possa in questa profonda de Architectura proceder per ordine et sapere discerner le generationi di edificii zoè Toscano, Dorico, Ionico, Corinthio et composito Havemo con laborioso studio et summa diligentia con misura disegnato li ditti ordini et sottilmente tagliato in rame*, et non solo li sopraditti ordini

[1] Quaritch, No. 36,711.
[2] See Copyrights, *sub an.*
[3] See Copyrights, *sub an.*
[4] Quaritch, No. 36,709.
[5] See Copyrights, *sub an.*
[6] Fulin, *op. cit.*, No. 209.
[7] Zani, *Enciclop. Metod.*, part i. vol. xiv. 338.
[8] 1504.
[9] 1508.

ma anchora intendemo stampare varii edificii, etc.[1] The plates are signed S. B. A. V. (Sebastian Bolognese and Agostino Veneziano).[2] In 1541 Gabriel Gioli obtained a copyright in his ornamentations and designs for Petrarch, the *Orlando Furioso*, and other works; and in the following year we meet with Francesco Peliccioli's *Disegni di lavoro di donne*, probably lace-pattern books. In 1548 Antonio Zantani applied for a copyright for the *Imagini delli Imperatori antiqui, con gli riversi trovati cosi in oro come argento et rame et la somma delle vite loro.*[3] In 1553 Giovanni Andrea Valvassore[4] had prepared *nove figure et nove additioni sopra Ariosto, Petrarcha et Boccaccio*, and sought for a copyright in them. In 1567 Titian sought for a similar protection for his copperplates, *Il Paradiso* and *La Santissima Trinità*, for which Fra Valerio Faenzi, Inquisitor, granted a certificate, declaring it to be *cosa degnissima et rapresenta degnamente la Santa Trinità.*[5] Twenty-three years later Titian's brother Cesare obtained a copyright in his well-known book, *Habiti antichi et moderni*, and for his engraving of *La città di Venetia con tre piazze et la corte Ducale.*

The Venetian press during the sixteenth century maintained the supremacy in Greek printing conferred upon it by Aldus and Caliergi. The long list of Greek printers to be found in Legrand abundantly proves that the publication of Greek books was a very important element in the Venetian book trade. The reason for this is not difficult to find. Venice was naturally the port at which Greeks coming to Italy would land. There was frequent communication between Corfu, Candia, Cyprus, and Venice. The revival of learning attracted a long line of needy Greek scholars and scribes to Italy; some of these rested in Venice instead of pushing further on. The majority of these Greeks were clerics, and looked for preferment in the Church, and their claims could be better urged at Venice, whose government had such widespread influence in the Levant. Apostolios, Musurus, Margounios, Severus, are examples of the success of this policy. Most of these Greek scholars on their arrival in Venice sought employment as editors, proof readers, correctors for the Venetian publishers, such as Aldus, Caliergi, Sessa, the Da Sabbio, Spinelli, Pietro, Bartolomeo and Cristoforo Zanetti. For this last, Guillaume le Bé, in 1548, cut a Greek type *pour imprimer des alphabetz, petites heures, qu'il nomme Horologi, et aultres fatras et histoyres en grec vulgaire pour apprendre les enfans a lyre.*[6]

1 Petition of Serli. Senato Terra, Reg. 18, Sep., 1528.

2 See Fisher, *op. cit.*, Append., p. 451.

3 Archiv. d. Stato, Senato Terra, Filza 7.

4 Said to be the engraver of the illustrations of the *Hypnerotomachia*.

5 Archiv. d. Stato, Senato Terra, Filza 48.

6 H. Omont, *Spécimens de Caractères Hebreux, grecs, latins et de musique gravés à Venise et à Paris par Guillaume le Bé.* Paris, 1889.

וילק ואין מספר: ויאכל כל־עשב
בארצם ויאכל פרי אדמתם: ויך כל
בכור בארצם ראשית לכל אונם:
ויוציאם בכסף וזהב ואין בשבטיו
כושל: שמח מצרים בצאתם כי־נפל
פחדם עליהם: פרש ענן למסך ואש
להאיר לילה: שאל ויבא שלו ולחם
שמים ישביעם: פתח צור ויזובו
מים הלכו בציות נהר: כי־זכר את־
דבר קדשו את־אברהם עבדו: ויוצא
עמו בששון ברנה את־בחיריו: ויתן
להם ארצות גוים ועמל לאמים יירשו:
בעבור ישמרו חקיו ותורתיו ינצרו
הללו־יה: קו
הללו יה הודו ליהוה
כי־טוב כי לעולם חסדו: מי ימלל

MARC' ANTONIO JUSTINIAN. *Psalter.* 1546.

ANTONIO GARDANO. ARCHADELT, *Madrigali*, lib. iii. 1539.

The Venetian press appears to have been as well known for its Hebrew as for its Greek type. We have seen how Fra Felice, in spite of a pressing invitation from the Pope to print in Rome, preferred to send his Hebrew works to the press of Daniele Bomberg and his companion, Hermann Liechtenstein. The government of the Republic showed little favour to the Jewish press in the city; it always displayed a deep suspicion on the subject. Bomberg had to face and overcome continued opposition, for the conduct of the government was hardly consistent, and, as he declares, it must have put him to serious expense and trouble. In the first place, it was only with difficulty that he could obtain permission to keep Hebrew compositors and readers. Fra Felice in his petition declared that for the proper publication of his works it was necessary to have four Jews to superintend the printing; but it would be impossible to induce them to come if they were obliged to wear the yellow cap, as they would be molested and insulted in the streets. He therefore begged that his readers might be allowed to wear a black cap. The government granted a grudging permission for four months only, and during their own pleasure. In the same year Bomberg applied to the College for a patent in his Hebrew type and for copyright in his Hebrew books, seeing that it had cost him *grande spese si del far excider le lettere hebree et attrovar persone doctissime in hebreo al componer et emendar ditti libri.* This petition was granted; and three years later, in 1518, Bomberg presented this concession to the Senate and begged for a renewal and confirmation of the same. This also was conceded by 113 votes against 17 noes and 7 doubtfuls. The copyright in Fra Felice's works ran for ten years, and this expired in 1525. In October of that year, we learn from Sanuto's Diaries, the Chiefs of the Ten moved to grant a privilege to *Daniele da Norimbergo*,[1] who is desirous of continuing to print Hebrew in this city, and offers one hundred ducats for the right to do so. "The motion was put to the vote and lost," says Sanuto, "and this for the second time; and it was well done, and I had a good hand in it; for he printed books in Hebrew that were against the faith." The next day the vote was put again with Bomberg's offer of one hundred and fifty ducats, and was lost. On March 8th of the following year a further effort was made to secure the privilege, Bomberg this time offering three hundred ducats; the motion was once more rejected. But on March 27th, on an offer of five hundred ducats, Bomberg secured a renewal of his privilege to print in Hebrew for ten years to come, and a copyright for all books in this kind. The religious scruples of the Republic were valued highly, but they were venal. Bomberg's business must have been a large one to enable him to pay so dearly for this privilege.[2] A further proof of the anxiety of the government on this

[1] *i.e.* Bomberg.

[2] Fulin, *op. cit.*, pp. 130, 131.

score is furnished by the privilege granted to Piero Galese in 1548 to print the Koran in Italian, provided he print the refutations, *per la traduttione dell' Alcorano di Arabo in Italiano, con le contradittione de' Teologi in margine, senza le quali non si possi stampare.* M. Omont, in his monograph on the types of Guillaume Le Bé, shows that Le Bé, who was a pupil of Robert Etienne, came to Venice in 1545, and there cut Hebrew type for Marc' Antonio Giustinian, a Venetian noble who owned a Hebrew press at the Rialto, in the Calle delli Cinque alla Justizia Vecchia. Le Bé talks of this type as *la première de mes ouvrages, aagé lors de 20 ans et huict moys.* Le Bé stayed in Venice till the year 1550, when he went to Rome for the jubilee of Pope Julius III. During his five years' sojourn in Venice he cut two kinds of Hebrew type for Giustinian and six kinds of Hebrew type for Mazo da Parenza.[1] The fourth and fifth of Le Bé's Hebrew types were cut *soubz l'adveu du magnifique messer Carlo Quirini, pour luy et les Mazo de Parensa, en une maison, size au bout d'une ruelle regardant sur le quay de la Madona de l'Orto.* The sixth character was cut *aussy en acier, faicte à Venise pour le dit May de Parensa, en une chambre que je tenoye à loyage à un ducat par moys, ayant veue sur le Camp de St. Lio, à coste de l'eglise.* Le Bé was in the habit of cutting his own name and that of Venice on the punches which he made there. His seventh Hebrew type was cast while he was at Rome for the papal jubilee, and his eighth was cut before the preceding character. But while Le Bé was absent from Venice *celui a qui je laissay mesdits poinsons en garde on a fait des frappes et tout mangé, ayant vendue et poinsons et matrices à un Allemant, ainsy que de Dansi*[2] *m'ont mandé.* While in Venice Le Bé made drawings and designs for various characters, which he preserved, and used in Paris as patterns for his fifteenth Hebrew type.[3] The name of Mazo da Parenza does not occur in the copyrights; the name of Marc' Antonio Giustinian is recorded in Cicogna's list of Venetian printers. The antagonism of the government towards Hebrew presses did not abate; and in the year 1571, 18th December, the Senate made a general order forbidding Jews to print at all: *non possa alcun hebreo lavorar di stampa ne far stampare libri, et contrafacendo incorrino in pena di perder la robba, et pagar ducati cento. Et quelli che facessero stampar sotto nome de Christiani incorrino nell istessa pena et li libri stampati si intendano esser et siano di colui in nome de chi fussero stati stampati.*

As regards the Arabic press and the printing of Oriental languages, we know that Democrito Terracina in 1498 applied for and obtained a monopoly for twenty-five years for all books printed in Arabic, Moorish, Armenian, &c. Democrito died without producing anything (*senza dar principio alcuno*), and his nephews Lelio and Paulo petition for and obtain

[1] Parenzo (?) in Istria. [2] Danzig (?).
[3] See Omont, *Spécimens de caractères Hébreux, etc.*, p. 13.

וזאת התור' אשר שם משה לפני בני ישר'

חמשה חומשי תורה

HEBRAICVS PENTATEV
chus latinus plané que nouus post
omnes hactenus æditiones euul
gatus ac hebraicæ veritati
quoad eius fieri potuit,
conformatus.
*Adiectis insuper e rabinorum commenta
rijs annotationibus pulchre & no*
ces ambiguas & obscuriora
quæq; elucidan-
tibus.

ITEM
Cantica Canticorum,
Ruth,
Threni,
Ecclesiastes,
Esther.
VENETIIS EX OFFI
cina Iustinianea MDLI.

תורה צוה לנו משה
מורשה קהלת יעקב

MARC' ANTONIO JUSTINIAN. *Pentateuch.* 1551.

MANOLI BLESSI
NELLA ROTTA
DELL'ARMATA
DE SVLTAN SELIN,
VLTIMO RE
DE TVRCHI.

GUERRA. MANOLI BLESSI. [1571?]

a renewal of their uncle's privilege. But no traces of works by the Terracinas are known to exist. The first Armenian book published in Venice appeared in the year 1565;[1] and De Rossi quotes a Koran in Arabic published by Paganini in 1530. In 1543-4 we find a patent granted to Antonio Bruccioli and companions for his Arabic type, though whether he issued books in Arabic we cannot say.

No branch of Venetian printing was more active during the sixteenth century than the musical press. The copyrights are rich in the titles of madrigals, motetts, masses, responses, psalms, composed by the masters who made the Venetian school of music famous. As an example, we have the copyright granted to Francesco Viola da Ferrara, for the series of new compositions (*musica nova*) by *Messer Adriano Viularet*. This collection numbers fifty-eight pieces.[2] Following close upon the privilege granted to Ottaviano de Petrucci, we have, in 1513, the petition of Jacomo Ungaro for a monopoly of all *canto figurato* for fifteen years to come. The petition was granted on condition *ne hoc præjudicetur concessionibus si quæ forte factæ fuissent antehac*, possibly a reference to the privilege already held by Petrucci. The next year Ottaviano appeared again before the College, and stated that in order to avail himself of the privilege granted to him he required capital, and that consideration induced him to enter into partnership with Amadio Scoto and Nicolo di Raffaele. This association had produced many volumes of music, but the recent wars had disturbed the course of business, the capital of the company was compromised, Nicolo di Raffaele had become almost blind, and the privilege would expire in four years' time. Petrucci and his partners therefore beg for a prolongation of the copyright for another five years, and obtain it. The next record of a musical press furnished by the copyrights is the privilege granted to Francesco Marcolini, in 1536, for a property in all music printed in metal types, and all music published by him. Marcolini states that *esser circa xxx anni che fu uno Ottaviano da Fossombrone, che stampava la musica nel modo che si imprimono le lettere, et è circa xxv anni che tal opera non si fa; alla quale impresa si è messa non pur la Italia ma l' allmagna et la franza et non lhanno potuto ritrovare, Io Francesco Marcolini, svisceratissimo servitor di quella, essendomi affatticato molti giorni et non con poca spesa in ritrovar tal cosa*, &c., and so he begs for a monopoly of all music printed *con charatteri di stagno* or *altra mestura*. This looks as though Ottaviano de Petrucci's method had been lost; and if Marcolini's statement is correct, it is clear that his musical press was the next to follow Petrucci's in Venice. Two years later we come across a more famous name than that of Marcolini.

[1] Fulin, *op. cit.*

[2] Senato Terra, Filza 28.

In 1538 Antonio Gardano presented to the Senate a petition, which was granted in the following terms, *che ad Antonio Gardano musico francese sia concesso quanto per la supplicatione soa el dimanda, intendendosi la gratia essergli concessa per anni x solamente et osservando le legge circa le stampe disponenti.* The supplication is lost, and so we do not know what were the first works for which Gardano begged a copyright. In 1542 Gardano patented his *novo modo trovato per lui di stampar musica.* But here again the absence of the file containing the petition prevents us from knowing what the new method was. Though other music printers, such as Troiano di Nano, appear in the field, yet from this date onwards it is Antonio Gardano whose name occurs most frequently in the copyrights, and who was the greatest musical printer in Venice. The Capella of San Marco and the great Conservatorii of Music helped to render the Venetian school world-famous; and we find such distinguished names as Palestrina,[1] Cyprian Rore, Adrian Villært,[2] Zarlino, appearing in the copyrights granted to one or other of the Venetian musical publishers.

There are other points, such as medicine, surgery, fortification, mathematics, upon which specialists may find useful information among the copyrights. The instances given above will suffice to prove that this collection, though it by no means records the whole movement of the Venetian press during the sixteenth century, contains much matter that is curious and valuable.

[1] 1572 and 1575.

[2] 1558.

IL QVARTO LIBRO

DI MADRIGALI D'ARCHADELT A
QVATRO VOCI COMPOSTI VLTIMAMENTE INSIEME CON
ALCVNI MADRIGALI DE ALTRI AVTORI NOVAMENTE CON
OGNI DILIGENTIA STAMPATI ET CORRETTI.

.A. G.

ALTVS. ALTVS.

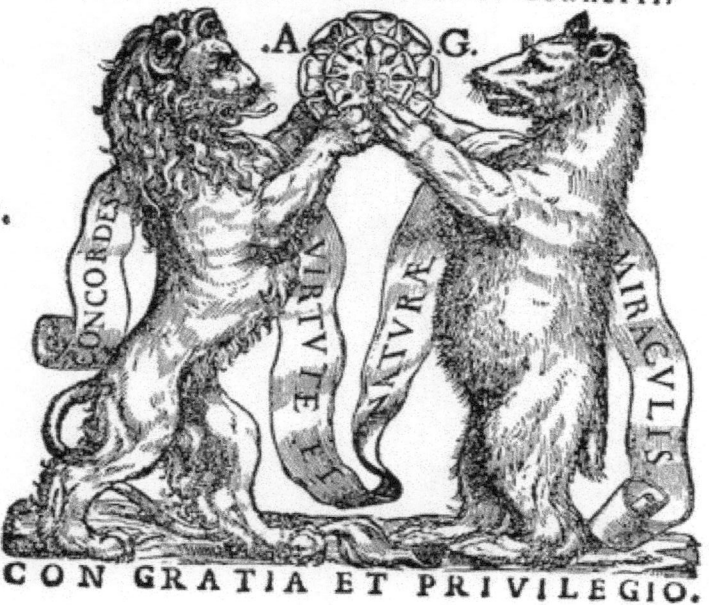

CONCORDES VIRTVTE ET NATVRÆ MIRACVLIS

CON GRATIA ET PRIVILEGIO. L

ANTONIO GARDANO. ARCHADELT, *Madrigali*, lib. iv. 1539.

PRIMO LIBRO DI MADRIGALI
D' A L F O N S O
DALLA VIOLA
NOVAMENTE
STAMPATO.

BUGLHAT, DE CAMPIS, HUCHER ET COMPAGNI. VIOLA, *Madrigali*, lib. i. 1539.

CHAPTER XIII.

1548—1593.

THE INQUISITION.

The Holy Office in Venice; its position and powers; the lay assessors—Composition of the tribunal—Archive of the Holy Office—Procedure—Penalties—The case of Francesco Stella.

EFORE going any further, we must consider for a moment the position and the operation of the Holy Office in Venice upon the subject of the press. The Inquisition had been admitted within the dominions of the Republic upon the basis of a concordat which carefully secured to the secular government its rights as supreme ruler of its own subjects. The Holy Office was not permitted to take separate and independent action; and, in theory at least, it drew all its powers in the dominion from the consent of the secular government, which was represented on the tribunal by three lay assessors in Venice, and by the civil governors in other cities, whose concurrence was necessary to the validity of all acts of the tribunal.[1]

The concordat upon which the position of the Holy Office in Venice was based, was that accepted by Julius III. in 1551. The terms of this concordat defined the position of the lay assessors on the tribunal. They were there not to take part in the discussions of the court, but (1) to hold, as it were, a watching brief on behalf of the secular government, in order to secure a fair trial for its subjects, and (2) to carry out the sentence, to serve as arm to the tribunal. They had authority to protest against actions of the court which were usurpations of temporal jurisdiction, or which might

[1] *E ciò essendo per antica consuetudine introdotto e praticato, fu poi finalmente concordato col pontefice Giulio III. Appunti sul Capitolare del S. Uffizio.* Ap. Cecchetti, *op. cit.*, ii. 8.

injure the State by causing tumult or scandal, or which were opposed to the just and proper liberties and rights of the subjects. They also had a right to insist that the action of the Holy Office should be strictly limited to cases of manifest heresy; and this power they exercised by refusing warrant of arrest, which they alone could issue, unless satisfied that the question to come before the court was one of heresy only. Every criminal suit was held to contain three parts:—First, the cognition of the quality of the crime imputed—was it heretical or not? This was, by the concordat, reserved entirely to the ecclesiastics of the tribunal, and the assessors had no voice. Second, cognition of the fact—did the accused hold such opinions? Upon this point there was divergence of view; the Venetians held that, as this part of the procedure affected the person of Venetian subjects, the lay assessors were entitled to a voice. Third, the sentence. This again the concordat reserved to the ecclesiastic members of the tribunal; but the execution of the sentence remained with the secular government.[1]

But although the action of the Holy Office was thus circumscribed, it was by no means a nonentity in the Republic. The archive of the Inquisition, with its 2,910 trials, and its 44,327 documents, proves that the activity of the tribunal was great.

The court was composed of ten members: the three lay assessors, the Nuncio, the Patriarch, the Inquisitor, the Nuncio's auditor, the Patriarch's vicar, the Inquisitor's commissary, and the Fiscal. The place where the court met is described as *la cappella di S. Theodoro appresso la chiesa di San Marco.* The prisons of the Inquisition belonged to the State, and the chief officer of the Holy Office was paid by the Council of Ten. The Republic aimed at securing the offices of Inquisitor, Inquisitor's commissary, and Fiscal, for Venetian subjects. And the necessity for the Ducal *exequatur* before the Inquisitor could act in the dominions of the Republic assisted the government to attain its object. The Patriarch of Venice was, as a rule, a Venetian by birth, so that the court of the Holy Office usually numbered seven Venetian subjects out of a total of ten.

The Holy Office trials for press offences begin in the year 1547—two years before the publication of La Casa's Index in Venice—and they continue down to the year 1730, when Giovanni Checcozzi's long trial for heresy closes the list. But the activity of the Holy Office on this subject varies very much. The sixteenth century gives us as many as one hundred and thirty-two cases, and that virtually in the last half of the century only; the seventeenth century furnishes fifty-five trials; and the eighteenth century only four trials. This remarkable difference in the number of Inquisition

[1] *Aspetta al magistrato secolare operare che siano puniti i detetti, &c.* Cecchetti, *loc. cit.*

cases points to one or other of three conclusions : either the hostile attitude of the government towards the Church of Rome, from the year 1596 to the year 1620, had crushed the activity of the Holy Office in Venice ; or the vigour of the press prosecutions during the last half of the sixteenth century had stamped out heretical and immoral publications in Venice ; or the Holy Office, finding itself thwarted by the attitude of the government, abandoned the method of prosecution in favour of other less overt methods. The great activity displayed between 1549 and 1592 is to be explained by the dread of Lutheran heresy and its propagation through the press. Holy Office prosecutions stop suddenly in 1592, and there is a blank of twenty-four years during which no press trials are recorded. It was during this period that the Republic came into open collision with the Church of Rome, the quarrel between Venice and Paul V. reached its climax in the Interdict, and Fra Paolo Sarpi defended his government against the claims of the Curia. These are reasons which sufficiently explain this period of inactivity on the part of the Holy Office. But how are we to account for the fact that the half of the sixteenth century furnishes nearly three times as many trials for press offences as the whole of the seventeenth century? It is true that by the opening of this century Italy generally had accepted the Catholic reaction ; the ferment of the Reformation died away, and the literary and intellectual vigour which accompanied it dwindled. This, however, is hardly sufficient cause to explain the phenomenon. Nor can we suppose that there were no infringements of the Inquisitorial regulations, no publications which would fall under the notice of the Holy Office, or only so few as are represented in the fifty-five trials recorded. It is more probable that the Inquisition in Venice, finding itself thwarted by the government and denied a free hand, refused to continue its labours openly by means of its own proper tribunal, and preferred to exercise its influence by such other means as lay within its power—the pulpit, the confessional, and the domestic chaplain.

The procedure of the Holy Office in Venice, in cases of trial for the possession or publication of prohibited or heretical works, as we gather from an examination of the trials themselves, was as follows :—On a denunciation, which was frequently anonymous or signed with a false name, being presented at the office of the Inquisition, the Inquisitori contra gli Heretici met, and, on the motion of the Fiscal, the denunciation was read, and an order made to search the house of the accused ; suspected books or writings were to be seized and handed into the court of the Office or to the auditor of the Legate. If the works seized were found to be incriminating, the court proceeded to examine witnesses as to the source whence the books came, and as to the character of the accused. If the court held that there was ground for prosecuting, the charges were formulated, and the accused was summoned to appear in person, within eight days from the publication of the summons in his place of residence, in order to purge himself; otherwise their Excellencies proceeded to judgment in contumacy, and to punishment in accordance with the powers received from the Council of Ten. In the majority of cases the accused allowed judgment to go by default.

The Holy Office in Venice was by no means harsh in its procedure. That it used torture is certain, even as late as the year 1693, but instances are not very common. Capital punishment was rarely applied, and then only by drowning, decapitation, or strangulation; never by fire. Nine cases of the infliction of capital punishment are recorded, and of these five are for heresies properly so called; the remainder for other offences of which the Holy Office took cognizance. But the most remarkable point in the procedure of the tribunal in Venice is the way in which every action of the court is taken ostensibly by the three lay assessors, and in the name of the secular government. The ecclesiastical members hear the case, but they do not issue warrants either for search or for arrest; nor do they execute the sentence, nor receive fines when imposed; their names do not appear individually nor corporately in the minutes of the trial. There is, however, no reason to suppose that they were not virtually supreme in their own court.

As an example of a Holy Office prosecution for the possession of prohibited books, we give a full abstract of the trial of Francesco Stella of Portobuffolè, in 1549.

Francesco Stella of Portobuffolè.[1]

I. The informer's accusation:[2]

Io non nominatomi altramente in questa mia Denuntia per gli respetti ben noti.

Denontio, dechiaro e querelo contra uno nominato Francesco Stella habita in porto buffale, homo perverso contra la fede appostolica et Sanita Del nostro Segnor Papa.

Quale essendo unito in ogni sua Trista e maledita luterana heresia con il crudo heretico Pietro Paolo Vergerio gia indegno Vescovo de Justinopoli.

Si potrano della sua Trista vita benissimo justificar . . . . e massime mandando subito alla sua casa fuori nel Borgo del Castello de porto Buffale si che per li suoi ministri con cauto modo siano tolti li libri e scritture.

In dita sua casa le Troverano gran copia de volumi heretici.

Similmente le potranno far cercar in casa de uno Ser Bernardo da Camin suo barba.

[1] Santo Uffizio. Processi. Busta 7.

[2] 16th Nov., 1549.

Also in the house of *Zuan Jacomo Sforza a San Samuele in le case da cha grimani.*

Also *in casa de Ser Andrea Arivaben libraro al insegna del pozo . . . perche questo tien tute le opinioni del ditto Vergerio.*

Et ancora far cercar . . . . in contra de S. Vido in casa de uno Antonio da Buchari over Schiavon.

(Signed) Il Zelator Del Nome Catholico.

II. Deposition of Bartholamio Soranzo before the Deputati sopra heretici :[1]

De vera scientia non so cosa alcuna per esser molti anni ch' io non sono stato in quel loco, ma per publica fama ho sempre udito adir che costui e heretticho anci capo de tal maledetta setta.

Et che li stette molti giorni il Vergerio.

Ho inteso ch'l havea una gran quantita de libri proibiti ; ma como ho detto non so questo se non per fama.

III. Specific charges against Stella :

Dice il pappa esser antechristo et la giesia Romano dice eser giesia del diavolo.

Non vuol che in casa sua pur sia nominata la nostra dona.

Niega il sacramento sacratissimo dell' altare et sopra questo intenderette di belle cose perche niega tutti i sacramenti ecetto il battesimo ma quello dice che non si puo dar da cattivi sacerdoti et che i sacerdoti sono tutti cattivi et per consequentia alcuno non è ben battizzato.

Dell oio santo dice alle persone che i vada ad unzearsi i stivalli con lui.

Del sagratissimo corpo del Signor dice che non si de adorare perche li è un pezzo di pane.

Non vuol che si vada a messa et dimanda le messe abominatione et santi non vuol che siano nominadi.

Vuol che in ogni tempo si manzi di ogni sorte di cibo, et non vuol che i homini sia obligadi a cosa alcuna che sia sta ordinada perche dice che sono ritrovati humani et molte altre cose che intendearete dall' esama de i testimoni i quali sarano.

IV. Note on Francesco Stella for use of Inquisition :

Uno francesco Stella da porto buffalè dotor di medicina . . . . fu condanato in pena pecunaria per haver portato libri lutherani.

[1] 9th Dec.

V. Receipt for Francesco Stella's writings and other effects given by Hieronimo Massara to the Sant' Uffizio.[1]

VI. Notice from Luca de Molino, Podestà of Porto Buffalè, that he has proclaimed Francesco Stella, as ordered by letters of 28th Nov. to 8th Dec.[2]

VII. The Inquisitors contra li Heretici cite Stella to appear in person within eight days before the Tribunal, *in la capella di S. Theodoro appresso la chiesa di San Marco a hora di terza*, to *expurgarsi delli libri heretici et prohibiti che gli sono stati trovati in una sua casella la quale lui haveva servato in casa de Ser Zuan Jacomo Sforza della contra de San Samuele.* Otherwise their Excellencies will proceed to punish in accordance with the decrees of the Ten.[3]

VIII. Charges against Francesco Stella and Francesco Pirrochin, repeating No. 3 in more formal language, probably based on No. 3. The heresy is spreading : *hanno suvertite diversi religiosi che . . . per le parole loro sono fatti lutterani et heretici marzi. Tenendo ridutto et sinagoga in casa di Francesco Stella.*

Witnesses to be called :

Il Magnifico Messer Bartholomio Soranzo.
Il Magnifico Messer Lorenzo Orio.
Il Magnifico Messer Zorzi Soranzo.
Monsignore Vicario di Ceneda.
Monsignore Messer Lodovico Conte di Brugnera.
Il Piovan di Mansoe.
Il suo Capellan.
Pre Altobello officia in Girandi.
Pre Troian.
Messer Francesco Orese.
Messer Federigo Arnoldo.
Messer Zuan Damiani.
Messer Antonio Schiavon biancheza ceré (moniere?) a S. Bartholomio alle dui Chiave.
Ser Fanto di Fanti.
Suo figliuolo.
Michiel de Tin.
Donna Marietta Padoana.

[1] 1550, 14th Jan.
[2] 1549, 14th Dec.
[3] 1549, 8th Dec.

IX. Minutes of the Court:[1]

Information read on request of the Procurator Fiscal, Alessandro Rugero.

The Deputati contra li Heretici, their third colleague, Alvise Contarini, Chief of Ten, being absent, order the Procurator Fiscal and officers to search the houses of the accused at once.

If books are found, they are to be handed in to the office of the Court, or to the auditor of the Legate, *si come è solito.*

Procurator Fiscal and officers appear in the office of the auditor, and make a notarial declaration that they have searched the house of Zuan Sforza. In the room of the said Zuan Sforza *hanno trovato un per de bisache piene de libri.* They found a box outside the room, and asked Sforza for the keys; he replied that he had not got them. Asked to whom the box belonged, he said he did not know who had brought it there. The box was broken open, and books found; all these were brought to the office of the auditor. The list follows:

Tenor inventarii librorum.

In le bissacche.

Tragedia.
Dialogo de merchurio.
Pasquino in estasi.
La 2da parte delle prediche de fra Julio de Milan.
L'esposition sopra la Epistola ad Galatas del ochino.
El cathechismo.
Martin luther de captivitate babilonicha.
Pie Christiane Epistole.
El summario della sacra Scrittura.
Le pie et Christiane prediche de fra Thomaso de Siena.
Una semplece dechiaration sopra li xii articoli de Maestro Piero Martire.
Prediche del Ochino.
Joannis Polii per Porti. (?)
De suscipienda Christiane reipublice propugnatione Jacobi Unsalii.
Conciliatio scripture divine authore Bartholomeo Vesternero.
Actorum Apostolicorum liber doctissimus per Erasmum Savarium.
La prima parte delle prediche de Maestro Julio.
Expositio super prima Epistola alli Romani sine authore.

[1] 1549, 16th Nov.

Nella cassa.

Commentarii del Bulingerio sopra il Testamento novo.
Acta Concilii Tridentini, Philippi Melantonis.
Pandette scripturarum.
Nova methodus, Erasmi Savarii.
Locorum communium divine scripture Erasmi Savarii.
Exortatione del Erasmo.
Cinque quinternetti a pena.
La polvere del mutio.
Dui libri coperte de carton scritti a pena, viz.:
    Del officio della madona.
    Delle feste.
    Ad un predicatore.
    La comparatione.
    Ceremonie del Diacono.
    Ceremonie del Vescovo.
    Vita de S. Hieronimo.
    Della Castata delli Apostoli.
    Della nativita.
        ?
    Quemadmodum desiderar.
    Che se habbia leger l' evangelio.
    Che se habbia star in la giesia.
    Del concilio.
    De alchuni abusi.
    Del libro chiamato miracoli della madona.
Sempronio Laura a Messer Hieronimo mutio scritto a pena
Aversus Berardum Billicum Veritatis inimicum.
Concilarii de bulengerio.
Lettere missive N° tredesi in un mazzo.
La conversion de la Maria Magdalena.
Celii secunda Curionis.
Sebastianus meger in Apochalipsim.
Prediche del Ochino in xii volumi.
Commentariorum evangelicorum per D. Johannem Draconitum.
Della afflictione et persecutione fatta sopra quelli de Capo d' istria 1548.
Acta ac decreta sacro sancti Tridentini.
Supputatio annorum mundi.
Opere Christiane de hieronimo Savonese.
D. Joachini Vadiani.

Educatio ? puerilis.
De Vocabulo fidei.
Epistola hieronimi lunensis ad Bernardinum Ochinum.
Sermones Bernardini Ochini.
Tre altre lettere missive.
Tre ligati de diverse scritture.
Una Camisa de tella.
Un per de Scarpetti.
Una camisola de bombaso.
Un zippon de tella Vecchia.
Una baretta chiamata Babban.
Profeta naum juxta Veritates hebraicas latine redditus per Theodorum Bibliandrum.
In Epistolas divini Pauli ad romanos annotationes a Joanni occholampadio.
Martini dorpii sante theologie professoris oratio.
Epitome Belli papistarum.
Pasquillus servi poete.
Acta sinodi novo Jan ?
De condemnatione Hieronomi in concilio Constantiensi.
Adversus Johannem fabrum Constantiensem.
Responsio ad Calumnias hieronimi D. D. friderici Davie.
Il cattalogo de libri fatto per il Vergerio.
Tragedie.
Le prediche del Occhino.
Trattato de Lorenzo Valla della donativa fatta per Constantino Imperatore.

X. Evidence taken before the Court :[1]

(*a*) Franciscus Argenta, living at San Samuele, in the house of Vettor Grimani, provedditor del mar.

Q. Were the books found on Saturday found in your house?

A. Yes, but in the part inhabited by Zuan Jacopo Sforza, for the house is occupied by us two separately.

Q. Whose books are they?

A. I don't know.

Q. Who brought the books?

A. Francesco Stella of Portobuffolè.

Q. How long ago?

[1] Die Martis 19 Nov., 1549.

A. Long ago; I don't remember.

Q. Did Stella bring anything else?

A. Not that I know.

Q. Did Stella say what was in the box?

A. No; he said nothing.

Q. How did Stella bring the box to your house?

A. He was a friend of the house, and used to stay there when he came to Venice. He said he wanted to leave the box in safe keeping, and so brought it.

Q. When Stella brought the box he said nothing about its contents?

A. No; no one in the house took note of what he did.

Q. Where was the box put?

A. First in the chamber that leads to the room of my father-in-law; then in my father-in-law's room.

Q. Who brought the bags, and whose are they?

A. I don't know.

Q. Were you present when the box was opened?

A. Yes.

Q. Do you remember what was in it?

A. Several books—I don't know how many—and I believe one or two shirts. One of the officers said, "I wish it had been cash."

Q. Was there any chain on the box?

A. No; and I never saw one.

Q. Do you know where Stella is? and how long is it since you saw him?

A. I do not know where he is. Friday evening he was with me.

Q. What sort of person do you take Stella for?

A. I hold him to be a good man as far as active life is concerned; but, as regards his contemplative life, I don't know what to say, for I have never talked to him on these subjects.

(β) Johannes Jacobus Sfortia:[1]

Q. Do you know Francesco Stella?

A. Yes, I have known him since my son-in-law Argenta came to stay in the same house. Argenta receives Stella when he is in Venice. I have my separate room. My son-in-law has the rest of the house.

Q. What do you think of Stella?

A. I don't know him beyond *Bon di, bon di, bon anno.* I don't know if he sells or gives away books.

Q. Why do you say that?

[1] Die Mercurii 20 Nov., 1549.

A. Because I have seen him handling books in a box.

Q. In what box?

A. The one that was seized on Saturday.

Q. Who brought the box?

A. I don't know; but Stella had the keys. The box was heavy; I gave the hammer to the officer who opened the box.

Q. How long had the box been there?

A. About a year and four months—two months after my son-in-law took the house.

Q. Do you know anything about a chain?

A. No, and I don't believe Stella had one ever.

Q. Have you seen Stella taking books in or out of the house?

A. I cannot read or write, but I have seen Stella with papers.

Q. To whom did the bags belong?

A. To one called the Bolognese; I think his name was Joseph.

Q. How came they in your house?

A. He owed me ten *marcellos* for rent.

Q. How long ago?

A. Two years, worse luck!

(γ) Dona Ursula Massara, daughter of Zuan Jacopo Sforza:[1]

Q. How long have you lived with Zuan Jacopo Sforza?

A. Fourteen years; and we have lived in various houses.

Q. Do other persons live with him?

A. No; nor does he let rooms.

Q. Who frequents his house?

A. No one; he is always alone.

Q. Whose is the box found in the house on Saturday?

A. Francesco Stella's. It is two years since he brought it. He often came and opened and shut said box. I don't know what he was about; for I attended to my own business and did not meddle with other matters. Stella was intimate with Messer Francesco Argenta. Stella keeps the wife of Argenta, who is his *comare;* and many times Argenta has tried to bring his wife home; but she would not. She is young and pretty. I don't know if there is any ill between them; but she has been three months with Francesco Stella, and he has no wife.

Q. Whose are the bags?

A. They belong to a Bolognese who was with us; I don't remember his name.

[1] Die Mercurii 20 Nov.

Q. How is it likely that you don't know his name?

A. I don't know it; if I remembered it I would say it; he was a stranger and a Bolognese.

Q. Had he any other goods?

A. No; he left them, saying, "I want to go home to fetch some papers, and I will come back and will take away my books." This is four years ago. He left on Ascension Day.

Q. What reputation has Stella?

A. On my faith, I don't know; I never talked with him.

Q. Have you ever seen other goods in the box—money, chains?

A. No; we thought the box must be full because of its weight.

XI. The Deputati sopra li Heretici cite Stella to appear in eight days.[1]

XII. Letter from Deputati to the Podestà of Portobuffolè.[2]

(Signed) FRANCESCO LONGO.
ALVISE CONTARINI.
GIOV. ANTONIO VENIER K.

XIII. The Herald's declaration that he has published the summons at St. Mark's.[3]

XIV. The Herald's declaration that he has published the summons at Rialto.[4]

XV. Evidence of Soranzo—same as No. 2.[5]

XVI. Declaration of Podestà of Portobuffolè that he has proclaimed Francesco Stella on the 8th inst.[6]

XVII. The sentence against Stella, published by the Deputati in obedience to a decree of the Ten.[7]

1. Books to be burned publicly in Piazza permeso la Gesia this morning.

2. Stella within ten days of the publication of this sentence is to pay fifty ducats fine into our office.

[1] Die Jovis 28 Nov.
[2] Die Martis 3 Dec.
[3] Alli 28 di Nov.
[4] Die Mercurii 4 Dec.
[5] Die 14 Dec.
[6] A di 9 Dec.
[7] Die Jovis 2 Jan., 1549-50.

3. If he fail to do so he is to be banished from Venice and from Portobuffolè for three years.

4. Fine to be exacted from his property.

5. If he break confines, six months in the prison called Liona.

XVIII. Publication of sentence in Venice and Portobuffolè.

XIX. Ser Valemino Croda of Ceneda appeared at the office of the Deputati contra Heretici in the name of Francesco Stella and paid fifty ducats.[1] And the notary of the office consigns to Hieronimo Massara, cousin of Francesco Stella, the box which contained the books; also the documents and other goods.

XX. Hieronimo Massara's receipt for Stella's effects.

XXI. Anastaso Zordan, *Prete titulato di Sant' Agnese*, represented in the office of Deputies that he had denounced Stella, and asked for the fifty ducats. Venier, one of the court, proposed to give them in accordance with Decree of Ten. But at the time the secret accusation was handed in, Venier declared to me, notary subscribing, that it was presented by a good man who wanted nothing for his reward, but did it only for the honour and glory of God. And as he has confessed and confirmed these words, the Deputies decree that he shall not have the fifty ducats. But *ex mera urbanitate* they make him a present of twelve ducats. The fifty ducats to be thus divided:

To Pre Anastaso . . .	Ducats 12.
To Inquisitor	,, 20.
To the Procurator Fiscal . .	,, 12.
To chief officer	,, 2.
To two constables . . .	,, 3.
To Pre Alvise	,, 1.

Die Martis 14 Jan., 1550 (*sic*).

[1] Die Jovis 16 Jan., 1550.

CHAPTER XIV.

1548—1593.

THE INDEX AND THE BOOK TRADE.

The crucial moment in the history of the Venetian Press—Part of a wider subject, the quarrel between the Church and the State—First independent censorial action on the part of the Church—Bishop Franco of Treviso—Earliest catalogues of prohibited books—Paris—Louvain—La Casa's Catalogue in Venice—Its true date—The Council of Ten take action to support the Catalogue—The Catalogue of the Venetian Inquisition, 1554—The Inquisition and the custom house—The Index of Paul IV., 1559—Its reception—The *Moderatio Indicis* of 1561—The Tridentine Index and the Ten *Regulæ*, 1564—The Tenth Rule and the press laws of Venice—Reception of the Tridentine Index—Its effect—First signs of disagreement between Venice and Rome—The Bull *in cæna Domini*—The Congregation of the Index, 1571—The Sixtine Index, 1590—Clement VIII., 1592.

WE have now reached the most decisive moment in the external history of the Venetian printing press—the moment when the art of printing and the book trade came into collision with the Church of Rome, and began to feel the influence of the Inquisition and the Index. It is at this period of the publication of Clement's Index and of the Concordat that the history of printing in Venice touches general history for the first time. The whole question involved is part of a larger question, the question of the relations between Venice and Rome, and belongs to the history of that great movement of which Paolo Sarpi was the champion—the movement which developed and expressed the modern conception of a State as a self-sustaining, autocratic, self-sufficing entity in opposition to the mediæval conception of a State with its dual dependence upon Emperor and Pope. The perennial sources of disagreement between Emperor and Pope, the definition of the limits of their respective powers, still continued; but the Empire as an idea had disappeared, leaving in its place a number of separate States to struggle for their absolute independence, in matters secular, with the Papacy, which still retained its life and all its vigour. The question was brought to an issue by the Church of Rome, not by the secular governments. It was the Bull *in cœna Domini*, with its vast claims to direction in such purely secular matters as taxation, and the acts of the Council of Trent giving form and substance to the Papal pretensions, which caused secular governments to look to their liberties, and raised the whole question to a burning point. Venice was not alone in her alarm and her opposition: in France, in Spain, in England, princes by their action declared their revolt against the Papal claims.

We have only to deal with this collision within the restricted region of books, and within the limits of Venetian history. The problem presented to the Venetian government was this: should the Venetian press, supported in its liberty by the government, continue to maintain its character as the freest press in Europe, and therefore one of the most copious, or should the government, by failing to support it, allow it to fall under the repressive influence of the Inquisition and the Index. The Church of Rome had always claimed a jurisdiction over the free publication of opinion on points which affected morals and dogma. As long as there was no divergence of opinion on the matter between Church and State, and as long as books remained in manuscript, it was comparatively easy to enforce this claim, to condemn and even to destroy all copies of offending works. But when, by the art of printing, books became indefinitely multiplied, this task almost exceeded the powers of the most perfect organization the world has ever seen. It became necessary to attack, not individual works, but whole classes of men who produced those works.[1] The result of the invention of printing upon the literary Inquisition was, in a large degree, to thrust that Inquisition a step further back, from the works of an author to the author who produced them. But the earliest Inquisition applied, as we have said, to morals and to dogma. In following the rise of the Index in Venice we shall see how this last heading of dogma came to be expanded till it covered the region of politics and of secular matters, and so brought about the collision between the Republic and the Church.

The earliest instance of a censorial order on the subject of books in Venetian territory,[2] and also in Italy, is the order of Niccolo Franco, Bishop of Treviso and Papal Legate. In 1491 Franco published a decree of his council, held at Treviso,[3] forbidding anyone to print, or to cause or permit to be printed, books which treat of the Catholic faith or of matters ecclesiastic—except the ordinary devotional works—without the express permission of the bishop or vicar-general of his dwelling-place. The decree proceeds

[1] *i.e. Primæ Classis* on the Index.
[2] Reusch, i. 58, 59.
[3] Mansi, *Supp. ad Concil. Luccæ*, 1752, vi. 681.

to name especially two works—Antonio Rosselli's *Monarchia*[1] and Pico della Mirandola's *Theses*[2]—which are absolutely prohibited, and are to be burned at the parish church or the cathedral within fifteen days from the publication of this decree.

At the very outset we are brought face to face with a vigorous and a wide-reaching order on the part of the Church. In the two books condemned to be burned there could be no question of immorality or of scandalous writing; the condemnation rested upon the unsoundness of the doctrine they contain.[3] The order tacitly makes a very wide claim; for if it were heretical to discuss the relative powers of the Pope and the Emperor in a sense at all hostile to the Curia, this would imply a right in the Church to revise, censure, and condemn, where it saw fit, any political writing in which the Pope and his authority play a part. In fact we find here implicitly a statement of the idea which forms the keystone of the ecclesiastical position as regards books that treat of politics—the idea that, in the case of the Church, politics and ecclesiastical dogma cannot be separated. An attack on the political position of the Pope is, *ipso facto*, an attack on the dogma of the Church. We must remember, however, that this vigorous action against the writings of Rosselli was the work, not of the Church generally, but of an individual bishop, and that Rosselli's tractate only stands in the Tridentine Index with *donec corrigatur*.[4] Although the work which was condemned to the flames had been dedicated to the Doge Francesco Foscari, the government, so far as I am aware, took no notice of the Bishop of Treviso's action.

As long as the Church confined its censorship to the questions of morals[5] and of dogma—what dogma might include had not yet been questioned nor defined—the Venetian government were willing to leave the matter in its hands, and ready to assist it in every way to carry out its prescriptions. The question of a censorship of morals was brought to a point and settled by the case of Cynthio degli Fabritii, on the initiative of the monks of Saint Francis, although the censorship remained in the hands of the Chiefs of the Ten or their delegates. But the religious censorship of the press was not formally acknowledged by law in Venice till the year 1547, and then only in

[1] *Sive de potestate imperatoris et papæ et de materia conciliorum.* On all Roman Indices after Trent, with *donec corrigatur.*

[2] *Conclusiones DCCCC dialecticæ morales*, &c.

[3] In the case of Pico's *Conclusiones*, a committee of theologians had condemned thirteen of the theses as heretical in tendency. Reusch, *op. cit.*, p. 59.

[4] Reusch, i. 3, explains the meaning of *donec corrigatur* as implying that the use of the book will be permitted on condition that the passages erased or corrected in the present edition be omitted or modified in the next.

[5] I think at first the government were willing to allow to the Church a concurrent censorship of morals, although they subsequently altered their position.

a modified form. In that year the three lay assessors who sat with the tribunal of the Holy Office were added to the Esecutori contro la Bestemmia to carry out the censorial law of 1542-3. No mention was made as yet of the Patriarch or the Inquisitor; but the presence of the three Savii sopra l' Heresia upon the Commission of the Ten shows us that the Inquisition *hæreticæ pravitatis* was tacitly recognized, and was beginning to make itself felt as an important element in the history of the Venetian printing press.

The University of Paris had published in the year 1544 a catalogue[1] of books which up to that date it had examined and judged worthy of censure.[2] The University of Louvain[3] followed in the year 1546 with a catalogue of books *reproved* (*gereprobeerde*) by its theological faculty. The year 1549 is usually given as the date of the first Italian Catalogue, published by La Casa in Venice.[4] No copy of La Casa's Catalogue is known to exist; our knowledge of it comes only from a critical edition of it published in the Graubünden by Pietro Paolo Vergerio on the 3rd July, 1549, under the following title: *Il Catalogo de Libri, li qvali nvovamente nel Mese di Maggio nell' anno presente M.D.XLVIIII. sono stati condannati et scomunicati per heretici, Da Giouan della casa legato di Venetia, et d' alcuni frati.* Zaccaria[5] maintains that La Casa's Catalogue was already printed in 1548, and that the date M.D.XLVIIII. in Vergerio's edition is an error. Reusch combats this proposition, and urges, on the contrary, that the one passage where Vergerio assigns the La Casa Catalogue to 1548 is a printer's mistake. But the Ducal decree published on July 19th, 1548, ordering that all heretical works are to be surrendered to the Savii sopra li Heretici within eight days, contains the expression *detti libri.* This seems to indicate that some list or classification of books had been already drawn up. The suggestion presents itself that this list was La Casa's Catalogue, and that the Ducal proclamation was intended to assist the Legate in giving effect to his prohibition of heretical books.

Reusch, moreover, does not explain what Vergerio meant by the word *nvovamente* in the title to his edition of La Casa's Catalogue. It may only mean recently; but then why should Vergerio have added the precise date? Or it may mean that La Casa published a second edition of his Catalogue in May, 1549. If this interpretation of *nvovamente* be correct, it would leave Vergerio's statements accurate, both in the passage where he says that La

[1] These early lists of censured books were called Catalogues, not Indices. Reusch, *op. cit.*, i. 2.

[2] Reusch, *op. cit.*, i. 147. *Catalogus librorum qui hactenus a Facultate Theologiæ Parisiensi diligenter examinati, censuraque digni visi sunt.*

[3] Reusch, i. 113.

[4] Reusch, i. 204.

[5] *Storia polemica delle proibizioni de libri*, Roma, 1777, p. 143.

Casa's Catalogue was published in 1548, and in his use of the date 1549 in the title to his critical edition of that catalogue.

The decree of the Council of Ten, 16th Jan., 1548-9,[1] appears to settle the question of the date of La Casa's Catalogue. From that document it seems that the Catalogue was compiled before January 16th, 1549, but not printed or published till after that date.

Whatever may be the correct date for the appearance of La Casa's Catalogue, the first prohibitive catalogue to appear in Italy was published in Venice. La Casa was Papal Nuncio, and therefore his Catalogue may to a certain extent be considered the act of the Holy See,[2] and in this respect different from the catalogues of Paris and Louvain. La Casa was not a learned theologian, and he called to his aid certain monks (*alcuni frati*) apparently very little better equipped than himself.[3] The result was a catalogue carelessly compiled and full of errors, which Vergerio found no difficulty in handling with satirical severity. La Casa's Catalogue is valuable, however, as furnishing the basis of the Index of Paul IV., upon which the majority of subsequent Italian indices are constructed. The Catalogue of La Casa was directed almost entirely against heretical works. Vergerio complains that there were no obscene publications such as La Casa's own *Capitolo del Forno* included in the condemnations. It is important to bear this fact in mind, for it throws light upon the way in which the Church made use of the repressive power of prohibitions, not so much in the interests of morality as in support of its own dogmatic claims.

As we have noticed, it is not improbable that we trace the result of La Casa's Catalogue in the Ducal proclamation of July, 1548. We must observe, however, that the surrender of heretical books, and the subsequent search for such works, is entrusted, not to the Patriarch or the Inquisitor or the bishops of the various dioceses, but to the three lay assessors, the representatives of the secular government on the tribunal of the Holy Office.

In the year 1549 the decree of the Council of Ten erecting the booksellers and printers of Venice into a corporation was published. The first and principal reason stated for taking this step is the difficulty which the Savii sopra l' Heresia found in checking the publication of scandalous and heretical works. This again is probably a proof of the pressure which the Church was bringing to bear upon the government in its desire to crush heresy. In all likelihood it was the action of the Church which brought about this most important step in the internal history of the Venetian press. But at the same time that it obeyed the pressure, the government did not officially recognize the hand of the ecclesiastical authorities, but only the

[1] See Appendix I., No. X. [2] Zaccaria, *op. cit.*, 144. [3] Reusch, i. 205.

advice and recommendation of its own three representatives. The government assisted the Inquisition as far as it could, but never intended to, and would not now recognize the Inquisition as a distinct and independent power when acting within the dominions of the Republic. The Venetians never swerved from their position that the Inquisitor, in so far as he had power in Venice, had it by delegation from the State.

La Casa published his Catalogue as Papal Nuncio, and without co-operation of the Venetian Inquisition. But in the year 1554 we find that Inquisition taking action in the matter of books. In that year, with the approval of the Nuncio, Filippo Archinti dei Salviati, Bishop of Saluzzo, and with the concurrence of the three Savii sopra l' Heresia, the Venetian Inquisition published a catalogue,[1] containing *nomina eorum qui male de fide scripserunt quorum scripta a catholicis legi prohibentur.* This Index is in fact nothing but an enlarged edition of Arcimboldi's Milan Index of the same year. It is an improvement upon La Casa's Catalogue,[2] and Paul IV. made great use of it for his own—the first Roman Index.

The Inquisition then, with this Index, begins openly and publicly to influence the history of the printing press and the book trade of Venice. Nor having once begun did it long remain idle. In the year 1558, 9th February, we find this important decree:[3] "The Reverend Monsignore the Patriarchal Vicar, and the Reverend the Father Inquisitor, with the assistance of the most illustrious Messer Bernardo Giorgio, Messer Andrea Barbarigo, and Messer Piero Sanudo, Nobles to this Sacred Tribunal of the most Holy Inquisition on Heretics, have resolved and determined, in order to avoid fraud upon this sacred tribunal, that for the future books brought into Venice cannot be taken out of bond until the consignees have deposited with this tribunal a list stating the number and the quality of those books." We must suppose that this order received the sanction of the government and became law. It was a strong measure; for though it did not claim to prevent consignees taking books out of bond after the presentation of the list describing those books, yet, if upon that list there were any books to which the Inquisition objected, this order made it easy for the Holy Office to seize them at the shops, and to open proceedings against the importer.

The Inquisition thus gained complete cognizance of one source of books in Venice—imported books; and with the cognizance also the control over that source. The law of 1562, associating the Inquisitor or his delegate with the public reader and a Ducal secretary as censors on behalf of the Rifformatori dello Studio di Padova, and making the inquisitorial

[1] Reusch, i. 217. [2] Reusch, i. 214, *et seq.* [3] Appendix I., No. XII.

testamur a *sine qua non* to a certificate from the office of the Rifformatori without which neither *imprimatur* nor copyright could be obtained, gave to the Inquisition a large share in the control of the other source of Venetian books—the home production. We see then that, by the year 1562, the Inquisition in Venice was openly and vigorously exercising its influence over the production, the importation, and the distribution of books, with the consent, approbation, and assistance of the government represented by, and in turn advised by, the three lay assessors to the Holy Office.

The first Roman Index was that published in 1559 by Paul IV. The title runs: *Index auctorum et librorum qui ab officio Sanctæ Romanæ et Universalis Inquisitionis caveri ab omnibus et singulis in universa Christiana Republica mandantur.*[1] The Index was divided into three classes: (1) The names of those authors each and all of whose works, published or to be published, are absolutely prohibited; (2) Names of writers certain of whose specified works are prohibited; (3) Titles of anonymous books prohibited. At the end of the Index a list of sixty-one printers' names was added, with a prohibition of all works printed by them. Among these sixty-one condemned printers there is only one Venetian, Francesco Bruccioli.[2] This arrangement of the Index into three series was continued throughout in the Indices of Rome, down to the pontificate of Alexander VII., when, in the year 1664, that pope broke the Index up into a continuous alphabetical order.

The Pauline Index was printed and published in Venice in 1559, 21st July, by Lilius and Company, after it had been seen, read, and collated with the Roman edition by Felix Peretti of Montalto, Inquisitor;[3] but it was not enforced with any rigour. Indeed everywhere, and not in Venice alone, the Index was received either coldly or with hostility. The Viceroy of Naples and the governor of Milan refused to allow it to be published in their dominions; and in Florence they waited to see how other countries would act.[4] Out of Italy it received even less attention. In Spain permission to print it was refused, and in Paris it was not published.

The dissatisfaction with the Pauline Index was felt even in Rome, and Paul's successor, Pius IV., instructed the Inquisitor General, Michael Ghislieri, to draw up a *Moderatio Indicis librorum prohibitorum*, which was published in 1561.[5] The *Moderatio*, though it afforded considerable relief from the severity of the Pauline Index, was not considered satisfactory, and in the year 1562 the Council of Trent turned its attention to the question of the book trade and to the construction of an Index with

[1] Reusch, i. 258, 259.

[2] Reusch, i. 267.

[3] *Frater Felix Perettus ex Monte alto Regens et Inquisitor vidit, legit, contulit et concordat cum Romano*, at the end of the Venetian edition. Reusch, i. 260.

[4] Reusch, i. 298, note.

[5] Zaccaria, *op. cit.*, 147.

rules for the guidance of the censor. The discussion on the question whether the Council should undertake the task was long, and called forth a variety of opinions.[1] Finally, a committee of eighteen members was appointed to draw up the decree. There were two Venetian prelates upon the committee, Giovanni Girolamo Trevisan, Patriarch of Venice, and Girolamo Trevisan, Bishop of Verona. The proposals of this committee were read in the eighteenth session of the Council, and afterwards sent to Rome to be submitted to the Pope. The Tridentine Index was published in Rome in March, 1564, under the title: *Index librorum prohibitorum cum regulis confectis per Patres a Tridentina Synodo delectos, auctoritate Sanctiss. N. D. Pii IIII. Pont. Max. comprobatus. Romæ, Apud Aldum Manutium, Aldi F.* 1564.

The Tridentine Index is based upon the Index of Paul IV., and both are directed more against heretical and anti-Curial works than against immoral publications. The most notable additions made by the Council of Trent are the Ten Rules for guidance in the formation and enlargement of the Index, and the introduction of the formula *donec corrigatur*, which signified a temporary or partial prohibition of a work not absolutely condemned, for the formula in its full meaning implied that the books so marked might be bought, sold, and used, provided that in the existing editions the corrupt passages were either blotted out or corrected by pen, and in all subsequent editions omitted or modified.

Of the Ten Rules the most important is the last—the rule which speaks in general terms of the censorship of books and of the relations between the book trade and the Holy Office. Some of the clauses of this rule call for consideration, especially as illustrating the extent to which the State-established censorship at Venice coincided with the ecclesiastical censorship now enjoined by the Council of Trent.

By Rule Ten it was provided:

1. That outside Rome the examination and approbation (*approbatio et examen*[2]) of books shall be confided to the Bishop of the diocese or his delegate, and to the Inquisitor. These are to sign the *testamur* with their own hands. A copy of the work, signed as authentic by the author, is to remain in the office of the examiner.

As far as Venice was concerned, this clause had been anticipated by the law of 1562, which required a triple censorship before the Rifformatori dello Studio would grant the necessary certificate.

2. Those who circulate books or pamphlets in manuscript, unless they have previously been examined and approved, shall be subject to the same penalties as printers of unexamined books. And those who possess such

[1] Zaccaria, *op. cit.* Reusch, i. 312.

[2] Not therefore necessarily an *imprimatur*.

books or pamphlets in manuscript, unless they declare the author, shall themselves be held to be the authors.

In Venice there was no law forbidding the sale of manuscript. The proclamation of the Esecutori contro la Bestemmia of October 10th, 1565,[1] formulated after the publication of the Tridentine *Regulæ*, distinctly and repeatedly refers to *Opere stampate*. The latter part of the clause, holding the possessor to be author unless he declared the author, was of course not thought of by the laws of the Republic.

3. The approval of the Inquisitorial censors must be printed or written at the beginning of books.

At this period the Venetian government did not require the publication of their *imprimatur*.

4. The Bishop's delegate and the Inquisitor are to make frequent inspection of printing presses and bookshops.

The Republic imposed this duty on the prior and officers of the guild.

5. All booksellers must have in their shops a list of the books which they have on sale, signed by the Bishop's delegate and the Inquisitor, nor may they have, sell, or in any way distribute other books than those on the list without permission of the aforesaid, under pain of forfeiting the books, and other punishment as shall seem fit to the Bishop or Inquisitor. Purchasers, readers, or printers of such books shall be punished by the same authorities.

Such a limit as this upon the freedom of the book trade, rendering it laborious and difficult to procure new books, or to know what was going on in the literary world, even though the books in themselves might be harmless, had never been even suggested in Venice.

6. Those who import books are to announce them to the Inquisitorial authorities; or in cases where there is a custom house, the customs officers shall announce the arrival of the books.

The decree of 9th February, 1558-9, published by the Patriarchal Vicar, the Inquisitor, and the Savii sopra l' Heresia, had already secured this point for the Inquisition in Venice.[2]

7. No one who has imported books may give them to another to read, nor may he part with them in any way, without permission.

This is an amplification of the powers granted under the preceding clause; it was new to Venice.

8. Heirs are to submit a list of the books they inherit before they may use or part with them.

This also was unknown in Venice.

[1] Appendix I., No. XIV.

[2] Appendix I., No. XII.

9. Bishops and Inquisitors General may, within their dioceses or provinces, forbid books which do not appear in this Index if it seem expedient.

The Venetian government had certainly never delegated such wide powers as this clause carried.

The Tridentine Index appears to have been recognized at once as the authoritative utterance of the Church on the subject of books, and to have been widely circulated. It was printed in Venice by the Aldine Press in 1564, the year of its publication, and ten times subsequently between 1564 and 1593.

The publication of the Tridentine Index and Rules by Pius IV. changed the position of the censorship of the press in Venice very considerably. In the first place, no mention is made of the co-operation or the approval of the secular authority, a point upon which the Venetian government had always insisted as necessary to the validity of the Inquisitorial action; and, secondly, the powers of the Inquisition in the matter of books were extended far beyond the limits which they had hitherto touched with the consent of the secular authority.

The stringent effects of the Tridentine Index and Rules soon made themselves felt generally in Europe. Reusch quotes two most interesting testimonies to this fact.[1] In 1581 the Dominican Bernardo Castiglione writes: "In Rome they are still very watchful about the books which come into Italy. The Inquisitors frequently publish an order forbidding the sale of this or that work. So the booksellers no longer take the risk of importing books, and very often they cannot sell those they have on stock. In Rome there must be several thousand scudi's worth of unsaleable books." And again, considerably earlier, in 1565, just after the publication of the Index, Josias Simler writes: "A new Index has appeared wherein so many books are condemned that a number of professors in the Italian universities complain that they cannot lecture if the edict remain in force. Frankfort and Zurich and other German States have written to the Senate of Venice, urging it not to accept the edict whereby the book trade will be ruined."[2] As a matter of fact, the Italian book traffic with Germany was all but destroyed, and the home book trade isolated and gradually starved. And the book business which suffered most was that of Venice. It was in close relations with Germany, and Venetian booksellers frequently made business journeys to Frankfort[3] and other German cities; and we see from Simler's letter that Frankfort and Zurich recognized the closeness of the relationship and its great importance.

[1] Reusch, i. 346. [2] Reusch, i. 346.

[3] It was in Frankfort that the Venetian bookseller Ciotti met Giordano Bruno.

Italy generally, and Venice with it, accepted the Council of Trent, and as a proof of the adhesion of the Venetian government we find that a statute for the regulation of the book trade was drawn up on the lines of the Ten Tridentine Rules, and published in 1567, with the approval of the Nuncio, the Patriarch, and the Inquisitor. The full import of the acts of the Council of Trent was not perceived at once by the world at large; acceptance of the Council was demanded and conceded before governments had had time to consider the probable results of the Council. So it was with the book trade in Venice. It did not immediately feel the full effects of the Index and the *Regulæ*. It may be that, as in the case of the Pauline Index, the Tridentine decree was not enforced with much vigour at first; though the cases of Christoph Senech,[1] a Mecklenburgher, tried for possessing and reading prohibited books, and the second condemnation of Baldo Lupatino,[2] prove that it was far from being a dead letter. The booksellers and printers did not complain at once to the government, and it took no steps to protect the liberty of the book trade. But if the book trade did not at once feel the pressure of the Index, it was because the Inquisition had not had time to make it felt. The number of Holy Office trials for press offences shows a steady increase, and during the next few years we shall see other signs[3] which induce us to believe that the pressure was slowly but steadily increased, until the printers and booksellers finally did cry out.

Although the Church of Rome and the Venetian Republic were as yet in full accord upon the question of the censorship of the press, there were not wanting signs of a nascent spirit of suspicion and hostility aroused by the growing claims of the Papacy. Julius II. had ordered the Bull *in cœna Domini*—the Bull which recited the various classes of persons and the special persons under excommunication—to be read solemnly at least once a year in all cathedrals and parish churches. La Casa threatened *excommunicatio major latæ sententiæ*[4] under the Bull, that is to say, excommunication from which the Pope alone could absolve, except *in mortis articulo*,[5] against all those who transgressed the orders implied in his Catalogue; and the Venetian Inquisitor announced the same penalty for infringement of the Pauline Index. As the

[1] Cecchetti, *La Republica di Venezia e la Corte di Roma*, Venezia, 1874, i. 407.

[2] Archivio di Stato. *Sant' Ufficio. Processi.* Busta 10.

[3] The rule requiring all Bibles to be sent to Rome for approval before being put on the market, for example.

[4] Excommunication *latæ sententiæ* is excommunication incurred by the very fact of committing the forbidden act, without further operation on the part of the authorities, *quæ sola criminis admissione infligitur*. Excommunication *ferendæ sententiæ* is that which is inflicted by a court after trial, *quæ statuitur infligenda per sententiam Judicis*.

[5] So in the Bull of Julius II.

Bull was flexible, capable of expansion, and as it appeared every year, the Curia made use of it to put forward claims on behalf of the Papal authority in matters secular, and of the Pope face to face with sovereign princes—such claims, for instance, as the right to dispense subjects from allegiance to their sovereign, and to absolve them from obligation to pay taxes under certain conditions. The Venetian government saw with disapproval the growth of these claims, and determined to make a stand for their rights. In the year 1569 the Senate forbade the publication of the Bull in Venice, and announced its decision to the Nuncio. This action seems to have been taken in concert with other powers, and probably upon a common understanding that a general resistance was to be offered to the Bull of 1568. Philip II. of Spain kept back the Bull, and declared that he would make representations to the Pope; in Naples the publication of the Bull was forbidden. In Venice the Senate subsequently explained that it would permit the publication of the Bull if accompanied by a Brief setting forth the rights of princes.[1] It was not till the year 1575, however, that the Council of Ten gave leave for the Bull to be published, once only, in the Church of San Pietro di Castello, the cathedral, but not the most important church of the city. This incident is the first sign of disagreement between the Court of Rome and the Republic—a flaw in their cordial relations which slowly widened and led to a complete rupture. The Bull and the acts of the Council of Trent placed the secular government on their guard, though they were willing, now as always, to support the Inquisition, provided its action were confined to the suppression of immoral and heretical books, and to the punishment of those who read them, with the concurrence and through the medium of the secular powers.

To return for a moment to Rome and the history of the Index previous to its settlement by Clement VIII. In the year 1571 Pope Pius V. erected the Congregation of the Index, for the special purpose of enforcing the Tridentine Index and *Regulæ*, and of dealing with all questions relating to the examination, prohibition, or expurgation of books, which had hitherto been entrusted to the Congregation of the Inquisition. The Congregation of the Index now created consisted of eight cardinals and seven consultors,[2] but the numbers varied. In the year 1588 Sixtus V. ordered the Congregation to draw up a new and enlarged edition of the Tridentine Index.

The new Index was compiled by Marc' Antonio Colonna, Girolamo Rovere, William Allen, Ascanio Colonna, and Federigo Borromeo.[3] The Sixtine Index not only contained large additions to the three classes of prohibited books, but it presented two new features—first, a list of heresiarchs

[1] Reusch, i. 78, 79. Cecchetti, *op. cit.*, i. 448.
[2] Reusch, i. 432.
[3] Zaccaria. Reusch, i. 503.

as distinguished from heretics, compiled upon the principles laid down by the Dominican Alphonse Chacon;[1] and, further, the ten Tridentine rules were amplified to twenty-two.[2] The Sixtine Index was printed by Paolo Blado in 1590, but the Pope died on 27th August of that year, and the publication of his Index was suspended. It had no effect on Venice, except in so far as it formed the basis for the Clementine Index, which brought matters to a crisis between the Republic and the Court of Rome.

Clement VIII., immediately on his succession to the Holy See, ordered the Congregation to set about the preparation of a new Index. In 1593 the Index was ready, but the Pope withheld the order for its immediate publication. There was a strong opposition to the Index, in which Venice, through her ambassador, Paolo Paruta, took a leading part. Paruta's despatches kept his government fully informed of all that was taking place in Rome, and the Venetians were forewarned and prepared to take steps in defence of the book trade when the Clementine Index appeared in 1596.

[1] Zaccaria. [2] Reusch, i. 510.

CHAPTER XV.

1593—1596.

CLEMENT VIII. AND THE REPUBLIC.

Paolo Paruta, Venetian ambassador at Rome—The case of Margounios, Bishop of Cythera—The Clementine Index prepared—Delayed—Paruta's remonstrance—The case of Domenico Bassa—The case of the Inquisitor of Bergamo.

THE incidents relating to the publication of the Bull *in cœna Domini*, in the year 1569, indicated that the relations between Rome and Venice were not perfectly cordial. And the divergence was continued and accentuated by several episodes, trifling in themselves, but all tending to strain those relations still further. At this period (1593) Venice was represented at the Vatican by Paolo Paruta, one of the ablest diplomatists the Republic ever possessed. In his vivid and lucid despatches[1] we can follow the whole course of the negotiations upon the points of divergence between the Pope and the Republic, and as they all bear upon and illustrate the history of the press in Venice, it is advisable to dwell upon them fully at this point.

Maximus Margounios, Bishop of Cythera, a Greek scholar and caligrapher, was at that time resident in Venice. He was engaged in editing numerous Greek works for the printer-publishers of Venice.[2] He had fallen under the observation of the Inquisition for his reputed heretical opinions on the procession of the Holy Ghost, and on account of a book sent to him from Germany by Frederick Sylburg. The copies of this work had been confiscated, and Margounios complained ὡς μόλις ἡμᾶς ἑνὸς ἢ καὶ δευτέρου ἐγκρατεῖς γενέσθαι. It is not surprising that Margounios had roused the hos-

[1] *La Legazione di Roma di Paolo Paruta. Dep. Storia Patria. Miscell.*, vol. vii.

[2] Legrand, *op. cit.*, Nos. 185, 220, 232, 234, &c. ; also vol. ii., p. lvii.

tility of the Inquisition, for among his inedited works we know that there were two pamphlets, *alterum in Franciscanos, alterum vero in Jesuitas, utrosque suis depinxit coloribus*. He was now summoned to Rome to answer for his opinions. But the Senate refused to give him up, and sent instructions on the subject to their ambassador. On the 3rd of July Paruta had informed his government that Cardinal Santa Severina had spoken to him at length on the matter of Margounios, explaining many things which the bishop had done to cause scandal, and promising to produce books printed by Margounios in Germany full of manifest heresies. The Inquisition, of which Santa Severina was head, desired to have Margounios at Rome, promising to treat him well, as their sole object was to save the bishop from his errors and to remove the possible cause of damnation for others. His Holiness made similar representations to Paruta, which were duly reported. In reply the Senate ordered their ambassador to urge upon the Pope the justice of recognizing the ancient rights of the Venetian Republic; at the same time to assure him that, as for Margounios, if he had done ought amiss or meriting castigation, they would not fail, on proof shown, to punish him as he deserved. Meantime the government ordered the rectors (the civil governors) of Padua to cause Margounios to surrender all his works printed in Germany or elsewhere, and to send them to Venice at once; also to inform Margounios that the government would not tolerate any scandals. On receiving his instructions Paruta sought an interview with Santa Severina, and reported that he had succeeded in persuading the Cardinal that it was impossible for the Venetian government to disgust and alarm the Greeks. Santa Severina replied that there were precedents for the extradition of ecclesiastics, and Paruta begs his government to furnish him with a complete list of all such cases, and to point out distinctions where they exist. "I took care," he adds, "to leave no illusions in Santa Severina's mind as to his ultimate success, and I trust I disabused him entirely, for his Holiness has not mentioned the matter again." On July 31st, however, Paruta again reports that he has had an interview with the Pope, in which he urged several considerations which might lessen the disgust his Holiness felt at the decision of the Senate After long conversation the Pope said, "Well, well, you will talk to Santa Severina about it; it is his business, for he is head of the Inquisition, and is better informed than I am." And here the matter of Margounios seems to have dropped. The Bishop of Cythera did not go to Rome. Just before his death he was collaborating with Sir Henry Saville in his edition of St. Chrysostom.

Throughout these negotiations with reference to the Bishop of Cythera the Venetian government showed itself very firm and carried its point. It is doubtful whether the reason alleged by Paruta, the unwillingness to alarm or disgust the Greeks, was the real reason for the refusal to surrender Margounios. It would hardly seem that disgusting the Greeks was as serious a matter as disgusting the Romans. It is to be regretted that the debates in the Senate have not been preserved; they would have shown us the true mind of the Republic. The instructions to Paruta merely tell him what he is to say to the Pope, and have a diplomatic colour. It is probable that the Senate was thinking far more of the ancient rights of the Republic than of the feelings of the Greeks; that it was defending the State against an interference between itself and one of its subjects which it considered to be excessive; and in this defence it proved successful.

On July 8th, 1593, Girolamo Bernerio, Cardinal of Ascoli, handed to the Pope the new Index drawn up by the Congregation of the Index. On August 14th, Paruta reported to his government that the Index had been presented to the Pope, but held back by his order; and seeing that his Holiness showed some hesitation on the subject, Paruta thought the moment favourable for putting forward the views of the Republic on the question of the press. He sought an audience of the Pope, and set forth the reasons which had induced him to broach the subject to his Holiness. These were: (1) The great commercial importance of the Venetian book trade, more flourishing in Venice than in any other city, not merely of Italy, but of Europe; for the present conditions of the press imposed by the Tridentine Index hampered the book trade in Antwerp, Lyons, and Paris. This was the reason why the Republic displayed such anxiety upon the matter. (2) The book trade in itself was worthy of protection and consideration. (3) A sufficient censorship was already exercised by the obligatory *imprimatur* from the Council of Ten, which was not conceded without the *testamurs* of various examiners, among them the Inquisitor; so that nothing *contra principi, nè contra buoni costumi, nè sopra tutto contra la religione cattolica* could issue from the press. (4) The publication of the new Index, which was not merely a revised, but an augmented edition of the Tridentine Index, would ruin many who, in all good faith, and believing themselves covered by the Index of Trent, had published books which now appeared upon the Clementine Index. Besides, many of these books did not, either mediately or immediately, touch upon religious questions, but were condemned for some triviality, such as the works of many poets, and an immense number of books on a variety of subjects which did not contain any attack on dogma, but in which the presence of a single word which might raise a scruple had been deemed sufficient to condemn them to an everlasting death. (5) Add to all this a general disapproval which reigns in Rome, and which, without doubt, will be felt everywhere by men of learning, whose authority is of value, as the Apostolic See knows to its cost, and whom it is therefore advisable, as far as may be, to preserve well affected and obedient to the Church.

One of Paruta's main objects, as he himself declared later on, was to save the Venetian trade in non-religious books—in the classics, the poets, the romancers. He therefore passes lightly over certain "trivialities" (*qualche vanità*) for which many of the most popular of these books had been placed on the Clementine Index, and rests upon the fact that Venice has taken and will take every precaution against works containing anti-Catholic dogma, thereby appealing to the major interests of the Papal Court. Not only was he diplomatic in so arguing, but he was following a line which Venice had always supported—a line of reasoning enunciated in the sittings of the Council of Trent by Daniele Barbaro, that it was absurd to condemn equally a work of youthful licence (*opus licentiæ juvenilis*) and an attack on the foundations of faith or the dogmas of the Church. Venice was not anxious to secure the purity of her press at the cost of hampering the press; but, as she said to Margounios, and earlier still to Cynthio degli Fabritii, she would not tolerate a scandal. "His Holiness," says Paruta, listened kindly to these vigorous arguments; "he recognized the force of what I urged about the great commercial importance of her book trade to Venice. The matter was one for the Congregation of the Index; but as he desired to consider the question fully, he had kept the new Index by him instead of causing it to be published. 'In the condemned books there must surely be something wrong,' he said. To which I replied, 'You cannot change the world and make everyone perfect. Nor is it to be expected that the prohibition of certain works not edifying to a Christian life will turn all men to the study of theology and sacred writings; indeed, it is quite possible that the time spent over bad books may be spent over worse actions. Furthermore, as regards doctrinal works, this consideration deserves attention, that the learned who at great cost and trouble have formed their libraries will be driven desperate, because they can never be sure that the very books bearing on their subjects of study will not be condemned; and if this prohibition of books be so widely extended, there is danger that it will not be obeyed.' The Pope was not displeased with my pleadings, to which I was urged by many people of weight here, who promised to follow up the suit if I would begin; for the proposal, generally speaking, is not approved even here in Rome."

To this long and interesting despatch the Senate replied on the 21st August, commending their ambassador's action, but pointing out that all he had hitherto urged had been put forward as a private individual, not as the representative of Venice. They now authorized him, should the Pope not make such modifications as were to be expected from his wisdom, to repeat his arguments in the name of the Republic. On September 4th Paruta was told that his Holiness intended to appoint a committee of the learned to examine the Index, but that he was hesitating owing to representations made to him that the Congregation would feel affronted by the appointment. Paruta at once sought an interview, in which he endeavoured to confirm the Pope in his resolution, praising his Holiness for having suspended the publication of the Index, and expressing a hope that some relaxation of the rigours of the new Index might be afforded. His Holiness replied that he was considering the question. "As this seemed too vague," says Paruta, "I returned to the charge, and called his attention to the fate which had overtaken the Index of Paul IV., which was so general in its terms, and so rigorous, that it was rejected not only abroad, but even in Italy itself." Nothing came of this interview. The Pope's hesitation continued for four months more. But in January of the next year the Congregation of the Index met before the Pope. Some of the Cardinals wished to maintain the Index in full, as drawn up by the Congregation. His Holiness, however, himself addressed the Congregation at length, showing that he was of another opinion. He made use of some of the arguments urged by Paruta in his audiences; chiefly the argument that by the publication of so severe an Index they were risking the reputation of the Holy See, and incurring the danger of being disobeyed. The Cardinal of Ascoli replied that this was no reason for shrinking; the Congregation must do its duty and leave the consequences of disobedience to those who disobeyed. The Pope, however, remained firm in his determination that the Index must be largely modified before he would sanction its publication. "So I hope Venetian interests will be satisfied," writes Paruta, "as the *libri vulgari* on the list will be reduced to almost nil. The Cardinal of Verona has been useful." Finally, on the 19th November, 1594, Paruta was able to report to the Council of Ten that at last the Congregation of the Index had resolved to print the Index of 1593, but much altered and diminished; particularly a whole class of books had been omitted which were all or in great part printed in Venice. "I must inform you, however," he continues, "that the Congregation complain that the censorship is not properly exercised in Venice. They call attention to the case of Mietti, the publisher, consignee of a box of books forwarded to Rome through him, which, when opened, was found to contain many books on the list of the First Class. They wished to prosecute Mietti, but I succeeded in pacifying them, and have heard nothing more of the matter. Venetian printers are also accused of forging the imprint on prohibited books. I should like, as the Congregation has been accommodating about the Index, to be able to promise them that the government will pay attention to these points." To which the Ten replied that the

Rifformatori have been ordered to prosecute all cases of forgery reported to them.

Two other causes of disagreement between the Republic and the Court of Rome tended to strain their relations still further. In the year 1594 Clement VIII. granted to a Venetian publisher, Domenico Bassa,[1] a copyright of a very extensive character. It ran as follows: *Universis et singulis librorum impressoribus ac bibliopolis tam extra quam intra Italiam sub excommunicationis latæ sententiæ pœna, nostræ vero et S. R. E. temporali ditioni mediate vel immediate subjectis etiam sub pœna quingentorum ducatorum auri fisco nostro applicandorum et amissionis librorum ipso facto absque alia declaratione cujusque judicis incurrendis inhibemus et interdicimus ne quis ullum ex supradictis libris aut cujuscunque generis qui vel nunquam antea editi fuerunt . . . ullo pacto ejusdem vel diversi characteris forma imprimere, vel ab aliis impressos vendere aut venales ponere et habuere audeant inter decennium a prima cujusque operis aut voluminis editione computandum.* The tenour of this privilege was to be printed in the books issued by Bassa. In February, 1594-5, the Venetian book trade petitioned the government against this privilege, as the phrase *tam extra quam intra Italiam* brought them within its terms. They urged that they could never be sure that Bassa would not publish some work upon which they also were engaged; in which case their edition must either lie idle for ten years, or they must take the risk of being excommunicated. Moreover, "the copyright to Bassa renders nugatory all efforts to comply with the regulations of the Council of Trent or with the laws of the Republic, and all to secure for one man and his heirs immoderate gain. Only two courses remain for Venetian printer-publishers, either to abandon their business or to migrate to Rome."

It is remarkable that the Venetian printer-publishers should have taken this matter so seriously. But, unless the whole petition were fictitious, put up on purpose to provoke a question with Rome, it is clear that they were alarmed, that they really thought that the privilege would operate to their injury, and that they were in lively dread of excommunication. The government of the Republic was not slow to reply to this appeal. On the 18th February, 1594-5, the Senate addressed the following strongly-worded protest to Paruta: "When this Papal Brief conferring a copyright upon Bassa first appeared, we thought it a forgery, or at least that it had been issued without due consideration by his Holiness. It is beyond all measure extravagant and intolerable that by the use of the pains of excommunication they should aim at destroying the arts and industries of our city. This Brief inflicts a wound upon the liberty and dignity of the laws and ancient constitutions of

[1] Cicogna, *Iscriz. Ven.*, iii. 64; iv. 639; v. 512, 513.

our temporal authority, conceded to us by the grace of the Lord God. If they pursue this course they may proceed to crush other industries, to say nothing of the important effect this Brief will have upon the activity of this market and upon the customs by injuring the trade in paper and other material employed in the book business." Paruta is instructed to beg his Holiness to withdraw the Brief altogether, as nothing short of this will avail, for everyone will refrain from printing and selling books through fear of incurring excommunication. And, further, Paruta is ordered to report upon the attitude assumed by the representatives of other powers in Rome. Paruta fulfilled his orders by appealing to the Pope upon two grounds: one a special ground, the consideration due to the Venetian and to all other presses; the other a general ground, that ecclesiastical weapons were being used in purely lay matters. The Pope replied that he was under the impression that Bassa's copyright applied only to books in the Vatican Library, but that he would refer the matter to a commission, which was naturally the Congregation of the Index. Paruta pointed out to his government, first, that the Brief did not receive the same wide interpretation in Rome as was put upon it by the Venetian publishers. The secretary who framed the Brief declared that it was designed merely to give Bassa a copyright in the notes and commentaries printed by him for the first time. Secondly, if the Pope's interpretation be correct, and the copyright applies only to books in the Vatican, that and the other Roman libraries "offer no material for good editions." Besides, Bassa himself was bankrupt through the failure of the Ubertini bank, so the Venetian printer-publishers need not fear his competition, and the ambassador expresses his private opinion that the copyright was granted merely as a blind to Bassa's creditors. To all this the Senate replied that the observations made by Paruta may be true, but they do not alter the aspect of the case. Venice is holding out on a matter of principle. The considerations at the close of Paruta's despatch are applicable only to the special case, and do not in any way affect the general aspect of Venetian interests as involved in the question whether his Holiness has the right to interfere in the matter of the lay arts and industries of the Venetian State, especially when he adopts the scandalous method of employing excommunication against lay persons in lay affairs. If excommunication, that tremendous weapon, be employed in trivial cases it will lose its terrors.

The Congregation of the Index, in considering Paruta's representations on the subject, showed itself willing to deal favourably with the question. The Cardinals professed themselves anxious upon the point of the correctness of Venetian editions of sacred works, but they declared that they would be satisfied if in the Venetian reprints of all such works the Roman text was adhered to; and this ought to be an advantage to the Venetian book market by insuring that none but good editions were published and sold in that city. The Congregation desired to be the sole source of copyright for Venetian editions of certain important ecclesiastical works, such as editions of the Councils. Paruta advised his government to reply that it will take every care that a proper copyright in such works is granted when sought for. He urges the Republic not to drive matters too hard. "We must avoid," he says, "bringing down on ourselves the reprisals which Paul IV. took against us when we refused to observe certain regulations in the matter of books, by forbidding the importation of books printed at Venice into the States of the Church. Rome can afford to do this, for she can bring her books from France and Germany; it is true they cost a little more, but they are far more beautiful and more accurately printed. I have heard, not from book printers but from book buyers, that unless the Venetian press uses more care than it has done for some time past, Venetian books will be prohibited by themselves, so serious are their imperfections."

Here the affair of Bassa ended. In all probability the Venetians were mistaken in attaching so much importance to the Papal Brief, and Paruta was most likely nearer the mark when he held it to be merely a show privilege to help Bassa to keep his creditors at bay. But all through the affair the Venetian government displayed extraordinary heat, while the Court of Rome maintained a conciliatory temper. Paruta thought his government was driving matters too far; but the Senate was in arms on a question of principle. It saw in the Papal Brief another proof of that spirit of encroachment upon the domain of secular princes which now characterized the Court of Rome, and it resolved to resist it. The indignation of the Venetian printer-publishers and their evident alarm seem to show that the Congregation of the Index was weighing heavily on the book trade and rendering it highly sensitive.

But a still more angry, though a shorter dispute between Venice and Rome was roused by the action of the Inquisitor of Bergamo. The Inquisitor arrested and tried a layman in that city without informing the civil governors or asking their assistance. This was, of course, a violation of the Concordat between Julius III. and the Republic. The Senate, on 18th February, 1594-5, instructed Paruta to go to his Holiness and to inform him of these disorderly proceedings on the part of the Inquisitor of Bergamo, and to tell the Pope that such conduct was a violation of the terms upon which Venice permitted the Holy Office to act within her dominions. Paruta is to urge the matter warmly upon the attention of his Holiness. The Senate then ordered the rectors of Bergamo to inform the Inquisitor there that the trial is null and void, and that he must go no further with it, as the rectors had not been invited to take a part in the proceedings. Paruta, at his audience with the Pope, informed him that the action of the Inquisitor of Bergamo was *contra le convenzioni, contra l' uso ordinario, e contra la ragione istessa*; to which the Pope replied that he had no information, and information must precede action on his part. Paruta answered that it was impossible to doubt the rectors of Bergamo's account, and that Venice only asked what was reasonable in claiming that each party should observe the proper limits of his action; to which his Holiness replied, smiling, "Certainly, it is only reasonable that they should observe their proper limits, but unfortunately they do not." This affair of the Inquisitor of Bergamo was quickly concluded, and in favour of Venice. The Court of Rome again showed itself conciliatory. The Bishop of Bergamo and the Inquisitor withdrew all proceedings against the layman, and the Senate returned them thanks on 11th March, 1595.

It has been necessary to dwell at some length on these various episodes, because they serve as important indications of how matters stood between Venice and Rome. We see how great the dread of excommunication still was, how strong the armoury of the Church. We learn how severe the strain between the two governments was growing, as Venice came to understand the nature of the claims put forward by the Papacy; how the book trade began to feel the hostile influence of the Index, and to resent it; how the government showed itself ready to support the press, and how the Republic gradually defined its position face to face with the Court of Rome, upon the lines which Sarpi subsequently developed and defended.

CHAPTER XVI.

1596.

THE CLEMENTINE INDEX AND THE CONCORDAT.

Publication of the Index; its date—The *Instructio*—The protest of Venetian printers and booksellers—The action of the Republic—The Concordat signed—Its terms—The attitude of Venice towards the Church.

AFTER three years' delay the Clementine Index was officially published in the year 1596.[1] It was largely based upon the Sixtine Index of 1590, but with very considerable modifications in severity. The original order and classification adopted in the Tridentine Index was preserved, and the Clementine additions to each class and letter were added in appendices.

By far the most important feature in the Clementine Index is the publication of a sort of appendix to the Ten Tridentine *Regulæ*, containing instructions to those who shall be engaged on the prohibition, the expurgation, and the printing of books (*instructio eorum qui tum prohibendis, tum expurgandis, tum etiam imprimendis diligentiam ac fidelem* (*ut par est*) *operam sunt daturi*). The substance of this Instruction is as follows:

On the Prohibition of Books.

1. Bishops and Inquisitors shall take care that, as soon as this Index is published, all persons under their jurisdiction shall bring to them a list of all

[1] The Brief of Publication is dated 17th Oct., 1596. Reusch, i. 533. But the Report of the Riffomatori to the Senate, 1765, gives 1595 as the year of publication. So, too, does Pietro Franceschi in his Report of 1761 (Cecchetti, ii. 256); and the terms of the Concordat of 14th Sept., 1596, seem to prove that the Index and Declaration were published before that date.

the books on this Index which are in the possession of those subjects. The Bishops and Inquisitors are to name a certain period within which this list must be presented. In Rome this duty is confided to the Master of the Sacred Palace.

2. In Rome the Master of the Sacred Palace, out of Rome the Bishops and Inquisitors, have authority to grant to pious and learned persons leave to have and to read one or more of the prohibited books which may be permitted by the rules of the Index.[1] Such permission was to be voted for three years only, and must be renewed every three years when required. The readers of these permitted books are bound to inform the Bishop or the Inquisitor of any passages which call for remark.

3. Outside Italy the Bishops, Inquisitors, and Universities shall draw up Indices of all books showing heretical or immoral tendencies which appear within their respective jurisdictions, and these books are to be prohibited.

4. The Apostolic Nuncios and Legates outside Italy, the Inquisitors and Bishops in Italy, shall send yearly to the Holy See, or to the Congregation of the Index or its delegate, a list of prohibited or censured works which have appeared in their districts.

5. The Bishops and Inquisitors shall examine all local Indices, with a view to considering whether books which appear only on those Indices should not be prohibited within their jurisdictions also.

6. Translations of books condemned by the Holy See are also condemned.

On the Correction of Books.

1. The Bishops and Inquisitors conjointly have the power to purge books, even in places exempt from their jurisdiction and belonging to no diocese. Where there is no Inquisitor, the Bishop alone shall discharge this duty. The purgation of books is to be performed by pious and learned men, usually three in number. After these censors have corrected and emended a work, the copy is to be submitted to the Bishop and to the Inquisitor for approval.

2. Censors are to pay attention not only to the text, but also to the notes, summaries, marginalia, indices, prefaces, and dedications. Then follows a list of points which especially require correction, including all ambiguous phrases,[2] all honourable epithets applied to heretics, and all praise of them, propositions hostile to the liberty, immunity, and jurisdiction

[1] *Qui ad prescriptum Regularum permitti possunt*, that is, books prohibited *donec corrigantur*.

[2] *Verba dubia et ambigua.*

of the Church,[1] propositions which, under appeal to the opinions, customs, or example of the heathen, favour political tyranny and support the ideas, falsely called reasons of State, which attack evangelical and Christian precepts.[2] Obscene drawings, even in capital letters and initials to chapters, are to be obliterated.

3. If in books published by Catholics after the year 1515 the correction can be effected easily by a slight alteration, the censors may emend the passage; if not, the whole passage must be erased.

4. In the works of the older Catholics nothing is to be altered unless it be passages corrupted by heretical editors or careless printers. Should any remarks be necessary, they may be added in the margins, or notes to new editions.

5. When the purged edition has been printed by order of the Bishop and the Inquisitor, those who possess the book may correct their own copy by the Inquisitorial one.

On the Printing of Books.

1. No book may be printed without the name, surname, and nationality of the author appearing on the title-page. If the Bishop and Inquisitor see good reason why the name should not appear, the name of the censor who approved the work shall be printed instead. Works of collaboration shall go by the name of the editor.

2. Regulars, besides the *imprimatur* of the Bishop and Inquisitor, require that also of their superiors, and both must be printed at the beginning of the work.

3. It is forbidden to use profane or indecent capital letters or illustrations in any work dealing with ecclesiastical or spiritual matters. The name of the printer, the place, and the date must appear in every book.

4. A full transcript of each new book or edition is to be left with the Bishop and the Inquisitor, and no copy of the printed work is to be sold until the edition has been compared with the transcript and found to agree absolutely.

5. The *testamur* of the examiners is to be printed along with the *imprimatur*.

6. Printers and booksellers are to take an oath before the Bishop and the Inquisitor that they will loyally obey the Rules and the Instructions of the Index, and that they will not wittingly admit to their art anyone who is suspected of heresy.

[1] *Propositiones quæ sunt contra libertatem, immunitatem et jurisdictionem Ecclesiasticam.*

[2] See Sarpi, *Opera*, iv. 443. Helmstat, 1763.

7. If a new and purged edition of a work which has been previously censured is to appear, a notification of that previous censure must be printed along with it in this form: *Bibliotheca . . . a Conrado Gesnero Tigurino, damnato auctore, olim edita ac prohibita, nunc jussu superiorum expurgata et permissa.*

In Clement's *Instructio* there was little that had not been already implied in the *Regulæ* of the Council of Trent, which the Republic had accepted. Three points, however, call for attention. By clauses 3, 4, and 5 on the Prohibition of Books, provision was made for the continual enlargement of the Index by the additions yearly sent to Rome from the dioceses of Italy and the Nunciatures at foreign courts. Clause 2 on the Correction of Books, perhaps the most important clause in the *Instructio*, advances claims to Inquisitorial jurisdiction over the debatable ground of political doctrine. The phrases *libertas, immunitas et jurisdictio Ecclesiastica*, contraposed to *ratio Status*, cover the whole ground upon which the battle of Church and State and their respective spheres was to be fought. Clause 6 on the Printing of Books required an oath of allegiance to the Index and its administrators from subjects of the Venetian Republic.

The Venetian government must have been informed early of the terms of the *Instructio*, or, as is more probable, the Clementine Index was published and in operation some time before the date of the Brief calling it into force,[1] for Venice took steps, early in 1596, to oppose the *Instructio* as it stood, and secured the Concordat a month before the date of the Brief.

We have seen that, between the years 1564 and 1596, the Inquisitorial censorship of books had been gradually weighing more and more heavily on the Venetian printers and booksellers. As proofs we have the attempt made to deprive Venetian printers of the right to print and publish bibles, breviaries, and missals, and to insist that such books shall be printed at Rome and nowhere else—an attempt which the government successfully resisted, with the help of Paolo Paruta. And, again, Luigi Grotto, Cieco d'Adria's appeal[2] to the commissary of the Inquisition in Venice on behalf of his 1588 edition of Boccaccio, for which no copyright from the Senate exists, would seem to show that publishers had more dread of the Inquisition than of their own government. The Indices which had appeared since La Casa's Catalogue had so increased the number of unpublishable books—many of them forming a large staple in the trade of Venetian printers and booksellers—that it seemed certain, if this new Index was enforced, as it was sure to be by the awakened activity of the Church, that the Venetian book trade would suffer

[1] 17th Oct., 1596. Reusch, i. 533.

[2] Reusch, i. 391.

severely. In spite of Paruta's opinion that Venetian interests had been sufficiently consulted, the printers and booksellers at once appealed [1] to the Senate for support against the new Index. The government was made anxious by the general attitude of the Church, and was still more alarmed by certain clauses in the *Instructio*, and resolved at once to make vigorous representations at Rome. The Pope charged the Patriarch of Venice, the Bishop of Amelia, and the Inquisitor of Venice to conduct negotiations with the Republic on his behalf. But the Curia was not anxious to conclude the matter quickly; it hoped that by delaying, the subject would be allowed to drop. To further this object, Clement talked of creating another Venetian a cardinal, in addition to the two already members of the College. In the meantime, however, Clement's commissaries in Venice had enjoined upon parish priests and confessors the obligation to carry out the Clementine Index, Rules, and Instructions in all their force, and to see that their congregations and their penitents observed the injunctions. This action on the part of the ecclesiastics, while the question was still pending, roused the Senate, who complained vigorously to the Pope, and ordered Venetian booksellers not to obey the injunctions of the clergy. The government also informed the Patriarch that in the State of an independent prince he had no right to take any steps affecting that State without the consent of the government.[2] In the face of this resolute attitude the Pope gave way, and on his behalf the Cardinal of San Giorgio wrote to the Cardinal Patriarch, Lorenzo Priuli, the Nuncio, Anton Maria, Bishop of Amelia, and the Inquisitor General, Giovanni Vicenzo Arrigoni of Brescia,[3] instructing them to sign the famous *Dichiarazioni delle Regole*, afterwards known as the Concordat, on the 14th September, 1596, the Senate having accepted both the Index and the Declaration two days previously.

The provisions of the Declaration were as follows:

1. The books on the new Index marked *donec corrigantur* may be sold unexpurgated to those who hold a licence from their Ordinary or from the Inquisitor to possess them.

2. Should a publisher desire to reissue one of the censured books, the correction may be effected in Venice; it shall not be necessary to send the book to Rome.

3. The printers are not obliged to hand to the Inquisitor a transcript of the work they intend to print; it is sufficient that they deposit the original

[1] Zaccaria, *op. cit.*

[2] *Che in casa di principe libero, e molto meno in quelle circostanze, non si doveva operare causa alcuna senza il publico beneplacito.* Report of Pietro Franceschi, 1761. Cecchetti, *op. cit.*, ii. 257.

[3] Cecchetti, *op. cit.*, ii. 10.

manuscript with the secretary of the Rifformatori dello Studio di Padova, who shall consign these manuscripts to a special chest in the Ducal Chancery, and shall enter the titles in an inventory to each chest. This is to apply only to new books or new editions of books marked *donec corrigantur*. In other cities of the Venetian dominion the manuscript shall be consigned to the Chancellor of the Captain [1] in each city.

4. In all books the *imprimatur* of the magistrates shall be printed on the verso of the first leaf, as at present by law established.

5. Printers are not to use lascivious woodcuts, but they may use profane ones provided they are not lascivious.

6. The booksellers shall draw up a list of all the books in their shops, and shall present it to the Inquisitor for this one time only, in order thus to clear the shops of all books on this new Index.

7. As regards the right of the Bishops and Inquisitors to prohibit books which are not on the present Index, it is declared that this refers only to books which attack religion, are printed out of Venice, or are issued with a false imprint. The right shall be exercised rarely, and only on just cause shown, and with the consent of the three lay assessors.[2]

8. The rule as to the oath of allegiance shall not take effect in the dominion.

9. All heirs shall give to the Inquisitor a list of the prohibited books which they find in their legacy within three months after succession, and until that be done they may not use nor alienate the prohibited or censured books.

The Concordat was signed, and one hundred and fifty copies [3] printed for distribution among the printers and booksellers of Venice; and then, but not till then, did the Republic permit the Index to be published with their consent. Some of the clauses in the Declaration refer to provisions of the Tridentine *Regulæ*, some are designed to counteract the Clementine *Instructio*. The three most important points in the *Instructio* were, as already stated, the oath of allegiance to the Holy Office, the continuous enlargement of the Index at the pleasure of Rome, and the introduction of purely political questions, under the heading of *jurisdictio Ecclesiastica* and *ratio Status*, as proper subjects for Inquisitorial censorship. The oath of allegiance was

[1] The Military Governor.

[2] *S' intende de' libri contrarii alla religione, forastieri, o con false et finte licenze stampati, e rarissime volte si darà il caso, nè si fara senza giustissima causa, e con partecipazione del Santo Offizio, et intervento de clarissimi Signori Assistenti, tanto in Venezia come nello Stato.*

[3] Reusch, i. 547, but the report of the Rifformatori in 1765 says sixty copies. I think Franceschi is right, for the same document states that there were 125 presses in Venice, and the Concordat was printed for circulation among them all. See Pietro Franceschi's Report. Cecchetti, ii. 256, 257.

abolished by the eighth clause of the Concordat; the preceding clause dealt with the other two points. The seventh clause is by far the most important clause in the Concordat. We shall find Paolo Sarpi and all the other partisans of Venice basing their resistance to the Index upon it. And indeed it contained such a curtailment of the powers of the Inquisition and the Congregation of the Index over books, that it is surprising to find the Court of Rome assenting to it. For it limited the ecclesiastical inquisition to purely religious questions, and to a supervision of books printed elsewhere than in Venetian territory or issued with a false imprint, thus excluding political and secular questions from its purview; and it provided that fresh additions to the Index should only be made rarely, on good cause shown, and with the assent of the lay assessors. And, though repeatedly requested to do so by Rome, the Venetian government declined to authorize the publication of any augmented Index till the year 1766,[1] wherein the new prohibitions are announced as *juxta formam concordatorum*.

The relief obtained for the book trade by the Concordat was very great, had the persons interested chosen to avail themselves of it. There was a tone of decision and sharpness about the clauses which indicate that the government was aroused and angry. And indeed, a few months before the settlement of the Concordat, and while the question was still pending, on the 14th June the Senate published the following decree, in effect an attack on the interference of Rome: "The printers and booksellers of this city have for some time past been in the habit of applying to Rome for privileges and *motu proprio*, conferring upon them sole rights in certain works to the exclusion of other printers and booksellers—a custom contrary to our laws, full of bad example, detrimental to the trade, and injurious to the public. Be it decreed, that all printers, our subjects or inhabitants of our city, who have obtained or enjoy such exclusive privileges or *motu proprio*, shall straightway renounce them, for the support and preservation of the art in this city and for other reasons; so that from this day onwards everyone is at liberty to print any books from which he has hitherto been debarred by such privileges and *motu proprio*, after he shall have obtained the licences declared necessary by our laws. Nor shall any subject or inhabitant, for the future, venture to seek either directly or indirectly, nor to enjoy such privileges, under pain of forfeiting all books printed upon such privileges, and a fine of ten ducats for each copy; one-third of the books and of the fine shall go to the accuser, one-third to the court, and one-third to charities."

The attitude of Venice towards the Church had changed very much

[1] Reusch, i. 547.

since it passed the law of 1562. Then the government was working hand in hand with the Inquisition; now its tone is suspicious and hostile. This change seems to have been brought about thus: when the government found itself face to face with the great problem raised by the new art of printing—the problem of the censorship of the press—it recognized the need for some check upon an industry which had the power to spread opinion so widely, unless the world was to be swamped by books hostile to religion, corrupting to morals, dangerous to government. It reserved to itself the censorship of politics and of morals, but it willingly yielded to the Church the position to which the Church was entitled, of censor on religious questions, only requiring that the Church should make use of the secular machinery for the enforcement of its censorship. That is to say, had the Inquisitor refused his *testamur* for a book, it is most unlikely that the Council of Ten would have granted its *imprimatur*, unless it believed that the Inquisitor had been actuated by motives other than dogmatic in the strict sense of the word. The government considered that its own and its subjects' reasonable liberties were sufficiently protected when it had secured the Concordat of 1551 with Julius III., securing the presence of three lay Venetian assessors at all sittings of the Holy Office, whose consent was essential to the validity of any action taken by the tribunal in Venice. But, as Sarpi points out, there came a moment when the divergence between the aims of the Church and the aims of the State began to manifest itself. The moment was marked by the pontificate of Paul IV.; the divergence was accentuated by the Lutheran heresy, and the new aims of the Church were formulated in the Council of Trent. Venice found that the Church, under the pressure of the Reformation and the necessity for strengthening its position, was beginning to put forward claims far wider than any it had explicitly advanced—claims to at least a concurrent jurisdiction on certain points which the government held to be secular, and in the abstract, to the universal authority of the Papacy over temporal princes; for the title, *Qui filii sint veri*, in the Decretal *Per venerabilem*, had been interpreted to mean that, and the doctrine *Papam habere potestatem in temporalia in ordine ad spiritualia* could be extended to cover incitement to rebellion and assassination. Moreover, Venice found that the Church was coming more and more to mean Rome. There was an attack on the liberty of Venice as a secular government, and there was an attack on her position of quasi-ecclesiastical independence. And this touched a chord deep down in the heart of the Republic, and stirred an ancient rivalry—the rivalry between the Evangelist and the Apostle, between St. Peter and St. Mark. The Venetians had believed themselves safe with three Savii sopra l' Heresia, and protected by the terms of their Concordat with Julius III. Now they found that

Rome was planting itself in the heart of the Republic under the guise of the Inquisition, and the discovery of this attack led Venice to take up the hostile attitude which we have noticed. We shall see how Venice stated her position, how she defended it, and how far she made her defence good, upon the subject of book-printing and book-selling in Venice.

CHAPTER XVII.

1596—1623.

THE ECCLESIASTICAL ATTACK ON THE CONCORDAT.

The position Venice desired to assume—Clause Seven of the Concordat, and the corollaries Venice deduced from it—Venice still Catholic—Double attitude the cause of weakness—The practical success of the Church.

NO doubt the position which Venice desired to assume was the position taken by Philip II. of Spain towards the Tridentine Index and its ten *Regulæ*. The King wrote to his ambassador that "Spain has her own special Index and her own special Rules on the prohibition of books. It can not be permitted to place her under general orders. Books which in one country may be innocuous, in another may be dangerous."[1] Venice was not hostile to a censorship and an Index, but it desired to have control over both. The Republic did not raise, as Philip did, any official objection to the Index and *Regulæ* of Trent, probably because she thought that, as the Index and the censorship were a part of the Inquisition, the question of her rights had really been settled when her position towards the Inquisition was defined. The Republic had always maintained that the Inquisition in Venetian territory was only operative through the consent of the government—that the Holy Office was by no means a separate and independent power in the State. And it based its argument upon the fact that the Papacy had not imposed the Inquisition upon Venice *nolens volens*, but had only succeeded in establishing it in the dominions of the Republic after consenting to specific agreements which the government dictated, and that one of these agreements rendered the Ducal *exequatur* necessary to the Inquisitor before he could act. When the government found that the

[1] Llorente, iii. 265, 272. Reusch, i. 318.

Church proposed to claim full and independent inquisitorial powers over the book trade, leaving the secular authority on one side, it took the active measures we have noted, to reassert its position by means of the Concordat.

The Venetians deduced two corollaries from the seventh clause of the Concordat—first, that all future prohibitions of books, in order to be valid in Venice, required a formal recognition on the part of the government. Though the wording of the clause is not very clear, yet the phrase, "with the participation of the Holy Office and the intervention of the three assessors," might be made to bear this meaning constructively, for the three assessors were subjects of Venice, amenable to her orders, removable by her, and triable for disobedience. This was undoubtedly the intention of Venice, though she clothed it in slightly ambiguous language, possibly in order to facilitate the consent of Rome.

The clergy in a body did their best to traverse this proposition in theory, and to render it abortive in fact. They maintained that prohibitions from Rome were binding on all good Christians, whether the government chose to admit it or not, and they constantly endeavoured to make additions to the subsequent issues of the Clementine Index which appeared in Venice.[1] As we have seen, the government remained firm, and the appendix to the first augmented edition in 1766 shows how very few books it had permitted the Inquisition to add to the Index. As a matter of fact, the Clementine Index remained the sole Index for Venice from 1596 to 1766.

The second corollary deduced by the Venetians from Clause 7 of the Concordat, the proposition that the duties of the Inquisitor shall be confined to questions of theology and of dogma, could be more easily evaded by the Church; for it raised the wide question—what is heretical? and brought into the arena the problem of the boundary line between temporal and spiritual spheres of action, between ecclesiastical dogma and secular policy. And it was in this region that the inherent weakness of the Venetian attitude lay. The government was quite clear as to the position it desired to maintain, and earnest enough in its endeavours to make that position good. Throughout the years from 1593 to 1596 it displayed a vigorous and even a violent temper on the question of its rights, and did what in it lay to protect its book trade, and to save it from those ruinous consequences which had overtaken the book trade of Rome, and, as Paruta declared, had injured that industry in Antwerp, Paris, and Lyons. It secured the Concordat from an unwilling Pope, and it enforced the provisions of the Concordat wherever its own action was possible; for example, it absolutely prevented the public and official enlargement of the Index inside Venice. Yet

[1] 1597, 1598, 1607, 1608, 1614, 1624, 1707. Reusch, i. 547.

if we turn to examine the conditions of the book trade itself, we find that the Index and the Inquisition are clearly operating with repressive vigour. The number of copyrights falls off suddenly, from twenty-four in 1596 to seven in 1597. The printers began to leave Venice in large numbers, and to carry away their instruments; and the Senate on February 20th, 1601-2,[1] was obliged to pass a law to stop this emigration, and, finally, there is a most remarkable decrease in the number of printing presses in Venice. Within a few months of the publication of the Index, and in spite of the protection of the Concordat, the presses of Venice fall from one hundred and twenty-five to forty. And the reason for this inefficiency of the government's attempts to shelter the trade is inherent in the relation of the Venetians to the Church. Venice had not broken with the Church, although it was at present in an attitude of hostility. It still acknowledged its spiritual allegiance; it had not the desire, nor in all likelihood the power, to become Protestant, to sever itself entirely from the Holy See. The very senators who wrung from the Pope the concessions of the Concordat, and who maintained that the Inquisitor drew his authority from the Doge, in their private life and in their cabinets admitted the authority of the Pope over their consciences, and obeyed the mandate of the Inquisitor. The very same printers who had complained to the Senate, and in whose behalf the Concordat was secured, admit in their complaint that they will not and dare not incur excommunication;[2] they knew that for their own peace of soul they required absolution in this life and the sacraments before death. It was impossible in this state of mind that the opposition to Rome should be vigorous, real, and effective. The Venetians were not sincere; there was a double attitude. The attitude of Venice as a State was hostile to Rome, and the attitude of the Venetians as individuals submissive to Rome. They desired with one part of their mind what they dreaded with the other, and the inevitable result was paralysis in action. How could men at this mental point of view combat an army perfectly organized, absolutely sincere, clear as to its object, positive and obedient? It was impossible. And the Church, though it yielded over the Concordat, never intended it and never permitted it to take effect. Almost the entire clergy laboured as one man to render the concession abortive.

The struggle was long drawn, and the means adopted to achieve this end were various. In the first place, as we have seen, the Roman party secured the publication of no more than 150 copies, and it was not difficult to cause many of these to disappear, while the Index was sown broadcast over Venice. They made use of that powerful instrument, the confessional; and fathers-confessors were ordered to announce to their penitents the prohibition of all the books

[1] Appendix I., No. XVIII.

[2] See p. 140, Paruta's Despatches.

condemned at Rome, in spite of the clauses in the Concordat which forbade such prohibitions. The result was that the books condemned at Rome could find little or no sale in Venice, and only among those who were more or less suspected and contemned for their unorthodoxy. The government replied by the expulsion of the Capuchins and Theatines, the principal offenders; but in vain, for in the Diocesan Synods the bishops took care to announce all the new prohibitions decreed by the Congregation of the Index. Rome caused its additions to the Index to be secretly printed and distributed to the book trade. The government arrested and severely punished a bookseller in Bergamo for having this list of additions in his shop. The Holy Office gave loose leaves containing the additional prohibitions to the Lent lecturers, with orders to read out the titles of forbidden books; though on the representations of the government this abuse was forbidden with the consent of the Nuncio. But by far the most powerful means for destroying the effect of the Concordat was offered by the laws of Venice itself, thereby illustrating the inherent weakness of the dual attitude towards Rome. By the law of 1562 the Inquisitor or his delegate was appointed one of the three government censors of books. Without his *testamur* the certificate of the Rifformatori could not be obtained, and without that an *imprimatur* would not be granted by the Council of Ten. All that the Inquisitor had to do was to take the latest edition of the Index of Rome, and to steadily refuse his *testamur* for any work whose title appeared therein. If the government pleaded Clause 7 of the Concordat, limiting new prohibitions to books *contrarii alla religione forastieri o con false e finte Licentie stampati*, the Inquisitor would not find it difficult to argue that any book to which the Church was opposed must necessarily be *contrario alla religione;* he could even point out that there was a difference between *contrario* and *contra*, and that a book might be *contrario alla religione* without dealing in any way with religious dogma. The government had conceded the Church's right to judge in this matter.

It is not till we come to the period when Venice acts under the inspiration of Fra Paolo Sarpi that we find the government making a stand on this point. When the Republic undertook the protection of the press in the year 1596, it should have removed the Inquisitor from his joint and concurrent action with the lay censors. This dual sovereignty of Church and State, the remnant of the mediæval idea, though not admitted in theory by Venice, was there in practice, and was sure to breed dissensions. But Venice could not remove the Inquisitor without incurring the charge of rebellion against the Church, and becoming suspect of heretical leanings. And how indignantly Venice repudiated such charges is proved by the Doge's exclamation when the accusation of Calvinism was brought against the State:

Che vuol dire Calvinista? siamo tanti Cristiani quanto il Papa, e Cristiani moriremo al dispetto di chi non vorria. And so it came about that while the Church yielded in appearance on the points of the Concordat, in reality it drove the Index, the *Regulæ*, and the *Instructio* home upon the Venetian printing press, with the result which many years after the government sorrowfully recognize, that in spite of every effort, *l'arte rimase priva di tutti que' Libri ch' erano segnati nell' Indice; o se alcuni ne adoperò gli ebbe così alterati e mutilati che ben presto negli altri Paesi s' estinse il credito delle nostre edizione, nè mai più si riebbe.* That the Church of Rome was not solely to blame for the extinction of the credit of the Venetian Press—that other causes, some general, such as the decline of Venice herself, others particular, such as the misdemeanours of the trade and the impotence of the laws, also contributed to this result, we shall have occasion to observe. But it is not too much to say that the blow dealt by the Index of Clement was a severe one, and contributed largely to that long decline which the government of Venice struggled vainly to arrest.

CHAPTER XVIII.

1605—1650.

THE INTERDICT AND FRA PAOLO SARPI.

The quarrel continued—The immediate causes of the Interdict—The adjustment of the quarrel—Fra Paolo Sarpi; his championship of the Republic and his views on the relation of Church to State—The attempt to suppress discussion of the Interdict—The case of Giovanni Battista Ciotto—Violation of the Concordat—Sarpi's *Consulta sulla regolazione delle Stampe*—The three classes of books created by the seventh clause of the Concordat; and examples—Sarpi's advice contained in the *Discorso sopra le Stampe* and the *Discorso sopra l' Inquisitione*—His conclusions—Resumé of Sarpi's position—Efforts of the government to make good this position—Success of the Church in defeating it.

THE quarrel between Rome and Venice was by no means concluded by the signature of the Concordat; but at the opening of the seventeenth century it assumed another phase. In the year 1601 the Court of Rome addressed a remonstrance to the Republic on the presence of the English ambassador in Venice, and the celebration of the Protestant service in his private chapel.[1] To this the Senate replied, thanking his Holiness for his vigilance, and assuring him that the government had taken all necessary precautions for the preservation of the Catholic faith, which was as much the care of the Republic as of his Holiness. More serious subjects of disagreement were in preparation. By a series of decrees passed in the years 1515, 1537, 1561,[2] and reaffirmed in 1603, the Senate had forbidden the erection of new churches, monasteries, and hospitals in Venice without the permission of the government. By a law passed in 1536,[3] and reaffirmed in 1605, the Senate had forbidden the alienation of lay property

[1] Romanin, *Storia documentata di Venezia*, Ven., 1853. This was a standing grievance against Venice at Rome. In 1594 Clement VIII. complained to Paruta of the English in Venice. Cf. *Legazione di Roma*, i. 265.

[2] Romanin, *op. cit.*, vol. vii. cap. 1. Cecchetti, *op. cit.*

[3] Romanin, *op. cit.*, vii. 20.

to ecclesiastical bodies. The government arrested, and resolved to send before a secular court, two ecclesiastics guilty of atrocious crimes;[1] and, finally, it had stated its position as regards the taxation of the clergy in the formula, *se il clero è protetto e difeso ch' essi contribuiscano alle spese che si fanno per loro sicurezza*, and more generally in Sarpi's second proposition as to the relation between secular and ecclesiastical subjects of a State, *che per leggi divine gli Ecclesiastici non hanno ricevuto alcun essentione dalla podestà secolare nè quanto alle persone nè quanto alli beni loro.*[2] The attitude of the Republic upon these points of building new churches, alienating lay property to ecclesiastical bodies, and secular jurisdiction over offending clerics, gave great offence at Rome, and when Camillo Borghese became Pope as Paul V., he sent Briefs to the Senate declaring their decrees against the building of churches and against ecclesiastical succession null and void, and requiring them to surrender the two ecclesiastics to the Nuncio.[3] As the Senate did not comply with these demands, Paul addressed a *monitorium* to the clergy of Venice, threatening excommunication to the Doge and Senate and interdict upon the Republic, if within twenty-four days they had not complied with the Briefs. The Doge forbade the publication of the *monitorium;* and the excommunication and interdict came into operation. The Jesuits, Capuchins, and Theatines, the orders which obeyed the interdict, were expelled. Venice was now in open rupture with the Pope, who seriously considered the possibility of reducing her by arms. Venice did not dream of separating herself from the Catholic communion; she still declared herself as spiritually subject to Rome, but she was fighting for her civil and secular independence. Her position is expressed by two phrases emanating from the Doge and from the Senate, *Siamo Cristiani quanto il Papa* and *Non sappiamo veder come si pretendeva d' impedire che un principe libero in casa sua non possa fare quelle disposizioni che stima necessarie per conservazione dello Stato suo.*[4] The Pope, on the other hand, had declared his position when he announced that he would not submit to be *Pope everywhere save in Venice.* There seemed little prospect of the quarrel being settled, for both parties were extremely obstinate. The government of Venice by its vigorous action avoided the worst inconveniences of an interdict; under threat of the gallows it compelled the priests to perform their functions of saying mass, baptizing, marrying, and burying. But after a year of negotiation the Cardinal de Joyeuse, the French ambassador, succeeded in arranging a compromise which both parties accepted. The two ecclesiastics were handed by the government to the French ambassador, with a declaration that the Republic still reserved

[1] Romanin, *op. cit.*, vii. cap. 1.
[2] *Consulta di Fra Paolo Sarpi*, ap. Cecchetti, ii. 302.
[3] Cecchetti, ii. 403.
[4] Romanin, *op. cit.*

its right to try criminal clerics; the decrees on the erection of churches and on the alienation of lay property were not withdrawn, but the Republic pledged itself to enforce them with its wonted moderation and piety. The Senate withdrew its manifesto against the censure, and the Pope withdrew the excommunication and the interdict. The Senate declined to receive the Papal absolution and benediction, but there is some reason for believing that it was delivered all the same, though covertly. The adviser and inspirer of the Venetian government all through its resolute opposition to Papal interference in secular matters was Fra Paolo Sarpi, and I have dwelt at length on the episode because it raised once more the question of literary censorship, and gave occasion to the great Servite to express his opinion on the whole subject.

Sarpi stands out as the most prominent figure in the whole of this struggle between Venice and the Court of Rome. He is the representative, the protagonist of Venice, and he is so because he had thoroughly caught the tone of Venice, understood her attitude, and sympathized with her action. Sarpi never had any intention of joining himself to the Protestant party; he had no wish to separate himself from communion with the Church of Rome; he too, like other Venetians, was *Cristiano quanto il Papa*, but, like many churchmen, he was strenuously opposed to the new departure which was proclaimed by the Council of Trent, and conducted by the new army of the Church, the Jesuits. He thought the Church was embarking upon a wrong course, and he held that the State was justified in resisting encroachments upon the rights of sovereigns in secular matters. He expressed his view in a notable passage, wherein he marks his conception of the respective spheres which Church and State ought to occupy, *La vera religione cristiana*, he says, *cammina per la via del cielo, non può incontrarsi ne urtare col governo politico che cammina per la via del mondo.* He believed that the Church of Rome was abandoning the true path of Christian religion for the dubious and perilous ways of a political power and a temporal State.

Sarpi was perfectly in accord with Venice, and he expressed simply, strongly, directly what Venice meant. There is little in Sarpi's arguments that had not been already implied in the action of the Venetian government; but the theories upon which those actions were based he put forth tersely and pungently, and supported them by close and subtle reasoning.

When the episode of the Interdict was concluded, Paul V. wished, as far as in him lay, to obliterate all traces of an event which had been so distasteful to the Church. The Inquisition cited Sarpi and the other Consultori di Stato to Rome, and prohibited all works, published or to be published, which dealt with the question in any way. The Republic considered this to be a breach of the seventh clause of the Concordat. Rome could not condemn in Venetian territory any books it thought fit; and the Republic urged that the question of the Interdict was a point in which religion played no part, that it was purely a matter of politics. Other causes of disagreement followed. While the quarrel about the Interdict was still in progress, the Venetian censorship granted permission for the publication of the fifth volume of Francesco Suarez' Commentary on Thomas Aquinas' tractate *De Censuris* only on condition that certain passages be omitted. At Rome this was resented, and the Congregation of the Index proposed to proceed against the censors, but confined itself to issuing the following decree: "The Venetian booksellers, Jo. Battista Ciotto and Jo. Battista and Jacopo de Franceschi, have published in Venice the fifth volume of Suarez' *De Censuris*, omitting many passages, and thereby incurring *crimen falsi*. As a punishment for such audacity, the Congregation of the Index forbids the said booksellers ever to print that work, under penalty of excommunication *latæ sententiæ*. The omitted passages are to be restored, and for the future no one is to buy this or other works from these booksellers, nor to possess them, but to hand them to the Bishop of the diocese."[1] Although the suppression of certain passages in Suarez' *Disputatio de Censuris* justified the Congregation of the Index in imputing *crimen falsi*, and proves that the secular government also were ready to use the censorship of books to further their own views and aims, still the action of the Congregation of the Index in punishing Venetian subjects directly, and not through the government or the Venetian Inquisition, was undoubtedly a violation of Clause 7 of the Concordat, which required the concurrence of the Venetian Inquisition and of the three lay assessors to every new act of prohibition, and, considering the severity of the penalty, was a high-handed act. The controversial attack on Venice by the supporters of the Curia grew in volume and violence, and the government had to consider what steps they would take upon this subject. Sarpi, in 1608-9, presented a report, pointing out the difficulties of the situation and advising how they should be met.[2]

Sarpi urged that the press is so important, owing to the facility it affords for the diffusion of doctrine, be it sound or be it pernicious, that it is absolutely necessary for the government to exercise censorship over it in matters of dogma, faith, politics, and morals. But this censorship should be employed with the greatest possible regard for the welfare of the trade (*il tutto però in tal maniera che l' arte faccia più negotio sia possibile*). On the points of faith and morals the supervision of the Fathers Inquisitors is sufficient, and the temporal authority need take no steps at present.

[1] Reusch, ii. 323.

[2] Cecchetti, ii. 234.

But the doctrine of the temporal independence of princes requires protection, for the Inquisitors will sanction any and every attack upon the temporal power of princes and any and every amplification of the temporalities of the Church.

The works of the Italian jurists, called forth by the question of the Interdict, are full of pernicious teaching on this point. But to prohibit such books altogether would be a serious blow to the trade.

And here arises a difficulty. If these books which attack the temporal authority of princes are printed and published in Venice, the world will say that they are published with approval of the doctrines they contain, for they have passed the secular censorship. It is inexpedient to refuse an *imprimatur* for the sake of the press, and it is inexpedient to grant it because of the doctrines which these books contain.

There are two remedies for this difficulty—either to alter the formula of the *imprimatur*, and to make it run "with the permission," instead of "with the approbation"[1] of the government, and indeed it is a serious matter to take upon oneself the *approval* of all books printed in Venice (*et veramente è gran cosa pigliar sopra se et farsi approbatore di tutti li libri che si stampano in Venezia*), or else to withdraw the law which compels the publication of the *imprimatur* along with the book, taking care, however, that the *testamurs* and *imprimatur* required by law are duly obtained.

Sarpi's tenderness for the book trade is remarkable. His object is to find a middle course, which shall relieve the government from some of the difficulties consequent upon the freedom of the press, and at the same time shall interfere as little as possible with the activity of that press (*senza restringere le facende dell' arte*). Sarpi was no friend to gagging the press; and in one of his later *Consulta* he even expresses a doubt whether it be possible to do so at a time when the violence of the attack on Venice made him ready to advise that step (*quando si potesse chiuder l' adito a queste scritture sarebbe il vero rimedio: questo non si potendo fare resta il rintuciarli il filo*).[2] It does not appear that the government adopted either of Sarpi's proposals. And the struggle with Rome was vigorously maintained on both sides.

The seventh clause of the Concordat as interpreted by the Venetians created three classes of books which came under the notice of the government: (1) books which both the Inquisition or Congregation of the Index and the government were willing to prohibit; (2) books which the Inquisition wished

[1] Albizzi, *De Inconstantia*, p. 279. This was a distinction which the Church had already drawn in the declaration by the Congregation of the Index, Dec. 10th, 1601, stating that in cases of doubtful books it was not sufficient to say "with the leave," but "with the approval" of superiors.

[2] Cecchetti, ii. 248.

to prohibit, but the government desired to see published; (3) books which the Inquisition wished to publish and the government wished to prohibit. At this burning point in the controversy several instances of both the latter classes came up for decision.

In 1611 Thomas Preston, under the name of Roger Widdrington, published his *Apologia Cardinalis Bellarmini pro jure principum adversus suas ipsius rationes pro auctoritate papali principes sæculares in ordine ad bonum spirituale deponendi. Cosmopoli,*[1] and in 1613, *Disputatio theologica de juramento fidelitatis. Albianopoli.* The first work was prohibited 10th May, 1613, and, by a special decree of the Congregation of the Index, both works were placed on the list on the 16th March, 1614, *nisi auctor quam primum se purgaverit.*

The Nuncio in Venice begged that the decree might be published and enjoined on Venetian booksellers.[2] The Senate called upon Sarpi for his opinion and advice in the matter. Sarpi gave his answer in a brief *Consulta,*[3] advising that the government should not allow the prohibition to take effect in Venice, for two reasons: first, in order to maintain the Concordat, which by its seventh clause allows prohibition only in cases where the faith is called in question, whereas "Widdrington's" book is eminently Catholic, and teaches doctrine most needful in these times; secondly, because it is necessary to eradicate the pernicious doctrine of the temporal authority of the Pope over princes, a doctrine which is the cause of an incurable suspicion between Church and State.

On the question of the second work by "Widdrington,"[4] Sarpi says that its doctrines are based partly on Thomas Aquinas, partly on Gerson; that there is nothing in the book which is hostile to religion, as it only treats of jurisdiction, and that in terms which are entirely Catholic. Sarpi's advice is to let the Nuncio's request fall through by delaying an answer; and should he press, the government may reply that the Concordat covers all books

[1] Reusch, ii. 333.

[2] He thereby appears to concede the point claimed by Venice, that no purely Roman prohibition was valid in Venice without the sanction of the government.

[3] Cecchetti, ii. 236. *Il libro è andato 3 anni per il mondo, comparse alle fiere et veduto dalli giesuiti nè però a Roma hanno pensato e censurarlo se non adesso per la causa che dirò di sotto.*

[4] Its occasion was a schism in the English Catholic party upon the proposal of the oath of allegiance. One party wished to accept it; the other, the Jesuit party, opposed, and obtained a Brief from Rome declaring the oath inadmissible on the ground that it was opposed to faith and salvation. The party in favour of taking the oath doubted the authenticity of the Brief, or, if authentic, maintained that it did not bear the meaning given by the Jesuit party, or if it did this, the Pope was misinformed, and obedience to a misinformed Pope was not obligatory. This is "Widdrington's" argument, and this is the reason why he came into collision with the Congregation of the Index.

except those which attack religion; if, however, anything of that nature is proved to exist in these books, it will be right to prohibit them.

A still more striking instance of the efforts of the Church to suppress a work which the Venetian government desired to see published is afforded by the case of Andrea Morosini's History.[1] Morosini in the course of his History dealt with the question of the Interdict, and when the time came for publication the Venetian Inquisition refused to sign the *testamur* which was needed before the Chiefs of the Ten could grant an *imprimatur*. Polo Morosini, who was in charge of his deceased brother's work, complained to the Senate. Thereupon the Senate declared that Morosini's History contained a true and veracious account of all that happened; that the Inquisitor drew his authority to act from no other prince than the Republic, and that authority extended only to the revision of books on questions of faith—questions which were not raised in the History; and the government ordered the immediate publication of the book without the Inquisitor's *testamur*, and with the words *Superiorum Permissu*.

These are two examples of the second class of books created by the Concordat. We may take two examples of the third, the class which the Church wished to publish and the State declined to permit.

Marc' Antonio de Dominis, Archbishop of Spalato, upon his return from England wrote and published a recantation of his heresies.[2] This recantation was to be published in Venice and elsewhere. The work was printed in Rome by the Apostolic printers in 1623, and the Senate requested the advice of Fra Fulgenzio, Sarpi's friend and biographer, on the question of letting it appear in Venice. Fra Fulgenzio, in a very spirited *Consulta*, arrived at the conclusion that Marc' Antonio's recantation should not be allowed to appear in Venice, on two grounds: first, because of the scandal which must result from announcing to the world that a prelate once held such monstrous doctrines; and secondly, because among the doctrines which Marc' Antonio abjures and anathematizes is this, that the Pope has not power in matters temporal with a view to matters spiritual, and this retraction leaves him declaring as an article of faith that the Pope has power in matters temporal with a view to matters spiritual.[3] On these grounds permission to publish the recantation should be denied.

[1] Reusch, ii. 322. Cecchetti, ii. 266.

[2] Reusch, ii. 401, *et seq.* Cecchetti, ii. 243. The title of the work is *M. A. de Dominis, Archiep. Spal., sui reditus ex Anglia consilium exponit.*

[3] *Per la quale retrattione resta da lui posta come articolo della nostra santa fede, Papam habere potestatem in temporalia, è vero che di sotto apporta questa limitazione in ordine ad spiritualia.* The origin of the term *in ordine ad spiritualia* is this. In 1215 Innocent III., in the middle of his struggles with Frederick II., took occasion to publish his decretal, *Per Venerabilem*. In the

The second example is that of Cardinal Sforza Pallavicini's semi-official History of the Council of Trent, written in answer to Fra Paolo Sarpi's History. Through the Venetian ambassador at Rome, Pallavicini begged the Senate to permit the sale of his History in Venice. The Senate replied that had the History been a purely historical work they would have raised no objection, but as it stands the History contains many sentiments noxious to the government of the Republic, and lacerates and injures the memory of a true and faithful servant, by stating that Pietro Soave Polano, the ostensible author of the History of the Council, is Fra Paolo Veneto; and the permission is accordingly refused.[1] The reply was both disingenuous and narrow. The government must surely have known that Sarpi was the real author of the History; and it proves that the Republic was also as ready as the Church to make use of the repressive powers of the censorship in order to stifle free discussion which was unpalatable to itself.

It was cases of this nature which induced the government to ask Fra Paolo Sarpi to place in writing his views on the whole question of the press. He obeyed, and presented to the government the *Discorso sopra le Stampe*. The *Discorso* is written with the lucidity and condensation which are characteristic of Fra Paolo. There is no declamation, but there is perfect plain speaking as between a trusted adviser and an honoured prince. The immediate occasion of the work is not stated, but at the outset Sarpi frees the question under discussion from all special and merely occasional colouring, and proceeds to deal with the issue in its main and general aspects as affecting the position of Venice and the whole future of the printing press.

Sarpi points out that, as long as the interests of the Church and of the State were identical, it was very right and proper that the censorship of the press should be left in the hands of the Inquisitor, who would take care that nothing was published hostile to true religion nor subversive of good government. "But about thirty years ago," he says, "the interests of the Church began to follow a different line from the interests of the State, and this divergence has gradually increased till it is now no longer possible to submit secular matters to the Inquisitors, for their interests are diametrically opposed to those of the State. This tendency on the part of the Church has in the last few years produced a whole series of books whose doctrines are entirely subversive of all secular government. They teach that no government but

title, *qui filii sint legitimi*, it is stated that the Pope has temporal jurisdiction in States not under his immediate temporal rule, *certis causis inspectis casualiter*. Around the proper meaning of *casualiter* a dispute arose, with the upshot that *casualiter* is glossed as *indirecte et in ordine ad spiritualia*. *Indirecte* was eventually dropped, leaving the dogma of Innocent as *Papam habere potestatem in temporalia ad spiritualia.*

[1] Cecchetti, i. 78. Senato Roma, reg. 62, c. 66to.

the ecclesiastical has a divine origin; that secular government is a thing profane and tyrannous, which God permits to be exercised upon his people as a kind of persecution; that the people is not in conscience bound to obey the secular law, nor to pay taxes nor public burdens; that it is enough if a man know how not to be found out; that the imposts and public subventions are for the most part iniquitous and unjust, and the princes who impose them excommunicated; that because of this excommunication of princes come death, want, and other public misfortunes. In short, princes and rulers are held up to view as impious, damned, and unjust; that man must fear them perforce, but in conscience he is free to do all that in him lies to break their yoke. The prince who first perceived the danger was Philip II. of Spain. He appointed a committee for the examination of all works except missals, breviaries, and school books—the only books which he allowed to remain entirely under the censorship of the Inquisition; his committee drew up rules upon the subject, and regulated matters as the interests of the government required. Venice followed a somewhat similar course. The censorship of such secular officials as the Rifformatori dello Studio di Padova was supposed to afford sufficient guarantee that freedom would be secured for all legitimate controversy, and that the interests of the State would not be sacrificed to the interests of the Church. But no sooner had the quarrel between Paul V. and the Republic been brought to a conclusion than the Court of Rome endeavoured to deprive Venice of the honour she had won. And to this end they sought by every means in their power to raise analogous questions, and to have them answered in favour of Rome, and to cause the works to be printed and circulated in Venice. The result of this will be that, in course of time, the Venetian press will have furnished a large number of books containing opinions adverse to her position in her struggle with Rome, and the world will argue that the Venetians themselves are aware that their cause was an unjust one, for, although they possess a political censorship of the press, they have allowed these works to appear."

"The truth is, that the system of political censorship as at present established, the censorship by a Ducal secretary, is defective. For the secretary has no code of general rules to guide him, and the want of such a code exposes him to the importunities of authors and publishers, and, further, frequently leaves such doubts in his mind that he has to refer to the College for an opinion."

"The most proper remedy for these defects is a code of general rules for the guidance of the secretary, drawn up by the government, and applying to all classes of cases. Behind such a code the secretary can shelter himself from the importunate, the interested, the over-zealous; the secretary himself will walk surely with the light of public wisdom before his eyes, and the College need not waste its time in judging upon the particular when it has already laid down the rule for the general."

In proposing the groundwork for these secretarial rules it is clear that Sarpi had in view the action of Rome in drawing up its Indices and *Regulæ*. He proposes, indeed, to follow the example of the Court of Rome, and as it applied its censorship in a sense favourable to the liberty and immunity of the Church, so he suggests that the government should apply its censorship in a sense favourable to the liberty and immunity of the State.[1] Following these lines, then, Sarpi distinguishes four classes of writers whose books ought to be placed upon the State Index: (1) those who attack the constitution of the Republic and its laws by name; (2) those who attack the laws and constitution adopted by the Republic without naming her; (3) those who in respectful terms and within the limits of fair controversy argue against the legislation of the State; (4) those who attack no laws of the State, but who broadly maintain the absolute and universal superiority of the ecclesiastical over the temporal authority. "In the correction of books which are open to censure, it is not advisable to follow the practice of the Church in 'raking through the entrails of many a good old author,' and altering the sense and the intention of whole passages, so that the writer is made to say the reverse of what he desired to say; first, because all the world stigmatizes such action as falsification; and secondly, because such conduct would bring upon Venice the infamous charge of castrating books; thirdly, because the Court of Rome claims to have the sole right to alter passages in books, as was proved by the case of Suarez' *De Censuris*.[2] As regards books written by a subject the author may most rightly be compelled to respect the interests of his State and of his prince. If the author be not a subject, rather than compel him to alter his work to suit the just requirements of the State, it would be better to refuse him an *imprimatur* altogether; for the government cannot prevent him from publishing the obnoxious passages elsewhere, with any comments on the Venetian government that may seem good to him. When it is necessary to make marginal notes or corrections, they should be made in a scholarly way and by scholars; they should not be mere negations or affirmations, but real corrections, supported by reference to authorities. If it be urged that this State censorship will prove prejudicial to the art of printing, the reply is this, that the Inquisitor, with his thousands of prohibitions, has not yet ruined the art, and so the secretary with his tens is not likely to do so. In formulating the secretary's rules

[1] The example of a selfish use of the Index by the Church had the inevitable tendency to induce a selfish use of the Index by the State.

[2] See above, p. 161.

due regard must of course be paid to the trade, but it is the very function of the government to draw a just line between public and private interests." In his *Discorso sopra l'Inquisitione* Sarpi returns again to the subject of the press. He insists that no new Index should be permitted to appear unless the terms of the Concordat are strictly observed by the Church of Rome, and he points out that the encroachments of Rome are effected in three ways: (1) by the prohibition of books which make for good government; (2) by prohibiting books which do not properly come under its jurisdiction; (3) by preventing the correction or suppression of sentiments hostile to good government. "In these ways the Church attempts to make itself *Padrona assoluta de Libri*, whereas her servant the Inquisitor ought properly to be a judge[1] of faith, not a censor of morals private or public, both of which belong to the jurisdiction of the secular power. The Church of Rome advances eleven grounds on which it claims to prohibit books; of these eleven, five do not pertain to ecclesiastical jurisdiction; they are *scandalum magnatum*, opposition to ecclesiastical authority, advocacy of tyranny, libel, and obscenity. It is quite true that books guilty of any of these charges should be prohibited, but such prohibition rests with the civil authorities; to assign this function to the ecclesiastical authority is to confound all order and balance of duties and powers. Yet from the basis of these eleven reasons for prohibition the Church has proceeded still further, and argues that the State may not and cannot by itself prohibit books; and in making this wide claim it is following out its ancient policy, *abbraciar tutto non risparmiar nulla; alla fine vi resta sempre qualche cosa dell' acquistato.*[2] This is a most dangerous doctrine, and it ought to be opposed for *le ragioni non usate in progresso di tempo si perdono, ed il contrario posto in consuetudine dà ragione di poterlo fare.*[3] Besides, the doctrine is condemned by all the teaching of St. Paul, who affirms often, but not sufficiently often, that God has given the order, the quiet, and the morality of States into the hands of princes."

Sarpi concludes by recapitulating the points of his discourse, and draws up ten propositions upon which he recommends the government to take action:

1. The Index of 1595 having received the consent of the prince, the books which appear upon it must remain there.

2. For the future no prohibition is to be permitted unless corroborated by public authority, as agreed on in the Concordat.

3. If ecclesiastics ask civil authorities for support in the prohibition of

[1] See above, p. 65, *et seq.*, on the position of the Inquisition.
[2] Sarpi, *Scrittura sop. la Probib. d. Libri.* *Opere*, Napoli, 1790, tom. viii. p. :7.
[3] Sarpi, *ut sup.*

heretical works, it must be granted to them after the works have been examined.

4. Under the title of heresy, dogmatical support of civil authority, in its own proper sphere, is not to be included.

5. Foreign books inimical to good government are to be absolutely prohibited.

6. In the reprints of books nothing favourable to good government is to be removed.

7. In issuing these reprints the old editions, before the ecclesiastical expurgations were made, are to be used.

8. In printing the Index of 1595 no new names are to be allowed to creep in.

9. The prohibitions of the Inquisitor shall be confined entirely to heretical works.

10. The Concordat shall always be printed along with the Index.

The policy which Sarpi suggested to counteract the "pregnant policies" of Rome, was this: strict and loyal adherence to the Concordat on both sides, and a clear definition and separation of the functions and duties of Church and State in the matter of censorship of the press; both are right and necessary, but there is a danger *di confondere il mondo* if their respective spheres are not clearly determined.

From the course of Sarpi's argument several points emerge. Neither Sarpi nor Venice are heretical; they do not desire to shelter heretical writings; the government is to assist the Church in the repression of heretical books; the censorship of such books belongs of right to the Church. *Non parlo*, Sarpi says, *de' libri proibiti per causa di Religione, perchè le ragioni di vietar questi sono giustissime, ed è necessario il farlo.* But Sarpi wished to define heresy so as to exclude political doctrine unpalatable to Rome. And here he laid his finger on the very knot and kernel of the difficulty. As long as those who had to judge of heresy had also the right to determine what heresy should imply and what it should cover, the danger that they would use their right and their power for their own benefit was inevitable. Yet it would have been illogical to refuse to the Church, the guardian of pure faith, the right to determine in what way that faith was endangered; accordingly Sarpi says the Church alone shall freely and absolutely determine upon matters of dogma and of faith, but it shall not touch upon that part of a man's conduct where dogma and faith do not enter, his duty to the State, his obligations as a citizen. This doctrine of the twofold duty of a man, his duty to the Church and his duty to the State, had never before been set out in such sharp antithesis. How far it could be supported in theory, how far it is possible to separate the two duties, is still an open question. But in practice, and at the moment of which we are speaking, Sarpi was right; in the face of the encroachments of the Church, and of the danger that it would monopolize all government, it was necessary to recall princes and subjects to a sense of the duties of a citizen towards his State.

It is remarkable how frequently the words "good government" occur in the course of Sarpi's argument. It seems as though he were developing around the phrase some new conception, some new ideal which had an equal and concurrent claim upon man's obedience and reverence with the older ideal of obedience and reverence towards the Church. I do not know of any passage where Sarpi has set forth what he exactly meant by good government, but it is clear that he has in view the united action of prince and subjects for the good of the State. The Church, then, was hostile to this ideal—it prevented the publication of books tending towards good government; it suppressed or altered passages of a similar tenour in the books which it allowed to be published. Sarpi saw, and saw to his sorrow, that at that time there was hostility between the two ideals; but he did not believe that they were incompatible, and his policy is governed by the hope of making their compatibility clear (*dandosi la mano l'un' l'altro per iscambievole ajuto*) through the determination and mutual observation of their respective spheres.

It is clear that neither Sarpi nor Venice could be accused of "introducing licence while they opposed licensing." They were, ostensibly at least, as anxious for the purity of the press as ever the Church was. To judge from the Indices the Church itself was not earnestly anxious on this point. The sole question was, which should exercise the censorship over certain offences—such as libel, *scandalum magnatum*, obscenity—the Church or the State. Sarpi distinctly states his opinion that all such books should be absolutely prohibited, and the government took abundant and even excessive care to carry out the moral censorship; its laws upon the subject were sufficient. That it did not succeed was the fault of its police, not of its intentions, and in part, no doubt, of its defective practice in legislation. Sarpi was right when he urged the government to frame laws based upon general principles, designed to include as many aspects of a case as possible, rather than special laws passed to meet individual cases as they arose. And, finally, he recognized the vigour and the ability of his opponents on the subject of censorship when he recommended the government to study the action of the Church in regard to the literature it desired to crush, and to take it as an example, either to avoid or to imitate, in regulating the State censorship of literature hostile to the Republic.

Such were the lines of Sarpi's policy. He thoroughly understood the danger which menaced his own political and ecclesiastical ideals. That danger threatened largely through the operation of the Index on the press. He dreaded lest, by the gradual expansion of the Index, all works in support of the temporal authority of princes, and the definition of the spheres of Church and State, would disappear, and that those who desired to take that line of argument would one day be told that their doctrines were new, heretical, unsupported by any authority, upon which the Church always set such store; that they would also be deprived of the very arsenal of their arguments, the views and opinions of those who had preceded them on the same side of the controversy. Furthermore, Sarpi dreaded lest the Concordat should disappear, be forgotten entirely, leaving the Venetian press completely under the control of the Inquisition, and deprived of the bulwark which the State had secured for its defence. In both these dreads Sarpi was partially justified. Although his reports were drawn up by order of the government and presented to the government, the Venetians never put their recommendations into practice. The heat of the quarrel died away; Sarpi's own personal influence began to wane as men of a younger generation came to the conduct of affairs, as acceptance of the counter reformation and intellectual apathy settled down on Italy. Above all, the insincere, the double position of Venice as regards the Church of Rome, rendered it impossible for her to act vigorously or thoroughly; *siamo tanti Cristiani quanto il Papa*, and that being the case, how could they strenuously oppose their spiritual chief? Occasionally the government was roused to a spasmodic assertion of its rights which it always maintained in theory, and the resistance to the encroachments of the Church was often vigorous in appearance. The Church was compelled to give way for the moment; but it had only to wait, and the innate catholicism of the Venetians soon rendered it mistress of the situation once more.

As early as 1612 the Senate had ordered an *imprimatur* granted by the Bishop of Vicenza to a printer of that place to be cancelled as a violation of the laws against *proprio motu*. And again, in 1623, a much graver question arose over the History of Andrea Morosini, to which we have already referred. The action of the Inquisitor in the matter of Morosini's History touched the pride of Venice, and the result was that the next year, 1624, the Senate proceeded to a regular reform of the innovations introduced by the Chief of the Holy Office. The Inquisitors had raised the fee which they demanded for the revision of books. This fee was fixed by the Venetian law of 1562 at the rate of one bezzo[1] for every sheet; now the Inquisitor demanded four soldi. This custom was not only an infringement of the laws of the Republic, but also was a breach of the tenth *Regula* of the Council of Trent, where we find the order that *probatio et examen ac cetera gratis fiant*. To correct this

[1] See p. 93, note 2.

abuse for the future, printers who seek the Inquisitor's *testamur* are ordered to send their books to a secretary of state, by whom the works shall be forwarded to the Inquisitor and his fee paid after revision. Further, the Inquisitor demanded a fee for licensing breviaries, missals, and works of devotion—an illegal demand; and, with a view to checking the abuse, it was declared sufficient that the printers should have the certificate of the secretary of the Rifformatori dello Studio di Padova. If the Inquisitor should raise any objection to the book or to passages in it, he must report these objections to the Rifformatori, who will see that the work is expurgated if necessary. The Inquisitor, instead of underlining obnoxious passages in the original manuscript, had undertaken to obliterate them entirely, so that it was impossible to tell how the passages stood. Such obliteration must cease; the Inquisitor shall only underline objectionable passages, and the Rifformatori shall examine the passages so marked, and take what action is necessary. In the *testamurs* of examination, the Inquisitor, being bound by the Concordat to deal with matters of faith and dogma only, shall confine himself to the words "nothing contrary to the Holy Catholic Faith," leaving the words "Princes and Morals" to the secretary. The Inquisitor may, if he think fit, cause the bales of imported books to be unpacked at the custom house, but at his own charges, in order that he may verify the lists consigned to him by law; for it is the firm intention of the Republic to suppress all heretical and prohibited works.

The very same day that this decree was passed the Inquisitor was summoned to the College, the abuses were pointed out to him, and he was ordered to abandon them at once, and for the future to follow closely the injunctions of the decree of the Senate,[1] which, for his better information, was read to him; the government expressed itself confident that he would obey the public commands, nor give fresh occasion for dissatisfaction or for taking further steps in the matter. A more vigorous assertion of independence could hardly be looked for; the resolution of the Senate is inspired by the spirit of Sarpi, and breathes his antagonism to ecclesiastical encroachment upon the domain of temporal jurisdiction. Yet these almost truculent assertions of authority, these sharp reprimands, seem to have affected the Inquisitor very slightly. They did not deter him from pursuing his own line of conduct; for in the following year we find that he had succeeded in publicly committing to the flames many books which had been condemned, among them Fra Paolo's *Considerazioni*[2] and a work by his friend, Fra Fulgenzio. Here again the

[1] Archivio di Stato. Senato Roma, Filza 47. *Dovete però astenervene, che così è volontà del Senato.*

[2] Sarpi's work was absolutely forbidden by an edict of the Inquisition, 20th Sept., 1606. Reusch, ii. 321.

Inquisitor was virtually the victor. It did not much matter how strongly the government protested; the fact, the patent fact, which impressed the public mind, remained—the Inquisitor had openly burned the books condemned by the Church. Again, in March and April, 1659, the Senate reminded printers that an *imprimatur* of the Inquisitor alone was not sufficient, and to enforce their orders they imprisoned a printer at Verona for publishing a sonnet with an *imprimatur* from the Inquisitor only. It was useless for the government to protest unless they were prepared to punish the Inquisitor, but this they shrank from doing. The Church, which made use of every opportunity that the spiritual allegiance of the Venetians placed in its hands, did not neglect the important medium of the pulpit. As we have seen, Lent lecturers were furnished by their ordinaries with printed injunctions, referring among other points to the prohibitions of books made from time to time at Rome, and insisting on the duty of denouncing such books to the Inquisitor; and the preachers were required to read these injunctions to their congregations. This was, of course, a violation of the Concordat, and the Senate declared these injunctions to be illegal; but we find no instance of a priest being punished for a breach of this law, and indeed we do not see how the law was to be enforced—who of all his congregation would denounce a preacher, when each member of that congregation in his private capacity acknowledged himself under the spiritual authority of that preacher? The Doge had declared the Venetians to be as much Christians as the Pope; the people had only to verify the words of their own government in order to render abortive any attempt to curb the authority of Rome.

These are some of the more prominent points upon which the Republic came into collision with the Church in the matter of the press and the book trade. They are landmarks in the course of that long struggle which began with the Council of Trent and outlived the Republic itself. Throughout the struggle the Venetians officially and publicly made large claims to independence, and the Church ostensibly, though reluctantly, made large concessions to those claims. But all along the line, as far as the real fact and substance goes, the anti-Roman party was defeated, the Church was victorious; she achieved her aim—the party that yielded was the party that won. The Venetian printing press felt the influence of the Index and the *Regulæ*, and suffered as all presses suffered which came under the operation of the Council of Trent.

CHAPTER XIX.

1600—1699.

PRESS LEGISLATION DURING THE SEVENTEENTH CENTURY.

Its inefficiency—Multifarious legislation—Official proof readers—The Senate ceases to be the fountain of copyright—The Guild takes its place—The rights of the Library of St. Mark—The Superintendent of the Press—The tariff of the official readers—The four groups of press laws in this century; their excellence and inefficiency—The reason for this.

THE quarrel between the Republic and the Church of Rome, which was in its most acute stage between the years 1593 and 1620, has detained us for so long because it is the point of greatest historical interest in the development of the Venetian press, and because this epoch marks the turning point in the career of that press. Down to the close of the sixteenth century the Venetian printing press had been for a time the most remarkable, and then one of the most remarkable, presses in Europe. After the year 1600, though not destroyed, it ceased to be exceptional. This change was due, no doubt, in part to the general decline of learning which was taking place in Italy, and to the general levelling of excellence which attended the diffusion of the art of printing, but in part also to the check received by the operation of the Index.

The book trade of Venice was, however, by no means destroyed; it was still an important item in the commerce of the Republic. The government did all that lay in its power to support and encourage the art. The steps it took to achieve this object, and the success which attended its efforts, call for attention.

The most remarkable feature in the press legislation of the seventeenth century is its impotence. The government in the preambles to its laws constantly laments the decadence of the art of printing, and expresses its desire to recover the pristine excellence of the Venetian press. But it does not appear to have known where the mischief lay, nor how to discover and cure it. Most of the laws of this century are repetitions of the earlier laws. The government seems to have felt that the armoury of legislation was exhausted, that nothing further could be done in that direction. Yet the perpetual repetition of the same laws proves how perpetually those laws were neglected or broken. In all probability the evil was beyond the powers of legislation to cure. When we come to deal with the history of the Guild of Printers and Booksellers during this century—the instrument which the government devised for the better preservation and regulation of the art—we shall see how ineffectively it worked.

In the year 1601 the Senate was seriously alarmed by the emigration of printers, who took with them the materials of their trade—type, presses, varnish, ink. The College and the Rifformatori dello Studio di Padova, after studying the subject, proposed a measure to the Senate framed to meet the danger. This law made it illegal for any printer to leave Venice, whether for another Venetian city or for a city beyond the dominions of the Republic, without a written permission from the Rifformatori. It enacted penalties for all those who sell or send out of Venice the materials and instruments used in printing, and for all those who, having left Venice, refuse to come back when summoned by the Rifformatori. This measure, however, was not sufficient to check the decline of printing; and in 1603 the Senate undertook a general reform of the art, which they say *è andata annichilando grandemente*. The reasons for this state of things are given in the preamble as (1) the continued emigration of printers from Venice; (2) the carelessness and avarice of publishers, who no longer pride themselves on the quality of the books which they produce, but aim at cheap workmanship and high prices; (3) the inferiority of Venetian editions owing to the want of good proof readers and correctors. The law now passed provided the following remedies:

1. The copy from which a new edition of any book is to be made shall be carefully revised before the printer begins his work.

2. The type, when set up, shall be read through by the compositor to the foreman and corrected in the forme. A proof shall then be cast off and sent to the reader; and after the proof has been read and corrected, a revise shall be cast off and submitted to the reader before the sheet is passed for press.

3. Official proof readers are to be appointed by the Rifformatori dello Studio, who, if necessary, shall fix their salary; and no one but an official proof reader may be employed by printers.

4. Manuscript copy and proofs are to be preserved, that it may be easily seen whether alterations have been made after the examination for an

imprimatur. The third reviser, the Public Reader, is abolished, and two only remain, the Ducal secretary and the Inquisitor.

5. A fine of at least twenty-five ducats for every printer who shall print the name *Venetia* on books not printed in Venice.

6. Publishers are to employ master-printers certificated by the guild, and to pay attention to the quality of paper, ink, and type; the paper should be of a weight corresponding to the nature of the book (*e bella Carta, la quale sia di pesso proporzionato alla qualità de' Libri*).

7. At the end of every book shall be an errata, with the name of the proof reader responsible for the correction of the proofs.

8. The prior and officers of the guild are to make frequent visits of inspection to all the bookshops and printing presses, and to report once every three months to the Rifformatori upon the progress of the trade.

9. Printers who are not matriculated in the guild are to pay to the corporation eight soldi grossi[1] for every ten reams of paper they use in printing, as the guild has to pay taxes which do not fall upon those who are not members.

10. In the case of first editions, when two or more printers have obtained the necessary *testamurs* and *imprimatur*, the first who registers his name with the officers of the guild shall enjoy the copyright, which is to run for twenty years.

11. In the case of books that have been printed elsewhere, in or out of Italy, but not in Venice, the printer or publisher who, after obtaining the necessary licences, shall register his name with the guild, shall enjoy a copyright of ten years. For books which have not been printed in Venice for the last twenty years a copyright for ten years may be obtained. For books which have not been printed in Venice for the last ten years a copyright of five years may be obtained. All these copyrights depend upon the condition that the printing is begun at once, and continued at the rate of half a folio every day at least.

12. Books issued by members of the guild under copyrights, if they are badly printed or full of errors, shall entail forfeiture of copyright.

13. Copyright for books which are to be printed out of Venice shall be granted only on a vote of five-sixths of the College and of five-sixths of the Senate, in a sitting of at least one hundred and eight members.

14. No one may put a book on the market until he has obtained from the librarian of St. Mark's[2] a certificate that he has presented to the Library a copy of the book bound in parchment.

[1] See p. 86, note 1.

[2] The Library lost this right under Austria. By decree of 10th August, 1853, it was conferred on the University of Padua. Cf. Castellani, *I privilegi di Stampa*, p. 11.

This was a very comprehensive measure, and should have proved of service in restoring the quality of Venetian editions, had its provisions been observed. The most striking points in the act are the creation of official proof readers; the abolition of the Public Reader as a censor of the press, and the delegation of his functions to the secretary, thus rendering the laborious process for obtaining an *imprimatur* slightly easier; the imposition of a tax on all printers who do not belong to the guild, thereby increasing the income of the guild, but at the same time recognizing a class which theoretically had no existence, for all master-printers were in theory supposed to belong to the guild, and affording us a curious example of that negligence and indifference which to a large extent accounted for the futility of the Venetian laws; the disappearance of the Senate as the fountain of copyright, and the substitution of the guild; the determination of the length of all copyrights for new works at twenty years, and the rendering attainment of copyright a purely mechanical process after the *imprimatur* had been secured; finally, the clause which records the rights of the Library of St. Mark for the first time. But this excellent law was not operative. In January, 1603-4, a deputation from the guild waited on the Rifformatori to complain of the infringements of copyright which constantly took place. The Rifformatori instructed the officers of the guild to inflict the customary punishment—that is to say, a fine of 300 ducats and forfeiture of books; and, to prevent the infringement of copyright by copies printed in other cities of the dominion, the guild is to furnish a list of all copyrights granted, to the chancelleries of the various towns, where on petition of the holder of the copyright the deed shall be registered for forty soldi.

As a natural result of the previous law which created the guild the fountain of copyright, the guild also became a sort of Stationers' Hall for the registration of copyright, although the register no longer exists, even if it were ever created, which is open to doubt. The government intended by clause 9 of the law of 1603 to increase the income of the guild by taxing non-matriculated printers and booksellers, but it gave the guild no power to enforce this tax upon recalcitrants. The guild found itself powerless to exact its dues, and in 1608 it was compelled to appeal for assistance to the Rifformatori, with the usual result that an order was issued threatening fines and penalties for non-compliance with the law; but no signs of obedience followed.

Six years later we meet for the first time a new official of the printing press added to the considerable number already in existence. This official is called the Superintendent of the Press, and his duties at first were confined to the examination of the exemplars to be used in the production of new editions, and to ordering their further revision by the official correctors should he think fit. This same law published the first tariff for these official correctors or readers; it is entitled, *Mercedi dei Correttori secondo la diversità de' Caratteri.*

Testin e Nonpariglia a Soldi 38 *il Foglio.*
Garamon e Filosofo a Soldi 28 *il Foglio.*
Antico commun, Lettura, Silvio, Testo d'Aldo Soldi 20 *il Foglio.*

This tariff indicates the kinds of character most commonly in use at the opening of the seventeenth century.

The frequent infractions of the press laws induced the government to apply the method of secret denunciations, which was at that time so much in favour with the Republic as a substitute for a proper police. Bartolamio Bertucci, notary to the Avogadori di Comun, was appointed to receive all secret denunciations of infringement of the press laws. But secret denunciations have seldom proved of any real value in enforcing laws; they may have been used as weapons of private revenge, and to such use they lent themselves, but they could not take the place of a proper police supervision. They were impotent to secure the observance of the law, and the frequent confessions of the inefficiency of the law prove it.

A further demonstration of this inefficiency is furnished by the general law of 1653, in which the government made another effort to check the abuses and defects in the trade. The preamble contains a lament over the inherent corruption of things human, *non è cosa per ottima che sia che dalla malitia degli uomini non venghi nel corso del tempo contaminata et guasta, come si esperimenta a' tempi correnti nell' istessa stampa.* Not only the manner of printing, the paper, ink, type, and correction are defective; but what is much worse, the clandestine press is issuing large numbers of scandalous and obscene works (*impressione clandestina di opere empie, obscene, malediche*). By way of remedy the following regulations were passed. The government return to the original idea of a powerful guild directing the trade, which shall be absolutely in the hands of the guild.

1. To strengthen the Guild of Printers and make it really universal, and thus to facilitate the punishment of offenders, the original idea of the guild shall be revived, and no one who is not matriculated in the guild may print in Venice.

2. The prior and officers of the guild are to make their inspection of ink, paper, type, and correction a real inspection, and are to report once a month to the Rifformatori dello Studio di Padova.

3. The rules about *testamurs* and *imprimatur* are to be strictly observed.

4. The owners of presses and shops are to keep these licences in files for inspection by officials.

5. Books which have already been printed with the necessary licences do not require the Inquisitor's *testamur* for subsequent editions, but the secretary's is necessary.

6. Copyright is frequently infringed by the importation of foreign editions. The custom house officer appointed to examine imported bales of books is now instructed to prevent foreign editions from passing the custom house.

7. The censorial secretary is frequently too much occupied with his other duties as secretary to the Senate to attend to the press. The Rifformatori shall appoint three or four fit persons to perform the secretary's duties in the revision of books, on whose report the secretary shall grant or refuse his *testamur*.

8. Books printed in Venice with the name of another place are to be suppressed.

9. The Inquisitorial *testamur* is to be presented to the secretary to the Rifformatori; and if within four months of its date the work of printing is not begun, any other printer may apply for an authentic copy of the *testamur*, and this shall be valid without further application to the Inquisitor, should that printer eventually complete the work.

10. Dangerous and scandalous foreign books are to be stopped by the custom house officers. Nor may any imported books be sold in Venice until the bookseller has presented a certificated list of titles from the custom house officer to the secretary of the Rifformatori, who shall then issue the permission to sell signed by at least two Rifformatori.

11. The prior of the guild is to see that the laws are obeyed; especially the law ordering a copy of each book to be presented to the Library of St. Mark and to the Library of Padua.

12. These laws apply to all printers and booksellers in the cities of the Venetian dominion as well as in Venice.

13. The tax on books imported, both by land and by sea, is fixed at the rate of sixteen ducats for every two hundred pounds weight.

14. In Venice the execution of this law is entrusted to the Rifformatori and to the Esecutori contro la Bestemmia; on the mainland to the rectors.

But the law was not respected. In 1655-6, February 4th, various provisions have to be re-enforced. Licences are not sought, as they should be, in every case; the Libraries of St. Mark and of Padua are defrauded of their due. And the same repetition of the law is necessary again in 1671, December 23rd. By this date the carelessness of the Venetian editions had become more scandalous; for we find that, besides a licence to print, the government now require a licence to sell, based on the *testamur* of the public proof reader, and to be granted by the secretary only after confronting the book with its original copy, either manuscript or printed. In 1671 the Libraries of St. Mark and of Padua were still neglected and ignored by the printers and publishers, and so again, in 1680 and in 1697, it is found necessary to renew the law in their favour, and each time without producing the desired effect. The law of 1671 also published a new tariff[1] for proof reading, in which a distinction is drawn between the correction of proofs of new works and the correction of a work already published, with a view to a new edition. No new kinds of type are mentioned—only those which appeared in the tariff of 1608; but the correction of missals, breviaries, and books of devotion is fixed at the rate of forty ducats a year for each press.

The press laws of this century fall into four groups: the laws of 1601, 1603, and 1608 in the first group; the laws of 1614, 1616, and 1622 in the second group; the laws of 1653 and 1655 in the third group, and the laws of 1671 and 1680 in the fourth group. Their number and the excellence of their provisions prove how anxious the government was to maintain the credit of the Venetian press. The general failure of the law to act, however, is patent, though the reason for this failure is not quite so obvious. Apart from general causes, such as "the decline of all things human," the fault probably lay in the fact that the government had constructed a machine which was too cumbersome to move, and all the minatory and penal laws which they created in order to make it operative were absolutely useless. If we consider for a moment the number of hands through which a book had to pass before it could see the light, the number of offices to which a publisher had to apply before he could put his wares upon the market, the inefficiency of the law becomes intelligible. By the close of the seventeenth century, the following process was necessary before a book could be published: *testamur* from the Inquisitor; *testamur* from the Ducal secretary; certificate from the Rifformatori dello Studio di Padova; *imprimatur* from the Chiefs of the Ten; revision by the Superintendent of the Press; revision by the public proof reader; confrontation of original and edition by secretary to the Rifformatori; certificate from the librarian of St. Mark's that a copy has been deposited in the Library; examination by experts appointed by the Proveditori di Comun to establish the market price of the book. It is clear that, with all these obstacles to overcome, many, if not the majority of them, would be ignored and neglected, especially when we remember that there was no police to enforce this excessive amount of law.

[1] *Mercedi dei Correttori secondo la diversità de caratteri, per la corretion di copia e stampa.*

CHAPTER XX.

1604—1699.

THE GUILD DURING THE SEVENTEENTH CENTURY.

Its powers increased—Its powers over the press of Venice—Internal difficulties and abuses—The income and the taxation of the guild—The guild hall.

TO return to the Guild of Printers and Booksellers. We left that body in 1586 nominally enjoying control over all printing in Venice, and supposed by the government to include among its members every master-printer and bookseller in the city—really struggling against the hostility and jealousy of the many printers and booksellers who refused to join the corporation. Although the government bestowed special advantages upon members of the guild, and allowed the corporation to tax non-matriculated printers, it was not till 1604 that sufficient powers were conferred upon the corporation to enable it to secure a monopoly of the trade in Venice. In that year the Proveditori di Comun empowered the members of the guild to seize all books printed or sold by those who are not matriculated, and to seal up their presses and their shops; even the street hawkers of books and pamphlets were forbidden to carry on their trade without a certificate from the prior of the guild. It might have been supposed that these powers would have proved sufficient; that the corporation would have known how to protect its obvious interests, and that, so armed, it would have secured in reality the monopoly of the Venetian book trade. Yet it is clear that this was not the case; for in 1653, as we have seen, the Senate was obliged to take cognizance of the large number of scandalous publications which were issued by the clandestine press, and to re-enforce the ancient statute which obliged every printer to enrol himself in the guild, under penalty of one thousand ducats, and of two thousand ducats for every work published clandestinely; and the execution of this act is entrusted to the Esecutori contro la Bestemmia. We find no further legislation upon this point, so we may suppose that the action taken in 1653 was effective; that the activity of the clandestine press was virtually suppressed, and that the guild secured the monopoly of the book trade.

The sale of loose literature and indecent pictures was common in Venice during the sixteenth century. The principal centre of this trade was the Merceria from the Piazza to the Rialto, and the time Sundays and holidays. A law of the Giustizia Vecchia, passed in 1565, forbade anyone on Sundays or holidays to have in his shop windows other books than *Epistile et Evangelii, lezende de Santi, offitii, bibie et simil opere divote et non libri immondi, Comedie et altra sorte, che siano profani . . . per la Marzaria veramente se possi tenir santi et Carte de disegni et depente de cose devote et honeste et non cose dishoneste et vergognose.* And in 1598, the law of the Giustizia Vecchia having apparently remained inoperative, the officers of the guild met to consider what steps should be taken to put down this abuse, which was not merely a breach of the law, but prejudicial to their trade, because members of the guild were by custom forbidden to open their shops on Sundays and holidays. They determined to ask for power to seize all such books as were offered for sale on those days, and at the same time for power to close all presses and shops of persons not members of the guild. Their request was granted; but it led to a lawsuit in which Alessandro de' Vecchi appealed against the rule twice over, once to the Proveditori di Comun, and once to the Quarantia Civile Nuova, but failed in both suits.

It is certain that the guild was not well governed by its own officers. The fact is made obvious by the long declaration of abuses which the officers of the guild themselves presented to the Proveditori di Comun in 1626. They begin by asserting that excellent rules are worthless if, as in their case, they are neglected. Many members of the guild refuse to pay their dues, some on the plea that they have been absent from Venice, others alleging that they have ceased to ply the trade; the Proveditori are asked to declare that as long as a member's name remains on the books he is liable for all subscriptions. The yearly election of officers is neglected, and it sometimes happens that the same officials remain in office for six years running. Further, St. John the Evangelist's day, when the elections should take place, falls in the great colds, when the days are short; it is impossible to finish the ballots till late at night, and for this reason many members do not attend, fearing *qualche pericolo di mal incontro nel ritornar a casa.* The guild accordingly propose to change the day of election from St. John's day to one of the feasts of Pentecost, and to make the guild year run from 1st July to 30th June. The syndics of the guild, with whom it rests to see that all the bye-laws of the guild are observed, do not fulfil their duties, possibly through inexperience; and so for the future no member shall be elected a syndic until he has held once at least some other office in the corporation. The matriculation list is falling into confusion, owing to the carelessness with which sons or heirs of members of the guild present themselves for registration; for the future they shall be bound to register themselves within three months of the death of parent or guardian.

The income of the guild consisted of entrance fees, annual dues, and fines upon the members; of fines upon those who exercised the trade without being enrolled in the guild; and of legacies.[1] Out of this income the guild, in common with all the guilds of Venice, was expected to pay the *tansa insensibile*, or tax for the maintenance of the armament, and occasionally an extra tax, such as that for the support of the nuns of Candia, driven out by the Turks. The imposition and collection of the armament tax gave rise to continual difficulties and abuses. The prior of the guild was charged with levying the tax, and was himself personally and directly responsible to the President of the Collegio da Mar for the whole amount for which the guild was assessed. But it frequently happened that the prior was either careless or fraudulent. In the first case, he spent the money on other objects before the tax fell due; in the second case, he was never at a loss to devise some means for appropriating part of the funds. As an instance, we have the case of the prior in 1688, who, to induce the magistrates to fix the quota at a higher rate per head than was necessary, presented a roll of the corporation where the names of several members were omitted; having obtained the order to tax at so much a head, he applied this to every member of the guild, with the result that there was a surplus at his disposal. In fact, as the government assessed the tax upon the roll of the corporation, and took the prior's word for the accuracy of that roll, frauds were constantly practised upon the roll itself.

In spite of mismanagement, however, the guild continued to flourish. In 1638 it was rich enough to contemplate the purchase of a guild hall or meeting-place for itself. Hitherto the guild had met, as occasion required, in the *Luogo de' Genovesi* in the Chapel of the Rosario at SS. Giovanni e Paolo. The corporation now appointed three of its members to find and to contract for a more suitable place, which should be entirely at their own disposal. In 1642 the committee of three reported that they had found such a place in a large magazine opening off the first cloister in the monastery of SS. Giovanni e Paolo, under the rooms of the novices, and next door to a similar magazine held by the Guild of Looking-glass Makers as a meeting-place. The chapter

[1] We have one instance, that of Siora Anzola de Maggi, who left 200 ducats to the guild.

of the monastery was willing to let this magazine in perpetuity, and the terms of the lease were drawn up by a notary public; the chapter of the convent was convoked by sound of bell, and the deed was signed by both parties on the 16th July, 1642. The lease was to be in perpetuity as long as the guild continued to pay the rent, which was fixed at thirty ducats a year, with the obligation to pay six ducats more for twenty-four masses, twelve of these to be said at the altar in the guild hall, and twelve at any altar in the church which the chapter of the convent might select. The guild had the right to open windows and doors in the magazine, provided that they were in harmony with the general architecture of the cloister. The guild had also the right to adorn the interior of the magazine in any way they thought fit; and should the chapter of the monastery be obliged at any time to pull down the magazine, the monks were bound to provide another suitable place, and to reimburse the booksellers and printers for damages done to the ornaments and fixtures.[1]

Early in the seventeenth century the conduct of the workmen in Venetian presses gave serious trouble to their principals, chiefly owing to the weakness of the master-printers themselves. It would appear from the law of 1616 that the journeymen demanded prepayment, or at least that prepayment had become customary. The result was inevitable; at the first word of reproof, or on the first impulse to take a holiday, the workman with his pay in his pocket walked out of his master's shop. It seems that he could readily find employment in another printing house whenever he chose to resume work—a fact which indicates that the press of Venice was active enough, or that there was a dearth of hands; the latter suggestion is the more probable, if we remember the previous legislation against emigrant printers. The abuse grew so serious that the government was compelled to pass a law ordering the imprisonment of any workman who left his master's shop till his contract was completed; and master-printers who received such fugitives should be obliged to refund to the first master of the man they had taken into their service the sum for which that man was debitor in labour.

[1] I do not know how long the Guild of Printers and Booksellers occupied this meeting-place; possibly till the beginning of the present century and the suppression of the monastery However that may be, the place now forms part of the town hospital of Venice.

CHAPTER XXI.

1700—1796.

PRESS LEGISLATION AND THE GUILD DURING THE EIGHTEENTH CENTURY.

The list of members—Taxation of the guild—The admission of bookbinders—Examination of candidates as binders, as booksellers, and as printers—Revival of the office of Superintendent—Efforts to restore the quality of printing—Tariff for printing in various types—Official examination of type-foundries—Attempt to regulate supply to demand—Efforts to restore the quality of paper and of ink—The end of the guild—Resumé.

THE history of the guild during the eighteenth century presents the same features as its history during the preceding century. We may follow that history under two aspects: first, as regards the internal economy of the corporation, and secondly, as regards the action of the government and its efforts to maintain the character of the Venetian press.

In the year 1695 the first list that I can find of the members of the guild was drawn up and entered in the minute-book. The list contains in all 290 names; but many of these, as the heading indicates, were added after the opening of the list. If we may judge by the character of the handwriting the number of those who belonged to the guild when the list was first formed was eighty-one.

All through this century the difficulty of taxation is an ever-present one; and we can hardly wonder at the fact, for the tax was heavy and steadily increased. In 1723 it is assessed at 192 ducats; in 1727 it is declared that the guild is responsible for the maintenance of ninety-two men at the rate of six ducats a head, *valore corrente;* and again, in 1752, it is assessed at 432 ducats. Whether it was this increasing weight of taxation which induced the guild to enlarge its numbers, or not, I cannot say; but the fact is that, in 1732, the guild enrolled among its members bookbinders as well as book-printers and booksellers. The more ancient portion of the guild, however, seem to have attempted to impose their will upon their new brethren. This led to a rupture, which was accommodated by the law of 1735, directing that, for the future, the bookbinders are to govern themselves; to form, as it were, a guild within a guild—to meet in chapter apart, and not to enter the chapter of the booksellers and printers. There was a double matriculation—one for printers and booksellers, and one for binders. The prior of the ancient guild, however, still remained head of the whole corporation, and the entrance fees and subscriptions of the binders were paid into the account of the whole guild. The immediate affairs of the binders' guild were conducted by a commission of six master-binders, namely, the chief, two examiners, two supervisors, and one councillor. It was the duty of this committee to superintend matriculation as an associate binder. The examination consisted in binding a missal in black cordovan, with gold tooling after a pattern proposed by the chief, and with gilt edges. This is the first occasion on which we hear of an examination in form, with test work, previous to matriculation; but later on, in 1767, the Guild of Printers and Booksellers published their examination paper, which we give in full.

Examination for those who seek Matriculation in the Guild of Booksellers.

1. Name the principal Bibles.
2. Name the principal Saints and Fathers, Greek and Latin.
3. Name the principal expositors of Holy Writ.
4. Name the principal theologians—controversialist and polemical writers.
5. Name the principal writers on ecclesiastical history.
6. Name the ancient writers on philosophy and history; also the principal poets, tragic as well as comic, in Greek and Latin.
7. Name the principal writers on the law of nature, the law of nations, on civil and canon law, on philosophy, metaphysics, and ethics.
8. Name the principal geographers, Greek, Latin, Italian, and French.
9. Name the principal historians, ancient and modern, letter writers, antiquarians, numismatists, mathematicians, physicians, surgeons, anatomists, jurists.
10. Name the principal writers on the fine arts—painting, sculpture, and architecture, civil and military.
11. Name the principal writers on natural history and botany.

Further, all candidates must be able to read and write Italian fluently, and must have a sufficient knowledge of Latin and of French. The examiners shall put some practical questions on the conduct of a bookseller's business.

The examination for admission as a matriculated printer is as follows:

1. How do you arrange the original copy from which you mean to print?
2. How do you place upon the table of press formes in 8vo, 12mo, 18vo, 24to, 32do?
3. How would you regulate the impression, and how do you arrange the registers of the sheets? and if they came out wrong, how would you put them right?
4. How would you remedy an unclean impression?
5. How do you set up a press?
6. How many kinds of type are there?
7. What means do you adopt for the correction of proofs?
8. How would you wet the paper that the impress may come out well?
9. How much lampblack and varnish do you use per pound for black ink? and how much cinnabar and varnish for red ink?

For the practical part of the examination the two examiners shall determine the *format* in which the candidate is to work. When the type has been set up in the forme, the candidate shall be required to read off the type, and then to cast off a proof; and this proof shall be presented to the officers of the guild by the examiners, who shall declare on oath that it is the proof set up and cast off by the candidate, and that he is capable of exercising his calling on all the points specified by the law of 1603. The candidate shall then be ballotted, and, if he obtain two-thirds of the votes, his name shall be enrolled. The examination shall be held in the guild hall or in some printing house to be named by the prior, and the examiners shall be present during the whole examination to insure its genuineness.

Indeed, throughout this century the guild took considerable pains to maintain itself in efficiency. Nor was the government remiss in supporting the guild by a series of provisions; the majority of these, however, are merely recapitulations of laws already in existence. By far the most important act on the part of the government—the act which closed the period of vigorous press legislation (1725 to 1734)—was the re-creation of the Superintendent of the Press. We have met with this officer before, during the previous century, but the office had been allowed to fall into disuse. It was now revived and conferred on Dr. Francesco Pivatti, with a salary of 100 ducats a year, payable by the Treasury. The duties of the Superintendent were to keep the volume in which all decrees relating to the press had to be registered; to see that these decrees were observed; to visit the workshops and to examine the quality of the paper, ink, and type, and the corrections of proofs, and to report all violations of the law to the Rifformatori dello Studio di Padova; he is also to be the councillor, guide, and referee of the printers and booksellers. In fact, it is clear that the government had abandoned the hope that the prior of the guild would fulfil his duties and watch over the interests of his trade, and so they appoint the Superintendent, to whom they assign duties analogous to those they had vainly imposed upon the prior of the guild. It is to the Superintendent that the orders of the magistrates are now addressed. But it is by no means certain that the Superintendent was more successful than the prior in enforcing the law and maintaining order in the guild; for after his appointment the repetition of rules and orders continues as actively as ever. For example, in 1767 the government was exercised by the bad quality of Venetian printing, which they ascribed to the greed of printers, who, in order to crowd more matter into a given space, make use of type which is thin and oblong or drawn up, instead of full and round (*caratteri gittati fuori del quadro naturale*). They proposed to compile a fixed tariff for each sheet printed in all the various kinds of type—thus rendering it futile to spoil the character in the hope of crowding more words into the sheet. The tariff is calculated on the number of letters in a sheet; and incidentally we learn that an edition usually ran to one thousand copies.

The tariff is as follows:

For a sheet containing from 20,000 to 21,000 letters of Silvio, Lire 15.10 for a thousand copies.

For a sheet in Philosophy or Antique, containing from 26,000 to 27,000 letters, Lire 16.00.

For a sheet in Garamon, containing from 34,000 to 35,000 letters, Lire 17.00.

For a sheet in Garamoncin, containing from 37,000 to 38,000 letters, Lire 18.10.

For a sheet in Small Text, containing from 48,000 to 50,000 letters, Lire 26.00.

The compositor's tariff is, for every 1,000 letters in Silvio, Antique, or Philosophy, Lire 4.10.

For every 1,000 letters in Garamon and Garamoncin, Lire 4.00.

For every 1,000 letters in Text, Lire 4.10.

The pressman's tariff shall be, for every two reams of ordinary paper, Lire 2.10.

For every two reams of royal, Lire 3.10.

The price for works in 16to, 18vo, 24to, and 32do; works with marginal notes; oriental character; figures or symbols, is to be arranged by contract. Printers are to give the work entrusted to them, not to apprentices, but to journeymen; no master-printer may keep uncovenanted apprentices, nor more than one apprentice at a time. Master-printers are to put their presses in full working order within six months. The types in ordinary use are to be founded in their natural proportions; and all type-founders, both in Venice and on the mainland, if they found a new type, must leave specimens of the fount with the magistrates for approval and for comparison with the fount used in the books printed in their type. And following upon this elaborate order to secure a good quality of type in the Venetian press, came an inspection of all the type-foundries, and a list of the founts which had received approval. From this list it appears that there were seven type-foundries in Venetian territory:

1. The foundry of Nicolò Bazzo and Giovanni Inchiostro .	26 founts.
2. The foundry of Andrea Burchicin	12 founts.
3. The foundry of Bassano	11 founts.
4. The foundry of Falconi	Not stated.
5. The foundry of Adami	,, ,,
6. The foundry of Andolfato	,, ,,
7. The foundry of Parolari	,, ,,

Exception was taken to some of the founts in all the foundries save those of Adami and of Andolfato.

In this same year, 1767, the Rifformatori turned their attention to the overcrowding and over-production in the book trade. They declare it to be their intention to regulate the supply to the demand, *onde si possa introdurre quel lavoro e quel numero e quantità di venditori che sono proporzionati al consumo.* The first clause of the law of July 29th forbids the articling of new apprentices for the next fifteen years. Sons and heirs may not enter the guild during the lifetime of their fathers, or of those whom they will succeed. If a candidate for admission to the guild has failed three times in examination, or has three times been refused the necessary two-thirds of the votes at the ballot, he may not present himself again. Those who are matriculated as printers may not trade as booksellers, and *vice versâ*, without passing the examination for printer or bookseller, as the case may be, but the entrance fee shall be exacted once only. Books printed under a copyright in Venice are to be strictly protected from foreign competition; all contraband copies are to be seized at the custom house. No member of the guild who owns a shop may sell books on street stalls; that is to be reserved for poor members of the guild, and only to be permitted in the case of second-hand books. No one may open a shop or a press without first satisfying the magistracy that there is room for and need for such shop or press. Booksellers or printers of the mainland who wish to enter the guild in Venice must close their mainland shop or press before they can be admitted. The four mainlanders at present members of the guild, Manfrè, Remondini, Conzatti, and Veronese, may remain. The copyright in new books, which, by the law of 1603, was fixed at twenty years' duration, is now extended to thirty years; and for reissues it is extended from ten to thirteen years. On the expiry of a Venetian copyright, no mainland printer may reissue the work; but mainlanders who, by the law of 1713, were deprived of all copyright, may now obtain copyright for new works to run for twenty years, and for reissues to run for ten years, but they are obliged to put the name of their own town, and not that of Venice, in the imprint. This was a law of a wide-reaching and vigorous nature; it was intended to strengthen the guild, and it would have done so, at the expense of the mainland printers, had its provisions been strictly observed. But they were not; for, in 1780, the prior and officers of the guild present a memorandum to the Rifformatori calling their attention to various abuses and disorders—the same abuses and disorders which have always hampered the art; the same inferiority of workmanship, assigned to the fact that for economy's sake master-printers entrust their commissions to prentice hands; the same careless correction of proofs; the same poverty of ink and type. Accordingly the Superintendent is once more called upon to visit the shops regularly, and to see to the nomination by the prior and officers of an expert who shall examine and, if he approves, sign the first sheets of all books which he considers sufficiently well printed to be put upon the market. One of the reasons for this bad workmanship, of which we hear so much, was the immense number of reissues which appeared the moment the copyright of a book had expired, and the consequent race to secure the market by speed and by cheapness, both implying poor workmanship. To meet this abuse it was decreed that the firm which held the first copyright for thirty years should be entitled to the second copyright for thirteen years if it applied for it, and provided that it began the printing of the reissue within two months of the expiry of the first copyright, otherwise any other printer may apply for the second copyright. If a firm desire to issue an *édition de luxe* (*ristampa di singolare nobilità, tanto per belezza di carta quanto per esquisitezza di caratteri, perfezione di correzione ed ornamenti*) he may infringe another firm's copyright, provided that he submits to the Rifformatori, through the Superintendent, a copy of the edition whose copyright he intends to infringe, and a copy of his own *édition de luxe*, pointing out its superiority. If the issue of a copyright edition be arrested by the death or bankruptcy of the holder of the copyright, another firm may continue the work, provided it has not more than six other copyright works on hand. Venetian printers must reach the market through Venetian booksellers only; they are not to sell to foreign booksellers, or to Venetian booksellers not members of the guild. A printer must place a copy of his contract with an author or editor, stating the number of copies he is to print, in the hands of the prior of the guild, that he may be kept to his contract, or punished and expelled if he print more than the number stated. If a private person, not matriculated in the guild, desire to issue an edition of a work, he must consult the prior, who will find out if any member of the guild has such an edition in view, and will also state the size of the edition which the private individual may place upon the market; nor may a private individual sell works which he has printed except through a Venetian bookseller. In order to assist the income of the guild the secretary to the Rifformatori is instructed to refuse a certificate to all who do not produce a receipt for their guild dues.

And yet all these elaborate provisions failed to achieve their object. In the very next year, 15th February, 1780-1, the Rifformatori had to consider the question of bankrupt members of the guild. A list was drawn up, showing on one side the solvent and on the other the insolvent members. The insolvent members were excluded from all active share in the guild until they could prove their solvency once more; but at the same time the government relieved them of their share in the public burdens of the guild, which was distributed among the solvent members. Solvency is to be proved by possessing a press worth five hundred ducats of capital, or a book-shop representing two thousand ducats of capital. I do not know how many of the guild found themselves on the black list, nor am I able to say what was the result of this purge; but the members on the bankruptcy list appealed to the government against their exclusion from the benefits of the guild; in vain, however, for the Senate ignored the appeal on June 5th, 1781.

The officers of the guild always showed themselves ready to assist the government with suggestions, however remiss they may have been in attending to the execution of the government rules. In 1782 they took into consideration certain new regulations which the government proposed to issue, and added certain suggestions of their own, which were embodied in the Ducal proclamation of that year. The regulations are divided into heads; one, on discipline, provides that no master-printer or bookseller may himself keep wine on sale, nor may he allow more than half a litre per head for the pressmen, nor more than a quarter of a litre per head for the compositors to be brought into the shop; and if they find a workman drunk, he must be made to stop printing for the whole of that day. No one may take a journeyman compositor into his service without a character from his last place, and a certificate that he is not in debt to his previous master. Articles of apprenticeship must be registered with the guild. Pressmen and compositors who leave Venetian territory for service abroad may never be received in any Venetian shop again, except on special licence from the guild. Fifteen days' warning is necessary on the side of master and of man. To encourage pressmen to work well, a prize of sixteen lire shall be given to every pressman who can produce certificates of two hundred well-printed sheets, the genuineness of the certificates to be guaranteed by the officers of the guild.

Under the heading *Materiali di Stamperia* the cashier of the guild is empowered to advance money to poor members who wish to put their presses and instruments in order. As to paper, the government is about to introduce a standard of quality below which no paper may fall, under penalty of confiscation of the edition in which the inferior paper is used. To augment the income of the guild the officers may exact a sum of twenty soldi for every certificate they issue; and in the external wall of the guild room the officers may cause to be made a slit and a box to receive secret denunciations. These denunciations shall be collected on the fourth Sunday of every month, and, after being read and annotated by the officials, they shall be forwarded to the Rifformatori dello Studio di Padova. If the accusation is proved, the accuser shall receive twenty per cent. of the fine.

But the usual failure of effect accompanied these last elaborate provisions; they received no more attention than their predecessors, and on May 1st, 1789, the Rifformatori again interfere, and repeat their vain task of attempting to govern by words.[1]

We come now to the last documents relating to the Guild of Printers and Booksellers in Venice. The guild survived the fall of the Republic, and no sooner was the provisional government established than the spirit of the revolutionary period made itself felt in the attack on the monopoly of printing all government papers enjoyed by the firm of Pinelli, the ex-Ducal printers. On the fall of the Republic the municipality had appointed Pinelli, Zatta, and Pasquale to carry out all official printing. These three printing houses employed eight or ten presses; but although they worked night and day, they were unable to keep pace with the orders they received. Thereupon ten other firms appealed to the municipality, offering their twenty presses and their hundred hands to do all municipal printing at a

[1] In spite of these perpetual difficulties, however, the press of Venice was not in an unprosperous condition, if we look at the number of workmen employed. Rossi (*Costumi Ven.*, tom. viii., c. 140) gives the following account of the trade in 1773: paper shops, 44, employing 92 foremen, 33 workmen, 25 apprentices; bookshops, 51, employing foremen 131, pressmen and compositors 310, workmen 318, apprentices 51.

reduction of twenty per cent. upon the prices of Pinelli, Zatta, and Pasquale, and they submitted a scheme for the rapid execution and the proper storing and arranging of all municipal orders. The Town Council, however, declined the offer, and Pinelli, Zatta, and Pasquale continued to print for the government of Venice. On the 23rd of March, 1799, the provisional government undertook the direct control of the press, re-affirming its ancient provisions and regulations on the matter of licensing books, of internal police, and of supervision; while, on the question of economy and of taxation, the guild was placed under the finance department of the municipality. Whether the guild was suppressed, or whether it died a natural death, we do not know. The last document in the minute-book is dated 1806, and after that date our knowledge ceases.

In surveying this last period of the history of the Venetian press the most notable feature is undoubtedly the constant lamentation on the part of the government that the art is decaying. Whether this was so or not may be doubted; the quality of the issue probably was not of a very high class, but the quantity must have been great.[1] There are, however, several indications which make us doubt whether the art was really as decrepit as the government believed. We hear much about the demand for cheap books; about the rush to republish a book whose copyright had expired; about the excessive number of presses and of bookshops; of 500 ducats as the minimum of solvency for a printer, and of 2,000 ducats as the minimum of solvency for a bookseller. All this does not look like indication of a trade in its decrepitude. It is probable that when the government referred to the decadence of the art, it was thinking chiefly of the quality of the work produced, not so much of the activity of the press; that it had in its mind's eye the ancient glories and triumphs of the art in Venice, and regretted that their like were not to be found in modern times; it longed for a series of Jensons or Johns of Speyer, and half believed that it could legislate them into existence.

Another point which is made clear by the legislation of the Republic during this century is the question of literary proprietorship. It is remarkable that throughout the Venetian laws on copyright it is not explicitly stated that the property in a work belongs to the author of that work. The government passed various regulations implying this, but had never stated it explicitly. That the government intended the property to reside in the author is made clear, however, by an act of the Senate passed on 11th March, 1780, in which it declares that *il privilegio prima d'essere perpetuo per suo posseditore, l'era per l'autore dell' opera, qualunque egli fosse, come si è sempre prati-*

[1] Cf. Rossi, *loc. cit.*

cato.[1] The last phrase proves that the government had always implicitly recognized the rights of the author. The question was absolutely settled by the sentence of the Rifformatori dello Studio di Padova, pronounced on 18th September, 1781, in the case of Pezzana and Company, where the Rifformatori rule that *il privilegio accordato alla stampa diventa dovuto premio all' autore.*[2]

The decree of the Rifformatori of July 30th, 1780, may perhaps be taken as conferring perpetual copyright,[3] by the phrase in clause vi., *per cio resta da noi risolutamente stabilito, che per l'avvenire il primo respettivo posseditore privileggiato possa egli solo, e non altri, ottenere la nuova licenza colle solite forme per la ristampa de Libri usciti di Privileggio e per cio resi comuni, e cio fin ch' egli voglia.* This could only constitute a perpetual copyright, however, by implication, not specifically, for the *nuova licenza colle solite forme* could only run for five years, and would then require renewal. The question was settled, however, in 1789, when the Rifformatori recall the law of 1603, whereby all books whose copyrights are exhausted become public property.[4]

And the third feature which distinguishes this period, as indeed it distinguishes all periods of Venetian press legislation, is the absolute inefficiency of the law, in spite of its constant interference and its many excellent provisions, to correct the abuses at which it aimed. This is due partly, no doubt, to the inherent indifference of the national character. The printers were capable of being roused, when in difficulties, to the serious consideration of evils and to the suggestion of many excellent remedies; but the warm fit soon passed off when things began to go better; *laissez aller*, or, as they would put it, *non combattere*, soon asserted itself, and matters fell back to their old bad ways. Besides, the Venetian printers would doubtless argue, with some show of reason, that it was the duty of those who passed the law to see that it was also observed. And this brings us to a second cause for the impotence of the press laws in Venice. There was no public opinion among the members of the guild; such a thing as public opinion among the people was of course out of the question in a close oligarchical constitution like that of the Republic. But the government had no apparatus to take the place of public opinion—they had no police. The Rifformatori dello Studio, the Esecutori contro la Bestemmia, and the Proveditori di Comun, the magistrates

[1] The Rifformatori, 30th July, 1780, clause vi. of their Decree (see Appendix), declare *intendendosi in oltre che la stessa libertà abbia, prima del posseditore (= editore) chiunque egli fosse, l' autore d' un opera, come si è sempre praticato.*

[2] On the whole of this question, see Castellani, *I privilegi di Stampa*, p. 12.

[3] See Appendix.

[4] Castellani, *op. cit.*, p. 14.

to whom was entrusted the execution of the press laws, endeavoured to make the members of the trade the police for the trade. No doubt they wondered why the members did not obey laws which were for their own good, and which in many cases they themselves had suggested. The printers and booksellers, on the other hand, wondered why the magistrates, the great nobles who had the whole control of affairs in their hands, did not see that their orders were obeyed and their rules respected; and so between the two wonders the law remained, for the most part, a dead letter.

And, lastly, there was a defect in the idea of the legislation: it was too officious, too paternal; it left nothing to the natural vigour of the art. The industry was nearly killed with kindness; it was choked by a multiplicity of laws relating to every conceivable phase of its existence. These laws come one on the top of another, not infrequently contradicting one another, and certainly confusing the minds of the printers and booksellers, till they resolved to go each his own way good or bad, and to leave the law to take care of itself—a thing that the law has never been able at any time to do.

CHAPTER XXII.

1765—1796.

LAST WORDS WITH ROME.

The report on the printing press presented in 1765—Official review of the history of the press in Venice; the causes of its decline, and remedies proposed—The position of the Inquisitor—Appointment of a Venetian subject, an ecclesiastic, to work with him—Opposition at Rome—Pietro Franceschi's opinion—Venice refuses to withdraw the order of 1765—Fall of the Republic.

HAVE left to the last a series of documents bearing upon the unsettled question of the relations between Venice and the Church on the subject of the Index and the censorship of the press. After the middle of the eighteenth century the whole question, which had been lying dormant for some time, entered upon an acute phase again. The publication of the Index, and its alteration in many respects by Benedict XIV. in 1758, helped, no doubt, to call men's attention to the subject once more. In the course of these documents we shall find, not only a very clear statement of the Venetian view as to the causes which retarded and nearly destroyed the art of printing in Venice, but also a masterly survey of the whole history of the Venetian printing press, which may properly conclude this study.

The facts of the case which led up to this new and final quarrel between the Court of Rome and the Republic are these:—The senate in 1765 was, as usual, much exercised by the poverty and inferiority of the Venetian press; and as, in spite of copious legislation, much of it excellent, no improvement took place, the Rifformatori dello Studio di Padova were ordered to draw up a report stating their view as to the causes for this deplorable condition of the press, and suggesting remedies. The report was presented in March, 1765;[1] it is a grave, weighty, profound document, and

[1] See Appendix. It was preceded by and largely based on a report by Pietro Franceschi, presented in 1761. Cecchetti, *op. cit.*, ii. 254.

deserves the praise subsequently bestowed upon it as *lavoro pregevole ed in tutta simmetria filato da mano Maestra*. The report states that the art of printing, once a source of revenue to the State and of livelihood to the population, is almost annihilated. As the Venetian press declines the press of other cities grows rich; for while the press of Venice retained its full vigour and activity there was not a press that could compete with it. The reasons for this superiority were the abundance and cheapness of paper, the moderate customs dues, the facilities for export, and the excellence of the workmen, who, thanks to the early development of printing in Venice, acquired a traditional skill and ability. The result of this superiority which Venice enjoyed was that most of the books intended for the Italian market were printed in that city, and the other towns of Italy became chiefly depots for the sale of Venetian editions. But now Leghorn, Lucca, Parma, Modena, Bologna, all print their own books, and, what is worse, they refuse Venetian editions in exchange for their own publications, and demand payment in money—a position which formerly Venice only could assume; and so Venice falls from her place as mistress of the book trade (*padrona del commerzio di libri*), and becomes merely a retailer (*rivenditrice*). Nor are internal proofs of this decline far to seek. In 1752 Venice possessed seventy-seven presses; in 1762 they had fallen to fifty-eight, and in 1765 to fifty. The matriculated printers, finding no work to employ their presses, abandon printing and take to bookselling; the trade of bookseller is congested, to the great harm of the ancient and well-established houses in that branch.

The Rifformatori made a long, profound, and careful study of the situation, in order to discover where the evil lay, and they came to the conclusion that the root of all the mischief was the want of new and good works to feed the press and to keep its activity fresh and vigorous. And to prove that this *mancanza de capi nuovi e buoni* is, and has always been, the real cause of decline in the trade, they follow the art of printing in Venice from its origin down to the time of their report, and demonstrate that wherever we find a period of decline or depression in the book trade, it is due to the want of good and new books to print, of which the press, for one reason or another, was deprived at that period. This was the case in 1517, when the early system of granting copyrights had nearly destroyed the Venetian press by confining the right to print the majority of valuable books to a few persons. From 1469 down to 1517 this difficulty had not arisen, for there were all the Latin classics to draw upon, and Aldus opened the way into another rich department of antiquity by his editions of the Greek classics. But by the year 1517 the evil had made itself manifest. The Senate remedied it by abolishing all existing copyrights, and regulating the issue of copyright for the future, thereby restoring to the press its natural aliment of books.

The sixteenth century was a period of great literary activity in Italy, and the press was kept abundantly supplied with works to print; till, in 1595, this source of life and vigour was suddenly dried up by the publication of the Clementine Index, the *Regulæ*, and *Instructio*. The fall in the Venetian press was made obvious immediately. The government tried to remedy the evil by securing the Concordat; but, for reasons which we explained in their proper place, their endeavours were of no avail. The seventeenth century was a period of great intellectual activity outside Italy, just as the sixteenth century had been remarkable for its intellectual activity inside Italy. And Venice was there, ready with her excellent press, her rapidity of work, her cheapness of production, to print all the foreign works as she had printed most of the Italian. But a secret cancer (*un tarlo celato*) prevented the government from ever being able to secure this vast trade for Venice. The Inquisitor, with the Indices of Rome by his side and his power of veto, prevented foreign works from being used to feed the Venetian press. The Concordat was evaded in the ways which we have seen; it became a dead letter, and the press was starved and pined. At first the government was hardly aware of the real reasons for this decline. But when they did discover the cause, they endeavoured to avoid and evade the tyranny of the Inquisitorial *testamur* by permitting Venetian printers to use a false date. They also, in 1695, suppressed the Inquisitorial *imprimatur*, which had been gradually and silently substituted for the *testamur*. The result of this, say the Rifformatori, was satisfactory, for the number of presses rose again, till in 1729 there were as many as ninety at work in Venice, thanks chiefly to the permission to use a false date. The Rifformatori are careful to declare that the precautions adopted by the Senate in granting this permission for a fictitious date worked so well, that they can confidently affirm that no book ever issued from the Venetian press with a foreign date which could in any way scandalize the most pious readers, nor had the Court of Rome ever raised any objection to this mode of procedure. All the same the Rifformatori, having set forth the causes of the decline in the art, and coming now to the question of remedies, do not recommend the continuance of this permission to use foreign dates, for several reasons. In the first place, by the constant use of a false name in Venetian editions, the press of Venice will begin to be forgotten, the name of Venice will disappear; secondly, there is a danger that publishers may use this pretext of a false date to print and publish in Venice scandalous books; thirdly, although the Court of Rome has raised no question as yet, it might do so upon the ground of the seventh clause of the Concordat, and such objections would be difficult to answer. The advice of the Rifformatori accordingly is, to print all books openly with the name of Venice on the title; to publish the Concordat and the Index of 1595, in order to prove that all works subsequently placed on the Index without the consent of the government are not prohibited in Venice, and may be freely printed, bought, and sold; to forbid printers and publishers to seek the Inquisitor's *testamur* for the reissue of foreign printed books in Venice, but to name faithful and learned persons, who shall examine those works from the point of view of faith and dogma, and license them. The great object of the Rifformatori was to secure for the Venetian press the large business of supplying the Italian market with editions of works which were appearing outside Italy, clearly indicating that the literary activity of Italy itself was, at that time, quite insufficient to keep the press alive. The embargo which the Inquisitor laid upon foreign books was the cause of the dearth of matter for the press, and it was to meet this difficulty, chiefly, that the Rifformatori aimed in their proposals. They close their report by assuring the government that action such as they suggest will prove the life and soul of the art, and without such action all other laws, though excellent in themselves, will prove useless.

The report made a deep impression on the government; it was indeed a most masterly summary of the situation, although it not unnaturally left too much out of sight the partial culpability of the Venetian printers and of the Venetian government. The decline in the art was not due solely to the action of the Inquisitor, and, even had it been so, the government would have been to blame for not taking the necessary steps to check the ruin the Inquisitor was said to be working. The report, however, had the effect of calling the attention of the government to the position of the Inquisitor, to his action, and to the question of what was to be done with him. Before adopting the advice contained in the report, the Senate submitted the document to their Consultori in Jure, Triffon Urachien and Fra Enrico de' Servi, who, in due course, presented an elaborate opinion on the advice given by the Rifformatori.[1] They recommend the publication of the Index of 1595, with the additions which the government of the Republic has subsequently sanctioned, and also of the Concordat, copies of which have almost entirely disappeared; and they advise a wide distribution of the Concordat, in order to calm timid and wavering consciences (*le più tenere et fluttuanti coscienze*). They also approve of the second advice given by the Rifformatori, the removal of the Inquisitor from the examination of books, and as this is the point upon which the government will probably come into collision with the Court of Rome, the Consultori are at pains to supply the Senate with sufficient arguments to justify their action. In the first place, the Inquisitor, in his capacity of reviser of books on matters of faith, was appointed, in

[1] See Appendix.

conjunction with certain lay revisers, by the government in 1562. The power that can appoint may also remove is an old maxim of canon law (*ejus est destitutio cujus est institutio*). Moreover, by this same law of 1562 a salary was assigned to the Inquisitor for the performance of his duties, and this salary accepted by the Inquisitor proves that he is in reality the paid servant of the secular government as far as the revision of books is concerned (*lo colloca in riga subalterno mercenario, ministro dipendente per intiero, in quanto appartiene all' esame de' libri, dalla superiorità del magistrato*). Finally, in 1623, the government of Venice had explicitly stated its own view of the Inquisitor's position. The Inquisitor is a reviser of books, not in virtue of his Inquisitorial office, but in virtue of a distinct delegation of power from the government—a delegation which the government may recall (*L' Inquisitor non tiene autorità da altri Principi che dai Magistrati della Repubblica di rivedere, per cause di Religione solamente, le opere che Stampano*). Armed with these arguments, the Consultori advise the Senate that they can fairly meet the Church of Rome; but although they have approved of the vigorous measure proposed by the Rifformatori, they themselves suggest a gentler method of dealing with the difficulty, by appointing other revisers to act concurrently with the Inquisitor, instead of removing the Inquisitor altogether. The Senate approved of this advice, and in August, 1765, they issued a decree setting forth that, as it is possible that the Inquisitor alone is not sufficient for the examination of works on the point of faith, the Rifformatori dello Studio di Padova are to seek out an ecclesiastic, a subject of Venice, but not belonging to any of the orders, who shall be associated with the Inquisitor as his equal; that is to say, that any work which has obtained the *testamur* of one or of the other may—as far as the religious censorship is concerned—go to press. Further, the Rifformatori are to publish the Index of Clement and the Concordat, and to see that it is circulated.

The publication of this decree caused considerable excitement at Rome. That court at once declared all books licensed by the newly-appointed Venetian officers as prohibited. It stigmatized the officers themselves as *persone illegitimamente intruse*, and forbade the entry into the Papal States of all books printed at Venice under their approval. The books are to be seized at the frontier and consigned to that part of the various convent libraries known as "the prison and hell of heretics."[1] In May, July, and November of the following year the Nuncio presented three protests against the action of the government, and demanded the withdrawal of the decree of August, 1765. The whole question now turned on the position of the Inquisitor in Venice, and upon this point the Senate took the opinion of

[1] See Gasparo Gozzi's report. Cecchetti, *op. cit.*, ii. 271.

P(ietro) F(ranceschi), who submitted his views in a long, though vigorously worded report.[1] Pietro Franceschi puts the point under discussion in a very clear light:—The Church of Rome argues that the Inquisitor is, on matters of religion, the judge and natural examiner of books in virtue of the power conferred upon the Church in all matters of faith; the Venetian government argues that the Inquisitor is a minister deputed by the temporal power for the revision of books, and dependent in this character upon the prince alone. The position of the Church on this point of censorship of the press is supported by twelve arguments, which P. F. sets forth at considerable length, with the answers which Venice may properly return. They are as follows:

1. The authority of Holy Writ, of the Fathers, and of the Councils proves that the ministry of the word is entrusted to the Church that it may keep the flock from poisonous food.

The answer is, that the question of the temporal authority of princes has nothing to do with the question of dogmatic orthodoxy.

2. The faithful have frequently condemned and burned books—an argument from custom.

The answer is, that to burn bad books is not the same as to suppress good ones.

3. Leo X. in the Lateran Council established the revision of books by the Inquisition.

The answer is, that the Lateran Council was not a general council, and therefore had no binding power on princes; nor was it legally promulgated in Venice.

4. This decree of the Lateran Council was necessary for the suppression of a corrupt press.

The answer is, that the Venetian government had itself provided for the purity of its press.

5. If the prince of his own authority may examine books on the point of political teaching, the Church on its own authority may also examine books on the point of faith.

The answer is, that this is an argument from analogy, and of little force, for politics and creed are not identical; but no one ever denied the Church's right to examine in matters of faith; all that is disputed is its right to inflict temporal penalties.

6. Heathen nations permit the suppression of books hostile to their religion.

The answer is, that Venice never opposed, but rather encouraged the suppression of irreligious books.

[1] See Appendix.

7. Other Catholic States permit such licensing by the Ordinary.

Answer: what other States may do does not necessarily bind Venice And the statement is not true of all Catholic States. Spain, for instance, does not permit the prohibition of any book by the Inquisition until it has stated its reasons and obtained the consent of the King; and the Catholic States of Germany, while they allow the Inquisition to condemn the book, reserve the penalties in their own hands.

8. The acts and decrees of the Nuncio in Venice established the practice.

The answer is, that these acts and decrees of the Nuncio are not canons of the Church accepted by Venice, but frequently abuses and claims which had no foundation in right.

9. The acts and decrees of the government of Venice acknowledge the authority of the Lateran Council.

The answer is, that if the decrees are examined one by one they will be found to be special, never general, in application; and that they frequently contradict one another; therefore, no argument as to the attitude of Venice can be based on them.

10. The fourth article of the Concordat provides that licences shall run in the name of the law, and the Court of Rome interprets law to mean the laws of Rome as well as the laws of the Republic.

The answer is, that the Church does not talk of its laws, but of its canons; and the Venetian government would have used that term had they meant the word *Leggi* to cover the orders of Rome.

11. Takes the form of a syllogism:

Powers on a given point can be deputed only by those who have jurisdiction on that point.

To the Church, by divine ordinance, belongs jurisdiction as legitimate judge and competent tribunal in matters of faith.

Therefore to the Church and not to the prince belongs the deputation of authority to revise in matters of faith.

The answer is, to demur to the conclusion; for though the Inquisitor is rightly deputed by the Church on matters of faith, he is deputed as an expert, not as a judge. His duty is to state the presence or absence of a given quality—that quality being conformity to dogma.

12. That in ancient times princes allowed the Church to condemn books.

The answer is, that Venice never opposed the condemnation of books; that she acknowledged the Church's right in Article VII. of the Concordat; all she opposes is temporal punishment inflicted by the Church in consequence of such condemnation.

The document ends with a list of cases in which the Venetian government had successfully opposed the encroachments of the Curia. Both this and the preceding documents are conceived in a spirit of great vigour, and couched in language that is clear, incisive, and often scornful. The voice and the spirit are the voice and the spirit of Sarpi; sometimes more on fire than that keen and adamantine spirit ever allowed himself to be, but still essentially the same. The outward, ostensible attitude of Venice has not changed one iota, she still claims to be *Principe libero in casa sua*. But no more had her internal attitude changed; she was the faithful child of the Church, *siamo Cristiani quanto il Papa*, and therefore it was useless for her to declare that *ejus est destitutio cujus est institutio*, when she never could venture to carry out the destitution, nor to insist on the dismissal of the representative of the Curia in her very midst. By way of reply to the decree of August 3rd, 1765, the Inquisitor proposed the following formula to be used by him in the censorship of books: "Seeing that many books which attack, deride, or undermine the Catholic religion have been secretly introduced into this most pious and religious State, the tribunal of the Holy Office condemns and prohibits all such. And since, among these books, some have been examined by the Holy Office and condemned, this tribunal now prohibits them by name, as containing doctrine false, rash, scandalous, wrong, impious, and heretical." Gasparo Gozzi, then Superintendent of the Press, was called on to give his opinion to the Rifformatori dello Studio di Padova. He points out that this formula, though alleged by the Inquisitor to conform to the seventh clause of the Concordat, is really a violation of that clause, and enters his vigorous and even bitter protest against the action of the Inquisitor and the admission of the formula he proposed. Venice certainly did not withdraw her decree of August 3rd, 1765, nor, so far as I know, did she admit the proposals of the Inquisitor; and the matter seems to have remained where it was till the fall of the Republic.

As regards the whole question between the Curia and the Republic, it is obvious that as it stood it was a question which could never be decided. Neither party is clear as to the meaning of the terms they use, for they use them in a sense which would not have been admitted by their adversaries. "Good" and "bad," "heretical" and "orthodox," become question-begging epithets on one side or the other; they had not even agreed upon the content of the term dogma—indeed, it was just here that the whole difficulty lay; it was round the import of this term that the battle should have been fought. Had Venice and Rome been agreed as to what dogma should mean, no difficulty would have remained to quarrel over; but until the import of that term had been defined, it was vain to marshal arguments and answers, both of which seem equally true and valid as viewed now from the standpoint adopted by Rome, now from the position assumed by Venice. Sarpi, with his singular acuteness and penetration, had touched the very core of the dispute when he urged the government to insist upon the exclusion of the temporal rights of princes from the content of the word dogma, and a clear statement of the respective spheres of Church and State, though it is doubtful if Rome would ever have agreed to such a restricted definition.

Venice did not withdraw her decree of August, 1765, and the place of the Inquisitor as censor of books upon matters of faith was taken by persons appointed by the Rifformatori dello Studio di Padova. In the year 1794 the Savii sopra l' Heresia requested an opinion from these censors of faith and dogma upon a work which had been censured at Rome in 1792,[1] with the result that, after considering all the grounds for that condemnation, the censors advised the government not to sanction the decree of the Congregation of the Index.

But Venice did not long enjoy this complete freedom from the press censorship of Rome. Three years later the Republic fell, and brought to a close the subject of this study, the history of the Venetian Printing Press.

[1] De Montazet, Archbishop of Lyons, *Institutiones Theologicæ*. Reusch, *op. cit.*, ii. 995, and Appendix.

DOCUMENTS.

I.

I.[1]

LAWS OF THE REPUBLIC RELATING TO THE PRINTING PRESS AND THE BOOK TRADE.

MDXVII. *Die primo Augusti.*

I. ato, Terra. Rº 20.]

SOLEBANT esse in hac urbe nostra impressores librorum in maximo numero, ex quibus haud modicum capiebatur vectigal publice, et privatim, praeter commodum studiosorum, qui ipsos libros vilius emebant, quo plures imprimebantur. Verum certo ab hinc tempore consuetudo invaluit, ut quidam gratias impetrantes à Domino Nostro, aliis viam occludant imprimendi quaedam opera; quarum gratiarum numerus adeo est auctus ut plerisque dictorum impressorum aliò migrare necesse fuerit, atque ob id hujusmodi artificium valde imminutum sit: unde et jactura publica privataque, et communis incommoditas successit: multoque magis successura esse proculdubio videtur nisi necessaria provisio fiat; Iccirco;

Vadit pars, quod auctoritate hujus Consilii, omnes gratiae à Dominio Nostro Concessae ad hanc diem usque, Impressoribus librorum aut aliis, ut quisque soli possint imprimere, aut imprimi facere opera quaedam, praeter illis quas hoc Consilium concesserit, revocentur, et pro revocatis habeantur, ita ut deinceps nullius sint vigoris, et omnibus liberum sit, illa imprimere, sive imprimi facere absque ulla contradictione, et sicuti aequum est, sine discrimine aliquo. Post hac vero hujusmodi gratiae amplius concedi, et fieri nequeant ullo modo, nisi per hoc Consilium, atque solum pro libris et operibus novis, nunquam antea impressis, et non pro aliis; et si aliter fierent, sint et intelligantur esse nullius valoris. Pars autem, sive gratia quae pro illis posita fuerit, non intelligatur capta, nisi tulerit duo tertia suffragorum hujus Consilii.

[1] This collection of the Venetian Press Laws has been taken from the *Raccolta de Parti prese in diversi Tempi, in Materia di Stampe. Stampata per Z. Antonio et Almorò Pinelli, Stampatori Ducali*, and revised from the originals, except in the cases where there is no marginal indication of their place at the Archivio di Stato, showing that I could not find them there.

MDXXVI. *Die* xxix *Januarii: In Con. X.*

II. [Cons. X. Com. R° 2.] Per la Licentia, che facilmente ognun ha de stampar Libri in questa Nostra Cita, se vede qualche volta ussir in stampa opere disoneste, et de mala natura; al che è da metter sufficiente ordine, et però:

L' andarà parte, che da mo in futurum non se possa stampar, nè stampata dar fuora alcuna opera, over libro da novo composto et non più stampato, si verso come prosa, et in qualunque Idioma se voglia, se prima non li sarà permesso da i capi de questo conseio, per termination de man loro sottoscripta; la qual permission però, et termination se habia à far dapoi che essa opera sarà sta veduta da do persone almeno, a cui parerà à loro capi de commetter che la debano veder et examinar, et referir la opinion sua in scriptis cum juramento: Ne altramente far se possi, sotto pena de perder le opere stampate, et de altratanto per pena, la qual sia delo inventor; et cussi sotto la pena soprascritta non se possa vender in questa Città alcuna opera composta da novo, etiam stampata fuora da questa terra senza licentia deli capi di questo conseio, modo ut supra. Dechiarando, che alcun non possi stampar libro alcuno da novo composto, over non più stampato, sel non vedera la licentia in scriptis, come è detto de sopra. Et lordine presente publicar se deba in Rialto à noticia de ciascuno.

MDXXXIII. *Die* iii *Januarii.*

III. [Senato, Terra. R° 27.] Vedendosi chiaramente come l' arte della stampa, che soleva esser grandissima in questa nostra città, è andata talmente in ruina che non se adopera quasi altri libri, se non quelli che vengono stampati de terre aliene, et tra le altre cause che hanno produtto questo, la principal è stà le tante gratie concesse alli stampadori per questo Conseglio de molti libri non più stampadi, i quali dapoi ottenute tal gratie, ò per non poter, ò per non voler stamparli, tengono oppressa larte, et levano la libertà alli altri stampatori, che quelli stampar non debbino, ita che ne seguita che tali libri sono poi stampadi in terre aliene, privando questa città della utilità publica, et li studenti della commodità universale, et li stampadori del beneficio commune; Però:

L' anderà parte, che per auttorità di questo Conseglio sia firmiter statuito, et deliberato, che quelli che hanno ottenute gratie da questo Conseglio, sia de che condition se vogli de stampar, ò far stampar libri, se in termine de anno uno proximo, comenzando dal zorno presente, non haverano date fuora tutte le opere stampate integre, et compite, et che in effetto publicamente se vendino, quale sarano nominate in la lor gratia, se intenda, passato il ditto anno, le lor gratie esser nulle, et de niun valor, et resti libertà à cadauno far quelle stampar à suo beneplacito, nè de caetero vaglia ad alcuno tal gratie, se non con tal conditione del ditto anno uno: ma se per caso l' opera fusse tanto grande, che secondo la commodità de stampadori, non se potesse espedire in uno anno dapoi ottenute le gratie, li sia in tal caso prorogato il termine, computado ditto anno uno, de tanto tempo quanto ditta opera se potra stampare ad un foglio integro al zorno, et non più.

Item non possi alcuno che ottenira da questo conseglio tal gratie, far stampar le opere altrove, cha in questa Nostra Città, et stampandole, non li vaglia la gratia: ne si possa dimandar gratia più de una volta del medesimo libro. Et la presente parte sia publicata sopra le schalle de Rialto, et di San Marco à notitia di cadauno

Et perchè molti, che hano havuto gratie de stampar le sue opere se fano licito de dimandar ogni precio excessivo, che li pare, è ben conveniente limitarli precio conveniente;

Però sia preso, che fornite (finite), che haveranno de stampar le loro opere, siano obligati ad portarne una a i Proveditori Nostri de Commun, inanzi che le diano fuora, i qual Proveditori havuto il parer, secondo per sua conscienza li parerà, de dui o più, periti in tal arte, per suo sacramento, li deputino il precio che haverano à vender ditte opere; havendo però rispetto alla qualità di esse: et il simile ordine se osservi in tutte le gratie, che de caetero si concederano à persone, che vorano stampar sue opere, over che le stamperano.

MDXXXVII. *Die quarto Junii.*

Perchè l' è introdutta una dannosa et vituperosa usanza da i stampatori di questa città, i quali soleano esser megliori che fossero in loco alcuno, et hora per far manco spesa nelle carte, le quali sono la più importante cosa che si adoperi in questo exercitio, le comprano si triste, che quasi tutti i libri, che ora si imprimeno in questa terra, non retengono l' inchiostro de chi vuol notar et scriver alcuna cosa in essi, come necessariamente si fa in ciascheduno, et per il più scompissano di sorte, che oltra, che è di danno alli lettori, che non possono cavar fuori quel che vogliono ne i margini d' essi libri, è anchora di gran vergogna et incarrico della patria nostra, che di fuori vengono libri stampati bellissimi, et di ottima carta, et in questa citade non si imprima et stampi più libro che buono sia; di che specialmente son cagione le gratie, che si concedono libere à tutti, et anchora de libri altra volta impressi, Per la qual cosa (acciò), in cosi utile arte, et al mondo necessaria delle stampe, non si incorra più in questo ignominoso, et dannoso disordine, et i libri siano qui boni, come in altri loci;

L' anderà parte, che non possano da hora inanzi per modo alcun quelli che haverano gratia da questo Conseglio stampare in questa città, ne in alcun loco delle terre nostre, libri che habbiano carte che scompissino, sotto pena alli stampatori di ducati cento, et a quelli che haverano havuto la gratia di perdere in tutto detta loro gratia, et tutti li libri stampati di quella stampa: li quali immediate siano arsi publicamente in Piazza di San Marco, nella qual pena si intendino esser incorsi quando si habiano ritrovati soli cinque libri di una stampa che scompissino in cinque fogli per uno, et per li avogadori nostri di commun, alli quali sia commessa la executione di tutta la presente parte, siano subito tolti li detti ducati cento, et in tutto essegnito quanto è dissopra detto, senza altro conseglio et senza altro processo, che della semplice prova delli detti cinque libri trovati con carte che non retengano l' inchiostro, mà passar lo lassino dall' altra parte di essa carta e scompissino, come è detto; delli qual danari la mità sia delli accusatori et l' altra mità delli detti avogadori de commun, che farano la executione; Nè possano essi avogadori sotto pena de ducati mille da esser applicadi al arsenal nostro, rimetter nè far gratia alcuna di detta pena, nè lassar di far arder tutti li detti libri, come è di sopra statuito; non si comprehendendo pero sotto 'l presente ordine le cose minute, che si vendessero fino alla summa di soldi 10 l' una.

Et perchè alcuna volta si da anchora gratia, et privilegio de libri altre fiate impressi, che è contra le lege nostre, et contra ogni dovere, che per poche correctioni che si aggiongono ad un libro, ch' era commune con tutti, sia data gratia di farlo speciale ad uno solo, il che fà poi, che quelli, che l' hanno, sapendo di non poter haver concorrentia d' altri, la qual acuisse l' industria in tutte l' arte, stampano gli libri in quella carta et in quel modo, che à loro viene meglio, Sia di novo preso, che la parte del 1517 che vole che non si possa dar gratia ad alcuno de libri, et d' opere, che non siano nove, et se fusse data, si intenda essere di nessun valore, sia in tutto, et per tutto confirmata, et per ditti avogadori esseguita; et se ad alcuno fosse per l' advenire mai conceduta tal gratia, possa nondimeno ciascaduno liberamente stampir tal libri, come se mai stata concessa non fosse.

Et la presente parte sia publicata à Rialto, et a San Marco ad intelligentia di cadauno, et non si possa revocar nè suspender, salvo per parte posta per tutti sei li conseglieri, et 3 capi de quaranta; la quale non si intenda presa, se non haverà i $\frac{5}{6}$ delle ballotte di questo Conseglio, congregato da 150 in suso.

MDXLII. *Die* xii *Februarii. in add.*

V. [Cons. X. Com. R° 15.]

Sono fatti cosi licentiosi li stampatori, et li botegieri di questa cità, che non stimando la poca punitione statuita dalle leze nostre a quelli, che fano stampar, o vendeno cose stampate de fuori, senza licentia di capi di questo conseglio, stampano, et etiam vendono libri, et opere stampate altrove publicamente, molte delle qual sono contra l' honor del Signor Dio, et della fede christiana, et molte inhonestissime, con tanto mal esempio et scandalo universal, quanto a tutti è noto. Al che essendo necessario proveder di gagliarda provisione;

L' anderà parte, che salve et reservate tutte le leze sopra ciò disponente, oltra la pena in quelle contenute de perder l' opere stampate, et altratanto più per pena sia aggionto etiam, che chi stampasse, ò facesse stampar de ditte opere senza licentia ut supra, immediate trovata la verità, pagar debba ducati cinquanta. Li venditori veramente, ò chi facesse vender, ò tenisse in casa, bottega, ò altro luogo, di tal opere, et libri, pagar debbano Ducati 25 li qual tutti siano dell' accusador, il qual sia tenuto secretissimo. Quelli veramente, che vendeno de tal libri et opere, pronostichi, historie, canzone, lettere, et altre simel cose sul ponte de Rialto, et in altri lochi di questa città, se loro, ò chi li farà vender, non haverà havuta la licentia dalli capi preditti, siano frustati da San Marco à Rialto, et poi star debbano sei mesi in preson seradi. Et se sarà trovato alcuno, che stamperà, o farà stampar opera alcuna in questa città, et farà apparer quella esser stampata altrove, sia in tal caso condennato à star uno anno in preson, et pagar Ducati cento quali siano del accusador, da esser tenuto secreto ut supra: nè possa uscir de preson, se prima non haverà pagato li danari preditti, et poi sia bandito in perpetuo da questa città, et destretto, con taglia in caso di contraffattion de pagar lire 500 à chi el prendesse, star uno anno in preson, et ritornar poi al suo bando ogni volta, chel sarà preso. Et questo istesso se intenda delle opere già stampate, se alcuno le venderà senza licentia, et contra la forma delle leze nostre. Il qual ordine si extenda et debba esser osservato in tutte le terre, et luogi nostri; et sia mandato alli rettori di fuora, aciò sia publicato, exeguito, et osservato. Et la execution della presente parte, per quanto aspetta a questa città, sia commessa alli Signori Executori sopra la Biastema con l' authorità che hano in altri casi commesseli da questo Conseglio, li quali Executori habbino etiam authorità di darli maggior pena della limitada, essendo tutti tre daccordo, secondo che giudicherano convenir alla transgressione del presente ordine nostro, et sia publicata sopra le scale de Rialto, et di S. Marco.

MDXLIIII. *Die* xxx *Decembris. In Cons. X.*

VI. [ons. X. Com. R° 16.] Preterea perche spesso l' accade ricercarsi alli capi di questo Conseglio licentie di stampar' opere composte, et suol esser in dubio à chi sia da commetter la ravision di quelle, si come per leze è statuito: Però sia preso, che ogni volta l' occorrerà, siano mandate tal opere alli [tre nobili nostri, che saranno] Refformatori sopra 'l studio di Padoa, che debbino vederle, ò far le veder, et far la relation soa, secondo la qual poi habbia ad esser il procedere de i preditti Capi nel fatto delle ditte licentie.

MDXLIIII. *Die* vii *Februarii. In Cons. X.*

VII. [ons. X. Com. R° 16.] È accresciuta in tanto l' audacia et cupidità di guadagno di alcuni stampatori in questa nostra città, che si fanno licito de imprimer quel che li pare, et nominar li compositori di quelle cose che stampano, senza alcuna loro scientia, anzi contra ogni loro voler: Essendo stà de ciò fatta querela alli capi di questo conseglio, con ricercar instantemente provisione, la qual si deve omnino far, et però;

L' anderà parte, che de cetero alcun' impressor in questa nostra città non habbia ardimento stampar, nè stampata far vender alcuna opera in cadauna lengua, sel non consterà per authentico documento alli Refformatori dello Studio Nostro di Padoa, à chi la cognition di tal cosa è stà deputata, l' autor di quella, over li sui heredi più congionti esser contenti, et ricercar, che la si stampi, et venda, sotto pena di pagar ducato uno per cadaun libro et auttor che stampassero contra il presente ordine, et di star mese uno serrato in preson, et che li sian brusati tutti li libri, che si trovessero stampati di tal sorte, et l' accusator per il qual si venirà in luce della verità, habbia la mità della pena sopraditta, et l' altra mità vadi all' hospedal della pietà; et la presente parte sia publicata sopra le scalle di San Marco et Rialto.

MDXLVII. *Die* xvii *Maii. In add.*

VIII. [ons. X. Com. R° 18.] Fu provisto per questo Conseglio del 1542 alli 12 di Febraro contra quelli che stampano, et vendeno libri, che trattano contra l' honor del Signor Dio, et della Fede Christiana, et non fù provisto contra quelli che conducono libri de simil sorte in questa città stampati in altri luoghi; Però;

L' anderà parte, che alla sopraditta deliberatione, la qual in tutto, e per tutto sia confirmata, sia aggionto et statuito, che se alcuno, sia chi esser si voglia, condurrà in questa nostra città libri della sorte preditta, cadi in pena di perde i libri, i quali siano fatti brusar publicamente, et di pagar ducati cinquanta, da esser dati all' accusador, il qual sia tenuto secretissimo. Et la essecutione del presente ordine sia commesso alli Essecutori nostri sopra la biastema, con l' auttorità, che li fu data di accrescer etiam la pena tutti tre d' accordo, si come in essa parte del 1542 si contiene; et etiam alli tre gentilhomini nostri sopra la inquisition delli heretici.

MD.XLVIII. *Die* xviii *Julii.* *In add.*

IX. [Cons. X. Com. R° 18.] Il Serenissimo Principe fà à saper, et è parte presa nell' Eccellentissimo Conseglio di X, à cadauna persona habitante in questa città, et destretto suo, cosi stampatori over venditori de libri, come cadaun' altro, sia de che condition et qualità esser si voglia, cosi clerici, come laici, che se alcuno di loro si ritrova haver libri, cosi stampati in questa città, come venuti da altri luoghi sottoposti, o non sottoposti al Serenissimo Dominio di Venetia, nelli qual libri sia scritto alcuna cosa contra la fede catholica, debbano in termine di giorni otto presentarli alli Clarissimi Signori Deputati sopra li heretici; perchè non obstante le parti dell' Illustrissimo conseglio di X contra quelli che tengono simil libri, non incorrerano in pena alcuna, ma passato che sarà il ditto termine, essi Clarissimi Signori farano diligentissima inquisitione, et ritrovando alcun contrafacente, li darano severissimo castigo, secondo l' auttorità concessali dal prefatto Illustrissimo Conseglio di X in questa materia. Et se alcuno accuserà qualche contrafacente, sarà tenuto secretissimo, et haverà il dono pecuniario promessoli dalle sopraditte leze.

MDXLVIII. *Die* xvi *Januarii. in add.*

X.[1] [Cons. X. Com. R° 18.] non detur exemplum. Fu fatta publicamente proclamar in questa città per deliberation di questo conseglio alli 18 luglio passato, che se alcuno havesse libri nelli quali si contenisse alcuna cosa contra le fede Catholica dovesse in termine de otto giorni presentarli alli tre dilettissimi nobili nostri deputati sopra i heretici senza incorrer in pena alcuna, et non fu dechiarito altramente li nomi de simil libri; Hora mò essendo sta fatto di ordine del Reverendo legato per il venerabile inquisitor con intervento et conseglio di tre p^li nobili nostri et di molti maestri in theologia un cathalogo o summario de tutti i libri heretici, et de altri suspetti, et de altri etiam nelli quali se contengono cose contra li boni costumi, è grandemente aproposito farlo publicar a notitia de tutti, Però;

L' andera parte chel sopraditto cathalogo sia fatto stampar, et per i ditti nobili ne sia dato uno a cadauno stampator, et venditor de libri, et se facci etiam che in una botega se ne vendi publicamente; et sia reiterato in questa cita il ditto proclama de 18 luglio con particolar menzione del presente cathalogo, et del libraro che li vendera, accioche se alcuno contrafara non habbi causa di escusarsi; il qual cathalogo sia

[1] This document does not occur in Pinelli's collection; the words *non detur exemplum* explain why. As far as I am aware it has never been published. It is unknown to Reusch and Zaccaria, and settles the question of the date and authorship of Giov. della Casa's *Catalogue*. Reusch, *op. cit.*, i. 105.

medesimamente mandato a tutti i rettori delle terre nostre principal da terra et da mar, con ordine chel faccino publicar per tutta la sua diocese, dando quel termine che li parerà de farseli presentar senza pena, il qual poi passato debbano proceder contra li inobedienti secondo li parerà meritar la temerita loro.

MDXLVIII. *Die* xviii *Januarii.* *In cons°. X.*

XI. Una delle principal arte di questa città et delle più importante per molti rispetti
[C. X. Com. è quella della stamparia; la qual nondimeno essendo quasi tutte l' altre ben ordinate, et
R° 18.] con le soe fraggie, et matricole, sola si ritrova senza ordine alcuno, di modo che essendo occorso più fiate alli tre deputati sopra li heretici di esser informati dalli authori et stampatori d' alcuni libri scandolosi et heretici per le cose pertinente al loro officio, non si ha ritrovato chi li habbi saputo render conto; et medesimamente occorrendo di giorno in giorno molti inconvenienti circa le stampe, che hano bisogno de emendatione, con difficultà per l' istessa cagione si può venir in cognitione della verità, non vi essendo alcuno che rappresenti la ditta arte, nè chi risponda per quella, onde avviene, che tutti fano à modo loro, con estremo disordine, et confusione; alle qual cose, essendo necessario far le debite provisione, prima per l' honore de Dio, et della religione, dapoi per l' honor della nostra città, et per altri rispetti publici, come sono de galeoti et simili nelli quali s' habbi con chi indriciarsi, Però;

L' anderà parte, che per auttorità di questo Conseglio sia preso, che se debbi levar una Schuola de tutti quelli, che fanno stampar et che tengono botege, et vendono libri in qualunque modo in questa città, et sia commessa alli Proveditori de Commune, che à questo effetto, et per la buona regolatione di essa Scuola, et de quella Arte, debbano poner quelli ordini, et far quelli capitoli, che li parerano convenir et esser espedienti.

Die 9 *Februari*, 1558.

XII. Li Reverendi Monsignor Vicario Patriarcale, et Padre Inquisitore, con l' assistenza delli Clarissimi M. Bernardo Giorgio, et M. Andrea Barbarigo, et M. Piero Sanudo Nobili Deputati a questo Sacro Tribunale della Santissima Inquisizione contra Heretici, hanno deliberato, et terminato per ogni buon fine et effetto, per fuggir la occasione che esso Sacro Tribunal non sia fraudato; Che de tutti li Libri, che de caetero saranno condutti per qualsivoglia persona in questa inclita Città di Venetia, non possano esser tratti di Dogna aliquo modo, se prima li Patroni di essi Libri non venghino a dar la Polizza della quantità et qualità di essi Libri a questo Sacro Tribunale; la qual polizza remagnir debba in l' Officio, per evitare le fraude, che si potriano commettere in Negozio de Libri. Et ita decreverunt, et mandarunt annotari.

1562. 19 *Marzo.*

XIII. Noi Refformatori dello Studio di Padova infrascritti, vedendo esser introdotto da alcuni anni in quà, che quelli, che vogliono far stampare alcuna Opera, la fanno vedere a chi più li piace; et portando Fede de doi, o tre, che non vi sia cosa contra le Leggi, ottengone Fede dal l' Officio Nostro secondo l' ordinario alli Eccellentissimi Signori Capi dell' Illustrissimo Conseglio di Dieci, et per conseguentie licenza di Stampare; dal che possono seguir moltò inconvenienti (come son già seguiti) alli quali si venirebbe a proveder quando li Libri fossero revisti da persone elette da Noi, dotte e Fedeli. Però terminiamo, che per il Segretario qual per tempora servirà all' officio Nostro, non possa esser fatta Fede alcuna per stampar qual si voglia cosa, se prima non sarà revista dal Reverendo Inquisitor, overo da uno delli suoi Vicarij, ò da altra persona Ecclesiastica, che habbia carico al Tribunal dell' Inquisitione; dal Nobil Homo M. Marc' Antonio Mocenigo, Lettor in Filosofia, overo da alcun' altro Lettor Publico, et da uno delli Secretarij Ducali, si che in tutto siano Tre, cioè uno Ecclesiastico, uno Lettore, et uno Secretario; et se da loro non haverà fede, che nell' Opera non s' attrovi cosa alcuna contro la Religione, nè contra Principi, nè contra li buoni costumi, et che meriti andar in luce; notando nella Fede il numero delle Carte, con una riga del principio et una del fine; et essendo più libri sia espresso il principio et il fine di cadaun libro. Li qual Revisori quelli però, che rivederanno le opere per la loro fatica habbiano un Bezzo per Foglio di Carta per cadauno di loro tre, da esserli pagato da chi vorrà stampare; et siano obligati quelli, che stamperanno portar una delle prime opere stampate all' Officio Nostro, avanti che diano fuori, acciocchè si possa in ogni tempo veder quel, che sarà stampato, e che non sia lecito poi aggiungervi cosa alcuna senza nuova Licenza.

D. Marinus de Cabalis Eques,
D. Petrus Sanutus,
D. Franciscus Balduarius, } Reformatores Gymnasij Patavini.

Capitolo estratto da una Proclama delli Eccellentissimi Signori Essecutori contra la Bestemia. Die 10. *Ottobre.* 1565.

XIV. De più si fà saper, che non sia alcuno, che ardisca stampar, ne far stampar, nè altrove stampati vender in questa Città Libri, Opere, Pronostichi, Historie, Canzoni, Lettere, o dell' altre simil cose, senza la Licenza ordinaria; sotto pena a chi stampasse, ò facesse stampar tal opere de pagar ducati cinquanta, et quelli che le vendessero, Ducati vinticinque. Quelli veramente, che vendessero Historie, ò altre simil cose stampate senza licentia sopra il Ponte di Rialto, et altrove per la Città siano frustati da San Marco a Rialto, e stiano mesi sei in Pregion serrati. Et se alcuno stampasse, over facesse stampar alcuna Opera in questa Città, et facesse parer, che fusse stampata altrove, sia condannato a star Anno uno in Pregion, et pagar Ducati cento, et in Bando perpetuo di questa Città, et del Destretto, et la pena Pecuniaria in tutti li casi sia dell' Accusador da esser tenuto secreto. Et oltra di questo, se parerà alli Tre Essecutori prefatti il delitto meritar maggior condennatione, gliela daranno secondo la forma della Legge dell' Illustrissimo Conseglio de Dieci con la Zonta de 12 Febraro 1542.

MDLXVI. *Die* xvii *Septembris. In Cons. X.*

XV. [Cons. X. Com. R° 27.] Per questo Conseglio fino del 1542, adi 12 Febraro fu deliberato, che gli Essecutori Nostri contra la Biastema havessero carico di castigar quelli che senza licentia stampano, et vendeno Libri, et Historie in questa Città; et perchè si vede, che contra gli Ordini predetti si stampano, et vendeno molte Opere senza licentia, che sono etiam prohibite dalle Leggi Nostre. Il che procede, che non havendo detti essecutori notitia delle Licentie, che vengono date, non possono exercitar l' officio loro; et (quod pejus est) molti stampano sopra le Opere, et dicono Con Licentia, ancor che non habbino havuta licentia di Stamparle, et à questo modo vengono ad inganar la Giustitia: però essendo da proveder a tali inconvenienti;

L'Anderà Parte che tutti quelli, che haveranno Licentie di stampar Opere, così dalli Capi di questo Conseglio, come dal Conseglio Nostro de Pregadi, debbano avanti, che le stampino presentar le Licentie, che haveranno havute nell' officio delli Essecutori Nostri contra la Biastema, quali senza spesa d' alcuno siano registrate sopra un Libro à parte, acciò de tempo in tempo le si possano vedere, et che quelli, che contra le Leggi, et Ordini stampano, et vendeno, siano castigati, giusta la Parte, et Ordini antedetti. Et la presente Parte sia Publicata sopra le Scale de Rialto, et ove farà bisogno per intelligentia universale.

MDXCVI. *Adi* xiiii *Giugno.*

Perche si vede essere introdotto da certo tempo in quà, che diversi Librari, et Stampatori in questa Città per impadronirsi dell' utile, che ricevono dal stampar soli diversi Libri con esclusione degl' altri, et rovina della Stampa di questa Città, hanno procurato d' ottener da Roma Motu proprij, et privilegij prohibitivi, che altri che loro non possano stamparli, senza curarsi delli Privilegij di questo Conseglio, contra la forma delle Leggi, con pessimo essempio, con detrimento dell' Arte, et anco danno Publico, non si deve restar di provedergli di quel modo, che ricerca una Materia così importante; Però;

L' Anderà Parte, che tutti quelli Librari, ò Stampatori sudditi, overo habitanti in questa Città, et in tutti lo Stato Nostro, che havessero fin' hora impetrato, overo godessero simili Privilegij prohibitivi, ò Motu proprij, come di sopra, siano tenuti sotto le pene infrascritte rinonciar immediatamente al beneficio, che da loro ricevono, et ciò per mantenimento et conservatione dell' Arte della Stampa in questa Città, ed altri rispetti sopradetti, conforme a quanto essi medesimi si sono offerti nel Collegio Nostro, si che dal giorno presente in poi sia in libertà d' ogn' uno di stampare tutti li Libri, che per tali Privilegij, et Motu proprij restavano impediti, et in libertà di alcuni soli, havute però prima le debite Licentie et servati gli Ordini statuiti per le Leggi in Materia delle Stampe. Nè sia lecito ad alcun suddito, o habitante in questa Città, et nello Stato Nostro, di ottener più nell' arvenire, ò per loro stessi, ò per interposta persona, nè goder simili privilegij, ò Motu proprij, sotto pena di perder irremissibilmente tutti li Libri che per virtù di tali Privilegij, o Motù proprij havessero stampati, et di pagar anco Ducati diece per ciascun Libro che havessero stampato, una parte de quali Libri et danari vada all' Accusator, una al Magistrato che farà l' essecutione, et la terza ad Pias Causas.

Et la essecutione della presente Parte sia commessa alli Proveditori di Commun, et alli Refformatori del Studio di Padova, salva sempre l' auttorità delli Avogadori Nostri.

DECHIARAZIONI DELLE REGOLE

dell' Indice di Libri proibiti, novamente pubblicato per ordine della Santità di N. S. Clemente Ottavo, da osservarsi nel Stato della Serenissima Signoria di Venetia, fatte dagl' Illustriss. et Reverendiss. Sign. Cardinale Priuli Patriarca di Venetia, et Vescovo d' Amelia Nuncio Apostolico per commissione di Sua Beatitudine come per Lettere dell' Illustrissimo et Reverendiss. Signor Cardinale S. Giorgio sotto li 24 Agosto, 1596—

Primo. Li Libri sospesi dal novo Indice, et che si devono espurgare si potranno vendere ancora innanzi l' espurgatione, a quelli che haveranno Licenza dall' Ordinario, over dall' Inquisitor di poterli tenere.

Secondo. Se li Stampatori vorranno ristampare li sudetti Libri sospesi, et faranno instanza per la Corretione, si correggeranno espeditamente in Venetia, et nell' altre Città del Stato senza mandarli à Roma, havendo sufficiente facoltà per il novo Indice li Vescovi insieme con li Inquisitori, et ristampandosi corretti, si venderanno liberamente a tutti.

Terzo. Useranno diligenza li Stampatori per conservare nel Miglior modo che potranno l' Originale Manuscritto de Libri che novamente anderanno alla stampa, et dopo doveranno consegnarlo al Segretario de' Clarissimi Signori Refformatori del Studio, acciò sia riposto in una Cassa sicura nella cancelleria Ducale per servirsene, quando farà bisogno, nella qual Cassa si tenghi un' Inventario de' Libri, che si riponeranno, et ciò s' intende solamente de Libri novi, et ancor de Libri sospesi, che si corregeranno et ristamperanno. Nelle Città poi del Stato li originali predetti si consigneranno al Cancelliero del Clarissimo Capitanio acciò li tenghi nel modo predetto, et si consegnino successivamente con l' inventario da Cancelliere à Cancelliere.

Quarto. Nel stampar de Libri s' imprima à tergo del primo foglio la Licentia solita del Magistrato, nella quale siano espressi li Nomi di quelli, che haveranno revisto, et approvato detti Libri, come è disposto per le Leggi.

Quinto. Avvertiranno li Stampatori, che nè Libri novi, che stamperanno, ò nè Vecchi, che ristampassero non usino figure, che rappresentino atti dishonesti, non essendo però prohibite le figure profane, che non contenessero dishonestà.

Sesto. Li Librari doveranno far l' inventario di tutti li Libri che si attrovano per espurgare in questo principio le Librarie da' Libri espressamente prohibiti nel novo Indice, et Presentarlo al Padre Inquisitore, et questo s' intenda per una volta solamente.

Settimo. Intorno la libertà, che vien concessa alli Vescovi, et Inquisitori di poter prohibire altri Libri non espressi nell' Indice, si dechiara, che s' intenda de Libri contrarij alla Religione, Forestieri, ò con false, et finte Licentie stampati, et rarissime volte si darà il caso, ne si farà senza giustissima causa, et con participatione del Santo Officio et Intervento di Clarissimi Signori Assistenti, tanto in Venetia, come nello Stato.

Ottavo. La regola del giuramento da darsi a Librari et Stampatori non s' esseguisca in questo Serenissimo Dominio.

Nono. Tutti li Heredi doveranno dar nota al Padre Inquisitore de Libri prohibiti et sospesi, che si ritrovassero nell' Heredità, et quelli Heredi, che non fossero abili a discernerli, doveranno loro, ò suoi Curatori chiamar persone intelligenti, che visitino tutta la Libraria per cavarne Nota delli prohibiti et sospesi, et presentarla, come di sopra, in termine di Mesi tere dopo che gli haveranno havuti in suo potere, et frà tanto non possano usare, ne in qualunque modo alienare li Libri prohibiti, o sospesi, et ciò sotto le pene et censure Statuite.

Per Fede et Corraboratione di tutto ciò li sudetti Illustrissimi Cardinale Patriarca, et Nuncio insieme co 'l Reverendo Padre Inquisitore di Venetia sottoscriveranno le presenti, et le affermaranno con proprij loro Sigilli commettendo per l' autorità datale da sua Beatitudine, che inviolabilmente si debbano osservare le predette dechiarazioni, tanto in Venezia, quanto in tutte le altre Città, et luoghi sudditi al Serenissimo Dominio. In quorum fidem etc.

Datum ex Palatio Patriarcali Venetiarum die 14 Septembris 1596.

LORENZO CARDINALE PRIULI Patriarca di mano propria.
ANT. MAR. VESCOVO D' AMELIA Nuncio.
FRATER VICENTIUS BRIXIENSIS Inquisitor G. Venetus.

MDCII. *Die* XX *Febraro.* *In Pregadi.*

XVIII. Essendosi per proponer a questo Consiglio una general provisione nella importante
[...tato, Terra. Materia della Stampa, la quale si è andata nel spatio de molti giorni dal Collegio
R° 72.] Nostro, et da' Reformatori del Studio di Padoa, maturando con tutti quei mezi che a ciò si sono conosciuti opportuni; et tra tanto essendosi scoperto, che di presente si tenta da varie parti di sviar à forza di danari parte de Professori di detta Arte, che sarebbe la destruttione di cosi utile pensiero;

L'Anderà Parte, che sicome fu da questo Consiglio a 10 Gennaro 1577 data auttorità contra simili perturbatori alli Cinque Nobili, che si eleggevano già dal Conseglio di X sopra le Arti di questa Città, cosi sia la medesima auttorità attribuita alli Reformatori sudetti, et tanto contra essi perturbatori et sviatori de Artefici di Stampe, quanto contra quei della medesima Arte, Matricolati, o non Matricolati, che ardissero partire di questa Città, per andar à lavorar altrove, et contra cadauno sia chi si voglia, il quale portasse, ò mandasse fuori alcuno di quei Materiali et Instrumenti, come Torchi, Caratteri, sotto nome di piombo lavorato, Inchiostro, ò Vernice liquida, et altro, che si appartenga al stampare, potendo contra questi tali proceder à pena cosi Pecuniaria, et di Prigione, come di Bando et di Galea, quando contrafacessero, sviando alcuno dell' Arte, et portando, o mandando i medesimi dell' Arte, et cadaun altro fuori di questa Città alcuno delli Materiali, et Instrumenti sopradetti dopo la Publicatione della presente Parte; et quelli parimente della predetta Arte, che essendo partiti, chiamati dai sudetti Reformatori non ritornassero al tempo prefisso. Dovendo etiandio contra quelli, che venissero in cognitione per lo passato haver commesso alcuna delle predette operationi indebite, et dannate dalle Leggi, proceder a quel castigo che giudicheranno convenir al loro demerito.

Ordine degl' Illustrussimi Signori Reformatori delle Studio di Padova.
1603. *adi* 10 *Marzo.*

XIX. De Ordine degl' Illustrissimi Signori Reformatori dello Studio di Padova, dall' Eccellentissimo Senato delegati nell' infrascritta Materia. Si fà Commandamento à cadauno Matricolato dell' arte di Librari, e Stampatori, et ad ogn' altro non Matricolato, come Gettadori de Caratteri, e Lavoranti di Stampa, et à qual si sia altra persona, che in pena di Prigione, Galea, Bando, perdita di robbe, e privatione dell' arte ad arbitrio di loro Signorie Illustrissime, non debbano partir per andar à lavorar in qualunque altro luoco, fuori di questa Città, tanto nel Stato, quanto fuori, Senza licentia in Scrittura delle loro Signorie Illustrissime, non essendo per mancar ad alcuno di essa Arte di quella Giustizia e Protettione, ch'è conveniente; E sotto tutte le pene predette si intima à cadauno delli Matricolati, e non Matricolati, et ad ogni altra persona, che non ardiscano sviare per se stessi, o per altri, alcuno dell' Arte, Matricolato o non Matricolato, nè meno condur fuori alcun Materiale, ò Instrumento pertinente alla Stampa, come Caratteri da Stampa, sotto nome di Piombo lavorato, ò altrimenti, Torcoli, Inchiostro, ò Vernise liquida, e Madri, con le quali si gettano i Caratteri, et ogn' altra cosa, come è detto, pertinente alla Stampa, ne meno favorir, e coadiuvar chi volesse sviar dei sopradetti artefici, e condur fuori dei sopradetti Materiali, et Instrumenti di Stampa, o haver con li Contrafattori secreta intelligenza, anzi denonciar cadauno, che sapessero, ò intendessero voler contrafar all' Ordine presente, sotto le medesime pene, quando non li palesassero, e di Ducati duecento, qual habbino ad esser dati al Denunciante da esser tenuto secreto. All' essecutione delle quali pene si protesta, che per loro Signorie Illustrissime, per l' autorità loro data dall' Eccellentissime Senato, si devenirà irremissibilmente contra gl' innobbedienti, di quel modo, che meritarà il loro eccesso. Et il presente Mandato sarà registrato presso il Secretario di loro Signorie Illustrissime per la sua dovuta essecutione, col nome di cadauno a chi sarà stato intimato, et Publicato etiandio sopra le scale di San Marco et di Rialto, acciò niun non ne possi pretender ignorantia.

M. Antonio Memo Proc. Reformator
Francesco Molin Cav. Reformator
Antonio Priuli Cav. Reformator

Paolo Ciera Secret.

MDCIII. *a* xxi *Maggio. In Pregadi.*

XX. [Senato, Terra. R° 73.] Frà le altre Arti, che maggiormente accrescono il splendore à questa Città, ha tenuto sempre luogo principale quella della Stampa, perche con molta accuratezza, et industria esercitata già per longo tempo da professori di essa, moltiplicò con molta reputatione Publica, e notabilissimo benefitio di tanti impiegati, et trattenuti in detto Lavoro. Questa al presente per la estrattione che si è andata facendo liberamente delle materie, et instrumenti di essa portati in Stati alieni con sviamento continuo de Maestri, et Operaij, si è andata annichilando grandemente, et per la poca cura et per l' avaritia de Stampatori, che non mettono più pensiero, che l' opere riescano ben stampate con buone Forme, e buone Carte, e (quello che importa) per mancamento de' Correttori sufficienti, riuscendo le Opere piene di errori, ha perduta quella riputatione, che solleva dar alli Libri di Venetia grandissimo aviamento; onde non dovendosi differir più in farvi la debita Provisione, e statuirvi quelle regole, che maggiormente possone levar li sudetti disordini;

L' Anderà Parte, che restando ferme, e valide quelle Deliberationi et Ordini, che si trovano sin hora statuiti in proposito di Stampe, non repugnanti alla presente, sia nell' avvenire osservato inviolabilmente quanto si contiene nelli sequenti Capitoli.

Che tutti li Librari, ò Stampatori Matricolati, che vorranno Stampare ò far stampare alcun Opera già Stampata, siano obligati di far prima veder l' esemplare, del quale haveranno a servirsi, e diligentissimamente corregger ogni incorretione, che in esso si trovasse.

Siano obligati di volta in volta far legger le forme in piombo con diligentia dalli Compositori, et farle ascoltar ò dalli Protti, ò da altre persone sufficienti, perchè la prima Correttione sia fatta in detto incontro sulla forma, e dapoi tirato il foglio in Torcolo far quello veder dal Correttore, dal quale debbano esser corretti gli errori, che troverà esser in esso foglio, e poi si habbi à tirar il secondo per assicurarsi, che siano stati acconci, e cancellati.

E perche dalla intelligenza e sufficienza de' Revisori, e Correttori depende principalmente la perfettione delle Stampe, e che l' opere non vengano, ò per malitia, ò per ignorantia alterate, ò contaminate, non possino per l' avvenire essercitar questo carico, di riveder e corregger se non quelle persone, che saranno approbate dalli Reformatori del Studio Nostro di Padoa, li quali habbino autorità ancora (se conosceranno necessario) di regolar l' ordinarie Mercedi di essi Correttori, e condennar li transgressori in quelle pene, che stimeranno convenienti alle transgressioni di quanto è sopradetto.

Siano obligati salvar le copie originali di tutte l' Opere nuove, e vecchie, e le stampe ancora, perchè si possi conoscer le Contrafattioni, e massime se dopo la revisione fatta di esse, prima di esserli stata concessa la Licentia di stamparle, sarà stato aggionto, o levatò alcuna cosa, ò postone alcun' altra di quelle, che saranno state cancellate, o depennate dalli Revisori deputati che saranno il Reverendo Inquisitore, et uno delli Secretari nostri con li soliti requisiti, e con giuramento, rimanendo del tutto per maggior sollevamento delli Stampatori, et Auttori delle Opere, levato il Lettor Publico, terzo Revisor, essendo a sufficienza la visione delli dui sudetti.

E sia servato l' obligo della medesima visione in tutte le Terre dello Stato Nostro, dove si stampano Libri; prohibendo espressamente il poterli stampar, se prima, oltre la Fede del Reverendo Inquisitore di quella Città, non si haverà havuta quella di uno delli Secretarij Nostri, e la Licenza sottoscritta almeno da dui delli Reformatori sudetti, altrimente siano puniti e castigati li Contrafattori, cosi dalli Rettori delle Città Nostre, come dalli Reformatori sopradetti, secondo parerà alla loro conscienza.

Che alli Libri stampati fuori di Venetia, non sia alcuno, che ardisca poner il primo foglio stampato, con la inscrittione del Stampatore, e della Città di Venetia, perchè apparino stampati in questa Città, sotto pene per il meno de Ducati vinticinque, e di quell' altre maggiori pene, avuto riguardo alla qualità della transgressione, che parerà alli Reformatori sudetti, e specialmente della perdita de' Libri, le quali pene siano applicate al Denonciante, da esser tenuto secreto.

Debbano quelli, che faranno Stampar, servirsi de maestri di stampa conosciuti per sufficienti dalli Deputati dell' Arte, e cosi parimente di bei Caratteri, e buoni Inchiostri, in modo che le lettere non solo siano corrette ma ben improntate nette e leggibili.

Siano tenuti far Stampar in fine di cadaun Libro nuovo l' Errata, et in tutti li vecchi, e nuovi il Nome del Correttore.

Si servino etiandio di buona, e bella Carta, la quale sia de peso proportionato alla qualità de' Libri, che haveranno a stampare, come dalli Reformatori sudetti sarà determinato, la qual non scompissi à modo alcuno, giusta la parte di questo Conseglio dell' anno 1537. E sotto tutte le pene contenute nella Deliberatione ultimamente fatta da esso Conseglio à 20 del Mese di Febraro passato, cosi li detti Matricolati come altri non Matricolati di detta Arte, non ardiscano di partir, ò sviar alcuno di essa Arte, per andar a lavorar fuori di questa Città, nè meno portar Materiali fuori, ò Instrumenti di qual si voglia sorte pertinenti alla Stampa.

E perchè si possi opportunamente conoscer, et oviar à quelle transgressioni, che si andassero commettendo in questa Professione, ma specialmente assicurarsi dell' osservanza di quanto viene ordinato; sia deliberato, che il Priore e Compagni della Banca de' Librari e Stampatori debbano andar spesso vedendo, inquirendo et osservanda, come venga esseguita la presente Parte, et almeno ogni tre Mesi venire a refferir alli predetti Reformatori quelle contrafattioni che haveranno potuto intendere, acciò vi si possi proveder della maniera, che ricerca materia tanto importante, come è la presente. Dovendo essi Reformatori haver in ciò quella medesima auttorità, che per la sudetta Parte di 20 Febraro passato, in proposito di sviar gli Artefici di Stampe, fu loro attribuita. E delle condanne, che facessero in danari, debbano come loro parerà, riconoscer le fatiche, et il sviamento, che haveranno convenuto patire dalli particolari Negotij loro, i sudetti Priore e Compagni; sendo tuttavia in facolta d' ogn' uno di denonciar qualunque avesse contrafatto à cadauno delli sopradetti Capitoli, con certezza di dover esser tenuto secreto, e con beneficio di Ducati vinticinque delli beni di essi transgressori.

Quelli, che non essendo Matricolati voranno far stampar alcun Libro in questa città, per contrattarlo debbano per ogni balla di vinti risme l' una pagar otto grossi all' arte sopradetta, convenendo ella sostener molte spese, e la gravezza de' Galeotti ch' essi non sostengono.

Quei dell' Arte sudetta Matricolati, che stamperanno da nuovo alcun Libro in questa città, non più stampato in luogo alcuno, havuto che haveranno il Mandato di poterlo stampare, dandosi in nota à quelli della Banca predetta, quello che sarà stato il primo, s' intendi aver senza altro Privilegio, che altri, che lui non lo possi stampare in tutto il Dominio Nostro, ò stampato venderlo in esso per anni vinti all' hora prossimi.

Di quelli, che saranno stampati in Italia, e così di quà, come di là dà Monti, stampandosi però con la Licentia detta di sopra, habbino privilegio per Anni dieci.

E se alcuno di essi Matricolati vorrà stampare alcun Libro di molta stima, come più volte è accaduto, qual non sia per Anni vinti à dietro stato stampato, habbi Privilegio per esso di Anni dieci. E per quelli non stampati per Anni dieci à dietro, di Anni cinque, con questa espressa conditione, che se questi tali non daranno principio a stampar dette Opere nel termine di un Mese, dopo haversi dati in nota, continuando fino al fine à farne ogni giorno mezo foglio almeno, e mancando, salvo giusto impedimento da esser conosciuto da quelli della sudetta Banca, del che debbano far relatione alli Reformatori sudetti, si intendino decaduti dal Privilegio, nel quale subentri quello, che darà la denontia, ò non vi essendo denontiante, quello, che parerà alli Reformatori predetti.

E se nelli Libri per li quali si concede a Matricolati, come di sopra, il Privilegio, si troverà errori, s' intendi senza altro da esso decaduto quello che l' haverà ottenuto, et il simile s' intendi riuscendo le opere mal stampate, et impróntate, non ben legibili, e con cattive Carte, et Inchiostri, cose tutte prohibite, et detestate nelli sopradetti Capitolo.

E perchè è grandemente à proposito che la prohibitione di conceder Privilegij di Opere, che si stampano fuori, e non in questa Città, resti nel suo vigor, per evitar li dannosi pregiudicij che da simili concessioni possono succeder alle stampe di questa Città, sia aggionto; Che non si possano tali Privilegij de' Libri stampati fuori per modo alcuno conceder, se la Parte non sarà prima presa nel Collegio Nostro con li cinque Sesti delle Ballotte, e posta poi da tutti gli ordini di esso Collegio, e presa con li cinque Sesti del Senato da 180 in su; dovendo inanzi la ballottatione esser sempre letta la presente Parte, altrimenti la concessione sia di niun valore, et come se fatto non fosse.

Siano etiandio obligati tutti quelli che stamperanno alcun libro così in questa Città come fuori nello Stato Nostro, consignar il primo di cadauna sorte de Libri che stamparanno, legato in Bergamina alla Libraria Nostra di S. Marco, nè possano principiar a vender quel tal libro, se non haveranno una Fede del Bibliotecario di detta Libraria di haverlo consignato. Et la essecutione della presente Parte sia specialmente commessa alli Reformatori del Studio sopradetti per l' intiera et inviolabile sua essecutione.

1603. 21 *Gennaro. In Pregadi.*

XXI. Havendo gl' Eccellentissimi Signori Marc' Antonio Memo Procurator, Francesco Molin Cavalier, et Antonio Priuli Cavalier Procurator, Reformatori del Studio di Padova inteso dalla espositione degl' Intervenienti dell' Arte de Librari, et Stampatori Matricolati di questa Città esser essi in qualche dubio che la Parte dell' Eccellentissimo Senato di 11 Maggio prossimamente passato in materia di Stampe, in quanto viene per essa in varii modi concesso (per commodo, et beneficio dell' Arte) Privileggio ad essi Matricolati di stampar Libri, così nuovi, come già stampati, et in questa, et in altre Città, et luoghi del Serenissimo Dominio: et in quanto etiamdio si prohibisce di condur fuori di Venetia Instrumenti, et Materiali pertinenti all' esercitio delle Stampe, possi facilmente da quelli, che poco timorosi della Giustizia, per avidità del proprio commodo tentano alle volte ogni illecito guadagno, mentre non sappino di dover riceverne castigo, non esserne obbedita, stampando l' opere ad altri concesse in Privileggio: et così anche arrischiandosi di condur fuori delli Instrumenti, et Materiali predetti da Stampa. Considerata da loro Signorie Eccellentissime l' honestà della Dimanda, et che ad essi viene dall' Eccellentissimo Senato raccomandata la totale essecutione di essa Parte, la quale espressamente di esso Senato è, che da chi si sia non debba esser in alcuna parte disubbidita, et che li transgressori della loro temerità ne habbino à riportar quella pena, che conviene.

Per la presente Terminatione hanno deliberato, et fermamente statuito, che alli transgressori di cadauno delli Privilegij dalli Presidenti dell' Arte assignati à qualunque de' predetti Matricolati in cadauno delli casi in essa parte specificati, non possi esser data minor pena di quella, che ordinariamente si suole apponer in ogni Privileggio di stampa, dall' Eccellentissimo Senato, tanto stampando, o facendo stampar l' Opera privilegiata in questa Città, ò fuori, quanto altrove stampata vendendola, ò conducendola per alcuna maniera in questa, et in cadauna altra Città, Terra, ò luogo del Serenissimo Dominio (la qual è di Ducati trecento) da essere divisi un terzo all' Accusator, un terzo alla Casa dell' Arsenale, et un terzo al Reggimento, ò Magistrato, che farà la essecutione, oltre il perder l' opere stampate, le quali siano di quello al Privileggio del quale sarà stato contrafatto. Dovendosi à tal fine dare summariamente notitia dell' Arte predetta co 'l mezo de suoi Intervenienti à cadauno Rettor di Città et Terre ove siano Stampatori et Librari, delli Privileggij che come di sopra si andaranno da lei assignando à predetti Matricolati, affine che ne appari memoria in quelle Cancellerie. Et volendo il Privileggiato far intimar à Stampatori, et Librari, e registrar il suo Privileggio in alcuna di esse cancellerie, non gli possi esser tolto più di soldi quaranta per ciascuno.

Quanto veramente a quei che transgredissero in portar fuori di questa Città Instrumenti, ò Materiali pertinenti alla stampa, oltra tutte le altre pene maggiori, che parerà à loro Signorie Eccellentiss. di darli, s' intendano come robba di contrabando aver persi li Instrumenti, et Materiali predetti, mentre siano da qualsivoglia Officiale ritrovati, senza che di essi ne possi loro esser fatta gratia alcuna, ordinando cosi dover esser notato.

Marc' Antonio Memo Proc. Reformator
Francesco Molin Cav. Reformator
Antonio Priuli Cav. Proc. Reformator.

Adi 22 *Agosto* 1608.

XXII. De Mandato degl' Illustrissimi et Eccellentissimi Signori Reformatori del Studio di Padova, per esecution della Parte del Senato 11 Maggio 1603. Sia intimato a tutti li Stampatori et Librari di questa Città, che in termine di giorni otto dopo l' intimatione del presente Mandato, debbano haver dato in nota al Priore et Consiglieri dell' Università de Librari, et Stampatori tutte le Opere, che hanno stampato, ò fatto stampare di ragione di qualunque persona, che non sia Matricolata in detta Università, con il numero di Fogli, et la quantità che di esse Opere havessero stampate ò non fatte stampare, ò tutte, ò parte di esse, dopo la sudetta Parte; et questo per poter riscuotere gli otto Grossi per Balla, che sono stati concessi alla detta Università [nella] predetta Parte, sotto pena à quelli che mancheranno di dar in nota, ut supra, di pagar del suo li detti Grossi otto per Balla, et di più Ducati cinquanta, la mità de' quali sia del Denontiante, et il resto ad arbitrio di sue Signorie Illustrissime. Et dopo havuta notitia di quelli non Matricolati che haveranno fatto stampar, ut supra, li sia intimato per ordine di sue Signorie Illustrissime, che in termine di giorni quindeci debbano haver pagato in mano di esso Priore, et Consiglieri quanto per tal occasione andassero debitori, sotto pena, oltre il loro debito, di Ducati cinquanta applicati ad arbitrio di Sue Signorie Illustrissime; ancora sia intimato à tutti li Librari, et Stampatori ut supra, che debbano dar in nota al Priore, et Consiglieri sopradetti tutte quelle opere, che al presente stampano, ò che per l' avvenire stampassero, o facessero stampare ad istanza di persona non Matricolata, come è detto di sopra, le quali opere finite di stampare, siano obligati quelli che le haveranno stampate, o fatte stampar, à dar in nota al detto Priore, et Consiglieri il numero delle opere Stampate, ne possino quelle consignar quovismodo à quelli che le haveranno fatte stampar, se prima non haveranno fatto constar di haver sodiffatto essa Università, sotto pena alli sopradetti Librari et Stampatori di pagar del suo, et altre pene ad arbitrio di sue Signorie Illustrissime. Et quelli Matricolati, che havessero servito o nell' avvenire serviranno del Nome loro a persone non Matricolate, per contravenir alla parte sudetta, et non pagar li otto Grossi per Balla, caschino in pena di Ducati cinquanta, la mittà della qual sia del Denontiante da esser tenuto secreto, et l' altra mità ad Arbitrio di Sue Signorie Illustrissime. Et oltre di ciò siano, et s' intendino decaduti dalli Privileggij, che havessero conseguiti, ne possino dopo tal fraude conseguir Privileggio alcuno.

Marc' Antonio Memo Proc. Reformator
Antonio Priuli Cav. Proc. Reformator
Andrea Morosini Reformator

Paolo Ciera Secr.

1614. *Adi 13 Aprile.*

XXIII. Terminatione degl' Eccellentiss. Sign. Reformatori del Studio di Padova, in Materia delli Fogli; et Copie, che devono esser consignati all' Eccellentiss. D. Zuanne Sosomeno sopraintendente alle Stampe, e del Bollino, co 'l quale deve esser segnato ogni foglio.

Non possa Stampatore alcuno, e sia chi si esser si voglia, publicar un' Opera stampata, ò fatta stampare in questa Citta, cosi picciola, come grande, eccettuate però quelle, che si dicono in rosso e negro, come Messali, Breviarij, Diurni, e cose simili, se non haverà una Fede dall' Eccellentiss. D. Zuanne Sosomeno sopraintendente alle stampe, di haverli portato tutti li Fogli di detta Opera, segnati col Bollino di S. Marco, che di Ordine Nostro egli ha fatto consegnare a tutti li stampatori, o Capi di stamparia, per esser adoperato, come più distintamente da lui nelli suoi Capitoli è stato dato ad intendere al Prior, Compagni, et a tutta l' arte di essi Stampatori, e parimente non li sia lecito fare la sopradetta Pubblicatione, se non haverà ancor fede di havergli dato tutte le copie, e fattogli vedere, che sono ben corrette, e tutto questo sotto quelle maggior pene, che pareranno a Sue Signorie Eccellentissime.

1614. *Adi 29 Ottobre.*

XXIV. Vedendo gl' Illustrissimi, et Eccellentissimi Signori Reformatori del Studio di Padova infrascritti li disordini, et abusi, che contra le Leggi et il Publico Servitio delle Stampe vengono commessi da stampatori. Per la presente Terminatione, deliberano di approbare li sottoscritti Capitoli, che concernano le necessarie provisioni in questa Materia, et hanno insieme approbati li sottoscritti per correttori delle Stampe con salario, che sarà qui sotto dechiarito. Li quali saranno obligati à quanto è disposto dagl' Ordeni in questa materia, nella quale è rissoluta volontà di loro Signorie Illustrissime, et Eccellentissime, che la presente et tutte l' altre Deliberationi siano inviolabilmente esseguite sotto tutte le pene espresse, et che saranno anco nell' avvenire ad libitum.

Siano obligati di volta in volta li stampatori far legger le forme in Piombo con diligentia dalli Compositori, et farle ascoltar, ò dalli Protti, ò da altre persone sufficienti sotto pena di Ducati 25 per ogni volta, che tralasciassero di legger, ut supra in Piombo, li quali siano applicati all' Accusator, qual habbia ad esser tenuto secreto giusta la parte 1603. 11 Maggio.

Debbano li Stampatori, perchè comodamente si possi legger, e corregger il Foglio di ciascuna stampa, quello far tirar in Torcolo, acciò possino esser corretti li errori, che in esso si troveranno, nè altrimenti ardiscano in conto alcuno tirar il secondo foglio, se prima non saranno stati corretti detti errori, et acconciata la stampa conforme alla correttione del Correttore, sotto pena alli contrafattori di Ducati venticinque da essergli irremissibilmente tolti, et applicati all' Accusator da esser tenuto secreto giusto la Parte sudetta.

Che tutti li Stampatori, ò Librari Matricolati, che voranno stampare, far stampare alcuna opera, siano obligati di portar l' esemplare, del quale se haveranno a servire al sudetto Sopraintendente Nostro alle Stampe, qual diligentemente vedutolo, consideri se quel tal' Esemplare habbi bisogni di esser corretto, nel qual caso non possi esser altrimenti principiato à stamparsi, se diligentemente non sarà stato corretto da uno delli Correttori approvati, sotto pena della perdita delli Libri, che senza simil Licenza fossero usciti in Stampa, li quali cedano a beneficio del denonciante, che sarà tenuto secreto.

Siano obligati di volta in volta, secondo che si anderanno stampando li libri, quelli portare al Sopraintendente, perchè trovatili conforme alle Leggi disponenti in Materia di stampe, di loro licenza di poterli vender, ne possino in conto alcuno Librari ò Stampatori, che haveranno stampato, ò fatto stampar alcun Libro, quello vender, ò dar fuori senza aver prima ottenuta la detta Licenza, sotto pena di perder li Libri, et di altre pene ad arbitrio di loro Eccellenze.

Et per maggior osservanza di queste presenti deliberationi, e di tutte le altre, tanto dell' Eccellentissimo Senato quanto dell' Illustrissimi Signori Refformatori, disponenti in Materia di Stampe, siino tutte stampate in un foglio grande, et affisse in ciascuna Stamparia una Copia à vista di ogn' uno, sotto pena à gl' innobedienti di Ducati 25 da esser dati all' Accusatore.

E acciochè si venga più facilmente à notitia de Contrafatori, e disobbedienti, sii Deputato il Fedel Nostro Bartolomio Bertucci Nodaro dell' Avogaria, nelli Atti del quale si potranno dare tutte le Denoncie, e Querele in Materia di Contrafatione di stampe, quale poi doverà di tempo in tempo portare le dette Denoncie, e Querele à Sue Signorie Illustrissime, perche possino ministrar Giustitia conforme a quanto vien disposto in dette Leggi.

Omessi li nomi de Correttori.

Mercedi dei Correttori secondo la diversità de' Caratteri, per la Correttion di Copia, e Stampa.

Testin, e Nompariglia à Soldi 38 il Foglio.
Garamon, e Filososofia à Soldi 28 il Foglio.
Antico Commun, Lettura, Silvio, Testo d' Aldo Soldi 20 il Foglio.
Lettura in Carta Reale à Soldi 28 il Foglio.

D. Alvise Zorzi Refformator
D. Nicolò Segredo Proc. Refformator
D. Nicolò Contarini Refformator.

Valerio Antelmi Secr.

Adi 22 Luglio 1616.

XXV. Si è introdotto da certo tempo in quà nelle Stamperie di questa Città un' pessimo abuso, che molti Lavoranti, Compositori, Torcolari, et altre si fatte persone, che servono nelle botteghe de Stampatori, ricevendo Soldi anticipatamente da Patroni, per dover quelli scontare in tanti Lavori, dopo che hanno havuto quel Danaro, che bisognava loro, senza aver finito di scontarlo, si partono dalle Botteghe alle quali servivano, et vanno a lavorar altrove, con molto pregiudicio, et danno, tanto de Patroni, che prestarono loro il Danaro, quanto delle Opere cominciate, che per tal mancamento di persone, non si possono proseguire: al qual disordine, essendo necessario provedere, Li Eccellentissimi Signori Refformatori del Studio infrascritti, per la presente loro Terminatione hanno terminato, et terminando dichiarito, che de caetero nissun Lavorante, Compositore, ò Torcorolaro, ò altra persona, che serve nelle Botteghe de' Stampatori, che habbi havuto Danaro da' Patroni di quelle per scontare in tanti Lavori, non possa partir dalla Bottega di quel Patrone da chi havesse ricevuti li Danari, se prima non haverà scontato tutto il suo debito, ò restituito al Patrone il restante di quello li deve: Ne' possi questo tale Lavorante, ò altro, esser ricevuto in Bottega di Stampatore alcuno, se non farà, co[n]stare al Patrone, dove anderà à servire, che non và debitore di cosa alcuna al primo Patrone, sotto pena a' Lavoranti ut supra, che non ostante la presente Terminatione ardissero andar à Lavorar altrove, di Mesi sei di Prigione, et alli Patroni, che li ricevessero a servitij loro senza la sudetta conditione di pagar a' primi Patroni quel tanto loro restassero debitori, et di più vinticinque Ducati di pena, da esserli tolti irremissibilmente per tal contrafatione, quali vadino anco à beneficio del primo Patrone dal quale questi tali fossero partiti. Et la presente sarà Publicata à notitia di cadauno. Essendo oltre di ciò obbligato ciascun Patrone di Botteghà, ancor che non vadi creditore del Lavorante, non volendo più servirsi di lui, avisarglielo almeno otto giorni prima, et cosi all' incontro il Lavorante, non volendo più servire in quella Bottegha, darne notitio, ut supra, al Patrone, perchè anch' esso habbi tempo di provedere à gli interessi suoi.

D. Antonio Lando Proc. Refformator
D. Nicolò Contarini Refformator
D. Agustin Nani Cav. Proc. Refformator.
Gio: Francesco Marchesini, Secr.

MDCXXII. Adi xvii *Settembr.*

XXVI. [...iato, Terra. R° 92.]

Per Deliberatione di questo Conseglio viene espressamente prohibito in tutte le Città, Terre e Luogi del Stato Nostro dove sono stampe, di poter stampare, se prima oltre alla fede dell' Inquisitore di quella Città, non si habbia parimente quella del Secretario del medesimo Conseglio à questo deputato, et la licentia sottoscritta almeno da dui delli Refformatori dello Studio di Padoa col mandato dei Capi del Conseglio di X[ci]. Vedesi nondimeno non esser osservato il sopradetto ordine, il che riesce di Publico importante pregiudicio per le consequenze gravissime, ben note alla prudenza di questo Conseglio, et essendo necessario abbollire cosi dannosa introduttione;

L' anderà parte, che debbano li Rettori Nostri, dove si trovano stampe con Publico Proclama al presente immediate, et nell' avvenire ogni principio del loro Reggimento, strettamente prohibire per ordine del sudetto Conseglio à cadaun stampatore, et sia chi si voglia, che senza la Licenza sopradetta dei Refformatori dello Studio di Padoa, con la previa relatione del Segretario à questo deputato, et senza il Mandato de i Capi del Conseglio di X sopradetti, ardiva stampare, opera ò scrittura di qualsivoglia sorte, qualità, o continenza, eccetto però quei soli ordeni, che per il buon governo delle Città e Territorio fossero da i Rettori Nostri, per questo bisogno solamente date le Licenze, et havessero per la intelligenza di cadauno necessità della stampa, escludendo ogni altra qual si voglia opera picciola ò grande, scrittura, discorso et ogni altra sotto qual si voglia titolo, continenza, ò pretesto, niuna eccettuata; et sia prohibito alli Rettori Nostri di darne la permissione, ò licenza, che in ogni caso doverà esser nulla et di niun valor, et il stampator che la esercitasse sia, non ostante essa permissione o Licenza, sottoposto alle pene sottoscritte. Al Proclama sopradetto debbia esser con l' autorità del sudetto Conseglio aggiunto, che all' accusatore ò accusatori, che saranno tenuti secreti, saranno dati ducati cinquanta in contanti de i beni di quello, che senza la Licenza ricevuta con l' ordine di sopra dichiarito, havesse fatto stampare, et l' opere siano perdute, et confiscate, oltre à quelle altre pene pecuniarie, et anche personali, che parerà alla coscienza del giudice, di dare al trasgressore, o trasgressori secondo la qualità dell' opere, che fossero stampate, nelle quali pene incorrino anche quei stampatori che in questa Città ardissero stampare contravendo all' ordine sopradetto; et di esse non possa esser fatta gratia, dono ò compensatione, se non con Parte presa prima nel Collegio Nostro, et poi in questo Conseglio con le solite strettezze dei quattro quinti ridotto al numero di cento cinquanta almeno, et con la previa lettura della Sentenza, et informatione delli Refformatori dello Studio di Padoa sopradetti.

La essecutione della presente deliberatione sia commessa alli Rettori delle Città, et luoghi dove si trovavano le trasgressioni, et anco alli Avogadori di Commun con il solito rito, et autorità di quel Magistrato, et parimente alli Refformatori dello Studio di Padoa. Sia la presente stampata, et accompagnata con lettere scritte con l' Autorità di questo Conseglio alli Rettori delle Città, Terre et Luoghi dello Stato Nostro, dove sono stampe, con ordine la facciano immediate pubblicare ne i Luoghi soliti, intimare à tutti li stampatori, e libreri, registrare nelle Cancellerie à perpetua memoria, et republicare come di sopra ogni principio di Reggimento, acciocchè abbia in tutti i tempi, et in tutte le sue Parti la debita essecutione, come anche in questa Città per quello si aspetta alli stampatori, e libreri, che habitano in essa doverà esser fatta intimare à chi farà bisogno, mà pubblicata, et intimata, o non, debba aver sempre et in ogni caso di transgressione la sua forza et vigore. Nell' avvenire sia posta nelle Commissioni de i Rettori sopradetti, et non sia dal Segretario deputato alle Voci, sotto pena di privatione del carico, permessa la espeditione delle commissioni à i Rettori dove sono stampe, se non la vederà registrata in esse, per levare con questo mezo transgressione al presente ordine nostro, sotto pretesto, che non li sia pervenuto à notitia.

MDCXXII. 2d Dec.

XXVII. [Senato, Terra. R° 92.] L' Anderà Parte, che non derogando ad alcun altra deliberatione in tal proposito, non possa alcun stampatore nell' avvenire, ò chi si sia, che farà stampare opera alcuna in questa Città, quella dispensar, vender, o far vender, se non haverà particolar Licenza sottoscritta da doi almeno de i Refformatori del Studio, nella qual sia espresso, che sia stato consegnato un volume ligato di tal opera, per metter nella Libraria Nostra, sotto pena à chi contrafacesse di ducati cento applicati un terzo all' accusator da esser tenuto secreto, un terzo all' Arsenal Nostro, et l' altro terzo ad arbitrio dei Refformatori del Studio, à chi resti commessa l' essecutione, con autorità di altre maggiori, pene à delinquenti, che meritasse la trasgressione: Et perchè si possa assicurar dell' effetto della Consegnatione, et che siano riposti nel luogo destinato, debbano i librari, ò altri come di sopra, presentar il libro al Secretario de li Refformatori del Studio, il qual habbia carico di darlo in mano al Bibliotecario, con farsene far ricevuta in Libro à questo tenuto, et aggionger in sua presenza nota nell' Inventario di essa Libraria da nuovo Regolato. Di quelle opere, che si stamperanno in altre Città e Luoghi del stato, sia fatta medesimamente la consegnatione di un volume legato come di sopra, al Rettore ò Publico rappresentante, qual debba mandarli di Mese in Mese con sue Lettere dricciate à i Refformatori del Studio, perche siano posti nella Libraria, come è predetto. Et della presente Parte sia mandata copia et ordine per l' essecutioni a i Rettori predetti, et dove farà bisogno, et publicata et intimata come sarà ordinato da essi Refformatori.

MDCLIII. 24 *Settembre.*

La stampa che è stata ritrovata dall' accutezza dell' ingegno humano à commun beneficio, per li molti et singolari commodi che da essa ne derivano, meritamente da Nostri Maggiori è stata ricevuta sotto l' immediata protetione et direttione Publica, col favor della quale è stata sempre custodita, et regolata con quei prudenti decreti che sono stati stimati proprij, per conseguirne (come fu fatto) il desiderato fine; essendo arrivata in questa Città la stampa medesima à somma perfezione con publico decoro, et vantaggio de particolari; ma perchè non è cosa per ottima che sii, che dalla malitia degli uomini non venghi nel corso del tempo contaminata et guasta, si che col mezzo d' abusivi sconcerti, et di odiose introduttioni divenghi pessima, come si esperimenta à tempi correnti nell' istessa stampa, che ben spesso da alcuni vien deturpata, con carte caratteri et inchiostri non buoni, con molti errori per difetto di buona corretione; et quello, ch' è peggio da stamparie prohibite resta grandemente pregiudicata, per l' impressione clandestina di opere empie, obsene, malediche et pregiuditiali all' honor del Signor Dio, decoro de Prencipi et interesse de privati; et perciò chiamata la pietà et prudenza di questo Conseglio à quelle più celeri et risolute deliberationi, che siino proprie et valevoli per reprimer non solo l' arditezza di chi con mali modi attenti sovvertire cosi gran bene, et pregiudicar intieramente alla Pubblica dignità, e tranquillità; ma ritornar la stampa in questà Città à quella perfettione che era à tempi passati. Per redimer dunque cosi pretiosa gemma, accio risplendi maggiormente a gloria del Signor Dio, et di questa Città, prese da Rifformatori dello Studio di Padova tutte le informationi, et lumi necessarij, et veduti lucidamente li disordini in questo rilevante negotio;

L' Anderà Parte, che salve, et riservate tutte et cadauna deliberatione di questo conseglio et di quello di X^{ci} fatte in varii tempi in tal materia, anzi quelle confirmando, et rinovando in quanto farà di bisogno per la loro pontuale essecutione in quello non fossere contrarie alla presente; sia fermamente decretato et stabilito quanto segue.

I. Che in questa Città possa alcuno, sia di che ordine, grado, conditione, niuno eccettuato, che ardisca haver, ò tener si Casa propria, o d' altri Torcoli, o Caratteri da Stampare, nè meno imprimer e stampar libri, scritture, ò altra cosa, benchè minima, di che materia, qualità, professione, scienza, lingua, verso, prosa, proffana, spirituale, ecclesiastica, ò di qualunque altra sorte immaginabile, che non sii descritto nella Matricola dell' arte de Librari, conforme alli Capitoli dell' Università de Stampatori, et Librari, approvati, laudati, et confirmati dalli Proveditori di Commun in essecutione di Parte del Conseglio di X^{ci} 18 Gennaro 1548, sotto pena à trasgressori di Ducati mille et in caso che stampassero cosa alcuna di Ducati due mille et altre maggiori anco corporali ad arbitrio del Magistrato della Biastema, havuto riguardo all' eccesso della trasgressione, et qualità del trasgressore, per il qual effetto già tiene ampla autorità; potendo ogn' uno denontiar questi con Polizze anco secrete, quali non doveranno esser palesati, et provata la reità guadagnino la mità della pena, l' altra mità sia applicata alla

Casa dell' Arsenale, non potendo esser fatta gratia, nè remissione ad alcuno delli detti trasgressori, trovati colpevoli di tutta, ò parte di essa pena, se non da questo Conseglio con le Strettezze di $\frac{4}{5}$ ridotto al numero 180 in su.

II. Sij commesso al Priore della Banca di Librari, e Stampatori, di andar spesso vedendo, et osservando, come sij ben lavorato da Operaij, si nel metter insieme li caratteri, come nella buona carta, inchiostro, correttione specialmente, et ogn' altro particolare, acciò riescano le stampe belle, buone, corrette, et habbino tutte quelle degne qualità, che sono necessarie, et opportune, per ridurle quanto più sij possibile à quella primiera riputatione, che soleva esser nelli tempi andati in questa Città, e sij tenuto riferir pontualmente il tutto à i Rifformatori ogni mese, perche possano andar applicando con la loro prudenza alla qualità dei disordini, li rimedij, et le correttioni aggiustate; et mancando il Prior medesimo all' adempimento di tal obligo, sij in arbitrio de Rifformatori medesimi il punirlo, et siano incaricati di dar buoni ordeni, et stabilir regole proprie per quello spetta alla correttione delle stampe stesse.

III. Non possi alcuno delli antidetti Stampatori principiar a far compositione alcuna, nè meno mettere in Torcolo, e stampare qualunque sorte di libro, scrittura, ò altro, come di sopra, che non sij stato più stampato, se prima non haveranno effettivamente ottenuta la Fede ordinaria dell' Inquisitore, e con essa il mandato del segretario de Rifformatori sottoscritto almeno da doi di essi, giusta le Leggi; con il quale all' hora et non prima li resti concessa la Licenza di poter far la stampa d' esso libro, ò altro, et publicarlo, et questo sotto quelle pene alli Patroni, che meglio pareranno ad essi Rifformatori.

IV. Doveranno li Patroni delle stamparie matricolati tener registro in filza di tutte esse Licenze, acciò in ogni occorrenza si possi saper con certezza, se quanto è uscito da qualunque stamparia sij stato fatto, servatis servandis, in conformità delle Leggi.

V. Possino ancora ristampar senza altra Fede dell' Inquisitori li libri Stampati nelle Città dello Stato Nostro, perchè di gia saranno stati veduti, et licentiati dagl' Inquisitori; siano però riveduti giusta la leggi dal segretario, per ricever il solito mandato, et sottoscrittione de Rifformatori.

VI. Viene talvolta dato privileggio da questo Consiglio à qualche stampatore o Libraro di questa Città, e Stato, di poter solo stampar alcun libro; tuttavia viene ristampato in luochi esteri, e introdotto in questo Stato, et venduto publicamente, si che cede in fraude d' esso privilegio, et grave pregiudicio del privileggiato; però essendo ragionevole proveder all' indemnità d' essi stampatori, e Librari Nostri sudditi, sij espressamente dichiarato che questi tali libri siino del tutto banditi dal Nostro Stato, et se ne capitassero per via alcuna, non possi il Deputato sopra l' estratione delli Libri di Doana licentiarli, siche siano estratti dal luogo dove saranno ricapitati, nè il Segretario farli mandato alcuno di poterli vender, ma siino perduti, et confiscati, puniti in oltre quelli à quali saranno diretti pecuniariamente, come stimeranno li Rifformatori più adequato à i termini di Giustitia.

VII. Et perche il Segretario d' essi Rifformatori è ben spesso occupato in altri negotij Publici nel Collegio, et in questo Conseglio, onde non può così facilmente attender alla revisione de libri, che giornalmente si stampano di nuovo, o ristampano, doveranno li Rifformatori senza Publico aggravio, deputar tre, ò quattro soggetti qualificati, di virtù, prudenza, esperienza, et integrità de quali possano valersi nel riveder dette opere, et con l' attestato loro in scritto farsi da esso Segretario il solito mandato in forma, da esser sottoscritto dagli stessi Rifformatori, come di sopra.

VIII. Vengono anco commesse varie, et gravi fraudi nell' impressione de libri à pregiudicio del Publico servitio, et degli stessi Librari, poichè sono alcuni, che ardiscono stampare di nuovo, ò ristampare senza le dovute licenze in questa Città, et mentitamente fanno apparire, che siano stampati altrove, e come tali si vendono publicamente; Però inherendo alla Parte del Conseglio di X[ci] 12 Febraro 1542 sij fermamente decretato, che se per denontia, inquisitione, ò altro modo si venirà in cognitione di tali temerarij trasgressori, debba il Magistrato della Biastema contro essi proceder con ogni rigore, non solo con farli perder li Libri, ma anco con Galera, prigione, corda, bando, et altre pene corporali, et pecuniarie, come meglio stimerà espediente, per reprimere l'ardire di questi tali, et per esempio ad altri di non attentar simili fraudi, tanto detestate da tutte le leggi.

IX. Sia dato obligo à Stampatori di presentar al Magistrato de Rifformatori in termine di giorni 15 tutte le fedi, che cavaranno di tempo in tempo dall' Inquisitore per dare alle stampe alcun libro, li quali habbino da esser custodite et registrate dal Segretario; et se nel spatio di mesi quattro susseguenti alla data delle fedi medesime, lo stampatore, che le haverà ottenute non habbi principiata e progredita la stampa, possi ogn' altro stampator che vogli stampar quel libro, ricercar al Segretario copia autentica d' essa fede, quale haver debba lo stesso vigore che l'esemplare, et ciò per divertir le collusioni à pregiudicio de stampatori di questa Città, et a vantaggio de' Forastieri; et terminato l' anno dalla fede possa ogn' uno, che vogli ristampare il medesimo Libro, sodisfarsi à suo beneplacito previa però la permissione dei Rifformatori.

X. Et perchè sono alcuni così temerarij, che da stati esteri ardiscono furtivamente introdur in questa Città et stato Libri, et altre opere contro l' honor del Signor Dio, et Religione Cattolica, et contro li Prencipi, [il] che oltre lo scandalo et mal esempio, corrompe anco li buoni costumi con tante altre pessime consequenze ben note ad ogn' uno; però essendo necessario estirpar quanto più sia possibile questa così pernitiosa introdutione, sia preso, che non possa alcun Mercante, Negotiante, ò altro che sij, al qual saranno inviati Libri forastieri per Mare, ò per Terra con Corrieri, ò altro modo, in balle, botte, ò fagotti, aprirli, o estraherli senza la presenza del Deputato all' estratione de Libri Forastieri, come di presente si prattica in virtu di Decreto di questo Conseglio 2 Gennaro 1631, ma estratti che sijno, non possino esser venduti, se non haveranno fede del medesimo Deputato, ch' in essi non si ritrova cosa alcuna contro le Leggi, stante la qual fede il Segretario farà un mandato, che doverà esser sottoscritto almeno da doi Refformatori, in virtù di che potranno pubblicarli et venderli; et se alcuno d' essi Mercanti, Negotianti, Librari, ò altri Patroni d' essi Libri trasgredirà in tutto, ò in parte questo preciso ordine et forma, che si deve inviolabilmente osservare da cadauno, le doveranno esser tolti, et confiscati li Libri, et puniti dagli stessi Rifformatori di quelle pene pecuniarie, che stimeranno necessarie et opportune, per contener ogn' uno nella dovuta obbedienza delle Leggi, affine, che non sijno introdotti Libri cattivi in questa Città, detestati da Dio et dal Mondo tutto.

XI. Doverà il Prior dell' Arte invigilar, come nel 3° Capitolo se le dà obligo, per l' intiero adempimento di tutte et cadauna delle cose premesse; et haverà particolar cura di far che dalli stampatori siano date doi copie di ogni Libro che stamperanno, uno per la Libraria Publica di questa Città, l' altro per quella di Padova, sotto le pene agl' innobbedienti, che pareranno à Refformatori.

XII. All' Osservanza degl' ordini, et regole sopradette, con le pene contro li Trasgressori in esse contenute, doveranno esser soggetti proportionabilmente anco li stampatori delle Città dello stato nostro, seben in quelle non fosse Compagnia, ò Scuola alcuna dell' arte de Librari, et Stampatori; et doveranno li Rettori d' esse città far di nuovo publicar la Parte di questo Conseglio de 17 Settembre 1622 presa in tal Materia, qual s' intendi in tutto, et per tutto confirmata et rinovata, et doverà esser ristampata nel fine delle presenti. Dovendo passar di concerto con detti Rifformatori in quelli emergenti, che alla giornata succedessero, per ricever quelle buone instrutioni, che fossero necessarie, et opportune per la buona direttione di Materia cosi importante.

XIII. Et perche si dolgono li Librari di esser aggravati da Ministri della Doana da Mar con pagamenti arbitrarij; sia preso, che tutte le Balle de Libri, per ogni Lire ducento di peso alla grossa, debbano esser stimate ducati 16 come si prattica alla Doana da Terra, acciò con questo uniforme pagamento restino sollevati da ogni molestia.

XIV. L' Essecutione puntuale della presente doverà esser raccomandata respettivamente per decoro, et servitio Publico alla vigilanza dei detti Rifformatori, et del Magistrato della Biastema, et nelle Città suddite alli Rettori di esse; sperando questo Conseglio, che con la virtù, et zelo loro siano per ridur questo negotio della stampa à quel buon fine, per il quale è stata ritrovata et ricevuta sotto la immediata protettione della Repubblica Nostra.

Et sia la presente Publicata, et Stampata a chiara intelligenza di cadauno.

PIETRO VIANOLI Seg[rio].

1655. *Adì 4 Febraro.*

XXIX. Intendendo gl' Illustrissimi, et Eccellentissimi Signori Refformatori dello Studio di Padova, che vengano da stampatori, cosi in questa Città, come in Terra Ferma, dato indifferentemente alle Stampe Libri et altro senza la loro necessaria permissione, contravenendosi espressamente al tenore delle Leggi in questo proposito, et a quella in particolare 17 Settembre 1622 rinovata l' anno 1653 à 24 Settembre, terminano però Sue Eccellenze, et fanno publicamente saper a tutti i stampatori sopradetti, che non debbano ardir di dare alle Stampe alcuna cosa senza la Licenza sopradetta; eccetto, che quei soli Ordini, che per il buon governo delle Città, e Territorij fossero da Rettori in Terra Ferma per questo bisogno solamente date le Licenze, et avessero per intelligenza di cadauno necessità della Stampa; et in questa Città, eccetto parimenti, le Parti, Ordini, Proclami, et altro, che fosse terminato da Consegli, e Magistrati per Publico servitio; escludendo ogn' altra qual si voglia Opera, piccola, o grande, Scrittura, Discorso, et ogn' altra sotto qual si voglia Titolo, Continenza; ò pretesto (parole istesse della sopradetto Parte 1622) che si publicano, perchè tanto più apparisca la risoluta volontà de detti Eccellentiss. Refformatori, et sia puntualmente eseguita da ogn' uno, sotto tutte le pene espresse nella medesima Parte de Ducti 50, perdita delle opere, et altre maggiori pecuniarie e personali, che pareranno convenirsi a Transgressori.

Sia parimenti commesso à tutti li detti Stampatori, di dover nel termine di Mese uno prossimo presentar due Copie d' ogni Libro, da loro dato alle Stampe nei passati tempi, et non fosse stato ancora da loro presentato, una nella Libraria pubblica di questa Città, et l' altra in quella di Padova, in conformità di quello, che dispongono le Leggi in questa Materia, della qual Consegna debbano quelli, che han la cura, et assistenza delle dette Librarie far capitar al magistrato Nostro Fede autentica de i Libri che li saranno stati presentati, per poterne far il riscontro con l' inquisitione molto diligente, che si anderà facendo, et con Note, che si conservano d' ordinario nel Magistrato.

Et per le Stampe, che si faranno in avvenire, siano similmente obligati li detti Stampatori a presentar sempre, et di tempo in tempo le dette due Copie nelle dette due Librarie, quelle di questa Città et di Padova nel termine di quindeci giorni, et quelli delle altre Città nel termine di un Mese doppo fattasi la Stampa; di che debbano pure li assistenti haver obligo di mandar le Fedi sopradette al Magistrato a capo ogni tre Mesi per lo stesso necessario rincontro.

Quelli Stampatori che mancassero in tutto, ò in parte d' essequire l' ordine presente, e le pontuali Consegne sopradette, incorrino per i Libri già stampati, in pena de Ducati 100, et per quelli che si stamperanno in Ducati 25 tutti applicati all' Accademia de Nobili, et in quelle maggiori ad arbitrio, per farsene immediate le più rigorose essecutioni alle Case, Botteghe, et contro le persone, nelle quali pene s' intenderanno essere incorsi sempre, che non imprimeranno in ogni stampa, e nello stesso Libro, così la Licenza di detti Eccellentissimi Refformatori, come quella del Padre Inquisitor Generale, perche sempre possa conoscersi, se quel Libro sarà stato stampato con la dovuta permissione, et così debba essequirsi.

Adì 23 *Decembre* 1671.

XXX. Conoscendo la prudenza degl' Eccellentissimi Signori Refformatori dello Studio di Padova, che i gravi pregiudicij, che hora rissente in questa Città l' arte della Stampa tanto necessaria e stimata, procedono principalmente dall' inosservanza di tanti Leggi saviamente stabilite per farla fiorire ad universale beneficio; diminuito per tale trasgressione considerabilmente il numero de' Torchi con notabile detrimento; e volendo l' Eccellenze loro procurar in ogni modo, che con l' osservation puntuale delle Leggi medesime si rimetta l' arte stessa nel suo stato primiero, hanno terminato, che dovendo restar nel loro intiero vigore tutte le Parti, e Terminationi in questo proposito, che haveranno ad esser da cadauno inviolabilmente essequite, siano registrate in stampa in un foglio specialmente gl' infrascritti particolari, compresi per la maggior parte nei sopradetti Decreti, e Terminationi per notitia di cadaun Stampatore, che doverà puntualmente osservarli, tale essendo la ferma risoluta volontà dell' Eccellenze loro, sotto le pene, che saranno qui sotto dichiarite, e mandate irremissibilmente ad essecutione contro cadaun Trasgressore.

Deputano in primo luogo, ed approvano li sottoscritti Correttori, i quali doveranno osservar tutti gl' ordini statuiti in questa materia, e riveder con diligenza tutti i libri di qualunque sorte che li saranno portati per stampare, ò ristampare, correggendoli, ed espurgandoli da qual si sia errore, con le Mercedi qui sotto registrate.

Tutti li Stampatori ò Librari matricolati, che vorranno stampare, ò far stampare alcun' opera, tanto nuova, quanto altre volte stampata, doppo riveduta dal Padre Inquisitore, e dal Segretario conforme il solito, ed ottenute le debite Licenze, siano obligati di portar l' esemplare, del quale haveranno a servirsi ad uno dei Correttori approvati, affinche sia da esso diligentemente corretti, ed espurgato come sopra.

Siano obligati di volta in volta far legger le forme in Piombo con diligenza dalli Compositori, e farle ascoltar ò dalli Proti, ò da altre persone sufficienti, perche la prima correttione sia fatta in detto incontro sù la forma, e poi non stampato con le mani, mà tirato in Torcolo il foglio, far quelle veder al Correttore, dal quale debbano esser corretti gl' errori, che vi trovasse; e s' habbi poi à tirar il secondo, per ben assicurarsi, che siano Stati cancellati et aggiustati.

Debbano quelli, che faranno stampar servirsi di Maestri di stampe conosciuti per sufficienti dalli Deputati dell' Arte, e così parimente di belli, e perfetti Caratteri, et inchiostri, in modo, che li libri non solo siano ben corretti, mà ben improntati, e netti.

Siano tenuti servirsi di buona, bella, e perfetta Carta, la quale sia di peso proportionato alla qualità de' Libri, che haveranno à stampare, e non scompissi in modo alcuno giusta la parte dell' Eccellentissimo Senato 3 Giungo 1573, e sotto tutte le pene in essa dichiarite.

Non possa da qual si sia Stampatore principiarsi la stampa d' alcuna sorte di Libro, se prima non haverà la licenza dei sopradetti Eccellentissimi Refformatori sottoscritta da due almeno, e se non lo haverà dato in nota al Prior dell' Arte.

Et ad oggetto di levar le occasioni à qualunque fraude scandalosa, che potesse esser commessa, non possa doppo stampato con le debite Licenze qual si sia Libro, nessuno eccettuato, nel quale doveranno restar sempre impresse la revisione del Correttore col di lui Nome, e la Licenza degli Eccellentiss. Refformatori, esser venduto se prima non sarà stato nuovamente revisto dal Segretario dell' Eccellenze loro, e suo Vicegerente, à fine, che possa egli osservar esattamente se doppo la Licenza di Stamparlo sarà stata fatta alcuna qual si sia imaginabile alteratione, e se non haveranno doppo presentate le due Copie legate in Bergamina per le Librarie Publiche di Venetia, e di Padova, conseguita una nuova Licenza sottoscritta da due Refformatori almeno, di poterlo Publicar e Vendere.

Sia tenuto il Prior de' Librari e Stampatori, che sarà di tempo in tempo, andar spesso vedendo, ed osservando come sia ben lavorato dagl' Operarij, così nel metter insieme i caratteri, come nel metter in opera buoni Caratteri, Inchiostro e Carta perfetta, e farsi buone Correttioni, e rifferir tutto puntualmente à sopradetti Eccellentissimi Refformatori ogni mese, perchè possano andar applicando ai disordini quei rimedi, e quei castighi, che stimeranno per propria prudenza.

Li Privileggi di stamparsi Libri fuori di questa Città non possano concedersi se non nella maniera che dispone il Decreto dell' Eccellentissimo Senato 11 Maggio 1603, cioè se la Parte non sarà prima presa nell' Eccellentissimo Collegio con li cinque sesti e poi posta per tutti gl' Ordini di esso, e presa pur con li cinque sesti dell' Eccellentiss. Senato da 180 in su, con precedente Lettura d' essa Parte 1603.

Ogn' anno il Prior de' Stampatori sopradetto sia tenuto a presentar al Segretario degl' Eccellentiss. Refformatori sopracennati, Nota distinta di tutti quelli che hanno permissione di stampare, et il luogo ove tengono le stamperie; affinche possa vedersi quelli che mancassero, ò di nuovo fossero nella Professione introdotti.

Caderà qual si sia Trasgressore di alcuno degl' ordini sopradetti in pena di Ducati vinticinque per ogni cosa, e per ogni volta, et in quelle altre maggiori, che à misura della Trasgressione pareranno alla prudenza degl' Eccellentissimi Refformatori predetti, da quali saranno mandate irremissibilmente ad esecutione.

Sia la presente Terminatione stampata, et intimata à cadaun Stampatore, e Libraro, con ordine ad ogn' uno d' essi di tenerla sempre affissa nelle loro stamparie, e librarie affinchè non possa da alcuno esserne pretesa ignoranza.

Ommessi li nomi de Correttori.

Mercedi dei Correttori secondo la diversità de' Caratteri, per la corretion di Copia e Stampa—

Per Correttion di Copia Testin, e Nompariglia il foglio .	Soldi 12
Per Correttion di stampa detta il foglio	Soldi 20

Per Correttion di Copia Garamon, e Filosofia il foglio . Soldi 8
Per Correttion di stampa detta il foglio . . . . . Soldi 12
Per Correttion di copia Antico Commun, Lettura il foglio Soldi 8
Per Correttion di stampa detta il foglio . . . . . Soldi 12
Per Correttion di Copia di Silvio, et Testo d' Aldo il foglio Soldi 6
Per Correttion di stampa detto il foglio . . . . . Soldi 8
Per Correttion di Rossi, e Negri per Copia, e Stampa in ragion di Ducati Quaranta all' anno per Torcolo.

Andrea Contarini, Cav. Proc. Refformator
Nicolò Sagredo Cav. Proc. Refformator
Pietro Basadonna Cav. Proc. Refformator.
Angelo Nicolosi Segr.

1680. 24 *Settembre.*

In Ordine à moltiplici rissoluti Decreti, e particolarmente del 1603, 11 Maggio, sono tenuti così li Stampatori e Librari di questa Città, come quelli di tutte l' altre Città del Serenissimo dominio à presentare nella Pubblica Libraria un' Essemplare legato in Bergamina d' ogn' uno de' Libri, che stampano, prima di Publicarli et esponerli in vendita. Mà perche s' è osservato non esser stata prestata intiera puntuale essecutione à Decreti medesimi, ha voluto l' Eccellentissimo Senato sotto li 12 del corrente Settembre incaricar Noi Refformatori dello Studio di Padova ad invigilare con proprie Ordinationi, perche in ciò resti esattamente adempita la Publica volontà, sotto le pene, che più da noi saranno credute aggiustate, obligando particolarmente li Stampatori, e li Librari à supplire al difetto in che fossero incorsi da vinti anni in quà.

Quindi è però, che con la presente nostra Terminatione, che sarà stampata, publicata, et intimata al Prior de Librari in questa Città, perche convocato il Capitolo la publichi ad intelligenza di cadauno dell' Arte e la registri nella sua Mariegola, come pur sarà trasmessa all' effetto stesso nell' altre Città di Terra Ferma, obblighiamo tutti li Librari, e Stampatori di questa dominante ad haver presentato per tutto il venturo mese di Novembre nella Publica Libraria un' Esemplare ligato in Bergamina d' ogni Libro, che havessero stampato, ò fatto stampare da vinti anni in quà, e che havessero omesso di presentarlo, sotto pena non lo essequendo dentro detto termine, della Confiscatione di tutti li Libri, de quali non fosse stato presentato l' Originale, e di quelle altre corporali, ò pecuniarie, che saranno stimate dal Magistrato Nostro convenienti, e che si manderanno summariamente ad esecutione rispetto alla qualità del Trasgresso.

E per l' avvenire siano strettamente tenuti sotto le pene precitate à non publicare, ne meno esponer in vendita qual si sia Libro di nuova stampa, se non haveranno una Licenza sotto scritta da due di Noi Refformatori, la qual Licenza doverà esser formata dal Segretario Nostro col fondamento d' una fede del Custode della Libraria medesima, da cui apparisca, che sia stata fatta la Consegna nella Publica Libraria dell' Esemplare legato in Bergamina come sopra.

Li Stampatori, e Librari di Terra Ferma doveranno supplire al debito, così del passato, come dell' avvenire del modo stesso, con le conditioni medesime, e sotto le pene di sopra dichiarite, consignando gl' Esemplari de Libri nelle mani de Rettori della Città, dove fossero stampati; il zelo de' quali viene da Noi vivamente eccitato à trasmetterli di quà di tempo in tempo al Bibliotecario, onde la mente dell' Eccellentissimo Senato resti pienamente incontrata.

Ne possa per questi di fuori, il Segretario Nostro formar la Licenza di publicarli, ò venderli, se non vi sarà l' avviso delli Rettori, che sia seguita la consegna in conformità etc.

Alvise Priuli Proc. Refformator
Nicolò Venier, Proc. Refformator
Silvestro Valier, Cav. Proc. Refformator.
Gio. Battista Nicolosi Segr.

1697. 9 *Marzo.*

XXXII. Trovandosi contro il tenore delle Leggi neglette intieramente da Librari delle Città suddite, le consegne delle Copie d' ogni impressione, et in gran parte delle Opere più principali defettive questa della Dominante, et essendo con Decreto dell' Eccellentissimo Senato 4 Novembre 1694 con l' oggetto di togliere tale essentialissimo disordine, eccitato il zelo degl' Eccellentissimi Signori Refformatori dello Studio di Padova, li proprii concerti con l' Eccellentissimo Bibliotecario di stringere in consonanza del Decreto 12 Settembre 1680, con quelle maniere, et cominationi di pene, che crederanno opportune, gli uni et gli altri à supplire al diffetto, et all' obligo, che le corre, hanno loro Eccellenze con la presente Termination stabilito, et ordinato, che non possi da Librari medesimi essere venduto alcun Libro, che uscira dalle Stampe, senza precedente fede d' haver consignato il Libro stesso nelle Biblioteche di questa Città et di Padova, sottoscritta dall' Eccellentissimo Bibliotecario destinato alla sopraintendenza della medesima qui in Venetia, et dal Co. Girolimi Frigimelica in quella di Padova, sotto pena della Confiscatione de Libri, che fossero stati stampati et di quelle, che pareranno all' Eccellenze loro, et che saranno irremissibilmente praticate contro Trasgressori, et della presente si data Copia al Custode della Pubblica Biblioteca, et al Priore di questa Città. Et sia pure mandata a Rettori della Terra ferma, perchè sia intimata à Librari della loro Giurisdizione per la sua pontuale inviolabile essecutione.

Ferigo Marcello Proc. Refformator
Ascanio Giustinian 2 Cav. Refformator
Francesco Cornaro Proc. Refformator.
Agostino Gadaldini Segr.

DOCUMENTS.

II.

Analysis of Monopolies, Patents, and Copyrights, 1469–1596.

Year.	Applicants.	Works named.	Average Length of Copyright.	
1469	1	Indefinite	5 years	
1486	1	1	Perpetuity	
1492	8	9	$8\frac{1}{7}$ years	Raphael Regius applied twice; once for a copyright, and once for the confirmation of the same. Francesco de Ravenna's copyright duration is not specified.
1493	7	10	10 years	Alessandro Calcedonio applied twice.
1494	17	38	$9\frac{2}{17}$ years	
1495	7	11	$9\frac{1}{2}$ years	Daniele Barbaro received a confirmation of copyright in his brother Hermolao's *Castigationes*.
1496	20	47	10 years	Including Aldus' monopoly of all Greek books, not yet published, which he shall publish, and Giorgio di Monferrato's copyright of unspecified duration.
1497	14	52	$10\frac{5}{14}$ years	
1498	16	64	$11\frac{3}{5}$ years	Including Ottaviano de Petrucci's monopoly for all *canto figurato*; and Vlastos' patent for his particular type; and Democrito Terracina's monopoly for all books printed in Arabic and Moorish; and Gabriel Brasichellensis' confirmation of privilege. Aldus' privilege incomplete.
1499	7	34	$9\frac{3}{7}$ years	Including Andrea Corbo's patent for his peculiar type. Confirmation of Giovanni Moretto's privilege. Marco Firmano's privilege, undefined length.
1500	10	32	$9\frac{9}{10}$ years	
1501	11	29	10 years	Including Aldus' patent for his *carattere cancellaresche*. Steffano detto Vosonio, neither time, penalty, nor works specified.
1502	10	31	$9\frac{1}{8}$ years	Including Aldus' patent for his *lettere greche et cancellaresche latinè*.
1503	9	37	$10\frac{5}{9}$ years	Francesco Bonhomini's copyright, time undefined. Alessandro Calcedonio's petition against infringement of his by subsequent copyrights.
1504	8	24	$10\frac{3}{8}$ years	
1505	6	16	13 years	
1506	8	17	10 years	Paulo da Canal's copyright was granted for the whole of his life (take it at 30 years).

1507	5	25	10 years	Includes Lucantonio's petition to Chiefs of the Ten for an *imprimatur*.
1508	6	19	11 years	Includes Gregorio de Gregoriis' petition to Chiefs of the Ten for an *imprimatur*.
1509	7	18	7$\frac{5}{7}$ years	Includes Leonardo Crasso's extension of copyright in the *Hypnerotomachia*, and Pietro Cirneo's petition to Chiefs of the Ten for an *imprimatur*.
1510	3	8	4$\frac{1}{2}$ years	Wars of League of Cambrai.
1511	1	9	10 years	Wars of League of Cambrai.
1512	4	14	13$\frac{1}{4}$ years	Includes copyright to Bernardino da Venezia from the Senate for Andrea Mocenigo's *Pantadapon*.
1513	3	3	20 years	Includes Jacomo Ungaro's patent for his musical type.
1514	5	9	9 years	Includes Ottaviano Petrucci's petition for prolongation of copyright.
1515	10	19	14$\frac{1}{5}$ years	Includes the permission to Sanuto to examine State papers, and Lodovico Ariosto's copyright for life (50 years).
1516	7	16	14$\frac{1}{8}$ years	Includes Lazzaro de Soardi's petitions for *imprimaturs* from Chiefs of the Ten, and Ugo da Carpi's perpetual monopoly for his new method of *chiaro oscuro*.
1517	4	7	7$\frac{3}{7}$ years	Includes Camillo Leone's petition to the Senate for the continuance of his copyright in spite of the law abolishing all copyrights.
1518	2	3	10 years	Includes Andrea Mocenigo's petition for an *imprimatur* from the Chiefs of the Ten.
1519	3	4	10 years	
1520	2	6	12$\frac{1}{4}$ years	
1521	6	6	10$\frac{1}{6}$ years	
1522	1	1	10 years	
1523	7	12	10 years	Includes Marc' Antonio da Bologna's patent for his new system of printing music. Copyright refused to Sigismondo Macasola for Socinus, *Opere*.
1524	8	49	11$\frac{5}{8}$ years	
1525	3	3	10 years	
1526	7	11	10 years	Includes Cola Bruno's petition for a rectification of his copyright.
1527	3	8	10 years	
1528	9	15	10 years	Includes confirmation of copyright to Lodovico Ariosto for his corrected edition of *Orlando Furioso*. Francesco Bonafede's copyright duration not specified (taken as ten years).

Year.	Applicants.	Works named.	Average Length of Copyright.	
1529	4	4	10 years	
1530	7	16	$13\frac{5}{7}$ years	Nicolo Liburnio's copyright duration undefined (taken as ten years).
1531	15	22	10 years	
1532	4	5	$10\frac{4}{5}$ years	
1533	21	52	10 years	In many cases it is impossible to count the number of works specified, as the formulas *prout supplicavit*, *quantum petiit*, &c., are used, and the *filze* containing the *Supplicationes*, where the works would be found, do not exist before 1543.
1534	6	12	$13\frac{1}{3}$ years	
1535	12	16	$10\frac{1}{11}$ years	Includes a confirmation of copyright to Alexandro Velutello.
1536	15	37	$11\frac{1}{3}$ years	
1537	12	15	$9\frac{2}{11}$ years	
1538	18	21	10 years	
1539	6	6	10 years	
1540	18	21	$11\frac{1}{11}$ years	Includes Troiano di Nano's perpetual patent for his new method of printing music.
1541	11	16	10 years	
1542	23	65	$10\frac{10}{17}$ years	
1543	16	30	10 years	
1544	33	82	$10\frac{10}{11}$ years	
1545	34	54	$9\frac{5}{17}$ years	Includes Roccho Bonicello's patent for his new method of printing.
1546	12	59	$13\frac{1}{4}$ years	
1547	28	63	$10\frac{1}{14}$ years	
1548	25	48	$11\frac{3}{5}$ years	
1549	25	88	$12\frac{3}{5}$ years	
1550	36	100	$10\frac{13}{18}$ years	
1551	31	72	$10\frac{7}{11}$ years	Includes Roccho Bonicello's patent for his printing frames; Vicenzo Valgrisi's *imprimatur* from the Senate; and a prolongation of Andrea Spinelli's copyright for four months.
1552	22	26	$12\frac{1}{11}$ years	But in this year many of the works specified were named in the original *suppliche* only, and these are not to be found in the *filze*.
1553	13	35	$14\frac{4}{13}$ years	Includes Marco Guazzo's prolongation of copyright for one year.
1554	24	52	$14\frac{1}{3}$ years	
1555	14	45	$17\frac{1}{7}$ years	

1556	29	67	10 years	
1557	24	75	10 years	
1558	26	69	$10\frac{1}{13}$ years	
1559	15	24	$12\frac{2}{3}$ years	
1560	30	67	$13\frac{1}{6}$ years	
1561	42	117	$13\frac{11}{21}$ years	
1562	25	66	$15\frac{1}{5}$ years	
1563	26	54	17 years	Includes the copyright refused to Francesco Sansovino for Alvise Pasqualigo's *Lettere Amorose*.
1564	24	39	$14\frac{1}{4}$ years	
1565	29	41	$16\frac{15}{29}$ years	
1566	23	57	$15\frac{10}{23}$ years	Includes Cardinal Borromeo's petition that the Senate should forbid the publication of the *Concilio Provinciale di Milano*.
1567	33	53	$18\frac{2}{11}$ years	Includes copyright to Titian for his *Paradiso* engraved on copper.
1568	41	92	$17\frac{11}{41}$ years	Includes Andrea Brugone's patent for his invention for printing.
1569	32	67	20 years	
1570	38	75	$18\frac{7}{19}$ years	
1571	30	45	$17\frac{1}{2}$ years	Prohibition of printing by Jews.
1572	34	59	$17\frac{11}{34}$ years	
1573	13	17	$10\frac{1}{13}$ years	
1574	41	79	$12\frac{1}{2}$ years	
1575	26	52	$14\frac{3}{13}$ years	
1576	23	33	$18\frac{15}{23}$ years	
1577				
1578	7	11	$17\frac{1}{7}$ years	Plague.
1579	8	16	$13\frac{1}{2}$ years	Plague.
1580				
1581				
1582	21	34	$17\frac{6}{7}$ years	
1583	22	52	$19\frac{6}{11}$ years	Including order to print Audebert's poem.
1584	26	39	$15\frac{6}{13}$ years	Including confirmation of Hieronymo da Udine's copyright.
1585	10	17	$16\frac{1}{2}$ years	
1586	32	62	$19\frac{11}{16}$ years	
1587	16	29	20 years	
1588	7	12	$18\frac{4}{7}$ years	
1589	27	57	$19\frac{2}{27}$ years	Includes rectification of Piero Gonzalez' copyright.
1590	20	39	$19\frac{1}{4}$ years	
1591	24	30	$21\frac{1}{6}$ years	Includes a patent to Marcello Scalino for his *caratteri cancellareschi*.

Year.	Applicants.	Works named.	Average Length of Copyright.	
1592	22	41	$22\frac{1}{11}$ years	
1593	18	31	20 years	
1594	13	19	$19\frac{7}{13}$ years	Including Giacomo Sostero's patent of citizenship.
1595	9	11	$19\frac{4}{9}$ years	
	24	53	$24\frac{7}{12}$ years	

DOCUMENTS.

III.

III.

MARIEGOLE DELLA SCUOLA DEI STAMPADORI E LIBRARII VENETI. 1548.

Capitoli dell' Università delli Stampatori, et Librari,
Approbati, laudati, et confermati dalli Clariss. Signori Proveditori di Comun.

In Essecutione della Parte Dell' Illustrissimo, et Eccelso Consiglio di X. sotto. XVIII. Genaro. M.DXLVIII.

IL Glorioso, et grande Iddio conceda gratia a noi Stampatori, et Librari che tenemo Botteghe et Case aperte in quest' alma Città, di poter fare et esseguir cose che siano per suo santo servitio, et a gloria et honor di questa Serenissima Repub. nel dar ordine et regola alle Cose dell' arte nostra, acciò che per l' avenire essa nostra Arte possa indrizar l' attioni sue a laude della Divina Maestà, et a beneficio comune, sotto la protettione della gloriosa Vergine Madre del Signor nostro Giesù Christo, et di questa felicissima et bene instituta Republica.

Capitolo Primo.

Sia creato prima un Collegio dell' arte nostra di Stampatori, et Librari che tengono Bottega, et vendono Libri li quali de presenti, siano obligati ritrovarsi tutti nella Chiesa di S. Giovanni et Paolo, luogo solito alle nostre congregationi, nella Capella del Sto. Rosario, et ivi far dire una messa del Spirito Santo da quelli Reverendi Padri all' altar della Vergine Maria nostra advocata, et protettrice, et alla Sagrestia di detti Reverendi Padri si debba dare una elemosina in detto giorno conveniente ad arbitrio delli presenti Presidenti, et in quel medesimo giorno, et Capella del Rosario, si habbia a far ridurre tutti quelli che sono del collegio de l' arte nostra, dove si habbia a far un Priore, dui Consiglieri, et sei di Zonta, nel modo che seguita, et ogni patrone di Stampa, et di bottega pagar debbia in detto giorno lire una e soldi quattro ogni anno per ciascuno, et al dir della detta messa siano sempre presenti il Priore, Conseglieri, et sei di Zonta, con il resto del collegio nostro. Et il Prior, Conseglieri, et sei di Zonta che de presenti saranno eletti habino a durar per tutto Febraro venturo. 1567.

Capitolo II.

Che ogni anno nella Festa di San Giovanni Evangelista siano eletti a bossoli et ballotte di tutto il corpo del Collegio dell' arte nostra de Stampatori, et Librari un Priore dui Conseglieri, et sei di Zonta delli piu atti et sufficienti al bisogno, et governo di questa Arte, et che non siano di menor età di anni XXX. I quali ellegger si debbano con l' ordine infrascritto, dovendo li sei di Zonta ridursi, et seder sempre con il Priore, et Conseglieri predetti.

Capitolo III.

Che ridutta che sarà l' Università, la qual s' intendi ridutta a numero perfetto quando saranno ridutti li doi terzi di tutto il numero de matricolati, li sindici nostri debbano dar giuramento a cadauno delli congregati di dover per sua conscientia eleggere, et voler li megliori, piu sufficienti, et utili alla nostra Università. Di poi sia in libertà di cadauno delli ridutti nominar uno secondo la sua conscientia, et tutti li nominati siano inbossolati, et uno per volta per sorte estratto, et ballottato. La qual ballottatione debba esser secretta per fino che tutti li nominati saranno stati ballottati, et poi si habbino ad aprir li bossoli et quelli che haveranno scosso piu ballotte dalli dui terzi in suso se intendano eletti, et rimasti. Li dui veramente che dalli dui terzi in suso haveranno piu ballotte sotto li predetti sei di Zonta s' intendano di rispetto, et intrar debbano in luogo di quelli che per qualche accidente non potessero ridursi. Li quali Priore, Conseglieri, et di Zonta entrar debbano nell' officio il primo di Marzo, et finire adi ultimo Febraro, et così di anno in anno.

Capitolo IIII.

Che nel medesimo modo et forma, siano eletti a bossoli et ballotte dui Sindici, li quali siano sempre assistenti, o almeno uno di essi, a tutte le ballottationi che si faranno nella nostra Università, et non si possa ballottare cosa alcuna senza la presentia di uno di loro et siano quelli che habbino a dar il giuramento al Priore, Conseglieri, et altri ministri nostri che saranno eletti, et a tutto il Capitolo della nostra università inanzi che si comincia a ballotare, et possino cosi separati come uniti sindicare nel nostro Capitulo tutte le operationi che a loro parerano fatte per alcuno di nostri officiali contra li nostri ordini. Et possino far convocar il Capitolo per placitar i loro Sindicati, et habbino quella auttorità che hanno li sindici delle Scuole Grandi.

Capitolo V.

Che quello che sara nominato per doversi ballottare ut supra, non possi farsi dispennar; ma il Priore, et Conseglieri siano obligati far che sia ballottato come gli altri, accioche non sia aperta la via che alcuno possa schifare le fatiche che li potessero toccare, et similmente dopo che alcuno sara rimasto, non possa refudare, sotto pena di pagar duc. X. diece.

Capitolo VI.

Che doppo l' elettione delli nostri Priore, Conseglieri, et sei di Zonta, ordinarij, et di rispetto, si debba con l' istesso modo per la nostra Università elegger un Scrivano, il quale habbia Carico et Officio di notare, et scrivere nel presente nostro Capitolare, tutte le Leggi, et ordini datti che per l' avvenir saranno fatti, et ordinati per li nostri Signori pertinenti alle Cose di stamparia et libraria, overo alla nostra università, et anchora tutte le cose che per il presente nostro Capitolare si dechiariranno. Et cosi tutti li ordini, et tutte le parti che si faranno per la nostra Università, et ancora tutte le cose che li saranno commesse dalli Ministri nostri, si come alla giornata et per varie occasione accaderà.

Capitolo VII.

Similmente dopo il Scrivanno, si elegga persona sufficiente ad esser nostro Bidello, con quel salario che parerà conveniente. L' officio del quale sia di convocare il Priore, Conseglieri, et Zonta, cosi ordinarij come de rispetto, et tutta la Università quando lì sarà commesso. La qual convocatione sia per lui fatta, ò personalmente, ò per poliza lasciata alla bottega, ò a casa, per la quale sia dechiarito il giorno, l' hora, et il luogo, ove si haveranno a ridurre, et debba rifferire al Scrivano la citatione di quelli che mancheranno di venire, et far che sia notata a fine di poter essequire li ordeni nostri contra quelli che chiamati non veniranno.

Che tutti li predetti officiali habbino contumacia de anno uno eccetto li dui di Zonta di rispetto, li quali possino esser ballottati l' anno sequente.

Capitolo VIII.

Che il nostro Priore sia deputato a tener conto della Cassa distinto, et regolato secondo si conviene, dechiarando particolarmente tutti li denari che entrano in cassa, et per qual causa, et similmente la dispensa, accio il dannaro della nostra Università sià conservato, et accresciuto. Et alla Cassa sopraditta siano poste tre serrature differenti, et delle tre Chiavi una sia datta al Priore, et le due altre alli dui Consiglieri.

Capitolo IX.

Che il Priore et Conseglieri per otto giorni avanti il suo finire dell' officio debbano render conto dell' administratione, et governo per loro fatta, *al Priore, et Conseglieri novi, et a quelli consegnar la Cassa con tutto il denaro che haveranno in essa, et con quello ancora che a lor si doveva pagare in tempo del loro officio,* restando i debitori alli quali haveranno essi fatto credenza per suo conto. Et debbano ancora consignare il capitolare et altre scritture che saranno della nostra Università. Delle quali consignationi ne sia fatta notta particolarmente sopra un libro a questo solamente deputato. La qual notta debba esser fatta per il nostro scrivano, sotto pena de ducati diece a cadauno di quelli per chi mancherà di fare esse consignationi. La metà della qual pena sia de luoghi pij secondo parerà alli Magnifici Signori Proveditori de Comune, et l' altra metà sia messa nella Cassa della nostra Università et il medesimo sia de tutte le pene, delle quali si fa mentione nel nostro Capitolare. Ma niuno della nostra Università che sarà debitore della nostra Cassa, per qualsivoglia causa possa entrare in Capitolo a ballottare, ne possa essere ancora ballottato ad alcun officio, finche non haverà pagato il suo debito, et siano obligati il Priore, et Conseglieri subsequenti, sotto debito di sagramento, astringere per justitia tali debitori a satisfar il loro debito.

Capitolo X.

Che ogni ballottatione che sarà fatta per la nostra Università se intendi presa quando passerà li dui terzi.

Capitolo XI.

Il nostro Priore, Conseglieri, et sei di Zonta, habbino carico et officio di comparire per nome dell' Università nostra avanti l' Illustrissimo Dominio, overo, avanti li Clarissimi nostri Signori, overo a qualunque magistrato, ove occorrerà per bisogno della nostra Università, et rispondere, et dar l' informationi in ogni occorrentia che li sarà dimandata o tutti in sieme, o la maggior parte di loro, et di essequire quanto per il nostro Capitolare, sarà commesso sopra di loro.

Capitolo XII.

Che quando il Priore overo alcun delli Conseglieri per qualche giusto impedimento non potesse intravenire in qualche attione per la nostra Università, debbia in luogo suo entrar uno delli aggionti ordinarij il piu vechio, et similmente quando mancherà alcuno delli aggionti ordinarij debba entrar uno de rispetto.

Capitolo XIII.

Che quando parerà al nostro Priore, Conseglieri, et sei di Zonta ordinarij trattare qualche cosa ardua, o di molta importantia, et per questo paresse a loro di haver insieme quelli di rispetto, possano per il nostro Bidello far intender alli predetti di rispetto, che si debbano ridurre, et unirsi con li ordinarij, et se recusassero, o, mancassero d' unirsi, et intervenire, caschino alla penna de ducati uno, salvo ogni giusto impedimento.

Capitolo XIIII.

Che in ogni caso di vacantia di Priore, Conseglieri, et di Zonta ordinarij, overo de rispetto, per morte over per altra causa, acciò la nostra università non sia derelitta del suo ordinario governo, si debba subito di ordine delli predetti ridurre la Università, et sia fatta elettione in luogo del vacante, secondo l' ordine et modo datto di sopra di una altra persona ut supra.

Capitolo XV.

Il nostro Priore, Conseglieri, et sei di Zonta siano obligati a ridursi tutti insieme per quel giorno, et hora che li sarà fatto intendere per il nostro Bidello di ordine della maggior parte, sotto pena di ducato uno, salvo ogni giusto impedimento.

Capitolo XVI.

Che cadauno della nostra Università quando sarà chiamato dal nostro Bidello secondo il modo sopra detto a doversi ridurre nel nostro Capitolo universale sia obligato venire sotto pena di grossi sie quando mancherà la prima volta, et di grossi dodese, quando mancherà la seconda, et la terza ducato uno, et sia privo la terza volta di ballottatione, per uno anno, salvo justo impedimento.

Capitolo XVII.

Quando il nostro Capitolo sara congregato, s' il nostro Priore, o alcuno delli Conseglieri proponerà, et parlerà, nissun' altro debba parlare, ne interrompere la sua proposta, ò il suo parlare, sotto pena de ducati dui, et nessuno della nostra Università ardisca di rispondere, o proponere cosa alcuna, se prima non haverà dimandato licentia, et mentre questo parlerà non sia da alcun' altro interrotto sotto pena di ducato uno à chi contrafarà, et così possa ogn' uno ordinatamente dire, et rispondere quello li parerà senza causare confusione com' è conveniente.

Capitolo XVIII.

Che ogn' uno dell' Università nostra sia chi si voglia sia tenuto portare rispetto et riverentia al nostro Priore, Conseglieri, et sei di Zonta in cadauno luogo, et non ardisca in modo alcuno in fatti, ne in parole ingiuriare, ne offendere la persona d' alcuno di detti ministri, sotto pena d' esser privo per anni dui di potter ballottare, ne haver officio alcuno, et pagare alla nostra Cassa ducati tre. Medesimamente essi ministri non ardiscano usar parole ingiuriose contra alcuno della nostra Università, così ridutto in Capitolo, come fuora, sotto pena d' esser privati d' officio, et di pagare ducati sei, et parimente ancora non ardisca alcuno altro della nostra Università, così ridotto in Capitolo come fuora ingiuriarsi in modo alcuno l' un l' altro, sotto pena di ducati sei.

Capitolo XIX.

Che nessun' altro possa proponere, ne metter parte nel Capitolo della nostra Università se non il Priore, et Conseglieri, et i Sindici ancora nelle cose pertinenti al loro officio.

Capitolo XX.

Niuno Matricolato nella nostra Università possa esser ballottato ne haver officio alcuno, se prima per anni cinque non haverà tenuto botega, overo in casa haverà venduto libri, overo haverà per anni cinque fatto stampar.

Et medesimamente tutti quelli matricolati che non eserciteranno la mercantia de libri, overo l' arte de stamparia non possino ballottare, ne haver officio alcuno.

Die 14 *Maij* 1567.

I Clarissimi. Messer. Francesco Donato. Messer Paolo Contarini. Messer Iacomo Marcello honorandi Proveditori di Comun iusta la parte presa nell' Illustrissimo Consiglio di X sotto di 18. Zenaro. 1548. per la qual, è commesso a loro officio, che per la regolatione dell' arte della Stampa et Libraria debbano dar quelli ordini che alle loro Signorie pareranno, veduta parimente l' instantia fattali per gli Illustrissimi Signori Capi di detto Consiglio, sotto di 29. Novembrio. 1566. passato, circa il dover far essequire essa deliberatione, et havuta sopra di ciò matura, et diligente consideratione, Vedute le instantie fatte alli Presidenti dell' arte sotto di 23 April passato, et uditili sopra i ricordi per loro presentati nec non, uditi similmente alcuni altri d' essi Librari, sue Signorie Clarissime per l' auttorità à loro concessa dalla prefatta parte, terminantes, hanno commesso, che li sopradetti ordeni per loro Magnificentie statuiti per il bon governo, et regimento di essa arte, siano inviolabilmente dalli Stampatori, et Librari osservati, sotto le pene in essi dechiariti, et sic ann. et cetera.

Francesco Donado Proveditor di Comun
Paolo Contarini Proveditor di Comun
Iacomo Marcello Proveditor di Comun
Ioannes Pulverinus Notarius Officij mandato.

DOCUMENTS.

IV.

IV.

MINUTE BOOK OF THE GUILD OF PRINTERS AND BOOKSELLERS.

1571 *a di Primo Aprile in Capitolo.*

No. 1. SSENDO redutto il nostro General Capitolo de Librari et Stampadori per elleger cinque homini dell' arte nostra per haver autorità di poter comparer ad ogni tribunal et officio per nome della Università dell' arte nostra et spender per giornata a beneficio universal di comun pubblico di questa arte. Et così andarà parte se questa tal deliberatione habbi haver effetto, et detti elletti possino spender sino ducati vinticinque per il presente, et che servino gratis et amore.

Il magnifico	Hier° Scotto	Priore
	Gabriel Giulitto Zuane de Varisco	Consiglieri.
	Zuane Griffo Pietro d' Affine	Sindici.
	Gasparo Bindoni	Scrivan.
	Di sì 33.	
	Di nò 18.	

1571 *a di secondo Settembre.*

No. 2. Considerando Io Hier° Scotto alli travagli dell' arte nostra per le tiranidi che li vengono usate però sicome parvegia al Capitolo nostro di creare cinque deputadi al beneficio et libertà di Essa arte così in conformità di tal deliberatione è paruto opportuno et necessario a me come Priore di mandar la presente parte, cioè

Che li predetti cinque deputadi come di sopra habbino autorità di provedere et spendere quanto farà bisogno per diffendere l' arte nostra in quanto loro parerà bisognevole et opportuno in mantenerla libera da ogni tiranide, opprenzione, inganno, usurpamento et d' ogni altra fraude che li venesse fatta da qualunque persona sia chi esser si voglia.

Et possano li predetti nostri deputadi spender nelle opportunità suddette si delli scossi che avanzassero dal presente armar, come metter una et più tanse, giusta la forma della tassatione già fatta, et quelle scuoder con ogni portuno rimedio, essendo però obbligati loro deputati tener particulare, giusto et reale conto delle dette spese.

Io Hier[mo] Scotto manu propria.

Io Zuane Guarisco come Consigliero affermo, esser passata ditta parte con conditione di spender fino a duc. cinquanta per liberatione di detta arte.

Io Giovanni Griffo affermo quanto di sopra.

Io Damian Zenaro affermo quanto di sopra.

Io Zuane Bariletto affermo quanto di sopra.

Io Lodov[co] Avanzo affermo a quanto è sopra.

Io Zuan' Antonio Bindoni affermo a quanto è sopra.

Et io Pietro da fino affermo quanto di sopra.

A di 2 Sett[e] 1571.

Fo balotado la sop[a] ditta parte et il Caplo. fu redutto al numero di sesanta sei, cioe, 66. et hebbe balotte de sì n° 45 et de nò n° 21.

Io Andrea Muschio Scrivano di detta Università.

Die 20 Augusti 1572.

No. 3. Li Clar[mi] Mr Domenego Corner et Mr Ant[o] Justinian hoñ Prov[i] di Comũ visto il tenor et continentia della oltrascritta Parte et le cose in quella contenute, per autorità del Off[o] suo Ter[ma] quella laudano approbano rattificano et confirmano come sta e jace, et sic annotari juss[t].

Sabba Mauroceno Not[s] Off[i] M[to].

Adi 27 April 1572.

No. 4. Fu gia fatto sotto il Priorato del Mag[co] Sr Jer[mo] Scotto mio precessore honõr, una buona et Santa deliberatione, che anco nel nostro General Capt[o] fu di commune consentimento presa, cioè che per le emergenti occasioni potessero li cinque deputadi al beneficio dell' arte nostra spender cinquanta ducati per diffender in giudicio essa nostra arte dalle tirannidi usurpationi et fraude da chi vie oppressa. Et perche le lite per tal causa incomminiciate sono indecise, anchor che ridotte alla speditione, et pare che più per mancamento de danari che per altra causa, essi nostri deputati siano ritardati da non poter far spedir tali cause.

Però seguendo il prudente ricordo di esso Mag[co] mio precessore è paruto a me Franc[o] rampazetto Prior di quest' anno 1572 mandar parte in esso nostro Caplo. che si possa al presente scuoder una meza tansa secondo l' ordine, et più successivamente quando bisognerà per poter dar fine alle suddette liti et altri opportuni remedij, per beneficio et libertà di essa nostra arte. Tenendose però appartato et fidel conto dei spesi. Però l' anderà parte.

Fu mesa la parte presente Adi 27 April 1572 nel Caplo. nostro de librari et Stampadori dove erano congregati de matricolati n° 54. fu presa de si ballotte n° 48 de no n° 4 et due quali non volsero ballottar, quai furono Mʳ Hier° Toresano et Mʳ Andrea Muschio; et il detto Caplo. era congregato in Sᵗᵒ Giovanni et Paulo nel loco di Genovesi.

Io Franc° Rampazetto Prior.
Io Vicenzo Valgrisio Consiglier affermer esser così.
Io Dominico Guerra Consiglier affermo ut supra.
Io Sigismondo Bordogna compagno alla banca affermo ut supra.
Io Julio Tamburino compagno alla banca affermo ut supra.
Io Bernardino Mazorino compagno alla Banca affermo ut supra.
Io Franc° di Fracᶦ compagno alla Banca affermo ut supra.
Io Dominico Nicolini Sindico affermo esser passada detta parte come di supra.

BORT° RUBINO Scrivan.

Die 20 *Augusti* 1573.

No. 5. Li Clarᵐᶦ Mʳ Domenego Corner et Mʳ Ant° Justiniano Honorᶦ Provᶦ de Comun visto el tenor et continentia della oltrascritta parte et le cose in quella contenute. Per auttorità dell' Offᵒ suo, Terᵉˢ quella laudano approbano ratificano et confirmano come sta e jace, et sic annotari jusserunt, ita Ref. Massario Officii.

SABBA MAUROCENO Not° Offᶦ Mᵗᵒ.

1572. *A di* 27 *April.*

No. 6. Considerando Io Franc° Rampazetto Prior di quest' anno 1572 quanta importanza sia questa nostra arte della stampa, la quale fabrica gli strumenti a tutte le scienze et all' oncontro vedendosi per poco ordine, quanti et quanti suscitano di continuo in essa arte, i quali grossamente credendo che l' esercitio della stamparia sia cosa di poca intelligentia, si fanno lecito entrar al maneggio di essa per poca cognitione et manco esperienza che ne habbiano. La qual temerità si vede anco nelli librari, il qual inconveniente oltre al gravissimo danno et vergogna a questa Inclyta citta di Venetia, partorisse ruina, precipitio et infamia ad essa arte nostra. Però è paruto a me opportuno rimedio a tanti mali mandar questa Parte:

Che per l' avenire alcuno che non sia matricolato non possa levar stamparia ne libraria di novo, ne impedirsi nell' arte nostra de librari et Stampatori in modo alcuno se prima non sarà stato garzone nella Città di Venetia per anni cinque scritto alla Justitia Vecchia, et doppo habbia servito per lavorante in questa Città anni tre continui et esaminati da periti eletti dal Prior et Banca nostra et conosciuto idoneo a tal esercitio, sia admesso et pagar debba per esser matricolato ducati cinque. Similmente che i forestieri che verranno per farsi maestri debbano prima lavorar nelle Botteghe nostre lavorante almeno anni cinque continui; et havuta fede di haver servito il detto tempo, et esaminati come di sopra, pagar debbano ducati dieci per ciascuno per esser matricolato. I quali denari siano messi a beneficio dell' Università nostra, Eccetuando però i figliuoli o heredi de matricolati esercitanti l' arte, i quali debbano esser accettati senza pagamento alcuno. Et se alcuno contrafarà alli nostri sopradetti ordini, così in metter stamparia come nel vender libri o carta stampata con lettere in qualunque modo, caschino in pena di pagar ducati cinquanta tante volte contrafaranno: La qual pena sia divisa in tre parti: una delle quali sia distribuita come più piacerà alli Clar^{mi} Sig^{i} Proveditori di Comun: l' altra alla casa dell' Arsenal: et l' ultima terza parte al beneficio dell' arte nostra.

1572 adi 27 April.

In Capitolo generale congregato in San Giovanni et Paulo, nel luogo de Genovesi al n° de 54, fu presa l' oltra scritta Parte a bossoli et ballotte con n° de si 51 de no n° 3.

Die 5 mensis Maii 1572.

No. 7. Li Clar^{mi} Mr Piero Bon, Mr Lod^{co} Memo et Mr Lorenzo di Priuli Honorandi P^{ri} di Comun, visto il tenor et continentia della oltra scritta parte, et aldito Mr Jer^{mo} toresan dimandante la revocation di quella in contraditorio juditio con il Prior et conseglieri dicenti petita minime fieri debere imo detta Parte dover esser laudata et confermata, onde sue Sig^{rie} omnibus bene intellectis terminantes hanno laudato approbato et ratificato detta Parte come sta et giace et sic annotari jusserunt.

Die 12 Augusti 1572.

Referi Annibal de Ventura comandador haver publicato il soprascritto ordine a San Marco et Rialto di ordine di S^{ri} P^{ri} di Comun.

SABBA MAUROCENO Not^{s} Off^{i} Ex^{ris}.

MDLXXIIII. *Di Primo April.*

No. 8. An order from the Presidents of the Collegio della Militia da Mar, addressed generally to all the Gastaldi of the various Guilds in Venice.

The tax levied for support of the Militia da Mar has been spent on lawsuits and other objects.

When the Presidents of the College call for it it is not forthcoming.

For the future the money accruing from the tax is to be deposited in a box with three keys; one key to be kept by the Gastaldo and the others by the two senior members of the Guild.

Every three months an account of the money in this box is to be presented at the office of the College. The penalty for disobedience is six months' imprisonment and a fine of fifty ducats; half of which is to go to the accuser, whose name shall be kept secret, and half to the Hospital of the Convict Prison at Sant' Antonio. This order is to be entered in the Mariegole of each Guild.

ZORZI PISAN } Presidenti.
MARCO CICOGNA }

The above order is followed by another, in date 23 June, 1581, confirming its predecessor and enjoining on the "Gastaldi et Compagni delle Arte di questa Citta che dobbiate eseguir ad unguem la Termination soprascritta."

No. 9. Terminatione delli Cl[mi] Sig. Prov[ri] di Comun contra li Governatori di Scole, cioè i Gastaldi et Sindici.

Die xxij *Novembris* 1581.

Seben è stato in diversi tempi fatte molte provisioni circa le regolationi delle scuole di questa Città sottoposte all' Officio nostro, et massime circa l' administratione di esse scuole, che li Guardiani over Governatori di quelle dovessero nel termine di giorni 15 doppo finito il suo officio, haver consignato al suo successore tutti li beni et danari di esse scuole, et similiter che li sindici di quelle, nel termine di giorni 30 doppoi finito essi Guardiani, Governatori over Gastaldi veder li suoi conti et administrationi loro, a fine che 'l danaro di esse scuole non fossero malmenato, sotto le pene come in esse deliberationi è dichiarito. Non dimeno chiaramente si vede che li beni di esse scuole da molti non vengono governati si come è l' intentione di esse leggi, ne li Sindici curano di veder l' administrationi di quelli che governano esse scuole, a tal che del continuo si vede molte male administrationi fatte da essi Governatori di esse scuole, con danno delli poveri et esterminio di esse scuole, et havendosi visto nelli giorni passati diverse male administrationi, et con tanti inconfusi, ne reso l' administratione per alcun di essi Guardiani di esse scuole in tempo debito al suo successor, ne etiam li Sindici curatosi di far la sua sindicatione in tempo debito, et precipue nella Confraternità de Librari et Stampatori, cosa in vero da non esser tollerada, per beneficio et augumento di esse scuole, imo inherendo alle deliberationi già fatte le quali restar debbino ferme et valide in cadaune sue parti, aggiongendo a quelle per la presente terminatione, Li Clar[mi] Mr Lazaro Moro Mr Bartolomeo Donado et Mr Zaccaria di Priuli honorandi Proveditori de Comun per l' autorità a loro concessa in virtu delle Leggi, Terminando Terminano che de cetero tutti li Guardiani, Governadori, Priori, Gastaldi et sia di che altro titolo esser si voglia, che haveranno la cura et maneggio dell' administratione et beni di esse scuole, nel termine de giorni quindici doppo compito il suo officio, debbano haver consignato al suo Successor, over Successori tutti li beni et danari et ogni altra cosa di ragione di essa scola, et il libro della sua administratione, con le partide dichiarite con millesimo, mese et giorno, et dichiarito in esse partide a chi haveranno pagato o esborsato danaro et per qual causa a fine che si possi veder la verità di tal administratione, et non tenir li conti confusi, si come si vede in molte di esse scuole ciò esser stà fatto; et similiter il successor di essi Guardiani debbi, immediate fattali la consignatione nel tempo sopradetto dal Guardiano che haverà finito, notar sopra del suo libro nel modo come di sopra è detto, tutto quello gli sarà consignato; et similmente li Sindici di esse scuole debbino, nel termine di Mese uno prossimo doppoi finito che haveranno li Governatori di esse scuole, veder l' administratione et poner la sua sindicatione in scrittura se essa administratione starà bene over se essa scola sarà creditrice, et lui Guardiano non haverà satisfatto a quanto era debitor; et trovando debito venir debbano nell' Officio di SS. Clar[me] a fine che sia astretti essi ministri et Governatori di esse scole a dover pagar quanto andarano debitori, sotto pena ad essi Gastaldi, Guardiani overo Governatori che non eseguiranno quanto di sopra si contiene, di pagar ducati cento applicati all' Arsenale, et di star mesi doi in prigion serrati, della qual non possi uscir se non haveranno satisfatto la pena sopradetta; et similiter se intendi esser incorsi alla pena sopradetta li sindici di esse scole et Guardiani ch' intraranno di tempo in tempo, e che non eseguiranno la presente deliberatione, come stà et iace, dechiarando che li sindici di esse scole, et cadauno di loro, habbino libertà et autorità circa li intachi et male administrationi di esse scole senza altra autorità del suo Capitolo et non ostante altri ordini in contrario, di poter comparere davanti SS. Clar^me^ et far convenir li debitori a far tutto quello facesse bisogno per far che esse scole siano satisfatte da quelli che andassero debitori, come è detto, per intachi o male administrationi; et sic annotari mandaverunt et la presente sii registrata in tutte le Mariegole delle Scole si di devotion come d' Arti.

Die 4 Septembris 1586.

No. 10. Chapters three and ten of the Mariegole amended.

Whereas a quorum of the University could only be formed by two-thirds of all the members, and every vote required a majority of two-thirds of those present before it could pass,

For the future half of all the members of the University shall form a quorum, and A vote may pass by a bare majority of those present.

Di sì 44.
Di nò 20.

Gli Eccell^mi SS^ri Ess^ri contra la Biastema Infras^ti.

No. 11 Tutto che le Leggi che prohibiscono il stampare o altrove stampata vendere cosa alcuna in questa città senza licentia, siano benissimo note per la loro frequentata publicatione et per altro, cosi che non può esser addotta iscusa d' ignoranza, hanno voluto non di meno quanto hanno commesso in voce a voi Prior del Collegio de Stampatori di questa città sotto quelle pene che riservano ad arbitrio di questo magistrato, specificarvi anco con il presente mandato, così a voi come a successori vostri, che con ogni diligentia debbiate doi volte all' anno almeno, in tempi che vi pareranno più opportuni avertire, o da altri deputati vostri far avertire l'osservanza di esse Leggi a tutti dell' Università vostra de Stampatori, cosi a Principali et Maestri come a lavoranti et garzoni, perche SS. Ecc^me^ vorrebbono pure che s' astenessero senza il castigo che li sarà dato irremissibilmente, dalle contrafationi, le quali succedono per il più da vendere senza licenza Historie et cose simili per le piazze, che sono o apparono stampate fuori di questa Città, perche cosi eseguiate faccendo registrar et conservar il presente per memoria de posteri vostri Priori del detto Collegio da quali doverà similmente esser esseguita.

Data nell' off^o contra la Biastema predetto. A 19 Novembre 1596.

Paulo Dandolo.
Franc^o Morosini.
Petro Lando.
Victor Barbarus Duc^s Not^s et Offi^ci con Blasph^ia coad^r.

A di 16 *Luglio* 1598 *in Venetia.*

No. 12. Redutta la Banca in casa del Mag^co Prior al numero di undici, et fu messa la sottoscritta Parte con balle nº dieci, et una di nò.

Ritrovandosi nella nostra Arte un grandissimo inconveniente per vendersi Libri nelli giorni festivi, che dà fomento et fà lecito a quelli che non sono di essa Arte matricolati goder li frutti di essa senza concorrer alli gravami et spese di essa, oltra che si fanno lecito contra le Leggi divine et humane vender Libri prohibiti et altro, che non stà bene, contra Dio, et vergogna di essa Arte,

L' anderà Parte che de cætero per vietar questo tanto scandalo niuno Libraro o Stampatore ne altri sia che si voglia, possa metter fuori ne vender Libri di niuna sorte in tempo di festa quando si serrano le Botteghe per la Città, sotto pena di perdere tutti li Libri che li saranno tolti inviolabilmente, da esser dati mezi alli Officiali et li altri mezi al Magistrato che farà l' esecutione; la qual Parte sia anco approbata dal Capitolo nostro Generale.

Riservandosi facoltà al Prior et Banca di poter conceder licenza a qualche povero matricolato dell' Arte nostra.

A di 25 *Agosto* 1598.

No. 13. Nel nostro Capitolo Generale Redutti al Nº 41 fu ballottata la sopradetta Parte con ballotte

Nº 29 de sì et
Nº 12 de nò } et così fu presa.

A di 26 *Agosto* 1598.

The rule approved by the Proveditori di Comun.

Die 6 *Maii* 1604.

No. 14. In support of the preceding order, the Proveditori di Comun empower any member of the University to seize or to cause to be seized all books printed or sold by those who are not matriculated in the University. The Proveditori also grant power to the University to seal up shops, presses, and type of those who are not matriculated; and to forbid their use under penalty of twenty-five ducats, to be applied to the building of the new prison.

Further, the University may seize all books sold on Festivals, whether by members of the University or by others; half of the books seized shall belong to the executing officer, the other half shall be deposited in the office of the Proveditori.

Antonio Malipiero.
Zuan Francesco Bragadin.
Francesco Donado.

Die prima Februarii 1611.

No. 15. A recapitulation of the preceding order.

PIERO EMO, Prov^r de Comun.
PIERO CAPELLO, Prov^r de Comun.

Coppia tratta dal Summario delle Leggi dell' Officio della Giustitia Vecchia publicato l'anno 1565.

No. 16. Item sotto il portego di Rialto della Drapparia non sia lecito ad alcuno di tenir in tal zorni salvo che santi et Libri de Epistole et Evangelii et lezende de Santi, Offitii, Bibie et simil opere devote et non Libri immondi, comedie et altra sorte che siano profani, et cosi altra sorte de Robba non s' habbi da vender sotto il detto portego.

Per la Marzaria veramente se possi tenir Santi et Carte de disegni et depente de cose divote et honeste et non cose dishoneste et vergognose, et cosi sotto il portego di San Marco.

1613 *a di* 18 *Luglio.*

No. 17. An appeal to the Proveditori di Comun made by Alessandro di Vecchi and others against the order of the Proveditori passed at the instance of the Prior and Council of the University, in date 26th August 1598.

The Proveditori uphold their order.

Die 14 *Augusti* 1613.

In Exc^mo Cons^o de xl^ta Ci. No.

Alessandro di Vecchi and others appeal to the Quarantia Civile Nuova.

His advocate moves that the order made by the Proveditori di Comun in date 26th August 1598 be quashed.

The court divided: "fuerunt omnes non sincere N° 27."

Die 19 *dicti.*

Case again before the Court:

"Fuerunt omnes non sincere N° 25."

Die 20 *dicti.*

Counsel addressed the Court on both sides. The court divided.

"Quod incidantur" N° 10.
"Quod sint bone" N° 15.
"Non sincere" N° 1.
"Et sic laudatæ remanserunt."

A di 26 *April* 1614.

No. 18. An order by the Proveditori del Collegio della Militia da Mar.

Seeing that the Gastaldi and Capi of the various guilds convoke their chapters and levy the galley money without the knowledge of the Collegio della Militia da Mar, it frequently happens that they levy more than is required for the public service, and apply the money to other purposes than that for which it was raised.

The Proveditori order that for the future no Gastaldo or Capo may summons his chapter to treat of the tax for the galley money and the mint deposit until he has obtained permission from this office, and stated the amount of the tax he proposes to levy; and within three days after the meeting of the chapter, the tax-gatherers who may have been elected shall appear at this office with their tax lists to be seen and approved.

A di 23 *Decembre* 1626.

No. 19. Comparsero avanti li Ill[mi] SS. Marc' Antonio Minoto, Nicolo Balbi et Domenego Moro, Hon. Proveditori di Commun li infrascritti della Banca dell' Università de Librari et Stampatori di questa città et come Rappresentanti di quella cioè Marco Ginami, consigliero, Aurelio Righettini, Marco Guarisco, Giovanni Salis, Giovanni Antonio Guiliani, di Zonta, Giovanni Gueriglio, Roberto Meglietti Sindici et Iseppo Imberti, Scrivano, et presentorono una scrittura del tenor infrascritto.

Illustriss. SS. Proveditori di Commun.

Poco importa che siano posti buoni ordini per la regolatione et conservatione d'un Arte, quando poi non siano rettamente intesi e giustamente eseguiti; Però havendo avertito noi Rappresentanti della Banca de' Librari e Stampatori alcuni disordini molto importanti che nascono per non essere i Capitoli della nostra Università osservati, come si conviene, il che succede per esser sinistramente interpretati, compariamo avanti VV. SS. Ill[me] a dargliene conto, e supplicandole che con loro autorità si degnino di porvi rimedio.

Nel capitolo primo di detta nostra Università vien disposto, che ogni patrone di stampa e di Bottega pagar debba ogni anno lire una soldi quattro per ciascuno, il qual pagamento communamente si dice la Luminaria, nondimeno molti si trovano scritti nella nostra Matricola, i quali vanno in resto, et non intendano di pagare, sotto pretesto o di essere stati fuori della Città, o di non haver per qualche tempo esercitato l' Arte, il che riesce a pregiuditio dell' Università nostra; Però riverentemente instiamo che circa il predetto primo Capitolo sia per VV. SS. Illustrissime dichiarato e terminato,

Che tutti li Matricolati siano tenuti a pagare la detta Luminaria per tutto quel tempo che il nome loro starà descritto nella Matricola; Et quelli che lascieranno d' esercitar l' Arte, così stando nella Città come andando fuori, e che tornassero a ripigliar il loro negotio di vender o stampar libri, debbano, nel termine di mese uno doppo ritornati, pagar intieramente tutto quello che andassero debitori per il tempo scorso fino all' hora; altramente non possano continuar a vender o stampar libri. Dovendo però il Prior fargli intimar per il nostro Bidello quanto sarà il suo debito, et astringerlo al pagamento. Sia però in libertà di quelli che volessero partire o lasciar d' esercitar l' Arte, di far dipennar il nome loro dalla Matricola, nel qual caso dal dì della dipennatione in dietro, non siano tenuti a pagar detta luminaria, e nondimeno ritornando essi o loro heredi possano di novo esser matricolati, pagando la Ben' intrada di ducati cinque et eseguendo gli altri ordini dell' Università nostra.

Nel capitolo secondo di detta nostra Università è ordinato che ogni anno nella Festa di San Giovanni Evangelista siano eletti a bossoli e ballotte un Prior doi Consiglieri e sei di Zonta et altri carichi, delli più atti e sufficienti al bisogno et governo dell' Arte; nondimeno alcune volte succede che la detta elettione non si faccia ogni anno, et quelli che si trovano ne' detti carichi non si curando, forse per qualche loro indebito fine, che sia fatto in loco loro, continuano anco il secondo ed il terzo a loro beneplacito, et vi sono di quelli che hanno continuato fino sei anni. Oltra di ciò faccendosi tal elettione nella Festa di S. Giovanni Evangelista, quando i giorni sono freddissimi e brevissimi, et non potendo finirsi le ballottationi se non a molte hore di notte, vi sono molti che o non possono per esser vecchi d' età, o non vogliono per fuggir il patimento, e qualche pericolo ancora di mal incontro nel ritornar a casa, ridursi al Capitolo. Di più se bene il Capitolo dice che siano eletti delli più atti e sufficienti, nondimeno non vi è regola ne distintion alcuna, e dalle cose predette risultano molti inconvenienti. Però riverentamente si insta che circa questo Capitolo sia da Vostre SS. Illustrissime dichiarato et terminato,

Che l' elettione predetta di Priore, Consiglieri, sei di Zonta et altri carichi, debba necessariamente esser fatta d' anno in anno, si che finito l' anno s' intenda anco finita l' auttorità loro, ne possano sotto qual si voglia pretesto continuar nel carico, se non fosse per qualche causa importante con Decreto di questo Illustris. Magistrato.

Che il Priore, il quale attualmente si troverà, sia tenuto di convocar e ridurre al tempo debito il Capitolo Generale, per far l' elettione de' Carichi predetti, et non potendo il Priore per giusti impedimenti far la detta ridutione sia tenuto a darne conto a Consiglieri, i quali debbano in tal caso haver carico di ridur il Capitolo per tal effetto.

Che non possa esser ballottato alcuno per Priore, il quale non sia stato almeno una volta di Banca.

Et che per più commodo commune, debba per l' avenire farsi detta elettione in una delle santissime Feste della Pentecoste, dovendosi in detto giorno far dir messa, pagar la Luminaria, et osservar tutto quel di più che per i Capitoli della nostra Università è disposto; Et il Priore, consiglieri, sei di Zonta et altri che saranno eletti habbiano ad entrar nel carico il primo giorno di Luglio prossimo susseguente, et finire l' ultimo di Giugno dell' anno venturo, et così d' anno in anno successivamente.

Ma perchè la prima elettione secondo l' ordine sopradetto haverà da farsi solamente alle Pentecoste dell' anno venturo 1627, e la nova elettione per la forma del detto Cap. 2do doverà farsi al presente S. Giovanni, oltra esser scorsi anni doi che non è stata pagata la luminaria; perciò sarà parte della prudenza di VV. SS. Illme terminar quello che a loro parerà più espediente che sia fatto per governo dell' arte nostra, fino al tempo predetto della nuova elettione.

Per il Capitolo quarto si elleggono due Sindici con gli obblighi et autorità come in esso, et particolaramente di sindicare tutte le operationi che fossero fatte contra gli ordini dell' Arte nostra, et per esser quello carico molta importante, et che ricerca persone pratiche et sufficienti, Però stimiamo bene et riverentamente instiamo, che per VV. SS. Illustriss. circa questo capo sia dichiarato et terminato,

Che non possa alcuno esser ballottato per Sindico, il quale non sia stato almeno una volta di Banca.

Item, che detti Sindici, i quali debbano haver cura dell' oservanza de gli ordeni dell' Arte, habbiano obbligo nelle proposte che saranno fatte nelle riduttioni dell' Università d' opponersi et contradire a tutte quelle cose che quovismodo fossero contra la forma de' Capitoli nostri o in qual si voglia maniera pregiuditiali all' Arte nostra.

Per il 20 Capitolo della nostra Matricola essendo disposto che nissun matricolato possa esser ballottato, nè haver offitio alcuno, se prima per anni cinque non haverà tenuto Bottega, o venduto libri in casa, o fatto Stamparia. Molte volte è nata difficultà se gli Figliuoli et heredi di Matricolati doppo la morte de loro auttori, sendo accettati in Scola senza pagamento, siano sottoposti a questa contumatia di non poter esser ballottati se non haveranno esercitato l' Arte per cinque anni, come di sopra; nel che, perche non caschi difficultà alcuna, instiamo che sia dichiarato e terminato,

Che de cætero li figliuoli o gli heredi di Matricolati esercitanti l' Arte, mentre che suo Padre o altri che rappresentassero siano stati notati in Matricola per anni cinque, possano esser ballottati et haver li carichi che conforme gli ordini nostri si conferiscono, mentre però siano de anni trenta conforme il 2do Capitolo della nostra Matricola. Ma se i loro auttori non fossero stati in Matricola per anni cinque, debbano essi loro Figliuoli o heredi haver contumatia per quel tempo che mancasse, si che fra essi et i loro auttori habbiano compito il detto tempo di anni cinque in tutto.

Et perche consti certamente del tempo predetto come anco per evitare altri inconvenienti che nascono dal non curarsi detti figliuoli o heredi de' Matricolati di comparire avanti il Prior et Banca per farsi matricolare come gli altri, sia dichiarato et terminato,

Che de cætero tutti essi figliuoli o heredi de' Matricolati che vorranno continuar l' Arte, debbano in termine di Mesi tre doppo la morte de' loro auttori, comparire avanti il nostro Prior et Banca, et farsi rolare nella nostra Matricola, dovendo esser rolati senza pagamento alcuno, giusto la Parte 1572, 27 Aprile; l' istesso far debbano tutti li figliuoli o heredi de' Matricolati morti per il passato, i quali non essendo notati in Matricola debbano, nel termine di Mesi tre doppo la publicatione del presente ordine, farsi matricolare, et mancando di ciò far, caschino in pena di ducati cinque, la quale gli debba esser fatta levare dal Priore con l' auttorità di questo Illmo Magistrato. Nè possano continuar a vender o stampare nè se gli possa notar Privilegio alcuno di libri da stamparsi, se non haveranno pagato essa pena e se non saranno Matricolati,

Dichiarando che non restino pregiudicati quei Figliuoli o heredi di Matricolati che non havessero il modo di poter far Stamparia o Libraria, i quali in ogni tempo che si trovassero commodità e volessero esercitar l' arte, possano et debbano esser accettati et matricolati senza alcun pagamento; Restando solamente sottoposti a pagar le luminarie scorse doppo la morte de' loro auttori fino al tempo che leveranno Stamparia o Libraria, et di continuar poi a pagarle come tutti gli altri; et esaminati da Periti e conosciuti idonei debbano esser ammessi et matricolati.

Ma perche gli inconvenienti tutti nascono dall' inoservanza de buoni ordini, et questi molte volte non sono eseguiti per non vi esser pena a chi gli trasgredisse perciò stimiamo necessario sopra tutte le cose che dall' auttorità di VV. SS. Illme sia terminato,

Che il Priore, Consiglieri, Sindici et ogni altro Rappresentante et Ministro dell' Arte nostra, debba inviolabilmente eseguire et far eseguire tutte quelle cose che per li

Decreti et ordeni di questo Illmo Magistrato et per i Capitoli et Parti della nostra Università è disposto et ordinato, ciascuno respettivamente quelle cose che aspettano all' offitio et carico suo, sotto pena a ciascuno che mancarà di ducati venticinque per volta, la mettà della quale sia distribuita come meglio parerà a gli Ill^mi SS. Proveditori, che per tempora si troveranno, et l' altra mettà a beneficio dell' Arte nostra; et nella medesima pena incorrino quel Priore, Consiglieri, Sindici o altri, i quali mancassero di eseguir quelle deliberationi che per il Capitolo Generale, e della Banca della nostra Università sino fin' hora sono state prese, et che per l' avenire si prenderanno per l' esecutione degli ordeni dell' Arte nostra, et per tutti quelli emergenti, che per benefitio di detta Arte possano occorrere; la qual pena debba esser levata a ciascuno che mancherà respettivamente al carico suo, et applicata come di sopra.

Et per chiara intelligenza d' ogn' uno le terminationi sopra dette siano registrate nella Matricola, et publicate nel Capitolo Generale dell' Arte, acciò che nessuno possa pretendere ignoranza, et habbiano la sua debita esecutione.

La qual scrittura essendo stata de verbo ad verbum letta avanti li prefatti Ill^mi SS. Proved. di Co: et da SS. SS. Illustrissime diligentemente discussa et considerata, trattandosi particolarmente della interpretatione, regolatione, osservanza et esecutione delli Capitoli spettanti alla sudetta Università de Librari et Stampatori, havendo il tutto bene et maturamente considerato, per l' auttorità a loro concessa per la Parte di 18 Genaro 1548 preso nell Ecc^so Conseglio di X di statuir et poner quelli ordini et capitoli che ad essi pareranno opportuni, come in quella, et fatti capaci e certi delli disordini che sono in detta Arte, l' hanno tutti tre concordi laudata, approbata et ratificata et successivamente hanno terminato che quella con tutte le terminationi, regolationi et dechiarationi in essa contenute, siano inviolabilmente osservate et eseguite da tutti a chi aspetta, sotto le pene come in quella esposte et specificate; et in oltre, che nel primo Capitolo Generale sia publicata et poi registrata nella Matricola di detta Arte a chiara intelligenza d' ogn' uno, con dichiaratione che cadauno di detta Università et Arte per il giorno di S. Giovanni Evangelista prossimo venturo, debba haver pagate le sue luminarie fin' hora corse et non pagate. Dovendo il Priore et Banca presenti durar fin' all' ultimo di Zugno sudetto, facendo le nove elettioni al tempo delle Pentecoste conforme ad essa scrittura.

A di 27 *Decembre* 1626.

Publicata in Capitolo Generale congregato in S. Gio. e Paolo nel luoco suolito de Genovesi conforme l' ordine sopradetto presente anco il Mag^co Prior, Consiglieri et Banca.

MDCXXVII. *a di* viii. *Marzo.*

No. 20. Redutto l' Ecc^mo Collegio di X Savii sopra le decime in Rialto al N° di 7.

Aldido Dno Lorenzo Magri per nome della Università di Libreri et Stampatori dimandando il taglio della sententia fatta per l' Ill^mi SS^ri Proveditori di Comun sotto di 27 Genero prossimo passato, come sentenza mal et indebitamente fatta a grave danno et pregiuditio di ditta Università per più ragion et cause, da una. Et dall' altra Aldido Dno Marco Genami Conseg^r per nome suo et per nome della maggior parte della

Banca et Università di Libreri et Stampatori, dimandante il laudo di ditta sentenza come bene et rettamente fatta per più ragion et cause.

Mette parte l' Illmo Sig^{r} Alessandro Marcello, ebdomadario, che ditta sentenza sii tagliata, cassata, et annullata come è stato richiesto, et dato giuramento al Collegio.

Bianco al Taglio N° 6 } Presa.
Verde al Laudo N° 1 }

A dì 11 Marzo 1628.

No. 21. Terminat^{e} delli Clar^{mi} SS^{ri} Prov. di Comun, in materia del prezo delli Libri nuovi che si stampano et che si sono fatto stampare da sei Mesi in qua.

Accioche li Librari et Stampatori di questa Città non si fanno lecito di domandar ogni pretio eccessivo delli loro libri fu disposto per parte del Ecc^{mo} Senato de di 3 Genaro 1533 che ogn' un che farà stampar qual si voglia libro, inanzi che quello dii fuori, debba portarlo al Magistrato nostro accio, secondo che vien decretato in essa parte, li sii deputato il pretio col quale dovera esser venduto; Et vedendo l' Ill^{mi} Signori Bernardo Dolfin et Andrea da Molin, Honorandi Proveditori di Comun, absente il suo terzo Colega, che detti Librari et Stampatori cominciano metter in desuso l' esecutione di detta Parte, il che non dovendosi per publica dignità più sopportare, hanno con la presente loro terminatione statuito et ordinato, che nel termine di giorni otto prossimi venturi, il Prior dell' arte predetta debba redur Cap^{o} et in quello far publicar l' esecut^{e} d' essa parte, acio per l' avenire nessun non habbia ardire di vender libri di sorte alcuna stampati di nuovo, se prima non saranno stati portati al magistrato di sue Sig^{e} Ill^{me} et da quello deputatoli il pretio, conforme alle leggi. Dovendo anco tutti quelli Librari et Stampatori far il simile, che da sei mesi in qua haveranno fatto stampar opere nuove, et cio sotto penna de Ducati 200, Bando, pregione, et altre penne maggiori ad arbitrio della Giustitia, da esser irremissibilmente eseguite contro li transgressori. Dovendo anco la presente terminatione esser registrata nella sua Mariegola per chiara inteligenza d' ogn' uno.

In Christi Nomine Amen.

No. 22. Anno ab ejusdem Incarnatione millesimo sexcentesimo quadragesimo secundo; indictione Decima, Die vero Mercurii Decima sexta Mensis Iulii.

Dall' Università, sive Arte, dei S^{ri} Librari e Stampatori di questa inclita Città, con Parte presa nel loro Capitolo Generale sotto di sei Decembre 1638, furono all' hora eletti tre S^{ri} Fratelli di essa loro Scola, cioè li S^{ri} Marco Ginami, Bernardo Giunti et Paulo Baglioni, con carico di cercare, veder et procurare di trovar un Luoco commodo et sufficiente per in quello riddursi a far il loro Capitoli, Banca e Zonta, prender Parti, et altre deliberationi e regole per il buon governo di detta loro Scola; alli quali tre Sig^{ri} fù anco nella medesima Parte concesso auttorità di trattar per tal causa con chi sia; Et essendo finalmente stato raccordato a detti tre S^{ri} un Luoco posto nel primo Claustro del Convento dei M^{to} R^{di} Padri di S^{ti} Giovanni e Paulo di quest' alma Città, da loro stimato proprio et adequato ai bisogni et hodierne occorenze di detta loro Scola; Fù perciò da essi tre S^{ri} rappresentato al detto loro Capitolo Generale. Et con altra Parte all' hora in esso Capitolo presa sotto di vintisette Decembre passato, fù di novo concessa auttorità alli già detti Ginami, Giunti et Baglioni al presente attuali di Banca, cioè il detto Sr Baglioni Priore, il detto Sr Giunti uno dei doi Consiglieri, et il detto Sr Ginami uno dei doi Sinnici, di concludere con detti M^{to} R^{di} Padri l' accordo del detto Luoco, con tutti quelli miglior patti che saranno possibili a benefitio di detta loro Università, et come più particolarmente si legge in detta Parte di vintisette Decembre passato, registrata nel Libro delle Parti di detta Università et rattifficata per l' Officio Illmo dei S^{ri} Proveditori di Comun di questa Città sotto di trenta dell' istesso; per vigor della quale havendo detti tre S^{ri} Ginami, Giunti et Baglioni per nome di detta loro Università, ricercato, trattato et finalmente concluso con detti M^{to} R^{di} Padri l' accordo di detto Luoco, con alcuni patti, dichiarationi et conventioni, da farsi fra l' una et l' altra Parte; Sopra di che, a maggior cautione d' ogn' una di esse Parti, et successori loro, dovendone seguir particolar instrumento di conventione et accordo in atti di publico Nodaro celebrato; De qui è, che alla presentia di me Nodaro, et delli testimonii infrascritti personalmente riddutto, et more solito a suon di Campanella, solennemente convocato et congregato il Venerando Capitolo delli già detti M^{to} R^{di} Padri di Santi Giovanni et Paulo, nella Sacristia della loro Veneranda Chiesa nel quale v' intervennero li seguenti M^{to} R^{di} Padri cioè,

Il M^{to} R^{do} Padre Frà Giorgio Bovio Priore.
Il Padre Maestro Santo Mariale.
Il Padre Maestro Remiggio Scrova.
Il Padre Maestro Marin Cerchiari.
Il Padre Maestro Gabriel Dominioni.
Il Padre Frà Gio: Carlo Fontana, sotto Priore.
Il Padre Frà Gioseppe Picini Baciliero.
Il Padre Frà Archangelo Mansueti, Predicatore Generale.
Il Padre Frà Paulo Girardi.
Il Padre Frà Benedetto Lioni, Predicatore Generale.
Il Padre Frà Tomaso Fontana, Predicatore Generale.
Il Padre Frà Tomaso Pillotto.
Il Padre Frà Vicenzo Maffei, Predicatore Generale.
Il Padre Frà Gio: Andrea Pratti, Lettore.
Il Padre Frà Lorenzo Christomolo, Lettore.
Il Padre Frà Nicolo Christomolo.
Il Padre Frà Bernardino Mutti, Lettore.
Il Padre Frà Pietro Martire Degna, Lettore.
Il Padre Frà Giovanni Premuda, Lettore.
Il Padre Frà Innocentio Pencini, Lettore.
Il Padre Frà Nicolò Gariboldi.
Il Padre Frà Antonio Moretti.
Il Padre Frà Giorgio Righetti, Predicatore Generale.
Frà Gio. Pietro Bortoletti.
Frà Giorgio Marturazza.
Frà Serafino Ciotti.
Frà Rimondo Redoi.
Frà Camillo Nascimben.
Frà Tomaso Rugolo.
Frà Marin Lazaroni.

Tutti li sopranominati M^{to} R^{di} Padri, presenti, che hanno facoltà et voce in detto loro Venerando Capitolo, et rappresentanti, dissero, la maggior parte di esso, Et spontanea et Volontariamente per nome di detto loro Venerando Monastero, et successori di quello in perpetuo, hanno dato et concesso si come veram^{te} in virtù della Parte presa, dissero, nel loro Consiglio sotto dì trenta Decembre passato, qui a piedi registrata, et in virtu del presente publico instrumento dano et liberamente in perpetuo concedono alli antedetti Mag^{ci} S^{ri} Marco Ginami, Bernardo Giunti et Paulo Baglioni, necnon alli S^{ri} Giulio Donadei, l' altro dei doi Consiglieri, Francesco Baba, l' altro dei doi Sinnici, Zuanne Vidali di Zonta et Zuanne Maria Misserini, Scrivan, tutti qui presenti, che con l' auttorità a loro ultimamente concessa, per parte presa nel detto loro Capitolo General sotto di tredici Instante, et rattifficata per l' Officio degl' Ill^{mi} S^{ri} Proveditori di Commun il giorno d' hoggi, per nome di detta loro Università Compagni et Successori di essa stipulano et accettano, Un Magazeno di Muro a pepian, posto et situato nel primo Claustro del detto loro Venerando Monastero, sotto il Novitiato, contiguo ad un' altro simile da essi M^{to} R^{di} Padri concesso alla Scola dei Specchieri di questa Città sotto dì venticinque Ottobre passato; Per abellimento del qual Magazeno et per special commodo di detta Università, detti M^{to} R^{di} Padri per nome di detto loro Monastero et successori di esso, hanno contentato et contentano, che detta Università possi et vaglia quello far fabricare, con porte, balconi et altre cose necessarie, come meglio le parerà et piacerà, mentre però non venghi interrotto l' ordine del Claustro et la cominciata Architettura; così che detta Università con li successori di essa, possi et vagli valersi liberamente del detto Magazeno, come sopra concessogli, et di quello disponer come di cosa propria, libera et espedita senza contradittione d' alcuna persona, et specialm^{te} delli M^{to} R^{di} Padri per nome di detto loro Venerando Monastero, et successori di quello in perpetuo; Ponendo detta Università et successori di essa circa il Magazeno come sopra concessogli, in ogni di detto loro Venerando Monastero, et successori di esso, luoco, ragion, grado stato et essere; Quella constituendo procuratrice irrevocabile come in cosa propria; Et concedendogli perciò di detto Magazeno l' attual, corporal et libero possesso; Così che possi et vogli di propria auttorità et senz' altro decreto d' alcun Giudice, in virtù del presente publico instrumento pigliar, et apprender detto possesso, Promettendo in oltre detti M^{to} R^{di} Padri per nome di detto loro Monastero et successori di esso in perpetuo, di mantener et conservar sempre detta Università et successori di essa in perpetuo nel quieto et paciffico possesso et godimento di detto Magazeno come sopra in perpetuo concessogli, et di quella difender in ogni caso di molestia contra qualunque contradicenti persone, in Giudicio et fuori, a tutte di detto loro monastero et successori di esso, spese, danni pericoli et interessi; Con decchiaratione che se in alcun tempo per causa di riffabricare il detto loro Monastero, o per qual si sia altra causa, fosse necessario anco di gettar a terra il detto Luoco come sopra concessogli, all' hora, et in tal caso, detti Molto R^{di} Padri per nome di detto loro Monastero et successori di esso in perpetuo, hanno promesso et promettono, si sono obligati et si obliganno di conceder a detta Università un' altro Luoco simile per special commodo et servitio di quella a sottisfattione et gusto particolare però di detta Università, et con obligo in oltre a detto Venerando Monastero di boniffìcar a detta Università tutte le spese che convenisse fare per abellimento del Luoco che in tal caso le fosse per detto Monastero concesso; Et perche l' Università et Arte predetta, con Parte presa nel detto loro Capitolo General sotto di vinticinque Genaro 1639, si è obligata di far Celebrare Messe doi al Mese per un Legato de ducati doicento lasciatogli dalla q̃ S^{ra} Anzola figliuola del q̃ Sr Constantin di Maggi, relitta in primo voto del q̃

Sr Pietro Giervason giusto al ponto del Testamento di detta q̃ S^{ra} Anzola, et come in detta Parte, registrata nel detto Libro delle Parti di detta Università, più particolarmente si legge; Per tanto li già detti M^{to} R^{di} Padri per nome di loro Monastero et successori di quello in perpetuo, hanno promesso et promettono, si sono obligati et si obligano, di celebrare et far celebrare le dette vintiquatro Messe all' anno, cioè dodeci all' Altare che doverà per detta Università esser fabricato, nel detto loro Luoco, come sopra concessogli, videlicet ogni Seconda Domenica di mese, et le altre dodeci nella loro Veneranda Chiesa all' Altare privileggiato del Crocifisso overo a quegli altri Altari, et in quelli giorni che a loro M^{to} R^{di} Padri meglio gradiranno; Et all' incontro detti Mag^{ci} Sig^{ri} Marco Ginami, Bernardo Giunti, Paulo Baglioni, Giulio Donadei, Francesco Baba, Zuanne Vidali, et Zuan Maria Misserini per nome di detta loro Università et successori di essa in perpetuo, hanno promesso et promettono, si sono obligati et si obligano, di dar, pagar et prontamente ogn' anno finito in perpetuo contribuire sive corrispondere al detto Venerando Monastero dei detti M^{to} R^{di} Padri di Santi Giovanni e Paulo, una recognitione sive elemosina de ducati trentasei correnti, da lire sei e soldi quatro per ducato, cioè Ducati trenta per la concessione perpetua di detto Magazeno, et gli altri Ducati sei per l' obligo predetto di celebrare perpetuamente le dette vintiquatro Messe ogn' anno; da principiarsi il dì primo Agosto prossimo, et finir debbi il dì ultimo di Luglio 1643, venturo; et così d' anno in anno finito in perpetuo, senz' alcun' immaginabil contradittione, ogn' eccettione et cavillatione rimmossa; Et quando che, per qualunque impensato accidente, mancasse l' Università predetta, overo che quella, con li Successori di essa, fosse deffetiva per qualche tempo considerevole di contribuire la detta corrisponsione annua perpetua al detto Venerando Monastero, all' hora et in tal caso li già detti M^{to} R^{di} Padri restino, et restar debbino liberi, et assoluti Patroni, come erano avanti la stipulazione del presente instrumento, non solo del detto Luoco ma anco degli abellimenti di esso affisi nel muro, potendolo nel detto caso tener per loro uso particolare, overo liberamente concederlo a chi più le parerà et piacerà; con patto special et espresso frà dette Parti fermamente stabilito, che quando detta Università sive Legitimi Intervenienti di quella assignassero al detto Venerando Monastero nell' Officio Illmo della Cecca di quest' inclita Città, overo in altro Luoco sicuro et di consenso del detto Monastero tanto capitale ivi esistente quanto che detti M^{to} R^{di} Padri potessero riscuoter ogn' anno li detti ducati trenta sei correnti, per la corrisponsione annua perpetua sopradetta, overo quando la detta Cecca s' affrancasse, investissero detto Capitale in un buon fondo idoneo, et sicuro, con il consenso del detto monastero, per la qual' investita riscuotesse similmente detti ducati trenta sei annui, ma però con la perpetua manutentione sempre et in ogni caso di essa Università; all' hora, et in tali casi, detta Università con li successori di essa resti, et restar debbi, a fatto libera et disobligata dalla detta corrisponsione annua, et goder debbi perpetuamente il detto Luoco ut supra concessogli, senz' alcun' immaginabil oppositione; et con espressa etiam decchiaratione che l' andito del Claustro dirimpetto al detto Luoco, come sopra per detti M^{to} R^{di} Padri a detta Università concesso resti, et restar debbi sempre libero, disoccupato et senz' alcun immaginabil impedimento; Per manutentione et osservanza delle quali tutte cose nel presente publico instrumento di conventione et accordo contenute, tanto detti M^{to} R^{di} Padri per nome di detto loro Venerando Monastero et successori di quello, quanto detti S^{ri} Ginami, Giunti, Baglioni, Donadei, Baba, Vidali et Misserini per nome di loro Università et successori di essa, in perpetuo, hanno obligato et hippothecato, obligano et hippotheccano tutti et cadauni beni mobili et immobili, presenti et futuri, in qualunque luoco posti et esistenti, Pregando me Nodaro a doverne far il presente publico instrumento.

Actum Venetiis.

In Sacristia Ecclesiæ suprascriptorum admodum Reverdorum Patrum Sanctorum Ioannis et Pauli, Presentibus ad predicta Perillustre et excellente Domino Paschalino Giavanelli filio Perillustris Domini Antonii, Medico Phisico Veneto, et Domino Carlo Filago filio Domini Lodovici de Rodigio, Testibus ad hæc specialiter vocatis et rog.

STEPHANUS SALA q̃ Dmi D LAURENTII publica auctoritate Venetiarum Notus de præmiss rogc scripsi, publicavi, meque hic in fidem subsst et signavi.

A di 28 *Marzo* 1664.

No. 23. Conoscendosi molto proprio et adequato al Servitio dell' Università de Librari e Stampatori, e con il riguardo al culto del Sigr Iddio, non sii permesso a chi si sii il giorno di Festa metter fuori Libri d' alcuna sorte che rende scandolo et poco decoro, et anco per ovviar alli dispendii et incomodi causati quotidianamente per tali disordini alla detta Università, perciò l' Illmi SSri Germo Zen, Almo Barbaro et Anto Molin Provri di Co: invigilando alla conservatione delle Leggi in tal proposito essistenti nella matricola di detta Università, et inherendo alla parte 16 Lugo 1598 stanno Terminando Terminato che siino casse e nulle tutte le licenze sin hora concesse a chi si sia, essendo risoluta volontà di SS. SS. Illme che siano santificate le Feste et osservati li decritti concernenti in tal proposito; et perchè vi sono alcuni poveri librari SS. SS. Illme hanno terminato che il prior di detta Università possi conceder licenza a qualche povero matricolato giusto alla Terminatione di SS. SS. Illme die 18 Zugo 1613, et confirmatione seguita li 20 Agto successivamente in 40 C. N.; alla quale in tutto et con tutto haver si debba l' intiera esecutione; qual licenza concessa doverà esser approbata et sottoscritta almeno da Due di SS. SS. Illme. Non intendendosi però che possi poner fuori altro che Libri Spirituali giusto alle Leggi in penna alli contrafacenti della perdita dei Libri et decaduti ipso facto di detta licenza; et se vi fosse alcuno ardito et temerario che in onta di questa terminatione volesse metter fuori le Feste, cadino in pena della perdita de Libri che li saranno ritrovati et altre penne ad arbitrio della Giustitia, da esser il tutto Decciso giusto le Leggi; et la presente sia registrata nella Matricola di detta Università et letta in ogni Capto Genale a chiara intelligenza di Cadauno.

GIRMO ZEN Prov de Co:
ALMORÒ BARBARO P. d Co:
ANTO MOLIN Pr d Co:

Die 11 *Genaro* 1665.

No. 24. L' Ill^mi S^ri Alvise Venier et Ascanio Giustiniã Honorandi P^ri d Comun udita l' instanza di bonifacio Ciera con la quale ha rapresentato li pregiudicii che trovano per occasione dal esser prorogati li tempi delli privileggi della stampa de libri da quelle persone che non sono li med^mi autori, essenduci con abuso introdoto che benche il med^o autore non facia alcuna instanza, ad ogni modo questi tali si arogano autorità di voler loro stessi appogiarsi li stessi privileggi di far stampare per se stessi li libri d' altri autori, il che non dovendosi tollerare, anzi essendo di necessità farne particolar provisione per beneficio universale di tutta l' arte de Libreri et Stampatori, per tanto SS. Ill^me per la presente terminatione hanno concesso et terminano, che fenito il tempo concesso, al proprio autore non ardisca alcun altro appropriar a se stesso libri d' alcuna sorte per farli stampare a suo utile et beneficio, ne vaglia alcun privileggio se non de Manuscriti, et ciò sotto pena di D 200 applicati al escavacion de Rii di questa Città, oltre altri D. 20 da esser applicati al denonciante secreto, se ne sarà, se non, alli ministri farano l' esecutione et altre pene ad arbitrio della Giustitia, et ciò affinche li detti Stampatori et Libreri possino universalmente tra loro haver quel beneficio et utile che li vien permesso dalle stampe et spese de med^mi libri.

1688. 11 *Gennaro.*

No. 25. The Presidents of the Collegio della Militia da Mar—seeing that the Gastaldi of the Guilds burden their brethren with excessive taxation by bringing to this office lists which omit the names of many members, and thereby inducing the President to sanction a higher taxation per head than is necessary—order that all sanctions shall be issued for the future on a printed form whereon shall appear the amount of money required.

Fifteen days must elapse between the presentation of the amount of the proposed tax and the ratification of the same, during which days the members of the Guild may appeal.

Marc Antonio Moresini.
Marco Loredan.

1704. 21 *Settembre.*

No. 26. Osservando gl' Illustrissimi et Eccellentissimi Signori Refformatori dello Studio di Padoa che contro il tenor de' Publici Decreti, et in particolare di quello 24 Settembre 1653, si prendono molti Librari e Stampatori temerariamente libertà di ristampare Libri, Canzoni, et altre carte senz' impetrarne la debita licenza dal magistrato, però l' Eccellenze loro, conoscendo perniciosissimo il disordine, hanno in ordine al preaccenato Decreto terminato, et terminando comandato che non possino ristamparsi Libri, Canzoni, ne altre Carte in questa Dominante senza precedente licenza del loro magistrato, in pena a Contrafacienti, oltre la perdita dell' opere ristampate, d' altre afflittive et pecuniarie che pareranno all' Eccellenze loro, ordinando, che la presente

Terminatione sia registrata nella Mariegola de Librari et Stampatori per la sua pontuale, et inviolabile essecutione.

FERIGO MARCELLO Proc. Reffor.
GIR. VENIER Cav. Proc. Reffor.
MARIN ZORZI Refformator
AGOSTINO GADALDINI Segr.

1704. 4 *Ottobre.*

No. 27. Rappresentando il Priore e Compagni dell' Arte de Librari e Stampatori invalso l' abuso che molti Lavoranti, et Matricolati, o Capi Mistri, che servono per Lavoranti, Compositori, Torcolari, et altri serventi, che s' essercittano nelle Botteghe de Stampatori e Librari, vanno diffetivi, et Debitori delle Tanse, che d' anno in anno vengono imposte dalla loro Università, come pure di Luminarie et altre Gravezze, di maniera che si rendono, e per la lunghezza del tempo e per la renitenza loro, inesigibili, con pregiudicio non solo al Publico interesse per la Tansa insensibile, e Gravezze spettanti all' Università medesima, ma anche alla specialità de Priori dell' Arte che devono soccombere all' Esborso, e col proprio Denaro supplire a pagamenti de' Salariati, et altri, ch' occorressero. Chiamato però il zelo dell' Illustrissimi et Eccellentissimi Signori Refformatori dello Studio di Padova a provedere a questo esentialissimo disordine, hanno con la presente terminato e terminando comandato, che tutti i Matricolati, Capi Mistri, Stampadori, Librari et altri che fanno lavorare cosi in Casa come fuori di Casa, tanto di stampe che di legar Libri, debbano al presente et in avvenire trattenere a quelli che rissultassero debitori delle preaccennate nature di maggior summa di Ducati cinque, Libre due alla Settimana sino all' estintione del debito loro, et a gl' altri che non eccedessero li Ducati cinque di Debito, Lira una alla Settimana.

Li sudetti denari doveranno di Mese in Mese essere esborsati a Priori dell' Arte pro tempore ad essere posti in Cassa sotto tre mani de Chiavi, giusta li Capitoli dell' Università sotto pena a detti Matricolati et altri come sopra che contrafacessero, di pagar del proprio, e de Ducati 25, da essere levati dal Magistrato, et applicati ad arbitrio di loro Eccellenze: E perche resti la presente Terminatione pontualmente osservata, non possi darsi ne riceversi lavoro alcuno, se prima da Lavoranti et altri non sarà portata fede de gl' attuali Priori che giustifichi se vi sia o non vi sia Debito, et la summa precisa dello stesso, da essere custodito da quel Libraro o Stampatore che darà da lavorare, e ciò sotto le sudette pene a chi contravenisse.

Et la presente sia stampata et registrata nella Mariegola dell' Arte a chiara intelligenza di cadauno.

FERIGO MARCELLO Proc. Reffor.
GIROL. VENIER Kav. Proc. Reff.
MARIN ZORZI Refformator.
AGOSTINO GADALDINI Segr.

1704. 11 *Ottobre. In Pregadi.*

No. 28. Confirmation of the above.

1704. 10 *Ottobre.*

No. 29. Gl' Illustrissimi et Eccellentissimi Signori Refformatori dello Studio di Padova, inherendo al Decreto dell' Eccellentissimo Senato de 11 Maggio 1603, et attese l' humilissime Instanze del Prior e Compagni dell' Arte de Librari e Stampatori di questa Città, hanno con la presente terminato, et terminando comandato, che volendo personne non Matricolate stampare alcun Libro in questa Dominante per contrattarlo, debbano pagar per ogni Balla di 10 Risme, come resta dal medesimo Decreto prescritto, Grossi otto all' Arte sopradetta, in pena a qualunque contrafaciente della perdita dell' opere da essere divise giusta le Leggi.

E perche conviene, che non resti defraudata l' Università di tale contributione, ch' è giusta, e che per il Decreto medesimo serve per sostentamento delle molte sue Spese, e della Gravezza del Galeotto, alla quale non soggiacciono li non Matricolati, siano parimente tenuti tutti li Librari e Stampatori dar in nota al Priore e Banca tutte l' Opere, che al presente si stampassero, o ristampassero, o si facessero stampare o ristampare da Particolari non Matricolati, col numero de' Fogli, rimosso qualunque concerto o Accordo che clandestinamente corresse con altri Nomi, in pena di pagar del proprio li sudetti otto Grossi per Balla, e di Ducati 25 da esser applicati ad arbitrio dell' Eccellenze loro.

Et la presente sia stampata, e fattone registro nella Mariegola dell' Arte.

Ferigo Marcello Proc. Reffor.
Girol. Venier Kav. Proc. Reffor.
Marin Zorzi Refformator.
Agostino Gadaldini Segretario.

A di 25 *Ottobre* 1704.

Publicate sopra le Scale di S. Marco, e di Rialto per Zuanne Pizzolato Comandador di sue Eccellenze.

20 *Aprile* 1700.

No. 30. The Proveditori di Comun, for the better preservation of Religion and for the good government of the Guilds recommended to their diligence, decree that:

1. Whereas in conformity with the order of 21 July, 1699, a public book, "sive catastico," has been opened, in which the income, expenditure, and property of the Guilds is registered; the Wardens, Gastaldi, or other heads of the Guilds are on their side to draw up an inventory of the income, expenditure, and property of their Guilds, and to bring it to this office to be compared with the Catastico.

The Gastaldi, on their election, are to sign a receipt for the property named in this Inventory.

The Gastaldi, at close of their term of office and before the Syndics pass their accounts, shall be obliged to make good any deficiencies in the Inventory.

2. In Chapter and Banca many resolutions are passed in a sense opposed to the standing orders, and are not brought to this office for ratification till many months and

sometimes years have elapsed since the date of their passing; in future all resolutions are to be submitted to this office within eight days after the meeting of the Chapter or Banca in which they were passed, under penalty of a fine amounting to fifty ducats.

3. Many salaried officials of the Guilds, as "Quadernieri, Nonzoli, Casselanti et altri," accept office "senza pieggeria di buon maneggio;" for the future within fifteen days of their election these officials shall deposit their caution money in this office and receive a certificate from our Notary that they have done so, under pain of a fine amounting to twenty-five ducats.

4. Many ex-officials of the Guilds, their ineligibility notwithstanding, are re-elected to office; in future anyone who proposes a man who is ineligible shall be fined fifty ducats.

These orders to be registered in the Mariegole of the Guilds.

MAR' ANTONIO MOLIN.
GIO: ANTONIO MORESINI.
GERMO FOSCARINI.

13 *Settembre* 1714.

No. 31. The Proveditori di Comun order—

1. That no Gastaldo or Head of a Guild shall convoke a Chapter, either General or Bancal, without obtaining permission printed on a form wherein shall appear all the business to be dealt with in the said Chapter. Our Secretary shall ratify no Chapter held without such permission.

2. The rules as to ineligibility are to be scrupulously observed.

3. The Heads of Guilds shall pay their caution money before entering office.

4. The three keys of the strong-box to be kept, one by the Gastaldo, one by the Vicar, and one by the elder Sindico.

5. The paid officials to be elected on the vote of two-thirds, not of the half, of the Chapter.

6. In cases where the Nonzolo is to have a voice in the management of the Banca, he must deposit a caution, which caution must be renewed every five years.

The above order to be registered in the Mariegole of the Guilds, "stampata dal Pinelli et aggiunta al libro e raccolta delle altre parti."

ANDREA VENDRAMIN.
AGUSTIN CONTARINI.
DANIEL DOLFIN.
GIO ANTONIO ALBINGONI (?) Nod.

1716. 30 *Giugno.*

No. 32. Rilevato dagl' Illmi ed Eccmi Sigri Reformatori dello Studio di Padova andar presentamente involendo uno grave disordine, che quantunque venga da un Revisore negata la Licenza della Stampa, e Ristampa de un Libro per l' eccezioni che la di lui attenzione s' è creduto in obbligo di farle, si prende in ogni modo l' Autore o il Stampatore la Libertà di riccurrere ad altro revisore per conseguirne l' intento. L' Eccte loro, conoscendo opportuno di troncare il progresso a tale pernicioso inconveniente, hanno terminato

Che fatte L' Osservazioni del Libro che sarà presentato al Revisore per la Licenza della stampa o ristampa, sia egli tenuto nello stesso far nota delle eccezioni che havesse in esso rimarcate, e di raccoglerle anche in suo particolar foglio diretto al Segretario del Magistrato, con esprimere li motivi che lo rendono persuaso a disapprovare in tutto o in parte il Libro medesimo.

Che ricevuta dal Segretario la nota stessa sia egli tenuto far tener copia delle eccezioni medesime agli altri Revisori, perche con tal lume debbono riggetare l' istanze che le fossero fatte per la concessione della stampa o ristampa, restando al solo Magistrato l' adito del ricorso per dipendere intieramente dall' Autorità e Prudenza dell' Ecc[ze] loro ordinando cosi doversi annotare.

Che della presente Terminazione sia data copia a' Revisori medesimi, a' Librari, e Stampatori per Lume e per l' esecutione.

Girolamo Renier K[r] Proc.
Marino Zorzi
Lorenzo Tiepolo K[r] Proc.
Agostino Gadaldini Seg[rio].

3 *Ottobre* 1719.

No. 33. The Proveditori di Comun.

The Senate by a decree of 12th December, 1716, confirming a previous decree of 6th November, 1648, ordered all the guilds of the city to contribute to the support of the nuns from Candia, at the rate of one ducat a year for each guild, which subvention gave a total of three hundred and fifty ducats applied to the support of four nuns and their chaplain for life, and after their death to the Hospital for Soldiers established on the island of San Servolo, and any surplus to the Convent of the Convertite on the Giudecca.

The Proveditori find that many Guilds are deep in debt for this subvention; and, in order to facilitate the payment thereof, they decree that

All Guilds for the future shall pay one ducat a year into the "Cassa dell' Escavation," in the office of this magistracy.

All Guilds that are in debt may extinguish that debt by a yearly payment of two ducats.

These payments fall due at the end of August each year. After that date the fine for non-payment shall be at the rate of twenty-five per cent., or one lira eleven soldi a ducat.

This decree to be registered in the Mariegole of the Guilds.

Gerolemo Polani
Gerolemo da Mula
Filippo Antonio Boldù.
Giulio Bonis loco Not.

Laus B. M. V. et Joanni de Deo. a di P^{mo} April 1695.

No. 34. A list of the members of the Guild at the above date, two hundred and ninety in number.

Nota de Matricolati che si trovano essere al presente, e che intrarano in avenire.

Judging as far as one can by the writing, the number of members at the date of opening the list was eighty-one.[1]

1 *Decembre* 1727.

No. 35. D' ordine degl' Ill^{mi} et Ecc^{mi} Sig^{i} Press^{i} et Ag^{o} al Coll^{o} della Militia da Mar et per essecutione di parte dell' Eccel^{mo} Sen^{o} 22 Nov. 1727, si da not^{a} a voi Gastaldo dell' Arte de Libreri a Stampa come l'Arte vostra e statta caratata per l' Armar delle Galerre Galeotti n^{o} trenta due, sop^{a} quali doverà a pmo Marzo pros^{o} venturo 1728, correre la Tansa Ins^{a} a detta vostra Arte in rag^{n} di ducati 6 v.c. per Galeotto, da esser di mesi tre in mesi tre antecipa^{te} da voi e successori vos^{i} contata in Cassa del pñte Mag^{o} et all' occorenze pur dell' Armar per q^{ta} portione quello vi spetta.

Ant^{o} Bragadin Nod^{o}.

1727. 4 *Settembre*.

No. 36. Avendo rilevato gl' Ill^{mi} et Ecc^{mi} Reff^{ri} dello Studio di Padova, che alcuni Librari, col mandato rilasciato dal loro Magistrato per la licenza della stampa d' un libro, si prendono la libertà, dopo il corso de molti anni, che n' è seguita la prima stampa, di farne del medemo altre ristampe, a loro arbitrio, e senza altro mandato di licenza, et conoscendo opportuno troncare il disordine e l' abuso invalso, hanno terminato che intendendo alcun libraro o stampatore ristampare lo stesso libro, dopo lo spazio di anni quattro sia obbligato a ricevere nuovo mandato per la licenza, previa la fede del Revisore deputato, sotto le pene pecuniarie che pareranno alle Ecc^{ze} loro.

E della presente Terminatione sia data copia al Priore de Librari perchè ne segua il Registro nella Mariegola a chiara intelligenza di Cadauno per la sua pontuale esecuzione.

Carlo Ruzini K^{r} e Proc.
Alvise Pisani K^{r} e Proc.
Gio Pietro Pasqualigo.
Agostino Gadaldini Seg^{rio}.

1728. 4 *Luglio*.

No. 37. Essendo stato da Antonio Mora stampatore senza la dovuta licenza, e in contravenzione de' Publici divieti, ristampata et venduta per la Pubblica Piazza la Carta

[1] The names in this list are contained in the Catalogue of Venetian Printers, Documents V.

intitolata ***Novissima istoria della Fondazione dell' inclita Città di Venecia con la Nascità, Vita e Morte di Pilato***, per gl' Ill[mi] et Ecc[mi] SS[ri] Refformatori dello Studio di Padova attesa la di lui miserabile povertà, et mitius agendo con la facoltà che tengono da' Pubblici Decreti di devenire summariamente a pene afflitive e pecuniarie, hanno condannato lo stesso in un candellotto di Cera di libbre una applicato alla Scuola de' Librari e Stampatori, dovendo della presente condanna esserne fatto nella medema registro per documento ad ognuno et ad intelligenza universale, che in casi simili di contravenzione si procederà a più pesanti castighi, ordinando così doversi annotare.

GIO: FRANCESCO MOROSINI Kav.
ALVISE PISANI Kav. Proc.
PIETRO GRIMANI Kav. Proc.

AGOSTINO GADALDINI Seg[rio].

1725. 15 *Gennaro.*

No. 38. Ordini degl' Ill[mi] et Eccm̃i SS[ri] Rifformatori dello Studio di Padova per regola delle Stampe, Stampatori et Librari di Venezia. In conformità di quanto dispongono le Leggi.

Considerata frà l' Arti principali, che accrescono splendore, et utile alla Dominante, anco quella della stampa, vi donò la Publica Potestà il suo Sovrano Patrocinio, e furono anco con providi decreti dell' Ecc[mo] Senato e con prudenti Terminationi del Magistrato degl' Illm̃i et Eccm̃i SS[ri] Rifformatori dello Studio di Padova, a' quali ne resta demandata la sopraintendenza, stabilite di tempo in tempo Regole aggiustate alla sua felice susistenza e diretione; nello scorgersi però, che dalla innoservanza delle medeme, e dalla facilità delle contraventioni vadano nel lavoro delle stampe invalendo li disordini, e ciò che si rende degno di riflesso, siasi avanzata la temeraria rilasciatezza d' alcuni Librari di far uscire da' Torchii Libri, Carte minute, et altre opere senza le dovute Licenze, e senza le prescritte Revisioni, et approvazioni che riguardano la Santa Fede Cattolica, l' interesse de Prencipi, e buoni Costumi, hà creduto opportuno la Maturità et il zelo di E.E. loro di raccogliere ad universale notizia, et intelligenza de medemi Librari e Stampatori nella presente Terminazione l' esentiale delle Leggi che contengono gl' ordini concernenti l' intraprendere le Stampe, e l' eseguirle, quali obblighi corrano doppo terminate, e li Privilegii dalla Publica Munificenza accordati, così che senza punto derogare all' altre Leggi in tal proposito disponenti, che s' intendano ferme nel loro vigore, ravvivata l' esecutione puntuale et intiera delle Publiche prescrittioni, sia troncato il pernicioso corso agli Inconvenienti, e tutto conspiri a rimettere nella sua antica estimatione e floridezza l' Arte medema.

Revisione avanti la Stampa.

Che in ordine a quanto viene Decretato dalle Parti dell' Ecc[mo] Senato 11 Maggio 1603 e 1653, 24 Settembre et altri ancora, qualunque Libro, Opera e Compositione qualunque siasi, et in ogni materia, niuna ecettuata, da stamparsi o ristamparsi debba esser da Stampatori e Librari Matricolati, è da ogni altro che vorà far stampare o ristampare, fatta vedere da uno delli Revisori deputati da SS. EE. perche dal medesimo con la diligenza, che si deve, sia riveduta, et esaminata, per quello concerne l' interesse de' Prencipi, e buoni costumi, per la licenza della stampa o ristampa.

Venendo da un Revisore negata la licenza della Stampa o ristampa di alcun Libro, per quelle eccettioni che la di lui attentione vi facesse, non possa l' Autore o stampatore ricorrere ad altro Revisore per conseguir l' intento, restando l' adito del ricorso al solo Magistrato di SS. E.E. Dovendo in tal caso il Revisore far tenere una nota del titolo del Libro al Secretario del Magistrato, il quale ne dovrà far tenere copia agli altri Revisori, perche con tal lume debbano rigettare l' instanze che gli fossero fatte per la concessione della Stampa, o ristampa del Libro stesso, et in resto con le formalità in tutto, come nella Terminatione del Magistrato 30 Gennaro 1716.

Se il compositore giudicasse che il suo Libro avesse bisogno d' alcuna Mutazione o Aggiunta, non possa farla senza essere quella riveduta et approvata, come sopra.

Licenze dopo la Revisione.

Che in ordine alla precitata Parte 24 Settembre 1653 et alla Terminatione di loro E.E. de dì 21 Settembre 1704 confermata con suseguente Decreto dell' Ecc^{mo} Senato 27 Settembre medemo, non possa alcuno delli Stampatori principiare a far compositione alcuna di Stampa, ne meno metter in Torcolo, o stampare qualunque sorte di Libro, Opera, et Compositione, se prima non haverà effettivamente ottenuta la Fede ordinaria dal P. Inquisitore, con la quale approvi il Libro et l' Opera per quanto spetta alla Cattolica Religione, e la Fede da uno delli Revisori Deputati, che non vi sia cosa alcuna contro Prencipi, e buoni Costumi, e poscia, col mezzo d' esse Fedi, il mandato dal Secretario di loro E.E. sottoscritto almeno da due d' essi giusta le Leggi, con il quale all' hora e non prima, gli resti concessa la Licenza di poter far la stampa d' esso Libro, Opera o Compositione qualunque si fosse, e questo sotto le pene che pareranno ad essi Rifformatori.

Per la Stampa però delle cose minute, e di poco momento, come Elogi, Sonetti, Canzoni, e cose simili, che non eccedano il num. di fogli tre, doppo esser state licenziate dal P. Inquisitore, basterà che previa la Revisione, siano sottoscritte dal Revisor e dal Secretario senza obbligo di prender il mandato de Rifformatori, giusto il Decreto dell' Ecc^{mo} Senato 1696, 25 Ottobre, e giusto il praticato in ordine al medemo.

Doveranno li Patroni delle Stamparie Matricolati tener in filza tutti li Mandati de Rifformatori, che avessero riportati per la Licenza della Stampa, acciò in ogni occorenza possa sapersi con certezza, se quanto è uscito da qualunque Stamperia, sia fatto servatis servandis in conformità delle Leggi.

Corretione per la Stampa.

Per la Corretione della Stampa inherendo S.S. E.E. a quanto resta disposto e comandato dll Ecc^{mo} Senato 1603, 11 Maggio, e Terminatione esecutiva del Magistrato di Rifformatori 1614, 29 Ottobre, hanno ordinato quanto segue.

Tutti gli Stampatori e Librari Matricolati che voranno stampare, o ristampare, o far stampare alcuna Opera siano obbligati di far vedere prima al Corettore l' Essemplare del quale voranno servirsi per dilligentemente coreggere ogni incorettione che in esso si trovasse.

Siano tenuti di volta in volta far leggere le Forme in piombo con dilligenza dalli Compositori, e farle ascoltare, o dalli Proti, o da altre persone sufficienti, perche la prima Corettione sia fatta in detto incontro su la forma, e doppo tirato il Foglio in Torcolo far quello vedere dal Corettore, dal quale debbano esser corretti gl' errori, che troverà in detto Foglio, e poi si abbia a tirare il secondo per assicurarsi che siano stati acconci e cancellati, E perche il Magistrato abbia la certezza della sufficienza dei Corettori, doveranno in avvenire li Corettori della Stamparie darsi in nota al Magistrato dell' Eccellenze loro.

Nella Stampa.

Debbano quelli, che stamperanno, ristamperanno, o faranno stampare servirsi di Maestri di Stampa conosciuti per sufficienti dalli Deputati dell' Arte.

Debbano servirsi di belli Caratteri, e buoni Inchiostri, in modo in modo che li Libri non solo siano corretti, ma ben improntati, netti, e leggibili.

Si servano di bella e buona Carta, con Colla sufficiente, la quale sia di peso proportionato alla qualità de Libri che averanno a stampare, la quale ritenga l' Inchiostro, e non trapassi nè scompisi in modo alcuno giusta la Parte dell' Ecc^me Senato 4 Giugno 1537, e sotto le pene in quella statuite.

Siano tenuti stampare in principio di cadun Libro il Mandato di Licenza de Rifformatori, et in fine l' Errata.

Siano tenuti il Priore de Librari e Stampatori, e quelli della Banca, che saranno di tempo in tempo, andar speso vedendo et osservando se vi sia la necessaria abilità negl' Operaii, e se suppliscano alli requisiti del Lavoro, nel metter insieme buoni Caratteri, usare buoni Inchiostri, Carte perfette, e farsi buone Correttioni, e riferir tutto pontualmente a Rifformatori ogni mese, perche possino essi andar applicando a misura de disordini, quei Rimedii e Castighi, che stimeranno giusti, in conformità di quanto resta disposto del preacenato Decreto 1603, 11 Maggio, e susseguente 1653, 24 Settembre.

Doppo la Stampa.

Siano obbligati li Stampatori doppo terminata la Stampa de Libri, raccoglier, e conservar appresso di se, almeno per il tempo d' un anno, gli stessi Originali, che saranno stati riveduti dal P. Inquisitore, e dalli Revisori Deputati, perche in questo fratempo possano con l' essistenza de medemi conoscere le Contrafattioni, e massime se doppo la Revisione fatta di essi, prima d' esser gli concessa la Licenza di stamparli, sarà stata aggiunta o levata alcuna cosa, e postane alcun' altra di quelle saranno state cancellate o depennate dalli Revisori, e ciò conformandosi alla precitata Legge 1603, 11 Maggio.

Se nello spatio di mesi quattro susseguenti alla Data delle sudette Fedi, lo Stampatore, che l' averà ottenute, non avrà principiata e progredita la stampa, possa ogn' altro stampatore, che voglia stampare quel Libro, ricercar al Secretario Mandato per poter stampare lo stesso Libro, che gli dovrà esser rilasciato, e ciò con l' oggetto di divertire le collusioni a pregiuditio degli Stampatori di questa Città, e vantaggio de Forastieri.

Terminato l' anno doppo la Data della Fede, possa ogni uno, che voglia stampare il medemo Libro, sodisfarsi a suo beneplacito, previa però la permissione de Rifformatori, e come nella precitata Legge 1653, 24 Settembre.

In ordine à più Decreti dell' Ecc^mo Senato, e Terminationi del Magistrato 24 Settembre 1680, e 9 Marzo 1697, siano tenutigli Stampatori, finita la Stampa, presentare le due prime copie di cadaun Libro legate in Bergamina nella Publica Libraria di Venezia, perche l' una serva per la stessa, e l' altra dà esser trasmessa nella Libraria di Padova, ne possano publicare ne vendere libro alcuno, se prima non sarà statta fatta la consegna come sopra, delle sudette due Copie, sotto pena della confiscatione di tutti li Libri stampati, et altre corporali e pecuniarie, che pareranno a E. E. loro.

Nelli Libri stampati fuori di Venezia, non sia alcuno che ardisca ponere il primo Foglio stampato con l' iscritione di Stampatore e Città di Venezia per fargli apparire stampati in questa Città, sotto pena per il meno di Ducati cento, et altre maggiori, che, avuto riguardo alla qualità delle trasgressioni, pareranno all' E. E. loro, e specialmente della perdita de Libri, li quali Ducati cento saranno applicati al Denonciante, da essere tenuto secreto in conformità in tutto della Legge 1603, 11 Maggio.

Perche alle volte vi sono stati alcuni cosi temerarii, che hanno ardito di stampar, e ristampare Libri senza le dovute Licenze in queste Città, e mentitamente hanno fatto apparire che siano stampati altrove, e come tali sono stati venduti.

Rimarcandosi però di molto peso, e degna di castigo la fraude, che tende egualmente a Publico pregiuditio, e dell' Arte, saranno contro questi giusta la dispositione delle Leggi, ricevute Denontie, e praticate Inquisitioni, e contro li liquidati Colpevoli sarà in conformità delle medesime proceduto con ogni rigore, non solo di fargli perdere li Libri, ma di pene pecuniarie et afflitive.

E mentre è della Publica Volontà che siano rimossi tutti li pregiuditii all' Arte, e che non siano distratti gli Artefici, ne che escano dalla Dominante, sotto titolo di piombo lavorato, materiali et altri Instrumenti inservienti all' uso delle stampe, doveranno in ogni caso di contrafattione essere eseguiti li Decreti 1602, 20 Febraro, e 1603, 11 Maggio.

Privileggiati.

Se il Privileggiato non darà principio a stampare l' Opera Privileggiata nel termine d' un mese, doppo averla data in nota, continuando sino al fine a farne ogni giorno mezzo Foglio almeno (salvo che se mancasse per giusto impedimento da esser conosciuto da quelli della Banca dell' Arte, e da medemi riferito a gl' Ecc^mi SS^ri Rifformatori) s' intenderà per la precitata Legge 1603, 11 Maggio, decaduto dal Privilegio, nel quale subintrerà quello, ch' averà dato la Denontia, e non v' essendo Denontiante, quello parerà all' E. E. loro.

Se nelli Libri per li quali si concede a' Matricolati Privileggio si troveranno Errori, quello che averà ottenuto il Privileggio s' intenderà senz' altro decaduto dal medemo, giusto il Decreto 1603, 11 Maggio.

Se li Libri per li quali si concede a' Matricolati Privileggio riuscirano mal stampati, et improntati, non ben leggibili, e con cattive Carte et Inchiostri, s' intenderà il Privileggiato incorso nelle pene, che per tale importante et essentiale difetto sono statuite dal' Decreto dell Ecc^mo Senato 1537, 4 Giugno, non comprendendosi però in questo ordine le cose minute sino a Fogli dieci l' una, come resta nel medemo Decreto dichiarito.

Non possa alcuno che ottenesse Grazie e Privileggio per la stampa di Libri, stampare l' Opere Privileggiate altrove che in Venezia, e stampandole altrove, non gli vaglia la Grazia, ne si possa dimandare Grazia più d' una volta del medemo Libro.

Se alcuno in onta del Privileggio, stampasse l' opere concesse ad altri in Privileggio, tanto stampandole, e facendole stampare in questa Città, o fuori, quanto stampate vendendole in questa Città o altre Città, Terre, e Luochi del Dominio, incorrerà giusto la Parte 21 Gennaro 1603, nella pena di Ducati 300, da essere divisi come in detta Parte, è ciò oltre il perdere l' opere stampate, le quali saranno di quello, al di cui Privileggio sarà stato contrafatto.

A preservatione de Privileggii, e dell' interesse de Privileggiati sarà lecito ad ogni Privileggiato, et a quelli dell' Arte dar notizia de Privileggii, col mezzo de suoi Intervenienti a cadaun Rappresentante delle Città e Luoghi ove fossero Stampatori e Librari, a fine che n' apparisca memoria in quelle Cancellarie.

Volendo il Privileggiato far intimare a Stampatori e Librari, e registrare il suo Privileggio in alcuna di quelle Cancellarie, non possano essere tolti piu di Soldi 40 per cadauno, come resta disposto nel preacennato Decreto 1603, 21 Gennaro.

Potendosi il Libro Privileggiato, come alcune volte è succeduto, ristampare in Luoghi esteri, et introdursi in questa Città, e Stato, et vendersi in fraude del Privileggio, e con grave pregiuditio del Privileggiato; a preservatione però dell' uno e dell' altro, mentre resta Decretato dalla Parte 24 Settembre 1653, quanto col Capitolo 6 occorre, doverà essere questa eseguita, così che tali Libri siano del tutto Banditi dallo Stato, e se ne capitassero per via alcuna non possa il Deputato all' Estratione de Libri dalla Dogana licenziarli, si che siano estrati dal Luogo ove saranno recapitati, ne il Secretario fargli il Mandato per venderli, ma siano confiscati, e perduti, et in oltre giusta detta Parte puniti quelli a' quali saranno diretti, come li Rifformatori stimeranno adequato ai termini di Giustitia.

Per le concessioni poi, che fossero supplicate de Privileggii d' Opere stampate ne Stati Esteri, sia a Carico del Secretario del Magistrato di raccordare nell' Informazioni, che saranno dall' E. E. loro prodotte, l' esecutione del Decreto 1603, 11 Maggio, perche le Ballottationi di tali Privileggii abbiano a farsi con li cinque sesti dell' Ecc[mo] Coleggio ridotto al suo intiero numero, e del Senato ridotto dalli 180 in sù, come resta dal medemo prescritto.

E la presente Terminatione sia stampata, e intimata a cadauno Stampatore e Libraro, con ordine ad ogni uno di tenerla sempre affissa nelle loro Stamparie, e Librarie, affinche non possa da alcuno esserne pretesa ignoranza.

Dat. li 15 Gennaro 1725.

Gio: Fran[co] Morosini Kav. Rifformator.
Andrea Soranzo Proc. Rifformator.
Pietro Grimani Kav. Proc. Rifformator.
Agostino Gadaldini Segr.

A di 5 Giugno 1730.

No. 39. Si è resa così osservabile la libertà che si prendono alcuni Auttori di Libri, Stampatori, e Librari di contravenire, nel proposito della Revisione di medesimi, a quanto fù dalla prudenza degl' Ill[mi] et Ecc[mi] Signori Refformatori dello Studio di Padoa prescritto, con Terminazione di 30 Gennaro 1716 e 15 Gennaro 1725, che trovano necessario per troncare il corso alla gravità del disordine che va invalendo, ravvivarne con la presente la dovuta esecutione. Essenzialissimo è il punto, che tutti li Libri, Opere e Composizioni, in ogni materia, niuna eccettuata, che saranno per stamparsi o ristamparsi, devono essere, prima che escano dalle stampe, in vigore delle Leggi, per li riguardi di Principi, e buoni Costumi, riveduti, e mentre a questa importante incombenza, in ordine a Decreti dell' Ecc^{mo} Senato 1603, 11 Maggio, e 1653, 24 Settembre, si trovano destinati soggetti d' integrità, virtù et esperienza col titolo di Deputati alla Revisione, restano anche incaricati a diligentemente praticarla, sopra qualunque Libro, Opera e Composizione che le sarà presentata, ne rilevando cosa alcuna contraria alle loro inspezioni, formeranno con chiare e distinte espressioni loro attestato, mentre dallo stesso dipende il rilascio del Mandato del Secretario, e susseguente sottoscrizione del Magistrato, per la Licenza della Stampa.

Nel caso che da' essi Deputati si rilevasse nelli Libri, Composizioni, et Opere cadute sotto il loro Esame, qualche eccezione, per la quale credessero di non concedere l' Attestato, e Fede per la Stampa o ristampa, sia e s' intenda prohibito agl' Auttori, Stampatori, e Librari, in consonanza delle preacenate Terminazioni, di ricorrere ad altro Revisore per conseguirla, ma sia preciso obbligo d' essi Revisori di far nota nel Libro, Opera e Composizione delle eccezioni che avessero rimarcate, e di raccoglierle in suo particolar Foglio diretto al Secretario del Magistrato, e spiegarle li motivi che lo rendono persuaso a disapprovarle in tutto o in parte.

Che ricevuta dal Secretario la nota stessa, sia egli obbligato a far tenere Copia a gl' altri Revisori; perche con tal lume, abbiano a rigettare l' Instanza per la concessione della Stampa, o Ristampa, restando al solo Ecc^{mo} Magistrato l' adito del ricorso per le Deliberazioni, che dall' Auttorità e dalla prudenza del medesimo fossero credute opportune.

E la presente sia Stampata e consegnata con l' altre a Deputati alla Revisione, alli Librari e Stampatori, registrata nella loro Mariegola per lume e per l' esecuzione.

CARLO RUZINI Kav. e Proc.
ANDREA SORANZO Proc. } Refformatori.
PIETRO GRIMANI Kav. Proc.
AGOSTINO GADALDINI Seg^{o}.

1730. 20 *Luglio.*

No. 40. Ricevuta sin nel suo nascere sotto il Publico Sovrano Patrocinio l' Arte della Stampa, reputata frà le Principali, et utile alla Dominante, et allo Stato, fu anche per la migliore, direttione, et per la più florida sussistenza munita di provide, e prudenti dispositioni che dall' attentione degl' Ill^{mi} et Ecc^{mi} Sig^{ri} Refformatori dello Studio di Padoa, a quali resta raccomandata s' è trovato necessario raccogliere e ravvivare nella Terminatione di 15 Gennaro 1725. Mentre però per renderle eseguite, s' è rilevato che ne tempi decorsi sia stato prescielto soggetto d' intelligenza, e pontualità, che con titolo di Presidente alle Stampe ci invigili, scorgono l' E. E. loro, anco ne presenti opportuno rinovare la pratica, e con tal oggetto conferire l' incombenza di Presidente alla Persona del Dr Gio: Fran^{co} Pivati, attuale Revisore di Libri, perche con l' abilità e virtù che possede, habbia ad essercitarla con le Comissioni che saranno in altra Terminatione espresse.

CARLO RUZINI Kav. Proc. Refformator.
ANDREA SORANZO Proc. Refformator.
GIO: PIET^{o}: PASQUALIGO Refformator.
AGOSTINO GADALDINI Segr^{o}.

1730. 20 *Luglio.*

No. 41. Appoggiata dagl' Ill^{mi} et Ecc^{mi} Sig^{ri} Refformatori dello Studio di Padoa alla virtù et habilità del Dr Gio: Fran^{co} Pivati Revisore de Libri con Terminatione di questo giorno la Carica di Presidente alle Stampe, resta anco alla di lui attenzione demandata la cura d' invigilare all' esecutione delle Leggi in varii tempi emanate per la migliore direttione dell' Arte stessa, e contenute nella Terminatione 15 Gennaro 1725, che se le consegna in copia portando al Magistratio ciò che andasse rilevando et occoresse.

Sarà sua particolar inspettione sopra le Stampe de Libri che con Decreti e Privilegii dell' Ecc^{mo} Senato vengono concesse, accudendo che pontualmente e per intiero siano adempite le condizioni prescritte, e de quali glene sarà eshibita la copia. A tenore d' essi Decreti dovrà esso Presidente andar di tempo in tempo, secondo gl' ordini del Magistrato, rivedendo li Fogli, che si anderanno da cadauno Privileggiato stampando per rincontro se siano conformi al primo Foglio, che sarà stato presentato nel Magistrato, e che dovrà sempre conservarsi per campion, e se corrispondano in esso gli' oblighi, che tiene d' ottima cartà, perfetti caratteri e diligenti correttioni, portando, in caso che diversamente risultasse, le relationi all' E. E. loro per gli opportuni compensi, onde escano le Stampe nella migliore perfettione e diligenza, con credito dell' Arte e benefitio del Commercio.

Per suo honorario dovrà da Stampatori che haveranno ottenuto dall' Ecc^{mo} Senato il Privileggio della Stampa, essere al medesimo corrisposto d' ogni Libro, e Tomo d' opera Privileggiata l' esemplare, onde conquesta honorifica e giusta rettributione resti riconosciuto l' impiego accurato e puntuale, che dalla di lui nota habilità si confida d' essigere.

Carlo Ruzini Kav. Proc. Refformator.
Andrea Soranzo Proc. Refformator.
Gio: Piet^{o} Pasqualigo Refformator.
Agostino Gadaldini Segr^{o}.

No. 42. Order to the Guild of Booksellers and Printers for the current tax.

"ciò pagheranno { Tansa Insensibile . . d. 252.
{ Taglion . . . . d. 200.

Data dal Collegio Ecc^{mo} Marittimo li 29 Dicembre 1732.

1733. 9 *Gennaro in Pregadi.*

No. 43. Quanto deriva dalla benemerita vigilanza delli Refformatori dello Studio di Padova, e volere con virtù e con zelo suggerito nella scrittura ora letta, onde promovere la maggior perfezione alle Stampe di questa Dominante rilevandosi molto consentaneo all' oggetto del represtinarsi il Carico di Sopraintendente alle stampe stesse tutto è ben degno de' loro studii e della pubblica approvazione.

Già però impartita facoltà alli Refformatori medesimi di devenire alla Scielta di Persona, che per la loro esperienza troveranno atta all' esercizio del Carico stesso, munendola di quell' istruzioni, et ordini, che per loro prudenza troveranno più accomodati e necessarii, onde se ne ritragga quel frutto che corrisponda alla massima, al vantaggio de Letterati et al maggior decoro dell' Arte.

Assentendo altresi l' equità pubblica, che al prescielto sia fissato l' annuale assegnamento di Ducati Cento al corrente valore della Piazza, e tanto più ch' è riuscito all' attenzione del Magistrato di conseguire a benefizio della Cassa un sopravanzo di Ducati 150 del sopraggio dell' annuali Stipendii (che) vengono contribuiti alli Maestri de' i Sestieri della Dominante, della qual summa sarà esborsato l' assegnamento stesso, che dovrà uscire dalla cassa stessa de Gramatici co i soliti mandati del Collegio Nostro.

VETTOR GRADENIGO
Nod° Ducal.

1733. 16 *Gennaro.*

Ben compreso dalla Sovrana prudenza dell' Ecc^mo Senato sopra zelante Scrittura degl' Ill^mi et Ecc^mi SSig^ri Rifformatori dello Studio di Padova, che a maggiore perfezione delle Stampe, et a mantenerle nell' antica estimazione, consenanteo sia il ripristinare il Carico di Sopraintendente alle medeme, instituito sin nel secolo passato et esercitato dal fù Zuanne Sozomeno, hanno l' E. E. loro, con la facoltà che le resta impartita dal Decreto 9 corrente, rivocando et intendendo per nulle le due Terminazioni di 20 Luglio 1730, come ce fatte non fossero, estese nella presente l' istruzioni et ordini che hanno riputati accomodati et necessarii all' esercizio del Carico stesso. In consonanza del medesimo Decreto, dovrà eleggersi un Sopraintendente alle Stampe, persona di Prudenza, di Dottrina e di pontualità, capace di esercitar l' impiego.

Al medesimo dovrà esser consegnato il Libro, in cui si contengono i Decreti e le Terminazioni concernenti le Stampe.

Sarà sua inspezione et precisa incombenza di acudire all' osservanza delle Leggi nel proposito delle Stampe, scoprire i diffetti e disordini che corressero, e siano per intiero adempite le condizioni prescritte et gli obblighi ingionti a Librari et Stampatori di valersi, particolarmente nei Libri a quali con Decreti dell' Ecc^mo Senato viene concesso Privileggio della Stampa, d' ottima carta, perfetto inchiostro, e caratteri ed accurate correzioni, e d' ogni mancanza e contravenzione portarne relazione al Magistrato per gli opportuni compensi, onde dalla di lui Sopraintendenza se ne ritragga quel frutto che corrispondi alla massima al vantaggio dei Letterati et al maggior decoro dell' Arte.

Siano al medesimo Sopraintendente assegnati in annuale stipendio Ducati Cento al corrente valore della Piazza, di esigerli con le forme e mandati soliti dell' Ecc^mo Colleggio, di sei in sei mesi, non potendo pretendere alcuna altra immaginabile utilità, e ricognizione, ne ingiongere per occasione del suo Offizio alcun aggravio o contribuzione a' Librari e Stampatori, bensi prestare tutta l' attenzione, per tenerli animati alla perfezione delle Stampe, onde non derivano stancheggi, ne dilazioni a rendere pregiudicata la riputazione dell' Arte.

Della presente Terminazione sia data copia al Priore di Librari e Stampatori perche ne siegua registro nella Mariegola dell' Arte, e sia ad essi notificata, e sortisca in ogni tempo la sua pontual esecuzione.

Sia parimente data copia del Decreto 9 corrente e della presente Terminazione al Magistrato de Governatori dell' Intrade C ssa di Gramatici, per la sua esecuzione nel proposito della corrisponsione dello Stipendio dell eletto Sopraintendente.

Gio : Fran^{co} Morosini Kav. Rifformator.
And^{a} Soranzo Proc. Rifformator.
Pietro Grimani Kav. Proc. Rifformator.
Agostino Gadaldini Segret^{o}.

1733. 18 *Gennaro.*

No. 45. Dovendo gl' Ill^{mi} et Ecc^{mi} SSig^{ri} Rifformatori dello Studio di Padova in ordine al Decreto dell' Ecc^{mo} Senato di 9 Gennaro corrente, devenire all' elezione di persona capace, di Dottrina, Intelligenza e pontualità ad esercitare il carico di Sopraintendenza alle Stampe, hanno con la facoltà impartita dal Decreto medesimo eletto il Dr Gio : Fran^{co} Pivati attuale Revisor de Libri, con lo Stipendio di Ducati cento al corrente valore di Piazza all' anno, da esigerli dalla Cassa di Grammatici et con gli obblighi et condizioni contenute nel preaccenato Decreto, et correlativa Terminazione di 16 corrente, ordinato cosi annotarsi.

Gio. Fran^{co} Morosini Kav. Rifformator.
And^{a} Soranzo Proc. Rifformator.
Pietro Grimani Kav. Proc. Rifformator.
Agostino Gadaldini Segretar^{o}.

173$\frac{4}{5}$. 23 *Gennaro.*

No. 46. Essendosi presentati con Riverente Supplica avanti gl' Ill^{mi} et Ecc^{mi} SSig^{ri} Rifformatori dello Studio di Padova il Priore Bancalli et Confratelli dell' Università de' Librari, nella quale premettendo Rassignatione et Ubbidienza al Divieto che ne' Libri da stamparsi in avvenire in materie Theologiche di Ius Canonico et simili, resti compresso il nome di questa Città et di tutte l' altre suddite, onde possi bensi spiegarsi quello di Città estere, Implorano di poter Unicamente dichiarire essere stampato il Libro a Spese di tal Libraro di Venetia, et ciò perche non rimangano Deviate le Commissioni che Ricevono, aggiongendo l' Instanza d' una permissione di questa Natura, sia a Cautione loro Rilasciata in scritto, SS. EE. trovano conveniente d' annuire al Ricorso, terminando che ne Libri dell' esposta condizione sia accordato all' occasione della stampa o Ristampa il ponervi la ricercata Dichiaratione, salva però la Proibitione antedeta, assentendo pure che di volta in volta venga in Carta concessa la Facoltà rifferita allo Stampatore, che stampare o Ristampare volesse Libri della condizione sudetta.

Gio : Pietro Pasqualigo. }
Michel Morosini. Cav. } Rifformatori.
Lorenzo Tiepolo Kav. Proc. }
Agostino Gadaldini Segretario.

17 *Marzo* 1736.

No. 47. Gl' Ill^{mi} et Ecc^{mi} Sig^{ri} Rifformatori dello Studio di Padova trovano proprio con la presente dichiarire che, essendo con Decreto del Ecc^{mo} Senato di 11 Maggio 1603 concesso ad ogni Libraro d' intraprendere la Stampa d' alcun Libro, o d' opera composta di più tomi il Privileggio d' anni dieci dal giorno che lo dà in nota, et potendo succedere che trascorrino quattro et anco anni cinque ad ultimarla, abbia et possi intendersi principiato il Privileggio dal giorno del compimento dell' ultimo tomo, che dovrà essere annotato nella stampa dal Libraro, con le pratiche che si stillano in Francia et Ollanda, et che tiene lo stampatore Comino in Padova, ma con l' obbligo al medesimo Libraro di stampare almeno ogni giorno un mezzo foglio, onde apparisca la continuazione della stampa, sotto pena in caso di trasgressione cominata nel Decreto dell' Ecc^{mo} Senato 1653, 24 Settembre, e Determinazione del Magistrato di 15 Gennaro 1725, et del Presente Capitolo sia data copia al Priore dell' Arte perche sia notificata a cadaun Libraro per la sua esecuzione.

Z. Pietro Pasqualigo. Rif.
Michiel Morosini. Kav. Rif.
Lorenzo Tiepolo. Kav. Proc. Rif.
Agostino Gadaldini Segr°.

1765. 29 *Agosto*.

No. 48. Pervenuti al Magistrato nostro con vera sorpresa alcuni Manifesti de' Libri Stampati e pubblicati senza le debite licenze dalli Libraij Pitteri e Storti, li quali notificano callo notabile di prezzo, l' uno per il Ricciardetto di Nicolò Carteromaco, e l' altro per la Biblioteca Ferrari, la stampa e publicazione de quali si trova contraria alle stabilite massime et alle Leggi, e reca sommo pregiuditio e sensibile danno alla Fede di Commerzio, et al Universale de Confratelli dell' Arte Tipografica, si fa determinare, operando con clemenza, al risoluto comando, che li detti Pitteri e Storti abbiano entro il solo termine di giorni otto a ritrattare con altri manifesti a stampa li viglietti suespressi come se fatti non fossero, precentando a medesimi di doverli presentare prima della stampa medesimo al Magistrato nostro per quelle osservazioni che convenissero, e per ottenerne la permissione della Stampa sudetta. E perche poi è supponibile che siano stati anche d' altri Libraij o Stampatori pubblicati con la Stampa altri avvisi o manifesti di tal natura senza la permissione nostra, si dichiara che questi siano nulli e di niun valore, come se usciti e pubblicati non fossero.

E la presente doverà esser consegnata al Priore de Librari e Stampatori per registrarla nella Mariegola dell' Arte, e da lui intimata a ciaschedun Matricolato per la sua pontuale et inalterabile obbedienza.

Angelo Contarini Pr. Riffor.
Francesco Morosini Kav. Pr. Riffor.
Girolamo Grimani Riffor.
Davidde Marchesini Seg^{rio}.

1737. 28 Aprile.

No. 49. Essendo stata nella pubblica Piazza di San Marco venduta la Predica intitolata "Passione di Gesu Cristo recitata nella Ducal Chiesa di San Marco nel Venerdi Santo dal Pr Serafino Petrobelli Capuccino de Lendenara," stampata nella stamperia di Steffano Tramontin, et di comissione d' Angelo Pasinello, Libraro, con annotazione di licenza di Superiori, ancorche non ottenuta dal Magistrato; Gl' Illmi et Eccmi SSri Rifformatori dello Studio di Padova, con la facoltà che le resta da pubblici decreti impartita d' essercitare in tali occasioni summariamente pene e castighi, mitius agendo, hanno condennato il medesimo Passinello in libre vinti di cera alli P. P. Rifformati, dovendo nel termine di giorni otto presentare al Segretario del Magistrato la ricevuta della sudetta cera.

Et della presente Terminazione sia data copia al Priore dell' Università de Librari, perche ne sia fatto registro, et resti la memoria della di lui trasgressione.

Gio: Franco Morosini Kav. Rifform.
Gio Emo. Proc. Riff.
Pietro Grimani. Kav. Proc. Riff.
Agostino Gadaldini Segretaro.

Illmi et Eccmi SSigri Proveditori di Comun li 30 Giugno 1736.

No 50. A solo fine di togliere gli abusi che si erano introdotti nell' accettar Fratelli, nel dar le loro Prove, e nel far le loro Cariche, nella nostra Università de' Librari, Stampatori e Legatori.

L' anderà Parte posta dal Magco Prior e Banca, che la Colonna de' Legatori sia regolata e governata da soli Capi Maestri Legatori, e che de cætero il Magco Prior e Banca de' Librari e Stampatori non abbia da ingerirsi nell' accettar Fratelli nè ballottar le Prove de Legatori nè far le loro Cariche, e così s' intendi regolata la Parte presa in Capitolo Generale li 10 Febbro $17\frac{35}{36}$.

Attesa dunque la sudetta Parte si dichiara che de cætero se alcuno Legatore desiderasse di entrare nell' Arte de' Librari e Stampatori non possi mai esser accettato in alcun modo se non averà li suoi giusti Requisiti, come accenna la Parte de 20 Decembre 1735, cio è che li sudetti Requisiti siano intieramente fatti che abbia servito un Capo Maestro Libraro. Così pure venendo il caso che qualche Libraro desiderasse di esser matricolato per Legatore, questo debba avere li suoi attestati tutti d' aver servito un Capo Maestro Legatore, e debba portarsi avanti la Banca de Legatori, la quale dovrà esser formata da sei Capi Maestri Legatori, cio è il suo Capo, li due Eletti sopra le Prove, li due sopra le contrafazione, ed un Consigliere da esser eletto da' soli Capi Maestri Legatori, e questi poi li destineranno la loro Prova spettante a Legatore, ciòe un Messale da esser legato con le carte dorate schiette, e coperto di Cordoan nero, lavorato la coperta di oro a piacere del Capo Colonna; e la sudetta Prova doverà esser peritata dalla sola Banca de' Legatori, e poi ballottata da tutti li Capi Maestri Legatori, e passando li due terzi delle balle resterà in tal modo matricolato per Capo Maestro Legatore.

Occorendo la sudetta Colonna de' Legatori di radunarsi per li loro affari, come sopra, si raduneranno nella nostra Scola di S.S. Gio: e Paolo, dichiarandosi che li sudetti

Legatori siino in avvenire sempre esclusi di entrare nelle Riduzioni, e Capitoli de' Librari, come facevano per il passato, e che essi Legatori sieno sempre soccombenti a quei giusti aggravii che li venissero gettati come erano per il passato, e s' intendi la sudetta Colonna solamente sciolta come sopra; E d' ogni volta che la detta Colonna accetterà qualche Capo Maestro Legatore dovrà il suo Capo consegnar subito la Benintrada ricevuta nelle mani del Mag^{co} Prior, ed insieme li Requisiti da esser posti in filza separata, e per farne registro in un libro a parte, che dovrà esser formato a tal fine per la sola Colonna de Legatori.

TOMASO MICHIEL. Proved. di C.

Terminazione degl' Illustrissimi et Eccellentissimi Signori Rifformatori dello Studio di Padova.

No. 51. Ritrovandosi scoperta al presente di Lire quattro mille ottocento e ottanta una l' arte de Librari e Stampatori di questa Città per crediti che ella tiene de suoi Confratelli in conto di Tanse, Taglioni, Luminarie ed altro, come apparisce dalla inserta nota formata dal' attuale Priore dell' Arte medesima, e venendo pur essa pregiudicata delle solite e già stabilite Lire tre e soldi due, che sborsar deve ogni Libraro al caso di dare in nota li Libri da stamparsi per il conseguimento del Privileggio, e ciò per ommettersi una tale annotazione sulla fede, che per l' instituito Registro de Mandati concedersi non possa dello stesso Libro a più d' uno la stampa, il che viene a farsi un equivalente del Privileggio suddetto, necessario conoscono gl' Illustrissimi et Eccellentissimi Signori Rifformatori dello Studio di Padova il provedere nell' una e nell' altra parte al disordine per benefizio dell' Arte suddetta, e per mantenerla in vigore, e nella capacità di reggere a suoi aggravii; E però

Hanno terminato, che non possa in avvenire il Segretario del loro Eccellentissimo Magistrato elevare Mandato alcuno per la Stampa di verun Libro, se unitamente alle consuete Fedi di Revisione non gli sarà esibito attestato dal Prior de Librari, pro tempore, che assicuri non esser debitore all' Arte stessa quello che ricercasse il Mandato, dovendo esso Priore rilasciar Gratis e senza stancheggio un tale attestato, onde in abuso non converta la provida disposizione.

Sarà poi detto Piore tenuto a presentare immancabilmente nel Magistrato di loro Eccellenze un foglio esatto di mese in mese, per il quale risultino tutti li Libri che entro quel mese fossero annotati, come sopra, in Privileggio, per eseguirsene sopra l' enunciato Registro il confronto col numero de Mandati ad oggetto delle opportune risoluzioni, dovendo esprimersi in detto foglio li nomi de Librari o Stampatori, che fatta avessero l' annotazione col pagamento delle predette Lire tre e soldi due all' incontro del nome che vi avrà suplito, e questo ancora per le deliberazioni che convenissero.

Et la presente dovrà esser stampata, e consegnata al Priore de Librari e Stampatori, per la sua esecuzione, e perchè l' abbia egli a render nota alla propria Università.

Dat. dal Magistrato de Rifformatori dello Studio di Padova li 31 Maggio 1742.

ALVISE MOCENIGO 2° Rifformator.
ZUANNE QUERINI Proc. Rifformator.
DANIEL BRAGADIN Kav. Proc. Rifformator.

AGOSTINO BIANCHI Seg^{r}.

1742. 11 *Settembre.*

No. 52. Riconosciutti dalla Maturità dell' Eccellentissimo Senato li molti e gravi inconvenienti che derivar possono dal diffondersi fuori della Dominante, e dall' introdursi nelle Città della Terra Ferma la Stampa de Rossi e Neri, che è quella de' Libri ad uso di Chiesa, ha con Auttorevole suo Decreto de di 28 Luglio ultimo passato stabilito che un tal genere di Stampa sia e s' intenda fissato nella sola Arte de Librari e Stampatori di questa Città di Venezia, cosiche in verun Luogo della Terra Ferma sudetta rimaner non possa esequito, e ne restino anzi sospese l' operazioni, che fossero incominciate. Essendo però stato dalla medesima sovrana Auttorità rimesso al Magistrato degl' Illustrissimi et Eccellentissimi Signori Rifformatori dello Studio di Padova di disponere gli Ordini necessarii per l' adempimento dell' accenata Deliberazione, trovano l' Eccellenze loro di rendere in vigor del presente Proclama pubblicamente noto,

Che cadaun Libraro o Stampatore Matricolato nell' Arte di questa stessa Città di Venezia possa liberamente, e senza impedimento veruno pratticare la stampa de Rossi e Neri nelle Stamparie qui esistenti, et in quelle pure, che qui fossero nuovamente aperte da Persone come sopra Matricolate, proibita essa Stampa intendendosi ad ogni altro che non si ritrovasse in detta Arte descritto, sotto le pene tutte quali sono già dalle pubbliche Leggi comminate a Contrafattori nell' universale delle Stampe.

Che alli Librari tutti e Stampatori di qualunque Città della Terra Ferma, ancorchè Matricolati in quelle lor Arti sia assolutamente vietato lo stampar Rossi e Neri per conto proprio, o per altrui commissione in poca o in molta quantità, dovendo in caso di trasgressione essere confiscate le stampe, e soggetti li Trasgressori a quelle pene pecuniarie et afflitive che pareranno a sue Eccellenze.

Che non possa alcun Libraro o Stampatore di Venezia prestare il proprio nome a Librari o Stampatore di Terra Ferma per la referita stampa de Rossi e Neri, ed ogni qual volta ciò venisse a scoprirsi, incorrerà tanto chi avesse commessa quanto chi data avesse mano ad una simile collusione nei più rigorosi castighi che a loro Eccellenze sembreran convenienti oltre la perdita anco in tal caso delle eseguite stampe.

Che debbano immediate restar sospesi, ne possano progredirsi i lavori de' Rossi e Neri in que' Luoghi di Terra Ferma, ove si trovassero incominciati, e per assicurare l' obbedienza sarà severamente punito chiunque contravenisse, sempre invigilare da sue Eccellenze dovendosi con mezzi opportuni per iscoprir le mancanze.

Et il presente dovrà esser stampato, consegnato al Prior de Librari e Stampatori di questa Città, e circolarmente spedito a pubblici Rappresentanti di Terra Ferma perchè ne promovano l' inviolabil esecuzione.

Z. Alvise Mocenigo secondo Rifformator.
Zuane Querini Procurator Rifformator.
Daniel Bragadin Cavalier Procurator Rifform.
Agostino Bianchi Segr.

A di 30 *Luglio* 1738.

No. 53. Giunto a notizia del Magistrato Eccellentissimo de' Signori Proveditori et Aggionti sopra danari, al quale da replicati Decreti è appoggiata la materia delle Stamparie Pubbliche di questa Città e della Terra Ferma, che in questa Dominante vi sono stampatori quali in pregiudizio del pubblico diritto, e con quelle maggiori conseguenze che possano succedere, si fanno lecito d' imprimer stampe attenenti alla Pubblica Stamparia in contraventione del prescritto da terminatione delli loro Precessori 1685, 15 Marzo, ma con abuso ancora più esentiale imprimer sopra di esse il pubblico segno di San Marco, lo che non è lecito, se non alli Stampatori Pubblici a quali con le dovute cautelle viene affidato il segno sudetto con il mezzo del quale potrebbero succeder rilevantissimi prejudizii alli pubblici interessi e riguardi.

Per tanto sue Eccellenze a divertimento di tale scandalosa introduzione hanno terminato, e con la presente ordinato, che non possa alcun stampatore di questa Città ingerirsi in alcuna sorte di Stampe attinenti alla Stamparia Pubblica, giusto a quanto viene prescritto dalla precitata Terminatione 1685, ma in oltre precisamente divietano a cadaun Stampatore il valersi e in qualsi sia modo imprimer stampe con il segno del San Marco in pena a cadaun contrafacente di Ducati 200 applicati alla Cassa d' Arsenal, e di quelle maggiori anche afflitive che fossero dovute a misura delle contrafazioni, e ciò in ogni e cadaun caso che contravenisse oltre l' obbligo di rissarcir la Stamparia Pubblica di tutto il danno che gli fosse stata inferito.

Dovrà la presente esser intimata al Prior dell' Arte dei Stampatori con obbligo di renderla nota a tutti li Confratelli di detta Arte, e di registrarla nella sua Matricola a cognizione perpettua, e per la sua dovuta esecuzione. Restando in oltre dichiarito che in qualunque caso di tali rillevate reità potrà cadauno del presente Eccellentissimo Magistrato levar la pena sudetta.

Lunardo Diedo Proveditor.
Gio: Priuli Kav. Proc. Proveditor.
Nicolò Corner Proveditor.
Vincenzo Pisani quinto Proveditor.
Antonio Olmo Nod e Segr.

1738. 13 *Agosto in Pregadi.*

Approval of the above.

Bortolamio Borghezalio Nod. Duc.

1749. 29 *Maggio.*

No. 54. Col oggetto di rimovere l' occazioni dei disordini che pur troppo insorger possono nella matteria molto gelosa delle Stampe, si è trovato necessario dagl' Ill[mi] et Ecc[mi] SS[ri] Refformatori dello Studio di Padova di ravivare gl' ordini nel proposito, in una nuova Terminatione capitulata, affinche, col loro pontual adempimento che convien confidare dalla Persona del Dr Gio: Fran[co] Pivatti, Pubblico Revisore de' Libri et attual sopraintendente alle Stampe, abbiano a riportare il loro effetto quelle provide e salutari ordinationi che altre volte furono dichiarate.

Quindi è che l E. E. loro con la presente ordinano, et ordinando comettono ad esso sopraintendente, non solo ma anco a tutti quelli che saranno nominati in progresso, per ciò che ha relazione al Carico medesimo, di dover ciascheduno dal proprio canto eseguire quanto segne;

P^{mo}. Sarà dal medesimo sopraintendente tenuto il libro a stampa in cui si contengono li Decreti e Terminazioni concernenti le Stampe, et averà ad unirsi gl' altri sucessive nel proposito.

2do. Inspetione particolare del medesimo Pivati, e sua precisa incombenza sarà l' accudire che riportino la dovuta osservanza le Leggi antedette nel proposito delle Stampe, e massimamente la Terminazione 16 Gennaro 1733, scoprirne li diffetti e li disordini che corressero, et invigilar finalmente se siano per intiero eseguite da Stampatori le Pubbliche Leggi nel proposito già Pubblicate, ed a lui note.

3^{zo}. Doverà ricopiare dal libro Mandati che tiene dal Segretario del Magistrato, per ordine di Alfabetto, il nome di tutti quei Stampatori e Librari di questa Città come della Terra Ferma, che d' anno in anno avessero ottenuta licenza di stampa, connotare all' incontro di cadaun nome con chiara disposizione li titoli de Libri che li fossero stati concessi, et annotarvi le variazioni che da nome a nome fossero soceduto de Mandati, affinche il tutto servir abbia per solo suo lume, e di fondamento per ritraere da loro l' Opere publicate, e per spiegar poi in scritto a lume delle ulteriori deliberazioni del Magistrato, l' omissioni in cui risultassero nelle consegne delle solite copie alla Publica Libraria di Padova.

4to. Ma perche sommamente importa per la riputazione delle Venete Stampe ch' esse procedino nella miglior maniera, averà egl' a ciò accudire con ogni cura giusto al Decreto di sua elezione, e sopraintendere assiduamente alle medesime, onde si ritragga quel frutto che si è prefisso l' Ecc^{mo} Senato dalla di lui cura et impiego pratticandolo con tutta la discrezione, col tenere animati li Stampatori alla perfezione, ma senza sturbare la quiete dell' Arte, e portandone in tempo opportuno, e sempre prima che sia publicata l' Opera le relazioni in scritto dei disordini, che mediante le continue sue diligenze averà osservati, e che meritassero compenso.

5°. Particolar avvertenza averà egli sopra i Libri a quali con Decreto dell' Ecc^{mo} Senato fosse stato concesso special Privileggio, affinche siano bene impressi in buona Carta, perfetto Inchiostro e Caratteri, con diligenti corretioni, e doverà portarne, anche di questi sempre in tempo opportuno in scritto le relazioni di chi fosse delinquente, et in che consistesse la mancanza perche si possa accorrere dall' E. E. loro con solleciti provedimenti et ordinazioni a correggere le delinquenze. Ad oggetto poi che possa il sopraintendente sudetto esatamente eseguire quanto anche in questo Capitolo gli resta prescritto, sarà egli tenuto procurarsi dal Segretario nostro le note de Libri concessi dall' Ecc^{mo} Senato in Privileggio a Stampatori cosi di questa Città come della Terra Ferma, et il tempo della Grazia il che agevolmente potrà e doverà adempire mediante l' esato registro che tiene di tali Privileggi il Segretario nostro, che lascierà al detto Pivati pratticare le note ommessegli.

6°. Doverà egli farsi consegnare dal Prior dell' Arte de' Librari e Stampatori la nota di tutti li Matricolati o siano descritti in detta Arte capaci di Mandati di Stampe e lavoranti delle Stampe di questa Città, distinguendo appresso che questi ultimi servissero, onde poter egli et il Prior de Librari connotare al margine le variazioni, i cambii delle persone di stamparia, o se mai alcuno partisse da questa Città, a lume di quelle deliberazioni e compensi che convenissero a tenor delle Leggi.

7mo. Perfetionato dal detto Sopraintendente Pivati l' Alfabetto commessogli negl' Articoli 3 e 5, che doverà pratticare con la maggior sollecitudine e diligenza non doverà il Segretario rilasciar più mandati ad alcuno se, oltre le solite fedi di revisione, non le sarà pur prodotta una fede dal custode della Publica Libreria di Venezia che dichiari che quel tale non è debitore de consegne de Libri Stampati alla detta Libreria di Venezia per mandati rilasciatigli; e così pure altra fede del detto sopraintendente che lo stesso spieghi per la Publica Libreria di Padova.

8vo. Et perche dalle Pubbliche Leggi è prescritto il termine a cadaun Stampatore per dar mano alla stampa doppo ricevuto il mandato e di compiere l' edizione per li libri di moderata grandezza dentro l' anno, e per gl' Altri di maggior molle et in più Tomi in ragione almeno di mezo foglio al giorno, salve l' escuzasioni col metodo stabilito dalle Publiche Leggi, così con tali avertenze si averanno dal custode e dal sopraintendente medesimo a segnarvi le sopra espresse fedi rilasciate con la connotazione del giorno e nome del Stampatore e Libraro averanno l' uno e l' altro imancabilmente a presentare nel Magistrato nostro, d' anno in anno la nota; come pure altra de Libri respettivamente ricevuti da esser custodite in filza a parte e numerate per li necessarii confronti a Publica e privata cauzione.

9°. A facilità de confronti medesimi resta prescritto all' Arte de Librari e Stampatore di questa Città di far imprimere Bolletini da esser distribuiti a cadaun Matricolato capace di Mandato ne' quali, lasciato in bianco il nome dello Stampatore et il titolo del Libro o Tomo, si esprima "Io N. N. ho publicato in questo giorno il Libro o Tomo . . . intitolato . . . giusto il Mandato degl' Ecc^{mi} SS^{ri} Rifformatori dello Studio di Padova de dì . . al N° . ." il quale Bolletino doverà essere consegnato prontamente al Segretario del Magistrato, e da lui custodito in filza a parte che intitolerà di Publicazioni de Libri, cominandosi la pena a Librari e Stampatori che ommettessero tal pronta presentazione di essergli depennati et annulati li Privileggii che avessero conseguito; le quali note e Bolletini non doveranno essere mostrati che al solo Ecc^{mo} Magistrato.

X^{mo}. Le copie poi de Libri Stampati appartenenti alla Publica Libreria di Padova, doveranno da qui inanzi essere consegnate dal solo sopraintendente Pivati, che di volta in volta rilascierà la ricevuta a cauzione de consegnatore; e di sei in sei mesi di tali ricevute ne porterà la nota con le distinzioni necessarie all' Ecc^{mo} Magistrato affinche raccolti in una conveniente quantità, se ne possa fare, con le solite formalità di Cassa serrata e sigilata, la spedizione alla Publica Rappresentanza di Padova, ritrarne le responsali da quel Bibliotechario, e aggiungerli al Cattalogo de Libri della medesima; e riconosciuti li resti astringere li debitori librari alla prescritta consegna. E queste note del sopraintendente si ingionge al Segretario di tenerle in Filza pur a parte, e sempre numerate come si è detto delle Altre.

XI. Averà il Pivati particolar avertenza di farsi conesgnar per l' intiero da' respettivi Stampatori diffettivi li Libri per quali fosse stato rilasciato il Mandato da primo Marzo 1739, tempo in cui incominciava l' instituto registro de' Mandati, sino al presente, senza pe ò ommettere le dilgenze per gl' anteriori, giusto alle Terminazioni già publicate, et a piena notizia de Stampatori medesimi.

E della presente perciò le spetta, sia fatta tener copia al Prior dell' Università de Librari e Stampatori di questa Città per registrarla nella Mariegola dell' Arte et ad ogni altro nominato in essa, ben certo il Magistrato che da ogn' uno per quanto le resta ingionto sarà prestata la dovuta obbedienza, et intiera esecuzione.

GIO EMO Proc. Riffʳ.
BARBON MOROSINI Kav. Proc. Riffʳ.
MARCO FOSCARINI Kav. Proc. Riffʳ.

No. 55. Li Illmi et Eccᵐⁱ SSʳⁱ Eⁱ contro la Bestemia infrascritti rillevando con sorpresa ed indignazione, che da *Librari* e Stampadori, ad onta delle antiche e recenti Leggi e Terminazioni, si persista tuttavia in una contumace negligenza di rassegnare li Mandati di Licenza e permissione delle respettive stampe, onde abbiano luoco li registri che sono prescritti dalle Leggi e che possono interessare per oggetti importantissimi la maturità e zelo del loro autorevole Magistrato, procedendo con rissoluzione non disgiunta da atto di clemenza verso gli innobedienti per il passato, terminano et accordano ad essi il termine di giorni 15 e non più, di suplire al loro dovere, e per il decetero vogliono a tutti noto, che a ciascheduno il quale sarà trovato diffettivo, e non averà obbedito dentro il predetto termine dal giorno della data del Mandato, sarà levata irremissibalmente la pena di ducati 25, et altre maggiori ad arbitrio di S.S. E.E. e successori, li quali avvenissero a circostanze agravanti la trasgressione medesima.

E la presente sia letta e data in copia al Prior de Librari e Stampatori alla presenza di S.S. E.E. con preciso comando di farla nota a tutti li Confratelli, di registrarla nella loro Mariegola, e di portar sollecitamente fede giurata al Magistrato di aver esatamente eseguito.

Dal Magistrato sudetto li 23 Ottobre 1771.

PAULO CONDULMER Esecutor.
ANTONIO DIEDO Esecutor.
ZUANE GRITI Esecutor.
PRŌ PISANI Esecutor.
ANDREA GRATAROL Segᵒ.

1755. 27 *Febraro.*

No. 56. Fatto seguire il fermo ed apporto degli esemplari in Nᵒ mille circa del libro intitolato—*Evangelica Tromba promulgata dal quondam sacro Dottare Maccario, che fu Maestro e Rettore del Colleggio esistente nell' Isola di Patmo, ora la prima volta data alle stampe, e portata in luce a spese di un certo pio et ortodosso e con la diligenza dell' eloquentissimo D. Efrem d' attene che presentamente è in Cipro sacro Predicatore. Nella celebre città di Olanda Amsterdam, anno di nostra Salute* 1754—stampato però in Venezia in idioma e carattere Greco da Gasparo Girardi, libraio e stampatore di questa Città senza veruna revisione e licenza, con aperta dettestabile innobbedienza e contravenzione alle publiche Leggi; Gl' Illᵐⁱ et Eccᵐⁱ SSʳⁱ Rifformatori dello Studio di Padova con l' auttorità loro impartita da publici Decreti, anno terminato e comandato, che tutti li detti esemplari sieno abbrucciati pubblicamente nella Piazzetta di San Marco, sicche si riducano intieramente in Cenere, e ciò segua presente il Comandador del Magistrato, e colle necessarie altre volte pratticate custodie.

Quanto poi alla persona del delinquente sunnominato Gasparo Girardi, cui giustamente conviensi il rigor delle pene dalle Leggi cominate, procedendo l' Eccellenze loro con atto di carità, e clemenza, terminano parimente, e comandano che esso Stampatore sia e s' intenda condannato alla pena pecuniaria di Ducati cento V. C. da disponersi come più parera all' Ecc^{ze} loro, dovendo il detto Girardi contare tal summa in mano del Priore di questa Università de Libraj e Stampatori, e sia e s' intenda pure obligato a soddisfare alle spese tutte occorse per il fermo ed apporto degli ennuntiati esemplari, e che occorrerano nella esecuzione del comandato incendio, al che sia tenuto suplire immancabilmente entro il periodo di giorni quindeci dal giorno della intimazione che le verrà fatta dal Comandador del Magistrato, passato il qual tempo, quando non fosse eseguito l' esborso e soddisfatte le dette spese, deveniranno S.S. E.E. a quegli ulteriori espedienti che saranno giudicati convenirsi.

E la presente sia data in copia all' ennuntiato Priore, per lume di quanto si ordinà, e sarà obbligo suo, spirato che sia il prescritto tempo, portare li responsali dell' eseguito, commettendosi di registrare la presente pure nella Matricola della Università a comune notizia, et ad altrui esempio.

E siano dati gli ordini necessarii al Comandador et a chi spetta, per la esecuzione in conformità.

Zan Alvise Mocenigo 2do Riff^{r}.
Zuanne Querini Proc. Riff^{r}.
Barbon Morosini Cav. Proc. Riff^{r}.
Giacomo Zuccato Seg^{rio}.

1756. 31 *Marzo.*

No. 57. Gl' Ill^{mi} et Ecc^{mi} SS^{ri} Rifformatori dello Studio di Padova inclinando per naturale clemenza a riflessi ed usi di Carità, e disposti a pratticarne gli effetti verso lo Stampatore Gasparo Girardi, cui per le irregolari reprensibili procedure ogni maggior severità si converebbe, devengono per atto di grazia ad ordinare che le siano restituite le cassette Caratteri da stampa fatte asportare dalla di lui Stamparia, ed esistenti nella dogana da Terra, e le siano levati i publici Bolli da Torchi, rimmettendolo cosi dalle penali cominate li 27 Febraro scaduto e 23 Marzo scaduto. Ordinano pure che del denaro per pena esborsalo dal detto Girardi nella summa depositata in mano del Priore di questa Università de Libraj e Stampatori, oltre quello che doveva a sodisfazione delle spese tutte occorse per occasione delle comandate esecuzioni, come appare dalla ricevuta presentata dal Priore medesimo, del detto denaro dunque sia fatto il ripparto seguente, cioè mettà all' Academia de Nobili alla Giudecca, e l' altra mettà sia giustamente divisa in Elemosina alla Fabrica della Chiesa di S. Giovanni Novo, e per titolo di ricognizione al Comandador del Magistrato.

Dovrà però rilasciarsi in conformità le convenienti comissioni a chi spetta, e darsi copia della presente al Sudetto Priore per le annotazioni occorrenti.

Zan Alvise Mocenigo 2° Riff^{r}.
Barbon Morosini Cav. D^{re} Riff^{r}.
Giacomo Zuccato Seg^{rio}.

1756. 7 *Settembre.*

No. 58. Essendo capitate in questa Dogana da Mar provenienti da estero Luogo alcune Balle Libri diretti alli Librai e Stampatori Francesco Pitteri, Nicolo Pezzana e Lorenzo Baseggio, tra li quali libri furono separati e trattenuti quelli che o per essere privileggiati in questa Città, o con mentito Frontispizio, o con altre abusive Macchie furono qui introdotti con aperta contravenzione alle Publiche Leggi replicatamente da tempo in tempo rinovate; Gl' Ill^mi et Ecc^mi SS^ri Refformatori dello Studio di Padova ad oggetto di promovere la dovuta osservanza alle Leggi medesime, e per togliere la reprensibile licenziosità di tali introduzioni che, contrarie ad ogni buon riguardo disciplina e di giustizia, feriscono l' interesse degli altri Veneti Privilegiati Libraj e Stampatori, con l' auttorità all' E. E. loro demandata da publici Decreti anno terminato e comandato che tutti li detti Libri che saran qui sotto descritti siano abbrucciati publicamente nella Piazzetta di San Marco, sicche si riducano intieramente in cenere, e ciò segua, com' è solito, presente il Comandador del Magistrato, e colle necessarie altre volte pratticate custodie.

Corpi 86. Lettere Critiche di C. Agostino Santi Puppieni, o sia dell' Avvocato Giuseppe Costantini.

Corpi 48. Apparatus Teologiæ Moralis etc. auctore Toma Francesco Lotario.

Corpi 48. Hermanii Boorlavve prelectiones Accademicæ cum annotationibus Alberti Haber sotto titolo Disputationes phisicæ medicæ, anatomicæ Chirurgicæ Alberti Haber.

Corpi 6. Sinonimi ed aggiunti Italiani raccolti da Carlo Costanzo Rabbi.

Corpi 25. Il Segretario Principiante etc. D' Isidoro Nardi.

E la presente sia data in copia al Prior dell' Università de Libraj e Stampatori perche abbia a farla registrare nella Matricola dell' Università medesima.

E siano dati gli ordini necessarii a chi spetta per la esecuzione in conformità.

Zuane Querini Proc. Riff^r.
Barbon Morosini Cav. Dr Riff^r.
Alvise Mocenigo 4to Cav. Dr Riff^r.
Giacomo Zuccato Seg^rio.

1756. 30 *Settembre.*

No. 59. Attrovandosi nella publica Dogana da Mar alcuni libri dirretti alli Libraj e Stampatori Veneti Nicolo Pezzana e Lorenzo Baseggio, supra quali furono riservate le convenienti deliberazioni, ed altri essendone pure capitati successivamente dirretti alli Libraj Giovanni Manfrè, Giambattista Pasquali, Giambattista Recotti, e Tomaso Bettinelli, gli uni e gli altri contrarj affatto alle Leggi, in aperta contravenzione alle medesime, con danno de' Veneti matricolati, li quali si trovano in possesso de' Privileggi, e con delusione de' buoni metodi; Gl' Ill^mi et Ecc^mi SS^ri Riformatori dello Studio di Padova eccitati da riflessi di Giustizia, e dalle istanze proddotte dal Priore della Università a nome pure de' Matricolati in essa, et ad oggetto di promovere e mantenere nel suo primo vigore la dovuta buona disciplina, da che derriva il felice andamento delle stampe, e l' avvantaggio reciproco de Librai e Stampatori, con l' auttorità all' Ecc^e loro impartita da publici Decreti, mitius agendo, terminano, e comandano che tutti libri qui sotto descritti sieno nella Piazzetta di San Marco publicamente incendiati, sicche si riducano intieramente in cenere, e ciò segua presente il Comandador del Magistrato, e colle solite altre volte pratticate maniere, e custodie

Corpi 36. Natalis Alexandri etc. in Evangelia.
Corpi 6. Arnoldi Vinnii.
Corpi 19. Vocabolario Pasini.
Corpi 20. Elementa Physicæ Muschenbrooek.
Corpi 20. Lettere critiche etc. del Costantini.
Corpi 5. Theologia Moralis Antoine.
Corpi 24. Heinecii de Jure naturæ et gentium.
Corpi 10. Il Segretario etc. del Nardi.
Corpi 8. Quaresimale del Padre Serafino da Vicenza.
Corpi 4. Vita di San Paolo.
Corpi 6. Plitcarnii Opera Medica.
Corpi 6. Lettere scielte del Chiari.
Corpi 200. Geografia Buffier.
Corpi 100. Martirio del Cuore.
Corpi 40. Felicità etc. del Muratori.
Corpi 70. Divon [= divotione] regolata del Muratori.
Corpi 15. Opuscula Haller.
Corpi 80. Giorno santificato del Siniscalchi.
Corpi 88. Comedie della sposa Persiana.

Doverà però darsene gli ordini a chi spetta in conformità di quanto viene ordinato.

E darsi pure copia della presente al Priore della detta Università per il suo registro nella matricola della Università medesima ad esempio e correzione.

Barbon Morosini Cav. Dr Riff^r.
Alvise Mocenigo 4to Cav. Dr Riff^r.
Giacomo Zuccato Seg^{rio}.

1761. *M. V.* 10 *Febb^r.*

No. 60. Sopra la stampa con le debite permissioni e licenze eseguita dal Libraro e Stampatore Simeone Occhi, dell' opera intitolata Compendio della Teologia Concina, e dall' altro Stampatore e Libraro Antonio Zatta ristampata sotto differente titolo e con pretesto di aggiunte, nacque tra li due Professori vertenza, il Primo reclamando perchè fosse leso il Privilegio da lui legalmente conseguito dall' Arte giusta le Leggi, e conseguentamente recato pregiudizio al proprio interesse assicurato dalla Fede del Privileggio medesimo; il secondo, cio è il Zatta giustificando la ristampa intrapresa per le aggiunte e per essere una copia della edizione seguita in Bologna. Rassegnato il ricorso d' ambo le Parti agl' Ill^{mi} et Ecc^{mi} SS^{ri} Rifformatori dello Studio di Padova, e dall' Ecc^e Loro attentamente udite le ragioni addotte dalle parti medesime, presente le persone ricorrenti, confrontati li fatti e viste le Leggi, con unanime consenso, e per effetto di retta equità deliberano e stabiliscono relativamente alle Publiche disposizioni nel proposito, che lesiva come è, e pregiudizievole al Legitimo Privileggio dello Stampatore Simeone Occhi la collusoria ristampa del Zatta, sia perciò lo Stampatore Zatta soggetto alla pena statuita. Tutti gli esemplari dunque (già fatti fermare dal Magistrato sotto publico Bollo) della detta ristampa e la ottenuta terminazione saranno prontamente dati al Libraro Simeone Occhi, che potrà usarli come proprie stampe, e resterà pure condannato, et obbligato il Libraro Antonio Zatta alla corrisponsione, ed intiero contamento di Ducati tre cento Valuta Piazza, giusta la Parte 1603, 21 Genn°, da essere tripartiti e riscossi giusta il Decreto 23 Febb° 1746, due terzi dal ricorrente, e Privileggiato Occhi predetto, e l' altro terzo dal N. H. Aggionto Cassier dell' Accademia de Nobili alla Giudecca, a beneficio di quella Cassa.

E della esecuzione della presente dovrà al Magistrato portarsene li riscontri, per il che sarà notificata rispettivamente et intimata alli suddetti Librari Occhi e Zatta.

Dovrà darsene copia per lume et esecuzione al N. H. Cassier riferito.

E sarà data parimente in copia al Priore della Università de Librari e Stampatori onde sia registrata in Mariegola e serva di esempio e correzione altrui.

Ordinando L' E.E. loro in fine che cosi sia annotato.

Marco Foscarini Cav. Proc. Riffr.
Alvise Mocenigo 4° Cav. Proc. Riffr.
Polo Renier Riffr.
Giacomo Zuccato. Segrio.

1767. 2 *Maggio.*

No. 61. Accertatosi il Magistrato nostro dopo maturi esami che il vizioso studio de Libraj nel diminuire ogni dì più la spesa dell' Edizioni, e specialmente nelle ristampe che fanno a concorenza l' uno dell' altro, è una delle Origini principali della pessima qualità delle Venete Stampe, faccendo essi accordi cosi scarsi e ristretti co' Padroni delle Stamperie che questi si trovano dalla necessità sforzati a valersi nello Stampare di mani imperite ed escluse dalle Leggi, e d' attrecci consumati dal tempo e guasti; ed inoltre essendosi per minorare ogni edizione di Fogli introdotta la pessima usanza d' ordinare con troppa avidità Caratteri gittati fuori del quadro naturale perche riescono con spalla ristretta, il che gli fà uscire dalla debita proporzione, e incomodi e dispiacevoli a chi legge, veniamo in deliberazione di commettere sopra questi due punti quanto segue.

1. Che i prezzi i quali saranno da qui in poi alle Stamparie accordati da chi fà stampare Opere licenziate dal Magistrato nostro con Mandato e dovranno cominciarsi ad accordare e pagare subito dopo publicata la presente Terminazione, non sieno minori di quelli che saranno in essa assegnati, ne possa dai Capi di Esse Stamparie alterarsi quella distribuzione di pagamento fra gli Operai, che sarà qui sotto stabilita, e anche essa dovrà cominciare al tempo destinato di sopra.

2. Nelle Opere soggette a Mandato tanto a penna quanto di ristampa in Carta Corsiva ordinaria di copie mille di lavoro usuale e corrente in Foglio, Quarto, Ottavo e Dodici paghinsi le Forme al Capo della Stamperia seguendo il calcolo delle migliaja di lettere che saranno in ogni Foglio contenute e secondo che per ogni spezie di Carattere nella sottonotata Lista è specificato e prescritto.

Per un foglio di Carattere detto Silvio, contenente Lettere frà venti e vent' una mila in carta e numero di Copie e sesti di Libro come sopra £15 10

Per uno in Antico, o Filosofia che contenga più che ventisei o ventisette mila Lettere £16
Per uno in Garamon di trentaquattro in trentacinque mila Lettere £17
Per uno in Garamoncin di trentasette in trentaotto mila Lettere £18 10
Per uno in Testino di quarantaotta in cinquanta mila Lettere . £26

3. E perche non rimangano senza la debita providenza i Compositori e gli altri Operaj che lavorano nelle Stamperie, ma possano fondarsi sopra una discretta utilità delle loro Fatiche sieno i Capi di quelle da qui avanti, tenuti a pagare ad ogn' uno di loro la Mercede qui sotto annotata.

Al Compositore per ogni migliajo di Lettere in Carattere Silvio, Antico, Filosofia nelle Carte Forme e quantità di Copie dette di sopra. [N.B. deve star soldi $4\frac{1}{2}$ ut Terminazione a stampa.] £4 10
In Caratteri Garamon, Garamoncin per ogni migliajo . . £4
In Testino [e qui deve star soldi 4 soli ut supra] . . . £4 10

Per due Risme in carta ordinaria.

Al Tiratore £2 10
Al Battitore £2 5

Per due Risme in carta Real da Stampa.

Al Tiratore £3 10
Al Battitore £2 10

4. Ma perche ci sono certe Opere che sogliono stamparsi in sesti difficili, quali sono in 16. 18. 24. 32. e alcune altre con notte di sotto o postille ai margini, o vi s' intrecciano caratteri Orientali, o vi si allargano margini, e cosi pure si fanno lavori di Matematica, Astronomia o Calendarj e altre Opere con numeri, per tutte queste si lascia libero il patteggiar prezzo per quel di più che meritassero fra Librajo e Capo di Stamperia come pure fra questo e i suoi Operaj secondo il minore o maggior ritardo dei Lavori.

5. Essendo però preciso debito delle Stamperie il corrispondere col perfetto lavoro alla Pubblica volontà e all' aumento del prezzo destinato dalla presente Terminazione sarà tenuto ogni Capo di quelle ad eseguire pontualmente quanto nelle passate leggi e spezzialmente nella Terminazione 23 Maggio 1766 fu ingiunto, cosi che nessuno di essi abbia più d' un Garzone accordato, ne faccia lavorare d' altri che da Lavoranti leggitimi dando esecuzione agl' ordini nostri sopra le Correzzioni, il pagamento delle quali però s' intenda a peso di chi fa stampare e non del Capo della Stamperia.

6. E se da qui avanti Stampatore veruno fosse cosi arditto che sotto qualsivoglia titolo tenesse Garzoni privi d' accordo, o avesse più d' uno accordato, o accettasse per Lavoranti persone escluse dalle Leggi, sia per ogni contrafazione di tal genere obbligato a pagare Ducati cinquanta, da essere presentati al Magistrato Nostro, la metà dei quali sarà dell' accusatore, e l' altra metà divisa fra i Lavoranti Leggitimi di quella Stamperia dove sarà stata scoperta la colpa.

7. Non bastando però alla perfezione delle Stampe ne al buon servizio di chi fa

stampare la Perizia delle Persone impiegate nelle Stamperie, ma richiedendosi che tutti gli ordigni inservienti alla stampa sieno di buona condizione, acciòche l' attività dei Lavoranti ottenga un esecuzione pontuale, determiniamo,

Che nel corso di mesi sei i quali comincieranno dal giorno in cui sarà pubblicata la presente i Torchi e tutte le parti che gli compongono si ritrovino buoni e bene allestiti e congegnati e di giusto e adattato servizio.

Tali ancora sieno dentro al detto termine tutti quelli attrecci che servono al lavoro della stampa e quel Capo di stamperia che si trovasse dopo il corso di detto tempo tenergli male in acconcio o consumati, caschi nella pena assegnata di sopra che sarà nella stessa forma distribuita.

8. Quanto è poi al secondo punto spettante ai Caratteri inerendo al Decreto 1603, 11 Maggio, il quale ordina che abbiano li Stampatori a servirsi di bei Caratteri, comandiamo,

Che gli usati ordinariamente quali sono Canon, Canoncino, Testoparagone, Testo d' Aldo, Silvio, Antico comune, Filosofia, Garamon, Garamoncin, Testino, Nompariglia sieno tutti gittati nel quadro loro naturale, con la proporzione fra lettere e spalla stabilita nei punzioni e nelle Madri. E se mai occorresse formarne alcuni d' una proporzione che abbia a stare fra l' uno e l' altro dei nominati di sopra, sieno sempre gittati in maniera che le lettere dette d' Asta lunga possano riscontrarsi dirittamente insieme tanto di sopra quanto di sotto senza addossarsi l' una all' altra e in maniera che l' Asta di tutte v' apparisca intiera e col suo finimento perfettamente compito.

9. E perche la Pubblica volontà non venga in ciò defraudata, ordiniamo che i Gittatori tanto di Venezia quanto di Terra Ferma, e così quelli che lavorano in Caratteri per Commissione di Stampatori e Libraj come quelli che gli formano per uso delle Stamperie proprie debbano ogni volta che viene loro occasione di gittarne, dar prima notizia al Magistrato Nostro della qualità e denominazione del Carattere da gittarsi, e della Stamperia e Librajo per cui s' avrà a lavorare per ottenere licenza somigliante a quella delle spedizioni di Caratteri per la Terra Ferma, ed acciocche si possa ad ogni occorrenza farne il confronto co' Campioni de respettivi Caratteri, che sono stati approvati per buoni e proporzionati e come tali segnati in fondo alla presente.

10. Se mai accadesse che il Carattere o Caratteri lavorati in qualsivoglia Gitteria della Dominante o dello Stato, non fossero corrispondenti in proporzione agli accettati con approvazione ne' Campioni, sia quel Gittatore che gli avrà fatti per altrui commissione, obbligato a rifondergli e lavorargli di nuovo a proprie spese senza poter pretendere risarcimento veruno, in pena dell' avere aderito ad una ordinazione contraria al nostro divieto; e chi avrà data l' ordine sia tenuto a sborsare tutto il costo del detto Carattere o Caratteri al Magistrato Nostro, da esser dispensato parte ai Lavoranti della Stamperia dove avea ad impiegarsi, e parte a quei Matricolati poveri che non hanno Stamperia ne Bottega, e allo stesso pagamento sieno soggette quelle Stamparie tanto di Venezia quanto di Terra Ferma che avendo Gitteria per uso proprio non ubbidissero pontualmente a quanto intorno ai Caratteri è da noi statuito.

Sebastian Zustinian Rif^r^.
Andrea Tron K^r^ Rif^r^.
Girolamo Grimani Rif^r^.
Davidde Marchesini Seg^rio^.

Caratteri approvati nella Fondaria in cui lavorano Nicolò Bazzo e Giovanni Inchiostro.

Canon, Canon Secondo con spalla, Canoncin più grasso Canoncin primo, Testo detto Paragon, il detto più grande, testo d' Aldo magro, un altro con spalla, un altro con più spalla, Silvio grosso, Lettura ordinaria, Lettura con più spalla, Garamon primo, altro più grosso, Garamoncin magro, altro più grasso, altro con spalla, Testin primo, Testin secondo, altro con più spalla, Nompariglia prima, seconda, terza, quarta, con spalla, Argentina, Filosofia.

S' eccettua il Silvio magro quando non sia gittato con la debita proporzione di quadro e d' occhio.

Caratteri approvati nella Fondaria in cui lavora Andrea Burchicin.

Canon, sotto Canon, Canoncin Silvio, Canoncin con spalla, Canoncin terzo, Canoncin Garamon, Canoncin Garamoncin sotto canoncino, Paragon grasso, Testo d' Aldo grosso, Testo d' Aldo grasso, Testo d' Aldo ordinario.

S' eccettuano quando non vengono lavorati colla debita proporzione di quadro e d' occhio Il Testo Aldino secondo, Testo d' Aldo stretto, Silvio grasso, Silvietto in Lettura, Silvio in Lettura, Antico Comun grasso, Antico comune, Garamon magro, Testin nompariglia grassa, Nompariglia ordinaria, Nompariglia.

Caratteri approvati nella Fondaria di Bassano.

Canon, Canoncin, Testo Paragon, Testo d' Aldo, Silvio, Antico comun, Filosofia, Garamon grasso, Garamoncin, Testin grasso, Testin grasso con spalla.

S' eccettuano se non vengono lavorati colla debita proporzione di quadro e d' occhio, il Garamon magro, Garamoncin magro, il Testo magro, la Nompariglia, la Filosofia denominata per il Francese, il Garamoncin per il Francese, il Testin per il Spagnuolo.

Caratteri approvati nella Gitteria Falconi.

Tutti fuorchè la Filosofia seconda se non viene lavorata colla debita proporzione di quadro e di occhio.

Caratteri approvati nella Gitteria Adami.

Tutti; e così quelli della Gitteria Andolfato.

Caratteri approvati nella Gitteria Parolari.

Tutti; a riserva del Testino ad uso di Fiandra, che si esclude affatto.

L'originale in filza del Prior 1781. N° 57.

1767. 29 *Luglio.*

No. 62. Importando di mettere in buono e regolato sistema la gelosa materia delle Stampe, e stabilir nelle medesime que regolamenti che sono adattabili alle circostanze de' tempi presenti, ed accomodare tanto alla Città di Venezia, quanto alla Terra Ferma quelle Leggi d' equità e di giustizia che all' una e all' altra convengono, onde si possa introdurre quel Lavoro e quel numero e quantità di venditori che sono proporzionati al consumo e non venga ulteriormente deluso lo spirito e la Lettera di tante Leggi da Predecessori nostri e dalla Pubblica Autorità del Senato con ottimi oggetti stabilite, sono devenuti Gl' Ill^mi^ et Ecc^mi^ SS^ri^ Rifformatori dello Studio di Padova all' estesa della presente Terminazione perche, approvata dall Ecc^mo^ Senato, sia pubblicata et immancabilmente eseguita.

P^mo^. Non possano le Botteghe e Negozj de Libri in Venezia per anni 15, i quali avranno principio dalla pubblicazione della presente, accordare nuovi Garzoni; intendendosi però anche nel corso di essi anni 15 aperto l' ingresso nelle sole stamperie ad un solo Garzone per una, con accordo conforme le Terminazioni 14 Luglio 1686, 2 Giugno 1752, e 23 Maggio 1766, appoggiata alla Parte 1572.

2do. Abbiano i Figliuoli de Padri Matricolati, e così i Figli de Figli la Consueta faccoltà d' entrare nel Corpo dell' Arte dopo la Morte paterna col metodo fino al presente usato, ma non possano in avvenire in alcun modo, neppure emancipati, essere accettati vivente il Padre.

3^zo^. Tutti gli altri che non sono Figli di Matricolati, e che abbiano compiuto il tempo dell' essere Lavoranti, tanto al presente quanto in avvenire, oltre li debiti requisiti per dimostrare i cinque Anni di Garzonato, e i tre di Lavorante, sicchè non vi manchi un giorno, abbiano ad assoggettarsi agli esami di Librari o di Stampatori qui annessi, secondo la professione che dichiareranno di voler esercitare, e venendo ritrovati idonei debbano esser ballottati da tutto il Capitolo, come ordina la Terminazione 23 Maggio 1766, intendendosi che saranno approvati quelli che avranno i due terzi de voti in favore, e seguendo la Terminazione 1752, 27 Aprile, quando saranno comparsi tre volte per essere esaminati e non verranno trovati idonei, o non avranno li due terzi de' voti sieno privi in perpetuo di entrare in detta Arte, ne possano mai più Matricolarsi. Ne sarà lecito a chi in avvenire sarà stato esaminato, ammesso e Matricolato per Stampatore esercitare l' Arte del Libraro, o vender Libri in altro modo, se prima non sarà esaminato, conosciuto idoneo, ammesso e Matricolato per Libraro, e lo stesso sia obbligato di fare chi fosse Matricolato per Libraro e volesse levar Stamperia ed impacciarsi in un Arte in cui non fosse stato prima esaminato, dichiarando che il pagamento dell' ingresso all' Arte debba farsi una volta sola.

4to. Libri stampati in Estero Stato e che si trovino stampati in Città, e privilegiati a Libraro o Stampatore veneto, non passano entrare in Città o nello Stato veneto, e se ne capitassero per via alcuna non possa il Deputato all' Estraditione de Libri dalla Dogana licenziarli sicchè siano estratti dal luogo dove saranno ricapitati, ne il Segretario Nostro fargli Mandato alcuno di poterli vendere, ma sieno perduti, e confiscati, puniti in oltre quelli a quali saranno diretti pecuniaramente come stimerà il Magistrato nostro più adequato a termini di giustizia conforme a quanto fu decretato dalla Parte 24 Settembre 1653 all' Articolo VI. come pure sotto le pene qui sopra espresse non potranno esser posti in vendita se non li Libri venuti per le Pubbliche Dogane a tenore della Terminazione 25 Settembre 1764.

5to. S' intenda ancora che Edizione Forestiera di Libro Stampato ed esistente in Venezia a sufficienza del rispettivo uso dell' Arte non possa avere ingresso nella Città e Stato Veneto, restando l' Autorità al Magistrato nostro di stabilire quelle ordinazioni che per giungere ad un tale oggetto stimerà conveniente.

6to. Non ardisca Matricolato alcuno ch' abbia Stamperia, Negozio in Casa, o Bottega di Libri in Venezia, di mettere Libri in Vendita sopra i Banchetti in nessun giorno dell' Anno, ma sia comportata tal qualità di vendita a soli matricolati poveri e per Libri vecchi solamente sotto la pena stabilita a contrafacenti dalla Terminazione 12 Luglio 1703, e sia proibito ne predetti Banchetti ogni cartello che dinoti Libro alcuno particolare.

7mo. Si stabilisce parimente che non sia lecito in avvenire a qualsivoglia persona, e a qualunque Direttore di Luogo Pubblico l' aprir Bottega o Stamperia in Terra Ferma, senza la Pubblica permissione, per ottener la quale dovrà constare la necessità d' aprirla o piantarla dalle informazioni del Pubblico Rappresentante e da quella del Magistrato nostro.

8vo. Si vieta con risoluto ordine e comando che nessuno possa in avvenire esser dall' Arte admesso alla Matricolazione il quale avesse Negozio di Libri o Stamperia in Terra Ferma, se non col preciso obbligo di trasportare in Venezia tanto il Negozio quanto la Stamperia, senza lasciar neppure un Torchio in Terra Ferma, ne s' intenda mai valere l' admissione all' Arte se non dopo pienamente eseguita questa inalterabile condizione. Ne possa mai questa Legge venir altarata a favore di chi si sia se non previa l' informazione del Magistrato nostro intesa quella dell' Arte, e con Parte sola, e co cinque sesti del Collegio e Senato. Considerandosi però che li quattro i quali al presente vi si trovano asscritti, Manfrè come agente rappresentante il Seminario di Padova, Remondini, Conzatti, e Veronese, hanno sotto la fede della ricevuta Matricolazione resi i loro Negozii base e stabilimento delle loro Famiglie, restano dalla pubblica Autorità approvati, e s' intende che i loro Figliuoli, mancati di vita i Padri, passino alla Matricolazione con quella felicità [facilità ?] e prerogativa ch' è statuita agli altri Matricolati Veneti, dovendo però tanto i suddetti quattro, quanto i loro Figli di Maschio in Maschio in avvenire osservar le regole tutte in questa Terminazione stabilite.

Nono. Essendosi col Decreto 1603, 11 Maggio, stabilito il privilegio d' anni 20 a Libri nuovi non più stampati in luogo alcuno, e d' anni 10 alle ristampe de Libri Forestieri, e comportando le circostanze de tempi presenti che questa materia de privilegj venga in altro modo regolata, si statuisce: che nella Città di Venezia il privilegio a Libri Manoscritti, e non più stampati in luogo alcuno, s' estenda dagli anni 20 ai 30, e alle ristampe de Libri Forestieri s' estenda dagli anni 10 a 15, dichiarando che dal giorno della presente Terminazione, di quelli che sono al presente in privilegio per Anni 20 s' estenderà la grazia agli anni 30, e di quelli che lo sono per anni 10, il privilegio s' estenderà agli anni 15, e tale facilità s' intenderanno godere i soli Librari e Stampatori di Venezia e che hanno Torchi e Botteghe in questa Città, esclusi anche li quattro Matricolati in Terra Ferma nominati di sopra e i loro Figliuoli in avvenire. Intendendosi però che i detti privilegiati debbano essere obbligati a tutti gli ordini espressi nel Decreto 1603, 11 Maggio, per la buona qualità delle Stampe, e soggetti a tutte quelle pene che sono statuite nel Decreto 1537, oltre la perdita del Privilegio, e allo stabilito dalle Terminazione del Magistrato Nostro 1766, 23 Maggio, e 2 Maggio, 1767.

Decimo. Libri i quali dopo la pubblicazione della presente usciranno in Venezia di privilegio, tanto quelli che ora vi sono notati quanto quelli che da qui in poi si noteranno, non possano essere più ristampato da nessun Librajo o Stampatore della Terra Ferma, e neppure da alcuno de quattro Matricolati che ora vengono approvati, e s' intendano tanto ad essa Terra Ferma quanto a Venezia comuni que soli che fossero fino ad ora usciti di privilegio, i quali potranno dall' una e dall' altra ristamparsi col metodo però ordinato dalla Terminazione 1764, che vieta il deterioramento delle ristampe dalle prime Edizioni.

Undecimo. Essendo stato poi col Decreto 11 Maggio 1713 stabilito che all' Opere che si stampano fuori di questa Città non si possa concedere privilegio di sorte alcuna, se non col vigore delle strettezze come nella parte medesima è dichiarito, e trovandosi a proposito in grazia delle presenti circostanze d' alterare sopra tal punto la detta Legge e d' animare l' industria della Terra Ferma a cercar Capi nuovi, tanto manoscritti quanto di Ristampe d' Opere Forestiere si stabilisce: che Librari di Terra Ferma tanto i quattro Matricolati quanto i non Matricolati i quali daranno primi il Mandato di Licenza in nota al Priore dell' Arte in Venezia, e pagheranno Lire 6. 4. goder debbano il privilegio delle Opere Manoscritte, e non più stampate in luogo alcuno d' Anni 20, e per le ristampe de Libri Forestieri d' Anni 10, intendendosi pero obbligati, tanto i quattro Matricolati, quanto i non matricolati a mettervi la Data de' proprj respettivi Paesi, come dalle Pubbliche Leggi è ordinato, e che quando essi Libri saranno usciti di privileggio possano essere ristampati tanto dalla Dominante quanto dalla Terra Ferma.

Sebastian Zustinian Rif^{r}.
Andrea Tron K^{r}. Rif^{r}.
Girolamo Grimani Rif^{r}.
Davidde Marchesini Seg^{rio}.

Esami da farsi a quelli che concorrono alla Matricolazione.

Quali sono le principali Bibbie.

Quali i Santi Padri Greci e Latini.

Quali gli Espositori della Sacra Scrittura.

Quali i Teologhi Controversisti e Polemici.

Quali li Scrittori della storia Ecclesiastica.

Quali gli autori antichi Filosofi, Storici, e Poeti, così Tragici come Comici Greci e Latini.

Quali gli Autori del Diritto di Natura e delle Genti, del Gius Civile e Canonico, quali i Filosofi, Metafisici e Morali.

Quali i principali Geografi Greci, Latini, Italiani e Francesi.

Quali gli Autori di Storia Profana Antica e Moderna, gli Epistolografi, li Antiquarii, Nummari, i Matematici, Medici Chirurghi, Anatomici, Leggisti.

Quali gli Autori delle Belle Arti, Pittura, Scultura, Architettura Civile, Militare e Nautica.

Quali gli Autori della Storia Naturale e Bottanica.

Saranno obbligati a saper ben leggere e scrivere la lingua Italiana, e d' avere quella cognizione della lingua Latina e Francese, che sia sufficiente.

Dovranno gli Esaminatori far loro alcune ricerche sull' intrinseco della Professione, e del Commercio de' Libri.

Esami da farsi a quelli che concorrono alla Matricolazione per Stamparsi.

In qual modo si compartiscono di Originali de' Libri da stamparsi.

In qual maniera porranno sopra le Tavole forme composte, cioè di ottavo, dodici, dieciotto, ventiquattro e trendadue.

In qual modo si possono aggiustare gli impronti del Torcolo, e i Registri de fogli al Torcolo: se non aggiustate in qual maniera si accomoderanno.

In qual modo si puo usare la bava al Torcolo, che si fa nello stampare.[1]

In qual modo metteranno in piedi un Torcolo.

Quante sorte di Caratteri da Stampa si trovano.

Qual diligenza debbasi usare perchè le Stampe vengono ben corrette.

Come si debbano bagnar le Carte accio riescano bene.

Quanto fumo e vernice anderà per Libbra nell' Inchiostro nero, e quanto Cinabro e vernice nel rosso.

Devanno i due Periti eletti dal Priore ordinar in qual sesto dovrà comporre il Lavorante e composta che sarà la forma dovrà esser letta in Piombo dal medesimo Lavorante, e messa in ordine conforme si deve, e farne una stampa, acciò con maggior facilità si veda il di lui operare, e questa dovrà esser presentata alla Banca, e al Capitolo dai suddetti Periti, i quali attesteranno con loro giuramento d' essere quella stata fatta dal suddetto Lavorante, ed esser egli sufficiente per esercitare l' Arte, in conformità della Parte presa nel 1603 in tal proposito, e dopo inteso da Periti l' attestato sarà messo alla ballottazione in Capitolo Generale, e con li due terzi de voti sarà descritto nel Libro de Matricolati.

Dovrà questa prova esser fatta nella Scuola de Librari e Stampatori, ovvero in qualche Stamperia dove parerà meglio al Priore e Sindici, alla quale prova dovranno essere assistente i due Periti, acciocche non fosse fatta d' altri in cambio di quello che volesse entrare nell' Università.

Approvata con Decreto dell Ecc^{mo} Senato 1767, 29 Agosto.

L'originale in Filza del Prior 1781. N° 58.

1775. 26 *Febraro in Pregadi.*

No. 63. In the year 1772, 17th Sept., the Senate appointed a commission to inquire into the best methods for regulating "le conseguenze del molto numero d' arbitrarie solennità per particolari consuetudine introdotte;" the commission presented their report, and upon that the Senate took the opinion of the Consultores in Jure, and resolved—

That the habit "solennizzare ad ogni tratto colla cessazione de' lavori molte

[1] The phrase *usare la bava* is difficult to explain. Sig. Visentini, a Venetian master printer, suggests reading *levare*—how would you remove the blur from an impression? or it may be rendered, how would you treat a blur?

feste particolari" is injurious alike to Church and State; and forbid all such special festivals upon week-days unless the week-day chosen be one of the canonical feasts.

The festival of the patron saint in each diocese shall be an exception to this rule.

The festivals of the patron saints of parish churches, guilds, and pious foundations, if they fall on a week-day, shall be kept on the Sunday following.

The bishops and the patriarch shall be invited to issue pastorals in this sense.

GIUSEPPE GRADENIGO Nod. Duc.

Nota di tutti li Matricolati dell' Università, regolata sotto il Priorato del Magn^co Sig^r Giŏ. Antonio Pinelli. L'Anno 1754.

No. 64. 137 names registered then, without the additions.

Nota di tutti li Matricolati che al presente s' attrovano sotto il Priorato di me Andrea Giuliani. L'Anno 1676.

No. 65. 99 names registered then, without the additions.

1780. 30 *Luglio.*

Terminazione degl' Ill^mi ed Ecc^mi Signori Rifformatori dello Studio di Padova.

No. 66. La somma cura, il costante impegno, e l' efficaci sollecitudini del Magistrato Nostro manifestate in più tempi con iterate regolazioni e necessarie providenze dell' Arte Veneta Tipografica, corroborate sempre dalle autorevoli sovrane deliberazioni, ci hanno condotti anche in adesso all' evidente conoscimento di varj disordini esposti nella intesa relazione del Priore dell' Arte stessa, e Bancali; quali con sommo pregiudizio la possono far più oltre decadere qualora prontamente non si accorra con nuovi efficaci rimedj et utili stabilimenti a farla risorgere dalla presente sua decadenza.

Datosi perciò serio e posato riflesso, non che praticati sodi esami sopra la natura delli correnti suoi mali, e sopra la qualità delle conseguenze, che in oggi l' addolerano siamo pur venuti a distinguere la forza delle providenze adattate, e confacenti al caso, per spiegarle e statuirle.

Vengono percio gl' Illustrissimi ed Eccellentissimi Signori Riformatori dello Studio di Padova a terminare, e terminare comandando.

I. Che riconosciuto il deturpamento delle Venete Edizioni aver principalmente origine dal pessimo lavoro, che si fa nelle Stamparie, per essersi in esse introdotta, in cambio di approvati Compositori, quantità di Garzoni abusivi, affato imperiti, inabili a quel Mestiere e replicatamente aboliti dalle Leggi tutte, e singolarmente da quella 13 Maggio 1767, perciò resta nuovamente, e risolutamente stabilito, che da qui inanzi non si abbia a tenere più d' un Garzone solo, dovendo chi di più ne avesse immediatamente licenziarli dalla Stamperia, sopra di che s' incarica il Sopraintendente Nostro alle Stampe a render conto al Magistrato Nostro della esecuzione, o inobbedienza al comando, portando la Nota al Magistrato stesso degli esistenti.

II. Ed affinchè le Stampe riescono di quella perfezione nelle correzioni, ch' è necessaria per far risorgere l' antico decoro d' esse nella nostra e nelle altre Nazioni, ed anche per facilitare un esito fortunato de' Veneti Libri; inerendosi perciò alle pubbliche ordinazioni, si vogliono tutti li Stampatori tenuti, per correggere le proprie Edizioni, a valersi di Correttori capaci et idonei, per i quali essi Stampatori si rendano responsabili al Magistrato nostro degli scoperti errori nelle loro Edizioni; assoggetati restando alla pena di perdere tutti i Libri stampati scorretti, privileggiati o comuni, senza eccezione, e ad altri castighi all' arbitrio Nostro riservati.

III. Al conoscimento di queste mancanze, viene espressamente incaricata la diligenza del Correttor Generale, ed eccitata efficacemente la di lui attenzione all' adempimento della propria incombenza.

IV. Sia da qui inanzi per maggior sicurezza della bontà delle Carte, Caratteri, Inchiostri e del buon lavoro mecanico delle Stampe, incaricato il Capitolo dell' Arte ad eleggere uno Stampatore intelligente, provetto, e d' integra probità, per esser in seguito da Noi approvato. Sarà incombenza di questo rivedere i primi Fogli d' ogni Opera privileggiata che si ristampa, ed assicurerà con esatta Perizia l' Edizioni da disordini sopraccennati. Sarà l' eletto proveduto dall' Arte in modi convenienti. L' esaminato foglio poi dovrà esser sottoscritto dal Perito eletto, e dallo Stampatore, e ne sarà fatto depositario il Sopraintendente nostro alle Stampe, a cui verrà consegnato per praticare i confronti d' esso primo modello col restante dell' Opera.

V. Per l' adempimento immancabile dei sopradetti Capitoli circa i Garzoni, Lavoranti e Correttori sia tenuto il Sopraintendente Nostro alle Stampe di visitare con frequenza le Stamperie, come prescrivono le Leggi della sua istituzione.

VI. Ma perchè, non meno intento, ed impegnato il Magistrato Nostro alla felicità delle Stampe Venete, ed alla buona disciplina di questa Università di Stampatori e Libraj, riconosce derivare simili pregiudiziali sconcerti negl' Individui di essa dall' incaglio de Corpi stampati e giacenti invenduti per la quantità eccessiva delle copie dei Libri usciti di Privileggio, ai quali per esser resi comuni si avventano molti ad un tratto per la ristampa, che difficolta di smaltire tanti replicati Esemplari di un' Opera sola; dal che ne avviene che si ricorre poi, e si fa uso di quei vantaggii detestabili, derivanti dal peggioramento delle Stampe, dalle Vendite illecite, dagli abusivi Partiti con Persone non dell' Arte ed anche Forestiere; cose tutte, vere cagioni, che collimano al generale deperimento dell' Arte stessa; perciò resta da Noi risolutamente stabilito, che per l' avvenire il primo respettivo posseditore privileggiato possa egli solo, e non altri, ottenere la nuova Licenza colle solite forme per la ristampa de' Libri usciti di Privileggio, e per ciò resi comuni, e ciò fin ch' egli voglia; intendendosi in oltre che la stessa libertà abbia, prima del posseditore, chiunque fosse, l' autore d' un' Opera, come si è sempre pratticato; e se per avventura ambidue rinunciassero ad un tale benefizio per la ristampa del suo Libro fino allora privileggiato, in questo solo identifico caso, e non in altro, lo ristamperà solamente quello che averà il primo conseguito il Mandato, nè altri potranno ottenerlo, nè prima nè dopo la sua Edizione.

VII. E come poi in questo luogo si tratta di ristampa, prefisso viene il termine di due Mesi allo Stampatore per incominciarla e proseguirla coll' opera al meno di un mezzo foglio al giorno, al che mancando potrà un' altro ricorrere per impetrare colle solite Licenze il possesso del Libro o non incominciato o non proseguito, e dovrà il sostituto al mancamento subentrare nella ristampa nel termine e nei modi comandati.

VIII. Nel solo caso però in cui intraprendesse qualche Stampatore o Librajo di produrre qualche ristampa di singolare nobiltà, tanto per bellezza di Carta, quanto per isquisitezza di Caratteri, perfezione di correzione, e d' ornamenti; conoscendo che tali Edizioni il cui scopo è la magnificenza, sono principalmente quelle che universalmente acquistano concetto e lode all' Arte Tipografica, ed alle Nazioni nelle quali viene esercitata; resta con fermezza deliberato, ch' esso intraprenditore di tale ristampa possa farla quando anche il Libro si trovasse in qualunque modo privileggiato. Sarà però suo obbligo di presentare tanto il primo foglio della stampa Privileggiata, quanto quello di tutti i miglioramenti della ristampa, all' eletto Esaminatore, il quale farà l' uno e l' altro presentare col mezzo del Sopraintendente alle Stampe al Magistrato Nostro colla dichiarazione delle differenze, perchè si possa confrontar l' Opera compiuta al proposta modello, e punire colla perdita delle stampe, e più gravi pene ad arbitrio Nostro, e spezzialmente quella dell' essere depennato dall' Arte, chi avesse mancato alla pontualità della sua promessa.

IX. Perchè però molti Libri si trovano che non possono tenersi per soggetti a Privilegiato primo veruno quali sono tutti quelli che furono stampati e ristampati senza Privilegio, tutti gli abbandonati o per impotenza di chi gli possedeva, o per mancanza di vita de' Capi di Negozi, e di Stampatori, o per altri umani irreparabili accidenti, inerendo Noi al Decreto 1603, 11 Maggio, che assegnò Privilegio a chi ricuperasse, colle ritampe Opere comuni di stima, concediamo unicamente a que' Libraj e Stampatori che non avessero almeno sei Libri in Privilegio, e non ad altri, che possano far annotare al Libro dell' Arte per anni dieci di Privilegio qualunque Opera di questo genere, della quale avrà ottenuto Mandato di ristampa, si ch' egli solo, o chi avesse causa da lui possa ristamparla per quel tempo, coll' espresso obbligo d' assoggettarne il primo Foglio all Esaminatore eletto, e di cominciare e proseguir l' Edizione co' metodi prescritti nell' Articolo VII.

X. Trovandosi poi nel soprallegato numero delle Opere comuni tutti i Testi Scolastici senza comenti ed altre Operette di piccola mole usuali del popolo che possono essere l' alimento d' alcune Stamparie di fortuna ristretta, e che sogliono di lavorare di Commissioni, le quali non sono sempre pronte; acciocchè possono mantenere negli intervalli vacui di quelle i loro lavoranti, commettiamo al Prior attuale, ed a suoi di Banca, che siccome fu già da loro eseguito nell' 1669, 6 Agosto, con loro spontanea Parte, sia da essi fatto un Catalogo di tal sorta di Libri comuni, e quello rendano pubblico, a fine che ogn' uno de sopraddetti Stampatori possa ripartitamente chiedere per se qualche capo, onde l' Edizione da lui fatta di quello, eseguiti prima gli ordini nostri del presentarne il primo foglio all' Esaminatore eletto, s' intenda privilegiata, e vietatane la ristampa ad ogni altro sotto le pene minacciate a chi ristampasse Libri in privilegio, ed altre ad arbitrio Nostro.

XI. Proscritta e totalmente condannata s' intenderà per l' avvenire la pessima usanza di quegli Stampatori che offeriscono Partiti di Libri o privilegiati, o di ristampe a Persone di Esteri Stati; per la qual fraude resterà irremissibilmente soggetto chi disubbidisse alla pena di essere escluso dall' Arte, e di chiudere la Stamperia; e lo stesso dovrà verificarsi sopra quegli Stampatori che offerissero Stampe a Partito a Persone non ascritte all' Arte medesima.

XII. Metodo fermo ed inalterabile delle Stampe denominate a *Partito* dovrà esser quello da qui inanzi, che lo Stampatore il quale le intraprendesse debba consegnare nelle mani del Priore pro tempore la nota di quella quantità di Esemplari che avrà stabilita di stampare, sicchè possa con facilità pervenire al Magistrato nostro in cognizione s' egli oltrepassasse il numero pattuito: il quale inganno, fatto in offesa della buona fede di un contratto, sarà punito coll' esclusione dell' ingannatore dall' Arte, e con altre pene convenienti a così abominevole delitto.

XIII. Se qualche particolare persona, e non Matricolata volesse per ajuto delle Stamperie tentare la ristampa di qualche opera possa ciò fare previo però l' avviso al Priore dell' Arte, il quale sarà obbligato a spedire il suo Bidello a tutti gli Individui di quella perchè resti deciso se fosse ad alcuno di questi opportuna la Edizione dell' Opera proposta, e ciò in tempo di otto giorni, e non più; e in caso che ciascuno ricusasse, resti in libertà della suddetta persona di farne pratticare la Edizione da qualunque Stampatore a suo piacimento purchè abbia Torchi in Venezia: intendendosi che essa però non possa negoziare il Libro in Baratti, nè farne, nè venderne più copie del numero stabilito.

XIV. Così pure se qualche persona che non fosse dell' Arte volesse introdurre a sue spese la Stampa di qualche Libro nuovo e non più stampato, sia lecito a questo d' intraprenderla a nome però di un Veneto Stampatore, supplito però prima a tutti i metodi che incombano per l' Articolo antecedente, tanto rapporto allo Stampatore quanto al Priore d' offrirne la Stampa a confratelli dell' Arte nel tempo di sopra prescritto, e col pagamento degli otto grossi per Balla.

XV. Sia in oltre proibito a Particolari non Matricolati l' aprir negozio, far Cambi e vendite al minuto su i Banchetti dei Libri stampati a loro conto, ma abbiano essi ad esibirli ai Veneti Libraj, per esser esposti alla vendita nelle loro pubbliche Botteghe; e siano pure obbligati gli Stampatori, che li stampassero, a non oltre passare il numero delle Copie pattuite, sotto pena di chiudere la Stamperia.

XVI. Restino assolutamente soggetti i venditori su i Banchetti di Piazza, od altri luoghi, a quanto è disposto nell' Articolo VI. della Leggi 1767, 29 Luglio, e debbano tenere un Banchetto solo, non raddoppiato colla giunta d' altri, a tenore della Terminazione del Magistrato Nostro 3 Ottobre 1778, nè possano vendere sopra Banchetti, se non Libri vecchj, nella serie e natura de' quali s' intendano essere i soli Libri legati, e colle Carte tagliate.

XVII. Ma perchè poi ai Matricolati dell' Arte devesi conservare il proprio diritto ed interesse, si rinnova con robustezza la sopraccitata Legge 3 Ottobre 1778, cioè che qualunque persona non Matricolata non ardisca di vendere, nè per le Botteghe, nè in publico nè occultamente Libri di qualunque sorte; la quale proibizione resta pure fissata per quelli che sono Matricolati, e ciò sotto tutte le pene nell' Articolo V. di essa Legge prescritte.

XVIII. Per l' indennità e risarcimento dell' Università Tipografica Veneta, ed ad oggetto di rendere men difficile ad essa la riscossione de debiti vecchi, de quali si trova in resto e difettiva per l' impontualità de' suoi Individui nel soddisfare alle Imposte a loro addossate dall' Arte, colle solite Tanse, resta persuaso il Magistrato Nostro di ravvivare il metodo prefisso dalla Terminazione 1742, in forza della quale sarà negato il Mandato di Stampa e ristampa, ad ogni ricorrente dal Segretario Nostro, a cui ciò si prescrive, allorche il ricorrente stesso non presentasse prima al suddetto Segretario la fede fattagli dal Priore o di non esser debitore all' Arte, o attesa l' abilità che ai debitore per le Quote vecchie sarà concessa, che li medesimi vadano di tempo in tempo redintegrando la Cassa Università con la Summa alla quale saranno stati prorogati dalla caritatevole condiscendenza del Magistrato Nostro.

XIX. Tutte le suddette Persone mancando o difettive essendo trovate a quanto loro s' impone e viene prescritto, saranno soggette ognuna alle pene comminate dalle Leggi sopra ogni colpa, e se le Leggi non provedessero, subiranno quelle ad arbitrio del Magistrato Nostro.

E la presente approvata che resti dall' Eccellentissimo Senato, sarà stampata e consegnata in varie Copie al Priore dell' Arte, il quale resta incaricato di farla spargere, e diffonderla col mezzo del Bidello a tutti gli Individui della medesima, a quali viene precettato di tenerla fissa a vista universale nella propria Bottega o Stamperia; volendosi, che per quanto a cadauno spetta, esiga immancabilmente la sua intiera perfetta osservanza ed esecuzione.

Data dal Magistrato Eccellentissimo suddetto li 30 Luglio 1780.

Alvise Vallaresso Rifformator.
Andrea Tron. Cav. Proc. Rifformator.
Sebastian Foscarini Cav. Rifformator.
Davide Marchesini Seg.

A di 9 Agosto 1780.

Approvata col Decreto dell' Eccellentissimo Senato.

Addi 24 *Agosto* 1780 *in Pregadi.*

No 67. Gl' inconvenienti che posson facilmente accadere nell' elezione del Proto Esaminatore dell' Arte Tipografica di questa Citta e che si rimarcano dedotti da quanto recentamente successe nel Capitolo dell' Arte siccome con benemerito impegno individua il Magistrato de Rifformatori dello studio di Padova determinano il Senato a secondare il riputato di lui sentimento espresso nell' ora intesa Scrittura, e però tagliando l' Articolo IV della Terminazione approvata col Decreto 9 corrente nella sola parte che demanda al Capitolo dell' Arte la detta elezione, e che in tutte le altre resta confermato, appoggia una tal incombenza alla desterità del Magistrato medesimo che ne rassegnerà al caso di ogni vacanza la nomina alla publica approvazione.

Davidde Marchesini Seg^{rio}.

1780. 27 *Agosti.*

Carlo Palese appointed by the Rifformatori Proto Esaminatore.
Confirmation by the Senate in the same month.

Terminazione degl' Illustrissimi ed Eccell[mi] *Signori Riformatori dello Studio di Padova.* 1780.

No. 68. Il Serenissimo Principe fà sapere, ed è per ordine suddetto.

Autorizzata dall' Eccell[mo] Senato col suo Decreto 9 Agosto passato la Terminazione di questo Magistrato 30 Luglio decorso a sollievo dell' Arte Veneta Tipografica si determinano gl' Ill[mi] ed Eccell[mi] Signori Riformatori dello Studio di Padova per togliere ogni mala interpretazione che possa esser data maliziosamente da qualunque Individuo della medesima Arte sopra alcuni Articoli della Terminazione suddetta, a spiegarli con maggior precisione e rischiaramento perche siano immancabilmente eseguiti a seconda ed in adempimento della Pubblica intenzione.

I.

Dichiarazione intorno alle Correzioni.

Che in esecutione dell' Articolo II. si lasciano in piena libertà Stampatori e Libraj di valersi di quali Corretori più credano a proposito, e d' usare que' metodi di Correzione che vogliono, perche degli errori che venissero scoperti nell' Edizioni, portino debitamente la pena prescritta alle Scorrezioni nell' Articolo II. della Terminazione 30 Luglio 1780.

II.

Intorno agli obblighi del Priore per esecuzione dell' Articolo VI.

Essendosi nel VI. Articolo dell' allegata Terminazione 1780 stabilito che un solo possa da qui in poi ottenere il Mandato per la ristampa d' un Libro uscito di Privilegio, e che in questo caso sia il prediletto il primo trovatore e posseditore di quello, sarà obbligo preciso del Priore, pro tempore, di non rilasciar alcuna Fede per la ristampa di Libri tali fuorchè al primo trovatore finch' egli voglia. E dovendosi come per essa Legge fù determinato, preferrire l' Autore, venga questo eccettuato se avesse alienata l' opera sua per Contratto.

E perche più volte è avvenuto che l' Autore d' un Opera ha fatte a quella delle Aggiunte, s' intenda che queste passino unite alla stessa; e quelle che non fossero dell' Autore restino in prelazione al primo Editor d' esse, ma sole e disgiunte dal Testo.

III.

Obblighi d' esso Priore per la custodia degli Articoli IX. e X.

Ha la pubblica Clemenza negl' Articoli IX. e X. riguardati con occhio paterno tutti gl' Individui dell' Arte suddetta; ma per dividere le sue beneficenze con somma facilità, furono formati per ordine Nostro, dal Priore due Fogli.

Si descrive nel primo l' Università degli Stampatori e Libraj, divisa in due Categorie, l' una continente i Matricolati che hanno Negozio e Stamperia, quelli che hanno Negozio senza Stamperia, o Stamperia senza Negozio, o Stamperia denominata da Bagaglie; L' altra Categoria e composta di Matricolati non esercenti perche si trovano a Servizio di Botteghe, o sono Lavoranti in Stamperie d' altri, o volanti per la Città, o esercenti per li Banchetti.

Il secondo Foglio contiene il Catalogo di tutti que' Libri che non possono giudicarsi per soggetti a privilegio veruno, ed insieme degl' abbandonati.

Per procedere però con la guida di questi due Fogli, senza parzialità nè gara, alla dispensa dei Libri in esso Catalogo compressi, saranno questi commessi alla sorte col metodo seguente.

Si convocherà per Commando nostro il Capitolo dell' Arte, s' imbossoleranno i nomi di quei Libraj e Stampatori unicamente che non hanno più di sei privilegj e sono nella Categoria prima descritti. Questi verranno quivi estratti pubblicamente alla sorte, ed ad alta voce secondo che escono promulgati e registrati in un Foglio affinche possa ognuno d' essi, seguendo l' ordine dell' estrazione, di mano in mano l' un dietro l' altro richiedere per se due Libri dei descritti in Catalogo nel Foglio commesso. E poiche nell' Articolo X. vennero assegnati alle sole Stamperie che stampano per commissioni, tutti i Testi scolastici senza Note, ed altre Operette di picciola mole dette usuali pel popolo, si trova cosa opportuna che dopo la disposizione dei Libri dell' Articolo IX. l' ordinare allo stesso Priore attuale di unirsi con alcuni pocchi de più assenati dell' Arte stessa e formare la Nota dei surriferiti Libri Scolastici e delle Operette popolari indicate, e di questi poi apparecchiare con equità un ripartimento distinto in tante divisioni ognuna segnata d' un numero che cominci dall' uno e segui fino a tanti che si pareggia alla quantità dei nomi dei Concorrenti, i quali saranno estratti da un Bossolo per ottenere ciascuno la divisione segnata col numero corrispondente alla volta della sua estrazione.

Fatti questi due riparti, avrà luogo quello dei Matricolati della seconda Categoria col metodo prescritto all' esecuzione dell' Articolo IX.

Si precetta parimenti a qualunque dei beneficati in questa Categoria seconda, che non possano cedere li acquistati Libri a chi avesse più di sei privileggi, ma debbano pubblicarli sotto il proprio nome, e per loro conto o almeno co loro interessi, e se mai venisse a notizia dell' Eccell^{mo} Magistrato che gli uni o gli altri facessero mal uso di questa beneficenza, rimangano per ciò privi del ricevuto Mandato, il quale incontinente passerà ad un' altro che ne facesse secondo la sua Categoria legale domanda; e rimarrà privo chi l' avesse occultamente acquistato, di tutte le copie se stampato l' avesse.

Qualunque poi de' beneficati d' ogni genere s' intenderà soggetto alla Legge generale dell' esame del Foglio primo, e del tempo di cominciare e progredire coll' Edizione.

E perche Libri che si chiamano usuali e comuni pel popolo da tempi antichissimi, detrattine sempre gli scolastici, alcuni pochi se ne ritrovano di piccola Mole, i quali vengono per uso de poveri Libraj di Terra Ferma stampati, sarà incombenza di esso Priore d' informarsi quali siano, e di presentarne all' Eccellentissimo Magistrato la Nota affinche le Stamperie, che non sono di Venezia, non rimangano prive di quelli, i quali s' intenderanno sempre comuni a Torchj delle Terra Ferma ed a quelli di Venezia.

IV.

Oblighi del Priore per la regola dell' Articolo XII.

In esecutione dell' Articolo XII, che mette regola pe' Libri che vengono stampati a *Partito*, s' incarica il detto Priore che prima di rilasciar la opportuna Fede, per ottenere il Mandato ritragga dallo Stampatore e Librajo proponente l' Opera a *Partito* il numero delle Copie ch' egli si sarà prefisso di stampare e ciò in una nota dall' Intraprenditore sottoscritta alla presenza del Priore, che sarà da lui tenuta in Filza a parte, perchè al caso le loro Eccell[e] possano con sicurezza venire in chiaro della fraude di coloro che avessero operato contro la buona fede de patti.

V.

Obblighi dell' Esaminatore de' Fogli per la buona regola dell' Articolo IV.

Essendo Stato nell' Articolo IV. decretato che l' incombenza dell' Esaminatore sarà la revisione del primo Foglio d' ogni Libro privilegiato, ed essendo in effetto col nuovo metodo privilegiati tutti i Libri dappoichè sono capaci di un solo Mandato, cosi per levare l' adito ad ogni arbitraria interpretazione sopra di ciò, s' incarica lo stesso Esaminatore di rivedere i primi Fogli d' ogni stampa e ristampa.

Queste sono le regole da dover esser costantimente eseguite come le opportune e sufficienti a guidare gl' individui della Università de Librai e Stampatori ad una corretta obbedienza dell' approvata Terminazione 30 Luglio 1780.

E la presente, confermata che sia dall' autorita dell Eccell[mo] Senato, dovrà esser stampata e consegnata al Prior dell' Arte sopradetta per esser difusa colle forme solite ad ogni individuo della medesima per la sua immediate ed inalterabile osservanza.

Data dal Magistrato Eccell[mo] Sud[o] li 28 Settembre 1780.

Alvise Vallaresso Riff[r].
Andrea Tron, Cav[r] Proc. Riff[r].
Sebastian Foscarini Cav[r] Riff[r].

Addi 5 *Ottobre* 1780.

Approvata con Decreto dell' Eccell[mo] Senato.

1780. 15 *Decembre.*

No. 69. Avendo il Magistrato de Rifformatori dello Studio di Padova riconosciuto e compreso che contro lo stabilimento di varie provide Leggi e specialmente della Terminazione 1767 Articolo IV. e V. dall' Ecc[mo] Senato approvata, molti Individui dell' Arte Tipografica di Venezia introducono furtivamente in questa Città di quelle Opere stampate in Esteri Stati che qui sono privilegiate a loro Confratelli o in abbondanza si trovano anche uscite di privilegio esistenti, onde con tal maliziosa e vietata introduzione impediscono e ritardano il commerzio dell' Edizioni qui publicate, e privano i Torchi Veneti di alimento, con danno universale de' commerzianti in Libri, de Capi delle Stamperie e de poveri Artisti che lavorano in quelle, viene in deliberazione di ravvivare gl' ordini in tal materia emanati, e di far risolutamente intendere e sapere.

Che per l' avvenire non si faccia lecito alcun Mercante, Negoziante, Stampatore o altri a quali saranno inviati Libri de Luoghi Forestieri, per Mare o per Terra, aprirli ed estraerli se non coll' Intervento del Deputato nostro alle Dogane, e con tutte le altre regole prescritte dalla Terminazione 25 Settembre 1764.

Ed affine che i publici ordini sieno con la possibile prontezza eseguiti, inerendosi al Decreto 1774, 14 Aprile, non che all' Articolo V. della Terminazione 1767 soprallegata, deliberiamo di dare una maggior assistenza al Deputato Nostro alle Dogane, Donadoni, per la ragione d' una maggior cautela e sicurezza, eleggendo a tale oggetto il Dr Don Giuseppe Cherubini a cui s' incombe, sempre però coll' assenso del Deputato suddetto, di difendere l' Edizioni privilegiate o l' altre anche non privilegiate ma in abbondanza esistenti nell' Arte Tipografica di questa Dominante, così che la sua attiva opera possa facilitare ed espedire con tutta la solecitudine le occorrenze de Libraj, ed assicurare contro ogni inosservanza le pubbliche Leggi.

Ed acciochè possa egli con soda cognitione agire sopra questa materia, avrà a prendere lumi necessari dal Priore di questa Università de Libraj, o da' due Sindici pro tempore, i quali, tanto uniti quanto separati, alla notizia che tenessero di ritrovarsi Libri che offendano i privileggi dell' Arte o altri in copia esistenti contra l' interesse de' Matricolati Veneti, o in questa Città o in qualunque altro luoco a portata d' essere furtivamente introdotti, dovranno per obbligo dell' Offizio loro e per bene degl' Individui della loro Università, avvertire il Deputato o l' eletta persona, col fine che sieno tratenuti e fermati Libri tali in qualunque luoco si trovassero, portandone in seguito la relazione in scritto al Magistrato per le susseguenti nostre Deliberazioni.

Ad esso Dr Don Giuseppe Cherubini, sulla cui fede, unitamente a quella del Deputato Donadoni riposa il Magistrato Nostro, per l' esatto adempimento di questa Ispezione, restano assegnati Ducati cento e venti annui eff' relativamente alla facoltà impartitaci dal Decreto 1774, 14 Aprile, sopra Cassa Grammatici, tenuta dagl' Ecc^{mi} Governatori dell' Entrate, il quale assegnamento dovrà aver principio da primo Gennaro venturo, di quattro in quattro mesi posticipati, netti da Decima ed ogni aggravio, co' soliti Mandati dell Ecc^{mo} Collegio, per l' effetto di che sarà fatta tenere al Magistrato de Governatori dell' Entrate la presente nostra Terminazione in copia, ch' è relativa al suddetto Decreto per lume e per la sua esecuzione.

E così ordinorono doversi annotare.

Alvise Vallaresso Rif^{r}.
Andrea Tron K^{r} Pr Rif^{r}.
Sebastian Foscarini K^{r} Rif^{r}.
Davidde Marchesini Seg^{o}.

1780. 8 *Gennaro.*

No. 70. A maggior spiegazione della Terminazione Nostra 15 Decembre prossimo passato con cui fu eletta dall' autorità del Magistrato Nostro in assistente al Deputato alle Dogane Donadoni, la persona dell' Abbate Don Giuseppe Cherubini per non ritardare il licenziamento dalle Dogane stesse dei Libri che capitano nelle medesime, si dichiara e si stabilisce che tali Libri non possano essere, o dal solo Deputato alle Dogane, o dal solo assistente, licenziati, ma che ambidue, in vista del Mandato di Licenza del Magistrato Nostro, abbiano a sottoscrivere l' attestato di rilascio dei surriferiti Libri, e che li Governatori delle respettive Dogane non possano mai far praticar la consegna dei Colli, Balle et altro se non quando si assicureranno che il detto attestato sii sottoscritto e dall Deputato e dall' Assistente medesimo.

E la presente sarà fatta tenere in copia alli Governatori delle respettive Dogane per lume et esecuzione.

Alvise Vallaresso Rif^r.
Andrea Tron K^r P^r. Rif^r.
Davidde Marchesini Seg^o.

1780. 30 *Decembre in Pregadi.*

No. 71. Nuovi motivi di compiacersi delle benemerite cure e solecitudini del Magistrato de Riformatori dello Studio di Padova ritrae questo Consiglio dall' ora letta diligente sua scrittura, mentre per essa e per gli accompagnati fogli rileva la pronta esecuzione prestata al Decreto 5 Ottobre decorso, ed incamminata con ordine e tranquillità la verificazione degli ultimi stabilimenti addottati per benefizio dell' Arte Tipografica di questa Dominante. Nel retribuirsi per tanto piena laude al Magistrato stesso e nell' animarlo alla prosecuzione delle benemerite sue applicazioni in un argomento così esenziale trovasi persuaso nel tempo stesso il Senato che tanto il Priore Marc' Antonio Manfrè, quanto il Sindico Simone Occhi prossimi al termine de loro attuali Offizj abbiano ad essere prorogati per anno uno susseguente nelle respettive loro Cariche, affinche in tal modo come riflette il Magistrato stesso, e si è pur praticato per qualche altra Arte, si tolgano più facilmente i disordini, e si assicuri colla costanza delle buone consuetudini l' esatta osservanza dei suindicati stabilimenti.

Davidde Marchesini Seg^rio.

1780. 15 *Febraro in Pregadi.*

No. 72. Per corrispondere in ogni parte alle Commissioni espresse nel Decreto 30 Dec. decorso, inerenti alle provvidenze e discipline da prefiggersi per il miglior governo dell' Università de Librai e Stampatori di questa Città, si rileva con quanto zelante impegno di esame, e di studj, si è prestato il Magistrato de Proveditori di Comun per riconoscere le Leggi e le regole stabilite sul proposito, immaginando, col Piano che accompagna, tutto ciò che può esser utile a promuovere il vero bene di questa Tipografica Università composta di due Classi di Matricolati, cioè l' una di Capitalisti, e l' altra d' Individui affatto sprovisti di Beni d' industria, su di che versò pure con aggiustate considerazioni la virtù delli Riformatori dello Studio di Padova.

E mentre riconoscono con uniforme sentimento li riputati Cittadini, dopo aver comprovati dal fatto gli esposti inconvenienti e disordini, utile e necessaria la gia eseguita divisione delle due Categorie de Matricolati descritti nel Foglio avvalorato dalla publica autorità, trovano poi molto corrispondente all' importanza dei contemplati oggetti ch' esclusi siano tutti li Matricolati della Seconda Categoria dalla voce attiva e passiva, non meno che dalle Cariche ed Offizj d' ogni sorte nella Banca e Capitolo, riducendo e questo e quella, al solo numero de Capitilisti descritti nella prima Categoria del Foglio sudichiarito, con la riserva però agli esclusi d' essere admessi nuovamente quallor siano provveduti degl' indicati Capitali, sollevandoli nel fratempo della loro admissione dell' Imposte publiche che rimaner dovranno frattanto a peso dei detti Capitalisti, e lasciandogli però intatti tutti gli altri diritti annessi alla Matricola.

Tale essendo il sistema delle providenze suggerite dal Magistrato de Proveditori

Comun, con quel più che riguarda il tempo delle loro adunanze, della distribuzione ed innovazione delle Cariche, e per ciò che concerne ancora all' esazione delle Imposte e del registro de Matricolati, il Senato che ravvisa in questa benemerita Opera investigati tutt' i mezzi li più salutari ed opportuni per presidiare la Tipografica Università da ulteriori sconcerti e disordini, accoglie e addotta il Piano stesso colle due modificazioni però ed aggiunte che dal conosciuto zelo ed esperienza dei Riformatori dello Studio di Padova vengono ennunciate.

Sarà pertanto effetto della vigilanza del Magistrato de Proveditori di Comun di sostituire in luoco della Ballottazione espressa nel Piano stesso, al caso di repristinare li Matricolati già ascritti nell' Arte, ed autorizzati dalle Leggi di poter piantare Negozj e Stamperie, che siano eletti dalla Banca due Periti, e verificata che sia da essi la summa de Capitali stabiliti, il riccorente dovrà esser tosto ascritto nella Categoria de Capitalisti e admesso nelle facoltà della medesima, senza che sia soggetto ad ulteriori Ballottazioni.

E sarà in pari tempo cura sua di dichiarare nel Piano stesso, che qualunque si creda in diritto di reclamare, esponer debba prima le sue ragioni alla Banca per conciliarle, o appoggiarle, scortandole a competenti Magistrati per la decisione, restando però sempre al riccorente libero l' adito di presentarsi in ogn' incontro alli surriferiti Magistrati.

Ridotto che sia, come se ne farà una particolar cura il Magistrato de Proveditori di Comun, il Piano sumentovato in Articolata Terminazione, con le prescritte aggiunte di ben intesa necessaria provvidenza, sarà quindi effetto dell' assidua vigilanza de riputati Cittadini di farla stampare, e consegnarla al Priore dell' Arte sopradetta per diffonderla a propri Individui, affinchè sia in ogni parte esattamente eseguita.

Davidde Marchesini Seg^{rio}.

Gl' Illustrissimi ed Eccell^{mi} SS^{ri} Proveditori di Comun Infrascritti.

No. 73. Avendo il loro Magistrato, in obbedienza al Sovrano Decreto dell' Eccell^{mo} Senato 30 Decembre decorso, prestati li di lui esami, e studj sopra le Leggi e le Regole stabilite per il Governo dell' Università de Libraj e Stampatori di questa Città, ha quindi rassegnato alla sua Sapienza ed Autorità il Piano 15 Gennaro prossimo passato di providenze e discipline da prefiggersi ad oggetto di promovere il vero bene di questa Tipografica Università composta di due Classi di Matricolati, cioè l' una di Capitalisti e l' altra d' Individui affatto sprovisti di Beni d' Industria.

Accolto ed addottato il Piano stesso dal suo susseguente Decreto 15 Febraro corrente, colle due modificazioni però ed aggiunte che sono prescritte nel Decreto medesimo, hanno altresì loro Eccellenze il Publico comando di ridurre esso Piano in articolata Terminazione, il quale perche resti prontamente adempito, divengono alla estesa della presente a norma di cui dovrà farsi la convocazione de' Capitoli d' essa Università, come della Banca sua rappresentante colle respettive sue facoltà.

I. Il Capitolo dovrà essere composto dei soli Individui Matricolati che hanno Stamperie in piedi, Bottega aperta in piedi per la vendita de Libri, o Negozio in Casa pure in piedi per la vendita dei medesimi, quali tutti sono raccolti nella prima Categoria delli componenti in adesso essa Universita nel Foglio rassegnato all' Ecc^{mo} Senato ed approvato dal suo Decreto 5 Ottobre prossimo passato.

II. Questi soli ancora potranno essere eletti alle Cariche ed Uffizj dell' Università.

III. Il Capitolo per l' elezione delle Cariche nuove che costituiscono la Banca dovrà radunarsi ogn' Anno immancabilmente nella prima Domenica di Febraro, affinche nella prima Domenica di Marzo segua il cambio e l' effettiva rinonzia della vecchia Banca alla Nuova.

IV. La Banca sarà composta dal Priore, due Sindici, due Consiglieri, due Aggionti attuali ed uno di rispetto, ed il Priore e Sindico più vecchio usciti, entreranno senza ballottazione nelli due Carichi di Conservatori alle Leggi, ed in oltre da un Scrivano.

V. Questi Matricolati descritti nella sudetta prima Categoria del suaccennato Foglio, qualora per disgrazia o per altra causa fossero assolti colle due terzi de Voti della Banca dal pagamento della Tansa, Taglione e Milizia, ed avessero un debito duennale di Tanse, Taglion, e Milizia, Luminarie e Gravezza Libri verso l' Università rimaneranno esclusi dalla voce attiva e passiva in Esso Capitolo, ed in conseguenza dalle Cariche ed Uffizj, venendo posti nella seconda Categoria del Foglio sopradetto di cui si dirà in appresso.

VI. Li Matricolati d' essa seconda Categoria saranno esclusi dal Capitolo, dalla voce attiva e passiva, e dalle Cariche ed Uffizj d' ogni sorte, sino a tanto che siano in grado di poter pretendere d' essere ammessi alla prima Categoria, avendo eretta o una Stamperia corrispondente al Capitale di Ducati 500 almeno, o una aperta Bottega in piedi col loro proprio Nome, o Negozio in Casa che contenghi almeno il Capitale di Ducati 2000. Essendo gl' Individui Matricolati di detta seconda Categoria nel caso di poter piantare Negozi o Stamperie si doverà dalla Banca eleggere due Periti, e verificata che sia da essi la summa de Capitali stabiliti, il Ricorrente dovrà essere tosto ascritto nella Categoria de' Capitalisti e ammesso nelle facoltà della medesima, senza che sia soggetto ad ulteriori ballottazioni, e sottosterà in allora alla Tansa, Taglion e Milizia, dovendo tutti quelli della seconda Categoria essere da oggi in avvenire esenti per le Tanse, Taglioni e Milizia che saranno imposte.

VII. Averanno bensì debito gl' Individui Matricolati della Seconda Categoria di pagare la Luminare annua di Lire 4 Viva e di Lire 3. 8 Morta, cioè senza candela, la Gravezza Libri ed i loro resti vecchi.

VIII. Accoglierà la Banca che verrà qui sotto destinata, li ricorsi che gli saranno prodotti da essi Matricolati della seconda Classe, quando fossero lesi nei diritti, prerogative e facoltà che gli restano riservate, e la Banca medesima per quanto alla stessa appartiene s' adopererà al loro mantenimento, rivolgendosi ancora agli Eccell[mi] Magistrati competenti, per la giusta loro difesa a spese dell' Università stessa.

IX. La Banca composta delli Carichi sopranominati averà il Governo esecutivo di tutte le Leggi di disciplina dell' Università, ed altresì quello dell' esazione verso d' Individui, tanto della prima Categoria che della seconda, in conformità di quanto praticavasi in addietro e che è tuttavia vigente appresso la Scola dei Marzeri, gli Uffizj dei Senseri, della Seda, e della Camera del Purgo colla subordinazione poi agli Eccellentissimi Magistrati competenti.

X. Qualunque degl' Individui Matricolati che si creda in diritto di reclamare, doverà esponere prima le sue ragioni alla Banca per conciliarle, o appoggiarle, scortandole ai competenti Magistrati per la decisione; restando però sempre al ricorrente libero l' adito di presentare in ogni incontro alli surriferiti Eccell[mi] Magistrati.

XI. Averà per tanto la medesima a radunarsi almeno una volta al mese la quarta Domenica per versare sopra gli affari dell' Università, ascoltare le Richieste degl' Individui Matricolati, e per sollecitare il Pagamento dei Debitori. Qualunque mancasse dei Bancali, non essendo da legittima Causa impedito, sarà soggetto alla pena di

Ducati uno V. C. applicabile alla Cassa dell' Università; ed il Priore che mancasse di chiamare essa Banca e d' intervenirvi incorrerà nella pena di Ducati 5 V. C. quando per intervenirvi non avesse giusto impedimento.

XII. Potranno essere consumati gli affari quando siano ridotti li Bancali al numero di sette e tutti a Bossoli e Ballotte; non averà però Voto il Scrivano in esse Riduzioni, perche egli averà l' incombenze di Cancelliere di scrivere e registrare le cose prese e stabilite.

XIII. Dovere indispensabile di essa Banca sarà un Mese prima del suo termine di regolare le due Tabelle, in cui sono descritti e separati li nomi de Matricolati si della prima che della seconda Categoria, che doveranno farsi in adesso dall' attuale Priore e Sindico più vecchio dietro al Foglio approvato dall' Ecce'l^mo^ Senato, ed essere esposte in luogo cospicuo della Scuola.

XIV. Si leveranno dalle medesime tutti quelli che fossero morti, si riporteranno dalla prima alla seconda Tabella li Debitori duennali, gli Assolti dalla Banca del pagamento della Tansa e Taglioni di Milizia, e si porteranno nella prima quelli che saranno stati dalla Banca ammessi.

XV. L' Esatore dell' Università avrà debito ogni quarta Domenica del Mese, giorno della riduzione metodica della Banca, di consegnare al Priore tutto il Dinaro riscosso dagl' Individui Matricolati accompagnata da Nota giurata, individuante le respettive Partite contate dalli Matricolati nominatamente, colle Base della qual Nota dovrà il Priore dar credito ad esse respettive Ditte, conservanda intatta a sua cauzione la Nota stessa.

XVI. Tutte le Leggi al presente Piano non deroganti doveranno essere intieramente eseguite; e come l' Eccell^mo^ Senato nel suo Decreto 30 Decembre scaduto ha riconosciuta necessaria la continuazione degli attuale Priore e Sindico più Vecchio anche per l' anno avvenire, onde con ordine e tranquilità s' abbia la verificazione de stabilimenti adottati per benefizio d' essa Arte Tipografica, così non potendo essi passare alli due Carichi di Conservatori saranno li Carichi medesimi eletti per questa sola volta dal Capitolo, che dovrà radunarsi coi soli Individui della prima Categoria, facendo provisionalmente sedere nei Carichi che ora sono occupati da quelli della seconda Categoria gli Matricolati della prima che hanno sostenute le Cariche di Priore e Sindico da essere estratti a sorte, come praticasi in tutte le altre Riduzione de' Capitoli, nelle quali mancano le Persone in attualità di Carico.

La presente sarà stampata e consegnata al Priore della sopradetta università per diffonderla a propri Individui, affinche sia in ogni parte esattamente eseguita.

Data li 19 Febraro 1780.

Giulio Ravagnin Prov^r^ di Co^o^.
Paulo Vallaresso Prov^r^ di Co^o^.
Zorzi Grimani Prov^r^ di Co^o^.
Pietro Ortali Nod^o^.

1781. 27 *Settembre in Pregadi.*

No. 74. Essendosi stabilito colla Terminazione del benemerito Magistrato de' Rifformatori dello Studio di Padova 1780, 30 Luglio, aprovata da questo Consiglio col Decreto 9 Agosto dell' anno medesimo, alcuni necessari regolamenti coll' oggetto di rimediare ai disordini invalsi nell' Arte Tipografica di questa Città, e per dar un qualche conforto e sostentamento ai poveri Librari e Stampatori della Dominante, fu sopra alcuni Articoli della Terminazione medesima ricercato ascolto dinanzi al Magistrato de Rifformatori dello Studio di Padova da alcuni individui dell' Arte stessa, e venendo ad essi accordato col Decreto di questo Consiglio 7 Aprile 1781, fu poi anche ricercato dal Prior e Sindico, unito ad altri Veneti Stampatori e Libraj innanzi al Magistrato medesimo, alli quali fu pure annuito coll' altro Decreto 3 Maggio 1781. Essendosi però dal Zelante Magistrato esaurito l' ascolto col mezzo degli Avvocati da una parte e dall' altra, e dopo aver diligentemente esaminate le rispettive allegazioni, tanto nell' una che nell' altra sentenza, spiega egli nell' ora letta scrittura il riputato suo sentimento al quale uniformandosi pienamente questo Consiglio, non trova motivo ne ragioni di far novità alcuna sulle stabilite regolazioni, e perciò riconferma in tutte le sue parti la Terminazione 30 Luglio 1780, dichiarando con ciò licenziata la supplica prodotta in Collegio nostro li 28 Marzo 1781 da Librari e Stampatori in essa nominati, come se presentata non fosse, e come nella supplica predetta e nelle Allegazioni dei ricorrenti aducono in loro favore la Legge 1767, 29 Agosto, così d' ora innanzi s' intenderà che non possa aver luogo nessuna interpretazione o spiegazione che dar si volesse ad essa ed ad altra Legge, che far potesse effetto contrario alla presente deliberazione. Nel raccomandarsi in fine al Magistrato de Rifformatori dello Studio di Padova l' esercizio della sua benemerita vigilanza per l' esecuzione di questa Legge starà in attenzione il Senato di essere dall' esattezza sua inteso degli effetti che saranno per derivare dall' osservanza delle providenze comprese nella Terminazione suddetta a vantaggio dell' Arte Tipografica, ed al comodo universale dei sudditi.

Davidde Marchesini Seg°.

1781. *7 Giugno in Pregadi.*

No. 75. Esauritosi dalla diligenza del Magistrato de Rifformatori dello Studio di Padova l' Ascolto comandato colle deliberazioni 31 Marzo decorso in via deliberativa innanzi ad esso, alla seconda classe de Stampatori e Libraj Matricolati di questa Arte Tipografica in confronto delli Matricolati della Classe prima sopra il nuovo Piano di discipline addottato dal Decreto 15 Febraro passato e relativa Terminazione, dopo il più attento esame donato alle ragioni e con la voce degli Avvocati e colle scritte allegazioni addotte dalle Parti esibisce nell' ora letta gradita scrittura il proprio sentimento nella vertenza di cui si tratta.

Al quale intieramente uniformandosi questo Consiglio coll' oggetto di assicurare l' ottenimento del vero bene ed utile che a benefizio di quest' Arte stà per derivarne dalla nuova regolazione suddetta tanto più che in tal modo vengono a ravvivarsi le Leggi fondamentali già sino da remoti tempi statuite nella Matricola di quella Università dall' abuso corrotte, e col tempo neglette, nel licenzar la Supplica della suddetta Seconda Classe prodotta come se stata presentata non fosse, conferma in ogni sua parte il surriferito Decreto 15 Febraro passato, non che il Piano ridotto in Terminazione che pur si avvalora, onde riportar abbiano inalterabile osservanza.

Davidde Marchesini.

1782.
Terminazione degl' Illustriss^mi et Eccellent^mi SS^i Riffermatori dello Studio di Padova.

No. 76. Il Serenissimo Principe fà sapere ed è per ordine degl' Ill^mi et Eccell^mi SS^i Sud^i.

Per la Disciplina.

Dopo aver provveduto con varie regolazioni ad alcuni disordini invalsi nell' Arte Tipografica di questa Dominante onde farla risorgere dalla sua decadenza, altri ne abbiamo rilevati col mezzo di scrittura presentata dalla Banca alle osservazioni e riflessi del Magistrato nostro, derivanti dalla mano d' Opera, da Materiali, che in alcune Stamperie sono ridotti quasi impotenti al Lavoro, e dalla pessima Carta nella quale s' imprimono l' Edizioni.

Occorrendo perciò pronti ripari e nuove provvidenze viene l' Autorità nostra a stabilire colli seguenti Articoli.

I. Per quanto riguarda adunque la mano d' Opera si commette che li Capi o Padroni di Stamperia o Proti, per se o sotto nome d' altri, non possano praticare la vendita di Vino per proprio conto ne permetter che altri portino in Stamperia maggior copia di Vino di mezza Libbra per Testa alli Torcoleri, e di un quarto per Testa similmente alli Compositori, obbligati volendosi li Padroni o Proti di osservare e riconoscere la quantità della mezza libbra o del quarto che respettivamente si stabilisce, e in caso per qualche maggior porzione furtivamente introdotta di Vino rinvenissero qualche Operajo Ubbriaco e disordinato, lo faranno tosto desistere per tutto quel giorno del Lavoro; e se non ostante il prescritto divieto li Patroni o Proti o altri Uffiziali di Stamperia non lo eseguissero, ed i Torcoleri o Compositori vi contravenissero, cadranno li primi in pena di Ducati Venti correnti, e li secondi di Ducato uno pure corrente per cadauno, da essere levati irremissibalmente dalla Banca ed applicati alla Cassa dell' Arte.

II. Niuno stampatore potrà prendere al suo servizio un Compositore senza il buon servire del Patrone della Stamperia da cui esce, e se il detto Compositore tenesse debito con il Padrone non possa andar al servizio di veruno dell' Arte senza aver prima soddisfatto il Creditore, e chi lo prendesse dovrà pagare per lui l' intiero debito al primo Padrone, ed in contravenzione, oltre il dover pagare per lui l' intiero debito al primo Padrone, cadrà nella pena di Ducati Venti correnti, tanto per il primo caso quanto per il Secondo, levati ed applicabili come sopra.

III. Sarà obbligata ogni Stamperia di Commissione avente due Torcoli, di allevare ed accordare un Garzon Torcoler per anni tre al consueto già noto prezzo, qual Garzone dovrà esser presentato dal suo Principale alla Banca per essere registrato l' accordo in un Libro che dovrà essere instituito dalla Banca stessa, ne veruno Stampatore potrà mai, sotto le pene di sopra enunciate, prendere al suo servizio alcuno di questi Accordati, se prima non averà compito l' accordo e non averà ottenuto il buon servire dall' Accordante; e se alcuni di questi Torcoleri, accordati passasse in qualche Stamperia di Terra Ferma, ciò rilevato, dovrà il Capo di quella Stamperia essere avvertito dal Priore pro tempore di licenziarlo subito dal servizio come Persona obbligata a quest' Arte, e a ciò mancando il detto Capo cadrà nella pena di Ducati trenta correnti applicabili come sopra, e sarà dal Priore e Banca implorato il presidio di questo Magistrato per il pagamento della stessa, e perche il detto accordato sia tolto da quella Stamperia.

IV. Affinche non manchi in Venezia il bisogno all' Arte de Compositori e Torcoleri, quelli che partissero di qua non potranno essere ricevuti d' alcun Stampatore della Terra Ferma se non previa una Fede del Priore e delli due Sindici pro tempore, quale spieghi non abbisognar l' Arte del medesimo, ed a questa stessa Legge saranno gli Allievi fatti nella Terra Ferma per accettarli nelle Stamperie di Venezia: che se poi questi Compositori o Torcolieri allievi di quest' Arte passassero a prender serviggio nel suo mestiere in Esteri Stati (locchè risolutamente si vieta) prescritto resta che qualor ritornassero nella Dominante non possano essere accettati in alcuna di queste Stamperie, sotto pena a chi li ricevesse di Ducati trenta Correnti applicabili come sopra, se non per grazia concessa con li due terzi de Voti dalla Banca per essere approvata dal Magistrato nostro, e previo anche il pagamento di quel tanto ch' essi fossero debitori verso il Padrone dal quale sono partiti.

Niuna Stamperia potrà da qui innanzi prendere per Compositore o Torcolero alcuno che non sia stato accordato per Garzone, Salvi, per altro, quelli che presentamente hanno dieci anni di serviggio e lavorano quantunque non Accordati.

Ogni Operajo poi o Compositore o Torcolero avrà debito di avvertire il Padrone giorni quindici prima quando volesse licenziarsi dal servigio, e cosi praticare dovrà il Padrone stesso verso il sopradetto, ma se questo scoperto fosse d' impontualità o di depravato Lavoro potrà essere immediate licenziato.

Ogni Padrone di Stamperia finalmente rassegnerà al' Priore e Banca li Nomi di tutti quelli Torcoleri e Compositori della respettiva Stamperia che sono oramai Vecchi ed impotenti affinche il Priore e Banca suddetta accordi a questi e non ad altri un Mandato sottoscritto da esso Priore da un Sindico e da un consigliere per poter vendere in Giro per le Strade della Città i soliti Libri Comuni e Stampe a Foglio Volante e questi Vecchj similmente ed impotenti parteciperanno dell' Elemosina che suol dispensarsi dalla Banca.

Tutti gli altri che non possederanno un tale Mandato, e che vendessero per le Strade, saranno considerati contrafacenti, e come tali verranno puniti irremissibilmente giusto alle Leggi: non compresi in questi i Banchetti, per li quali si confermano li Comandi già emanati.

V. Dovendo poi il Magistrato essere appieno assicurato che ogni Edizione corrisponda intieramente al suo Campione che tenuto viene uno dal Proto Esaminatore, e l' altro dal Sopraintendente alle Stampe a confronto sempre dell' Opera Stampata, resta stabilito che il detto Proto Esaminatore ripeta dallo Stampatore un terzo foglio del detto Campione, e numito dalle statuite sottoscrizioni debba consegnarlo ogni volta al Priore pro tempore.

Questo terzo Foglio di Campione valer dovrà di confronto all' opera compita, la quale non potrà mai pubblicarsi nè vendersi, se lo Stampatore o Librajo o Autore o Proprietario non la presenterà prima al Priore ed alli due Sindici pro tempore, da quali tre praticati li necessarii esami e riconosciutala uniforme al Campione verrà approvata con un Attestato giurato da Consegnarsi al Proprietario, la qual copia restar dovrà in soddisfazione di quella per le Leggi dovuta all' Arte.

Di questi attestati si farà Registro dalla Banca in un apposito Libro, e se ne presenterà copia al Magistrato nostro, onde rilevar e punire severamente le pubblicazioni de Libri che si facessero senza avere chiesta ed ottenuta l' approvazione dei sopradetti Priore e Sindici i quali se la negassero dovranno darne conto al Magistrato.

Si dichiara in oltre che qualor succedesse una qualche collusione tra il Priore e

Sindici collo Stampatore o Librajo o Autore, dalla quale derivasse una illegittima approvazione sopra di che sarà da noi inquisito per rilevarla, punita sarà l' infedeltà con Ducati trenta per cadauno di essi, applicabili come sopra.

Che se i Libri o Opere da pubblicarsi saranno di ragione delli Priore e Sindici pro tempore, dovranno queste essere presentate col metodo sopra enunciato al Priore e Sindici usciti per l' istesso effetto.

VI. E come poi conviene animare la mano d' Opera delli Torcoleri per ottenere l' utile e decoroso fine della buona e ben travagliata Stampa, resta persuaso il Magistrato che il Priore e li due Sindici debbano approvate che siano le Stampe, consegnare ad ognuno delli rispettivi Torcoleri Lavoratori di esse un Viglietto di Laude con specificazione del Numero de Fogli, perche giunti a duecento da calcolarsi sopra una o più Opere, conseguisca il Torcolero in premio Lire sedici dalla Cassa dell' Arte.

Sopra tutti gli enunciati Articoli sarà sempre però aperto ed accolto il ricorso nel Magistrato Nostro agli aggravati per gli ulteriori atti di Giustizia.

Per li Materiali di Stamperia.

Da esatta relazione del Sostituito al Sopraintendente alle Stampe viene a sapersi che varie connotate Stamperie non possono ridurre al voluto buon Lavoro l' Edizioni, o perche li Torchj sono con imperfezione piantati, o perche gli Attreccj necessarj compariscono difettosi e quasi inservibili; sopra un si essenziale Articolo proveder volendo il Magistrato stabilisce: Che, eccettuate le Stamperie denominate da Bagaglie, debba l' Arte medesima far dar mano di tempo in tempo con il Soldo della sua Cassa, per via d' imprestanza, ai ripari necessarj in quelle Stamperie che appartengono a poveri Proprietarj Matricolati, quale imprestanza poi risarcita esser dovrà da medesimi Matricolati Poveri in quei modi che verranno dalla Banca ed al respettivo Soccorso Stampatore conciliati ed accordati.

Di quelle altre Stamperie poi spettanti a Matricolati non bisognosi, li quali tengono li loro Materiali ed Attreccj non montati a dovere, obbligati restano li Padroni entro il termine di due Mesi dalla pubblicazione della presente di rimetterli al voluto buon Lavoro il che sarà riconosciuto o dal Sopraintendente alle Stampe o dal Sostituito colle diligenti personali visite prescritte da tempo in tempo dalle Leggi, e se per avventura rilevato venisse non adempito il Comando, verranno gl' inobbedienti dal Magistrato nostro con pene ad arbitrio castigati.

Per la Carta.

Derivando in molta parte la buona riuscita della Stampa dalla qualità e natura della Carta, si risserva il Magistrato di fissare un Campione della qualità di essa sotto alla quale non sarà permesso a chiunque di far uso nell' Edizioni in pena della confiscazione degli Esemplari: e fra tanto si commette alla Banca di suggerire dentro due Mesi, i modi più facili e di più sicura esecuzione per verificare questo regolamento.

Per la Economia della Cassa.

Si vuole in oltre che ogni Individuo Librajo o Stampatore si di questa Città che delle Terra Ferma non potendo ottenere il solito Mandato di Licenza nè di Stampa nè di ristampa senza la consueta fede del Priore quale assicuri che il Manoscritto o Libro non offenda il Privilegio di alcuno, contribuisca nella consegna e ricevere della Fede stessa soldi venti alla Cassa dell' Arte de Libraj per dargli con questo tenue aggravio un qualche soccorso.

Dovendo perciò questa Cassa supplire, come si è di sopra stabilito, ai ripari de Materiali nelle Stamperie povere ed alli premj di sopra indicati, e non tenendo modi sufficienti a si utili effetti si da facoltà alla Banca colla pluralità de Voti di potersi servire dei Civanzi della stessa dei Soldi venti per ogni rilascio delle Fedi, e di quanto entrerà nella medesima di ragione di pene.

Per Facilitar l'Azione della Banca.

Provveduto in tal modo con nuove discipline, e stabilimenti ai scoperti disordini e volendo di tempo in tempo il Magistrato nostro sapere se le cose deliberate abbiano il loro effetto, così resta permesso alla Banca in sequela del diritto accordatogli dalla Terminazione 19 Febraro dell' Anno decorso relativa al Decreto 15 dello stesso Mese di aprire una Fessura semplice all' esterno del Muro della sua Scuola, affinche ognuno possa ponere nella medesima Fessura avvisi o Denunzie sopra qualunque contraffazione alla presente ed alle decorse emanate Leggi, quali Carte saranno raccolte dal Priore, che tenerà le Chiavi, e saranno comunicate alla Banca ogni quarta Domenica del Mese, e sarà poi Carico della Banca suddetta di rassegnarle alle osservazioni del Magistrato Nostro accompagnate da sua relazione per indi dipendere dagli ulteriori ordini nostri. Quando si conoscerà verificata la colpa verrà accordato al Denunziante, che sarà tenuto Secreto, li venti per Cento sopra la pena a cui sarà il contrafacente condannato dall' Autorità del Magistrato, ed il rimanente restar dovrà a benefizio della Cassa dell' Arte.

E la presente dovrà essere stampata e pubblicata ad universale notizia, e dovrà pure ogni Individuo tenerla affissa nella propria Bottega o Stamperia in luoco della sua Maggior vista.

Data li 6 Marzo 1782.

Andrea Querini Riform^r.
Niccolò Barbarigo Riform^r.
Girolamo Ascanio Zustinian Cav. Rifform^r.
Davidde Marchesini Segrio.

Addi 16 *Marzo* 1782.

Pubblicata sopra le Scale di S. Marco e di Rialto.

1782. 16 *Aprile*.

No. 77. Riflessibile di molto comparendo al Magistrato Nostro la innobbedienza di alcuni Libraj e Stampatori di questa Arte Tipografica alla Legge 15 Gennaro 1725, che fu anche ravvivata e repubblicata alli 21 Maggio 1745, in non consegnare le due prime copie di cadaun Libro ch' esce stampato, l' una alla Pubblica Libreria di Venezia, e l' altra a quella di Padova, resta risolutamente prescritto che ogni Librajo, o Stampatore, o Autore o Proprietario del Libro stampato quale per la Legge 1782, 6 Marzo, ultimamente emanata, deve presentare al Priore e Sindici una Copia del Libro stampato che serva di confronto con il Foglio di Campione per essere approvata prima della sua pubblicazione, sii obbligato a dover consegnar nello stesso tempo nelle mani del medesimo Priore le due Copie suddette, onde ambedue le Pubbliche Librarie non restino prive delle volute Edizioni; e caso che non eseguissero il Comando resterano soggetti alle pene ad arbitrio del Magistrato predetto.

E la presente dovrà essere consegnata al Prior dell' Arte onde la registri nella sua Matricola e la rendi notificata a tutti li suoi Individui.

Andrea Querini Rif^r.
Niccolò Barbarigo Rif^r.
Girolamo Ascanio Zustinian Kav^r Rif^r.
Davidde Marchesini Segret^o.
L' Originale in filza N° 97.

28 *Aprile* 1782.

No. 78. Registro di Torcoleri e Compositori vecchi ed impotenti a quali spetta il mandato di andar per la Città vendendo Libri comuni e Stampe a Foglio volante et a quali spetta di partecipare della Limosina che suol dispensarsi dalla Banca giusta la Terminazione degl' Ill^mi et Ecc^mi SS^r Rifformatori dello Studio di Padova sei Marzo 1782, pubblicata sopra le Scale di S. Marco e di Rialto li 16 pure Marzo 1782.

Antonio Quesuolo detto Capella Torcoler.

Paulo Rossini detto Paulone Torcoler con fede di Giuseppe Fenzo e di Ant^o Gislon proto del Coletti.

Osvaldo Mazucco comp^r.
Valentin Turi Torcoler.
Lorenzo Bossi Torcoler.
Vettor Brentello Torcoler.
Agostin Biffi Torcoler.
Girolamo Petroi detto Bonvicini.
Giorgio Travi.
Bortolo Calegari.
Gio: Batta: Marchiada.
Felice Rusca.
Alvise Poli compositore.

Il Serenissimo Principe
fà Sapere
Ed è per ordine degli Illustrissimi ed Eccellentissimi Signori
Riformatori dello Studio di Padova.

No. 79. Fù sempre un oggetto delle attente cure del Magistrato l' invigilare al buon andamento di questa Arte Tipografica coll' accorrere di tratto in tratto all' emenda dei disordini, e degli abusi che s' introdussero, de quali riconosciuta l' importanza, i Precessori Nostri prescrissero nelle Terminazioni 1767, 29 Luglio, e 1780, 30 Luglio, quei presidj che parvero loro opportuni.

Ma come l' esperienza fa conoscere, che le emanate provvidenze pienamente nel fatto non soddisfano le viste contemplate, il Magistrato trova opportuno di rinovarle con quelle modificazioni di disciplina, e di buon' ordine, le quali saranno per l' avvenire di norma alla inalterabile esecuzione dei respettive Individui dell' Arte medesima.

I. Datosi riflesso alla Classe dei Garzoni Compositori, si stabilisce, che non potendo supplire un Garzone solo a tutti li rapporti delli Lavori delle rispettive Stamperie, che hanno tre Torchj in effettivo Lavoro, possano li Principali delle medesime tenerne due accordati giusto alle Leggi; e gli altri Principali che non avessero il numero suddetto di tre Torchi in lavoro non abbiano a tenerne che un solo accordato, con la condizione, per altro, che si vuole osservata, ciò che sappiano ben leggere particolarmente il Manoscritto.

II. Obbligo delli suddetti Garzoni sarà di star fissi per un Quinquennio a terminare il loro Garzonato nella respettiva Stamperia; e qualor passassero in altra senza legittime cause, da esser riconosciute dal Magistrato Nostro, non verrà loro computato il servigio prestato nella prima, ma ricominciare dovranno il Quinquennio suespresso.

Terminato il loro Garzonato si prescrive che non possano passare ad essere Lavoranti, se prima non avranno fatto un' altro Anno, a seconda del praticato, per *Lavorantino* nella stessa Stamperia, oppure sotto un altro Principale; dietro il quale Anno dovranno far la Prova per essere certi della loro abilità, cioè dovranno presentarsi all Priore dell' Arte pro tempore, acciò destini loro una Stamperia per comporre una Forma, quale dovrà essere esaminata dal suddetto Priore, ovvero da chi esso destinasse, e risponder dovranno a tutte quelle altre interrogazioni che venissero loro fatte rapporto al Mecanico Lavoro della Stampa e sopra gli altri punti de sapersi da un Compositore per essere approvato Lavorante.

E quanto alli Garzoni Torcoleri che si vogliono pure soggetti alle stesse discipline dei Garzoni Compositori suddetti, con la sola differenza di un Triennio a compire il loro Garzonato, mentre si riconferma per gli uni e per gli altri il risoluto divieto prescritto nella Terminazione 1782, 6 Marzo, all' Articolo IV, di non esercitare l' Arte loro in Stati Esteri, sotto le pene comminate, si dichiara però che, volendo, possano qualor abbiano terminato il loro Garzonato, trasferirsi nelle Stamperie della Terra Ferma.

III. Riconoscendosi poscia gli abusi, e le dannose conseguenze che sono derivate dagli accordati Privilegj perpetui agl' Individui Libraj e Stampatori di detta Arte sopra ogni Classe de Libri, si prescrive che i Libri tutti usati volgarmente e comunemente da ogni condizione di Persone, cioè Scolastici, e Ascetici ed altri di piccola mole che non soprapassino il prezzo delle *Lire due*, non possano d' ora innanzi essere coperti da Privilegio; ma sieno per sempre posti in Libertà, sicchè ogni Stampatore di Commissione, o Librajo Veneto di scarsa fortuna possi stamparli, e ristamparli, sempre però colle debite Licenze e colla comandata condizione di esibirli a *Partito* a quei prezzi che veranno prefissi con equità dalla Banca dell' Arte; alla quale viene commesso tanto sopra questi Libri, quanto sopra tutte le altre opere di stampa e ristampa, di far un equa Tanza del prezzo conveniente sul fondamento della Stampa del primo Foglio, che gli verrà prodotto di chiunque stamperà o ristamperà Libri; dichiarandosi però sempre aperto il ricorso competente al Magistrato a qualunque Stampatore che non fosse Contento delli fatti apprezzamenti.

IV. Ogni Librajo e Stampatore, che stamperà Opere a *Partito*, non potrà esibirlo agli Esteri Libraj, sennon nel solo caso, che non trovasse l' esito del numero delle Copie, che avesse prefisso di stampare; il qual numero di Copie dovrà denotarlo al Priore dell' Arte, il quale viene incaricato di farne il dovuto registro, e di difondere la notizia a tutti gli Individui.

E come la Terminazione 1788, 27 Maggio, prescrive che qualunque Librajo o Stampatore al quale viene esibito il *Partito*, abbia a notificare sul Foglio a stampa, che prodotto gli verrà dall' Imprenditore, *il numero delle Copie che gli occorresse*, oppure spiegarsi di *non volerne*; così si precetta tanto alli Libraj e Stampatori di ciò esattamente eseguire, quanto all' Imprenditore di verificare l' esibizione nel modo sopraccennato, onde possa il Magistrato essere al fatto di riconoscere se adempito venghi il voluto comando.

V. E quanto agli altri Libri di maggior prezzo degli enunciati nell' Articolo III, li quali avevano goduto il loro privilegio per il tempo solito concedersi prima della Terminazione 1767 suddetta, e così pure quelli che dopo la Legge stessa avessero compito e compissero in avvenire il termine della medesima accordato; tutti questi si dichiara che d' ora innanzi possi chiunque Librajo e Stampatore, previe le debite Licenze, ristamparle, come ciò si faceva prima della Terminazione 1780, 30 Luglio, soprallegata.

VI. Si statuisce poi che li Libri Manuscritti, e non più stampati in luogo alcuno, e parimente le Ristampe de' Libri Forastieri, abbiano in avvenire a godere il privilegio, in correlazione al Decreto 1603, 11 Maggio, di anni 20 li Manuscritti, e di Anni 10 le Ristampe Forastiere; dichiarandosi però che un tal privilegio verrà accordato a quei soli Libraj e Stampatori Veneti che dopo ottenuto il Mandato di Licenza dal Magistrato Nostro per la stampa dei surriferiti Libri, faranno annotare nel Libro dell' Arte, previo l' esborso a questa delle consuete Lire 3 : 2, l' opera in Privilegio, quale s' intenderà aver principio dalla Data del Mandato stesso.

VII. E come si vuole che una tal concessione di privilegio colla suespressa modificazione di tempo e di epoca relativa al giorno del rilascio del Mandato, si estenda anco sopra tutti li Manuscritti e Ristampe nuove Estere, delle quali ottennero li rispettivi Libraj, e Stampatori Veneti il Mandato dopo la surriferita Terminazione 1780, 30 Luglio, sino in presente, così si dichiara che debbano far annotare nel Libro dei privilegi dell' Arte li loro rispettivi Mandati per godere del privilegio in continuazione fino allo spirato periodo degli anni di sopra stabiliti; passati li quale potrà qualunque Stampatore e Librajo Veneto liberamente ristamparli, sempre però colle debite Licenze e colle seguenti condizione; cioè d' incominciare la Stampa e Ristampa de' Libri entro due Mesi, e di progredirla coll' Opera almeno di un mezzo Foglio al giorno; al che mancando gli resterà sospeso e ritirato il Mandato.

VIII. E siccome le imprese che si assumano i Libraj, o Stampatori di dar alla Luce *Opere per Società*, servono di molta utilità all' Arte stessa, e di comodo a Letterati; perciò per correggere gli abusi che ben speso emergono con indecoro della Nazione e sulla qualità delle stampe, e sull' arenamento delle Opere, si stabilisce, che ogni Stampatore o Librajo che voglia stampare un' *Opera per Società*, debba prima prendere le solite Licenze, e successivo Mandato Nostro del primo Tomo, quale dovrà averlo Stampato prima di publicare il Manifesto.

Sarà parimente obbligo dello Stampatore o Librajo Imprenditore delle suddette *Opere per Società*, di presentarsi nella Segretaria del Magistrato Nostro per annotare

Gratis un formale Costituto, nel quale dichiari e si obblighi di proseguire, e terminare la Edizione dell' *Opera per Associazione* con le condizioni espresse nel Manifesto, e per esibire idonea Pieggieria, da essere riconosciuta e ammessa dal Magistrato, per un terzo del prezzo di tutta l' Opera; da soddisfarsi dal Pieggio in giusto risarcimento degli Associati qualunque volta mancasse agli obblighi assunti nel Manifesto medesimo.

IX. Importando poi che le stampe e ristampe di qualunque Libro riescono di quella perfezione nelle Correzioni che fu sempre l' oggetto primario della vigile cura del Magistrato per far risorgere l' antico decoro di esse, e facilitare in pari tempo un esito felice de' Libri Veneti, per ciò si stabilisce, in coerenza alla costante pubblica volonta che tutti li Libraj e Stampatori siano rissolutamente obbligati a fornirsi di Correttori capaci ed idonei per Correggere le proprie Edizioni, sotto pena di esser soggetti alla perdita di tutti gli Esamplari stampati con privilegio o comuni senza eccezione, non meno che ad altri castighi riserbati all' arbitrio nostro a proporzione dei diffetti che si rinvenissero.

X. Al conoscimento di queste mancanze viene espressamente incaricata la diligenza del Correttor Nostro Generale, ed eccitata efficacimente la di lui assidua vigilanza per l' esatto adempimento delle proprie ispezioni.

XI. Obbligo sarà pertanto immancabile, per la voluta inalterabile osservanza de sopradetti Articoli relativi a Garzoni, Lavoranti e Correttori del Sopraintendente Nostro alle Stampe di visitare con frequenza le Stamperie tutte, come gli viene risolutamente prescritto dalle Leggi di sua Istituzione, e di assoggettare ogni Bimestre al Magistrato il risultato delle scoperte mancanze, o del buon andamento delle respettive Stamperie.

XII. Per assicurarsi poi che il Campione di ogni Libro che si stampa o ristampa, corrisponda e per la qualità della Carta, degl' Inchiostri e dei Caratteri a quei importanti oggetti che si sono sempre contemplati per il miglioramento delle stampe, si prescrive l' obbligo a cadaun Librajo e Stampatore dopo aver ottenuto il Mandato di Licenza di presentare non solo al Proto Esaminadore, che si vuole sussista sempre un tal carico, il Campione stesso per essere da lui approvato, ma eziandio di produrlo al Sopraintendente Nostro alle Stampe, il quale viene incaricato di prestarsi attento per riconoscere se la qualità della Carta e dei Caratteri corrisponda, oltre il Mecanico Lavoro, al merito dell' Opera che si vuol difondere colla Stampa, e trovandolo uniforme, lo approverà egli stesso, e lo terrà appresso di se per praticare i necessarj confronti di esso primo Modello col restante dell' Opera.

Compiuta che sarà questa, e riconosciuta del tutto simile al Campione dal Sopraintendente suddetto, al qual obbligato sarà lo Stampatore di presentarla per ottenere, prima di darla alla luce, il comandato *Pubblicetur*, verrà questo soltanto firmato, e rilasciato dallo stesso Sopraintendente e dal Priore dell' Arte *pro tempore* senza altre sottoscrizioni.

XIII. Ma perchè qualche particolare Persona non matricolata potrebbe indursi di far stampare o ristampare qualche Opera coi Capitali propri, locchè servirebbe di maggior soccorso a questa Arte Tipografica, perciò si stabilisce che sia essa in piena libertà di farlo, sempre però col mezzo di un Stampatore Veneto, e con le condizioni di non poter negoziare la stampa o ristampa in Baratti, ne far egli la vendita di questa, ma valersi di un Librajo, o Stampatore Veneto; obbligando però lo Stampatore, che stampasse per particolari Persone, di farsi pagare per la Cassa dell' Arte Grossi 18 per ogni Balla.

XIV. Sia in oltre proibito a Particolari non Matricolati l' aprir Negozio, far

Cambi o Vendite al minuto su' i Banchetti de' Libri Stampati per loro conto, ma abbiano essi ad esibirli ai Veneti Libraj e Stampatori per essere esposti alla Vendita nelle loro Pubbliche Botteghe.

XV. E quanto ai Venditori dei Libri sopra i Banchetti di Piazza, od altri luoghi, si prescrive, che saranno essi assolutamente soggetti a quelle condizioni ed obblighi, espressi già nell' Articolo VI. della Terminazione 1767, 29 Luglio; volendosi in oltre, a tenor dell' altra 3 Ottobre 1778, che tener debbano un Banchetto solo, non raddoppiato coll' aggiunta d' altri, ne possano vendere sopra Banchetti, sennon Libri Vecchj, nella serie e natura de quali s' intendono essere i soli Libri legati, e colle Carte tagliate.

XVI. Ma perchè ai Matricolati dell' Arte devesi preservare il diritto proprio, ed interesse, si rinova fermamente il comando emanato dalla sopraccitata Terminazione 3 Ottobre 1778, cioè che a qualunque Persona non Matricolata sia risolutamente vietato di vendere, nè per le Botteghe, nè in Pubblico, nè occultamente Libri di qualunque sorte; il qual divieto si vuole pure eseguito anche per quelli, che sono Matricolati; sotto tutte le pene dichiarite nell' Articolo V. della sumentovata Terminazione.

XVII. Presente pure al Magistrato le solite Tanse, che addossate sono dall' Arte colle prescritte norme agl' Individui della medesima, perciò si determina di voler adempito il metodo prefisso dalla Terminazione 1742, tanto per la riscossione de Debiti Vecchj, quanto per le annue contribuzioni della Tansa, in forza della quale sarà negato il Mandato di Stampa o Ristampa ad ogni Ricorrente dal Segretario Nostro, qualor non gli presenti prima l' Attestato del Priore dell' Arte *pro tempore*, o di non essere Debitore, o attesa l' abilità concessa a' Debitori dell' Arte stessa, non si presti puntuale di tempo in tempo al prescritto respettivo pagamento.

XVIII. Sopra tutte le sopradette provvidenze viene incaricato il Priore dell' Arte *pro tempore* d'invigilare perchè venghino adempite, e di riferirne di quando in quando il risultato al Magistrato Nostro della prestata obbedienza.

E la presente, approvata che sia dall' Eccellentissimo Senato, annullando la surriferita Terminazione 1780, 30 Luglio, non che l' altra 28 Settembre susseguente, sarà stampata, e consegnate ne varie Copie al Prior dell' Arte, onde le faccia diffondere col mezzo del Bidello a tutti gli Individui della medesima, a' quali viene precettato di tenerla affissa a vista universale nella propria Bottega, o Stamperia; volendosi che per quanto a cadaun spetta riporti immancabilmente la sua intiera perfetta osservanza ed esecuzione.

Dat dal Magistrato Eccellentissimo suddetto primo Maggio 1789.

Piero Barbarigo Riformator.
Girolamo Ascanio Giustinian Cav. Riformator.
Francesco Pesaro Cav. Proc. Riformator.
Marcantonio Sanfermo Segr.

Addì 10 *Giugno* 1789.

Approvata con Decreto dell Eccellentissimo Senato.

Il Serenissimo Principe
fà sapere, ed è per ordine degl' Illustrissimi ed Eccellentissimi Signori Rifformatori dello Studio di Padova.

No. 80. All' oggetto di rendere sempre più provida ed operativa la Terminazione primo Maggio prossimo passato, autorizzata dall' Eccellentissimo Senato col susseguente Decreto 10 Giugno prossimo decorso.

Gl' Illustrissimi ed Eccellentissimi Signori Riformatori dello studio di Padova dato il conveniente riflesso alle divote istanze prodotte dalla Banca dell' Arte Tipografica, si determinano di aggiungere alcune altre rischiarazioni di buon' ordine, e di disciplina per vieppiù assicurarsi della possibile perfezione del lavoro delle Stampe, ch' è l' oggetto primario, a cui dirette sono le applicazioni del Magistrato Nostro.

I. Obbligo sarà pertanto di ogni Matricolato dell' Arte, che voglia tener Garzone di accordarlo giusto alle Leggi, e di notificarlo entro il termine di Mesi sei alla Banca dell' Arte colla relativa dichiarazione in iscritto, che dovrà esser registrata; con la condizione però che il Garzone non abbi minor età degli anni 12, nè maggiore delli 17.

Che tanto li Garzoni, che li Lavoranti, istrutti che saranno unicamente nelle loro respettive Professioni, qualora volessero conseguire la Matricolazione, si dichiara che non potranno essere ammessi alla medesima, se non quando faranno constare colla scorta dei soliti requisiti alla Banca dell' Arte di essere provetti, e capace nel loro Mestiere a tenor della Terminazione 1767, 29 Luglio.

II. A maggior dilucidazione poi dell' Articolo III. della Terminazione 1789, e coll' oggetto di animare la produzione delle Opere nuove, si dichiara che queste qualor oltrapassino li Fogli quattro di Stampa quantunque apprezziate meno delle Lire 2, avranno a godere il privilegio di Anni 20 li Manuscritti, e di Anni 10 le ristampe nuove Estere; sempre però colle prescrizioni espresse nell' Articolo VI. della suddetta Terminazione 1789.

E perchè la Libertà di stampare, e ristampare li Libri a Partito enunciati nella surriferita Terminazione all' Articolo III. venne concessa solamente alli Stampadori di Commissione, o Libraj di scarsa fortuna, così per togliere gli abusi, e le malizie, che ponno esser introdotte in offesa di questa provvidenza si aggiunge l' obbligo preciso al Priore dell' Arte pro tempore di rassegnare a cognizione del Magistrato ogni Semestre la nota di que' Libri del prezzo delle Lire 2 in giù, che non fossero stati accolti e riprodotti alla stampa entro il suddetto termine di sei Mesi dalli Stampatori e Libraj anzidetti, onde si possa in questo solo caso, concedere al Librajo Proprietario de medesimi di poterle ristampare, restando però anco liberi essi Libri a qualunque altro Librajo di scarsa fortuna, o Stampatore di Commissione che li ricercasse per farne l' Edizione.

III. E quanto a tutte le altre Opere di Stampa, e Ristampa, che dovranno essere apprezziate dalla Banca dell' Arte, a tenor del summentovato Articolo III., si prescrive che qualunque Librajo, o stampatore, presentar debba alla medesima il Libro impresso prima di darlo alla luce, affinchè essa, riconoscendo il numero delle Copie stampate, le spese ordinarie ed estraordinarie, che avesse esso incontrate anche fuor dell' Edizione, da essere fedelmente espresse in una nota, possi con equità farne il prezzo; al che contravvenendo l' Imprenditore, avrà il Priore a rassegnare la notizia al Magistrato per gli opportuni ripari.

IV. Abbisognando egualmente di essere rischiarato l' Articolo IV. della suddetta Terminazione relativo alle Opere, che si stampano a Partito per le viste in esso contemplate, viene pure ingionto l' obbligo alla Banca dell' Arte, nell' incontro di rilasciare il Foglio a stampa per la formazione del Partito, di riconoscere effettivamente se il Ricorrente sia Stampatore di Commissione, o Librajo di scarsa fortuna, per concedergli elo, qualora però si verifichi che abbia Bottega aperta, o Negozio in Casa; escludendo tutti gli altri Matricolati non compressi in dette due Categorie, a' quali vietate sono le ristampe a Partito.

Sarà però debito dell' Imprenditore, ottenute che abbia le solite Licenze per la ristampa del Libro a Partito, di presentare alla Banca il primo Foglio stampato prima di proseguirne il Lavoro, dando alla medesima il conto preciso delle Spese, e numero delle Copie, affinchè la stessa possa fissarne il relativo apprezziamento.

Che eseguito il Partito colle sottoscrizioni di ciaschedun Librajo, o Stampatore, che volesse farne acquisto, come pure di quelli che non lo volessero, inerentemente alla Terminazione 1788, 27 Maggio, dovrà l' Imprenditore consegnare al Priore il Foglio suddetto per essere conservato, e per rassegnarne un' esemplare al Segretario del Magistrato, onde riconoscere se adempito venghi il preciso Comando.

Vigile però esser dovrà la Banca stessa, affinchè non si facciano contemporaneamente moltiplici Ristampe di un' Opera medesima a Partito, al qual oggetto si stabilisce, che l' anzidetta Banca, concisa come esser ne deve dell' esito, e del bisogno Nazionale, decider abbia co' suoi Voti se convenga o nò aderire alla ricerca d' altra ristampa, oppure differirne l' assenso, rendendone il dovuto riscontro al Magistrato; intendendosi però esclusa da questa regola la prima Edizione di qualunque Opera uscita di Privilegio, la quale potrà sempre essere ristampata a Partito, e dichiarata al Priore, nel momento di ottenere l' attestato, con tale condizione dalli Stampatori di Commissione, e Libraj di scarsa fortuna.

V. Necessaria rendendosi per il miglioramento delle Stampe la susistenza del Carico di Proto esaminadore, a cui incombe la conoscenza di tutti li Campioni di ogni Edizione in conformità del prescritto nell' Articolo XII. della stessa Terminazione 1789, si stabilisce, che tolta la perpetuità della Persona nel medesimo impiego, il Generale Capitolo dell' Arte, osservando li consueti metodi di buon' ordine, e disciplina, debba devenire a nuova elezione di altro Individuo, scegliendo il più abile, probo ed imparziale della Classe però dei Stampatori, il quale eletto potrà pure coprire altro Carico, a cui fosse destinato, e presiedere alla Banca colla voce attiva e passiva come gli altri Individui, che la compongono; e così di Anno in Anno dovrà essere eseguito dal Capitolo colle solite ballotazioni, ed al caso non rimanesse alcuno delli nuovi nominati, potrà essere proposto alla riconferma l' antecedente che copriva l' impiego; intendendosi però sempre levato dalla Banca l' intervento del Scrivano, attesa la inutilità del medesimo.

VI. Volendosi poi che sussista la conformazione delle due Categorie de' Matricolati, già da molto tempo osservata, e per la quale hanno soltanto il libero intervento nelle occasioni tutte della convocazione del Generale Capitolo dell' Arte gl' Individui della prima Categoria, si riconferma questo stabilimento, che si vuole inalterabilmente eseguito.

VII. Provedutosi di tal modo ad ogni rapporto del Mecanico dell' Arte, non che a togliere le malizie, e gli abusi che potevano essere introdotti da taluni in offesa delle fissate provvidenze per il possibile risorgimento dell' Arte, siccome sarà debito preciso del Priore pro tempore di invigilare per l' esatto adempimento delle medesime, le quali dovranno essere costantamente eseguite da tutti gl' Individui dell' Università Tipografica come le più opportune ed adattate per la dovuta osservanza della Terminazione 1789 anzidetta, così si farà un particolar impegno del Sopraintendente alle Stampe in conformità degli obblighi ingionti al suo impiego colla Terminazione suaccennata, e coll' altra 1749, 29 Maggio, di riconoscere frequentamente se li Lavori delle respettive Stamperie corrispondano per intiero al confronto dei Campioni; al qual oggetto, dovendo esso munirsi di tutti li Titoli de' Libri che furono e saranno da Noi rilasciati co' Mandati alli Libraj e Stampatori, avrà a senso dell' anzidetta Terminazione 1749, ad extraerne dal Registro esistente nella Segretaria Nostra di tempo in tempo la Copia per li necessarj esami, ed osservazioni, che gli si richiedono da fare nelle Stamperie, onde ritrarre da queste quel frutto desiderabile di perfezione da Noi voluto nelle Edizioni.

E la presente, confirmata che sia dall' autorità dell' Eccellentissimo Senato, dovrà essere stampata e consegnata al Prior dell' Arte sopradetta per esser diffusa colle forme solite ad ogni Individuo della medesima per la sua immediata, ed inalterabile osservanza.

Data dal Magistrato Eccellentissimo suddetto li 30 Novembre 1789.

Piero Barbarigo Riformator.
Francesco Morosini 2° Cav. Proc. Riformator.
Girolamo Ascanio Giustinian Cav. Riformator.
Marcantonio Sanfermo Segr.

Addì 12 *Decembre* 1789.

Approvata con Decreto dell' Eccellentiss. Senato.

Venezia 23 *Marzo* 1799.

No. 81. La Università de' Stampatori, Libraj e Legatori di Libri era soggetta all' Epoca 1796 all' ex Magistrato de' Riformatori dello Studio di Padova in quanto apparteneva alle discipline della Stampa, censura e vendita de Libri ed a tutto ciò che vi aveva rapporto, ed alli ex Magistrati dei Proveditori di Comun, e della Milizia da Mar negli articoli concernenti la interna economia, e polizia, come anche il pagamento della Tanza. Non avendo però alcun posteriore Decreto diversificata l' essenza di queste Leggi egli è da ritenersi per conseguente risultato, che debba anche per il senso del Proclama 27 Settembre passato essere riservato alle ispezioni del Governo tutto ciò che si riferisce alla prima parte concernente le discipline della tipografia, censura e vendita di Libri, e che riguardo alla seconda debbano sopravegliarvi quei Dicasteri a quali resta col suddetto Proclama demandatta la cura sopra le Arti di questa Città. Di tanto rende il Governo intesa la Congregazione delegata a risoluzione del quesito propostogli colla Consulta 24 Ottobre decorso.

Pellegrini.

Gradenigo Seg°.

Venezia 13 *Novembre* 1805.

No. $\frac{18433}{1587}$.

No. 82. Accogliendo il R. Capitaniato il memoriale prodotto dal Priore dell' Università dei Libreri e Stampatori, poichè lo trova appoggiato a viste di Giustizia, delibera in quanto alla prima parte che sieno richiamate alla esatta loro osservanza le tre Terminazioni 19 Febbraro 1780, primo Maggio e 30 Novembre 1789, incaricando il Priore e Banca *pro tempore* di rendere avvertiti tutti gli Individui, non chè d' invigilare, perchè dai medesimi venghi prestata indiminutamente esecuzione alle Terminazioni stesse, mentre per quello riguarda la seconda ricerca se la parola *Chiunque* voglia significare di ristampare li Libri previa prima ricognizione dello smercio, e del nazionale bisogno; oppure se la parola *Chiunque* significhi la permissione della Ristampa in ogni momento, ed a quanti la ricercassero si rivolge il Capitaniato stesso all' Ecc. R. Governo perchè dalla sua maturità venghi data quella interpretazione che crederà alla parola stessa.

Per impedimento del R. Capitano.
Del Maino Vice-Capitano.

VINCENTI FOSCARINI, S.R.

Venezia 12 *Gennajo* 1806.

No. $\frac{823}{15}$.

No. 83. Ad intiera evasione del Ricorso prodotto a questo R. Capitaniato dal Priore dell' Università de Stampatori e Libraj li 2 Novembre decorso, lo si rende inteso per regola sua e dell' Università stessa nella Ristampa de' Libri, che l' Ecc. R. Governo accogliendo il Capitanale Parere con venerato suo Decreto 7 Gennajo corrente N° 26332, dichiarò che la facoltà accordata dalla Legge Primo Maggio 1789, a chiunque Librajo e Stampatore di ristampare i Libri a prezzo superiore a Lire Due, previe le debite Licenze, non deroga punto alla Legge qual proibisce la Simultanea Ristampa de' Libri, cosicchè in un istesso momento non potrà venire accordato il permesso per la Ristampa di un medesimo Libro, qualunque ne fosse il prezzo a quanti fossero per ricercarlo, e dovranno anche relativamente a' Libri di prezzo maggiore delle Lire due osservarsi le discipline e provvidenze prescritte dalle relative Leggi.

Per impedimento del R. Capitano.
Del Maino Vice-Capitano.

ALBERTI. Seg° R.

Venezia li 8 *Marzo* 1806.

No. 1229.

No. 84. Il Magistrato Civile della Provincia di Venezia al Priore e Banca dell' Università de Libraj e Stampatori.

Accogliendo il Magistrato le zelanti rappresentazioni dei Bancali della predetta Università, per cui viene di rilevare il malizioso ritrovato, onde deludere con scandalosa impudenza le più sacre Leggi, e ad infermare le salutari emanate discipline, prescrive, che ritenute nel suo vigore le une e le altre tanto per le Stampe che per le Ristampe di Libri, qualunque Stampatore che avesse Esemplari difettivi, e desiderasse completarli debba portarsi alla Banca per ricercare il permesso di stampare uno o più Fogli quiditando il tempo nel quale dovrà farne seguire l' impressione sotto la cominatoria di quelle pene pecuniarie che saranno credute opportune, oltre la perdita degli Esemplari al caso fosse rinvenuta una qualche trasgressione. Ed affinchè sia rilevata la contrafazione sarà premiato chi accuserà il Contrafattore con la metà della multa che sarà stata levata, rimanendo l' altra metà a beneficio della Cassa dell' Università il di cui Priore riceverà le Denunzie, tenendo però secreto il Denonziante, e dovrà tosto portarsi nella Stamperia che gli verrà indicata onde riconoscere la verità per quindi riferirne le risultanze al Magistrato perchè sieno assoggettati li Trasgressori alle multe che saranno cominate ed alla confisca dei Fogli abusivamente stampati. Della esecuzione della presente Deliberazione restano incaricati sotto la loro responsabiltà li Priore e Banca attuali, e pro tempore, dovendo essere legalmente notiziata a cadaun Matricolato.

Erizzo.

PIETRO VINCENTI FOSCARINI Seg^rio R.

Progetto delli Stampatori delle Stampe del Foro Civile alla Municipalità Provisoria di Venezia.

5 Termidore Anno Primo della Libertà Italiana.

Per il Cittadino Marcellino Piotto in Rio Terrà San Benedetto Al. N. 7.

No. 85. Libertà. Eguaglianza.

Li Stampatori Progettanti alla Municipalità Provisoria di Venezia.

Al momento dell' istallazione di questa Provisoria Municipalità godevano ancora li Fratelli Pinelli l' ereditato odiosissimo jus privativo di stampare tutte le pubbliche Carte, cioè tutte quelle marcate collo Stema di S. Marco.

L' importanza di rilevantissimi affari, che interessavano le più attente cure di questa Provisoria Municipalità, e l' importanza del pari d' una pronta, e sollecita stampa, e promulgazione delle provide sue deliberazioni, non permettevano al benefico fraterno zelo della stessa di occuparsi al riconoscimento del dannoso Privilegio per rimediarvi, ma dovelte continuare a dirigere le sue commissioni alla Stamperia Pinelli, supposta forse allora necessaria.

Se ne accorsero dal fatto quegl' illuminati individui Municipalisti, che coprivano il Comitato di Salute Pubblica, che non potendo supplire otto o dieci Torchi, che gemevano giorno e notte, alla pronta diffusione de' pubblici Editti, tanto erano affluenti; osservando altresì quant' era pernicioso il ritardo della promulgazione, e finalmente l' ingiustizia di continuare a somministrare ad un solo (ed a uno che per qualche Secolo innanzi ha già goduto il privativo dritto di questo genere di Stampe) con suo rapporto 8 Pratile (27 Maggio pass. V.S.) demandato al Comitato Municipale unitamente all' asserto Decreto per la sua approvazione contemplo ampiamente la necessità d' una Sollecita Stampa, non che l' ingiustizia del Privativo.

La diligenza delli Cittadini Stampatori Antonio Zatta e Giustin Pasquali, il quale non ha neppure Stamperia, fece sì che l' oneste lodevoli mire di questo Comitato, con un apparente oggetto di proposta utilità alla Cassa Nazionale, deviasse il Comitato medesimo dall' importanza del suo rapporto mentre in vece col sunnominato Decreto di scegliere dieci Stamperie, le quali hanno venti Torchi inoperosi atteso l' arenamento assoluto delle Stampe del Foro, e cento e più Operaj che languiscono dalla fame*

* Alcuni di questi Lavoratori sonnosi prodotti al Comitato di Salute Publica con una petitzione,

sciegliesse per questo lavoro col primo articolo del suo Decreto Zatta e Pasquali doviziosi Mercanti, occupati da infiniti intrichi di Edizioni e di Stampe per loro conto, perchè stabiliti questi in massima in unione al Pinelli, il Comitato Finanze far dovesse il suo rapporto sopra la progettata illusiva utilità da questi ingegnosissimi Mercanti proposta.

Chiamato il Comitato Finanze a formare il suo rapporto sopra le sole proposizioni delli sudetti già decretati Stampatori, consistenti nella più energica promessa di una pronta e sollecita diffusione delle pubbliche Carte, e nel ribasso del 20 per $\frac{0}{0}$ col ragguaglio de' prezzi dell' estinto Governo, non poteva il Comitato medesimo rigettare tali proposizioni, che conciliavano apparentamente li eminenti oggetti di *Sollecitudine*, e di *Economia* dal Municipale Decreto contemplati, ma doveva anzi appoggiarle, anco se fossero stati minori.

Per questo poi il Comitato Finanze fu sordo alle querule voci degl' infelici Stampatori delle Stampe del Foro, quali inscienti di tale impercettibile maneggio si produssero contemporaneamente con una petizione al Comitato medesimo, implorando susistenza col mezzo del lavoro delle Stampe de' pubblici Editti, esibindo le loro Stamperie, i loro Torchi e cento e più man d' opere ad un tale importantissimo serviggio.

Penetrata finalmente la ragione di questa secreta predilezione delle scelte Stamperie Pinelli, Zatta e Pasquali, si produssero li Cittadini Stampatori Marcellino Piotto, Pietro Sola, Isodoro Borghi, Francesco Andreola, Fratteli Casali, Nicoletto Fenzo, Andrea Milocco, Pietro Valvasense, Zuanne Bernardi e Andrea Martini al Comitato Municipale, come Organo della Municipalità, e Comitati porgendo un' utilissimo Progetto riguardante le pubbliche Stampe. Fu accolta la Petizione, e fu commesso il Rapporto al Comitato di Pubblica Istruzione. Prestatosi questo Comitato ad eseguire le commissioni, ricercò alli Stampatori Nazionali li conti e Note delle Stampe da medesimi fino all' ora eseguite, sull' appoggio delle quali formare un' identico quadro dell' utilità proposta dal piano de' Progettanti, ma in un mese e più non potè avere se non una sola capricciosa nota da detti Stampatori Pinelli, Zatta e Pasquali artifiziosamente composta.

Nel peculiar interessantissimo argomento, nel quale si tratta della Economia delle Finanze Nazionali, pur troppo da tanti secoli male amministrate, e della sussistenza di cento e più Famiglie di poveri onorati Cittadini, si produssero li progettanti Stampatori di nuovo al Comitato Municipale perchè venisse dal Comitato Finanze obbligati li Stampatori Pinelli, Zatta e Pasquali alla produzione delle Note e Conti delle Stampe, almeno per un mese dalli medesimi stampate. Fu decretata la Petizione per urgenza li 21 Mietitore (9 Luglio corr.) e fu commesso al Comitato Finanze e Zecca la formazione del suo rapporto nel termine di giorni dieci.

Contemporaneamente il Comitato d' Istruzione fece ricerca con sua Petizione al Comitato Finanze delli suddetti ricercati conti, nè questi sono ancora stati presentati.

La folla degl' affari, che vi occupano, con bastano credetemi, o Cittadini, di giustificare tanta lentezza in argomento così importante, ne la Nazione può indolente osservare cosi poco curato un affare, la remora del quale fa accrescere di giorno in giorno li aggravj alla sbilanciata pubblica sua economia.

Degnatevi, o Cittadini, di confrontare l' adottato Progetto Pinelli, Zatta e Pasquali, col nuovo esibitovi, e decidetevi.

colla quale imploravano che nella dispensa delle publiche Carte fossero anch' essi contemplati unitamenti ai Venditori per ritrarre un qualche miserabile modo di sussistenza.

Per conciliare li interessanti premurosi oggetti di *sollecito serviggio nelle Stampe, e di Economia pubblica* offrirono detti Stampatori le proposizioni seguenti.

I. Ogni Comitato in libertà di sciegliere una delle dette Stamperie, accompagnerà al manoscritto da Stamparsi l' apposita commissione della qualità, e quantità delle Stampe.

Vi prego a rimarcare che per questo primo Articolo non può, nè deve essere arbitrio ne' Stampatori, nè nella qualità nè nel numero delle Stampe.

II. Si dispensano del carico di un Corretore, ed adossano il peso della correzione delle Stampe ad un Ministro de' respettivi Comitati.

III. Creano un Archivista per ogni Comitato, e li adossano de' seguenti doveri.

I. Che debbano questi Archivisti ricevere le Stampe dalli Stampatori, e cautare li Medesimi con ricevuta.

II. Che debbano li medesimi dispensarle alla Municipalità, Comitati ed Ufficj adetti.

III. Far seguire la dispensa per le Contrade.

IV. Consegnarle alli Venditori per esser vendute per la Città.

Rimarcate già chiaramente, che anche questo Articolo tende ad aggravare il Ministro occupato in affari più importanti, ed a sollevare se medesimi.

Col quarto Articolo finalmente, dispensati da qualunque aggravio Ministeriale, propongono il ribasso del 20 per % calcolato col ragguaglio de' prezzi del passato Governo, obbligandosi di passare mensualmente le Polizze colle respettive Commissioni alli Comitati ed Ufficj che saranno destinati, onde sieno queste soddisfatte.

Ora, o Cittadini, che raccolto avete l' adottato Progetto, osservate la sua esecuzione dall' asserta Nota prodotta nello Spirato mese Mietitore al Comitato d' Istruzione, dietro le ricerche del Comitato medesimo dalli sudetti Stampatori.

Se per il primo Articolo del Progetto si obbligarono di stampare la sola quantità di copie, che fossero da' Comitati ordinate e se col terzo Articolo la dispensa di queste copie deve esser fatta da' respettivi Archivisti de' Comitati, come regge dunque la Partita di 3000 copie al giorno, ora ridotte a 480 che troverete nella Nota sunominata al Num. 5 nella Classe delle dispense ordinarie.

Trovarete nelle dette dispense ordinarie al Num. 4 della detta Nota una Partita di 250 copie per ogni Editto per affiggerle alle Vedute principali, ed alle Botteghe di Piazza. Trovarete altresì nelle dispense estraordinarie al Num. 6 simile Partita di Copie 500, per affiggerle alle Contrade, e diffonderle alle Botteghe.

Se ogni giorno per ogni Editto venissero affisse 750 Copie, che a soli tre Decreti al giorno importarebbero 2225 copie, li muri delle Strade sarebbero tutti coperti di Carta.

Osservate pure nella dispensa estraordinaria la Partita di Copie 1500 a Parrochi delle Contrade, la quale non fu mai, nè deve essere maggiore di 200.

Dopo queste picciole riflessioni lascio a Voi illuminati Cittadini di esaminare più attentamente la condotta delli Stampatori Pinelli, Zatta e Pasquali nella esecuzione del loro progetto col confronto delle Commissioni de' Comitati, e Ricevute degl' Archivisti, non ancora potute vedersi.

Analizzato così quasi astrattamente per mancanza de' Registri delle Commissioni fin' ora eseguite dalli Stampatori Pinelli, Zatta e Pasquali, non rimane però dubbio che il nuovo esibitovi Progetto da un mese e più non fosse di gran lunga migliore.

Vi proponeva questo il sollievo delle spese di tutte quelle Stampe pubbliche che vengono diffuse per la Città e Vendute a Cittadini, li quali dopo di averne rissentito il danno per la Stampa di queste colla Cassa Nazionale, devono soggiacere a un nuovo esborso per l' acquisto delle stesse; risservava alli decretati Stampatori quel solo prescritto numero occorente alla Municipalità, Comitati ed Officj adetti, che a norma della più volte accennatavi Nota erano in numero di circa 1200 colla Partita del N. B. ed il sollievo proposto è di copie 4500 c. per ogni Editto, li quali Editti essendo per lo meno tre al giorno viene a risparmiare la Cassa Nazionale di sola carta Risme trenta al giorno, che importano almeno £300 oltre £300 almeno per la Stampa, non computando le fatture di maggior rimarco, e li Libri dell' Organizzazione del Foro Civile, e Criminale, impegnandosi anche di farle vendere da' soliti Venditori.

Giacchè, benemeriti Cittadini, non risparmiate Studj e fatiche per felicitare questo Popolo, la di cui sovrana Autorità è da Voi rappresentata, raccoglietevi a versare sollecitamente sopra il nuovo Progetto che dieci onorati Patrioti Stampatori vi porge, il quale assolutamente concilia li da Voi grandiosi contemplati oggetti *di sollecita promulgazione, e di Pubblica Economia.*

Progetto.

Col terzo Capitolo del Decreto 8 Pratile (27 Maggio pross. pass.) del Comitato Municipale, ricercate ad oggetto di sollecitudine un giusto riparto d' affari tra le tre scelte Stamperie; e col Capitolo quinto bramate due Torchi in seno alla Casa della Municipalità, (cioè nel Palazzo Nazionale) quali due Torchi non sono ancora andati alla sua residenza, anzi questo Articolo lo veggo intieramente abbandonato dall' adottato Progetto Pinelli, Zatta e Pasquali Stampatori del Governo.

Niente di meglio poteva immaginare quel saggio Comitato di Salute Pubblica per la sollecita promulgazione delle Stampe, che bramare le Stamperie in seno alla Municipalità; sono più pronte le consegne, ed in conseguenza più pronta l' esecuzione, e l' emenda in caso di errori: sono più sicure le pubbliche Carte onde non vadino smarrite, e sempre eguale la distribuzione tra Stampatori anco se fossero cento.

Dietro perciò a' Vostri desiderj, e per il bene della Nazione ecco il primo Articolo del Progetto.

I. Dal giorno che avrete Decretato, ed assegnato un luogo nell' interno del Palazzo Nazionale capace ad errigere una Stamperia, si obbligano li Progettanti nel termine di giorni 20 di costruirvi una Stamperia con numero di Torchi e quantità di Caratteri quanti potranno occorrere alla più pronta esecuzione delle Vostre Commissioni, ed a quelle de' Comitati ed Uffici adetti.

II. Tutte quelle Stampe pubbliche, che serviranno ad uso della Municipalità, Comitati, ed Ufficj a norma delle commissioni de' medesimi saranno stampate a medesimi prezzi ch' ora le stampano li Stampatori presenti del Governo.

III. Tutte quelle Copie ch' ora vengono diffuse per la Città stampate a spese della Cassa Nazionale, saranno queste stampate a proprie spese de' Progettanti, e fatte vendere per loro conto ai soliti prezzi, e da' soliti Venditori, onde questa misera gente non restino sprovisti del solito lucro che ritraevano dalla Vendita delle stesse.*

IV. Dovrà però essere proibita a qualunque la ristampa in qualunque forma delle

* Le carte publiche che vengono vendute dai soliti Venditori venivano prima consegnate al cosidetto Capo di Piazza, il quale ritraeva da detti Venditori un prezzo per cadauno a norma del numero delle Copie che ai rispettivi Venditori veniva da lui accordato.

stampe che sortiranno dalla Stamperia centrale del Governo (eccettuato solo l' uso Giudiziario) altrimenti non resterebbe piu salva la proprietà ne' Progettanti, che sollevano la Cassa Nazionale di qualche migliaja di Ducati al mese, assumendosi l' obbligo di stamparle a proprie spese.

V. Dovrà la Municipalità da quindeci in quindeci giorni dare le opportune Commissioni alli Comitati cui spettano perchè sieno soddisfatte le Polizze, che verranno dalli Progettanti legalmente al Comitato Municipale ogni quindeci giorni prodotte.

VI. Accettato che sia il Presente Progetto, dovrà continuare fino a tanto continuera la Municipalità Provisoria.

Cittadini se bramate un sollecito servigio per la pronta promulgazione de' Vostri Decreti, Eccovelo procurato; se bramate di conciliare a questo la Economia delle Pubbliche Finanze, questa vi viene pure proposta senza il danno di alcuno.

Se togliete alli Decretati Stampatori la commissione della Stampa, non mancate per questo alla Vostra parola, mentre coi Vostri Decreti non avete decretato alcun tempo preciso. Se essi hanno servito per tre mesi, è ben giusto che quest' utile servigio venga prestato da altrattanti onorati Cittadini, li quali da mezzo secolo e più hanno li loro negozj piantati in questa Città.

Se inibite la ristampa de' pubblici Decreti, non togliete per questo la proprietà ad alcuno; nessuno può acquistare proprietà sopra le Stampe Pubbliche. Il diritto di stampare li pubblici Editti, li Decreti, li Statuti ed ogni altra pubblica Carta è diritto Sovrano, come quello del conio delle Monete, e perciò è della Nazione, o di chi legittimamente la rappresenta; se dunque la ristampa di questi fosse di danno alla Nazione, come lo è nel caso presente, il Nazional interesse, ch' è l' interesse di tutti, esclude assolutamente il parzial interesse di alcuni, e perciò avete un diritto legittimo d' inibirne la ristampa senza offendere, ripeto, le proprietà di alcuno.

Al bene della Nazione conciliate insieme il bene delle Famiglie de' Progettanti, e quello de' loro Operaj rimasti tutti senza modo di sussistenza atteso il fortunato Cambiamento di Governo.

Nell' attendere perciò li stessi di gustare li beni di questo fortunato Cambiamento, autorizzano quanto con il presente vi umiliano colle loro firme. Salute e Fratellanza.

Marcellino Piotto. Pietro Valvasense.
Iseppo e Fratelli Casali. Andrea Milocco.
Andrea Martini. Nicoletto Fenzo.
Pietro Sola. Francesco Andreola.
Isidoro Borghi. Zuanne Bernardi.

Libertà. Eguaglianza.

Il Comitato di Salute Pubblica.
Alla Municipalità Provisoria Veneziana.

No. 86. Ne' Governi in rivoluzione la rapidità delle misure, e l' energia de' mezzi ha spesso salvate le Nazioni dalle più orribili catastrofi.

La Stampa sollecita delle Carte Pubbliche, ed i mezzi pronti di diffonderle, e porle alla portata di tutti, sono oggetti si grandi e necessarj, che sovente senza di essi si potrebbe fare la disgrazia dello Stato piuttostochè il bene del Popolo.

Quindi è che il nostro Comitato di Salute Pubblica, avendo esperimentati i tristi effetti della tardanza nel diffondere le Carte, e volendo in seguito possibilmente evitarli; e considerando innoltre, che se l' oggetto della Stampa è utile agli Stampatori, importa che questo bene sia diviso in alcune Famiglie e non concentrato in una sola vi eccita all' adesione del seguente Decreto.

La Municipalità Provvisoria di Venezia.

Inteso il rapporto del Comitato di Salute Pubblica, considerando essere urgente per l' interesse del Popolo che le sue deliberazioni sieno subito Stampate, e diffuse

Decreta

I. Le Stamperie destinate Municipali sono tre; prima la Stamperia Pinelli: seconda la Stamperia Zatta: terza la Stamperia Pasquali.

II. Ciascun Comitato si sciegliera fra queste la propria.

III. Ogn' una di esse Stamperie abbia una quantità d' affari corrispondenti all' oggetto di sollecitudine, ed al reciproco interesse.

IV. Saranno responsabili li Stampatori della pronta diffusione de' Rapporti, Decreti, Ordini ed altro.

V. Risiederanno provisoriamente due Torchi in seno alla Casa della Municipalità per suo uso.

VI. Non potranno esser vendute le Carte pubbliche dai dispensatori al maggior prezzo di un soldo per grandi che sieno.

VII. Il Comitato di Salute Pubblica Veglierà sull' osservanza di tutte le discipline stabilite negl' Articoli suespressi.

Data li 27 Maggio 1797, V. S. Anno prima della Libertà Italiana.

Approvata in quanto alla massima, e quanto alle Stamperie demandato al Comitato Finanze per gl' oggetti Economici.

Progetto delli Stampatori Pinelli, Zatta e Pasquali.

Libertà. Eguaglianza.

Cittadini del Comitato alle Finanze e Zecca.

No. 87. Li Stampatori Pinelli, Zatta e Pasquali eletti dalla Municipalità, incontrando li due oggetti di sollecito *servigio nelle stampe* e di *Economia Pubblica* vi offrono il presente Piano.

Ciascuna stamperia servendo il rispettivo Comitato, a cui fosse prescielta, sarà da quello munita del Manoscritto da stamparsi con l' apposita commissione indicante la quantità e qualità delle Stampe.

Per togliere gl' equivoci sarebbe ottima cosa che il primo informe esemplare fosse corretto da uno delli respettivi Ministri della Municipalità o Comitati.

Riflettesi necessaria l' elezione di un Pubblico Archivista, che risieda presso la Municipalità con li seguenti doveri. Riceverà egli dagli Stampatori le Stampe eseguite relativamente alle Commissioni cautando i medesimi con ricevuto sotto le Commissioni stesse. Dispenserà le Stampe alla Municipalità, Comitati ed altri Ufficj adetti, farà seguire la diffusione per le Contrade, e consegna ai Baroni[1] soliti a non comprar quelle Stampe che vendono per la Città, essendo stato questo un contemplato provedimento a tal classe di misera gente. Potrà coll' avanzo delle Stampe servire immediatamente alle ricerche della Municipalità, Comitati ed Ufficj di tutte le Carte in addietro stampate, che formerano centro, e raccolta dell' Archivio suddetto.

Per poi secondare l' eccitamenti del Comitato nell' Articolo della Pubblica Economia, li Stampatori suddetti con promessa dell' ottimo servigio con la condizione, e di andar esenti di qualunque aggravio, e spesa Ministeriale offrono un ribasso del venti per cento in confronto de' prezzi attuali, che con tal base dovranno essere regolati; le Polizze veranno mensualmente esibite al Comitato, ed ufficio destinato all' incontro col fondamento delle respettive Commissioni rilasciate, e delle coerenti Ricevute dell' Archivista per essere dalla Tesoraria Nazionale di Mese in Mese pagate. Salute e rispetto.

Libertà. Eguaglianza.

1797. 27 *Maggio.*

Alla Municipalità Provisoria di Venezia il Comitato di Finanze e Zecca.

No. 88. Cittadini. Dietro le deliberazioni della Municipalità Provisoria 22 cadente, che rimette al Comitato Finanze l' esecuzione di quanto spetta all' Economia della fissata massima, che ne' Stampatori Pinelli, Zatta e Pasquali debbano esser divise le disposizione, e li profitti per le Stampe Nazionali, che occorrono alla giornata di render pubbliche alla cognizione dei Cittadini per ordine della Municipalità stessa, e dei respettivi suoi Comitati con oggetto anche di rendere più sollecita e pronta l' esecuzione, si è fatto sollecito il Comitato suddetto di raccoglier lumi da detti Cittadini Stampatori, e di eccitarli a proponere un piano d' accordo che conciliasse in un tempo stesso la sollecitudine del servigio, con li riguardi del dovuto possibile risparmio. Deve però il Comitato in conseguenza delle prestate attenzioni, prestar, o Cittadini, a vostri riflessi inserto nella presente Piano che ci hanno li tre suddetti Stampatori prodotto, col quale offrono d' assumere l' impresa della Stampa delle Carte Nazionali alle condizioni e metodi nel Piano dichiariti, e col ribasso per la sola misurata quantità delle Stampe occorrenti alla Municipalità, Comitati ed altri Ufficj adetti, del 20 per % in confronto de prezzi del passato Governo. Vantaggiosa per tanto e per l' esattezza, e sollecitudine del Servigio, e per gl' economici riguardi, riputando il Comitato la proferta de prescielti Stampatori, egli l' assoggetta a vostri riflessi ed approvazione se la trovate conforme a' sudichiariti riguardi, al qual fine vi offre la formula del seguente Decreto.

La Municipalità Provvisoria di Venezia.

Inteso il Rapporto del Comitato Finanze sul Piano presentatogli dalli tre prescielti Stampatori Pinelli, Zatta, e Pasquali, che si riconosce conciliante i riguardi di rispormio con quelli di sollecitudine e di esattezza di servigio, quello approva in tutte le parti, e sarà cura del Comitato stesso di procurare l' immediata sua verificazione.

[1] Baroni, *i.e.* gamins.

DOCUMENTS.

V.

V.

REPORT OF THE RIFFORMATORI DELLO STUDIO DI PADOVA ON THE VENETIAN PRESS. 1765.

"CONSULTA" OF TRIFFONE URACHIEN AND FRA ENRICO DE' SERVI ON THE REPORT OF THE RIFFORMATORI.

OBSERVATIONS OF P(IETRO) F(RANCESCHI) ON THE OBJECTIONS RAISED AT ROME TO THE APPOINTMENT OF AN ECCLESIASTICAL REVISOR OF THE PRESS.

REPORT ON THE "INSTITUTIONES THEOLOGICÆ" OF THE ARCHBISHOP OF LYONS. 1794.

REPORT ON THE "GIORNALE ECCLESIASTICO DI ROMA." 1794.

1765. 3 *Agosto.* *In Pregadi.*

RILEVA con rincrescimento il Senato dall' esatte, e benemerite Scritture[1] del Magistrato de' Riformatori dello Studio di Padova, e de' Consultori in Jure la decadenza dell' Arte Tipografica in questa Dominante, ove prosperamente fiorì ne' passati tempi, ed ove per le oportunità preferibili ad ogni altro luogo nei prezzi, e nella perizia e nella prontezza di stampare dovrebbe giornalmente aumentarsi. Rilevata pure la causa di questo deperimento procedente dalla mancanza de' Capi nuovi stampabili, vuole il Senato per i gravi rispetti del Principato provvedervi co' modi valevoli a farla risorgere. E perchè nel cercarsi la moltiplicazione delle Stampe può non esser bastante a supplirvi la sola Opera del P. Inquisitore destinato già ne' passati tempi da questo Consiglio alla Revisione in punto di Religione; s' incarica perciò il Magistrato Sudetto a rintracciare, esclusi i Regolari, Ecclesiastico dotto, probo, e fedele Suddito Nostro, per una simile Revisione nell' oggetto stesso, di modo che

[1] See next page.

qualunque libro ottenga la Fede di licenziamento, o da l' uno, o dall' altro de' Revisori possa passare col metodo, che corre in presente, e che si conferma, a quella de' Revisori già destinati per le cose de' Principi, e buoni costumi, per ottener poi il Mandato de' Refformatori per eseguirne con la data di Venezia, e con le solite forme la Stampa; sistema questo, col quale sarà tolto l' abuso introdotto di finta data, per cui prescindevasi dalla Revisione, ed uniforme alle provvide disposizioni del Decreto 1603, 11 Maggio, che in ora confermasi. Questo stabilimento pertanto dovrà esser fatto noto dal Magistrato a' Stampatori, e Librai per direzione loro nel prodursi alla Revisione.

Alla maturità del Senato convenendo pure dar pensiere a que' disordini, che per la lunghezza del tempo introdotti si fossero alteranti le solenni convenzioni nel proposito de' Libri proibiti, si commette al Magistrato de' Reformatori dello Studio di Padova di repubblicare a commune notizia, ed inparticolare a quella de' Stampatori, e Librai, l' Indice 1595 con le Aggiunte accettate da questo Consiglio unitamente al Concordato 1596; e sia pure incaricato di far esaminare, e raccogliere la nota di tutti quei Libri, che non compresi nell' Indice Sudetto meritassero per rispetti di Religione, e di Stato d' esser proibiti, spiegando a questo Consiglio il sentimento loro, et il modo, con cui si dovesse procedere per assicurare li stessi importanti oggetti.

Resa in tal modo più facile, e più sicura l' esecuzione della Stampa, ne succederà in conseguenza, che que' Libri riconosciuti per admissibili, i quali in adesso ci provengono da Paesi Forastieri, potranno essere ristampati facendo venire i soli esemplari con escludersi quelle copie, che in ora con l' asporto del soldo proprio c' inondano, e convertendo in attivo quel passivo commercio, che presentemente si soffre.

Acciò poi assicurati rimangano gli oggetti avuti sempre a cuore da questo Consiglio si rinnovano con la presente Deliberazione le ottime Leggi che custodiscono il Traffico nostro dall' ingresso in Venezia di que' libri che contengono cose contrarie alla Religione, ai Principi, et ai buoni costumi, con la pratica commessa nel Decreto 1653, e ravvivata dal Magistrato con Terminazione a stampa 23 Settembre dell' anno scorso.

Accudirà il Magistrato de' Riformatori, che il tutto esattamente si adempia, dandosi merito con la vigilante sua attenzione di disporre dietro ai stabiliti principj tutto quel più, che contribuir possa alla prosperità di un' Arte costituente uno de' più fruttuosi rami di Commercio, ed assai avvantaggiosa all' impiego del Popolo.

Serenissimo Principe.

L' Arte della Stampa dalla Germania passata in Venezia verso il 1461, venne dall' Ecc^{mo} Senato giudicata, al suo primo apparire, una delle industrie più opportune all' impiego del popolo, e al commerzio, e perciò accolta, e animata con singolari benefizj, e favori.

La speranza de' Maggiori di VV. EE. non riuscì vana. Impiegaronsi Scrittori, Traduttori, Copisti, Gittatori di Caratteri, Compositori alle Casse, Torchiaj, Legatori, e Venditori di Libri; e col tempo Professori di Dissegno, Intagliatori in Legno, e in Rame, Torchiaj da Rami, e Miniatori; sicchè gran numero di famiglie trasse la propria sussistenza da quest' Arte. Il Traffico de' Libri s' allargò presto anch' esso fra le Nazioni. Non se ne confinò l' uso fra i Dotti soli. Le scienze diffuse destarono una curiosità universale. I libri divenuti un mezzo facile per far conoscere le invenzioni, l' arte, le idee, i tratti d' ingegno, e i costumi d' una Nazione ad un' altra, invogliarono di se quasi ogni condizione di gente in ogni luogo.

Ma se il tempo ne' secoli trascorsi verificò le conghietture dell' Ecc^mo Senato, sicchè molto fu l' impiego del popolo nella Tipografica, e fiorito il traffico de' Libri; al presente siamo costretti con nostro sommo rammarico a confessare alla Serenità Vostra, che quest' Arte in Venezia è quasi annichilata; e che la sua rovina è quell' unica sorgente, da cui l' altre Città d' Italia traggono un continuo aumento di Torchi, e per conseguenza del Commerzio loro di Libri.

Finchè quest' Arte lavora vigorosamente in questa Città, l' altre dell' Italia non possono tentare d' ingrandire le stamperie proprie. Tanta è l' abbondanza della Carta fra noi, cosi agevoli sono le navigazioni, e sì moderati i Dazii per introdurla in Venezia, e tale è la perizia, e prestezza de' nostri Artisti, che le Venete Edizioni vincono nel buon mercato tutte quelle degli altri Paesi. I Librai forestieri non hanno ardimento di starci a fronte, abbandonano il pensiero de' Torchi, e trovando maggior utile nel rivendere i Libri nostri, che gli stampati fra loro, danno le commissioni a Venezia d' ogni loro occorrenza.

Oggidì, che l' Arte in questa Città è giunta ad un' estrema declinazione, siamo ridotti a segno, che Livorno, Lucca, Parma, Modena, e Bologna stampando assai, sono fatte ritrose al cambio de' proprii Libri co' Veneti. Mandarano prima danari per ottenerne, ora pretendono contanti da' Librai di Venezia per mandarci le loro edizioni. In tal forma la nostra Città stessa aumenta i Torchi loro co' suoi contanti, e di padrona del Commerzio di Libri è divenuta rivenditrice.

Napoli, che spargeva l' edizioni Venete in tutto il Regno, ora lo sazia con quelle ch' escono de' suoi Torchi. Ristampa i nostri Capi migliori, e proibisce per conseguenza l' ingresso alla maggior parte de' nostri. Trieste pochi anni fà ha piantata Stamperia, Lugano, e Losanna Stampano assai; ogni luogo ci minaccia. Il minoramento cotidiano de' Torchi in Venezia ci avvertisce dell' aumento d' essi in altri luoghi.

Venezia nel 1752 ne avea 77, nel 1762, 58; oggi 50, e di questi molti incerti d' aver lavoro fra pochi giorni. Compositori, e Torchiaj domandano impiego, e nol trovano. I matricolati, i quali la legge concede tanto di poter essere Stampatori quanto Librai, non trovando più di che alimentare i Torchi passano quasi tutti a fare i venditori di Libri. Questa turba, ch' apre botteghe ogni dì con Libri incagliati, disusati, e morti al traffico, inquieta i negozii migliori: interrompe il loro privilegii: Sollecita i forestieri a ristampare i Capi di Venezia; ottiene privilegii di Libri, che non stampa; vende talvolta gli stessi privilegii a' Librai di Terra ferma, contro le leggi: minaccia di volere far ristampare per atterrire i Negozii buoni; e in fine le basta di venire ad un aggiustamento per cavarne qualche summa di contanti. All' incontro i Negozj migliori con aggiunte inutili, note, prefazioni, frontespizii alterati, prolunganși i privilegii di Libri fatti comuni, e tengono oppressi i confratelli dell' Arte. Questa divisa in due fazioni di sei o otto da un lato, e tutti dall' altro, fà istanze cosi diverse, che si veggono uscire da due volontà nemicissime. Ognuno de' partiti dipinge con lamenti per ben universale della Tipografica Veneta, e del Commerzio quello, ch' è puro interesse privato; chiede, o ricorda un rimedio giovevole a se, non a tutti. Tale è il vero sconcerto della Tipografica Veneta al giorno d' oggi, sperimentata pel corso di qualche secolo assai vantaggiosa all' impiego del popolo, e per uno de' più fruttosi rami di commerzio.

Obbligati noi da quell' Offizio, di cui fummo onorati, a vegliare sugl' interessi d' un' arte così benefica, e presi da sincera compassione, che un' industria di tanta utilità abbia portati quasi tutti i suoi vantaggi fino alle men colte Nazioni, lasciando qui solo un' amara memoria dei beni posseduti per essa un tempo, ci siamo applicati lungamente a farne un attento, e maturo esame del suo Stato, e delle Leggi, che la reggono, per comprendere la vera sorgente del suo sconcerto, e stabilirne i ripari più efficaci, e più pronti. Una diligente osservazione di tutte le cause, che produssero tanto i suoi passati, quanto il presente sconcerto, ci guidò finalmente a scoprire, che la principale origine della sua decadenza fu la mancanza de' Capi nuovi e buoni da stampare, i quali oggidì più che mai essendole mancati sono la percossa più grave, da cui viene atterrata: nè senza il provvedimento di questi, si può usare altro rimedio giovevole a ricuperarla in parte, non che a ridurla in vigore da abbattere le stamperie forestiere; dalle quali verrà certamente nel corso di pochi anni affatto distrutta.

Perchè l' EE. VV. conoscano ad evidenza, che mai quest' Arte non andò in decadenza, se non per la difficoltà d' ottenere capi nuovi, e buoni da stampare, rappresenteremo con brevità le due principali epoche del suo decadimento.

La Prima del 1517.
La Seconda del 1595.

Quest' Arte fino al 1517 non avea leggi. Riconosceva solamente dall' Ecc^{mo} Senato licenze, e privilegii per la pubblicazione de' Libri. Li capi stampabili non le mancavano, in un tempo, in cui si traevano da' soli manoscritti antichi non ancora pubblicati co' Torchi. Aldo il Vecchio, che fu il primo a stampare i Codici Greci, e a fare altre scoperte, aperse alle stamperie nuovi fonti d' abbondanza di capi. N' ebbe perciò singolari privilegii. Ma l' esempio suo imitato da molti gli fece degni d' essere privilegiati anch' essi. Intanto i manoscritti mancarono, quasi tutti i Capi si trovarono obbligati ad alcuni pochi Librai; il comune degl' impiegati in tale industria rimase senza capi da alimentare i Torchi. Subito nacquero gli sconcerti segnati nel Decreto 1 Agosto 1517; prima Legge dopo 56 anni dall' introduzione della Tipografica in Venezia, fino a quel tempo feconda, e felice. Con tal Decreto furono sciolti i Capi stampabili dalle mani di pochi, e restituiti al comune; e solo lasciati i privilegii all' opere nuove, e non più stampate, per animare i Librai all' introduzione d' altri Capi.

Alla sapienza del Decreto si congiunse la fortuna de' tempi. Fiorirono per tutto il Secolo del 1500 gl' ingegni Italiani sopra gli altri. Venezia era piena d' uomini dotti, di fautori di lettere, di Letterati ad essa concorsi. I Torchi Veneti prosperarono tanto, che le nostre edizioni presero voga per tutti i paesi col traffico in grande abbondanza fino al 1595. Poche ordinazioni dell' Ecc^{mo} Senato bastarono dal 1517 fino al 1595 per mantener l' Arte in fiore. Non sarebbe decaduta, se non le fosse avvenuto caso tale, che la privò affatto della maggior parte de' Capi stampabili, che già possedeva, e le troncò quasi tutte le vie d' acquistarne di nuovi. Questa fu l' Epoca Seconda del suo decadimento.

Nel 1595 uscì un Indice di Libri proibiti dalla Corte di Roma. Fu così grande questa percossa sopra i materiali, che qui si stampano, che in pochi mesi, non sapendosi più che dare per alimento alle Stamperie, i Torchi nostri, ch' erano 125 si ridussero a 40 Stampatori e Librai atterriti rappresentarono la loro repentina desolazione alla paterna clemenza dell' Ecc^{mo} Senato, il quale mosso a pietà della nuova miseria d' un' Arte tanto giovevole all' impiego del popolo, e al commerzio, e pochi mesi prima tanto florida, che teneva in soggezione le stamperie degli altri paesi lontani, e vicini, adoperò i più risoluti maneggi con la Corte di Roma, per sollevarla dalla sua calamità improvvisa. Nè mai accettò con suo consenso l' Indice nel proprio Dominio, se non dopo lunghi trattati, e con un Concordato in più articoli diviso, il cui settimo articolo importa, che non senza difficoltà, e rare volte, e senza partecipazione al Principe, non possano essere vietati Libri nel suo Dominio, fuorchè i contenuti nell' Indice 1595. Fu ciò accordato nel 1596. Niente di manco l' Arte rimase priva di tutti que' Libri, ch' erano segnati nell' Indice ; o se alcuni ne adoperò, gli ebbe così atterati, e mutilati, che ben presto negli altri Paesi s' estinse il credito delle nostre edizioni, nè mai più si riebbe.

Non passarono cinque anni, che l' Arte non potendo più sostenersi, si sconcertò, e diede que' medesimi segni di mancanza de' Capi, che avea dati nel 1517 cominciando i matricolati a partirsi da Venezia, e a sviarsi gli Artisti verso altri luoghi. L' Ecc^{mo} Senato fece il Decreto 20 Febbraro 1602 per arrestargli, promettendo nuovi provvedimenti. Nel 1603, 11 Maggio, gli effettuò, e tali gli fece, che mostrano principalmente la mira di riparare alla mancanza de' capi, riconosciuta per origine della rovina dell' Arte. Perchè dove in tutti i Decreti anteriori privilegiava le sole opere nuove, e non più stampate, in questo allarga il benefizio alle stampate qui altre volte, e principalmente alle ristampe de' Libri forestieri. Un provvedimento così pieno di sapienza per allettare i matricolati all' introduzione di capi nuovi, era quel solo, che potea bastare a ristorar l' Arte in Venezia, se un illegittimo, e occulto ostacolo, quale appresso diremo, non si fosse sempre opposto agli ottimi effetti, che avrebbe certamente prodotti.

In tutto quel secolo le Nazioni forestiere pubblicarono opere famose. Le ristampe di quelle avrebbero mantenuta in Venezia quell' abbondanza, ch' era stata somministrata a' nostri Torchi dal 1517 fino al 1595 dagl' Ingegni Italiani, fra quali, come s' è detto, fiorirono le dottrine in tutte il secolo Decimosesto. I Libri forestieri avrebbero non solo con l' aumento de' Torchi impiegato maggior numero di persone, ma reso sempre più vivo, e affaccendato il Commerzio. Pel moderato costo delle stampe Venete sarebbero entrati nel traffico più facilmente vendibili di tutte l' edizioni degli stessi libri fatte nè paesi d' Oltremante, e nell' altre Città d' Italia. Avrebbero col buon mercato impedito il corso all' edizioni forestiere, e mortificate in gran parte le stamperie degli altri luoghi. In somma l' Ecc^{mo} Senato non potea meglio riparare a' danni di quel tempo, nè aprir la strada a' maggiori vantaggi per l' avvenire.

Ma un tarlo celato, come accennato abbiamo, s' oppose allora, e sempre all' esecuzione di tal provvidenza ; la quale salvò bensì la Tipograficâ Veneta dall' interna rovina, ma non potè mai farle tutto quel benefizio, a cui mirava la pubblica paterna volontà. Rimase anche dopo il 1603 la stessa penuria di Capi. Ne dà indizio il poco impiego del popolo accennato nella Terminazione 22 Luglio 1616. Lo di mostrano i Libri stampati a spesa di Librai Veneti in Paesi forestieri, ed altre trasgressioni segnate nel Decreto 1653, e finalmente la diminuzione de' Torchi annotata nella Terminazione 1671. Nè mai da quel Secolo fino a' presenti giorni, per quante Leggi uscirono, e per quante diligenza furono usate dal Magistrato nostro per farle osservare, si potè più far risorgere al suo primo stato quest' Arte, e liberarla da' continui sconcerti. Questi sono di tal sorte oggidì, che l' hanno quasi atterrata, ma sono nello stesso tempo tante manifeste prove, che la sua distruzione deriva appunto dalla mancanza de' Capi stampabili.

La Prima prova è la trasgressione d' alcuni pochi Libraj più potenti, i quali cercano con molti artifizii di prorogarsi i privilegii anche dopo il tempo limitato da' Decreti. Se ci fosse facilità d' aver capi nuovi, e buoni non cozzerebbero così spesso con le Leggi, nè vorrebbero ogni giorno litigi co' Matricolati.

La Seconda prova è il tentativo de' Libraj minori di trafugare qualche privilegio a' più potenti prima, che ne sia spirato il termine. Andrebbero più cauti nell' offendere le Leggi, e i più potenti, de' quali hanno bisogno, se potessero facilmente aver buoni Capi nuovi da stampare.

Non sono trasgressione, ma cosa legittima le ristampe de' Libri usciti di privilegio; pure sono la terza prova della mancanza de' Capi, e con essa va congiunto il continuo pensiero de' più potenti d' opporsi contro le Leggi a tali ristampe. Sarebbe impossibile, che tanto chi vuol ristampare quanto chi s' oppone, mettesse tutta la sua speranza in Libri che da tempi immemorabili in quà non sono altro, che moltiplicazioni d' una massa di Medici, Legali, e Teologi, stampati, ristampati, venduti, rivenduti, e quasi scordati in un traffico largo, se non ci mancassero capi nuovi, che meritano privilegio, destano la curiosità nè lettori, e apportano utile maggiore.

Quarta prova è l' improvviso aprimento di botteghe, che succede spesso. I matricolati, che come è detto, sono tanto Stampatori, che Librai, vedendo vuoti i Torchi, intraprendono di signoreggiare sotto un' insegna prima fallita, ch' esposta. Chi vuole aprir bottega chiede a credenza a molti Libraj una porzione di quegl' infiniti Libri incagliati che inondano Venezia. Gli trova, ne guernisce la bottega, è debitore a tutti. Fitti, vestire, bisogno di cotidiano vitto l' assediano tutto il dì. Vende in fretta, e con preghiere, per 20 quello che val 100. Chiude la bottega fallito: l' Arte perde il concetto. Se i Matricolati avessero qualche buon capo nuovo, o non si partirebbero da Torchi, che avendo lavoro danno un pane sicuro, e senza pensieri; o anche partendosi potrebbero pagare col cambio d' un capo o due nuovi, i Creditori, e starsi in bottega con onore.

Quinta prova è la negativa del cambio di Libri fra Libraj della Città, primo movente di questo commerzio. Con la forza sola d' un' interna commutazione di carta stampata ogni Librajo di Venezia può provvedersi de' Libri degli altri, e tutti gli altri possono avere de' suoi. Ognuno in tal guisa forma quell' assortimento, che conviene alle commissioni, che suol avere di fuori. E quel, che in Venezia era solo Carta stampata, e commutata fra Libraj, spedito fuori le apporta contanti. Al presente i Negozii più potenti, possessori di quasi tutti i Capi, negano il cambio a' minori; e allegano per ragione, che non ritrovando da loro capi buoni a barratto, non gli vogliono impinguare co' proprii buoni, per averne de' tristi o nulla. Sicchè pretendono da' confratelli danari al banco col ribasso del 20 per 100, e non più. I minori obbligati a sborsar contanti tralasciano d' ubbidire alle commissioni di fuori, perchè fra i ribassi pretesi da' forestieri, Dazii, portature, e altro vi perdono. I Libri, che qui commutati hanno spaccio presto, ritenuti da pochi vanno lenti, e per poche vie; e quel, ch' è peggio, i forestieri non soddisfatti in quello, che domandano, ristampano que' pochi nostri Capi migliori, che ci restano, danno più grave di tutti. Se ogni Librajo, anche de' più infimi, avesse qualche Capo nuovo, e buono, i Negozii più potenti non solo gli consentirebbero il cambio, ma lo pregherebbero a volerlo fare.

Sesta prova non solamente della mancanza de' Capi buoni, ma d' un' inondazione de' disutili, è il ribasso di 30, 40, e fino 6 per 100 preteso da' forestieri ne' contratti de' nostri Libri. I Capi buoni, nuovi, non ristampati da molti, e da molte Città si sostengono con decoro, e vantaggio. Quelli, che si trovano moltiplicati, e in ogni luogo, deggiono soggiacere a qualsivoglia pretenzione di ribasso. Oggidi la gara principale fra nostri Librai è quella di chi sà dare i Libri quasi per nulla, nè possono far meglio, perchè non hanno più capi buoni e apprezzati.

Settima prova sono le querele, che fa l' una fazione, e l' altra de' Libraj, l' una per opporsi alle ristampe de' Libri comuni, l' altra per ristamparli. Dice la prima: Perchè si tenta con pertinacia di ristampare i nostri Libri? Non ha forse il Decreto 1603, premiata l' industria, privilegiando i Capi nuovi? Perchè questa non si risveglia? Perchè si vuol vivere a danno de' nostri assortimenti? Dice la Seconda: Perchè vogliono ritenersi Libri renduti comuni dalle Leggi? Trovino Capi nuovi privilegiati dal Decreto 1603. Intanto nè l' una fazione, nè l' altra ne stampa. Ognuna crede, che derivi da ostinazione, e tirannide del partito avversario quello, ch' è impossibilità d' eseguire il Decreto 1603, citato per benefico dall' un partito, e dall' altro.

Crediamo d' avere esposto a sufficienza alla Serenità vostra la miseria dell' Arte Tipografica Veneta, e gli sconcerti del commerzio Librario, nel tempo stesso, che siamo andati numerando le prove della mancanza de' Capi, dalla quale nascono tutti i danni presenti di questa Arte.

E vero, che i passati Decreti s' oppongono ad una parte de' suoi disordini; ma la pratica dopo il 1603 fino a' giorni nostri ha dimostrato tanto agli Antecessori nostri quanto a noi, che senza l' acquisto di nuovi capi è nociva tanto l' esecuzione, quanto l' inesecuzione dell' altre Leggi, se non è posto nell' intera sua attività il Decreto di quell' anno nell' articolo, in cui privilegia le ristampe de' Libri forestieri. Senza un tale soccorso, tolerando le proroghe de' privilegii contro al sentimento delle Leggi a' Negozii meglio assortiti, questi in pochi anni s' impadroniscono di quella massa limitata di Libri, che si stampano, e ristampano sempre. Il comune dell' Arte non ha più impiego, il commerzio si chiude fra pochi.

Se vengono levate le proroghe, secondo le leggi, e renduti i Libri comuni a chi gli vuole, la stessa massa in breve giro d' anni và alle mani di tutti. I negozii ben fondati, e che soli ancora fanno qualche commerzio largo, e lontano, perdono gli assortimenti. L' abuso degli aprimenti di botteghe non si può frenare senza impiegare i matricolati nelle stamperie con nuovi capi. I cambii interni, anima di questo commerzio, non si possono comandare. I soli capi buoni, e nuovi compartiti fra tutti farebbero nascere la necessità de' cambii, destando negli animi una spontanea disposizione a fargli. Fino le ottime provvidenze dell' Ecc^{mo} Senato sopra la buona qualità delle Stampe, se non acquistiamo capi nuovi, sono di pericolosa esecuzione. Finchè non si fà altro che ristampe sopra ristampe di libri invecchiati, che non destano più la curiosità, venduti, rivenduti, sparsi in ogni paese, lo stampar bene è disutile. Il solo buon mercato che nasce dal peggioramento ravviva qualche poco nel traffico questo rancidume di libri, e contrasta con le ristampe, che n' hanno fatte gli esteri peggiorate anch' essi. Sono però così pieni di sapienza gli emanati Decreti, che se ne può avere un intero profitto mettendogli in esecuzione, quando ugualmente ad essi sia reso operativo il sopraccitato Articolo del Decreto 11 Maggio 1603, intorno alle ristampe de' libri forestieri. Ma per fatale disgrazia, questo solo, che provvede all' acquisto de' Capi nuovi, rimedio principale, e senza di cui gli altri non hanno sopra che operare con vantaggio, è occultamente legato da tale impedimento, che la somma provvidenza degli antecessori dell' EE. VV. non è messa ad esecuzione.

Non avrebbero essi pensato mai, dopo tanti maneggi, e patti solennemente stabiliti, che gl' Indici di Roma posteriori a quelle del 1595 s' opponessero in Venezia, quantunque non accettati, nè mai assentiti, all' acquisto de' Capi nuovi, e che il Concordato s' incamminasse all' inesecuzione, come osservò, e in parte predisse il P. M. fra Paolo. Molti in ogni tempo furono i modi tenuti dalla Corte di Roma per inestarsi nelle stamperie di Venezia con quell' Autorità, che spetta solo al Principe naturale. Anche prima che fosse nel 1596 accolto l' Indice, cioè fin dai principii del 1500 privilegiava Libri in Venezia, che secondo il linguaggio di quella Corte è quanto dire licenziargli. E pure a que' tempi l' Ecc[mo] Senato riteneva appresso di se solo la facoltà de' privilegii, e delle licenze. A fronte del suo Decreto, che nel 1517 sciolse tutti i privilegii per l' impiego del popolo, e bene del commerzio, usci un Libro a Stampa in Venezia nel 1518 con un privilegio Romano.

Questo abuso così contrario al dritto del Principe andò avanti fino al 1596, 4 Giugno, quando tai privilegii proibitivi di Roma detti *Motu proprii* furono da un Decreto affatto aboliti. Dopo l' accettazione in Venezia dell' Indice col Concordato, in forza del quale non possono nel Dominio di Vostra Serenità essere proibiti altri libri, che i contrarii alla Religione, e questi ancora con la partecipazione al Principe, incominciarono diversi altri modi di quella Corte per scapolare dall' accordo.

Domandò prima, che sole 60 copie del Concordato fossero stampate, mentre che dell' Indice andarono attorno infiniti esemplari. Così volle, che si cominciasse dal far conoscere il Concordato a pochi, l' Indice a tutti.

Dopo non passò quasi mai anno, che in Roma non si facessero aggiunte all' Indice di nuove proibizioni. Nè furono già in esso notati que' libri soli, che sono contrarii alla Religione, ma tutti quelli, che contengono materie spiacevoli ad essa Corte, e sopra tutto opinioni favorevole al Diritto de' Principi. Ma perchè il Concordato non lasciava, che la forza delle proibizioni aggiunte dopo senza saputa di Vostra Serenità valesse nel suo Dominio, principiò quella Corte ad usare occultamente l' opera de' Confessori, perchè obbligassero li coscienze ad ubbidire anche alle aggiunte. S' oppose l' autorità del Governo col far carcerare, e scacciare dagli Stati suoi quelli, che servivano di mezzo ad insinuare questo errore nelle coscienze.

Furono fatte inserire ne' Decreti de' Sinodi Diocesani, che sogliono celebrarsi da' vescovi, parole, che dessero corso, e vigore alle nuove proibizioni. Nel 1616, vennero fatti regolare quelli del Sinodo di Trevigi.

Furono da quella Corte fatti stampare nello Stato Veneto i Decreti Romani delle proibizioni qui non accettate. Il Governo nel 1624 fece ritenere un Librajo in Bergamo, che gli avea stampati, per dar esempio agli altri col suo castigo.

Il Sant' Officio diede biglietti a Stampa a' Predicatori della Quaresima per annunziare al popolo, che temesse quelle proibizioni. Furono aboliti anche col consenso del Nunzio per Decreto del 1665.

Vennero inseriti da' Padri Inquisitori negl' Indici, ch' erano di tempo in tempo pubblicati in Venezia, molti libri, la cui proibizione non era mai stata proposta, nè Decretata. Vi fu posta avvertenza, e tralasciato di stampar l' Indice.

In somma di tempo in tempo si destarono nuove opposizioni al Concordato, alla difesa del quale vegliò però con risoluzione l' Ecc[mo] Senato. E se mai i Ministri di Roma fecero querela, che qui si volesse far esame di Libri proibiti in quella Città, questo sempre rispose, ch' era necessaria qualche notizia intorno alla qualità de' Libri, che qui si vogliono avere per proibiti, così ricercando il debito del mantenere il Concordato, che s' annullerebbe, quando si proibisse ogni sorta di Libri senza vedergli.

Mancati a quella Corte tutti gli altri modi illegittimi di frangere il Concordato, si valse finalmente del più occulto, lasciandone la cura segreta al solo Padre Inquisitore del Sant' Officio. Questi, il quale fu eletto la prima volta dal Magistrato nostro nel 1562, 19 Marzo, per uno de' Revisori quanto alla Religione, e a cui fu stabilito prezzo della Revisione: questi che fu confermato dal Decreto 1603, 11 Maggio, e dichiarato da un Decreto 19 Marzo 1623, per dipendente dal Governo con queste parole: *L' Inquisitore non tiene autorità da altri Principi, che dai Magistrati della Repubblica di rivedere per cause di Religione solamente l' opere, che si stampano:* questi, che secondo le leggi dello Stato non dee ritenere la stampa d' altri Libri, che di quelli dell' Indice 1595, e di quelli, la cui proibizione fu assentita dall' Ecc^mo Senato alle richieste di Roma, può arrestare la stampa di qualunque Libro segretamente, e annullare il Concordato da se solo.

Quando un Librajo gli si presenta, acciocchè esamini un Libro, e gli faccia l' attestato per poter ottenere licenza da pubblicarlo, se non ha cose contrarie alla Religione; quando egli lo trova nell' immense aggiunte dell' Indice Romano, postovi anche per qualunque altra causa, che di Religione, senza farne altro esame, e senza renderne conto, nega l' attestato. O se lo concede, vuole, che sia mutilato il Libro, quantunque spesso non abbia altra macchia, che quella di dispiacere a Roma per le buone opinioni, che contiene a' favore de' Principi. VV. EE. veggono, che con tale difficoltà di mezzo non può aver mai esecuzione la provida mira del Decreto 1605 d' acquistar Capi nuovi, e buoni con le ristampe de' Libri forestieri. E se si stampano mutilati non giovano più al Commerzio nè come Libri nè come Carta; oltre alla perdita del concetto della Tipografica Veneta pur troppo derisa per le stampe mutilate. Furono questi maneggi tutti, e spezialmente quest' ultimo, quelli che arrestarono sempre le clementi intenzioni del Decreto 1603, 11 Maggio.

Vennero intanto accusate della decadenza della Tipografica nostra ora le insidie d' una fazione de' Librai contro all' altra; ora le Spedizioni de' caratteri in Paesi forestieri, le quali pure senza offesa dell' Arte si fecero fino a' principii del 1600 liberamente; e tal volta fu anche incolpata la meschinità delle Stampe nostre. Si fecero leggi, s' eseguirono; e tuttavia l' Arte rimase col notabile detrimento d' una gran diminuzione nel numero de' Torchi, dalla Terminazione 1761 chiaramente annotata.

Gli Antecessori nostri nel Magistrato de' Riformatori commossi alla vista di tanto danno, conoscendo il sicuro rimedio essere riposto nel Decreto 1603, che anima le ristampe de' Libri forestieri, e vedendo, ch' era stato renduto vano dalla Corte di Roma per 70 Anni co' maneggi indicati, rinnovarono fra il 1671 e il 1681 la pratica di far esaminare i libri, stabilita prima del 1562 cioè prima, che fosse stato eletto l' Inquisitore per uno de' Revisori del Magistrato nostro. E con la revisione di *Dotte*, e *Fedeli persone* che attestassero il Libro esser netto da massime contrarie alla Religione, a' Principi, e a' buoni costumi concedevano con una Terminazione la licenza di Stamparlo con Data di Città forestiera.

Questo metodo tenne in vita l' Arte, ma usato di rado, di nuovo fra 48 anni in circa essa ritornò alle consuete estremità. Ripigliato nel 1729 con qualche frequenza, e continuato per qualche tempo, nel corso di 20 anni ridusse i nostri torchi al numero di 90; e il commerzio Librario florido, e grande.

Con tutto ciò possiamo affermare all' EE. VV., che non usci mai Libro in Venezia con data forestiera, il quale scandalizzasse i Lettori anche più pii; nè la Corte di Roma ebbe mai animo d' opporsi a tal risoluzione. Nè scandalo alcuno potea avvenire con l' ottime Leggi, che custodiscono il traffico nostro dall' Ingresso in Venezia di que' Libri, che contengono cose contrarie alla Religione, a' Principi, e a' buoni costumi.

L' Ecc^{mo} Senato ha divisi quelli, a' quali è conceduto l' Ingresso, da quelli, a' quali è vietato. Ha instituito un Revisore alle Dogane, e Fontico, perchè i vietati si rimandino al Librajo estero, che gli ha spediti. Perchè faccia la nota di volta in volta di quelli, che entrano nelle Dogane, e quella presenti al Magistrato Nostro attestando, che sono degli accettati dal Principe. Vostra Serenità ha commesso di più nel Decreto 1653, che non possano esser pubblicati, nè venduti ancora, se i Libraj non hanno un mandato di Licenza sottoscritto almeno da due de' Riformatori dello Studio di Padova; pratica ravvivata, e ricordata pubblicamente con la Stampa del Magistrato Nostro addi 25 Settembre dell' anno Scorso.

Qual macchia possono avere libri tali, entrati in Venezia con tante cautele, se vengono ristampati previa ancora una revisione di Dotte e fideli persone? E come mai se possono entrare in Città in qualsivoglia numero, esser pubblicati, e venduto coll' assenso del Principe nelle botteghe, non potranno poi passare a' Torchi Veneti, solo perchè il Padre Inquisitore del Sant' Offizio gli trova segnati nelle Giunte degl' Indici di Roma? Per questa sola ragione dovranno i nostri Librai, mandar sempre à forestieri i proprii danari; per aver Libri dall' altre Città, e rinforzare i Torchi esteri col comperarne una gran quantità d' esemplari? dovranno esser sempre rivenditori a prò degli altri paese, in cambio d' impiegare il contante nelle Venete Stamperie, impiegare il popolo, vantaggiare il commerzio, come fu intenzione del Decreto 1603, 11 Maggio?

Si può, è vero, per acquistar tali Capi, proseguire coll' uso della Data forestiera. Ma prima questa è un solo rimedio eventuale, che non vien sempre adoperato con ugual vigore: e venendo per intervalli or tralasciato, ed ora ripreso, non fà mai abbondare i Capi quanto abbisogna, per sostenere continuamente i Torchi, i quali quando all' improvviso cessano d' aver lavoro, lasciano in una subitanea miseria molte famiglie.

In secondo luogo, se la data forestiera fosse anche frequentata assai, a lungo andare quella di Venezia si perderebbe, o resterebbe solo in alcuni pochi libri vecchi; sarebbe di ritardo al commerzio l' incertezza de' compratori forestieri intorno al vero luogo dell' edizione; verrebbero deviate le commissioni. Potrebbere inoltre i Librai, renduti baldanzosi dal lungo uso d' una Data Coperta, prevalersi d' essa in qualche stampa clandestina, o introdurre più facilmente Libri Stampati altrove contro i privilegiati. Finalmente questo metodo pratico spesso potrebbe anche ricevere qualche sofistico disturbo dalla Corte di Roma con cavillose interpretazioni dell' Articolo settimo del Concordato, che parla di false, e finte licenze.

Per acquistar dunque capi stampabili, acciocchè l' Arte torni al suo primo splendore, con impiego del popolo, e utilità di commerzio, il metodo più confacente alla grandezza, e autorità naturale del Principe, il più giovevole a rendere celebre il nome della Tipografica nostra, e agevolar il traffico de' Libri, il più atto a somministrare lavoro non interrotto a' Torchi, e il non soggetto a malizie di Librai, o ad altri cavilli, è quello d' usare apertamente nelle ristampe de' Libri Forastieri la Data di Venezia, togliendo via quell' ostacolo, che impedisce il salubre provvedimento del Decreto 1603, 11 Maggio.

Per la qual cosa crediamo di necessità, che la Serenità Vostra decreti in primo luogo una ristampa del Concordato coll' Indice del 1595, e con quelle sole aggiunte, che dall' Ecc^{mo} Senato vennero da quel tempo fino a' giorni nostri assentite alle richieste di Roma, dichiarando a pubblica notizia che nel Veneto dominio altri Libri non s' intendono vietati, fuorchè i contenuti in esso; acciocchè sappia ognuno, che i proibiti aggiunti in Roma senza saputa del Principe naturale non aggravano le coscienze de' Sudditi suoi.

Stabilisca appresso, che dopo d' essersi Vostra Serenità opposta a tutte le insistenze di Roma, e a' tentativi occulti usati in varii tempi da quella Corte per frangere il Concordato 1596 riconoscendo, che questo viene offeso dal P. Inquisitore del Sant' Offizio, coll' ubbidire in segreto alle aggiunte qui non accettate degl' Indici Romani, e col sottrarsi celatamente a quella dipendenza, che ha da' soli Magistrati della Repubblica, da' quali fu eletto alla revisione de' Libri, sicchè fa impedimento all' esecuzione del Decreto 1603 in quella parte, che incoraggisce le ristampe de' Libri forestieri, sia deliberato, che da qui in poi non sia alcun Librajo, che vada ad esso Padre Inquisitore a chiedergli attestato per tali ristampe tanto originali quanto tradotte; ma vengano elette Persone dotte, e fedeli dello Stato, alle quali debbano essi Librai presentarsi per la Revisioni di si fatti Libri, che dopo saranno qui pubblicati con la Data di Venezia; lasciando quell' ispezione al detto P. Inquisitore sopra altri generi di Libri che gli fu conferita dagli anteriori Decreti.

Una tal massima decretata sarà certamente l' unico riparo a' mali presenti dell' Arte Tipografica e del Commerzio de' Libri. Questa è l' anima che può dar vita a tutte l' altre Leggi, che senza essa non possono giovare. Il Magistrato nostro incoraggito da così stabile fondamento può aprirsi tutte le vie da risuscitar un' Arte quasi perduta. Può subito assistere all' erezione d' una Stamperia in originale Francese, la quale pel buon mercato della Stampa Veneta sazierà certamente tutta l' Italia almeno, e arresterà per essa il corso de' Libri assai cari, commessi in paesi lontani. La prestezza nelle spedizioni, e il poco prezzo de' suoi Libri rendono Venezia sicura di tutto il vantaggio sopra gli altri. Può con l' acquisto di Capi nuovi mantenere una divisione di Libri proporzionata frà matricolati: costringere potenti, e minori ad un' esatta, e fruttuosa obbedienza circa i privilegii, e le proroghe. Gli uomini occupati con frutto nelle Stamperie perderanno il pensiero d' aprir botteghe, nocive agli altri, a sè, al concetto dell' Arte. Il bisogno vicendevole de' Capi nuovi stampati risveglierà i cambii interni. Il commerzio si farà attivamente con edizioni Venete in gran numero, accreditate per l' integrità, e bontà delle stampe, che allora potrà risolutamente valersi dalla pubblica autorità a tenore delle Leggi, senza timore d' arrestare il traffico de' Libri, come avverrà, finchè non abbiamo altro che le solite ristampe de' nostri, i quali si mantengono in vita, e in giro a forza di quel buon mercato, che nasce dal peggioramento. Grazie.

Dal Mag^{to} de' Reformatori dello Studio di Padova 16 Marzo 1765.

Angelo Contarini Proc^{r} Rif^{r}.
Alvise Vallaresso Rif^{r}.
Francesco Morosini, 2° Cav^{r} Proc^{r} Rif^{r}.

Serenissimo Principe.

No. 2. Negozio di grande importanza pongono sotto le ponderazioni della Serenità Vostra gli Ecc^mi Riformatori dello Studio di Padova; mentre in assai diligente Scrittura, lavorio pregevole, ed in tutta simmetria filato da mano Maestra, le rappresentano dedotta sino dalli suoi primordj con alterazion di vicende per andamento successivo di tre Secoli l' odierna costituzion della Veneta Tipografia. Alla serie istorica dei fatti, e all' industriosa scoperta de' gravi suoi disordini, al ragguaglio della primiera fortuna, e alla vista della presente sua decadenza, (affine di redimerla dall' estremo pericolo, che le sovrasta) internatisi con profonda indagine nella radice delli di lei malori vi accoppiano consiglio quanto provvido, altrettanto zelante di rimedj necessarj, non meno che salutari.

Il primo consiste in comandare, che abbia a ristamparsi l' Indice de' Libri proibiti del 1595 da Papa Clemente VIII.; insieme unito al Concordato, dopo varj maneggi stabilito tra la Repubblica Serenissima, e quel Pontefice nel susseguente anno sotto il di 14 Settembre.

Giacchè pochi ormai n' esistono gli esemplari dell' edizion primigenia, la quale non senz' artificioso dissegno si cercò di restringere a soli sessanta, onde nella scarsezza de' medesimi riescisse più facile e più sicura la mira di sottrarneli non pur alla cognizione, ma agli occhi altrui; complirà pertanto il reimprimerlo puntualmente in numero più copioso, coll' Appendice di quelle Opere altresi, le quali a richiesta di Roma fossersi per avventura dappoi proscritte dall' autorità dell' Ecc^mo Senato.

La diffusion di tal lume, esposto a notizia universale, rischiarirà le tenebre dell' ignoranza per vie clandestine nodrita nell' oppinion del volgo offuscato sotto simulacro di pietosa osservanza da fallaci capziose idee; e valerà a mettere in calma colla lucida comparsa della verità le agitazioni eziandio delle più tenere, e fluttuanti coscienze.

Per disinganno proprio verranno quindi desse ad apprendere, non dover credersi lecita, nè perciò obbligatoria dalli Sudditi di questo Dominio la proibizione di verun altro Scritto, neppur in materia di Religione, il quale non vi si vegga segnato nell' Indice ammesso per li concordi assensi dell' una, e dell' altra parte contrattante, oppur aggiuntovi successivamente per l' Offizio di questa Inquisizione coll' intervento dell' Assistenza Secolare.

L' evidente riscontro di così dimostrativi monumenti dileguerà le caligini di quegli errori Popolari, tra cui involta la mente di taluni oltre misura superstiziosi sen giace nella cieca persuasione, che la conoscenza, e il voto decisivo sopra si fatti Articoli dipenda unicamente dal giudizio degli Ecclesiastici, senza che possan intromettersi ad avervi consorzio Magistrature Civili.

Quanto rilevi la cura di sradicare una credenza cotanto perniciosa dagli Animi, che ne fossero miseramente preoccupati o per debolezza di spirito, o per malizia di suggeste insinuazioni, lo ravvisò in prevenzione il perspicace ingegno di Maestro Paolo, quando in diversi Consulti egli lascia un giudizioso arricordo, che come Vostra Serenità troverebbe sempre mai intenta la Curia Romana non pur a sopprimere dal canto suo l' *Indice* per toglierlo affatto (se fia possibile) dalla memoria degli uomini, e deluderne con tale obbliqua maniera la pattuita esecuzione, ma a seppellire in oblio perpetuo li regolamenti sù di esso capitolati; così non dovrà dalla Pubblica vigilanza, e sollecitudine ommettersi mai pari premura di ripulsar, e rendere vani li tentativi avversarj con reiterare di tratto in tratto a stampa le sue promulgazioni.

Dietro la scorta d' un Direttore sì avveduto convien dire espediente ai Sovrani riguardi il passo, che libero d' ogni difficoltà interiore ed estranea, viene additato dall' EE. Sue per l' accreditata loro prudenza.

Sperar giova non minore il vantaggio, che ne deriverà dall' uso del secondo suggerimento, ed è di sostituire nelle veci del P. Inquisitore per la disamina de' Libri l' esattezza di Persone dotte, e fedeli, col cui attestato si permetta di stamparli, qualora queste affermino in scritto, non contenervisi cosa contraria alla Religione, ai Principi, nè a' buoni costumi.

Praticavasi infatti metodo simile anche avanti il 1562; nel qual anno appunto con Terminazione dell' Ecc^mo Magistrato 19 Marzo ne fu pure appoggiata l' incombenza all' attenzion del P. Inquisitore, assegnandosegli per tal incarico la Tassa d' una difinita mercede.

Quest' Atto invigorito poscia dalla Serenità Vostra con suo speciale decreto caratterizza, e lo colloca in riga di subalterno mercenario Ministro, dipendente per

Marzo 1623. intiero (in quanto appartiene all' esame de' Libri) dalla superiorità del Magistrato.

Trito è l' assioma del Jus Canonico, per cui resta disposto, che chiunque esercita ministeriale temporaneo Impiego, può esserne leggittimamente ammosso per quella mano istessa, che glielo ha conferito. *Ejus est destitutio, cuius est institutio.*

Questo Religioso non è Revisor ordinario in conseguenza del suo Inquisitoriale Offizio; ma egli è meramente commesso per ultronea delegazione in virtù di revocabil Mandato.

Non v' ha perciò titolo fondamentale di perpetuarsi in lui questa peculiar, separata, ed accessoria Deputazione, la qual all' incontro può essergli onninamente tolta, ed almeno modificata a Pubblico beneplacito, e volere.

Modificazion certamente esigono le di lui eccedenze; poichè reso egli instrumento servile delle Curiali macchinazioni di continuo rivolte all' intacco, e defraudo della Temporale per l' accrescimento dell' Ecclesiastica giurisdizione, alieno dal contenersi tra le innocenti riserve di Esaminator mero, e spassionato de' Libri; si è intruso, ed eretto nella figura d' arrogarsene l' arbitrio d' assoluto dispositore.

Esso osserva con inflessibil durezza qual Canone sacro, ed inviolabile la massima di ricusare cervicoso, e pertinace a' Libraj la licenza di qualunque impressione, sia tradotta, favorevole, e difensiva della Potestà Laica; sebben pura nel resto, ed immune da qualsisia macchia, ed offesa di Religione.

Quest' è un' aperta infrazione del Concordato, per la qual il destino delle Venete Stamperie messo al coperto da ogni pregiudizio di fuori con le di lui saggie provvidenze dipende dalle altrui voglie, e dall' abuso di forastier dispotismo.

Sorgiva è questa del fatale deliquio, e scadimento, in cui quivi languisce a' giorni Nostri l' Opifizio Tipografico; dacchè in questa Pianta nelle età trascorse molto feconda di ubertosi annui proventi per le manifatture de' suoi cultori, per la nutritura del Popolo, e per l' estension del florido Commerzio attivo, vi si asconde un tarlo, che intestinamente la corrode; e togliendole la facoltà d' alimentarsi colla produzion di Libri buoni, e nuovi vieppiù la inarridisce nella totale deficienza del vitale suo succo.

Persuasa la maturità dell' Ecc^mo Senato di così efficaci, o piuttosto urgenti motivi, vorrà in seguito di quanto espongono accuratamente, e di quanto insinuano con aggiustatezza d' opportuno ripiego gli Ecc^mi Riformatori, decretar all' avvenire, che le opere tutte imprimibili, cioè le non interdette dalla Legge del suo Concordato, siano di volta in volta rivedute per il di loro licenziamento da' Soggetti di dottrina e di Fede, scielti per destinazion del Magistrato, l' attestazione de' quali sia requisito bastevole ad autorizzare col consenso di SS. EE. la legittimità delle ricercate edizioni.

Dubbio non v' ha, che inspezion tale potria di pieno diritto levarsi al P. Inquisitore, cui ella compete, per investitura non già reale, inerente al suo Carico, ma per collazion fattane alla di lui Persona, e perciò abdicabile da essa a genio, e piacere del Collatore. *L' Inquisitor* (sono voci della Serenità Vostra) *non tiene autorità da altri Principi, che dai Magistrati della Repubblica di rivedere per cause di Religione solamente le opere che si stampano.*

Decreto, 19 Marzo 1623.

Tutta volta se tornasse a maggior grado il moderato partito di non dargli onnimodo esclusiva da tal Ministero, conseguirebbesi forse il medesimo intento coll' assentirne la prosecuzione dell' esercizio; giammai privativamente in rapporto alla di Lui Persona, ma bensì cumulativo colla nomina d' altri Revisori, de' quali valesse a tenerlo in freno fra giusti limiti del dover la capacità, e la riputazione, il timore, e la censura.

Egual moderazione di temperamento la troviam usata dal vivente Monarca delle Spagne in Regio suo Editto, che fà divieto a quella Inquisizione Generale d' impedir contro alle regole del suo Concordato le Stampe di qualsivoglia autore, senza renderne prima conto, e senza farne inteso il Segretario di Stato, ed altri primarj Uffiziali della Corte; coll' obbligo in appresso d' impetrar il placito della Maestà Sua; e di rilevarne in opposito le ragioni di chi potria pretendervi interesse.

Di quest' esempio autorevole non meno, che recente in somiglianza di circostanze non rifiuterà Vostra Serenità di mostrarsi imitatrice.

Intorno alla terza provvisione, che osservano spiegata nella Scrittura in forma concludente, e precisa, non vi aggiungeremo parole; si perchè tale Articolo vi si scopre in quella cribrato con la più fina purgatezza di criterio, e di senno, sì perchè la provvisione istessa conferisce non poco ad imprimere nel concetto delle Estere Genti una onorevole fiducia in riguardo al Candor Pubblico, e alla rettitudine dell' inalterabile suo istituto.

Si consiglia d' apporvi in fronte ciascun libro la Data, e 'l nome del Luogo dalli cui Torchj egli esce impresso alla luce del Mondo erudito, onde si abolisca l' illegittima supposizione di Paesi immaginarj, o fittizj, che nel coprire l' originalità delle Edizioni col velo d' imposture mendaci, stornano a danno non lieve del traffico la influenza delle commissioni, ed invece di allettare illudono con simulata indicazione il desiderio de' Compratori, segnatamente dei più lontani.

Ripugna inoltre, e contravviene al Capº VII. del Concordato inibitivo di località falsificate quest' abusiva consuetudine, talchè potria ella fornire di pretesti le cavillose, e sottili interpretazioni de' Curiali a schierare in Campo contro di questa mala fede, tolerata dalla Pubblica connivenza, non irragionevoli querele.

Anderebbesi a rischio di rinforzar le medesime per la incidenza di qualche sconcerto eventuale, non impossibile a succedere in punto tal volta di Religione: giacchè la stampa di tai Libri pseudonimj và esente (in vigor di Magistral Terminazione, per cui ella si permette) dalle osservazioni Inquisitoriali, ch' estender non si possono alli travisamenti suoi, nè alle sue mentite apparenze.

La verità prevaler dee alla finzione, perciò non dissentirà Vostra Serenità d' adottare l' ingenuo parere dell' EE. Sue, col por argine al corso progressivo di tali falsificazioni, ed inibirne l' abitudine, quanto meno giustificabile, altrettanto più azzardosa, ed indegna di lode.

Seppur una distaccata dall' altra le cauzioni proposte dalla sperienza, e zelo esimio del Magistrato non bastassero al conseguimento delle commendevoli sue, e proficue intenzioni, val a dire al ricupero, e alla salvezza d' un' Arte poco discosta dal suo naufraggio; Noi felice presagimo, e ne attendiamo il successo dalla pratica simultanea, ed individua di tutti, e tre li suggeriti provvedimenti. *Quae non prosunt singula, juncta juvant.*

Nella sapienza delle deliberazioni supreme rinchiudesi lo stato di molte, e molte miserabili famiglie. La penuria, e mancanza de' Capi nutritivi del loro giornaliero lavoro; cioè l' arbitraria, e dispotica esclusione di stampabili, e comercievoli Libri, inceppa le mani, e tiene oppressa da violente schiavitù, dall' ozio, e dall' indigenza una turba d' operarj mendici, perchè inoperosi; senza che possano per l' altrui superchievole impedimento impiegare la propria industria a sostegno di se medesimi, e dei Figli; non che a prò della Società, alla quale vagabondi, e poveri riescon' anzi d' aggraviò, nè di rado pericolosi.

Per non turbare il cuore paterno della Serenità Vostra colla rimembranza di moleste immagini; non ripeteremo i discapiti eccessivi quindi promossi all' Università di questi Stampatori, e Libraj per il ristagno, ed interclusa Circolazione al giro, ed avvanzamento de' sui Capitali.

Dappoichè gli Ecc^mi^ Riformatori ne l' hanno ennunciati con la più individuale, cattegorica, e distinta descrizione; noi nè sapressimo, nè oseressimo restringerne entro cerchio angusto la dolorosa Iliade; contenti sobriamente di rammemorare, e riferire; che dal cumulo di 125 Torchj, de' quali era provista la Città dominante (emporio all' ora letterario a tutte le più colte Regioni) sonoci oggi esinaniti, e ridotti a soli 50 colla caducità di 75, de grado pur troppo convincente gl' infortunj, e la sorte deteriorata dell' Arte.

Ella è costretta di procacciarsi, e di mercare a viltà di prezzo la sua sussistenza, con peggiorare Caratteri, inchiostri, correzioni, e Stampa. La necessità ce la spinge ad una tal coruttella, non senza smacco, nè indecoro dell' onor nazionale: cosichè Gaspare Scioppio Tedesco, uom di grido, e di Letteratura insigne, s' avanzò ad inveire, ed a pubblicare con acrimonia di stil acerbe doglianze per l' opere quivi stampatesi malconcie di Cicerone, non temperatosi la di lui pena dal protestare, che era condannabile al fuoco quella deforme Edizione; che meritava patiboli la furberia del malizioso stampatore; e che alla gravità del Senato conveniva il provedervi in guisa, che garantita venisse l' indemnizazione di chi compra, e particolarmente degli Stranieri, da sì fatte baratterie. *Ciceronis Venetæ Editiones flammis aboleri debebant: Cruces vero figi Typographis, ut documento sint alijs, ne tam improbo furto emptores argento emungere et depeculari audeant. Senatui certe Veneto curæ esse oportet, ne iste Typographorum Fraudes tam deformem Veneto nomini maculam inferant.*

Porterà certamente riparo a tutte queste jatture d' utilità, e di credito la riforma dissegnata dalle benemerite applicazioni, e dalla soda intelligenza d' un cospicuo Triumvirato. Vostra Serenità, ottimo Principe, clementissimo Padre, coll' approvarla ristorerà per l' innata carità sua una moltitudine de' Sudditi, che periscono di fame, e rintuzzerà stessamente per la somma sua prudenza li colpi di lingue malediche, vibrati ad ingiuria, e contro la fame della Nazione. Grazie.

Um^mi^ Dev^mi^ Ser^vi^

Triffon Urachien Cons^r^.

Frà Enrico de' Servi Cons^r^.

Osservazioni di P. . . . . . . F. . . . . . .

Sopra le Scritture di Roma circa il Revisore Ecclesiastico delle Stampe.

No. 3. Con un Memoriale 2 Maggio 1766 prodotto da Monsignor Nunzio Apostolico, con un lunghissimo Promemoria, o sia pretesa Allegazione in quello inserita, e con altri due Memoriali 26 Luglio, e 22 Novembre dello stesso anno si forma grave doglianza dalla Corte di Roma sopra il Decreto 3 Agosto 1765 del Senato Veneziano, per cui oltre al Padre Inquisitore fù aggiunto un Sacerdote Secolare in Revisore delle opere, che si stampano in questa Città, affinchè questo Sacerdote al pari del primo possa rispondere al Principe dei riguardi dovuti alla Religione Cattolica. Lascieremo di riferire i motivi urgenti, che indussero la necessità, e la giustizia di tale provvedimento, perchè stanno a sufficienza espressi nelle scritture degli Ecc^mi Riformatori dello Studio di Padova, e perchè il pubblicarli farebbe poco onore a quei Reverendi Padri, che ne hanno data l' occasione, e che sono gli artefici veri del Promemoria, e di tutti que' maneggi, che industriosamente hanno poi saputo coprire col nome rispettabile del Sommo Pontefice per meglio sorprendere l' altrui pietà.

All' intento nostro basterà mostrare semplicemente, che queste mosse non tanto sono dirette a pugnare colla persona del Revisore nuovamente eletto, il quale è Sacerdote, e Teologo al pari dell' altro, quanto ad invadere il Gius Regale di destinarlo negli Stati della Ser^ma Repubblica. Il qual tentativo sebbene al suono delle parole comparisce vestito di oggetti spirituali, nondimeno spogliato della corteccia, e bene esaminato nell' effetto suo mira propriamente ad introdurre nell' Arte della Stampa una Podestà Forastiera, la qual in apparenza sia bensì cumulativa, e simultanea con quella del Principe, ma nella sostanza diventi l' arbitra e la padrona del tutto.

A questo fine la Corte di Roma domanda nelli suoi Memoriali il *ritiro* del Decreto 1765, perchè sia restituito appunto l' *arbitrio* di prima al Padre Inquisitore, e si arroga cortesemente il vocabolo imperioso di *diritto*, e di *potestà*, parole incognite nel linguaggio dei primi secoli della Chiesa, quando parla di se medesima, ed usa l' altro meno efficace di *autorità*, quando parla dei Sovrani, e Signori Terreni. Per tal guisa ella indossa le veste altrui, e si mette in vantaggio, ben conoscendo che ciò, che si ha per *diritto* proprio, non è limitabile, nè rivocabile, a differenza di ciò, che si ha per concessione altrui, che è soggetto a limitazione, e rivocazione ad arbitrio del concedente. Ma in progresso di queste osservazioni ognuno agevolmente potrà comprendere, che tutto ciò, che di *diritto* in questa materia fosse accordato all' Ecclesiastico, si toglierebbe al Principe, e al Magistrato; e che il cedere a una parte del negozio sarebbe far apertura per cedere al tutto; mentre due padroni, e con interessi opposti non possono lungamente, nè con tranquillità insieme albergare, ma è forza che uno di loro soccomba, e ruini. Si potrebbe ancora aggiungere qualche riflesso sopra lo stile assai franco di quelle Carte, sopra la loro affetata prolissità, e sopra alcuni degli autori in esse citati. Ma sarebbe far via troppo lunga con danno della materia, e con noja de' leggitori. Ogni uomo può da se conoscere quanto allo stile, che i Curiali, e li Regolari del ceto Inquisitoriale non sogliono prendersi gran cura del Galateo autore poco stimato nelle loro Scuole, eziandio quando parlano delle Maestà Supreme; che la lunghezza è un' astuzia per disviare, e colpire con un perpetuo giro di argomentazioni equivoche, e cavillose lo spirito de' meno accorti; e che tra gli autori citati non potranno avere gran fede in questo proposito, per esempio il Sig^r Cardinale Bellarmino, che nei suoi scritti ha depressa la Podestà de' Principi per inalzare di soverchio quella del Papa; il Sig' Cardinale Albizzi, che molto infelicemente si è opposto all' opera della Inquisizione scritta da Fr. Paolo Sarpi Teologo della Repubblica; e il nome di Erasmo da Roterdam uomo sempre tenuto di credenza dubia dai Cattolici, ed oggidì nel Promemoria annoverato dai Romani tra i Padri della Chiesa. Potrà inoltre accorgersi, che si esagerano i mali, e si lasciano sotto silenzio i beni, che ne derivano dalle Stampe; che l' erudite cognizioni sono per la maggior parte male applicate; e che si portano in trionfo gli speziosi vocaboli di *Diritto*, e di *Fatto* in favore della nuova pretesa, quando nè l' uno, nè l' altro regge alle prove.

Insomma tutto lo sforzo è diretto a stabilire nella Stampa sotto pretesti spirituali, e per la via de' sofismi l' ingerenza degli Ecclesiastici, e principalmente della Corte Romana, la quale può avere interesse contrario al nostro e per la qualità dei Libri, e per la ragione del proprio traffico. Ma ormai è noto al Mondo, che da quei Cortigiani si usa di far querele, e di metter in questione eziandio le cose più certe, perché la questione confonde l' idea degli affari, la confusione promove il negozio sopra la merce altrui senza arrischiare la propria, il negozio invita il componimento, e nel componimento la Corte per lo più trova il guadagno. Noi all' opposto per strade molto più ingenue, e più brevi entraremo di fronte nel vero centro della controversia proposta, contenti soltanto di rischiarare, e ridurre a ordine di tempi, e di cose ciò, che fu dall' altrui malizia con disordine, e confusione collocato, potendo paragonarsi il promemoria Romano alle Fabbriche Gottiche, le quali sono piene di piccole bagattelle, e di gusto così corrotto, che niuno Architetto si degna più d' imitarle.

Tutto dunque lo scopo di Roma è quello di provare, che il Padre Inquisitore del Sant' Officio nel punto di Religione è Giudice, ed esaminatore ordinario de' Libri, che si mandano alle Stampe in questo Dominio per vigore della Podestà conferita alla Chiesa nei giudizi della Fede; e che però dai Vescovi, o dal Pontefice deve attendersi la destinazione.

Per contrario tutto lo scopo di Venezia è quello di provarlo Ministro deputato, e dipendente dal solo Principe nella incombenza di rivederli in vigore di suo mandato, che può modificare, ed anco rivocare a misura dell' esigenza, e che però dal libero Diritto di esso Principe, e non da altra Potestà ne deriva la sua destinazione.

Gli argomenti principali sparsi confusamente, e con nojose repliche nei cinquantadue Articoli del Promemoria, e ritoccati in parte nell' ultimo Memoriale 22 Novembre si riducono in sostanza a soli tredici, a ciascuno de' quali aggiungeremo per maggiore facilità la risposta, affinchè nel confronto sia meglio conosciuta la forza loro, e la verità del preteso Diritto Ecclesiastico, e dei fatti introdotti.

Il primo è tratto dall' autorità delle Divine Scritture, de' Santi Padri, e de' Concilj per mostrare, che il Ministero del Verbo fu consegnato ai Pastori della Chiesa: Che a questa appartiene il guardare la greggia dai pascoli velenosi: Che li maggiori Santi fuggirono i colloquj degli Eretici, e ne proibirono ogni pratica: Che le prediche di costoro come pericolose furono sempre vietate; e permesse soltanto quelle de' Cattolici, purchè intervenga la licenza del Papa, o del Vescovo del luogo: Che finalmente i cattivi Libri sono un fonte perpetuo di sovversione, e un mezzo facilissimo per guastare le Provincie.

Si risponde, che tutto questo magnifico apparato di erudizioni, e di timori non ha che fare colla immaginata questione, nè col Decreto Veneto 3 Agosto 1765, perchè qui nessuno contende alla Chiesa il Ministerio del Verbo. Anzi il Senato Veneto, e tutti i buoni Cattolici desiderano, che di quello ne facciano i Sacri Pastori l' uso prescritto in edificazione, e non in distruzione della Greggia di Cristo, e che la guardino pure attentamente dai pascoli velenosi colla sana predicazione, colle pie istruzioni, e coll' esempio de' Maggiori Santi, che è la pratica delle morali virtù. La questione proposta versa tutta sulla facoltà di deputare un Ispettore, il quale vegga, che nelle cose, che vanno alla stampa, niente passi di contrario alla Religione. Una tal ispezione non è certamente nè predicare il Vangelo, nè insegnare la dottrina Cristiana, nè decidere i dubbj della Fede, nè amministrare i Sacramenti, nè stendere la mano all' Incensiere; e però non si arroga il Ministerio del Verbo consegnato alla Chiesa. Ma è vedere soltanto, e osservare ciò, che si vuol stampare e far pubblico, per farne relazione al Principe, al quale dalle Divine Scritture, dai sacri Canoni, dai Santi Padri e dagli Statuti più venerandi è raccomandata la custodia, e la protezione della Religione, e dalla Chiesa medesima, siccome per moltissimi e notissimi documenti si potrebbe mostrare. Dunque una tale ispezione è occhio, è voce; non è giudizio, e sentenza. Essa è anzi un guardiano perpetuo, che sta vigilante in ajuto e difesa della Santa Fede, e non esce da quei limiti, e da quei doveri, che competono alle potestà Secolari. Di lei non si trova parola in tutti i Libri usciti nello spazio di quindici Secoli; ed in questi tempi di tanta luce è ben infelice l' artifizio di farla supporre figliuola di quei Padri antichi, che non l' hanno mai nè sognata nè generata. Questo è propriamente assomigliare coloro, i quali fingono l' Uffizio de' Frati Inquisitori instituito da Dio nel Paradiso Terrestre, e fanno discendere li Carmelitani dal Profeta Elia. La ragion poi del peccato fu sempre un pretesto generale per estendere la giurisdizione Ecclesiastica, e farla entrare in tutti gli affari, e le professioni del Mondo. E pure ognuno sà, che la Chiesa è giudice di ogni peccato soltanto nel Foro interno, quando il peccatore se ne accusa, o anche nell' esterno, quando il delitto è pubblico, e scandaloso, e che non può far uso che di pene spirituali, mentre più oltre non s' estende l' autorità conferitale dal Divin Redentore. E inoltre principio certo, che la Stampa è un' Arte Laica venuta in Italia verso l' anno 1460, e che ha luogo principale in Venezia tra quelle, che alimentano il Commercio. D' allora in quà fu sempre governata colle Leggi della Repubblica, e non con altre anche nel punto di mantenere salvi li riguardi dovuti alla Religione, siccome più a basso sarà mostrato. Quando gli Ecclesiastici sotto il pretesto dei mali o dei beni, che possono avvenire allo Spirito umano, giungessero ad acquistarne ingerenza per diritto proprio, e non per quella sola ispezione, che loro accorda la pietà de' Principi secondo i varj rispetti, e le varie costumanze de' proprj Stati, a poco a poco la farebbero tutta sua, o almeno pretenderebbero di averne egual parte che i Principi stessi, e forse col progresso del tempo questi ne sarebbero anche esclusi, siccome avvenne in altre materie. Un tale pretesto invero è tanto generico, che potrebbe sottoporre all' arbitrio degli Ecclesiastici tutte le cose temporali del Mondo, il governo delle Famiglie, quello degli Stati, il traffico, e le Arti eziandio più comuni. Le guerre, e le paci dipenderebbero dal loro cenno, siccome dipendevano al tempo delle Crociate, e di qui Pontefici bellicosi, che per questo mezzo esposero a gravissimi travagli la Germania, la Francia, la Sicilia, l' Italia ed altre Provincie dell' Europa. Gli Osti, li Locandieri, e li Venditori di tutta la vittuaria sarebbero fatti soggetti al loro imperio, perchè possono dar occasione di peccato nei loro ridotti, o per la qualità delle persone, che albergano, o per la natura de' cibi vietati, che vendessero, siccome pretendono in alcune Città gli inquisitori del Sant' Offizio. Il traffico medesimo con Nazioni di credenza diversa resterebbe impedito, perchè i fedeli possono contaminarsi, quando non intervenga una dispensa del

Papa, siccome si usava con gravissimo dispendio de' Mercadanti innanzi il 1300 per le Provincie d' Oriente, o quando il P. Inquisitore non lo permetta sotto alcune condizioni, siccome fu tentato d' introdurre nel fine del Secolo decimosesto, e nel principio del decimosettimo per gl' Italiani, che viaggiavano in Provincie Oltramontane. Niun governo ora è più così cieco, che non conosca gli oggetti arcani di tali pretese, e quali conseguenze funeste ne derivarebbero a tutti gli Stati e alla Società Civile, se queste dottrine trovassero albergo. Li Santi poi citati nel Promemoria, i quali raccomandarono di fuggire i colloquj, e la pratica degli Eretici e degl' Infedeli, diedero consigli, e non precetti, ed intesero di parlare di quella pratica, e di que' colloquj, che sono perniciosi, e di eccitare con santo Zelo gli uomini alla perfezione, alla quale però non tutti possiamo arrivare. Ma non per questo poterono conferir alla Chiesa ingerenza legale in professione alcuna del mondo, e molto meno nella Stampa, che a lor tempi non era ancor nata. E se altrimenti fossero intesi, non si potrebbe secondo la regola del moderno autore parlare in Roma cogli Ebrei, nè in Venezia coi Turchi, nè in Germania coi Luterani. Inoltre la Stampa non è nè un' uomo Eretico, nè una nazione infedele; ma è un' Arte Laica al pari di tutte le altre; e come tale fu sempre difesa robustamente contro le invasioni degli Ecclesiastici, siccome appare da molte deliberazioni del Senato, che si lasciano per oggetto di brevità. Per essa si comunica agli uomini ciò, che si farebbe in iscritto per mezzo de' Copisti. Sopra l' industria di questi la Chiesa certamente non ha facoltà, nè la esercita se non nel foro dell' anima, quando sia male usata, siccome la esercita sopra i peccati de' Medici, degli Avvocati, de' Mercadanti, di tutti i Fedeli, e de' Principi stessi Cattolici. Il peccato dell' uomo è bensì sottoposto all' emenda spirituale della Chiesa per i mezzi stabiliti da Cristo, che è fondatore infallibile della Religione, ma non già le Arti, le professioni, e i governi, coi quali il mondo si regge. Altro è l' Arte, ed altro è l' uomo, che la esercita; siccome altro è la persona del Principe, ed altro la potestà sua. Nemmeno poi ha che fare col nostro proposito il divieto di ascoltar le Prediche degli Eretici, o il debito de' Cattolici di farle sempre colla permissione del Papa, o del Vescovo locale. Il Decreto 1765 parla di Stampe, e non di Prediche; nè il Senato si prende la noja di sapere, se il Padre Predicatore abbia la licenza, o no di mostrare la penna dell' Angiolo Gabriello, o li carboni, che arrostirono San Lorenzo. Che in fine li cattivi Libri siano un fonte perpetuo di sovversione, ed un mezzo facilissimo per guastare le Provincie, ne siamo più persuasi dell' autore medesimo del Promemoria. E per impedire appunto i mali che da quelli possono derivare, la Repubblica, con saggio provvedimento ha destinati i suoi Revisori per la Religione, per il Principe, e per i Costumi, ed ha instituiti i suoi Magistrati, perchè avessero cura non meno della disciplina degli Artefici, che della qualità delle opere, che sono consegnate alle Stamperie. Fu destinato tra i Revisori l' Inquisitore come Professore approvato nella Facoltà Teologica, e il Segretario come Perito negli interessi de' Principi per rispondere al Governo colla rispettiva scienza, vale a dire non per decidere, e giudicare, ma per opinare, e riferire, chiamati ad esercitare un opera puramente ministeriale nella stessa guisa, che da un Medico si farebbe opinare sopra una malattia, da un Legale sopra una controversia forense, o da un Antiquario sopra qualche monumento o medaglia. La loro incombenza pertanto non è giudiziale, o giurisdizionale, come accortamente si dà a credere nel Promemoria quanto alla persona del Padre Inquisitore, ma solamente un esame del fatto, e una opinione dottrinale, la qual rende testimonianza al Principe, che l' opera da imprimersi non contiene cosa offensiva dei rispetti sopraccennati. Per questo al solo Magistrato appartiene dar la *Licenza*, che è l' atto di Giurisdizione, e si chiama *Fede*, e *attestato* la cognizione fatta dai Revisori, perchè sono suoi Ministri e non Compagni. Questa verità riluce in tutti i Mandati impressi nè Libri, che sono alle Stampe; e per questo modo legittimo il Principe toglie il corso ai Libri, che sono veramente cattivi, e salva tutti gli oggetti con tanta esuberanza predicati dall' autore del Promemoria. E manifesto dunque, dalle cose dette, che l' uffizio di rivedere un Libro, se contiene cosa contraria alla Religione, per farne relazione al Principe e al Magistrato Civile per quella cura, che loro compete di custodirla, non è lo stesso, che istruire i popoli, predicare, definire la dottrina, e amministrare i Sacramenti, che sono gli uffizj raccomandati alla Chiesa ed ai Sacri Pastori, e che dall' autore Romano si cammina ingegnosamente per la via de' sofismi con fine di spaventare, confondere, e ingannare con false immagini la mente de' semplici.

Promem. Rom. Art. XIII. XIV. XV. e Memoriale 22 Nov^e 1766.

Il secondo argomento è dedotto dall' esempio di alcuni Libri cattivi, che furono abbruciati o volontariamente dai Fedeli, ovvero in ordine a condanne fatte nei Concilj.

Si risponde, che la Storia è bensì vera, e mostra anco l' erudizione immensa dello Scrittore, ma che non fà al presente proposito, e che è falsa la deduzione, che egli ne vorrebbe cavare. Imperciocchè l' abbrucciare i Libri, o il condannarli, quando sono cattivi, e ingiuriosi, non è lo stesso che rivederli perchè siano stampati, quando sono buoni e innocenti. L' una azione è molto diversa dall' altra. Può ognuno voluntariamente privarsene, ed abbrucciarli ancora per iscrupolo proprio, o per consiglio del Confessore o per altra ragione, siccome può fare anco d' una Pittura, d' uno Scritto, e d' una Veste, quando gli rechi molestia allo Spirito. Si poteva aggiungere a questi documenti, che Andrea Navagero dotto Senator Veneziano soleva in un determinato giorno dell' anno alla presenza di molti suoi amici abbrucciare un grosso fascio di Marziali, e di somiglianti libri da lui creduti cattivi. Dunque sarà questo un atto di giurisdizione, e farà esempio, perchè il Magistrato non possa farli rivedere, e licenziare per la stampa, se li trova buoni? Le azioni private degli uomini quantunque lodevoli possono bensì esigere laude, e anco premio, ma non hanno giammai vigore di legare l' autorità, che è pubblica, e indipendente. Non ha poi nemmeno che fare colla questione proposta l' abbrucciamento de' Libri, che fosse fatto in ordine a condanne promulgate nei Concilj; poichè oggidì non si tratta di abbrucciare Libri, che fossero legittimamente condannati, ma di rivedere le opere, che i Concilj non condannarono e che possono essere degne di Stampa. L' oggetto vero, e solo di questa revisione e di tutte le Leggi, che l' hanno instituita, e confermata, è quello d' impedire che niente di offensivo alla Cattolica Religione sia divulgato. E se il Libro approvato da cotali Revisori averà cosa offensiva, resta tuttavia nella Chiesa la facoltà di condannarlo, e nè principi quella di vietarlo, perchè l' approvazione del Revisore è tenuta per semplice opinione di un Ministro deputato a vedere, e riferire, e il divieto de' Tribunali Ecclesiastici, o Secolari è un giudizio formale di chi è vestito di legittima autorità. Così l' opera del primo tende ad impedire la divolgazione, e quella dei secondi toglie l' errore già divolgato. Non si vuol per altro menar per buona l' opinione sparsa con industria nel Promemoria, che la pena dell' incendio pubblico competa giuridicamente alla Potestà Spirituale della Chiesa. Imperciocchè la Giurisdizione Ecclesiastica non ha da se diritto di far abbrucciare Libri quantunque scandalosi. La ragione è, perchè la pena della combustione non può eseguirsi se non in qualche Territorio, e però non può aver effetto se non dalla mano di quello, a cui è commessa la Sovranità Territoriale, e l' esecuzione delle pene capitali.

iem. Rom. t. XVI. XVII. Memor. Nov° 1766.

Il terzo argomento di queste Scritture è tratto da una costituzione pubblicata del Pontefice Leone X. ai 4 Maggio 1515, nel Concilio di Laterano chiamato il quinto, per la quale fu ordinato, che niente si stampasse se non riveduto, ed approvato dagli ordinarj e dagl' Inquisitori de' luoghi. Si citano in appresso altri successivi Concilj Provinciali, quello generale di Trento, e alcuni sinodi particolari, che fecero la medesima ordinazione del Lateranense.

Si risponde, che essendo questa la prima Costituzione in tale preposito a buon conto si confessa assieme con noi, che per quindici secoli, non si parlò di stampe, nè sopra quelli si fecero statuti nella Chiesa. Quanto poi a quel Concilio di Laterano con dispiacere bensì, ma per necessità di Argomento, si devono accennare alcune cause, per le quali egli non fu tenuto per Generale, nè ricevuto giuridicamente dai Principi, nè di lui si fece in Venezia una legittima promulgazione. La storia c' insegna, che fu convocato da Giulio II., nel 1512, vale a dire poco dopo i primi successi della famosa guerra di Cambrai promossa alla Repubblica da quel Pontefice intraprendente in tempo, che una partita di Cardinali ne aveva chiamato un' altro in Pisa, che fu poi trafferito a Milano sotto la protezione di Lodovico XII., Re di Francia. Cominciò egli dall' essere il Papa intitolato il Principe di tutta la Terra dall' Arcivescovo di Spalatro Bernardo Zane, che fece la prima orazione; dal disapprovarsi tutte le cose dell' altra assemblea; dal pubblicarsi una confederazione col Re d' Inghilterra, e dalla minaccia di un Interdetto sopra il Regno di Francia. Fu continuato in mezzo alle armi, e alle turbolenze da Leon X. suo successore, che promulgò in esso oltre un Decreto, che vieta a' Principi il far alcun sequestro sopra le rendite Ecclesiastiche, ed oltre una Bolla circa i Monti di Pietà, quella ancora delle stampe citata nel Promemoria, la qual contiene molte esorbitanze, come sono la perdita de' Libri, l' abbrucciamento loro, la sospensione de' Librai dall' impiego, e il pagamento di denaro applicato alla Fabbrica di S. Pietro in Roma, che sono tutte pene temporali. Ebbe termine poco dopo la venuta improvvisa in Italia di Francesco I., Re di Francia, che disfece l' esercito Pontificio, e stabilì in Bologna col Papa il famoso concordato, per cui fu confermato nel Re la nomina de' Vescovati, e data regola alle Appellazioni delle Cause fuori del Regno. Da ciò ognuno può considerare, qual Concilio fu quello, e di quanta efficacia sia il Decreto de' Libri in esso pubblicato. E sebbene v' intervenne assieme con altri Oratori anco l' Ambasciatore della Reppubblica, tale intervento però non importa recivimento legittimo del Concilio, nè delle Bolle promulgate dal Papa in quelle radunanze, perchè i Ministri non hanno facoltà rinonciare alle ragioni de' loro Sovrani. Anco in Trento intervennero gli Ambasciatori de' Principi, e ciò non ostante il Concilio da molte Provincie non fu ricevuto nel punto della disciplina, e in altre fu ricevuto con qualche limitazione, e sempre con atto espresso dal Governo Civile. Resta dunque manifesto, che un tale Decreto, il quale è di semplice disciplina, non essendo in questo Dominio Stato ammesso con pubblicazione giuridica, non induce obbligazione veruna. Molto meno inducono obbligazione li Concilj Provinciali, e li Sinodi particolari fatti in Spagna, in Germania, nel Messico, e in altre Provincie con bella, e industriosa schiera decantati nel Promemoria con fine di gettare la polvere negli occhj a chi non li avesse letti: Poichè quelli non hanno corso oltre i confini della respettiva Diocese, e Provincia, e niente hanno che fare con questo Stato. Quello di Aquileja, che solo potrebbe in parte applicarsi allo Stato Veneto, perchè oltre le Provincie Austriache ne abbraccia alcune della Repubblica, non comprende la Dominante, dove è la sede di questo negozio, nè si vede approvato dalla Pubblica potestà.

Se poi il Lateranense avesse obbligato per tutto il Mondo, e per tutti i Libri, non era bisogno, che altri facessero la medesima ordinazione di propria autorità senza riferirsi a lui, siccome fecero alcuni, e specialmente quelli tenuti in Francia. Ciò anzi prova, che egli non fu tenuto per Generale, nè ricevuto da tutte le Chiese Cattoliche.

Si prega inoltre osservare, che essi Concilj non fanno tutti lo stesso stabilmento, ma che sono tra loro assai diversi, siccome appare dal confronto de' testi, che sarebbe troppo nojoso il ripetere in questo luogo, e che ognuno può leggere nei fonti originali stampati. Nè quei Concilj medesimi possono anco avere maggior vigore di quello, che il Principe rispettivo ha loro accordato; nè alcuno avrà mai accordato di perdere l' autorità, che è propria, e inalienabile, e che ha in deposito per tramandare illesa ai suoi successori. Senza andare a Magonza, o al Messico basta leggere quello di Trento appunto nella Sessione quarta, citata dall' autore, e si vedrà che la ordinazione del Lateranense non si applica ad ogni genere di Libri, ma soltanto alla impressione della Scrittura Santa, e dei Libri che trattano delle Cose Sacre, e che fu raccomandato l' esame ai Vescovi, che sono i veri Pastori della Chiesa, e non ai Padri Inquisitori, che sono i Ministri dei Processi. Nè può anche riputarsi in questo capo ricevuto il detto Concilio in Venezia almeno quanto alle Stampe, all' esame de' Vescovi, ed alla pena della scommunica, e del denaro, essendo esso stato ricevuto con parola di Pio IV.; che restino salve le consuetudini dello Stato, e non essendo egli perciò in osservanza in diciotto e più capi di disciplina, tra i quali si annovera appunto questo. Imperciocchè è verità manifesta che qui la stampa anche dopo l' accettazione del Concilio medesimo continuò sul piede delle consuetudini, e Leggi anteriori, che sono quelle emanate dal Principe, e che da niuna altra Potestà ella si riconobbe dipendente. Nè in questo capo il Concilio si poteva mai eseguire, senza abolire appunto una consuetudine anteriore fondato nell' autorità naturale del Principe. E parimente fatto certo, che qui li Vescovi non presero mai alcuna inspezione sulle opere, che passano ai Torchj; che alle Scommuniche non si dà facile il corso; e che la emenda in denaro essendo pena temporale non ha luogo nelle Curie Ecclesiastiche senza il braccio Secolare. E ritornando al Concilio Lateranense, si può aggiungere, che egli non è tenuto, nè deve tenersi per Generale, mentre in esso fu anco determinata la superiorità del Papa al Concilio: E pure il dubbio resta tuttavia nella Chiesa di Dio, siccome è notorio, e lo attesta lo stesso Cardinale Bellarmino; il che prova, che quella radunanza non fu creduta da tutti per la unione della Chiesa universale assistita dallo Spirito Santo, le di cui decisione sono infallibili. Finalmente per prova, che nè l' uno, nè l' altro di questi due Concilj riguardo alle stampa fu mai riconosciuto ed ammesso nel Dominio Veneto; potranno servire tutte le Leggi Pubbliche emanate in questa materia, nelle quali si è sempre fuggito di nominarli, e si è sempre parlato colla sola autorità, e linguaggio di Principe Supremo; e per tutte può bastare la Terminazione 1562, 19 Marzo, de' Riformatori dello Studio di Padova, e la Deliberazione del Senato 1624, 3 Decembre, nelle quali si assegna, e si conferma la mercede del Revisore Ecclesiastico, cosa direttamente opposta alle disposizioni emanate nei detti Concilij, che ne inibiscono ogni emolumento.

Il quarto argomento è tratto dall' esempio di alcuni pii, e santi uomini, i quali presentarono i proprii scritti a Romani Pontefici per averne la loro approvazione prima di publicarlè. . . .

Si risponde che li documenti citati predicano Libri scritti unicamente in materia di religione, e che non è per questo legata l' autorità de Principi. . . .

Promem. Rom. Art. XXIII. XXIV. Il quinto argomento si sforza di mostrare la necessità del Decreto di Leon X. pubblicato nel Concilio di Laterano, perchè per mezzo della Stampa si diffondono più facilmente i Libri cattivi, e si conservano le perniciose dottrine.

Si risponde, che questa necessità medesima ha indotta anco la Repubblica di Venezia a formare le sue Leggi, e ad instituire i suoi Revisori; e che appunto nell' aver fatto tutto questo senza far menzione nè del Decreto di Leone, nè di alcun' altro regolamento Ecclesiastico ha voluto significare, che intendeva ella pure di provvedere al bisogno, ma non giammai di perdere l' autorità sua coll' introdurne una Forastiera.

m. Rom. XXV. Il Sesto dal Diritto del Principe di far esaminare i Libri per gl' interessi del Principato deduce quello della Chiesa di un simile esame per le cose della Religione.

Si risponde, che essendo questo un' argomento di similitudine, non è di veruna forza nemmeno nelle stesse Scuole de' Regolari, che perfettamente conoscono tutte le cabbale del sillogismo. Nessuno contende alla Chiesa Santa, che non faccia esame, se nè Libri si contengano errori offensivi della Fede Cattolica. Ma si sostiene, che lo deve fare per quei modi, che sono della sua competenze, e non per quelli del Principe. E questi modi per Venezia sono chiaramente spiegati dall' Articolo settimo del Concordato 1596; cioè nel Tribunale del Santo Offizio con l' intervento degli Assistenti Laici, rarissime volte, e per materie di Religione; ma non già nella Cella del Padre Inquisitore, solo, senza intervento di Magistrato alcuno, sempre, e sopra i Libri di ogni argomento. La Paternità sua non è la Chiesa, ma membro semplicemente della Chiesa; E se mai volesse rappresentare la Chiesa fuori del suo Tribunale, taluno facetamente gli risponderebbe, che non può farlo altrimenti che con la giunta di un Campanile. Nella incombenza pertanto di rivedere i Libri l' Inquisitore non è Giudice della Fede, nè il Segretario è Giudice dei Principi. Ma ambedue sono Ministri di quella Potestà, che li ha deputati per rispondere l' uno colla Scienza Teologica, l' altro colla Politica del contenuto del Libro, siccome altrove più ampliamente sarà mostrato.

m. Rom. XXVI. Il settimo argomento reca l' esempio di nazioni Idolatre, che davano ai suoi Ministri il Diritto di opporsi al corso dei Libri contrarj allo loro credenza.

Si risponde, che il diritto, o per meglio dire il dovere di opporsi al corso dei Libri nocivi alla Religione non è per la Dio grazia nè conteso, nè tolto all' autorità Ecclesiastica. Ma che questa lo deve esercitare per i modi legittimi, come si è detto, cioè per Concilio Generale in tutta la Chiesa, e per condanna fatta nel Santo Offizio coll' intervento Laico in Venezia. Piace poi di vedere dopo i Romani collocati tra gl' Idolatri i Nestoriani, e i Calvinisti, quasi chè l' erudito Scrittore parli qui cogl' Indiani, o coi Chinesi, dove nelle Missioni Apostoliche potrebbe vendere ogni merce a suo talento. E poichè tanto si trastulla negli esempi di queste sette, si avverte con ogni riverenza che l' ordine citato dei Calvinisti è poco dissimile dal Decreto fatto nella sessione quarta del Concilio di Trento, e che non per questo egli darà mai a credere nè a loro nè a noi, che essi abbiano ricevuto quel Concilio, siccome non darà a credere ai' Veneziani di aver ricevuto la Bolla di Leone per una accidentale somiglianza di Leggi, che si trovano fatte dalla Repubblica. Ma tutti saremo bensì persuasi, che ogni Potestà a provveduto e provvede in proporzione de' Suoi bisogni, e che guidata da questi principj ha formati i rispettivi stabilimenti. Ciò che attiene al Governo delle cose Temporali, fu consegnato da Dio Monarca Supremo alla Potestà de' Principi. E se alcun Principe ha voluta imparte, o in tutto dar esecuzione ad una costituzione Pontificia, ovvero addottare la consuetudine di altri governi in qualche punto di disciplina, può anco ritirarsene, quando l' effetto cada in diminuzione della sua potestà, o lo ricerchi la mutazione delle circostanze.

Ciò si vede nella pratica giornaliera, perchè l' esempio altrui può bensì consigliare, ma non obbligare. Dunque perchè dieci portano il cappuccio, tutti devono averlo?

Promem. Rom. Artic. XXVIII. e Memor. 22 Nov^{e}. 1766.

L' ottavo argomento si pianta sopra le ordinazioni fatte da diversi Principi, e sopra le pratiche di molti Stati che perciò egli chiama veramente Cattolici, le quali vogliono, che nelle opere da stamparsi preceda la revisione dell' ordinario Ecclesiastico, o de' suoi Deputati.

Si risponde, che ancora questo è un' argomento di similitudine, e si ripete che la Legge, o la pratica di uno Stato non induce obbligazione all' altro; altrimenti in ogni luogo tra Dio e il Principe intervenirebbe un' altra Potestà, nè alcuno sarebbe Supremo. Ogni Stato si regola secondo i proprj istituti; e uno istituto, che sarà buono in Spagna, come per esempio l' Inquisizione, la Bolla della Crociata, e simili, non sarà buono in Francia, nè in Germania, e così vice versa. E per venire ad un paragone assai più basso si domanda all' autore, se la Regola dei Capuccini simile alle altre nella professione dei tre voti induca la medesima osservanza anco nei Domenicani, e negli altri ordini Regolari? Egli dirà, che ognuno li osserva secondo le pratiche, e le Leggi introdotte nell' ordine rispettivo, e da se abbracciate. E dirà bene, e lo stesso diciamo noi non solo di ogni Governo, e società ma anco di ogni famiglia particolare. Poteva pur aggiungere, che in altri Dominj gli Uffizj Ecclesiastici danno ancora la licenza per istampare, e adoperano la formola dell' *Imprimatur*, dopo la quale si sottoscrivono li Magistrati Regj. E noi avressimo risposto, che questo uso quasi universale non ha trovata buona accoglienza singolarmente in Venezia, donde ne fu cacciato nel 1688, e nel 1693, perchè qui si volle conservare questa autorità nel solo Magistrato senza farne parte, e dividerla coi Padri Inquisitori, che sono uomini sudditi bensì per origine, ma Forastieri per dipendenza. Nè l' universalità di questo uso ha mai avuto forza di persuadere il Senato ad abbracciarlo; nè da tale rifiuto n' è derivato alcun danno alla Cattolica Religione. Egli li ha sempre voluti tenere in grado di Suoi Ministri, e non di Giudici in questo Articolo di disciplina; e perciò esigge da loro Fedi, e Attestati, non Sentenze, e Decreti. Per altro si vuol avvertire il dotto Scrittore, che se vorrà compiacersi di fare uno giusto, ed imparziale esame sopra le addotte ordinazioni delle altre Provincie egli troverà:

I. Che alcune riguardano sottanto le opere, che espressamente trattano di Religione, e non comprendono quelle di altro argomento. II. Che non tutte si fondano nel Concilio Lateranense nè prendono legge da lui. III. Che per la maggior parte nacquero per occasione dell' Eresie de' Luterani, e Calvinisti, e nelle Provincie, che più dell' altre si trovavano esposte a quella infezione. IV. Che ne furono incaricati gli Ecclesiastici, perchè creduti periti di quella Scienza, che era necessaria a questo oggetto, senza immaginar mai, che potessero fame abuso, e un capo di Commerzio in danno dei Principi. V. Che in molti luoghi l' esame è commesso alle Università. VI. Che queste ordinazioni mostrano appunto, che non erano sufficienti gli ordinamenti Ecclesiastici, e provano la potestà legislativa, che sta nei Principi in questa materie, e l' esercizio della medesima sempre da essi mantenuto in vigore. VII. Che siccome hanno potuto farne l' instituzione per giusta causa, così possono per giusta causa farne ancora la destituzione. E invero sappiamo, che appunto Filippo II° Re di Spagna citato dall' Autore fu il primo di tutti nei suoi Regni, che sottrasse la Stampa dalla ingerenza degli Ecclesiastici sottoponendola ad un Consiglio particolare, avendo lasciata loro soltanto la cura de' Messali, Breviarj, e delle Carte da insegnare a' Fanciulli la Grammatica. Vediamo ancora, che in altre Provincie Cattoliche la pratica ha limitate oggidì le ispezioni degli Ecclesiastici, mentre escono infiniti Libri con la sola approvazione di Revisori di volta in volta destinati dal Re, dal Magistrato Civile, e dalle Università, siccome si può vedere nelle Stampe di Germania, Portogallo, Francia, Napoli, Milano, Lucca e di altri Dominj. Nè primi tempi era buona la cura degli Ecclesiastici, perchè esercitavano il carico lodevole. Ma scoprendosi nuove offese è necessario usare anco nuovi modo di difesa.

m. Rom. XXIX. XXI. (XII. XIV. V. XL.

Il nono argomento è cavato da Atti, Ordini, e Decreti fatti da due Nunzj Apostolici in Venezia, e dal Tribunale dell' Inquisizione, coi quali fu prescritta la licenza de' Vescovi per stampare, fu stesa la mano degli Ecclesiastici alla revisione nelle Dogane, e furono fatti stampare particolari Indici di libri proibiti; il che secondo l' autore prova non meno l' autorità, che l' esercizio della Chiesa in questa materia anco in Venezia.

Si risponde che tutti questi non furono Canoni, nè Sanzioni della Chiesa, ma pretese, abusi, ed attentati commessi dai Ministri della Corte Romana in pregiudizio della Potestà Civile, e che un millione di tali atti fatti clandistinamente, o senza l' assenzo, e spesse volte contrarj alla Potestà naturale del Principe non fanno prova di legittima autorità, nè di retto esercizio della medesima in favore degli Ecclesiastici. Venendo alli due Nunzj citati Monsignor Nicolò Franco Vescovo di Trevigi, e Monsignor Giovanni dalla Casa l' istoria ci ricorda, che il Franco si avanzò ai più coraggiosi attentati contro il Governo per la stessa via indicata nel Promemoria di pubblicare le sue ordinazioni nella Chiesa Patriarcale di Castello, mal profittando della stupidezza, o della connivenza de' Patriarchi di allora. Tra queste una fu di pubblicare nel 1486 una imposizione sopra il Clero a favore del Papa contro la espressa volontà del Governo. E quanto al Catalogo de' Libri fatto Stampare dal Casa nel 1548, egli non può essere obbligatorio, perchè deriva da uno, che non ha legittima facoltà di proibire, e può reputarsi effetto di zelo in uomo di Chiesa per insegnare ai fedeli i libri, che dovevano fuggirsi. Di cotali Catalogi ne usci più d' uno in quel Secolo formato da persone dotte, e zelanti. Però devono considerarsi come una pia istruzione, un avviso, e niente più. E stato stampato anche il Capitolo del Forno scritto dallo stesso Casa, mentre era Nunzio in Venezia, per cui si crede aver perduta il Cardinalato. Sarà dunque per la regola di questo autore ancora quello un canone ricevuto? Il Catalogo poi 1554 dell' Inquisizione di Venezia al pari del Catalogo del Casa mostra i Libri già stampati, che meritavano di fuggirsi, ma non parla di Revisione, o di Revisori, nè impone, nè poteva imporre alcun obbligo ai Librai, e Stampatori di pigliare la *Licenza* dagli Ecclesiastici per stampare, essendo questo un' atto di giurisdizione propria del Magistrato Civile, che ha la cura e l' autorità sopra l' Arte della Stampa, che è Laica, come l' ha sopra la Pittura, e le Scuole Pubbliche. E gran miracolo, che anco sopra queste professioni l' Ecclesiastico non estenda le sue pretese per li rapporti, che possono avere colla religione. Nemmeno a forza di legge, nè ha che fare colla Revisione l' Indice de' Libri proibiti fatto stampare in Roma dalla Congregazione del Santo Officio nel 1559, e ristampato da un' Librajo di Venezia nello stesso anno, e nemmeno l' altro 1564 di Pio IV. parimente stampato, e ristampato qui colle Regole aggiunte dalla Corte Romana, perchè anche in quelli si vuol introdurre *la licenza* dell' Ordinario, o dell' Inquisitore per istampare. Imperciocchè la Congregazione è un Magistrato per Roma, e non per Venezia; e la stampa, e la ristampa di un libro in Venezia non ha vigore di accettazione dei Decreti, e delle dottrine in quello inserite. Si stampano anche i Bollarj, e ne seguirà per questo, che tutte quelle immense Bolle s' intendano ricevute? Così i Concilj, tanti Libri di Morale, il Bellarmino, il Sanchez, il Busembaum, ed altri autori. Si diranno perciò ammessi tutti quei Concilj, accordata al Papa la superiorità nel Temporale de' Principi, fatto lecito ogni atto, anche illecito tra

Coniugati, e permesso il Regicidio? Si stamparono negli anni passati anco gl' Indici di Roma. Ne è venuta per questo la conseguenza, che fosse abolito l' Indice pubblicato nel 1596, e che s' intendessero ricevute le proibizioni aggiunte da Roma? Fu creduto, che quel cotale fosse un Libro da Commercio, e fu lasciato stampare. Ma l' esperienza avendo insegnato, che la permissione di un male usata dalla industria Ecclesiastica tendeva a chiudere la circolazione a tre mille, fu rivocata la licenza, e fatto stampare nuovamente l' Indice vecchio del Concordato 1596, che solo può dar norma in questa materia alle coscienze de' Sudditi. E questa risoluzione fatta collo stesso Decreto 3 Agosto 1765 si riconosce per legittima, e giusta del Memoriale medesimo 22 Novembre 1766 della Corte di Roma. L' accettazione, dunque e la pubblicazione giuridica è quella, che obbliga, siccome anco di sopra si è detto, e fu provato da gravissimi autori, e specialmente dall' insigne van Espen. Quanto sia poi alli Capitoli fatti dall' Università de' Librai, e confermati dal Nunzio, dal Patriarca, e dall' Inquisitore nel 1567, hanno essi tutto il lor fondamento nell' opera scritta dal Sig^r Cardinale Albizzi contro Fra Paolo, anzi contro questo Governo. Perciò una tale autorità non è di veruna fede, e non può essere accolta con molto favore in Venezia. Non si scorge poi nemmeno per la citazione medesima, che si legge nel Promemoria, cosa contengano essi Capitoli nel proposito presente. Se per altro si citano con fine di mostrare l' ingerenza Ecclesiastica in quest' Arte, perchè li ha confermati con suo decreto, si risponde che tale conferma non fa prova di legittima autorità, perchè gli Ecclesiastici a lor talento per lo stesso modo possono confermare tutti gli Statuti del Mondo, li Contratti Civili, e anco l' Alcorano. Ciò si fa da loro per arrogare a se ogni materia. Non pretendono i Papi di Confermare in oggi anco gl' Imperadori, quando anticamente gl' Imperadori confermavano i Papi? Non viene per questo, che senza il Papa non possono essere eletti? Nell' ultima Dieta dell' Imperio non si volle nemmeno ammettere il Nunzio, perchè gli Elettori conobbero, che il Papa non dovea aver parte in quella elezione. Venendo finalmente ai Decreti dell' Inquisizione di Venezia 1558, e 1582, per insinuarsi nelle Dogane è noto ad ognuno, che essendosi in esse introdotti con Pubblica condiscendenza li Padri Inquisitori ne furono anco qualche tempo dopo rimossi per il loro indiscreto procedere, e che colle due Leggi del Senato 1631, 2 Gennaro, e 1653, 24 Settembre, ne sono tuttavia tenuti lontani; il che prova la inefficacia di cotali Decreti. E se ha bastato nè tempi andati, e basta oggidì la revisione del solo Deputato dal Principe anche per gli oggetti della Religione, perchè quei Libri vadano in Commercio, e sotto gli occhj di tutti, perchè non potrà bastare, perchè siano anco ristampati? L' un modo sebben' è diverso dall' altro, l' effetto però è lo stesso per mandarlo alla cognizione degli uomini. Li Decreti poi del Santo Offizio 1660, 23 Novembre, e 1683, 23 Giugno, e 16 Luglio, i quali prescrivono la Licenza, o la Fede degli Inquisitori prima di stamparsi cosa alcuna furono messi a campo la prima volta nel 1688 dal Padre Rovetta Bresciano Inquisitore di Venezia, che fu fatto Vescovo di Lesina: in premio di aver fatto un tentativo simile a questo. Di essi prima di allora non si era intesa notizia veruna, e furono anco allora tenuti per falsi, e per nulli, perchè davano a questi Frati ciò che è del Magistrato Pubblico, e facevano Giudice l' Inquisitore, quando è soltanto Ministro nella incombenza della Revisione. L' Autorità del Principe non è prescrivibile nella minima delle azioni, che le competono; altrimenti cessarebbe d' esser Principe. La Chiesa in altri tempi o per concessione, o per acquiescenza de' Principi stese la mano, come riflette il Fleury, nelli giudizj Civili, nelle Arti Teatrali, negli Spettacoli pubblici, nella creazione dei Tutori, ai Minori e ai Mentecatti, nella detenzione dei

Prigioni, nell' impiego del denaro pubblico, ne' Testamenti, nelle Usure, nei Contratti. Ne fece Canoni, e Decreti sopra queste materie. Ne viene per questo la conseguenza, che ella ne avesse un diritto proprio di governarle nel Foro esteriore, e che possa a suo talento ripigliarlo sotto pretesto d' impedire i danni, che possono derivare alla Religione? Non certamente, perchè la sua autorità è tutta spirituale, e deve usarla nel Foro dell' Anima, e per li mezzi, che le furono dati da Cristo Signor Nostro, e additati dagli Apostoli Santi.

Il decimo argomento è dedotto dagli Atti, Leggi, e Decreti della Repubblica fatti in varj tempi per esiggere dai Padri Inquisitori la revisione di ciò, che deve stamparsi, in punto di Religione, supponendo, che tali Decreti essendo venuti al mondo dopo quelli fatti dalla Corte di Roma siano in certa guisa figli del Concilio Lateranense, ne comandino la di lui esecuzione, e tolgano al Senato per trasferire negli Ecclesiastici la facoltà di destinare si fatti Revisori; e tutto ciò per la massima addotta dalli Cortigiani, che li Principi devono seguire, e far osservare li giudizj, e le Leggi della Chiesa.

Si risponde a uno a uno dei documenti citati con quella esatezza di Epoche, che l' Autore diligentissimo vuole negli altri, ma non osserva in se stesso. L' Atto de' Capi del Consiglio de' Dieci 1516, in cui si fa buoni l' esame, anzi la concessione fatta dal Patriarca, e dall' Inquisitore per la stampa di un Libro, non è gia un Decreto, ovvero una Formola, come suppone l' Autore, ma una di quelle Licenze, che dava allora quel Tribunale. Non si vede poi, donde sia cavata, e sarà forse un unico esempio, che non ha vigore di Legge, e che è contradetto e distrutto manifestamente da infiniti altri essemplari di tenore affatto contrario, che si rincontrano nei libri vecchj stampati, e ne' registri Pubblici di quei tempi. E se quella Licenza fosse figlia, o una conseguenza del Lateranense Concilio, si domanda, perchè questo Concilio non si nomina in essa, e non si vede mai giuridicamente pubblicato? E se quella fu una Formola per metterlo in esecuzione, perchè non fu in progresso continuata? Anco i Giuristi più meschini sanno, che per fondare un Jus con il possesso non basta, che si principj a metterlo in pratica, ma che è necessario continuare; altrimenti la stessa pratica senza la debita continuazione si ha, come mai fosse stata per la ragione da loro addotta, che non si dice nato chi subito è morto. Inoltre si rifletta, che ciò, che quei accorda il Tribunale de' Capi del Consiglio de' Dieci, è concessione sua, e non d' altri; e però limitabile, e revocabile ad arbitrio suo, se giusta causa intervenisse di farlo. E si nega assolutamente, che un Decreto fatto da una Potestà posteriore a quello di un' altra induca la conseguenza, che il secondo prenda vigore, e sussistenza dal primo. Le Potestà essendo da Dio distinte con diversità di Uffizj, ognuna provvede ai suoi bisogni, secondo i proprj rispetti, e la sola somiglianza del provvedimento non rende l' una serva dell' altra. Quanti Canoni non fece la Chiesa in sequela delle Leggi Imperiali, e quante Leggi non fecero gl' Imperadori in sequela degli ordinamenti Canonici? Se l' anzianità del tempo che è cosa accidentale cagionasse questi effetti, i Romani sarebbero divenuti servi dei Greci, perchè da loro presero le Leggi, e così Norimberga de' Veneziani. Molte Chiese specialmente nei primi Secoli presero da altre, e riportarono nel proprio Codice l' ordine, e i regolamenti della disciplina. Ciò fecero l' Africana, la Francese, e quella stessa di Roma, siccome è noto per la Storia Ecclesiastica. Ma non per questo alcuna di esse si sognò mai di diventar Figlia, o serva dell' altra. Tutte sapevano di aver sortita una egual parte di Sacerdozio nella cura del Gregge Cristiano, siccome i Principi Supremi conoscono di aver sortita una egual parte d' Imperio sopra i popoli a se commessi. Nemmeno è l' autore favorito dalla Terminazione dei Riformatori 1562, perchè nemmeno essa fà parola del Concilio Lateranense, nè poteva farla non essendo qui giuridicamente accettato. Si legga anzi attentamente questa Carta, che è la pietra fondamentale della Revisione data dal Padre Inquisitore, e si vedrà a chiare note, che l' Inquisitore non è introdotto per autorità di Concilio alcuno, o di Papa, ma per quella sola di Principe: Che non al solo Inquisitore si da' questa Incombenza, ma ancora ai suoi Vicarj, e alle altre persone Ecclesiastiche, le quali abbiano carico al Tribunal dell' Inquisizione: Che il metodo anteriore al 1562 lasciava libertà allo Stampatore di far vedere le opere *da chi più gli piaceva*: Che inavvenire si vogliono persone elette da *Noi*, cioè dal Magistrato. Che allora si stabilirono tre Revisori, e non due: Che un *bezzo* per Carta fu loro accordato di Mercede, vale a dire con stipendio per tale fatica, rendendoli così tutti eguali. Questo documento solo ben considerato è bastante a confutare tutti gli argomenti introdotti dall'autore del Promemoria. Molto meno ancora lo favorisce il Decreto del Senato 11 Maggio 1603; in cui si dice, che li Revisori *deputati saranno* l' Inquisitore, ed uno de' Segretarj Pubblici, tolto il Lettor Pubblico, che era il terzo Revisore. Questa Legge, che è la prima del Senato nel proposito della Revisione, al pari della Terminazione de' Riformatori stà contro l' autore; perchè nemmen ella prende sostanza dal Concilio, ovvero dal Concordato, e prova anzi, che quanto alla deputazione de' Revisori per le stampe la facoltà continuò sempre liberamente nel Magistrato Civile, e non in altri, come a quello, a cui appartiene la giurisdizione, e il governo sopra l' Arte della Stampa. Si noti inoltre la parola *saranno*, la quale predicando di tempo futuro denota piuttosto una deputazione nuova, che la confermazione di una antica; e si rifletta all' altra *deputati*, la qual ci presenta la deputazione, che fa il Principe, e non quella di un' altro. Più a cotali deputati si da l' obbligo del giuramento. Il giuramento importa subordinazione, e soggezione ad un superiore; il che maggiormente dimostra la dipendenza dell' Inquisitore dal Principe in questa incombenza. Si cita poi dall' autore una questione mossa da Paulo V. nel 1615; e una riposta fatta dare dal Senato al Nunzio con promessa di mantenere la facoltà della Revisione negl' Inquisitori. Manco male, che egli non cita il fonte di questa sua erudizione; poichè si nega assolutamente questo fatto, di cui non apparisce vestigio negli Archivj Pubblici, che sono fonti assai più esatti, e più veri di quelli dai quali egli l' avrà cavata; non essendo probabile, che se l' abbia immaginata, quando sia uomo d' onore. Avrebbe con più verità potuta citare l' altra controversia mossa da Paulo V. dieci anni prima, cioè nel 1605, e terminata con tanta gloria dalla Repubblica nel 1607, quando senza far uso dell' Inquisitore si stamparono moltissimi Libri con la revisione di alcuni Teologi, che furono dal Governo particolarmente deputati. E pure a quel Pontefice gelosissimo de' suoi diritti non parve di trovarne alcuno per se in questo proposito, nè in Bolle di Papi, nè in Concilj, nè in Concordati, nè in Leggi Venete, o Forastieri. Non giova al suo intento nemmeno il Decreto 17 Settembre 1622; non essendo quello che una ripetizione in questa parte dell' altro 1603; siccome apparisce dal suo proemio. Anzi comincia dall' intimare, che un tal ordine sussiste per *deliberazione di questo Consiglio*, cioè del Senato, e non del Papa, o del suo Concilio di Laterano. Lo stesso può dirsi dell' altro Decreto 24 Settembre 1653, perchè ancor questo si riferisce alla disposizione dei precedenti, e non fa menzione di Concilio veruno. Non sono parimente di gran soccorso alla pretesa Romana le due Terminazioni de' Riformatori 1655, 4 Febbraro, e 1665, 9 Maggio, per le quali è prescritta la Fede de' Padri Inquisitori prima di stamparsi cosa alcuna. Poichè nemmeno queste si fondano in sanzione Ecclesiastica, ed essendo figlie dei soli Decreti Pubblici a quelli solamente devono riferirsi, e non possono attribuire alle loro Paternità maggiore ispezione di quella, che ha Comandata il Senato, essendo il Magistrato in questo affare un semplice Delegato, che non può uscire dai termini della sua delegazione. La differenza parimenti insorta nel 1688, e continuata per lo spazio di sette anni sta contro l' autore. Imperciocchè il punto vero della questione non era la Fede, ma l' *Imprimatur*, che aveva introdotto l' Inquisitore. La Fede lo costituisce Ministro; ma l' *Imprimatur* lo faceva compagno del Magistrato, essendo un termine significativo di autorità. Anco in allora riuscì al Padre Inquisitore d' impiegare gli uffizj della Corte di Roma a favore della sua pretesa, e furono adoperati quasi li medesimi argomenti di oggidì per sostenerla, siccome appare da un Memoriale del Nunzio 11 Gennajo 1693. Ma con Decreto 29 Settembre 1695 l' *Imprimatur* in fine fu abolito, restando la Fede solita, di cui si prescrisse dal Senato una formola, la qual servisse di norma così al Segretario come al frate, che sono i due Ministri della Revisione deputati dal Principe, e non da altri, rendendo ai suoi Magistrati, e non ad altri, conto della propria condotta. E se con esso Decreto fu stabilita anche la forma di nominare una tal Fede nei Mandati, o sian Licenze del Magistrato, ciò è seguito per sola deliberazione del Principe, e non d' altri; e però a lui solo compete l' interpretarla, o modificarla. Fu instituita per regola del Magistrato nell' esprimere il nome dei Revisori voluto dal Concordato 1596; di cui qui appresso si parlerà. Si notarono l' Inquisitore, e il Segretario, perchè allora non esistevano altri Revisori, nè per questo è tolto al Senato l' arbitrio di aggiungerne quanti a lui piace. E per altro falsa l' asserzione dell' autore, che in quei sette anni siano stati oziosi li Torchj Veneti, perchè si trovano molti libri stampati nello Stato in quel frattempo. E poi ancor sagace l' industria sua di chiamar *diritto di revisione* quello, che è ministerio per ritornare per gradi all' *Imprimatur*, cioè ad una veste di autorità. Pretende finalmente rinnovata nel 1725, 15 Gennaro, la Legge 1653, e questa rinnovazione non fa per lui certamente prova maggiore di quella della Legge 1653. Tutta questa catena pertanto di Atti, Leggi, e Decreti Pubblici in luogo di esser Figlia, o serva della Bolla di Leon X., o di altra Costituzione Forastiera mostra anzi l' avvertenza sempre usata dal Governo di declinare da qualunque regolamento ecclesiastico, e di mantenere dipendente dalla sola Potestà Secolare questa preziosa parte del suo Commercio. Quanto sia infine alla massima generale de' Cortigiani replicatamente ricordata nelle loro Scritture e male applicata all' argomento presente, che i sovrani tengono obbligo di Seguire, e far osservare i Giudizj, e le Leggi della Chiesa; la Repubblica, che è Governo *veramente Cattolico;* seguendo l' esempio de' Suoi Maggiori, e di altri Santissimi, e religiosissimi Principi ha sempre distinte le materie di Fede da quelle di Disciplina, e di Giurisdizione. Nelle prime ella si ha fatto un impegno cospicuo in tutti i tempi di ricevere, e far osservare esattamente le definizioni dei Sacri Concilj Generali, dalla unione de' quali è rappresentata la Santa Chiesa, e quelle ancora dei Sommi Pontefici promulgate nella debita forma della Cattedra, come dicono i Teologi. Ma nelle Seconde ella si è creduta in dovere di conservare illese le ragioni della propria Sovranità, li Riti, e le costumanze lodevoli de' suoi Stati. E invero come mai potrebbe un Principe ammettere per esempio la costituzione *Unam Sanctam* di Bonifazio VIII.; che stabilisce la superiorità del Papa nel Temporale dei Principi; la *Bolla in Coena Domini*, che per altro modo sovverte tutte le Polizie della Terra; il *Mare Magnum* delle Concessioni fatte ai Regolari, che ha ingoiata quasi affatto l' autorità de' Vescovi, gran porzione de' Tributi Pubblici, e la miglior parte delle sostanze de' Laici; le Decretali, che arrogano alla Dataria Romana le disposizioni de' Benefizj anche di Giuspadronato; e quelle, che estendono la Immunità Ecclesiastica sino alle Concubine dei frati?

Li Principi eziandio li più timidi, e Santi si sono opposti a sì fatte esorbitanze per il debito, che hanno, di tramandare illesa ai suoi successori la potestà ricevuta da Dio, di allontanare ogni oppressione da suoi sudditi, di render loro giustizia, e di mantenere la Pubblica tranquillità. Per queste ragioni è stato introdotto il Regio *Exequatur* in tutti gli stati *veramente Cattolici*, onde aprire, o chiudere la porta alla Carte di Fuori, avendo l' esperienza fatto conoscere, che altro è Chiesa di Roma, ed altro Corte; altro la Santa Sede Apostolica; ed altro la Dataria, Cancellaria, e Camera Pontificia. Per queste medesime ragioni lo stesso Concilio di Trento non è in osservanza in molti capi di Disciplina non solo nelle Provincie Oltramontane, ma ancora nel Dominio Veneto, come sono quelli, che riguardano li debiti Civili degli Ecclesiastici, le visite degli Ospitali, la commutazione de' Testamenti, le amministrazioni delle Scuole, i Monti di Pietà, l' esame de' Notaj, il castigo degli Adulteri, e delle Concubine, li Sinodi Provinciali, la pubblicazione delle Scommuniche, la punizione de' Regolari dimoranti fuori del Chiostro, l' economia de' Monasteri, le pene pecuniarie, la confiscazione de' beni alli Duellisti, e somiglianti Decreti, tra i quali l' autore del Promemoria non dovrebbe più scandalizzarsi, se sente francamente annoverato ancora quello delle Stampe, che pure non abbraccia tutti gli oggetti della sua impresa. Egli, come altrove si è detto, non parla che de' Libri soli di Sacro Argomento, e ne commette l' esame agli ordinarj. Li Prelati Veneti non ne presero mai ingerenza per l' attenzione usata dal Magistrato; e se mai avessero tentato di poner la falce in questa messe, li primi a sostenere l' inosservanza del Concilio, e a discacciarli col braccio del Principe sarebbero stati i Padri Inquisitori medesimi, i quali in caso tale sarebbero venuti in campo col soccorso delle Leggi Pubbliche, e colla veste di Ministri del Principe, e non di Roma. Così a misura de' loro interessi fanno valere, e non valere tutte le Leggi del Mondo.

Promem. Rom. Art. XXXVI. Memor^e. 22 Nov^e. 1766.

L' undecimo argomento è tratto dal Capitolo IV. del Concordato 1596; il quale ordina, che nei Libri sia stampata la Licenza solita del Magistrato con *i nomi* di quelli averanno revisto, ed approvato detti Libri, *siccome è disposto per le leggi*, pretendendo, che sotto questo nome di Leggi si comprendano tanto le ordinazioni Ecclesiastiche, quanto le Civile della Repubblica, che dispongono a favore del Padre Inquisitore.

Si risponde, che il nome di Leggi come imperioso e significativo della forza Civile dell' Imperio, fu aborrito dalla Chiesa, la quale ha dato ai suoi regolamenti il nome più modesto di Canoni; e che nel senso commune, e naturale, la Legge è propria de' soli Principi, che sono i Legislatori Terreni. Però in questo Capo del Concordato il nome di Leggi stà in favore della Repubblica, e non degli Ecclesiastici. E quando un Principe vuol dar vigore di Legge a qualche ordinamento della Chiesa, lo fà con atto espresso, e con cognizione della cosa, che ammette. Qui non fu fatto nè l' uno, nè l' altro a favore dei Decreti Pontificj, che vogliono l' Inquisitore Giudice della Fede privativamente ad ogni altro nelle opere da stamparsi; e però non sono attendibili, nè possono venire sotto il nome di Leggi se non le Leggi della Repubblica. Lo scopo vero, ed ingenuo di questo Capo bene esaminato, e senza passione, o sofismo, è quello d' impedire le Stampe arbitrarie, che si fanno dai Libraj; e si vuol espresso *il nome* de' Revisori Pubblici per togliere le revisioni privati, che a proprio talento si procuravano dagli autori, e dai Libraj, come ci assicura la Terminazione 1562, dalle quali ne sorgevano molti inconvenienti. Le leggi poi anteriori al Concordato circa i Revisori de' Libri sono quella 1526, 29 Gennaro, del Consiglio de' Dieci, in cui la facoltà di destinare i Revisori è data ai Capi di quel Consiglio, ai quali in allora era raccomandata l' Arte della Stampa, e non erano legati a condizion di persone, ma al solo numero di due almeno col debito di riferir l' *opinion sua in scriptis cum juramento.* L' altra legge era quella 1544, 30 Decembre, dello stesso Consiglio de' Dieci, la qual raccomanda la Revisione de' Libri alli Riformatori dello Studio di Padova, perchè li *vedano*, o li *facciano vedere*. La terza finalmente era la citata Terminazione 1562 di essi Riformatori, i quali in luogo di destinare di volta in volta i Revisori, e le mercedi per cadaun Libro, cosa per se fastidiosa, fecero tre Revisori stabili, uno Ecclesiastico, uno Lettore Pubblico, e uno Segretario con l' assegnamento del Bezzo per Foglio; alla qual terminazione si riferisce poi anco un Decreto 1593, 12 Maggio, del Consiglio de' Dieci. Queste pertanto essendo le Leggi anteriori al Concordato devono per conseguenza essere anco quelle intese dal medesimo, e non altre. In esse non si pianta fondamento in ordinazione veruna Ecclesiastica, nè il Principe li spoglia dell' arbitrio di conferire tale incombenza a chè più gli piace. Dunque è chiaro, che il Concordato si riferisce a quelle, e che non limita, ne poteva limitare una tale autorità, che anzi fu resa salva dalla studiata generalità de' termini, coi quali si espresse appunto nel Capo Quarto. E se quelle parole avessero fatto effetto di limitarla, il Principe non avrebbe potuto far poi il minimo cangiamento in niuno dei Revisori, e la Corte attentissima ai suoi vantaggi avrebbe alzata le grida, quando senza ricevere, nè attendere il di lei consenso il Senato da se levò il terzo Revisore, che era il Lettor Pubblico di Filosofia. E pure ciò seguì in molta vicinanza del Concordato, mentre dal Settembre 1596 sino al Maggio 1603, non erano corsi che sei anni, e sette mesi circa. Le avrebbe alzate nel 1623, quando a fronte della ripugnanza del Padre Inquisitore fu data la licenza di stampare la storia di Andrea Morosini. Così nel 1624, quando il Senato ammonì esso Padre, e gli comandò di render conto ai Riformatori dello Studio di Padova e non ad altri nel fatto della revisione de' Libri.

Queste Leggi pertanto, e quelle, che vennero di poi, mostrano anzi la libertà, e la potestà legislativa del Principe; e quante più sono, tanto più ne provano l' esercizio. Perciò in vigore di questo Capitolo basta, che nelle Licenze del Magistrato sia espresso il nome de' Revisori, e non più. E se avesse forza di stabilire il Segretario, e il Padre Inquisitore per Revisori perpetui de' Libri con gius privativo, ne verrebbe l' effetto terribile, che il poterli o non poterli stampare dipenderebbe dall' arbitrio loro. Il Segretario certamente non ha questa pretesa, nè professa alcun jus quesito in quel Concordato. Nè di tanto errore possono imputarsi quegli avveduti Senatori intervenuti nel medesimo, i quali avendo ristretta colle molte avvertenze apposte la facoltà di proibire nel Tribunale Ecclesiastico, e di prender ingerenza nelle Stampe sarebbero stati poi così ciechi di abbandonare alla volontà di un solo, Frate, e Ministro anco di Roma il destino di questo Traffico, e de' suoi Mercadanti. Quando tale fosse l' effetto, il Padre Inquisitore avrebbe conseguito un Tribunale da se solo, e un Regno proprio, e un' altra Giurisdizione in casa del Principe feracissima di gravissimi disturbi, perchè chiuderebbe la porta ai Libri, che difendono la ragioni de' Sovrani, e la spallancherebbe agli altri, che le opprimono, ed ampliano all' infinito le pretensioni degli Ecclesiastici, cosicchè per gradi il Mondo ritornerebbe allo stato della ignoranza, o non avverrebbe altra scienza se non quella, che fosse commoda agl' interessi del Clero. Questo Capitolo dunque lasciò l' Inquisitore, e gli altri Revisori nella qualità, e condizione in cui si trovavano allora, cioè di ministri dipendenti dalle Leggi della Repubblica, e destinati dal Magistrato, sociabili con altri, e amovibili ancora. Nè un Magistrato, che ha autorità limitata, e rivocabile da un superiore, che è il Senato, poteva dar loro un potere illimitato e irrevocabile. Adunque esso capitolo è pienamente eseguito, quando nelle Licenze de' Riformatori sono spiegati i nomi di coloro, che dalle Leggi sono destinati alla Revisione.

Promem. Romano. Art. XLVII.

Il duodecimo argomento esibisce un sillogismo in forma secondo l' uso delle Scuole. La maggiore è, che la deputazione in ogni causa deve farsi da quelli, ai quali per diritto spetta la Cognizione. La minore è, che appartiene alla Chiesa per instituzione Divina il conoscere, e decidere come Giudice legittimo, e Tribunal competente le materie di Fede. La conseguenza è, che dunque alla Chiesa e non ai Principi appartiene il deputare le persone, che rivedano, ed approvino i libri in punto di Fede, e di Religione.

Si risponde brevemente, che siamo d' accordo nella maggiore, e nella minore, ma che si nega la conseguenza: Perchè la deputazione di Revisori per le Stampe non è una deputazione di Giudici in Causa di Fede, e di Religione, come suppone accortamente l' autore, ma una destinazione di Ministri, i quali soltanto guardano, se nel Libro si contiene cosa offensiva al Dogma, come consta ad evidenza dal testo delle Leggi, e del fatto. E non trovandola lo approvano col farne l' attestato consueto, e trovandola lo disapprovano col negare esso attestato. E in questo senso si dice il loro approvare, e disapprovare. Nè questa visione, o revisione, com' è chiamata dalle Leggi, tiene luogo di giudizio formale, ma di semplice opinione. Poichè se fosse giudizio Canonico, il Padre Inquisitore con assurdità intolerabile sarebbe fatto eguale, ed anche superiore a Monsignor Patriarca nel maneggio di quelle Chiavi Celesti, che Gesù Cristo vero, e solo nostro Signore, ha volute affidare soltanto agli Apostoli Suoi, ed ai Vescovi lor Successori. Inoltre ne seguirebbe un altro inconveniente anco nell' ordine stesso Forense della Chiesa, poichè il Padre Inquisitore non potrebbe condannare sedente al Santo Offizio il Libro da se approvato con tale giudizio, siccome talvolta è avvenuto; ma sarebbe necessità di attendere la condanna da un Tribunale superiore al suo, e forse instituirlo, perchè l' Inquisizione del Santo Offizio in questo Dominio è il Giudice definitivo nella condanna de' Libri per materia di Fede, siccome dispone il Capitolo Settimo del Concordato 1596. L' approvare dunque, e disapprovare di questi Revisori deriva da instituzione umana e non Divina, e nello Stato della Repubblica Veneta è ministero, e non autorità in quel modo stesso, che si farebbe approvare la sodezza di una Fabbrica dall' Architetto, la bontà di un Fucile dall' Artigliere, uno stromento da un suonatore, dove ciascuno in sua scienza dà un giudizio di Perito, e non di Giudice, di discernimento e non di giurisdizione.

Promem. Rom. Art. XLVI. XLVIII. XLIX. L. LI. LII. e Memor^e^, 22 Nov^e^. 1766.

Il decimoterzo argomento finalmente si piglia dall' esempio di alcuni antichi Principi, che lasciarono alla decisione della Chiesa la condanna dei Libri in punto di religione, e dall' autorità di alcuni Santi, e dotti Scrittori, che vissero nei secoli bassi, e che furono d' opinione di doversi riferire al Papa i disordini in materia di Fede, e di assoggettarne al di lui esame gli scritti, che si vogliono divolgare.

Si risponde, che la questione presente non versa sulla facoltà di condannare, ma in quella di rivedere i Libri in punto di Religione. Però gli esempj addotti non hanno che fare più della luna coi gamberi. La condanna in punto di Religione, che è giudizio, e atto giurisdizionale, fu lasciata alla Chiesa anco dalla Repubblica di Venezia, siccome appare cospicuamente dall' artic. VII. dello stesso Concordato, e delle condanne fatte in questo Santo Uffizio in relazione al medesimo, delle quali industriosamente non se ne cita pur una. E se l' Inquisitore in questo farà le parti sue, farà cosa utile al Servizio di Dio, e grata ad un Principe religioso, qual' è appunto questa Repubblica. Si potevano per altro citare dall' autore gli esempi ancora di quegl' Imperatori, che lasciarono bensì alla Chiesa la censura Canonica, cioè il decidere delle opinioni, ma che vollero far essi di propria autorità il divieto de' Libri, e la condanna dell' incendio loro, che è pena temporale. E quanto all' opinione dei privati Scrittori sebben essa è rispettabile, non fa però Legge per chi si sia, e molto meno per i Principi supremi, che non hanno Superiore dopo Dio. Che i disordini in punto di Fede siano recati a notizia del Pontefice, è cosa buona, e anco debita, perchè egli tiene il primo luogo tra i Sacri Pastori, affinchè colla sua autorità, col suo consiglio, e coll' opera de' Vescovi suoi Confratelli trovi il rimedio occorrente. Ma non si sa poi come conciliare il Santo rigore, che si mostra per mondare gli altrui stati dai Libri proibiti, colla facilità, che si vede introdotta di venderli in Roma. Non è libro, quantunque proibito, e scellerato, che non si trovi vendibile in quella Città sotto il Manto di alcune Concessioni Apostoliche. Se queste siano un preservativo benedetto per impedire le contaminazioni degli spiriti, e se in ciò si contenga mistero alcuno di Fede, o piuttosto di Traffico, essendo varia l' opinione degli uomini, se ne rimmette ai più dotti, e meno interessati la spiegazione.

Dalle cose pertanto esposte ognuno agevolmente comprende, che alcuni degli argomenti adoperati nelle Romane Scritture niente hanno che fare colla questione immaginata da quei Cortigiani, e che gli altri, e per il Diritto, e per il fatto agiscono anzi contro di loro. Ora è tempo di mostrare, che l' Inquisitore Veneto in questa incombenza è Ministro deputato, e dipendente dal solo Principe in vigore di suo mandato; il che si farà colla maggior brevità, e con poca fatica.

Si è già veduto, che in tale inspezione egli non è collocato per ordinazione Divina; o per Canone alcuno legittimamente ricevuto. Anzi si è mostrato, che la sua instituzione prende radice, e sostanza dalla sola Legge del Principe, la quale lo ha deputato non per Giudice, ma per Ministro, e con mercede assegnata. Le leggi, che fanno la prova indubitata di una tale deputazione, sono quelle citate dal Promemoria medesimo, cioè la Terminazione de' Riformatori 1562, e li Decreti del Senato 1603, 1622, 1653, e 1695. A questi si possono aggiungere ancora li Decreti 1623, 19 Maggio, e 1624, 3 Decembre, dello stesso Senato, poichè in ambedue lucidamente l' Inquisitore nella qualità di Revisore di Libri è dichiarato e riconosciuto Ministro della Repubblica, e non di altra Potestà; si correggono gli arbitrj, che egli commetteva o negando l' attestato consueto per le stampe, o eccedendo nella esazione delle sue mercedi; e si obliga a render conto delle difficoltà, che incontrasse, al Magistrato come a suo Superiore in questa incombenza. Ma giovava all' autore di dissimularli come poco favorevoli alla sue impresa, e noi li aggiungeremo nel fine di queste osservazioni per suo conforto. Lo stesso Maggior Consiglio colla Legge 1628, 25 Settembre, nell' atto di raccomandare la materia delle Stampe al Magistrato sopra la Biastema dichiarò, che la *Revisione*, e *la Licenza* appartiene ai Riformatori. E sebbene nel 1688 il Padre Rovetta mosse arditamente la pretesa dell' *Imprimatur*, nella quale impegnò gli Uffizj della Corte di Roma, e ne ottenne un Vescovato; il Senato nondimeno rimise l' Inquisitore al Magistrato, di cui lo riconosceva Ministro, nè quella Paternità sebben Reverendissima ebbe coraggio di sottrarsi dall' ubbidienza a tal Superiore. Tutto ciò prova ad evidenza, che un simile Revisore non conosce della dottrina di un Libro nel Foro Spirituale, e non fa giudizio Canonico, ma che indaga estragiudicialmente, e vede di un fatto per renderne conto a quello, che in tale uffizio lo ha costituito. Nè la potestà della Chiesa rimane offesa da tale provvedimento, poichè resta qual era prima, cioè libera di poter formare la sua Censura, e di pronunciare il suo giudizio Canonico non meno sopra le dottrine stampate, che sopra ogni scritto, e detto di uomo Cristiano in punto di Religione, quando proceda colle forme prescritte dai Sacri Canoni, o dai Concordati, come si è detto; e potrà sempre senza veruna difficoltà dichiare Eretico non solo un Libro, ma un uomo ancora. Il Principe nelle Stampe non giudica della dottrina Cattolica, ma conosce del fatto per mezzo de' suoi Revisori deputati, onde impedire il corso a qualunque errore, per il debito, che incombe anco ai Principi e per comando Divino, e per ragione Politica di difendere la Religione. Le Legge 1562, e successive emanarono in tempi innocenti, e furono utili, sinchè li Padri Inquisitori non abusarono della incombenza, e non la convertirono in danno del Principato. Il Principe con insigne toleranza in luogo di castigarli si contentò di usare moderazione, e di andare con temperamenti assai blandi di tempo in tempo incontro alle loro fraudi. Ma oggidì vedendo totalmente deluse le sue rette intenzioni, e fatto abuso della pietà sua, fu in necessità di venire alla provvisione promulgata a' 3 Agosto 1765. Non si vede poi, come possano derivare cattivi effetti dalla Revisione di un Prete, il quale è Teologo di una Università Cattolica, ed approvata dal Papa, e non da quella di un Frate Inquisitore, o dal suo Commissario, quando peravventura li Frati nell' assumere il gradi di Ministri non si pretendessero fatti miracolosamente participi della infallibilità Pontificia. Qui invero non sono mai stati creduti partecipi, e molto meno si crederanno inavvenire, dopocchè nel principio di Maggio decorso fu negato dal Prete Teologo l' attestato, e fu benignamente concesso dal Frate Commissario al Sig^r Conte Stefano Carli per la stampa di certo Foglio, che sovvertiva il timore dell' uomo verso Dio, e tutta l' autorità della Divina Scrittura. Il fatto nacque a un parto medesimo col Promemoria Romano, e il Magistrato si trovò in necessità di correggere il Frate, e di comandare al Conte una pubblica ritrattazione. Se la Fede di cotal Revisore fosse stato un giudizio Canonico, e non opinione, avrebbe egli autorizzata una bella dottrina nella Chiesa di Dio? Provvida poi si ravvisa anco la destinazione di un sacerdote secolare attesi li diversi, ed opposti sistemi, che si professano dalle Scuole de' Regolari, specialmente nelle questioni Morali, e Teologiche, dove un arcano del proprio Istituto, o lo spirito di partito inseparabile dalla umana condizione impedisce talvolta molte produzioni utili alle Scienze, e alla Società. Gli Uffizj delle Inquisizioni sono divisi quasi per eredità tra li due Ordini de' Domenicani, e dei Francescani, e tutti gli altri Regolari ne sono disgiunti. L' Inquisitore pertanto Domenicano non abbandonerà agevolmente i principj difesi dalle sue Scuole, nè il Franciscano quelle delle proprie; e l' uno, e l' altro con l' arma pubblica della Revisione possono commettere molte vendette private sopra i suoi avversarj, e sopra li medesimi suoi Confratelli, siccome tal volta è accaduto, e ne sono state fatte doglianze al Magistrato. E ragionevole all' incontro, che il Prete Revisore non essendo legato cogl' interessi di alcun partito, ed avendo meno di attaccamento colli Ministri della Corte Romana sia tutto Ministro del Magistrato, e più Confidente. Questa circostanza è quella, che più duole ai Cortigiani, perchè egli opera col lume retto della ragione, e del proprio discernimento senza parzialità, e senza attendere l' oracolo della Congregazione, come fà l' altro. La stampa, come altrove si è accennato, è un' Arte Laica, per cui in luogo de' Libri scritti a mano si communicano agli uomini le opere degli Scrittori; così che non è cambiato l' effetto, ma il modo è reso anche più facile di communicare le dottrine, e le Scienze. Prima di essa erano in uso grande i Copisti, nè si trova memoria che sopra il mestiere di questi, che pur teneva il luogo della Stampa, abbia mai la Chiesa presa ingerenza nè preteso mai di vedere le opere, che copiavano. Venuta al mondo quest' Arte verso l' anno 1460 fu considerata sempre Laica; e se gli Ecclesiastici tentarono d' introdursi per varj modi, e sotto varj pretesti, la Repubblica li volle esclusi, ben considerando le dannosissime conseguenze, che ne sarebbero derivate all' autorità sua, a questa riguardevole porzione del suo Traffico, ed ai Sudditi Suoi, che sarebbero fatti servi degl' interessi altrui, ed impediti insieme di apprendere le scienze nella loro purità. E cosa notoria, che gl' Inquisitori lasciano correre facilmente que' Libri, nei quali si conculca la fama dei Principi, si avvilisce la giurisdizione loro, e si fà il Papa padrone, e Monarca non solo delle cose Spirituali, e Divine, ma eziandio delle Temporali, e Civili, e ciò per Diritto non umano, ma Divino contro il sentimento della Scrittura Santa, e della Chiesa antica. Però il lasciar, che trovino corso le dottrine solamente dei Romani, e nascondere gli autori, che quelle confutano, e difendono i Principi, sarebbe lo stesso che voler ruinare, perchè il mondo s' imbeverebbe di sediziose opinioni. Posto pertanto il negozio in questi termini si trova la Repubblica in una invincibile necessità di non poter far atto, che offenda in minima parte la libertà del suo governo. Mossa da questa necessità medesima ella ha sempre governata questa materia indipendentemente da ogni stabilimento Ecclesiastico, nè ha voluto legare a Concordati il suo Diritto Supremo. Per la qual ragione il Concordato 1596 non da al Padre Inquisitore nella revisione de Libri prerogativa alcuna particolare, e distinta dagli altri Revisori, ma lo lascia alla comun condizione, qual lo ha trovato, cioè capace di compagni, e amovibile ancora, quando non corrisponda all' oggetto delle Pubbliche intenzioni. Li due altri Concordati 1289, e 1551, che formano la regola dell' Uffizio Inquisitoriale in questo Dominio, non contengono parola nel proposito de' Libri, e non conferiscono sopra di essi al Padre Inquisitore facoltà alcuna particolare. Il Breve di sua elezione esibito al Governo non fà questo effetto, ed egli non può far uso di autorità non conosciuta dal Principe. Nemmeno l' autorità di Padre Maestro nella sua Religione non lo autorizza a questo; perchè sarebbero autorizzati tutti i Frati Maestri. Le Regole dell' Indice, che potrebbero in parte soccorrerlo, non hanno maggior forza in questo Dominio, nè intelligenza diversa di quella, che da loro il Concordato 1596; il quale in questa parte non stabilisce altro, che l' espressione dei nomi di chi ha revisto il Mandato dei Riformatori, come si è veduto. L' oggetto dunque arcano del tentativo presente non è di ricuperar al Padre Inquisitore cosa propria, e legittima, la qual fosse perduta, o diminuita, ma di mettere in schiavitù il Governo per far proprio ciò, che è del Principe, per diventar di Ministro Giudice, per ritornare nelle Dogane, e impadronirisi di tutto. Quando la revisione fosse accordata al Padre Inquisitore come sua propria, non renderebbe più conto al Magistrato, come è tenuto per le Leggi, ma a Roma, ed avrebbe in mano un modo facile di frangere li Concordati, come ha tentato, e di far valere tutte le proibizioni Romane a suo *Arbitrio*. In somma egli non sarebbe più Ministro del Magistrato, ma Tribunale della Corte Romana, uomo non più dipendente, ma indipendente, inamovibile, Giudice, e Sovrano non meno della dottrina, che del traffico. In tal guisa egli solo avrebbe quel potere, che non ha tutto il Tribunale del Santo Officio unito con l' assistenza del Magistrato Secolare. Ognuno consideri, se la prudenza degli antichi Legislatori ha voluto mai introdurre un effetto così terribile, e pernicioso alle massime fondamentali di questo Governo colla introduzione d' un semplice Revisore di Stampe. Questo negozio si potrebbe paragonare all' altro dell' Inquisizione contro gli Eretici, in cui essendo a principio stata accordata agli Ecclesiastici dagl' Imperadori, e dalla Repubblica una podestà cumulativa coi Magistrati Civili, essi a poco a poco se la pigliarono tutta con esclusione di questi. Entrino gli Ecclesiastici anco nella Stampa con titolo proprio, e non dipendente, e se ne proveranno gli effetti. Contro gli scrittori, e le opere loro resta nella Chiesa tuttavia intatto il giudizio, che è suo; nè la giunta di un Revisore di più, nè di cento leva a lei questo potere. Le decisioni di Fede, e Religione devono esser appoggiate all' autorità infallibile della stessa Chiesa, e non all' opinione ambulatoria, ed al giudizio arbitrario di privati Dottori, qual sarebbe in sostanza quello voluto oggidì dalla Corte di Roma.

Il Padre Inquisitore distaccato dal Tribunale del Santo Offizio non veste alcuna prerogativa nella materia de' Libri, che gli sia stata concessa da altri che dalla Repubblica. E questa prerogativa è di semplice Teologo da lei deputato, perchè colla sua perizia Teologica riconosca il fatto, e coll' attestazione assicuri il Governo per dare, o negare la permissione della Stampa. In Roma stessa la revisione è raccomandata al Padre Maestro del Sacro Palazzo, che certamente non è grado di girarchia nella Chiesa di Dio, e che però non toglie a quelle Congregazioni la facoltà di giudicare, e proibire le opere da se licenziate. In Parigi si stampano i Libri anco di argomenti Dogmatici colla sola revisione di un Dottore della Sorbona, o di un' altro Perito Ecclesiastico destinato dal Regio Guardasigilli, o dal Cancelliere del Regno. Ma non perciò que' Ministri si stimano fatti Giudici della Fede, nè quei Prelati hanno riguardo di promulgare colle lor Pastorali la Censura, e il giudizio competente alla Chiesa. Dal che è chiaro, che cotali Revisori non hanno la veste di Giudice Canonico, qual si dipinge con accortezza nel Promemoria, ma sono unicamente osservatori di quelle cose, che per loro opinione possono offendere la Religione. Il Sovrano pertanto, da cui deriva una tal facoltà, può communicarla anco ad altri, e toglierla eziandio a chi l' ha data. Non si è egli spogliato, nè poteva spogliarsi della libertà naturale d' investirne qualunque altra persona, in cui alle qualità di uomo probo, dotto, e fedele trovi congiunta la Perizia, o scienza che gli abbisogna. Il Principe per ragion del suo imperio ha dritto di regolare in quel modo, che più crede conveniente, la disciplina dello Stato suo. E questa potestà deve usarla a misura dell' esigenze, nè può ricever da altri il rimedio, che ha nelle mani, senza diminuirla. Poteva pure la Repubblica di Venezia rimovere da questa incombenza il Padre Inquisitore, che ne aveva dato il motivo, essendo indubitato per tutte le Leggi, che chi può instituire può anche destituire. Imperciocchè questo Religioso non erigge qui Tribunale sopra le opere da stamparsi nè in vigore della Potestà conferita da Cristo alla Chiesa, nè in conseguenza del Suo Inquisitoriale Offizio, nè di Concordato, o Canone ricevuto; ma le esamina nella sua Cella come Revisore, e Dottore, che si occupa in un impiego ministeriale, temporaneo, e mercenario, conferito e dipendente dalla superiorità del Magistrato Civile. Ma seguendo ella l' indole clementissima del Governo volle usare un nuovo atto di benignità, lasciandolo nella primiera incombenza, resa soltanto comune con un' altro Ministro fornito di egual dottrina, e pietà con fine di assicurare i rispetti suoi, di togliere i ritardi delle impressioni, e di non lasciare nell' *arbitrio* di un uomo solo, e dipendente dalle commissioni segrete di altro Principe il destino delle Stampe, che forma un ramo importante del proprio Commercio, e l' alimento principale di molte Arti in questa città, come sono Carta, Torchiaj, Gittatori di Caratteri, Professori di Disegno, Intagliatori in Legno, e in Rame, Copisti, Traduttori, Correttori, Legatori e Venditori di Libri.

Instituì il nuovo collo stesso diritto, e potestà, colla quale destinò il vecchio indipendentemente da qualunque ordinazione Ecclesiastica, cioè di propria libera autorità, ben conoscendo che la società d' un' altra era pericolosa, e col progresso avrebbe discacciata la prima. Così mostrò che la ispezione data a' questi Padri dal Principe non è di tal modo, che non possa riassumerla alle occorrenze; e che il Sacerdote Secolare nuovamente destinato alla revisione non è un intruso, come fu dato a credere a Monsignor Nunzio, ma che fu destinato da legittima Potestà. E se li Ministri Romani passando dal dritto d' eleggere alle qualità dell' eletto imputano d' incapacità quest' uomo, e quindi credono che si apra il corso à Libri di perniciose dottrine; mostrano di non sapere, che egli è Dottore in Sacra Teologia, e dell' ordine degli aggregati al Collegio de' Teologi di Padova, il che importa esami più rigorosi, e prove più solenni. Mostrano di non sapere, che quel Collegio di Teologi fu approvato, e autorizzato nel 1363 da Urbano V., e nel 1424 più ampiamente confermato da Martino V., ambedue Sommi Pontefici; che il Vescovo stesso è il Capo di quel Collegio; che la Laurea viene conferita per autorità Pontificia; che il Laureato dinanzi al Vescovo, e a tutto il Collegio fà la solenne professione della Fede Cattolica; che dopo un tal atto e dopo l' approvazione di un tal Collegio non può aver luogo il sospetto ingegnosamente sparso nei Memoriali prodotti, perchè la presunzione Legale, e canonica, che milita per il Revisore Teologo, non si potrebbe distruggeve che con l' evidenza de' fatti contrarj. Ma se si vorrà esaminare la persona, si troverà irreprensibile e nella dottrina e ne' costumi. Mostrano ancora di non sapere le facoltà conferite per la medesima autorità del Pontefice ai Dottori Teologi, di spiegar le Divine Scritture, di tener Cattedra di Teologia, insegnare, disputare, e altre clausole piene d' ampiezza, e d' autorità, come si vede nell' ampulloso Diploma dei Teologi Laureati, i quali finalmente altro non sono che Maestri in Religione. Adunque il Papa ha sparsi per le Provincie Cattoliche tanti Maestri di Religione, quanti furono dichiarati per di lui nome, e autorità Dottori in sacra Teologia. Ora è cosa troppo mostruosa, che il Pontefice con tanta solennità proponga Maestri in materia di Dogma, e poi non sia lecito usarli, interrogarli al bisogno, e riposare alle loro risposte: È più ancora mostruosa, che il privato possa ricever lume da loro, e operare con morale certezza dietro alle loro dottrine, e decisioni, e il Principe non possa altrettanto. Che altro ha fatto il Governo con questa destinazione, se non far scelta d' uno di que' tanti Maestri di Dogma, che il Papa stesso ha autorizzati? Si fa lo stesso nella scelta d' un Teologo Consultore, lo stesso nella scelta d' un Confessore. Basta, che abbia i caratteri d' approvazione. Sarebbe ridicolo un Vescovo, che dopo aver approvati nella sua diocesi più Confessori Sacerdoti Secolari, e Regolari non lasciasse poi ai Penitenti la libera elezione, e volesse obbligare a valersi più dei Frati che dei Preti. Dal che s' intende quanto sia irragionevole la querela, e la pretesa dei Memoriali. Pertanto il Principe quando ha destinato alla Revisione un Sacerdote Secolare, non gli ha conferita alcuna di quelle facoltà, che non possono emanare se non dal Sommo Pontefice, non gli ha conferita la Laurea Teologale, non gli ha data autorità d' interpretar le Divine Scritture, e di trattare, ed esporre in voce, o scritto le Cattoliche dottrine. Ma trovando in lui queste facoltà per approvazione d' un Collegio di Teologi, e per autorità dei Pontefici stessi, ha deliberato di valersi di lui, e di riposare con moral sicurezza alle sue risposte, ed a' suoi attestati.. È poi cosa assurda, che un Dottore in Teologia possa insignare, interpretare, disputare in Materia di Religione, e non possa mettere in iscritto il suo privato giudizio sopra un libro per quanto spetta ai Dogmi, quando venga interrogato o da un particolare, o da un Principe. Ed è assurdo parimenti, che da tanti maestri in Teologia nell' esercizio si vasto, e si geloso delle loro legittime facoltà Dottorali non s' abbia a temere alcun pericolo alla Sanità della

Religione, e s' abbia a temerlo solamente nel caso della Revisione, come le scritture di Roma accennano di temere con grave ingiuria di tutte le Università, alle quali ogni principe è tenuto di conservare i lor Privilegj.

Resta dunque concluso e per il Diritto e per il Fatto che la Revisione è ministerio e non autorità: Che qui è stabilita dalle Leggi Civili, e non da Canoni e Bolle: Che non invade gli Uffizii Sublimi del Sacerdozio, ma serve unicamente a quelli del Principato: Che un tal Ministro non decide della Dottrina, ma opina unicamente sopra le opere da Stamparsi: che non definisce il Dogna, poichè la definizione di questo appartiene alla Chiesa; Ma guarda, dove sta scritto l' errore, o l' offesa alla Religione, e la denoncia a chi è in debito di defenderla. Il primo sarebbe giudizio; il secondo è un nudo conoscimento del fatto. E se in questo fatto erra per volontà egli è responsabile a Dio, al Principe, e alla Chiesa stessa, a cui resta libera la facoltà originaria di condannare colle debite forme qualunque errore, che fosse corso. Dal che tutto ognuno in fine potrà essere convinto, che la questione non tanto è mossa alla persona, quanto al Pubblico Diritto, di cui non si può far parte all' Ecclesiastico senza toglierla al Principe, e al Magistrato, e senza esporre la libertà propria, i sudditi, e il commercio a molestissime difficoltà. Nelle contese di giurisdizione il cedere una volta dà pretensione, che sia ceduto per sempre, e chi non può ferire nel capo può ferire in un piede di ferita mortale. Venezia 3 Febbrajo 1766. M. V.

P. S.

Resterebbe a farsi alcuna osservazione sopra l' Elenco posto in fine del Promemoria, il quale contiene una serie di condanne, e proibizioni di Libri fatte dai Concilj e dai Papi con pene eziandio di fuoco in diversi tempi prima della introduzione della Stampa. Ma si vuol passare per buona tutta quella fredda leggenda, sebbene alcuni fatti sono riferiti in senso diverso dalla verità; perchè nè la Repubblica, nè alcun altro principe Cattolico ha mai negata, nè impedita, come sogna l' autore, la facoltà e il dovere della Chiesa di denunciare ai Fedeli i Libri di dottrina perniciosa alla Religione; nè questo ha che fare colla stessa questione sognata dalla sua fantasia, che è l' opera di rivederli, e non l' atto di condannarli. Anzi si potrebbe comporre un altro Elenco di varie Proibizioni fatte dai Principi, e di eccitamenti dati dal Senato Veneto ai Padri Inquisitori, purchè questi per umani rispetti, per interessi di Corte o per raggiro di Frati mancavano ai proprij doveri. Ma si lasciano queste istorie per carità Cristiana, e per non farne arrossire l' Autore, se pure un mostaccio incallito ad ogni cimento è suscettibile di vergogna. Si replica soltanto che la pena del fuoco essendo temporale, sebben talvolta fu usata dalla Chiesa, non è proprio della Chiesa, ma del Principe, che da Dio è costituito Signore del Territorio. Si potrebbe anco ricordargli, che per più secoli l' autorità Ecclesiastica non usci dal limite di condannare le dottrine perverse, e d' indicare gli autori, e i Libri, che le contenevano, lasciandone ai principi la cura della proibizione, e del castigo; e che l' aversi arrogato la pena del fuoco fuori degli stati possessi con diritto di Principe, è uno di quei tanti attentati, che ha prodotto la confusione delle due Potestà.

Si erano i Papi arrogata la pretesa di deporre anche i Re, e gl' Imperadori, e tal volta vi riuscirono per que' mezzi funesti, che si raccontano dagl' Istorici. Ne hanno perciò acquistato un legittimo diritto? E sarebbe questa una sana, e tranquilla dottrina? Ma poichè egli ama cotanto le giunte, noi lo vorremo pur gratificare, aggiungendo alla sua immensa erudizione un breve Elenco di alcuni modi tenuti dagli Ecclesiastici per insinuarsi nelle Stampe Venete, che furono repressi dalla Repubblica.

1573, 21 Novembre. In Pregadi. A Roma si difende l' Arte de' Libraj, e la Giurisdizione Pubblica per la Stampa de' Messali fatta in Venezia, che la Corte di Roma pretendeva avvocata al Solo Pontefice invigore del Decreto del Concilio di Trento.

F^a^ Roma, N° 6, e Reg° I. Esp^ti^ Roma @ 129.

1596, 4 Giugno. In Pregadi. Decreto, che leva i Privilegj detti *Motu Proprj*, che si davano in Roma ai Nostri Libraj, e fatto risponder al Papa sotto li 20 Luglio, che ciò si è fatto, perchè la Stampa è mera Laica.

Filza Roma, N° 18.

1596, 17 Agosto. In Pregadi. Offizio grave al Patriarca, che unito al Nunzio, e all' Inquisitore avea commesso ai Piovani, Frati, e Confessori di dover eseguir l' Indice Romano di Clemente VIII. colle Regole aggiunte, e detto. "Che in casa di Principe libero, come noi siamo, non si conviene operare cosa alcuna senza il nostro beneplacito."

Filza Roma, N° 18.

1612, 1 Settembre. In Pregadi. A Roma. Fatta resistenza agli Indulti e *Motu Proprj* concessi dal Pontefice, e dai Generali delle Religioni per far dipendente da loro la stampa de' Messali e Breviarj.

Filza Roma, N° 35.

1612, 5 Febbraro. In Pregadi. A Vicenza. Fatto cancellar un Privilegio dato da quel Vescovo a certo Librajo per la stampa delle cose sue con minaccia di Scommunica agli altri, che le avessero stampate.

Filza Roma, N° 35.

1623, 19 Maggio. In Pregadi. Fatta stampar la Storia di Andrea Morosini a fronte delle repugnanze più forti del Padre Inquisitore, che si riconosce in qualità di Ministro della Repubblica nella incombenza della Revisione.

Filza Roma, N° 45.

1625, 4 Novembre. Scrittura di Frà Fulgenzio, e Dottor Lonigo Consultori per attentato del Padre Inquisitore di Venezia, che fece abbrucciar in pubblico molti Libri, tra i quali le considerazioni di Frà Paolo, e le confermazioni di Frà Fulgenzio Scritte a difesa delle Leggi Pubbliche.

Tom. 4 @ 165.

1659, 22 Marzo, 5, 19 e 26 Aprile. In Pregadi. Circolari, per levar l' abuso di stampar piccole operette, come sono Sonetti, Orazioni, Spirituali, e simili cose con la sola licenza dell' Inquisitore, e si ordina quella dei Rappresentanti. Filza Roma, N° 101.

1659, 26 Aprile. In Pregadi. A Verona. Fatto carcerar uno Stampatore per un Sonetto, e stampa di Sanità sottoscritta dall' Inquisitore. Ibid.

1665, 5 Marzo. In Pregadi. Abolite le Stampe di alcuni Ordini, fatte seguire dal Padre Inquisitore per darle ai Predicatori con fine di far avvertito il popolo con termini ambigui di non praticar con Eretici, e di dover denonciar i Libri.

Filza Roma, N° 113.

1688, 1 Settembre.
1690, 5 Luglio.
1695, 29 Settembre. } In Pregadi. Rimossa la pretesa dell' *Imprimatur* introdotto dal Padre Inquisitore, perchè dinotava autorità, e licenza di Stampare.

Filze Exp^is di detti anni.

1708, 28 Luglio. In Pregadi. A Rovigo. Abolito l' *Imprimatur*, e levata l' ingerenza dei Vicarj dell' Inquisizione.

Filza Exp^is di detto anno.

1623, 19 *Maggio*. *In Pregadi*.

Ha riferito nel Collegio il Diletto Nob^r Nostro Ser Polo Morosini, che dall' Inquisizione di questa Città li è difficoltato il sottoscriversi per la permissione alla Stampa della Istoria Veneziana per ordine pubblico scritta dal già Dilettissimo Nob^r Nostro Morosini suo Fratello; dicendo la Inquisizione, che trattandose in essa di quanto successe per occasione delle controversie con Roma li anni 1605 et 1606 per causa dell' Interdetto, non vedeva come potersi fare stante massime qualche ordine, che l' aveva ricevuto in detto proposito. Nè dovendosi per questo rispetto tralasciar di stampare la detta Istoria, che contiene una veridica narrazione delle cose in diversi tempi seguite, *et l' Inquisitore non tiene autorità da altro Principe, ma da Magistrato della Repubblica Nostra di rivedere* per causa solamente di Religione le opere, che si stampano, et in quella Istoria non vi è parola, che possa pregiudicare alla Religione predetta, ma la semplice serie molto veridica, et cavata da Scritture autentiche di quanto particolarmente seguì nei suddetti anni, e *non vi è alcuna necessità della Sottoscrizione dell' Inquisitore*. Però

L' anderà parte, nonostante, che non vi sia la sottoscrizione sopradetta, così *convenendo alla dignità et autorità della Repubblica, di ordinare quello li piace si stampi nel stato di lei*, che sia commesso a chi spetta di dover con l' autorità di questo consiglio far stampare la sopradetta Istoria, e portarla col mezzo dell' Impressione alla notizia di cadauno, et vi sia nel fine di essa posta l' infrascritta Inscrizione: *Superiorum Permissu*.

F^a Roma, N° 45.

1624, 3 *Decembre, in Pregadi.*

Sono molto importanti li disordini, et gli abusi da certo tempo in qua introdotti dalli Padri Inquisitori di questa Città, et al presente con più rigore delli passati, contrarj alle Leggi Nostre, al Concordato a' 14 Settembre 1596, et a grave danno, et pregiudizio dell' Arte dei Stampatori, e Libreri, rappresentati con Scrittura ai Riformatori del Studio di Padova, et da essi passati alla consulta de' Savj del Collegio Nostro, che ora sono stati letti a quel Consiglio. Onde se non si ferma il corso a tante dannose introduzioni, si renderiano infruttuosi gli ottimi, e prudentissimi ordini del detto Consiglio con notabile danno pubblico, et dell' Arti sopradette: Però

L' anderà parte, che acciocchè non passi più avanti l' alterazione introdotta dalli Inquisitori per la revisione dei Libri, che si hanno a stampare, ma sia ricevuto solamente quello è limitato per legge, che è un *bezzo* solo per ogni foglio di carta, terminato à 19 Marzo 1562; che ora si pretende soldi quattro: Siano nell' avvenire tenuti li Stampadori, et Libreri portare quei Libri, che vorranno far imprimere in mano del Segretario deputato alla revisione di essi, il quale sia tenuto riceverlo, e con opportuno mezzo farlo capitare all' Inquisitore per la visione, che dovrà esser dal medesimo Segretario diligentemente sollecitata, e segondo il solito sia soddisfatto il bezzo per foglio, nè si debba in alcun modo alterare quell' antico uso di pagamento. Si intende anco essere stato introdotto altro ingordo pagamento per ogni impressione de' Breviarj, Messali e Diurni, et accostumato in modo, che quando viene difficoltato, si stentano le licenze con maniere certamente insopportabili: Però resti nell' avvenire abbolito qualunque pagamento per la detta causa; e senza che abbiano li Stampatori o Librai a trattare con l' Inquisitore sia usata la diligenza debita per la espedizione col mezzo del Segretario delli Riformatori sopradetti. *Sempre che li Inquisitori ovvero i Suoi Vicarj* avessero qualche *dubbio*, che alcun Libro fosse proibito, et non si potesse vender, *non facciano il giudizio da se stessi*, ne si facciano lecito, come hanno introdotto, di comandare alli Librari, che portino alla sua Camera quella sorte di Libri, et se li tengano senza renderli, a di cui sono: ma *debbono farlo sapere* alli *Riformatori Nostri*, ovvero per maggior facilità al Suo Segretario in Scrittura, o in voce, come ricercasse la materia, che portatane da lui la relazione al Magistrato *debbasi da essi Rifformatori ben mutare le cose, et toltone il parere da chi a loro paresse, terminar quello, che giudicaranno conveniente*, ben certi, che colla loro prudenza averanno la mira, che si deva a tutti li rispetti con particolar considerazione, che non sia delli stampati dell' Indice, et sia osservato in tutte le sue parti il Concordato 14 Settembre 1596 sopradetto. Si è ancora introdotto contro l' antico, et sempre osservato uso in luogo di lineare semplicemente le cose, che stimano l' Inquisitori, che non siano stampate, cancellarle di maniera nelli originali, che non si sa quello, vogliano dire; però sia nell' avvenire strettamente proibito il cancellare alcuna qualsivoglia opera, ma semplicemente lineare quella parte, che non si crede conveniente stamparsi, perchè osservate dai *Rifformatori si faccia quello, che da essi sarà giudicato giusto, et conveniente.*

L' introduzione del rivedersi i Libri, che si hanno a stampare, *dall' Inquisitori, è stata per solo pubblico Decreto senza che alcun altro se ne abbia ingerito con fine*, che osservassero quelle sole cose, che si appartengono ai Dogmi, et alla Religione Cattolica; che *così ha voluto la Repubblica Nostra* per la sua natural somma pietà, e zelo verso la medesima Religione: Ora nondimeno accostumano essi Inquisitori osservare anco di quelle materie, che non si appartengono al suo carico: però debba l' Inquisitore nelle sue attestazioni dire solamente, non aver trovato cosa contraria alla Santa Fede Cattolica, lasciando quell' altre parole, Principi, e buoni costumi, che doveranno esser dette dal Segretario a questo Deputato, poichè non è ragionevole, che nelle materie di Stato alcun altro che un Nostro Ministro vi si debba ingerire, le quali attestazioni dal presente Inquisitore, e successori suoi siano fatte, secondo l' uso de' precessori intieramente di propria mano; e se per loro commodo vorranno far veder l' opera a qualche suo confidente, tengano la relazione per sua particolar cauzione. Ma le inserizioni et li attestati siano fatte dall' Inquisitori solamente secondo l' antico uso per levar l' occasione a inconvenienti gravissimi, e molto pregiudiziali al pubblico, et privato interesse, come lo hà mostrato l' esperienza in diverse occorrenze.

Et essendo nel sottoscrivere le liste de' Libri, che vengono a Doana, alterato quello, che fu ordinato a' 9 Febbraro 1558; vedendosi nondimeno l' introduzione sopradetta in qualche parte ragionevole resti coll' autorità di questo Consiglio dichiarito, che sempre che stimassero a proposito l' Inquisitori, che si sbalino a Doane li Libri alla loro presenza, o de' suoi Viccari, per osservare, che nelle liste non vi sia inganno, li sia permesso di poterlo fare, perchè per tutti li rispetti è conveniente, che sia usata ogni estraordinaria diligenza, che non siano portati in questa Città, nè in altra parte dello Stato Nostro Libri proibiti, et dannosi alla Cattolica Religione, che fù sempre, et è intenzione costantissima della Repubblica Nostra, che non siano admessi sotto qual si sia pretesto, dovendo il tutto seguire senza spese de' Libreri.

Sia commessa l' esecuzione della presente parte alli Rifformatori dello Studio di Padova, et col mezzo della seguente scrittura fattone consapevole nel Collegio Nostro il presente Padre Inquisitore.

Fª Roma, N° 47.

1624, 3 *Decembre*, *in Pregadi.*

Che fatto venir nel Collegio nostro il Padre Inquisitore in questa Città li sia letto, quanto segue.

Sono pervenute a nostra notizia diverse introduzioni dannose agl' interessi così pubblici, come particolari dei nostri Sudditi Stampatori, et Libreri, che abitano in questa Città, così nel ricevere i pagamenti contra l' uso ordinario, e terminato per le *nostre Leggi* come nel far le Fedi della Revisione de' Libri per altra mano che per la vostra, et sempre si è accostumato, come anco nel levarsi dalle Botteghe di propria autorità sotto pretesto di proibizioni alcuni libri, che nel Concordato de' 14 Settembre 1596, fu dichiarato, che li Librari potessero vendere, et appresso in luogo di lineare semplicemente le cose, che non pareva si dovessero stampare, al presente si cancellano di maniera li Originali, che non si sà quello vogliano dire: Operazioni tutte, che come molto pregiudiziali sono anco da noi sentite con molto discontento.

Doverete però astenervene, che così è volontà del Senato, e per l' avvenire eseguir intieramente, *quanto abbiamo in questo proposito terminato*, et che per maggior intelligentia vi sarà anco letto; sicuri, che obbedirete alla Pubblica volontà per non ci dar nuova occasione di mala soddisfazione, e necessità di capitare a quelle risoluzioni, che fossero conosciute necessarie.

Fª Roma, N° 47.

Serenissimo Principe.

1794, 30 Aprile.

No. 4. Dalla ossequiata Commissione 8 Febbraro passato degli Eccm̃i Signori Savj ci troviamo incaricati di prendere in maturo esame l' Opera in Tomi otto uscita dai Torchi di Simone Occhj intitolata: *Institutiones Theologicae auctoritate DD. Archiepiscopi Lugdunensis ad usum Scholarum suae Dioecesis editae*, insieme con una Carta relativa ad essa opera, perchè versando sopra le dottrine contenute nelle medesime abbiasi a produrre il nostro divotissimo parere sopra ciò, che convenga farsi, ed aggiungere tutti quei riflessi, che si riputassero opportuni.

L' edizione a noi consegnata del Libro è la quinta uscita in Venezia nell' anno 1792 con la Permissione de' Superiori e Privilegio. La Carta Manoscritta è un Foglio di Proposizioni, in numero di nove imputate, a questo Libro, senza aggiungervi qualificazione veruna, la qual è necessaria per riconoscere la ragion dell' accusa, essendo differente in alcune questioni il sistema delle Scuole Teologiche, e per conseguenza lo spirito di partito. Congiuntamente ci fu consegnato anche un Decreto a stampa 17 Decembre 1792 pubblicato in Roma dalla Sacra Congregazione dell' Indice, in cui si legge annoverata colle opere in esso proibite anche questa volgarmente chiamata la Teologia di Lione. Perciò in tre parti dobbiamo dividere le riverenti nostre considerazione seguendo li dettami del Sommo Pontefice Benedetto XIV.; che nella Bolla 8 Luglio 1753. *Sollicita:* raccomandò in tali esami la Cristiana discrezione, la buona fama degli Autori, e l' avvertenza di ben ponderare ciò, che precede, e ciò che seguita alle Proposizioni accusate.

Gli otto tomi stampati dall' Occhj comprendono un corso regolato di Teologia per la uniforme instituzione de' proprj Chierici prescrittosi da Monsr di Montazet allora Arcivescovo di Lione, che lo mandò in luce nell' anno 1780 in quella Città. L' Opera trovò molto accoglimento presso gli uomini imparziali, e sensati a grado, che ne fu introdotto l' uso anche in Italia in qualche Vescovile Seminario. Il metodo degl' insegnamenti procede gradatamente, ed instruisce con facilità gli studiosi della Divina Scienza, illustrando ogni argomento con le autorità più rispettabili, e maneggiando nel tempo stesso con la temperanza e modestia la più religiosa. Tal è il carattere genuino dell' opera, nella quale non si è affacciato alla breve nostra intelligenza passo alcuno, che offenda la santità della Religione, l' integrità del Costume, o li riguardi del Principato. Nel Paragrafo quarto della Pastorale posta in fronte di questa quinta Edizione il Prelato anche dà conto delle molte diligenze, cautelle, ed esami attentissimi fatti praticare sopra ciascuno dei Trattati da più eruditi Teologi innanzi di commetter l' Opera alla Stampa, e di proporla al suo Clero.

Il foglio poi manoscritto contiene li novi Capi delle Odierne imputazioni segnate in questa Opera, le quali sebben possono credersi figlie di un eccedente zelo, esiggono però quella ponderazione matura, che è propria di questo Serenissimo Governo. Siccome ciascuna risguarda un soggetto diverso, ed è applicata a differenti luoghi dell' autore; così fa di mestieri conoscerla ad una ad una particolarmente col lume della verità, che è la guida sicura della giustizia. Avvertiremo, soltanto per la dovuta esattezza, che li passi citati in questa Carta sembrano presi da un' altra Edizione, non corrispondente nel numero dei Tomi citati. Quindi al margine segnaremo in ciascheduno il Tomo, e la Pagina, dove si legge nella quinta Edizione Veneta, che ci fu consegnata.

Tom. II. *de Locis Theol.* Dissert. V. Cap. 6. Prop. 2 @ 272.

La prima delle imputazioni è data all' asserzione, che li Decreti dei Concilj, anche Generali, che appartengono alla *Disciplina* ossia Governo esteriore, non obbligano senza l' approvazione del Principe. Deve notarsi che l' autore nella prima proposizione immediate antecedente avea provato, che le Definizioni di *Fede* emanate dal Concilio, il quale è il Tribunale Supremo ed infallibile della Chiesa, obbligano anche senza l' approvazione del Principe. In questa seconda, che riguarda soltanto la Disciplina esterna, viene denunciato il solo titolo, e questo nemmeno ne' termini, coi quali è preposto dall' Autore. Egli dice, che li Decreti dei Concilj anche Generali senza l' approvazione dei Principi non sono obbligatorj in *quelle cose, che sono soggette alla loro autorità.*

La denoncia in qualche modo altera il testo, quando il testo essendo in questo genere di accuse il corpo del delitto, come dicono li Dottori, deve essere allegato secondo le regole di ogni sana Giurisprudenza, e degli stessi Teologi colla più severa precisione e veracità.

La Proposizione viene provata dall' autore cogli esempj delle istanze fatte dal Clero Gallicano, e dai Sommi Pontefici, perchè il Concilio di Trento fosse promulgato in Francia; il che non poterono ottenere da quei Re per li Capi concernenti la Disciplina, sebbene li canoni definitivi del Dogma col fatto erano stati ricevuti, e posti in osservanza senza eccezione veruna. Lo stesso Concilio fu accettato, e pubblicato in questo Serenissimo Dominio, con previa parola del Pontefice Pio IV., che fossero sempre salve la Giurisdizione, e le consuetudine della Repubblica. Infatti quanto alla Disciplina esteriore non si osserva in alcuni Capi nemmeno in Roma; in alcune Provincie della Cristianità non fu accettato; in altre come nelle Fiandre, nel Regno di Napoli, e nello Stato Veneto, dove fu promulgato, molti Decreti Disciplinari trovarono gravissimi ostacoli, e con Ordini particolari non furono giammai amessi all' esecuzione. Qui non si è concesso l' assenso Pubblico per esempio alle facoltà dei Vescovi d' imponer Pene pecuniarie, di visitar Ospitali, Monti di Pietà, ed altri luoghi Pij Laici, di vederne i loro Conti, di privar li Notaj per colpe del loro uffizio, di castigare gli Adulteri e li Concubinarj, di cacciar le Donne prostitute fuori della Diocese, di scommunicar li Magistrati, che entrassero nella Clausura delle Monache, o che non osservassero nella sua estensione l' Ecclesiastica Immunità. Li Vescovi stessi potrebbero col fatto proprio somministrar molte prove della loro inosservanza in alcuni Capi Disciplinari dello Stesso Concilio, come sono quelli dei Concilj Provinciali, dei Sinodi Diocesani, delle visite Pastorali alle Chiese, nella scelta de' Ministri per il Santuario, ed in altri punti di grave importanza, che la riverenza non permette di ricapitolare in questo luogo.

Se li Concilj antichi fossero tenuti per obbligatorj anche nella Disciplina, come intenderebbe il Denunziante, o Censore che sia di questa Proposizione, e si volessero eseguire a fronte della universal Consuetudine contraria, si farebbe uno strano rivolgimento nel mondo, e succederebbe una confusione enorme in ogni stato Cattolico, perchè le circostanze odierne sono affatto differenti dalle antiche. Fà di mestieri in questi tempi calamitosi pregar Dio, che resti la Fede, e che la Disciplina si osservi nelle cose più sostanziali del culto Sacro, e del buon Costume. La Fede è immutabile in ogni tempo è luogo; ma la Disciplina, che non la offende, può variare secondo i tempi, i luoghi e le circostanze. Molte discipline sono venute al mondo, quando i Sacerdoti erano d' Oro, e li Calici di Legno. Ora per contrario nell' età nostra si veggono molti Calici d' Oro, e troppi Sacerdoti di Legno.

Alla Proposizione in oltre, che li Concilj non ricevuti non obbligano quanto alla

Disciplina esteriore il testo aggiunge in *quelle cose, che sono soggette all' autorità del Principe*; le quali parole, che fanno ancora più chiaro il senso, vengono ommesse nell' Estratto. La condanna di questa Proposizione farebbe l' effetto di condannar la Podestà de' Sovrani, di confonder il Governo Civile, di abbattere il *Regio exequatur*, e di stabilire due Sovranità in un medesimo Stato con un assurdo non più inteso, ed opposto alla pace Cristiana, e sicurezza comune.

Lo stato esterno della Religione stà legato strettamente colla costituzione politica, e perciò non può sottrarsi dalle naturali inspezioni di chi governa tutto il corpo della Civil Società.

La Podestà ai Principi è data da Dio secondo l' insegnamento delle Divine Scritture, e de' Santi Padri, nè al retto uso di quella può alcuno rinunziare senza cessar d' esser Principe. La lezione sola degli antichi Concilj basta a documentarci, che li Principi della più illustre pietà lasciavano bensì ai Vescovi come a successori degli Apostoli nelle Sante Assemblee della Chiesa la libertà pienissima di definire le regole della Fede, e della Morale. Ma ciò che era stato in forma canonica deciso, e giudicato, veniva poscia munito della lor autorità Secolare con Leggi, e Sovrani Editti per comandarne l' osservanza e regolarne l' esecuzione esteriore. Dall' esercizio di questo potere necessario alla tranquillità della Religione e dello Stato, ed usato sino dai primi Imperatori Cristiani, ne parlano gli stessi Scrittori Ecclesiastici, che sarebbe lungo il riferire; e per molti secoli que' Sovrani ricevettero dai Sommi Pontefici, e dai Pastori della Chiesa applausi, benedizioni e ringraziamenti. E fatto ancora troppo notorio, che li quattro ultimi Concilj di Costanza, Basilea, Fiorenza e Trento incontrarono eccezioni, e difficoltà in molti luoghi; sicchè negli articoli della Disciplina o non vennero ammessi, o dove furono ammessi, la osservanza soggiace a diversa limitazione secondo li aspetti delle differenti Nazioni. Se il consenso de' Principi non fosse stato necessario per obbligare, li Pontefici non avrebbero fatte tante instanze ai Principi stessi, acciò fosse ricevuto da loro il Concilio di Trento. La storia ci ammaestra, che per molti secoli ne' Concilj intervennero li Principi, e che nei Concilj degli ultimi tempi vi sostennero la loro rappresentanza gli Ambasciatori.

La seconda imputazione contra questa Opera accagiona l' altra asserzione, che il Concilio di Fiorenza non viene ammesso da tutti, e specialmente dai Francesi per Ecumenico, e perciò esser maggiore l' autorità del Concilio di Costanza. Che il Concilio di Fiorenza abbia sofferte molte vicende, anche quando fu convocato dal Pontefice Eugenio IV. prima in Ferrara e poscia trafferito in Fiorenza, è fatto notissimo nella Storia di quel tempo, e di quel travaglioso Pontificato. Lo stesso Papa aveva precedentemente convocato l' altro di Basilea, che poscia voleva sciolto; per lo che a vicenda seguirono minaccie Spirituali di poca edificazione dall' una e dall' altra parte.

In quello di Fiorenza si disputò assai fra i Teologi delle due Chiesa Orientale ed Occidentale, e si operò molto per la unione de' Greci coi Latini, la qual ben presto fatalmente restò sciolta per li rumori suscitati da Marco d' Effeso. La sua definizione sull' autorità del Papa dai Latini fu intesa in senso di Superiore anche al Concilio generale, sebben in questo si rappresenta tutta la Chiesa congregata nello Spirito Santo. Ma li Greci, ed alcune Provincie d' Occidente con qualche Teologo Latino di molta riputazione tengono il Papa per inferiore al Concilio, allegando gravissime autorità, e fatti cospicui; sicchè la questione resta indecisa fra li Teologi e fra le Nazioni. Il testo del Fiorentino in questo particolare trovò discordi li Dottori nella Traduzione, e quando in Trento si trattò di farne uso, li Francesi vi si opposero, perchè non tengono il Fiorentino per Universale, nè ammettono la intelligenza, e la Traduzione dei Romani. Gli Oltramontani trovano restrizioni, ed oscurità in esso testo, e coll' autorità del Concilio singolarmente di Costanza, che ha deposti tre Papi in un colpo, e dato alla Chiesa Martino V., riguardano il Pontefice per soggetto al Concilio.

Nel 1626 essendo state spedite in Candia dalla Congregazione di Propaganda due Casse del Concilio di Fiorenza scritto nell' Idioma Greco e Latino, e molti Libretti della Dottrina Cristiana composti dal dottissimo Cardinal Bellarmino Gesuita, l' Arcivescovo Stella ha creduto di soprasedere, piuttosto che eseguire la distribuzione. E da credersi, che la condotta di quel Prelato non dispiacesse in Roma stessa, poichè successivamente venne promosse a Vescovato di Vicenza, e poscia a quello di Padova, dove morì. Communicata quella spedizione all' Eccmo Senato li due consultori Dottor Gasparo Lonigo Prete e Piovano di San Giovanni Decollato, e Frà Fulgenzio de' Servi Successori di Fra Paolo fecero tre scritture consigliando, che fosse impedita quella novità. Perciò con le Ducali 1626, 25 Settembre, e 1627, 5 Giugno, si laudò la prudente condotta dell' Arcivescovo, e fu data una risoluta commissione al Provveditor Generale in quel Regno d' impedire non solamente qualunque distribuzione, ma d' imporre eziandio un assoluto silenzio intorno alli suddetti Concilj. Sembrano sufficienti questi pochi cenni per intendere la verità contenuta nella asserzione del fatto storico allegato dal Libro, e quale fallacia si nasconda nel tentare oggidì la condanna, quasi chè offendesse un Dogma definito, e una Regola della Fede. Resta tuttavia in controversia fra cattolici il punto della Superiorità del Papa al Concilio, e del Concilio al Papa; ed entrambi li partiti combattono con buone ragioni, e con antesignani illustri per santità, e per dottrina.

Tom. II. *de Locis Theol.* Dissert. VI. Cap. 2. Coroll. 2 @ 310.

La terza imputazione è data alla conclusione dell' autore nel secondo suo Corollario di quel medesimo Capo, perchè reputa lecite, e qualche volta anche necessarie le Appellazioni dal Romano Pontefice al Concilio Generale. Sono molte le ragioni premesse in quel lungo Capo per la Superiorità del Concilio Generale, essendo ancora questa una delle questioni indecise nelle Scuole della Teologia, come si è detto. Rinforza il suo assunto con due autorità, l' una tratta dal Vangelo, e l' altra da una lettera di Santo Agostino, e cogli esempj delle tante appellazioni interposte, che egli omette per oggetto di brevità. Quando però il Denunciante avesse fedelmente considerato tutto ciò, che è permesso in quel Capo, e ciò che susseguita ne' Corollarj, secondo il dettame di Benedetto XIV., avrebbe risparmiata la fatica di porre isolato anche questo articolo con l' astuzia di far condannare le Appellazioni al Concilio, e così dar nuovo corso ad uno de' casi riservati della Bolla *in Coena Domini*, sebbene eliminata per le sue esorbitanze da quasi tutti gli Stati Cattolici dell' Europa, e dai Decreti antichi, e recenti dell' Eccmo Senato.

Sono ventiquattro almeno dall' anno 1239 sino al secolo presente le Appellazioni interposte dal Papa al Concilio con Instromenti, ed Atti solenni da Imperatori, da altri Principi, da Università, da Corpi Ecclesiastici, da Vescovi, e da medesimi Cardinali. Il Padre Generale de' Frati Minori di San Francesco appellò dal Sommo Pontefice Giovanni XII. alla Chiesa Cattolica, ed al futuro Concilio, per la controversia della Povertà di Cristo da osservarsi nell' Ordine suo. Anzi l' affare andò tanto innanzi, che li Frati sostenuti dall' Imperatore Lodovico il Bavaro fecero deporre quel Pontefice, e sostituire in suo luogo un altro, che fu l' Antipapa Fra Pietro di Corbara lor confratello. E celebre il caso di Gregorio XII. Pontefice Veneziano, detto prima il Cardinal

Angelo Corraro, il quale non volendo rinonciare il Pontificato secondo l' obbligo preso, nell' assumerlo, la Repubblica seguì le Deliberazioni del Concilio ridotto in Pisa, sottraendosi dall' ubbidienza di esso Gregorio, e riconoscendo Alessandro V. sostenuto dal Concilio. Restano le memorie di quel successo nelle Ducali, e Decreti suoi degli anni 1409, e 1410; e nei castighi allora adoperati sopra alcuni Ecclesiastici di riguardevole grado. Per opposto nel 1436, si appellò dalle Censure del Concilio di Basilea al Pontefice Eugenio IV. per le pretensioni mosse in quella radunanza dal Patriarca di Aquileja sopra il Friuli. Ma par altro opposto sono ancora assai note le solenne Appellazioni della medesima Serenissima Repubblica al Concilio ne' tempi di Sisto IV., e di Giulio Secondo; ed è recentissimo il divieto qui fattosi nel Settembre nel 1793 di alcune Tesi, che difendevano la Superiorità del Papa al Concilio sul fondamento della Bolla *Execrabilis* di Pio Secondo, che forma il tema di un Capo dell' accennata *Bolla* della Cerca, così detta, perchè si pubblicava nel Giovedì Santo.

La quarta imputazione ha preso di mira le ultime parole d' una *Osservazione* dell' Autore, posta dopo un lungo esame, ed un Corollario sull' argomento della Grazia e del Libro Arbitrio da lui maneggiato con le dottrine tratte dai medesimi fonti, ai quali sogliono ricorrere li partiti Teologici, che sono impegnati nella questione. Il passo estratto, e contenuto nel Foglio, non è per verità riportato nè precisi termini del Libro a noi consegnato, come prescrivono le regole di tali Censure. Egli è copiato con alcune alterazioni, che importano parole ommesse, altre cangiate, ed altre aggiunte; sicchè quello non essendo più il vero testo della Veneta Edizione, che è la quinta, manca la prima, i fondamental base della Denunzia, e per conseguenza la ragione di farne giudicio alcuno. In questo genere di accuse le sentenze degli Autori devono trascriversi con la più scrupolosa esattezza, perche formano il corpo del Delitto, come dicono i Giuristi; altrimenti non sarebbe più il senso dell' Autore, ma quello del Denunziante il soggetto della procedura in ogni tribunale del mondo.

Ciò premesso genera sorpresa il testo del Libro variato nella Copia dei punti estratti dal medesimo, quasi che l' accusa, e l' accusatore potessero scappar dal confronto.

Il testo dice, che nell' uomo privo della Grazia queste due cose insieme sono associate; la naturale possibilità del bene, e la impotenza volontaria, donde avviene, che per l' affezione predominante egli non operò se non male, e che dalla perversa volontà costretto al vizio non operi il bene, che pure gli è naturale di potere. Questa è la traduzione litterale del testo qui stampato, il di cui senso genuino ritiene la dottrina Cattolica circa il libero Arbitrio. Ma la variazione consiste nelle parole forse copiate da qualche altra Edizione, le quali nell' uomo privo della Grazia di Cristo la possibilità naturale del bene vi aggiunsero la spiegazione, *ossia la facoltà di sua natura idonea a sceglier il bene.* Questa giunta potendo causar equivoco non conforme al sentimento della Chiesa, fa dire al Libro ciò, che nondice. La scelta del bene non potendo farsi dalla volontà senza l' ajuto della Grazia, non può attribuirsi alle sole forze naturali dell' uomo, che si trova da quella abbandonato, come può cavillarsi in questa giunta. Perciò l' imputazione manca di fondamento, ed ha il carattere della illusione la più manifesta. Le altre meno importanti, ma sempre arbitrarie, variazioni introdotte nella Copia si trapassano per non recar troppa noja a V.V. E.E.

Anche la quinta imputazione sullo stesso argomento della Grazia non è la più fondata, ne la più sincera. Il testo dice, che la concupiscenza, la qual nell' uomo abbandonato dalla Grazia, domina con più d' imperio, e che in esso è come un' altra natura, *per lo più* lo induce a dirigge l' opera anche in se stessa onesta allo scopo o del piacere, o di qualche altro fine vano, e massimamente di umana lode. Sin qui il testo genuino del Libro si conforma al sentimento di Santo Agostino, ivi immediatamente allegato, che fa menzioni a questo proposito delle Azioni lodevoli e generose degli antichi Romani. Il Censore per altro nella Copia ha cambiato il *per lo più* induce, che è termine di modificazione, in un *sempre*, che è termine assoluto. In oltre nel fine alla riflessione della lode umana contemplata vi aggiunse del proprio: *benchè talvolta soltanto virtualmente.* Senza entrare negli oggetti delle introdotte variazioni stà in fatto l' alterazione del Testo anche in questa parte della Copia; sicchè risulta al pari della precedente un' affettata viziatura del testo per aggravare indebitamente l' autore del Libro.

Le controversie sulle operazioni della Grazia Divina, e sulle forze dell' arbitrio umano sono molto antiche ed ostinate, nè bastarono le dottrine di Santo Agostino, e di San Tommaso, non l' autorità di qualche Concilio, non quella di più Sommi Ponteficì, e nemmeno la possanza dei Sovrani per imporre l' ultimo termine al Teologico susurro. Molti rami delle questioni si trovano bensì recisi da questa pianta fatale; ma ne restano tuttavia degli altri conosciuti nelle Scuole sotto li nomi di Grazia Efficace, e di Grazia Sufficiente. Le Passioni, e gli umani interessi ebbero sempre molta influenza nel mantener la scissura delle opinioni e delle dispute, che recarono grandissimo travaglio alle Provincie Oltramontane, e molta persecuzione ad uomini d' illustre pietà con molto discapito del servizio di Dio, e della Santa sua Chiesa. Fra Paolo Sarpi nel principio del secolo passato e Fra Paolo Celotti nell' anno 1726, ambedue Consultori Pubblici, ed insigni Teologi dell' Ordine de' Servi, in due Scritture all' Eccmo Senato esposero con molto zelo e chiarezza le vere cause, e gli effetti perniciosi della scolastica discordia senza che da noi si aggiunga di più.

Dopo l' anno 1773 le questioni medesime compariscono alquanto riscaldate in Italia, dove li Teologi si torturano miseramente il cervello per intenderle, e per risolverle secondo il differente sistema delle proprie scuole e del partito adottato. Gli argomenti maneggiati con molta sottigliezza, e calore spesse volte oltrepassano li termini della religiosa moderazione; intrigano l' intendimento dei Cristiani, che non sono Teologi; inquietano singolarmente li paesi oltre il Mincio; e dopo tutto ciò le questioni restano sempre indecise. E perchè non abbiano a finir mai, si usa l' istromento pericoloso dei Giornali Ecclesiastici, nei quali il giornalista lavora a capriccio proprio, o per soggestione altrui una indiscreta censura, che manda impunemente alle stampe, sopra ogni Autore di Chiesa, e che serve a mantenere con tale astuzia le animosità fra i dotti e la confusione fra gl' ignoranti. La singolare prudenza di Vostra Serenità ben comprende, a qual segno di turbamento possono essere condotti li suoi buoni Sudditi da queste pratiche, e divulgazioni, e quanto importi l' imporre al grave disordine quel forte ed imparziale riparo, che ristituisca la calma se non nello spirito almeno nelle parole, chiamando li disputanti a religiosa temperanza, ed opponendo un argine al corso infesto di somiglianti Giornali.

Tom. V. *de Censur.* Cap. 8. Art. 1 @ 455.

La sesta imputazione è data al sentimento dell' autore, che le *scomuniche latae sentiae*, come le dichiarano le Scuole, furono affatto incognite all' antichità. Ma quella riflessione è una risposta al quesito, se anticamente fosse in uso quella forma di Censura Ecclesiastica, ed in quai tempi venisse introdotta. Dunque la risposta non riguarda punto alcuno di Fede, ma un Fatto unicamente di semplice Storia; il quale è sostenuto colle ragioni ivi allegate, e coll' autorità del Van-Espen dottissimo canonista.

Quindi non contenendosi nell' asserzione un' argomento di Dogma, ma un punto di Storia, dove a tutti è lecito di opinare, diviene insussistente, e poco onesta l' accusa.

Li Teologi dividono la Scommunica in Maggiore e Minore; ed alla prima attribuiscono l' efficacia di escludere lo scommunicato da tutti li beni della Chiesa, col separarlo dalla Società dei Fedeli. Alla seconda, che è la Minore, assegnano l' effetto soltanto di privarlo di alcuni, cioè del partecipare de' Sagramenti. Dividono pur la scomunica in altre specie, l' una chiamata di *latae*, e l' altra di *ferendae Sententiae*. Quella di *latae Sententiae*, ossia di delitto già sentenziato dalla Legge insegnano incorrersi issofatto, cioè immantinente, che è commesso il peccato senza bisogno di nuova sentenza di Giudice. L' altra specie all' incontro di *ferendae Sententiae*, cioè del Giudicio da pronunziarsi domanda, che si osservi l' ordine Canonico per la regolar procedura. Della prima specie l' Autore parla in questo Capo, e la crede incognita ne' primi tempi della Chiesa, non trovandone fatta menzione dagli scrittori di allora. Poscia riferisce li concigli del Cardinale San Pietro Damiani al Papa Alessandro Secondo e del Sommo Pontefice Benedetto XIV. alli Vescovi, perchè l' uso ne fosse meno frequente, e più moderato.

La settima delle imputazioni nota la proposizioni: che li matrimonj contratti contro la volontà dei genitori dai Figli, che sono minori degli anni venticinque, per il Dritto di Francia sono dichiarati invalidi non solo quanto agli effetti Civili, ma ancora quanto alla sostanza del contratto. L' Autore in questo capo espone al suo Clero ciò, che si praticava per Legge Civile nel proprio Paese, non ciò, che si avrebbe a praticare.

Quanto colà si praticava, e la ragione per cui si praticava, abbondantemente è da lui narrato, citando in prova gli Editti di quei Re, le Interpretazioni di quei Magistrati, e li Giudizj conformi di quelle Supreme Curie. Non ho lasciato ancora di prender in esame gli obbietti secondo la Giurisprudenza, che vigeva in quel Regno, quando scrisse, prima delle ultime rivoluzioni. Il consensò paterno per li Matrimonj dei figli di Famiglia era colà stabilito per una delle condizioni essenziali alle Nozze Pubbliche, sicchè mancando questa la congiunzione si riguardava per clandestina, siccome tra noi si riguarda dopo l' accettazione del Concilio di Trento, quando manca l' intervento del Parroco e de' Testimonj. Per tale difetto si dichiarava colà nullo dal Giudice il Matrimonio dei figli Minori.

Finalmente l' Autore tra gli obbietti, che si affacciavano a quella pratica, sebben fondata sulla Podestà Legislativa de' Sovrani, e sulle ordinanze e consuetudini particolari del Regno, mette in considerazione il Decreto del Sacro Concilio di Trento in cui si condanna la opinione, che teneva invalidi li Matrimonj contratti dai Figlj di Famiglia senza il consenso dei Genitori, ed attribuiva ai Padri la facoltà di potere per quella ragione renderli validi, o nulli. Col metodo Scolastico allega anche le varie interpretazioni, che venivano date a quel Decreto, e come si pensava in Trento, quando fu proposto di farlo. In ultimo luogo abbandona prudentemente la questione senza aggiungervi alcuna formal conclusione del proprio; il che poteva bastare al Denonziante per intendere ciò, che l' autore aveva proposto in fronte del quesito da riferirsi agli effetti Civili, e alla sostanza del contratto secondo il Dritto Gallicano, e non secondo il Dritto di altri Dominj.

Oggidì pertanto questa fatica di Storico e non di Teologico insegnamento, serve alle Scuole di cognizione erudita di quanto altrove si accostumava senza entrare nella parte del Sacramento, che li Dottori sogliono distinguere da quella del Contratto, come lo distingue anche l' Autore. Dalle fatte osservazioni e confronti resta dileguato ogni motivo di giusto reclamo in linea di Dogma offeso.

Tom. VI. *de Matr.* Dissert. IV. Cap. 2. Art. 2 @ 313.

La ottava imputazione è rivolta all' altra proposizione sul Matrimonio degl' Infedeli, perchè l' Autore asserisce, che quando è contratto legittimente non può mai disciogliersi quanto al vincolo, neppure se uno de' Coniugj essendo convertito alla Fede l' altro non voglia vivere pacificamente con esso. A questa Proposizione l' autore ha premesso il quesito, se il Matrimonj degl' Infedeli possano sciogliersi, essendo cosa certa presso tutto il mondo, che sono tenuti per validi, allorchè si contraggono secondo le Leggi del Dritto Naturale, e Civile. Al qual passo di ciò ne rende qualche ragione; e soggiunge, che nei casi delle Sante Conversioni vi è disputa tra i Teologi, se il matrimonio possa disciogliersi, e darsi libera facoltà al Coniuge Fedele di contrarne un altro. Avvisa inoltre, che il numero maggiore sostiene lecito lo scioglimento nei tre casi ivi specificati, e che il numero bensì minore, ma che sembra il più forte nel peso delle ragioni, insegna l' opinione contraria. Dopo tale avvertenze propone gli argomenti, che militano per questa seconda, traendoli dalla Scrittura dai Padri, e dalle ragioni Teologiche, ed esaminando gli obbietti colla maniera delle Scuole. In fine conclude col mandar tutti a leggere due Volumi Stampati sopra questa quistione l' anno 1761.

Assai rari per altro nei Pubblici registri sono i Casi, nei quali dai Sommi Pontefici sia stata dato mano a tali scioglimenti; il che prova il molto riguardo da loro avuto in questa materia, e ci ammaestra insieme di non far decisione, dove non fu fatta nemmeno dalla loro sapienza, e di lasciar intatto lo stato della Controversio. Quando però si affaccia la necessità di qualche provvidenza, sogliono far prima interpellare il Conjuge Infedele, assegnandovi un termine di mesi a dichiarare, se vuol convertirsi, ovvero coabitare con l' altro conjuge convertito senza contumelia del Creatore. Di questa precauzione vi è l' esempio in un Editto prodotto sotto il giorno 24 Febbrajo 1711 alla Revisione de' Brevi.

Tom. VII. *de Eccl. Praec.* Cap. 1 @ 108.

La nona, ed ultima imputazione è data alla risposta dell' Autore sopra il quesito, se li fedeli nelle Domeniche, e Feste maggiori siano tenuti ad ascoltar la Messa Parrocchiale. Egli inclina per l' affermativa attesa la legge Ecclesiastica, e ne porta alcune ragioni dedotte dalla disciplina antica, dalle sanzioni di Concilj, e da Bolle Pontificie. Una immagine di tal disciplina resta tuttavia nella Chiesa Greca, e nè Villaggi Latini, dove i Parrochi inculcano al Popolo di frequente l' intervento alla Messa Parrocchiale, perchè in quella si fa la spiegazione del Vangelo colle istruzioni della Religione. L' autore per altro dopo aver ragionato, con erudite considerazioni se ne spedisce, anche qui mandando tutti a leggere un Libro, che tratta dell' intervento alle Messe Festive nelle Chiese de' Regolari.

Questo articolo dunque non contenendo senso veruno contrario al Dogma, anzi non appartenendo di sua natura nemmeno al Dogma, non può cadere sotto le inspezioni consuete del Santo Officio, perchè sarebbe fuori de' Casi assegnati dai Concordati a quel Tribunale. L' Autore ne fa l' esame secondo la legge Ecclesiastica; e il decidere con altre autorità, che deve aversi per erronea l' opinione dell' obbligo d' intervenire alla Messa del Proprio Parroco, che è il Pastore del secondo ordine, causerebbe nella fantasia di molti una intelligenza assai poco favorevole alla pietà, e alla miglior disciplina, di cui tanto abbisognano li nostri tempi.

Fra le carte, chi ci furono consegnate viene in ultimo luogo il Decreto a stampa

17 Novembre 1792, pubblicato in Roma dalla Sacra Congregazione dell' Indice, nel quale con altri Libri si legge vietata anche questa Teologia conosciuta nelle Scuole col nome di Lione. La ragione per cui è stato proibito il Libro, resta del tutto ignota, perchè non la dice il Decreto, siccome non la dice neppure degli altri nel medesimo enunciati. Ma vostra Serenità non ammette giammai questo genere di condanna senza esserne prima debitamente informata; e la fà sempre seguire coi metodi prescritti dall' altro Concordato 1596, 14 Settembre, nella materia dei Libri. Se tutte le proibizioni di Roma si ammettessero ciecamente, sarebbe inofficioso, e distrutto il Concordato con turbamento delle coscienze, colla rovina dei Librai, e con molto pregiudizio all' ordine del Governo Civile.

L' Indice de' Libri proibiti sotto colore di Religione ebbe il suo principio al tempo del Pontefice Paulo IV. nel 1559; e fu compiuto dall' altro Pontefice Pio IV.; a cui l' affare era stato rimesso dal Concilio di Trento. Il Primo Catalogo dell' anno 1564 ridotto a classi conteneva il numero di 985 autori vietati; il secondo dell' anno 1595 di Clemente VIII. pervenne a quello di 2154; il terzo stampato nell' anno 1765 ammontava al numero di 4992, così che si erano clandistinamente seminate entro il Dominio della Serenissima Repubblica in numero di 2788 le proibizioni vaganti fuori del Concordato. In quest' anno fu scoperto il disordine, e col Decreto 1765, 3 Agosto, venne comandata e poscia eseguita la ristampa dell' Indice accettato nel 1596 insieme con quel Concordato, e coll' appendice aggiunta delle pochissime Proibizioni, che si erano trovate al livello del Concordato. Ma l' intenzione degli Ecclesiastici tentò sempre di raccoglierne con gran diligenza gli esemplari Veneti, acciò fosse dato luogo alla dispersione dei Romani accresciuti di molto numero ancora dopo quell' anno. Se li rispetti del Principato, e l' Arte della Stampa ricevano discapiti da questa inondazione, e quali cautele altresì occorrano a frenare l' ingresso dei Libri perniciosi, sono tutte provvidenze riserbate all' alto discernimento di VV. EE. Il condannare per altro senza imputar la colpo e senza dar luogo alla difesa non sembra accordato nè dai Sacri Canoni, nè dalla Divina Scrittura, nè da giustizia alcuna della Terra, com' è dimostrato da gravissimi Autori.

Negl' Indici stampati in Roma, si trova un numero immenso di Libri proibiti in ogni facoltà, per ogni altra causa che per quella della Santa Fede. Gli Scrittori Legali spesse volte sono censurati, perchè difendono la podestà Temporale delle pretensioni della Corte, e fermano la Ecclesiastica tra li suoi giusti confini. Si vietano molti storici, perchè scoprono qualche fatto particolare, che li Cortigiani desiderano resti occulto, o dimenticato. In una parola si mette mano ad ogni genere di scritti, eziandio Grammaticali, di Medicina, di Alchimia, e di Lotti con fine di ampliare la propria giurisdizione sopra ogni argomento, e talvolta ancora con quello di rendere odioso il nome dell' Autore per qualche arcana veduta. Basta trascorrere li Cataloghi stampati per esser certi di questa condotta.

L' esame è raccomandato ad alcuni Teologi, chiamati da quelle Congregazioni col titolo di Qualificatori, o di Consultori, i quali essendo per lo più degli ordini Regolari secondo lo spirito di partito, e la diversità delle loro Scuole, regolano le censure. Poi sulla fede di quelle relazioni non sempre libere da privati affetti si formano le condanne senza la parsimonia, la circospezione, e la carità desiderate dai Pontefici Sisto V., Benedetto XIV.; cosichè oggidì non vi è più Libro, che non possa soggiacere a simil destino, nè Autore sicuro da questo attacco. Quindi avviene che si veggono proibiti Libri, che prima furono colà permessi, ed altri permessi, che prima furono vietati. In ciò non andò esente nemmeno il Breviario; poiche

Urbano VIII. avendo aggiunte a quel Libro le lezioni di Santa Catterina da Siena la Congregazione dell' Indice dopo alcuni anni spedì un suo rigoroso Decreto 22 Gennaro 1642 agli Inquisitori di Sant' Offizio acciò facessero togliere le parole, che dicevano essere la Famiglia Benincasa discendente da un medesimo stipite colla Borghese. Quella della Santa era creduta di origine bassa, e perciò poco degna di andar del pari colla Borghese, ch' era Pontificia. Così gli umani rispetti si vestono tal volta con l' abito di religione. Per contrario non si vede usata la stessa attenzione in alcuni libri di Autori Ecclesiastici, le dottrine dei quali sono dissimulate, e lasciate in corso nelle Scuole e nei Circoli letterarj, come se fossero approvate, Cattoliche, e sane. A tutti è noto il nome rispettabilissimo del Sig' Cardinal Bellarmino; ma non può esser lodata da tutti l' opinione, che insegna, di portar l' autorità Pontificia sopra il Governo Politico, e li temporali Diritti dei Sovrani. Di poca edificazione riuscirà ad altri il Sanchez, dove parla, e quasi instruisce degli usi della lascivia nei congressi matrimoniali. Il Busembaum con alcuni suoi seguaci sarà sempre infesto alla pace Cristiana, e Civile negl' insegnamenti favorevoli al Regicidio.

Procedendo con troppa facilità le Proibizioni succede, che molte condanne si credono provenire dal maneggio umano, e non dalla ispirazione Divina. Quindi pur avviene, che non sono più tenute per infallibili, ne riportano la riverenza, che era loro prestata nè primi tempi. Gli Autori, che sono offesi nella fama, non cessano di reclamar contro li divieti, e d' invocar la giustizia di Dio, e dei Principi, onde non soccombere sotto questo nuovo genere di oppressione. In fatti è desiderabile una maggior temperanza nel far le censure, e la sapienza di Benedetto XIV. non trascurò di promoverla, e di raccomandarla efficacemente, come si è detto. Nella Opera Teologica di Lione agli occhi nostri imparziali non si è affacciata Proposizione alcuna contraria alle regole della Fede, o del Costume, o della Pietà, e perciò nel comandato esame non ci è risultata la parte degna di essere condannata che la cattiva stampa qui fatta di un' Opera buona. Le nove Imputazioni contenute nel foglio Manoscritto essendosi poste all' ingenuo confronto del Libro nei luoghi citati cadono da se stesse, come abbiamo rispettosamente considerato.

Ciò, che dalla Chiesa non è deciso con le debite formalità di Giudizio nei punti di controversia Dogmatica, rimani sempre nello stato di questione disputabile nelle scuole con libera facoltà ai Teologi di seguire l' opinione, che più loro piace, di battersi religiosamente quanto vagliono con gli argomenti, e di non trovarsi mai nè vittoriosi, nè vinti. Le Pubbliche, e private Librerie, e li Negozj de' Libraj abbondano degli autori dell' uno, e dell' altro partito stampata colla buona fede delle consuete approvazioni, e licenze. Con gli stessi requisiti, che nello stato delle Cose non potevano essere negati nè dalli Revisori, nè dal Magistrato Eccmo de' Riformatori dello Studio di Padova, seguì la Stampa ancora di questo Libro, il quale non si potrebbe condannare oggidì senza intendersi condannati insieme con lui tutti quelli, che ritengono la stessa dottrina, con gravi conseguenze per il susurro Scolastico, e per il Commercio Libraio.

Non è forse da trascurarsi la osservazione, che in Roma se ne fece il divieto, mentre in Venezia si dava in luce un' altro libro di Teologia egualmente però incensurabile, e dotto. In quel Giornale Ecclesiastico, ristampato in Bergamo sotto il giorno 16 Febbrajo 1793 si mandò innanzi il Decreto 17 Decembre precedente, che proibiva la Teologia di Lione; e passato un mese venne poscia enunciata sotto il giorno 16 Marzo susseguente la edizione Veneta dell' altra Teologia, il di cui uso dal Giornalista si bramava sostituito a quello di Lione. Noi lasceremo di entrare nelle gare de' Teologi, e dei Librai. Ma per il debito dell' uffizio nostro non possiamo dispensarci dal ricordare che nello Stato Veneto non possono tenersi esposti, e molto meno stamparsi li Decreti di Roma proibitorj de' Libri, e che appunto in Bergamo con le Ducali 1624, 2 Marzo, fu ordinata la retensione del Librajo Cantoni per aver tenuto in luogo esposto della sua Bottega alcuni Decreti di Roma sopra la proibizione de' Libri. Le proibizioni di Roma per la forza del Concordato 1596 non hanno luogo nel Serenissimo Dominio. Quando nasce l' occorrenza di proibire, intesa prima la volontà dell' Eccmo Senato, le proibizioni per le materie di Eresia si fanno dal Tribunale di Sant' Offizio con l' assistenza del Magistrato Secolare; e quelle per altri rispetti sono promulgate dai competenti Magistrati, e Rappresentanti secondo il particolare comando ricevutone da Vostra Serenità, e con la Facoltà ordinaria loro concessa dalle Pubbliche Leggi.

Nel caso presente sembra non occorrere l' uso nè dell' una, nè dell' altra Potestà, perchè manca in tutti li punti accusati il soggetto da condannarsi. Perciò non resta che la opportunità di molto laudar il plausibile zelo di chi ha creduto con egregia intenzione, e singolar merito di far note al Governo le apprensioni concepite nel colore alquanto fosco di quella Denunzia. Nasce insieme l' altra opportunità di far sentire il giusto conforto, che non risulti motivo ragionevole di far passo alcuno ulteriore sopra questo emergente, che la singolare prudenza di VV. EE. vorrà posto in un perfetto, ed inalterabile Silenzio. Grazie.

Serenissimo Principe.
Illmi ed Eccmi Sigr Inquisitori di Stato.

1794, 30 Aprile.

No. 5. La necessità di leggere, e riscontrare gli ultimi Fogli usciti in Bergamo, col titolo di Giornale Ecclesiastico di Roma, non ci ha permesso di umiliare prima di questo giorno le riverenti nostre osservazioni sopra il medesimo in ubbidienza del vocale comando ingiuntoci da questo Tribunale Supremo.

Il Giornale Ecclesiastico di Roma è un Foglio periodico il quale da otto anni circa si stampa in quella Città, e si ristampa in Bergamo da Francesco Locatelli; così che di settimana in settimana partendo da un punto e portandosi all' altro trascorre velocemente quasi tutta l' Italia, e si diffonde per tutti gli stati intermedj, e conterminanti. Egli è una di quelle Gazzette Letterarie, che escono al mondo colla promessa di somministrar la cognizione imparziale, ed instruttive de' Libri nuovi, ma che tal volta si convertono in istromento pericoloso per isfogar le private passioni per diminuire il credito di qualche Autore, o per imprimere le opinioni professate dai Giornalisti, e Gazzettieri.

Per tal mezzo le Gazzette instituite a principio per dare gli avvisi degli avvenimenti più notabili delle Guerre, e di altri notorj fatti da un paese all' altro, oggidì sono cadute in molti abusi, perchè i loro Scrittori v' innestano le considerazioni lavorate a capriccio, e collo spirito di partito. Presero il nome di Gazzetta da una Moneta allora usata per comprar ciascun Foglio. In presente li Fogli di tali avvisi, come si fa de' Balsami, vengono mascherati con nomi diversi; e non essendovi Libri, o Carte più lette di queste, l' impressioni si spargono per tutte il popolo con poco servizio della Chiesa e del Principato.

Il presente Giornale ha preso voga nell' occasione che fu soppresso nello Stato Veneto un altro Foglio Letterario, il quale si distribuira col titolo: *Dai Confini d'Italia.*

Allora fu creduto, che a quella soppressione avesse dato motivo l' indiscreto ritratto, che si faceva di un Professore di Padova, ora morto. Ma nell' effetto anche quel Foglio aveva degenerato in molti arbitrj, che offendevano la reputazione, e la fama altrui. Nel carattere di quasi tutti gli scrittori di somiglianti Gazzette si trova la pretenzione di eriggersi in Censori, e Giudici non solo delle Opere pubbliche, come sono le Stampe, ma delle Persone ancora di ogni grado imputandole bene spesso di qualche difetto ancorchè non vero, o non provato, o da non pubblicarsi, donde provengono poi gli odj, le animosità e le tristi conseguenze delle fazioni.

Il giornale di Roma, per quanto risulta dai Fogli del passato anno 1793, e da alcuni pochi del presente 1794, che si sono procurati, spiega due oggetti. L' uno è quello di riscaldare in Italia li questioni della Grazia Divina, e dell' Arbitrio Umano; questioni che furono pur troppo fatali alle Fiandre, e alla Francia, e che nel giusto esame di quei lagrimevoli successi ammaestrano il mondo, quanto alimento abbiano somministrato in quegl' incendj. L' altro oggetto è quello di portare in questi tempi l' autorità Ecclesiastica e singolarmente la Pontificia fuori dei termini suoi spirituali e celesti per farla valere in tutti gl' interessi Temporali, e Terreni.

La controversia della Grazia è tanto antica quanto Santo Agostino, che ha confutato robustamente con la dottrina di San Paolo, e col nome della sua grandissima scienza gli errori dei Pelagiani, e Semipelagiani.

La sua Dottrina fu ricevuta da tutte la Chiesa, e San Tommaso l' ha rinforzata nel sistema della propria Scuola. Ma negli ultimi tempi li Teologi sottilizzando i termini per intendere più di qui Santi le operazioni della Grazia di Nostro Signor Gesu Cristo, e misurare le forze dell' Umano Arbitrio si sono divisi in due feroci partiti, l' uno dei Padri Gesuiti detto anche dei Molinisti per il nome celebre del Padre Lodovico Molina, primo autore di quella scissura, e l' altro delle Scuole Domenicane, ed Agostiniane, che si oppongono alla dottrina dei Padri Gesuiti. Quantunque ambedue le religiosi fazioni sieno concordi nel detestare le cinque Proposizione in questa materia condannate dai Sommi Pontefici, ed attribuite al Libro intitolato *Augustinus* di Cornelio Giansenio Vescovo d' Ipri nelle Fiandre; nondimeno viene mossa da alcuni la questione di fatto, se sieno, o non siano in quel Libro, e se sono, o non sono condannate nel senso dell' autore. Da questo particolare dissidio nel quale hanno avuto sempre molta influenza altri interessi, che non sono di Teologia, è derivato il nome di Giansenisti per caricare di odio con l' equivoco di tal denominazione arbitraria tutti coloro, che non seguono la scuola dei Padri Gesuiti, o che si oppongono in qualsivoglia modo eziandio il più giusto e riverente a qualche impresa della Corte Romana, la qual è cosa diversa della Santa Chiesa di Roma.

Premessi questi pochi cenni per ben discernere lo spirito, ed il linguaggio dell' odierno Giornale non può negarsi, che tutto lo sforzo del medesimo, sebben maneggiato in varie guise tratta sempre, e sostiene con modi alquanto focosi, ed intemperanti la sola opinione della estinta Compagnia di Gesù, senza dar luogo a verun' altra per quanto sia lecita e permessa dalla Chiesa stessa Cattolica in Stato di questione indecisa, e non definita. A questa, sia lecito il dirlo, soperchieria li giornalisti di Roma, che mandano sempre innanzi le loro opinioni, e combattono quelle degli altri coll' abusato nome di Giansenisti, hanno l' attenzione indescritissima di aggiungervi molte contumelie, e riflessioni oltraggiose contro i Vescovi, Capitoli, Parrochi, e Professori delle Università, l' onore dei quali tutti stà in protezione del Sovrano rispettivo.

Il tolerare in vero, che un partito parli, ed offenda, espone alla conseguenza, che anche l' altro sciolga il silenzio, e si difenda. L' attacco e la difesa nelle passioni umane rare volte hanno misura; e quando la malattia delle opinione ha preso incremento, è difficilissimo il rimedio senza generar convulsioni mortali nel Corpo Civile; e per lo più riesce con inutilità, o con infelice riuscita. Per questa riflessione insegnata dalla Storia di tutti i tempi, e verificata miseramente ancora nei nostri, li saggi Politici hanno paragonate le malattie degli Stati a quelle degli Etici, e de Tisici, le quali sono di facile guarigione, se sono conosciute a principio, ma impossibili a curarsi, quando per non esser conosciute, e medicate presero forza nel Corpo umano.

Al Giornale oltre i Fogli periodici vanno congiunti altri fogli col titolo di Supplemento distinto per Mesi, stampato egualmente in Roma, e ristampato in Bergamo dal Locatelli. Questi accessorj fedelmente ritengono la stessa natura del principale, e si fanno servire ad accrescere la semina dell' opinioni, e delle ingiurie contro li Teologi dell' opposto partito, senza risparmiare la critica e la mordacità nemmeno verso li Sovrani più sfortunati, le intere Nazioni, ed altre rispettabilissime Figure. Affinchè però VV. EE. ne abbiano sotto l' occhio un estratto fedele dei passi più notabili da rimarcarsi, nei soli Fogli degli ultimi quattordici Mesi, si è fatta la descrizione in due distinte Classi.

La prima avvisa i luoghi, e li termini usati rispetto a Principi, e la seconda rispetto a Persone, colla indicazione in margine del numero del Foglio, e della Pagina rispettiva. L' alto discernimento del Tribunale ne farà il suo sapientissimo giudicio.

Sono circa venti anni, che questo fermento Teologico serpeggia per l' Italia, singolarmente nella Toscana, e nella Lombardia. Nello Stato Veneto la Città di Bergamo sembra la più travagliata dalle scissure Ecclesiastiche; e da chi vengano coltivate, VV. EE. hanno pronti li mezzi di risaperlo. Uno però degl' istromenti per tenerle vive si può rinvenire nella ristampa di questo Giornale coi suoi supplementi, che si và dispensando a poco a poco per le altre Città. Sarà della gravissima loro maturità il ponderare se impedita affatto la Ristampa Bergamasca, abbia più a lasciarsi ingresso alla Stampa di Roma, poichè il disordine sussisterebbe tuttavia colla giunta di un altro danno, che recherebbe l' uscita del denaro fuori di Stato. Nelle Scuole tutte le Sentenze, che non sono condannate, possono aver luogo, come avviene in altri punti di sublime Teologia. Ma fuori delle Scuole, e nelle Stampe le dispute non hanno mai cagionata la felicità della Religione, e del Principato e facilmente confondono gli spiriti deboli senza convincer punto li forti.

L' obbligo di servire al comando non permetteva di trascurare questi rispettosi ed ingenui riflessi per quel peso, che potessero meritare nel grandissimo oggetto della Pubblica quiete. Grazie.

DOCUMENTS.

VI.

VI.

LIST OF VENETIAN PRINTERS AND BOOKSELLERS FROM 1469-1799.[1]

Aborelli, Gueriglio. 1574.
Accademia Veneta. 1502.
Accademia Veneta. 1558-1561.
Accademia Pellegrina. 1552.
Achates, Leonardus. 1472.
Adam de Ambergau. 1471.
Adam de Rotwill. 1471.
Adami. 1767.
Affine (d'), Pietro. 1571.
Alaris (de), Eneas. 1573.
Albanesoti, Bernardino. 1492.
Albanesoti, Marco. 1492.
Albani, Giovan Giacomo. 1563.
Alberti, Bartolomeo. 1544.
Alberti, Filippo. 1638.
Alberti, Giacomo. 1754.
Alberti, Giovanni. 1507.
Alberti, Giambatista. 1610.
Alberti (degli), Marco. 1605.
Alberti, Oliviero. 1616.
Albertinus. 1499.
Albertino de Lisbona. 1501.
Albertino. 1501.
Albertis (de), Giovanni. 1599.
Albirelli. 1594.
Albrizzi, Almorò. 1749.
Albrizzi, Andrea. 1778.
Albrizzi, Angelo. 1778.
Albrizzi, Giambatista. 1723.
Albrizzi, Giambatista, q. Angelo. 1795.
Albrizzi, Girolamo. 1693.
Albrizziana, Società. 1730.
Aldus Manutius. 1494.
Aldo e Andrea Suocero. 1534.
Alexander (di), Giorgio. 1486.
Alexandrinus, Gerardus. 1476.
Alexandria (de), Antonius. 1481.
Alexandria (de), Tomasius. 1477.
Alessi (di), Stefano. 1552.
Alessandro. 1587.
Alessandro Cretese. 1486.
Aloisianus, Jacob-Baptista. 1504.
Alopa, Lorenzo Francesco. 1494.
Alvise de Contrata S. Luciæ. 1492.
Amadi, Francesco. 1538.
Amadino, Ricciardo. 1591.
Amadoro, Marco (v. Simbeni). 1569.
Ambrosini, Cristoforo. 1647.
Ammano, Giovanni. 1487.
Anastasi, Pasqualin. 1717.
Andolfato. 1767.
Andrea d' Ascoli. 1485.

[1] This list is based entirely on Cicogna's unpublished *Elenco di Stampatori e Librari tanto Veneti che Forestieri et di quelli ad istanza de quali si pubblicarono Libri in Venezia* (Museo Civico, Cod. 3044). The names and dates, with some exceptions, are those given by Cicogna. Other catalogues of Venetian printers are to be found in Hain, Panzer, the *Archivio Veneto*, and Castellani. Cicogna's notes, which accompany his *elenco*, are of value to the student of Venetian printing.

Andrea d' Asola. 1487.
Andrea Calabrese. 1489.
Andrea Catharensis. 1476.
Andrea de Corona. 1476.
Andrea de Parma. 1485.
Andrea da Pavia. 1484.
Andrea de Platasichis. 1478.
Andrea de Valentia.
Anesi, Gervasio. 1627.
Angeli, Giuseppe Nicolò. 1703.
Angelieri, Agostino. 1607.
Angelieri, Giorgio. 1574.
Angelieri, Giovanni (?).
Animamia, alias Gug. Cereto. 1486.
Annibale da Parma. 1487.
Antignano, Christophorus (v. Quaieti). 1492.
Antonellus a Moneta. 1478.
Antonelli, Giovanni. 1727.
Antonelli, Giuseppe. 1740.
Antonelli, Leonardo. 1799.
Antonii (degli), Giannantonio. 1578.
Antonius de Alexandria de Paglia. 1481.
Antonius, Bartholomeus, de Bologna. 1476.
Antonio da Bologna. 1472.
Antonio da Guzzago Bergamasco. 1497.
Antonio da Pavia. 1482.
Antonio de Strata. 1481.
Antonius de Valentia. 1481.
Antonius de Regio. 1484.
Antonius Venetus (v. Graesse, *Tresor*, ii. 240).
Aquila, Lorenzo d'. 1475.
Arbe (d'), Nicolò. 1529.
Aristotele, Nicolò. 1528.
Aristotele, Nicolò di. 1547.
Arnoldus, Christophorus. 1472.
Arrivabene, Andrea. 1547.
Arrivabene, Cesare. 1518.
Arrivabene, Cornelio. 1527.
Arrivabene, Cornelio. 1485.
Arrivabene, Giorgio. 1585.
Arubaris, Vettore (? Ravani). 1539.
Ascoli (d'), Andrea. 1485.
Asola (d'), Andrea de Torresani. 1487.
Asola (d'), Francesco. 1544.
Aste (d'), Giovanni. 1523.
Astolfi, Antonio. 1695, cir.
Astolfi, Giuseppe. 1772.
Astolfi, Giovanni. 1794.
Astolfi, Luigi. 1797.
Avanzo, Lodovico. 1556.
Aurelio (di), Pietro. 1568.
Aurl, Leonardus. 1472, 1473.
Augusta (de), Joannes. 1472.

Babba, Gabriello. 1673.
Baba, Andrea. 1621.
Baba, Francesco. 1627.
Baba, heirs of. 1673.
Baco. 1600.
Bactibovis (de), Antonius. 1485.
Badagio, Andrea. 14 (?).
Badoara, Accademia. 1558-1561.
Baglioni, Paolo. 1637.
Baglioni, Tommaso. 1680.
Baglioni, Tommaso. 1608.
Baglioni, Giambattista. 1695.
Baglioni, Giambattista. 1749.
Baldarfer, Cristoforo. 1470.
Baldini, Vittorio. 1552.
Balissi, Nicolò. 1730.
Ballarini, Tommaso, de Ternengo. 1535.
Balleoni (v. Baglioni).
Baltibovi (v. Bactibovis).
Barba (dalla), Francesco (detto Imperador). 1550.
Barboni, Michelangelo. 1671.
Barca, Scipione. 1699.
Barezzi, Barrezzo. 1592.
Bariletto, Antonio. 1636.
Bariletto, Francesco. 1598.
Bariletto, Giovanni. 1561.
Bariletto, Lelio. 1565.
Barnasconibus (de), Antonellus. 1485.
Baroni, Andrea. 1687.
Baronchello, Bortolo. 1746, cir.
Baronchello, Giacomo. 1793.
Barreo, Giovanni, e Fratelli. 1542.
Barrevelt, Gerardus (v. Egmont). 1494.
Bartholomæus, Justinopolitanus. 1498.
Bartolommeo (di), Antonio. 1476, 1486.

Bartolommeo da Cremona. 1472.
Bartolommeo. 1543.
Bartolommeo da Fossombrone. 1485.
Bartua (de), Petrus. 1477.
Baruc, Cornelio. 1528.
Basa, Bernardo. 1584.
Basa, Domenico. 1588.
Bascarini, Nicolo. 1541.
Baseggio, Gasparo. 1749.
Baseggio, Lorenzo. 1711.
Baseggio, Lorenzo. 1731.
Baseggio, Lorenzo. 1794.
Baseggio, Giacomo. 1784.
Baseggio, Nicolo. 1754.
Baseggio, Basilius. 1695, cir.
Bashan de Ventura. 1571.
Bassaglia, Pietro. 1730.
Bassaglia, Giovan Andrea. 1797.
Bassaglia, Pietro. 1764.
Bassaglia, Giammaria. 1765.
Bassaglia, Leonardo. 1782.
Bassanese, Antonio. 1729, cir.
Bassi, Dionisio. 1784.
Basso, Pietro. 1676.
Basso, Zuanne. 1725, cir.
Bastian, Vicentino. 1532.
Batista e Stefano, cognati. 1549.
Batti, Francesco. 1695.
Batti, Giacomo. 1663.
Batti, Giovanni. 1689.
Batti, Pietro. 1695, cir.
Battibove, Antonio. 1485.
Battibove, Nicolaus. 1486.
Battifoco, Domenico. 1768.
Bazzo, Nicolo. 1767.
Bazetto, Iseppo. 1676.
Bedafini, Francesco. 1532.
Bellori, Francesco. 1796.
Bellotti, Veneziano. 1750, cir.
Beltrame, Bortolo. 1676.
Benacense (v. Paganino). 1517.
Benalius, Bernardinus. 1483.
Benalio. 1577.
Benalius, Vicentinus. 1493.
Bendolo, Jacopo. 1587.
Bendoni (v. Bindoni). 1535.
Benedictis (de), Nicolaus. 1498.
Benedetti (de), Platone. 1483.
Benedetto Fontana. 1495.
Benedictus, Genuensis. 1480.
Benetti (de), Andrea. 1484.
Benvegni, Marco. 1770.
Benvenuti, Rinaldo. 1783.
Beretin Convento. 1477.
Bergamasco, Pietro. 1487.
Bergamasco, Antonio. 1497.
Bergamo (da), Giovanni. 1495.
Bergamo (da), Giampietro. 1487.
Bernardi, Giovanni Antonio. 1785.
Bernardi, Giovanni. 1785.
Bernardon, Pontio. 1681.
Bernardon [Monsù]. 1680.
Bernardus, Pictor. 1475.
Bernardinus Venetus de Vitalibus. 1480.
Bernardinus Vercellensis. 1495.
Bernardinus Rizus. 1485.
Bernardino de Cremona. 1490.
Bernardinus Stagninus. 1483.
Bernardus de Choris, de Cremona. 1491.
Bernardin Milanese. 1541.
Bernardino e Matteo de Vitali. 1498.
Bernardino da Luere. 1484.
Bernardino Rizus de Novaria. 1484.
Bernardino da Trino. 1484.
Bernasconi (v. de Bernasconibus). 1485.
Berni, Michiel. 1589.
Berro (il). 1589.
Bertacagno, Giambatista. 1553.
Bertagli, Giannantonio. 1575.
Bertagni, Gregorio. 1676.
Bertano, Antonio. 1586.
Bertani, Giacomo. 1698.
Bertano, Giannantonio. 1572.
Bertano, Pietro. 1607.
Bertano, Piermaria. 1585.
Bertano (il). 1678.
Bertani (li). 1640.
Bertani, Valentin. 1676.
Bertani, Zuanne. 1676.
Bertazzoni, Leonardo. 1794.
Bertella, Giuseppe. 1747.
Bertelli, Donato. 1564.
Bertelli, Lorenzo. 1590.
Bertelli, Donato. 1571.

Berthocus, Dionisius. 1484.
Berthocus, Dominicus. 1486.
Bertini, Giambatista. 1605.
Bertoni, Giambatista. 1600.
Bettanin, Omobon. 1738.
Bettanin, Antonio. 1748.
Bettanin, Pietro. 1796.
Bettanin, Francesco. 1770.
Bettinelli, Nicolò. 1784.
Bettinelli, Giambatista. 1762.
Bettinelli, Francesco. 1786.
Bettinelli, Giuseppe. 1731.
Bettinelli, Tommaso. 1743.
Bevilacqua, Nicolò. 1558.
Bevilacqua, Simon. 1485.
Bianchi (de), Tommaso. 1477.
Bianchi, Domenico. 1676.
Bianco, Zuanne. 1470.
Bianconi, Vincenzo. 1786.
Biascon, Biasio. 1768.
Biave (v. de Blavis).
Biffi, Agostin. 1782.
Bindoni, Giannantonio. 1571.
Bindoni, Agostino. 1525.
Bindoni (de), Alexander. 1516.
Bindoni (de), Benedetto. 1499.
Bindoni, Bernardino. 1538.
Bindoni, Francesco. 1524, 1526.
Bindoni, Gasparo. 1563.
Biondi, Francesco. 1525.
Biondo, Francesco. 1548.
Biondo, Girolamo. 1494.
Biondo, Girolamo Fiorentino. 1495.
Biondo, Michelangelo. 1549.
Biretis (de), Johannes Antonius. 1488.
Biscarini (de), Nicolò. 1554.
Bissolus, Johannes. 1498.
Bisuccio, Daniele. 1605.
Bivilaqua, Simon. 1485.
Bizardo, Giorgio. 1612.
Blasto, Nicolò. 1499.
Blavis (de), Bartholomeus de Alexandria. 1479.
Blavio, Girardo da Alexandria. 1476.
Blavio, Girolamo da Alexandria. 1472.
Blavio, Tomaso da Alexandria. 1477.
Blondus, Hieronymus. 1495.
Boaria, Liga (cf. Virgilii, Opera, s. a. Museo Civico, E. 233).
Bochini, Andrea, e Fratelli. 1571.
Bodio, Angelo. 1674.
Bolani, Francesco. 1480, 1488.
Bologna (da), Antonio. 1472.
Bolzetta, Francesco. 1610.
Bomberg, Daniele. 1515.
Bolis, Giacomo. 1695, cir.
Bolis, Benedetto. 1571.
Bon, Altobello. 1626.
Bon, Manfrino da Monferrato. 1505.
Bona, Domenico. 1695, cir.
Bona Pace, Domenico. 1680, cir.
Bona Pace, Pasino.
Bonadio, Giovanni. 1562.
Bonardi, Giovanni. 1502.
Bonarrigo, Carlo. 1716.
Bondeno, Benedetto. 1526.
Bonelli, Giammaria. 1552.
Bonelli, Giammaria, Eredi di.
Bonellis (de), Manfredus, de Strevo de Monferrato. 1481.
Bonelli, Michele. 1576.
Bonelli, Valerio. 1579.
Bonettis (de), Andrea de Pavia. 1483.
Bonfadino, Giambatista. 1586.
Bonfadino, Giammaria. 1620.
Bonfadio, Angelo. 1582.
Bonfante, Giacomo. 1684.
Bonfante, Gabriele. 1695, cir.
Bonfante, Giovanni. 1668.
Bonfante, Matteo. 1702.
Bonfanti, Giovanni e Gabriele. 1680, cir.
Bonibelli, Marcantonio. 1596.
Bonibelli, Michele (?). 1595.
Bonifacius, Joannes. 1494.
Boninis (de), Boninus. 1478.
Bonino (v. Paltasichis). 1484.
Bonino, Pietro. 1735.
Bono, Manfredo. 1508.
Bonomo. 1749.
Bontognale, Angelo. 1683.
Bonvicini, (Petroi) Girolamo. 1782.
Bonzio, Giovanni. 1609.
Bordogna, Sigismondo. 1555.
Borghi, Domenico. 1746, cir.

Borghi, Zorzi. 1754.
Borgofranco (de), Giambatista. 1542.
Borgofranco (de), Giacomo. 1529.
Borgominero, Camillo. 1563.
Borgominero, Rutilio. 1560.
Borselio (de), Manfredo. 1493.
Bortoli, Antonio. 1705.
Bortoli, Camillo. 1658.
Bortoli, Giacomo. 1655.
Bortoli, Giovanni. 1654.
Bortoli, Girolamo. 1741.
Bortoli, Giuseppe. 1738.
Bortoli, Girolamo.
Bortoli, Cristofolo. 1676.
Bortoli, Francesco. 1781.
Bortoli, Francesco.
Bortoli, Giammaria.
Boselli, Matteo. 1571.
Bosello, Pietro. 1556.
Bosio, Antonio. 1696.
Bottieta, Tommaso. 1546.
Bovis, Giambatista. 1676.
Bracius, Gabriele, Brasichellensis. 1498.
Bragadini (li). 1749.
Bragato, Valentin. 1765.
Braida, Antonio. 1607.
Brazzetti, Giuseppe.
Brenta, Nicolò. 1507.
Brentello, Vettor. 1782.
Bressanino, Bortolo. 1571.
Briganti, Giampietro. 1567.
Brigna, Giambatista. 1668.
Brigonci, Giampietro. 1660.
Brigonci, Giambatista. 1676.
Brigonci, Pierantonio. 1687.
Brino. 1543.
Britannicus (de), Angelus et Jacobus Fratres. 1491.
Britannicus, Jacobus. 1481.
Brixiensis, Gabriel. 1491.
Brogiollo, Mar' Antonio. 1627.
Brogiollo, Giambatista. 1676.
Brogiollo, Francesco. 1665.
Brogiollo, Mar' Antonio. 1572.
Brognollo, Gioachino. 1582.
Brognollo, Benedetto. 1598.
Brucioli, Alessandro. 1542.
Brucioli, Alessandro, e Fratelli. 1545.
Brucioli, Antonio. 1530.
Brucioli, Francesco, e Fratelli. 1542.
Brunello, Francesco. 1799.
Brunetti, Giambatista. 1752.
Brunetti, Carlo. 1781.
Bruni, Bortolo. 1666.
Bruno, Maestro. 1477.
Buono, Manfrin. 1508.
Buonarrigo, Carlo. 1716.
Burchian, Andrea. 1767.
Burciensis, Martinus de Czeidino. 1484.
Burciensis, Andrea de Corona. 1484.
Buscha (de), Hercules. 1480.
Busetto, Francesco. 1674.
Businello, Giovanni. 1602.
Butricis (de), Maximus de Papia. 1491.
Buzzardo, Giorgio. 1610.

Cagnan, Domenico. 1730.
Cagnacini, Giulio Cesare. 1583.
Cagnolini, Giovanni. 1679.
Calabrese, Andrea da Pavia. 1485.
Calapo, Cristoforo. 1754.
Calapo, Girolamo. 1680.
Calcedonio, Alessandro. 1505.
Calegari, Bortolo. 1782.
Caleoni, Antonio. 1676.
Calepino, Girolamo. 1550.
Calleoni, Giovanni. 1638.
Calliergi, Zaccaria. 1499.
Camozzi, Gianfrancesco. 1569.
Camporese, Agostino. 1747.
Candiotto (v. Alessandro Cretese).
Canocio, Manfrè. 1571.
Canziani, Cristoforo. 1793.
Canziani, Antonio. 1785.
Capcasa, Mattheus da Parma. 1482.
Capellato, Giacomo. 1754.
Capodistria (da) (v. Justinopolitanus).
Cappello, Silvano. 1530, cir.
Cappello, Antonio. 1530, cir.
Carampello, Bortolomio. 1581.
Carcano, Giacomo. 1774.
Cardano. 1641.
Cardueti, Lodovico. 1598.
Carenzello, Bartolomeo. 1581.

Cargiani, Marco. 1759.
Cargnoni, Marco. 1750.
Cariletti (? Bariletti). 1596.
Carlo (de), Bartolomeo. 1474.
Carnioni, Marco. 1750.
Carminati, Pietro. 1754.
Caroboli, Giacomo. 1783.
Cartolari, Girolama, Perugina. 1544.
Casali, Antonio. 1779.
Casali, Giuseppe. 1789.
Casali, Giambatista. 1759.
Cassiolina, Pierantonio. 1799.
Casterzagense, Bartolomeo, da Brescia. 1536.
Castilione (de), Pietro. 1483.
Castro (de), Antonio. 1748.
Catalanus, Benedictus. 1481.
Catanellus, Marcus Schavicolla. 1480.
Catani, Giambatista. 1668.
Catarense, Andrea. 1476.
Catarense, Jacobus. 1476.
Cavalcabò, Jeronimo. 1568.
Cavalcalovo, Domenico. 1563.
Cavalcalovo, Alessandro. 1606.
Cavalcalovo, Girolamo. 1564.
Cavalli (de), Giorgio. 1560.
Celeri, Bernardinus de Luere. 1478.
Cellebrini, Giambatista. 1766.
Cereto (de), Joannes de Tridino. 1492.
Cereto, Guglielmo, de Tridino de Monteferrato. 1486.
Ceruti, Giovanni. 1613.
Cesano, Bartolommeo. 1550.
Cestari, Giambatista. 1647.
Cha Grande (v. Beretin Convento). 1477.
Chalierges, Zaccaria. 1499.
Chandoce (da), Alessandro. 1486.
Chandoce (da), Zeinico. 1486.
Chataro (v. Andrea da).
Chellero, Bernardo. 1787.
Cheris (sive Choris), Bernardino. 1488.
Chiarello, Giambatista. 1706.
Chiesa (della or dalla), Giovanni. 1539.
Chiesa (dalla), Giovanni. 1571.
Choris (de), Bernardinus. 1488.
Chreger. 1557.
Chrigero, Giovanni. 1539.
Christophorus de Cremona. 1491.
Cieco, Cristoforo da Forlì. 1574.
Ciera, Bonifacio. 1599.
Ciera, Nicolò. 1695, cir.
Ciera, Pietro. 1606.
Cioci (?), Giambatista. 1587.
Ciotti, Francesco. 1606.
Ciotti, Giambatista. 1583.
Ciotti, Pietro. 1606.
Cirneo, Pietro. 1482.
Clagera (? Claseri).
Claseri, Marco. 1597.
Clementino, Patavino. 1471.
Clichi (v. Glichi).
Codeca (de), Joannes, da Parma. 1493.
Codeca (de), Matteo, da Parma. 1493 [1482].
Colleoni, Giovanni. 1630.
Collosini, Giambatista. 1604.
Coletti, Sebastiano. 1719.
Coletti, Nicolò. 1795.
Coletti, Nicolò. 1762.
Colombani, Paolo. 1760.
Colonia (de), Joannes. 1471.
Coma, Stefano. 1567.
Combi, Giambattista. 1618.
Combi, Bastiano. 1605.
Combi, Giambattista, e La Nou. 1621.
Combi e La Nou. 1660.
Combi, Carlo Giuseppe. 1785.
Combi, Giampietro. 1785.
Comin da Trino [de Monferrato]. 1540 [1535].
Comin, Antonio. 1784.
Comin, Giulio Antonio. 1788.
Cominotti, Angelo. 1792.
Comitibus (de), Marco. 1476.
Compagnia Grande. 16th cent.
Compagnia Piccola. 16th cent.
Compagnia Minima. 1596.
Compagnia degli Uniti. 1585.
Contarini, Gasparo.
Contegna (de), Nicolò. 1483.
Conti (de), Marco. 1476.
Conventus Minoritanorum. 1477.
Convertite, Convento delle. 1558.
Convento di San Spirito. 1597.

Conzatti, Carlo. 1666.
Conzatti, Giambatista. 1720.
Conzatti, Zaccaria. 1662.
Conzatti, Francesco. 1735.
Conzatti, Giovanni Antonio. 1784.
Conzatti, Carlo. 1792.
Conzatti, Francesco. 1784.
Conzatto, Giambattista. 1631.
Coppa, Jacopo. 1547.
Coradi, Bernardo. 1729.
Coradizzi, Gasparo. 1664.
Cordella, Simon. 1789.
Coris (de), Bernardino. 1488.
Cornetto, Giacomo. 1578.
Corona (da), Andrea (v. Corvus). 1476.
Corona, Giuseppe. 1716.
Corona, Spinardo. 1676.
Corona, Agostino. 1754.
Corona, Antonio. 1695, cir.
Corona, Giuseppe. 1716.
Corona, Domenico. 1754.
Cortese, Alessandro. 1676.
Corvus, Andrea burciensis da Corona. 1476.
Costantini, Giacomo. 1799.
Costantini, Angelo. 1754.
Costantini, Baldassar. 1543.
Cremonensis, Bartholomæus. 1472.
Cremona (da), Bernardino. 1490.
Cremona (da), Cristoforo. 1494.
Cremona (da), Pietro. 1480.
Creston, Anzolo. 1680.
Cretensis (v. Laonicus). 1486.
Cretensis (v. Alexander). 1486.
Crisero (?), Giacomo. 1569.
Cristofoli, Angelo. 1799.
Cristoforo da Cremona. 1491.
Cristoforo (detto Stampon). 1531.
Cuna (di), Andrea di Patrasso. 1544.
Cuogia, Carlo. 1695, cir.
Cuori (de), Bernardino. 1488.
Curti, Francesco. 16 . . .
Curti, Stefano. 1672.
Curti, Antonio. 1799.
Curti, Giovanni Antonio. 1786.
Curzio, Trojano. 1565.
Czeidino (de), Martinus. 1484.

Da Fino, Pietro. 1571.
Da Trino, Comino. 1571.
Dalla Chiesa, Zuanne. 1571.
Dalla Madonna, Domenico. 1571.
Dalla Speranza, Gasparo. 1571.
Dall' Ercole, Francesco. 1571.
Dalmatinus, Georgius. 1482.
Damiano de Gorgonzola. 1493.
Daniel, Pietro. 1557.
Darè, Antonio. 1782.
Danza, Paolo. 1534.
Danza, Julio. 1547.
Danza, Bastian. 1571.
Dauvome, Joannes Persan. 1483.
De Borgo, Zorzi. 1754.
De Castro, Antonio. 1748.
De Faris, Antonio. 1571.
De Grandis, Giambatista. 1762.
De Lenis, Francesco. 1571.
De Luchi, Pietro. 1695, cir.
De pane e vino (v. Verolengo). 1492.
De Paoli, Zuanne. 1676.
De Polo, Leonardo. 1695, cir.
De Prà, Giacomo. 1720.
De Tofolo, Cristofolo. 1680.
De Tomaso, Francesco. 1571.
Dedini, Giacomo. 1688.
Dei, Ambrogio. 1610.
Dei, Bortolo. 1614.
Dereghi, Domenico. 1746.
Dereghi, Giambatista. 1749.
Desio, Valentino. 1613.
Deuchino, Evangelista. 1606.
Deuchino, Pietro. 1578.
Deuchino, Eredi di Pietro. 1586.
Diamanti, Vilio. 1571.
Dinali, Stefano. 1494.
Dinali, Bernardino. 1494.
Dinflaken (de), Jordanus. 1505.
Divineur (?), Giovanni. 1519.
Domenico (de), Lucas Venetus. 1482 [1480].
Domenico alla Speranza. 1571.
Domenico, de Piero. 1571.
Donadei, Giulio. 1642.
Donato, Gregorio. 1584.
Doni. 1540.

Doriguzzi, Zuanne. 1676.
Dramin, Bernardo. 1676.
Duranti, Girolamo. 1493.
Durigoni, Girolamo. 1749.
Dusinelli, Pietro. 1588.
Dusinelli, Pietro. 1597.
Dulcigno (da) (v. Olchiense). 1517.

Eberardi, Antonio. 1680.
Eberardi, Corrado. 1676.
Egmont (de), Federicus. { 1494.
Egmont, Federigo. } 1487.
Emerich, Giovanni. 1487.
Emilio, Iseppo. 1680.
Enea d' Alaris. 1573.
Ercole (dall'), Francesco. 1571.
Erasmiana, Stamperia (v. Valgrisi).
Erbipoli (d'), Francesco Teodoro. 1480.
Ersog (v. Hertzog).
Ertz, Gabriele. 1721.
Ertz, Jacopo. 1646.
Ertz, Michele. 1710.
Ertz, Gianjacopo. 1678.
Ettore (di), Benedetto. 1506.

Fabri, Uberto. 1620.
Fabris, Ignazio Lorenzo. 1754.
Fabris, Michele. 1754.
Fabris, Giammaria. 1782.
Fabris, Bernardo. 1717.
Fabro, Antonio. 1786.
Facchini, Bortolo. 1789.
Facchinetti, Pietro. 1588.
Facolo (?) (de), Pietro. 1543.
Falconi. 1767.
Fama (della), Accademia. 1558.
Farina, Bernardo. 1729.
Farina, Giovanni. 1592.
Farrei, Giovanni. 1542.
Farri, Domenico, da Rivoltalla. 1556.
Farri, Giovanni. 1540.
Farri, Giannantonio. 1572.
Farri, Onofrio. 1559.
Farri, Eredi di Domenico. 1607.
Farri, Pietro. 1621.
Fassina (il). 1648.
Favai, Luca Antonio. 1762.

Fei, Bartolommeo. 1478.
Felixe de Consorte. 1503.
Feltrini, Natale. 1713.
Fenio (da), Annibale da Parma. 1485.
Fenzo, Modesto. 1738.
Fenzo, Giuseppe. 1779.
Fenzo, Nicolò. 1784.
Ferno, Michele. 1497.
Feroben (?), Giovanni. 1519.
Ferrarese, Giovanni Bernardo. 1530.
Ferrari, Antonio. 1580.
Ferrari (de), Giolito Gabriele. 1544.
Ferrariis (de), Nicolaus de Pralormis. 1492.
Ferrarin, Giovanni. 1780.
Ferrarin, Domenico. 1754.
Ferretti, Giacomo. 1680.
Ferretti, Ognibene. 1651.
Ferretti, Giambatista. 1658.
Fialetti. 1596.
Fiandra (da), Gerardo. 1477.
Filadelfo, Giovanni. 1556.
Filippi, Marco. 1668.
Filippo, de Piero. 1474.
Filippo e Gabriele de Piero. 1472.
Finazzi, Girolamo. 1774.
Finazzi, Giambatista. 1706.
Finozzi, Bortolo. 1774.
Fine (da), Pietro. 1562.
Fiorentino, Francesco. 1532.
Fiorentino, Domenico. 1577.
Fiorina, Giovanni. 1592.
Fiorina, Vincenzo. 1616, 1607.
Fivizzano (da), Jacopo. 1472.
Flandria (de), Gerardo. 1477.
Foglierini, Antonio. 1766.
Foglierini, Andrea. 1768.
Foglierini, Domenico. 1792.
Foglierini, Giannandrea. 1789.
Foglietta, Girolamo. 1575.
Fontana, Bartolommeo. 1626.
Fontana, Benedictus. 1492.
Fontaneto (de), Guillielmus. 1518.
Fontaneto (de), Guglielmo di Monteferrato. 1577.
Fontanotto, Vincenzo. 1748.
Forcatini, Alvise. 1676.

Foreseno (?). 1547.
Foresti e Bettinelli. 1797.
Foresto, Iseppo. 1558.
Formaleoni, Vincenzo. 1781.
Fossati, Giorgio. 1757.
Forli (da), Giovanni. 1494.
Forli (da), Giovanni e Gregorio Fratelli. 1497.
Fortunato, Guglielmo. 1516.
Fosio, Annibale da Parma (v. Foxius). 1487.
Fossombrone (da), Bartolommeo. 1485.
Fossombrone (da), Ottaviano de' Petrucci. 1500.
Foxius, Annibal Parmensis. 1485.
Fozzano, Domenico. 1574.
Framotti, Costantino, Eredi di. 1695, cir.
Francesco, Jacopo. 1479.
Francesci, Camillo. 1528.
Franceschi (de), Domenico. 1570.
Franceschi (de), Francesco Senese. 1562.
Franceschi (de), Giacomo. 1614.
Franceschi (de), Girolamo. 1596.
Franceschi (di), Pietro. 1574.
Franceschi (de), Zuanne. 1541.
Franceschini, Camillo. 1566.
Franceschini, Francesco. 1564.
Francesco d' Asola. 1544.
Francesco dall' Ercole. 1571.
Francesco de Tommaso. 1571.
Francfordia (de), Nicolo. 1473.
Franchi. 1567.
Franciscus, Lapicida (Tagliapietra). 1494.
Franciscus, Lucentis Presbyter. 1499.
Franer, Giacomo. 1601.
Franco, Jacopo. 1579.
Frari (v. Beretin Convento). 1477.
Franzini, Giovanni Antonio. 1601.
Franzoso, Francesco. 1591.
Freghetti, Zuanne. 1680, cir.
Frigiolo, Domenico. 1676.
Furlanetto, Lodovico. 1725.
Furlivio (de Forli), Giovanni. 1481.

Gabis (de), Simone. 1487.
Gabriel, Brixiensis. 1491.
Gabriel, Petrus de Tarvisio. 1472.
Gabriele, de Petri. 1475.
Gabriele e Filippo de Piero. 1472.
Gabrielli, Federico. 1594.
Gafarotto, Giambatista. 1695, cir.
Galignani, Giambatista. 1599.
Galignani, Giorgio. 1598.
Galignani, Simon. 1574.
Galignani, Simon, Eredi di. 1590.
Gallico, Jacopo. 1473.
Gallina, Comeno (?). 1615.
Gallus, Guillelmus. 1477.
Ganassi (di), Silvestro. 1535.
Gara, Giovanni. 1590.
Gara (de), Simon. 1491.
Garanta, Nicolo. 1526.
Garbin, Santo. 1748.
Garbiza, Francesco. 1749.
Garbiza, Iseppo. 1676.
Garbiza, Francesco. 1658.
Garbiza, Giuseppe. 1736.
Garbiza, Teodoro. 1754.
Garbo, Francesco.
Garbo, Gianfrancesco. 1763.
Gardano, Anzolo. 1585.
Gardano, Alessandro. 1578.
Gardano, Antonio. 1539.
Garizzo, Giuseppe. 1767.
Garon, Francesco. 1527.
Garone, Giovanni. 1527.
Garzoni, Marco. 1652.
Gasparo dalla Speranza. 1571.
Gatti, Giovanni. 1770.
Gatti, Silvestro. 1783.
Gatti, Pietro. 1788.
Gava (da), Simone. 1497.
Gaza (li). 1560.
Genuensis, Benedictus. 1480.
Georgius, Dalmatinus. 1482.
Gerardo de Fiandra. 1477.
Gerardi, Gasparo. 1732.
Gerardus, Alexandrinus. 1476.
Geremia, Angelo. 1730.
Geremia, Geremia. 1765.
Gerretzem (de), Johann Manthen. 1473.
Gesù (del), Nicolo. 1578.

Gesù (del), Domenico. 1578.
Gesuati, i Frati di San Girolamo. 1528.
Ghedini, Jacopo. 1580.
Gherardo, Paolo. 1543.
Gherretzem, Joannes. 1473.
Ghidioli, Giacomo. 1580.
Ghirardengus, Nicolaus, de Nove. 1479.
Giacomazzi, Giampaolo. 1607.
Giacomini, Iseppo. 1676.
Giacomo di Borgofranco. 1529.
Gianicolo, Tolomeo. 1529.
Gianicolo (il). 1547.
Giannalvise da Varese. 1493.
Giantomaso, Napolitano. 1539.
Giavarina, Bartolomeo. 1723.
Gidini, Giacomo. 1580.
Giglio, Domenico. 1551.
Giglio, Girolamo. 1559.
Giglio, Domenico. 1538.
Ginami, Francesco. 1655.
Ginami, Marco. 1621.
Ginami, Zuanne. 1676.
Giolito, Gabriele. 1542.
Giolito, Gabriele di Ferrari. 1544.
Giolito, Giovanni da Trino. 1529.
Giolito, Giovanni di Giovanni. 1579.
Giolito, Gianfrancesco. 1565.
Giolito (il). 1543.
Gioliti (i). 1569.
Gionta (v. Giunta).
Giovanni, Bartolommeo d'Aste. 1523.
Giovanni, Bonifacio. 1494.
Giovanni, da Cereto, da Tridino. 1492.
Giovanni de Colonia. 1471.
Giovanni Enrico da Spira. 1494.
Giovanni da Forlì. 1494.
Giovanni de Gerretzem. 1473.
Giovanni de Lorenzo da Bergamo. 1495.
Giovanni di Augusta. 1472.
Giovanni Matteo. 1477.
Giovanni da Spira. 1469.
Giovanni da Trino. 1496.
Giovanni da Villavecchia. 1494.
Giovanni Andrea da Varese. 1499.
Girardengo, Francesco. 1479.
Girardengo, Nicolò. 1479.
Girardi, Gasparo. 1738.
Girardo, Alessandrino. 1476.
Giudecca (v. Convertite della).
Giuliani, Andrea. 1671.
Giuliani, Baldisera. 1619.
Giuliani, Giannantonio. 1643, 1626.
Giunta, Antonio. 1512.
Giunta, Bernardo. 1582.
Giunta, Filippo. 1589.
Giunta, Lucantonio. 1489.
Giunta, Lucantonio, Eredi di. 1542.
Giunti, Bernardo. 1585.
Giunti, Tomaso.
Giunti, Filippo. 1580.
Giunti e Baba. 1647.
Giustiniani, Marcantonio. 1546.
Glichi, Nicolò. 1742.
Glichi, Michiel. 1789.
Glichi, Nicolò. 1676.
Gnoato, Silvestro. 1789.
Gobbi (de), Orazio. 1508 (?).
Gobbi (de), Orazio. 1580.
Godini, Jacopo. 1577.
Gonzatti (v. Conzatti).
Gorgonzola (de), Damiano. 1493.
Grandi (de), Giambatista. 1763.
Grandi, Marco. 1625.
Grassi, Domenico. 1680.
Grassis, Gabriel de Papia. 1485.
Graziosi, Antonio.
Gregolin, Marco. 1788.
Gregorii (de), Gregorio. 1480.
Griffio, Alessandro. 1581.
Griffio, Cristofolo. 1577.
Griffio, Giovanni. 1518.
Griffio (il). 1629.
Grillo, Santo. 1618.
Groppo, Beltrame. 1695, cir.
Groppo, Eredi. 1695, cir.
Groppo, Antonio. 1719.
Groppo, Francesco. 1697.
Guadagnino, Giannandrea (v. Valvasore). 1565.
Gualtero. 1553.
Gualtieri (li). 1560.
Guarisco, Marco. 1598.
Guarisco, Zuanne. 1571.

Guazzo, Marco. 1534.
Gueraldi, Bernardino da Vercelli. 1502.
Guerigliana, Stamperia. 1643.
Gueriglio, Federico. 1574.
Gueriglio, Paolo. 1676.
Gueriglio, Giovanni. 1596.
Guerino, Geremia. 1477 (?).
Guerinus, Juvenis. 1477.
Guerini, Santo. 1557.
Guerra, Domenico. 1574.
Guerra, Domenico e Giambatista. 1562.
Guerra, Domenico e Giambatista. 1578.
Guglielmo da Trino. 1486.
Guilielmus, Gallus. 1477.
Guillelmo, Giuseppe. 1578.
Gulnafor, Anabiet. 1680.
Gunzago, Antonius. 1497.
Guzzago (da), Antonio. 1497.
Guzzo, Francesco. 1680.
Gyrardengus, Franciscus de Papia. 1484 [1479].

Hailbrun (de), Francesco Renner. 1471.
Hailbrun (de), Johannes Santritter. 1480.
Hallis (de), Johannes. 1476.
Hamman, Johannes de Landoja. 1487.
Harlem, Henricus. 1483.
Herasmius, Bernardinus. 1491.
Herbort, Joannes. 1487.
Hercules de Buscha. 1480.
Hertz, Michele. 1695, cir.
Hertz, Giovanni Gabriello. 1711.
Hertz, Giovanni Cichario. 1693.
Hertz, Gabriele. 1746.
Hertz, Giangiacomo. 1649.
Hertzhauser, Francesco. 1733.
Hertzog, Joannes de Landoja. 1487.

Jacobus, Andreas, da Cattaro. 1476.
Jacobus de Fivizano. 1477.
Jacobo, Gallico. { 1473.
Jacobo, Francese. { 1473.
Jacobo da Lecce. 1497.
Jacopo, Britannico. 1483.
Janiculo, Tolomeo. 1548, 1529.

Jenson, Nicolaus. 1470. [1461.]
Jesù, Nicolaus. 1526.
Jesù, Domenico. 1526.
Imberti, Domenico. 1587.
Imberti, Giandomenico. 1588.
Imberti, Gherardo. 1611.
Imberti, Gherardo e Giuseppe. 1622.
Imberti, Giovanni. 1656.
Imberti, Giuseppe. 1628.
Imperatore, Bartolomeo detto. 1544.
Imperatore (de lo), Francesco. 1557.
Inchiostro, Giovanni. 1767.
Indrich, Giambatista. 1680.
Indrich, Giambatista. 1752.
Indrich, Giammaria. 1695, cir.
Insegna dell' Albero. 1560.
" dell' Agnello. 1686.
" dell' Ancora.
" dell' Angelo di Tobbia.
" dell' Aurora.
" d' Apolline.
" dell' Aquila. 1547.
" di San Bernardino.
" del Castello.
" della Carità.
" del Cavaletto.
" del Centauro.
" della Cognizione. 1548.
" della Colomba. 1597.
" della Colonna.
" del Diamante. 1535.
" della Elefanta. 1573.
" dell' Elefante.
" della Fede.
" della Fenice.
" della Fortezza.
" della Fortuna.
" delle Frezze.
" della Gatta.
" dell' Ipografo. 1582.
" dell' Idra. 1590.
" di Laocoonte. 1530.
" della Minerva.
" del Monte Parnasso.
" della Nave.
" del Nome di Dio.
" della Pace.

Insegna del Re.
„ di Roma.
„ della Religione.
„ della Salamandra.
„ alla Sapienza.
„ del Serpente.
„ della Sibilla.
„ della Sirena.
„ della Speranza.
„ della Stella.
„ della Torre.
„ della Providenza.
„ della Verità.
„ del Sol.
„ all' Italia.
„ alla Piramide.
„ della Geografia.
„ dell' Hercole.
Joannis (v. Bonifacius).
Joannes (v. Cereto).
Johannes (v. Hallis).
Johannes (v. Leodio).
Johannes (v. Noederlingen).
Joannes (v. Varisco).
Johannes (v. Villa Vetteri).
Johannes Antonius de Papia. 1483.
Johannes Emericus de Udenhem. 1487.
Johannes de Lorenzo, da Bergamo. 1495.
Johannes Herbort de Selgenstat. 1481.
Johannes Patavinus. 1534.
Johannes de Rheno.
Isoardis (de), Lazaro. 1490.
Isola di San Spirito.
Itechem, Pietro. 1542.
Junta (v. Giunta).
Justinopolitanus, Bartholomæus.
Justiniane (Case Nove). 1536.
Juvenis Guerinus. 1477.

Karera (de), Eredi di Simon Galignani. 1585.

Lamberti, Bernardo. 1722.
Lamberti, Zuanne. 1730.
Lambillionus, Antonius. 1492.
Lampugnano, Odoardo. 1525.
Lanau, Girolamo. 1680.
La Nou, Zuanne. 1676.
Landoja (v. Hammann de).
Landucci, Orazio. 1601.
Laonicus, Cretensis. 1486.
Lapicida, Francesco. 1494.
Laros, Giovanni. 1589.
Latomi, Pietro. 1494.
Laurentius, Presbyter de Aquila. 1475.
Laurentius, Rubeus, de Valentia. 1482.
Laurentino, Francesco. 1562.
Lauro (de), Lucantonio. 1489.
Lazaro de Soardis. 1490.
Lazaronibus (de), Martino, da Rovado. 1492.
Lazaroni, Giammaria. 1734.
Lazaroni, Felice. 1753.
Lecco (da), Jacopo. 1491.
Lecco (da), Jacopo. 1522.
Lecco (da), Pencio. 1528.
Lega Boaria.
Legieri. 1532.
Leichtenstein, Pietro. 1496.
Leni, Giammaria. 1567.
Leni, Matteo. 1642.
Leniana e Vecelliana, Stamperia. 1643.
Leno (de), Francesco. 1566.
Leodio (de), Johannes. 1483.
Leon de Wild. 1478.
Leonardi, Antonio. 1607.
Leonardo da Basilea. 1473.
Leoncini, Jacopo. 1547.
Leoviller, Giovanni de Hallis. 1487.
Lessona (de), Bernardinus. 1522.
Leuco (da), Jacopo. 1496.
Lexona (de), Bernardinus. 1522.
Liechtenstein, Hermann. 1473.
Liechtenstein, Pietro. 1497.
Liga Boaria.
Ligname, Antonio. 1533.
Lignano, Johannes Antonius. 1494.
Lilio, Presbyter Hieronymus. 1558.
Lironcurti, Giovanni. 1758.
Lissona (de), Albertinus. 1500.
Lissona (de), Bernardinus de Vianis. 1504.
Locatello, Bonetto. 1473.

Locatelli, Antonio.
Locatelli, Francesco.
Locatelli, Giambatista. 1786.
Locatelli, Giuseppe. 1786.
Locatelli, Bartolommeo. 1742.
Lodovico da Venezia. 1488.
Londuzio (?), Lodovico. 1589.
Longo, Giambatista. 1772.
Longo, Francesco. 1797.
Longo, Pietro. 1579.
Lorenzini, Francesco da Trino. 1556.
Lorenzino (v. Laurentino). 1562.
Lorenzo (de), Johannes da Bergamo. 1495.
Lorenzo degli Orefici, da Vicenza. 1523.
Lorio, Lorenzo de Portes. 1525.
Lorii (de), Lorio. 1585.
Loslein, Petrus de Langencen. 1476.
Lovere (de), Simon. 1490.
Lovisa, Domenico. 1701.
Lovisa, Giuseppe. 1733.
Lovisa, Gasparo. 1797.
Lucas Venetus. 1480.
Lucensis, alias Luchese, Franciscus. 1499.
Luchi (de), Pietro.
Luciani, Giovanni.
Luciani, Bernardo. 1680, cir.
Luciani, Giuseppe. 1788.
Luciani, Giambatista. 1676.
Luciani, Zuanne. 1676.
Lucilius, Joannes (v. Santritter). 1480.
Luere (da), Bernardino. 1484.
Luere (de), Comino. 1528.
Luere (de), Simon. 1489.
Luere (da) (v. Celeri).
Luna (da), Otino da Pavia. 1496.
Lunensis, Jacobus. 1477.

Madiis (de), Franciscus. 1485.
Madonna (della), Domenico. 1571.
Maestro Bruno di Piemonte. 1477.
Maffei, Giulio. 1719.
Maggi (v. Madiis). 1485.
Magiorino, Bernardino. 1569.
Magnanzio, Pietro. 1542.
Magnus (v. Herbort de Selegenstat).
Magni, Francesco. 1676.
Magno, Stefano Maria. 1680.
Mainelli. 1594.
Malachin, Giovanni. 1721.
Malaspina, Marcantonio. 1580.
Maldura, Biagio. 1678.
Maldura, Francesco.
Maldura, Domenico. 1604.
Maldura, Giovanni. 1749.
Manassi, Nicolò. 1619.
Mandello (de), Cristoforo, de Pensis. 1492.
Manetti, Giovanni. 1695, cir.
Manerbi, Nicolò. 1477.
Manfer, Pietro. 1483.
Manfrè, Giovanni. 1718.
Manfrè, Marcantonio. 1784.
Manfrè, Giovanni. 1793.
Manfrè, Zuanne. 1680.
Manfrè (de), Manfrino. 1502.
Manfredi, di Monferrato di Sustreno. 1481.
Manfrino de Monferrato. 1490.
Mangius, Benedictus. 1498.
Manilius, Sebastianus Romanus. 1494.
Mantelli, Giuseppe. 1567.
Manthen, Johannes da Gheretzem. 1473.
Manutius, Aldus. 1494.
Manuzio. 1555.
Manuzio, Antonio. 1554.
Manuzio, Paolo. 1533.
Manzolini, Michele de Parma. 1481.
Manzoni, Andrea. 1695.
Marca, Francesco. 1538.
Marcello, Iseppo. 1610.
Marchesan, Pietro. 1736.
Marchetti, Silvestro. 1599.
Marchettini, Antonio. 1792.
Marchiada, Giambatista. 1782.
Marcolini, Francesco. 1536.
Marcolini, da Forlì. 1538.
Marcolini, al segno della Verità. 1544.
Marconi, Girolamo. 1751.
Marcucci, Pietro. 1784.
Maria (de), Marco. 1565.

Mariani, Giuseppe. 1754.
Marin (de), Giannantonio. 1575.
Marinello, Curzio. 1581.
Marinelli, Pietro. 1589.
Marinoni, Giuseppe. 1788.
Marini, Giambatista. 1600.
Marino, Bartholomæus. 1485.
Marino, Hanibale. 1485.
Marinus (v. Saracenus). 1478.
Marsini, Silvestro. 1754.
Martini, Andrea. 1784.
Martini, Antonio. 1792.
Martinelli, Pietro. 1589.
Martinelli, Zuanne. 1676.
Massarini. 1545.
Mattio (Pagan) dalla Fede. 1550.
Matteo, Giovanni. 1477.
Matthæus Venetus. 1498.
Maufer, Petrus. 1480.
Mazo (de), Domenico. 1791.
Mazo de Parenzo. 1548.
Mazzorini, Bernardo. 1571.
Mazucco, Osvaldo. 1782.
Mediolanus. 1493.
Megietti, Giambatista. 1601.
Megietti, Antonio. 1601.
Megietti, Paolo. 1578.
Megietti, Roberto. 1594.
Menafoglio, Abbondio. 1671.
Menegatti, Sebastiano. 1699.
Mercurio, Andrea. 1695.
Messarolo, Orlando. 1571.
Micheli, Giandomenico. 1575.
Michielucci, Giacomo. 1713.
Milano (da), Damiano. 1493.
Milli, Giovanni.
Milli, Francesco. 1792.
Milli, Antonio. 1695.
Milli, Cristino. 1754.
Miloco, Alvise. 1784.
Miloco, Andrea. 1787.
Miloco, Pierantonio. 1746.
Miloco, Benedetto. 1745.
Miloco, Giuseppe. 1695, cir.
Miloco, Benedetto. 1658.
Miloco, Domenico. 1673.
Miloco, Francesco. 1645.
Miloco, Michele. 1667.
Miloco, Pietro. 1616.
Miloco, Domenico. 1684.
Minima, Compagnia. 1596.
Minoritorum, Conventus. 1477.
Misserini, Francesco. 1551.
Misserini, Giammaria. 1638.
Misserini, Giovanni Antonio. 1637.
Misserini, Giovanni Maria. 1637.
Misserini, Nicolò. 1601.
Molin, Giovanni. 1697.
Molinari, Giuseppe. 1799.
Molinari, Vincenzo. 1745.
Moneta (della), Antonellus. 1478.
Monferrà (da), Guglielmo. 1543.
Monferrà (de), Manfredo. 1493.
Monsù, Bernardino. 1680.
Monti, Panfilo. 1537.
Monti, Stefano. 1713.
Mora, Antonio. 1718.
Morando, Giannantonio. 1554.
Moretto, Antonio. 1492.
Moretti, Nicolò. 1583.
Moronis (de), Bernardinus da Lecco. 1482.
Mortali, Valentino. 1665.
Murari, Giambatista. 1680.
Murari, Zuanne. 1676.
Muschio, Andrea. 1565.

Nallis (de), Stephanus. 1494.
Nallis (de), Bernardinus. 1494.
Nanti, Francesco. 1730.
Nanti, Domenico. 1701.
Napolitano (v. Giantomaso). 1539.
Natto, Domenico. 1750.
Navò, Curzio Trojano et Fratelli. 1538.
Negri, Giambatista. 1791.
Negri, Zuanne. 1676.
Negro (dal), Giandomenico. 1492.
Nicolaus, Benedictus. 1481.
Nicolaus et Dominicus.
Nicolaus de Franckfordia. 1473.
Nicolini, Pietro. 1536.
Nicolini, Francesco. 1676.
Nicolini, Dominicus. 1570.

Nicolini, Domenico. 1560.
Nicolini (de), Domenico et Cornelio. 1572.
Nicolini (de), Johannes Antonius. 1516.
Nicolini (de), Pietro. 1541.
Nicolini (de), Giammaria. 1549.
Nicolo d' Aristotele. 1508.
Nicolò di Franckofordia. 1474.
Noerdlingen (de), Johannes. 1483.
Nou, La. 1621.
Novara (da), Bernardino. 1485.
Novaria, Rizzus de. 1485.
Novelle, Jacopo. 1564.
Novelli, Giambatista. 1784.
Novimagio (de), Rinaldo. 1477.
Numeister, Giovanni. 1472.
Nus (?), Giambatista. 1618.
Noctua. 1474 (cf. the *Duranti*, Bologna, 1474).

Occhi, Giambatista. 1784.
Occhi, Simon. 1784.
Occhi, Andrea. 1784.
Occhi, Carlo Antonio. 1784.
Occhi, Giambatista. 1763.
Occhi, Domenico. 1784.
Occhi, Domenico. 1789.
Occhi, Antonio. 1749.
Occhi, Bortolo. 1712.
Occhi, Domenico. 1735.
Occhi, Giovanni. 1749.
Occhi, Simone. 1735.
Oddoni, Guglielmo. 1642.
Olchiense, Luca. 1517.
Olmo, Innocenzio. 1557.
Olmo, Antonio. 1572.
Olzati, Tomaso. 1695, cir.
Omiciano, Giammaria di Monferrato. 1491.
Orio, Lorenzo. 1554.
Orlandelli, Giuseppe. 1788.
Orlandi (d'), Pietro. 1686.
Orlandini, Giambatista. 1784.
Orlandini, Stefano. 1749.
Orsetti, Angelo. 1685.
Osanna, Francesco Bernardino. 1573.
Ostio (ab) (v. Porta). 1578.
Otinus de Luna, Papiensis. 1496.

Padovani, Domenico. 1688.
Padovano, Clemente. 1471.
Padovano, Giovanni. 1535.
Padovano, Giovanni, Eredi di. 1555.
Pagano, Marco (? Mattio). 1553.
Pagano, Mattio. 1552.
Paganinus, Alexander da Toscolano. 1491.
Paganinis (de), Jacobus, Brixiensis. 1490.
Paganinis (de), Hieronymus, Brixiensis. 1492.
Paganinis (de), Paganinus, Brixiensis. 1485.
Paganino, Pietro. 1589.
Paganino, Giambatista. 1639.
Palamides, Giammaria. 1539.
Palazogo (de), Petrus Johannes. 1492.
Palese, Carlo. 1784.
Paltasichis (de), Andrea Catharensis. 1476.
Panizza, Paolo. 1610.
Pantaglioni, Giambatista. 1748, cir.
Paoli (de), Zuanne. 1676.
Paoli (de), Giovanni. 1749.
Paolo (de). 1518.
Papia (de), Johannes. 1483.
Papiense, Ottino. 1496.
Papiensis, Petrus. 1500.
Papini. 1585.
Parè, Giovanni. 1676.
Parè, Michele. 1695, cir.
Paretti, Bartolommeo. 1535.
Parma (da), Andrea. 1485.
Parma (da), Annibale. 1487.
Parma (da), Matteo. 1493.
Parolari. 1767.
Paron, Paolo. 1680, cir.
Pasinello, Angelo. 1737.
Pasini, Nicolò. 1571.
Pasini, Agostino. 1619.
Pasini, Maffeo. 1524.
Pasquali, Giambatista. 1733.
Pasquali (de), Perigrino, Bolognese. 1483.

Pasquali (de), Peregrino e Socii. 1485.
Pasquali, Giambatista. 1784.
Pasquali, Giuseppe. 1784.
Pasquali, Giovanni Antonio. 1784.
Pasquali, Pietro. 1784.
Pasquali, Giovanni. 1787.
Pasquali, Giustino. 1790.
Pasqualino, Antonio da San Germano, 1476.
Pasquardo, Donato. 1630.
Pasquati, Lorenzo. 1603.
Patavinus, Clemens. 1471.
Patavinus, Johannes. 1535.
Patriani, Francesco. 1574.
Pavese, Antonio. 1682.
Pavese, Simon. 1487.
Pavesi, Cesare. 1580.
Pavia (da), Ottino. 1496.
Pavia (da), Andrea. 1484.
Pavin, Francesco. 1754.
Pavin, Alvise. 1784.
Pavino, Alvise. 1696.
Pavoni, Taddeo. 1642.
Pauli (de), Giovanni. 1717.
Pecora, Carlo. 1740.
Pecori, Santo. 1727.
Pedemio (detto) (v. de Prà). 1720.
Pederbonis (de), Mapheus de Salodio. 1481.
Pedon, Giovanni. 1754.
Pedrezzano, Giambatista. 1527.
Pegolotto, Andrea. 1539.
Peladin, Girolamo. 1754.
Peladin, Zuanne. 1676.
Pellegrini, Nicolo. 1784.
Pellegrini, Pellegrino. 1571.
Pensa (da), Cristoforo da Mandelo. 1488.
Pensa, Crisostomo. 1499.
Pentius, Jacobinus de Leucho. 1495.
Penzio (de), Giacobino. 1598.
Penzio (de), Girolamo da Lecco. 1528.
Penzon, Nicolò. 1494.
Pepoli, Conte Alessandro. 1794.
Peregrino e Bergamasco. 1540.
Peracino, Grazioso. 1568.
Peri, Nicolò. 1590.
Perlini, Antonio. 1695.
Perlini, Antonio. 1754.
Perugino, Biagio. 1543.
Persan, Joannes Dauvome. 1483.
Petenei, Giacomo. 1573.
Petraccini, Silvestro. 1784.
Petri, Philippus condam. [1472.]
Petroi, Girolamo, detto Bonvicini. 1782.
Petrus de Bartua. 1477.
Petrus Bergomensis. 1498.
Petrus Papiensis. 1500.
Petrus, Gabriele. 1475 [1472].
Petrus Cyrneus da Corsica. 1482.
Pezzana, Nicolò. 1667.
Pezzana, Francesco. 1784.
Pezzana, Giovanni Antonio. 1784.
Pezzana, Nicolo. 1784.
Pezzana, Lorenzo. 1794.
Pezzana, Antonio. 1788.
Pezzana, Francesco. 1768.
Pezzana, Nicolo. 1774.
Pezzana, Zuanne. 1684.
Pezzana, Lorenzo. 1695.
Pezzedo, Gervaso. 1676.
Philippus condam petri. 1472.
Piacentini, Francesco. 1736.
Piasio, Pietro da Cremona, detto Veronese. 1480, 1479.
Piasis (de), Tommaso. 1492.
Piazza, Zuanne. 1784.
Piccajo, Jacopo.
Picini, Angelo. 1695.
Pictor, Bernardus. 1476.
Piero de Chusa. 1501 (v. Arch. d. St. Testam. Malipede, 718, No. 121).
Pietro de Domenego. 1571.
Pietro da Fino. 1571.
Pietro (di), Aurelio. 1568.
Pietro Bergamasco. 1487.
Pietro da Bertua. 1477.
Pietro Cremonese detto Veronese. 1479.
Pietro (di), Filippo. 1472.
Pietrasanta, Plinio. 1554.
Pilolini, Andrea. 1571.
Pinardo, Giammaria. 1526.
Pincio, Aurelio. 1530.

Pincio, Filippo. 1473.
Pincio, Mantovano da Lonato. 1492.
Pincio, Pietro. 1480.
Pincius, Philippus de Caneto Mantovano. 1490.
Pinelli, Antonio. 1700.
Pinelli, Pietro. 1700, cir.
Pinelli, Antonio. 1610.
Pinelli, Giampietro. 1633.
Pinelli, Giannantonio. 1696.
Pinelli, Almorò. 1696.
Pinelli, Pietro. 1749.
Pinelli, Giannantonio. 1784.
Pinelli, Giampietro. 1799.
Pinelli, Figliuoli di Giannantonio. 1741.
Pinese, Bastian. 1754.
Pino, Bernardinus da Como. 1483.
Pinso da Lecco. 1496.
Piotto, Pietro. 1784.
Piotto, Marcellino. 1784.
Piotto, Giuseppe. 1789.
Pipini, Carlo. 1595.
Pitteri, Francesco. 1728.
Pitteri, Giuseppe. 1784.
Pittoni, Bernardino. 1476.
Pittoni, Giambatista. 1479.
Pittoni, Leonardo. 1689.
Pittoni, Leonardo. 1715.
Pittoni, Giampietro. 1676, cir.
Pittore, Bernardo. 1475.
Pittore, Girardo. 1477.
Pittorghetto. 1568.
Piuti, Girolamo. 1626.
Pizzolato, Pietro. 1784.
Plano (de), Guglielmus. 1485.
Platachiscis (de), Andrea. 1478.
Plateo, Antonio. 1740, cir.
Pleunich, Michele. 1735.
Poggio, Angelo. 1784.
Poletti, Andrea. 1680.
Poletti, Giandomenico. 1684.
Poletti, Orazio. 1684.
Poletti, Pietro. 1726.
Poletti, Giuseppe. 1755.
Poli, Alvise. 1782.
Polidoro, Antonio. 1705.
Polo, Alessandro. 1620.
Polo, Girolamo. 1589.
Polo, Nicolo. 1602.
Polo (de), Lunardo. 1695, cir.
Pompeati, Domenico. 1726.
Ponzio (v. Bernardon).
Porro, Girolamo. 1597.
Porta (dalla), Giambatista. 1578.
Porta (da), Giambatista. 1584.
Porta, Giambatista. 1581.
Portenaris, Francesco. 1560.
Portenaris, Francesco da Trino. 1556.
Portese (da), Agostino Zani. 1527.
Portesio (de), Bartolomeo de Zanni. 1486.
Portolan, Giambatista. 1745.
Pradotto, Lorenzo. 1663.
Pralormis (v. Ferrariis).
Prati, Fioravante. 1586.
Presegni, Comino. 1595.
Pretigiani, Giovanni. 1754.
Pretigiani, Giambatista.
Prodocimo, Giuseppe. 1676.
Prodotti, Giacomo. 1700.
Pulciani, Giambatista. 1606.
Pulissi, Zuanne. 1754.

Quaietis (de), Antignano Cristophorus. 1492.
Quarengis (de), Petrus Joannes de Palazogo. 1492.
Quarengi (di), Giovanni. 1497.
Quarengi, Giampietro. 1506.
Quartarol, Zuanne. 1676.
Quati, Matteo. 1606.
Quesuolo, Antonio. 1782.
Queti, Stefano. 1693.
Quieti, Pietro. 1700, cir.

Rabanis (sive Ravanis) (de), Victor, et Socii. 1532.
Radici, Vincenzo. 1784.
Radici, Giovanni. 1723.
Raffai, Luca. 1784.
Ragazo (de), Joannes de Monteferrato. 1490.
Ragazzola, Egidio. 1573.

Rotwil (de), Adam. 1474.
Rovado (de), Martinus de Lazaronibus. 1492.
Rota (de), Andrea da Leucho. 1527.
Rubeus, Joannes. 1486.
Rubeus (sive Rossi o Rosso), Jacobus Gallus. 1472.
Rubeys (de), Alovisius. 1499.
Rubeys (de), Franciscus. 1499.
Rubeo (sive Rossi), Jacopo. 1473.
Rubini, Bartolommeo. 1573.
Rubini, Eredi di Bartolommeo. 1586.
Ruffinellis (v. Johannes Patavinus).
Ruffinelli, Angelo. 1578.
Ruffinelli, Venturino. 1535.
Ruffinelli, Giacomo. 1571.
Ruinetti, Giuseppe Maria. 1703.
Rusca, Felice. 1782.
Rusconi (de), Elisabetta. 1525.
Rusconi (de), Giorgio. 1500.

Sabini, Baldo. 1551.
Sabini, Claudio. 1548.
Sabbio (da), Giovanni Antonio. 1516.
Sabbio (da), Pietro. 1549 [1538].
Sabbio (da), Steffano. 1524.
Sabbio, Cornelio. 1549.
Saigo (v. Suigus), Jacopo. 1498.
Sala, Iseppo. 1676.
Sala, Giuseppe. 1695, cir.
Sale (de), Aloysius. 1473.
Salerini, Francesco. 1676.
Salicata, Altobello. 1572.
Salicata, Eredi di Altobello. 1643.
Salice, Giovanni. 1628.
Salii, Giovanni. 1619.
Salis, Eredi di Giovanni. 1641.
Saltarello, Giambatista. 1695, cir.
Saltarello, Domenico. 1784.
Saltarello, Carlo. 1747.
Saltarello, Pietro. 1784.
Salvatori (dei), Ventura. 1583.
Salvadori, Angelo. 1633.
Salvazzo, Giovanni. 1487.
Salutin, Giacomo. 1700, cir.
Salviani, Baldo Venetiano. 1577.
San Bernardino (al). 1537.
Sanctis (de), Hieronymus. 1487.
Sanese, Francesco. 1562.
Sani de Florentia. 1487 (v. Arch. d. Stato. Test. Malipede, No. 578).
San Spirito, Frati di. 1603.
Sano, sæc. XV. (v. Cod. Cic. 2113).
Sansoni, Francesco. 1784.
Sansovino, Francesco. 1558.
Sansovino, Jacopo. 1569.
Santi, Domenico. 1784.
Santini, Francesco. 1762.
Santritter, Joannes Lucilius de Heilbronn. 1480.
Sanzonio, Paulo Antonio. 1695, cir.
Saracenus, Marinus. 1478.
Sarè, Giovanni. 1687.
Saro, Nicolo. 1686.
Saro, Spiridion. 1686.
Sartori, Giambatista. 1784.
Sarzina, Jacopo. 1623.
Sarzina (il). 1640.
Savioli, Agostino. 1738.
Savioni, Giammaria. 1668.
Savioni, Girolamo. 1749.
Savioni (dei), Marchesino, Milanese.
Savioni, Pietro. 1784.
Savioni, Domenico. 1784.
Savioni, Pietro. 1796.
Savioni, Gianfrancesco.
Savioni, Francesco. 1754.
Scaglia, Giacomo. 1629.
Scalvinoni, Giambatista. 1676.
Scanna (?), Giambattista. 1648.
Schavicolla (v. Catanellus). 1480.
Schiratti (li). 1681.
Scheffer, Pietro da Magonza. 1541.
Scolari, Stefano.
Scotto, Girolamo. 1540.
Scotto, Eredi di Girolamo. 1601.
Scotto, Gualtiero. 1552.
Scotto, Ottaviano. 1480.
Scotto, Girolamo. 1571.
Scotto, Ottaviano. 1542.
Scotto, Brandino. 1540.
Scotto, Eredi di Ottaviano. 1500.
Sebastiano di Verelengo. 1492.
Seffer (v. Scheffer).

Segati, Antonio. 1750, cir.
Segno del Leon d' Oro (Vaglierino).
„ dell' Albero (Avanzo).
„ del Pozzo della Samaritana (Arrivabene).
„ dell' Ancora.
„ della Croce (Bindoni).
„ del Cavaletto (Stefano di Alessi).
„ della Fama (Accademia Veneta).
„ d' Aldo (Manasse).
„ della Salamandra (Basaglia).
„ del Pozzo (Bart. Cesano).
„ del Pellegrino (Bertoni).
„ della Minerva (Combi).
„ della Carità (Farri).
„ della Virtù Coronata (Feltrin).
„ della Venezia (Lovisa).
„ delle Colonne (Marinello).
„ della Colonna (Zaltieri).
„ dell' Italia (Occhi).
„ della Fortuna Trionfante (Pitteri).
„ delle Frezze (Trino).
„ delle tre Rose (Vecchi).
„ della Cognitione (Trino).
„ della Regina (Franceschi).
„ dell' Angelo Raffaele (Bindoni). 1532.
„ di San Bernardino (Stagnino). 1537.
„ della Chiave. 1543.
„ di Erasmo (Valgrisi). 1551.
„ di San Giorgio. 1553.
„ di San Zorzi (Bart. Imperador).
„ di San Girolamo. 1550.
„ del Griffio. 1543.
„ della Luna Crescente.
„ di San Moise (Bertacagno).
„ dell' Hercole.
„ dell' Orso. 1543.
„ del Pozzo. 1550.
„ del Salamandra. 1570.
„ della Sibilla. 1560.
„ della Speranza (Bindoni). 1542.
„ della Verità (Marcolini).
„ della Gatta.
Senese, Francesco. 1562.
Serona, Pietro. 1525.
Sessa, Alvise. 1588.
Sessa (da), Jo. Baptista. 1490.
Sessa, Giovanni. 1486.
Sessa, Battista. 1491.
Sessa, Giambatista. 1561.
Sessa, Giovanni Bernardo. 1564.
Sessa, Giambatista e Marchio Fratelli. 1560.
Sessa, Giambernardo. 1597.
Sessa, Marchio. 1502.
Sessa, Eredi di Marchio. 1567.
Sgava, Giambatista. 1648.
Sibyllinus Umber. 1475.
Siligenstat (v. Johannes).
Siliprandus, Dominicus. 1477.
Simbeni, Jacopo. 1574.
Simon de Gara. 1491.
Simon de Luere. 1489.
Simon da Pavia. 1487.
Simon da Fiorenza, sæc. XV. (v. Cod. Cic. 2113).
Singrerio, Giovanni. 1529.
Sirena, Pietro. 1525.
Sisto. 1526.
Soardis (de), Lazarus. 1490.
Soardo, Lorenzo. 1511.
Società Albrizziana. 1730.
Società Boaria (v. Liga Boaria).
Società degli Uniti. 1585.
Società Veneta. 1610.
Sola, Pietro. 1784.
Solda, Antonio. 1748.
Solda, Giuseppe. 1700, cir.
Soldon, Antonio. 1700, cir.
Somasco, Giovanni e Fratelli. 1570.
Somasco, Giambatista. 1583.
Somasco, Giovanni Antonio. 1603.
Somasco, Gian Jacopo. 1606.
Somasco, Jacopo Antonio. 1602.
Somasco, Vincenzo. 1618.
Sonzonio, Paulo Antonio. 1695.
Soziis (de), Andreas Parmensis. 1484.
Speranza (dalla), Gaspero. 1568.
Spineda, Lucio. 1599.
Spinelli, Andrea. 1551.
Spinelli, Giacomo. 1551.
Spira (de), Joannes. 1469.

Spira (de), Joannes Emericus. 1487. –
Spira (de), Vindelino. 1470. –
Spora, Antonio. 1695.
Stachel, Conradus de Blaubern. 1484. –
Stagnino, Bernardino de Tridino de Monteferrato. 1482. –
Stagnino, Bernardino. 1508.
Stagnino, Filippo. 1585.
Stagninus, Guglielmus. 1486. –
Stagnino, Filippo. 1546.
Stamperia a San Bartolomeo. 1556.
Stamperia Gregoriana. 1522.
Stamperia Nuova. 1584.
Stampon Cristoforo. 1571.
Stanchis (de), Andrea de Valentia. 1486. –
Stendal (de), Albertus. 1473. –
Stella, Antonio. 1680, cir.
Stella, Antonio Fortunato. 1792.
Storti, Francesco. 1653.
Storti, Francesco. 1724.
Storti, Eredi di Francesco.
Storti, Gasparo. 1686.
Storti, Gasparo. 1784.
Storti, Francesco. 1784.
Storti, Giacomo. 1784.
Storti, Gasparo. 1759.
Storti, Giacomo. 1796.
Strata (de), Antonius Cremonensis. 1480. –
Strada, Giacomo. 1557.
Strevo, Manfredo da Monferrato. 1481. –
Suigus, Jacobinus de S. Germano. 1498. –
Surian, Giambatista. 1641.

Tabacco, Domenico. 1741.
Tacco, Marco. 1792.
Tacuino, Giovanni de Trino. 1494. –
Tager, Giovanni. 1743.
Tagliapietra, Francesco (v. Lapicida). 1494. –
Taja (de), Agostino. 1509.
Tamburini, Giulio. 1572.
Tandoni (?), (li). 1547.
Tarsi (di), Alvise. 1539.
Tavernini, Giovanni. 1749.
Tebaldini, Nicolò. 1603.
Teodoro, Franco. 1480. –
Teodoro de Rheinsburg. 1477.
Teodosio, Demetrio. 1761.
Termengo. 1534.
Thomas de Alexandria de Blavis. 1477.
Theodoricus de Reynsburch. 1477.
Tivani, Antonio. 1594.
Tivani, Antonio. 1685.
Tivan, Lunardo. 1747.
Todaro, Pietro. 1760.
Todero, Carlo. 1784.
Tofolo (de), Cristofolo. 1680.
Tommaso (de), Francesco. 1571.
Tommaso d' Alessandria. 1477.
Tommaso di Venezia. 1495.
Tommasini, Giuseppe. 1754.
Tommasini, Alessandro. 1480.
Tommasini, Cristoforo. 1637.
Tommasini, Antonio. 1620.
Tommasini, Giacomo. 1704.
Tommasini (il). 1633.
Tortis (de), Baptista. 1481.
Torti (de), Luigi. 1534.
Torresanus, Andreas de Asula. 1480.
Torresani, Andrea e Maffio. 1480.
Torresani, Francesco.
Torresani, Federico. 1528.
Torre, Pietro. 1784.
Torris (de), Raffaelle. 1484.
Torri. 1555.
Tossello, Pietro. 1784.
Tosi, Francesco. 1789.
Trajani, Curzio di Navo. 1541.
Tramezzino, Michele. 1543.
Tramontini, Bartolommeo. 1669.
Tramontini, Giambatista. 1697.
Tramontini, Giuseppe. 1684.
Tramontini (il). 1749.
Tramontini, Francesco. 1695.
Tramontin, Felice. 1784.
Tramontin, Gregorio.
Tramontin, Gianfrancesco. 1793.
Tramontin, Stefano. 1737.
Travi, Giorgio. 1782.
Trentino, Nicolo. 1554.
Trevisano (il). 1476.
Trevisan, Reginaldo. 1613.
Tridino (de), Johannes. 1490.

Tridino (de), Stagninus. 1483.
Tridino (de), Guglielmo. 1486.
Tricavallus (?). 1534.
Trino (da), Comin. 1541.
Trino (da), Giovanni. 1496.
Trojano, Curzio (v. Trajani).
Tuin, Domenico. 1754.
Turi, Valentin. 1782.
Turini, Antonio. 1592.
Turini, Antonio. 1651.
Turrini, Giacomo. 1674.

Udenhem (v. Johannes Emericus).
Ugolini, Giambatista. 1588.
Ugolini, Paolo. 1592.
Ugolini, Fratelli. 1584.
Umber, Sybillinus. 1475.
Uniti, Societa degli. 1585.
Usci, Domenico. 1625.
Usci, Pietro. 1625.
Uscio (v. Porta), Giambatista. 1588.

Vadagnino (v. Guadagnino).
Vadeli (?), Jacopo. 1574.
Vaglierino (?), Giambatista. 1639.
Valcenese, Albertino. 1501.
Valdarfer, Cristoforo. 1470.
Valentia (de), Antonius. 1481.
Valentini, Giorgio. 1615.
Valentini, Matteo. 1592.
Valgrisi, Erasmo di Vincenzo. 1549.
Valgrisi, Felice. 1583.
Valgrisi, Francesco. 1584.
Valgrisi, Giovanni.
Valgrisi, Vincenzo. 1541.
Valla, Brunus, Pedemontanus. 1477.
Valla, Giovanni. 1501.
Valle, Sebastiano. 1789.
Valvasenese, Alvise. 1695.
Valvasenese, Pietro. 1784.
Valvasenese, Pietro. 1784.
Valvasenese, Andrea. 1754.
Valvasenese, Domenico. 1703.
Valvasenese, Francesco. 1644.
Valvasenese, Stefano. 1749.
Valvassore, Andrea. 1550.
Valvassore, Florio. 1541.
Valvassore, Giannandrea. 1532.
Valvassore, Giannantonio. 1565.
Valvassore, Luigi. 1564.
Valvassore, Eredi di Luigi. 1565.
Vardello, Giovanni. 1784.
Varese, Giannandrea. 1499.
Varisco, Giorgio. 1599.
Varisco, Giovanni. 1564.
Varisco, Eredi di Giovanni. 1594.
Varisco, Giovanni e Compagni.
Varisco, Marco. 1599.
Varisio (di), Joannes Aluisius. 1493.
Vasalini, Giulio. 1587.
Vavassore (v. Valvassore).
Vecchi, Alessandro. 1597.
Vecelli, Giovanni. 1643.
Vecelliana, Stamperia. 1643.
Vedelago, Domenico. 1676.
Venetiano, Bernardinus. 1480.
Venetiano, Vidal. 1480.
Venetiano, Matteo. 1494.
Venetus, Lucas. 1480.
Venezia (da), Vincenzo di Paolo. 1521.
Veneziano, Francesco. 1544.
Venier, Antonio. 1669.
Ventura de Salvador. 1586.
Ventura (de), Bastian. 1571.
Vercellensis (v. Albertinus).
Vercellese, Giovanni. 1486.
Verolengo (de), Sebastianus, de pane et vino. 1492.
Veronese, Antonio. 1784.
Veronese, Giuseppe. 1791.
Veronese, Albertino de Lisbona. 1500.
Veronese, Pietro. 1481.
Viani, Giulio. 1676.
Viani, Viano. 1613.
Viani (de), Alessandro. 1556.
Vianis (de), Bernardino, da Lexona. 1513.
Viani, Vincenzo. 1576.
Vicentino, Zorzi. 1571.
Vicenzi, Jacopo. 1588.
Vico, Andrea. 1554.
Vidal, Zuanne. 1642.
Vidali (de), Bernardino. 1506.
Vidali (de), Matteo. 1528.

Vidali, Jacopo. 1574.
Vidali, Jacomo. 1573.
Viezzeri, Bonifacio. 1712.
Viezzeri, Ilario. 1784.
Viezzeri, Giampaolo. 1784.
Viezzeri, Giuseppe. 1764.
Viezzeri, Felice. 1680.
Viezzeri, Zuanne. 1676.
Viezzeri, Leonardo. 1680.
Vilio dal Diamante. 1571.
Villavecchia (da), Giovanni. 1494.
Viller, Giovanni (v. Leoviller). 1488.
Vincenti, Martin. 1700.
Vincenzi, Girolamo. 1588.
Vincenzii, Giacomo. 1604.
Vincenzii, Sebastiano. 1532.
Vincenzo de Paolo. 1518.
Vindelino da Spira. 1470.
Violati, Giacomo. 1615.
Viotti, Antheo (?). 1591.
Viotti, Erasmo. 1594.
Visomio, Pietro. 1676.
Vitali (de), Agostino. 1533.
Vitali, Antonio. 1668.
Vitali, Bernardino. 1500.
Vitali, Zuanne. 1642.
Vitali, Jacomo. 1575.
Vitto, Giovanni. 1784.
Vuoman, Francesco. 1695.
Volpini (de), Giovanni Antonio. 1540.
Volpini (de), Domenico. 1540.
Voltolin, Vincenzo. 1759.

Windischgretz (de), Matteo. 1487.
Walch, Georgius. 1479.
Wiest, Michele. 1676.
Wiest, Giacomo. 1695, cir.
Wild (de), Leonardus de Ratisbona. 1478.

Xilt (? Wilt, s. Wild), Leonardo. 1483.

Zaltieri, Bolognino. 1555.
Zaltieri, Marcantonio. 1584.
Zambon, Apollonio. 1706.
Zamboni, Pierantonio. 1676.
Zamboni, Giovanni. 1784.
Zanardi, Giacomo. 1799.
Zanchi (de), Antonio. 1497.
Zane, Domenico. 1788.
Zane, Francesco. 1754.
Zane da Portesio. 1486.
Zane, Francesco. 1725.
Zanetti, Bartolommeo, da Brescia. 1536.
Zanetti, Cristoforo. 1547.
Zanetti, Daniele. 1606.
Zanetti, Fabrizio. 1601.
Zanetti, Michele. 1584.
Zanetti, Matteo. 1595.
Zanetti, Giacomo. 1754.
Zanfretti, Paolo. 1583.
Zani, Agostino, da Portesio. 1508.
Zanni, Bartholomæus de Portesio. 1486.
Zanoti (?), Figli di, da Monferrato. 1475.
Zantin (?), Bartolommeo. 1504.
Zanizza, Paolo. 1617.
Zappa, Adamo. 1784.
Zarabini, Pierantonio (?). 1661.
Zarotto. 1484.
Zatta, Alessandro. 1663.
Zatta, Antonio. 1711.
Zatta, Giacomo.
Zatta, Antonio. 1784.
Zattoni, Giacomo. 1670.
Zazzara, Stefano. 1564.
Zenari, Giovanni. 1596.
Zenari, Girolamo. 1584.
Zenaro, Damiano. 1573.
Zenaro, Zaccharia. 1571.
Zenaro e Fratelli.
Zeni, Eredi del. 1599.
Zerletti, Girolamo. 1700, cir.
Zerletti, Guglielmo. 1784.
Zerletti, Bortolo. 1754.
Ziletti, Francesco. 1540.
Ziletti, Eredi di Francesco. 1587.
Ziletti, Giordano. 1556.
Ziletti, Giovanni. 1574.
Ziletti, Girolamo. 1562.
Ziliolo, Alessandro. 1650.
Zini, Jacopo. 1672.

DOCUMENTS.

VII.

Trials before the Holy Office for Press Offences, 1547-1730.

No.	Date.	Name.	Habitation.	Busta.	Number of Documents.
1	1547	Claudio, Marco		7	3
2	1549	Comino	Monferrato	7	3
3	1549	Leon, Angelo	Venezia	7	3
4	1549	Steffanelli, Steffano	Piove di Sacco	7	4
5	1549	Stella, Francesco	Porto Buffolè	7	63
6	1549	Vitalba, Nicolò	Bergamo	7	10
7	1550	Dolfin, Landolfo	Svizzera	8	2
8	1551	Costantini, Baldissera		14	1
9	1552	Cocco, Pietro	Asolo	10	
10	1552	Macaluffo, Francesco	Marostica	10	1
11	1552	Rana, Gianjacopo	Marostica	10	1
12	1552	Rosello, Lucio Paolo	Padova	10	44
13	1553	Tomitano, Bernardino	Padova	11	28
14	1555	Contarini, Luigi	Vene	12	1
15	1555	Fra Marin, Inquisitor of Venice	Venice	12	20 [for absolving Lutherans]
16	1555	Stella, Laura	Venice	12	43
17	1556	Caravia, Alessandro	Venice	13	5
18	1556	Tarsia, Andrea	Monfalcone	13	7
19	1556	Olmo (dall'), Faustino		14	1
20	1556	Reietto, Girolamo		14	1
21	1556	Craia, Ippolito	Veglia	15, 21	
22	1558	Doria, Giovanni Bernardo	Genova	13	9
23	1558	Formentino, Nicolo	Gemona	14	1
24	1558	Franceschi (de), Domenico		14	1
25	1558	Francesi, Giovanni		14	3
26	1558	Freschi, Fra Michele	Vicenza	14	2
27	1558	Giulio, Fra	Brescia	14	1
28	1558	Ulova, Alfonso	Spagna	14	2
29	1559	Valgrisio, Vicenzo	Venezia	14	3
30	1559	Martinello, Pietro	Venezia	15	2

31	1560	Muzio		15	
32	1560	Scudieri, Francesco	Cremona	15	49
33	1561	Pellizzari, Benedetto	Schio	17	3
34	1563	Agostino (Medico)	Modena	17	3
35	1565	Giolito, Gabriele	Ferrara	20	16
36	1565	Senech, Cristoforo	Mecklenburg	20	2
37	1565	Ventura, Samuele	Città di Castello	20	15
38	1566	Craia, Ippolito	Veglia	15, 21	104
39	1566	Massimi, Massimo	Padova	21	67
40	1566	Tussignano, Pietro	Padova	21	1
41	1567	Avogari (degl'), Alessandro	Verona	22	
42	1567	Giacomo	Roma	22	
43	1567	Tommaso	Francia	22	26
44	1568	Bonaldi, Dre Francesco		23	2
45	1568	Sbais, Santo	Friuli	23	26
46	1568	Calepin, Girolamo		25	2
47	1568	Zachis, Domenico	Castelfranco	25	33
48	1569	Bertoldi, Vicenzo	Oderzo	26	40
49	1569	Borello, Fra Eusebio	Napoli	26	4
50	1569	Calegari, Carlo	Murano	26	1
51	1569	Mara, Emmanuele	Candia	27	88
52	1570	Nicolo	Venezia	27	1
53	1571	Andriana	Venezia	29	3
54	1571	Arrivabene, Andrea	Venezia	30	14
55	1571	Oderzo (Comunisti)		30	12
56	1571	Ziletto, Francesco		30	10
57	1572	Aquila	Cittanova	32	4
58	1572	Bruno, Matteo	Tolmezzo	32	20
59	1572	Rocca, Francesco	Venezia	32	
60	1572	Trissino, Giulio	Vicenza	32	26
61	1572	Vitali (de), Paolo	Brescia	32	1
62	1572	Sforza, Bartolo		33	4
63	1573	Caliari, Leonzio	Campiglia, Vicenza	33	16
64	1573	Florida, Benedetto	Cittadella	35	11
65	1573	Lancilotto, Biggio	Brescia	35	
66	1574	Valgolio, Marcantonio	Brescia	37	8
67	1574	Giustiniani, Antonio	Venezia	37	11
68	1574	Sabio (de), Bartolomeo	Salò	37	3

No.	Date.	Name.	Habitation.	Busta.	Number of Documents.
69	1574	Volterra, Antonio	Cadore	37	6
70	1574	Sanudo, Giov. Batt.	Venezia	37	11
71	1574	Leonardo, Fra	Venezia	38	9
72	1574	Lezze, Leonatello	Mantova	38	4
73	1575	Faris (de), Pietro		39	8
74	1575	Gomez, Giovanni	Ferrara	39	3
75	1577	Andreis (de), Tranquillo	Trau	41	37
76	1578	Lorenzi, Domenico	Venezia	43	16
77	1578	Zennaro, Girolamo	Venezia	43	1
78	1579	Baroni, Bartolomeo	Venezia	43	2
79	1579	Maranta, Domenico	Grumagna	44	30
80	1580	Bindoni, Stefano	Venezia	46	18
81	1580	Galeazzi, Lodovico	Venezia	46	2
82	1580	Savorgnan, Federico	Udine	46	1
83	1581	Valvasore, Fra Clemente	Bergamo	47	47
84	1581	Chemer, Bartolomeo	Lovanio	48	7
85	1581	Ippolito, Fra	Bagnio	48	25
86	1582	Giletti, Francesco	Venezia	49	9
87	1582	Pavese (dal), Giov. Antonio	Venezia	49	1
88	1582	Renerio	Francia	49	5
89	1582	Vitrino, Girolamo		49	3
90	1583	Cazzola, Tommaso	Como	50	5
91	1583	Ciera, Bonifacio	Venezia	50	5
92	1583	Gobbi (de), Orazio	Salò	50	7
93	1583	Graziano, Fra	Venezia	50	27
94	1583	Grazioli, Teodoro	Brescia	50	9
95	1583	Putei (de), Giovanni	Venezia	50	2
96	1583	Simottini, Guidone	Venezia	50	8
97	1583	Renato, Eusebio	Ferrara	51	7
98	1583	Sessa, Melchiori	Venezia	51	1
99	1584	Zefiro	Venezia	53	12
100	1585	Marii (de), Alessandro	Cesena	54	3
101	1585	Azzano (d'), Gaspare	Venezia	55	7

102	1586	Minio, Antonio	Venezia	57	6
103	1587	Boroni, Broccardo	Venezia	59	8
104	1587	Brugnoli, Gioacchino	Venezia	59	2
105	1587	Claudio	Savoia	59	21
106	1587	Valgrisio, Giorgio	Venezia	59	9
107	1587	Loredan, Paolo	Venezia	60	10
108	1587	Mileto, Roberto	Venezia	60	4
109	1587	Pisani, Chiara	Venezia	60	23
110	1588	Longo, Pietro	Venezia	61	2
111	1588	Percatino, Grazioso	Venezia	61	3
112	1588	Bozzuola, Orazio	Brescia	62	1
113	1588	Fregonio, Bernardo	Spilimbergo	62	11
114	1588	Meietti, Roberto	Venezia	62	2
115	1588	Rizzo, Giulio	Padova	62	
116	1588	Venzoni, Oswaldo	Venezia	62	7
117	1588	Zennaro, Girolamo	Venezia	62	
118	1588	Rampaceto, Giovanni Antonio	Venezia	63	6
119	1588	Zanelli, Camillo	Venezia	63	
120	1589	Longo, Giovanni	Venezia	63	2
121	1589	Cabalino, Gaspare		64	2
122	1589	Canal, Domenico	Venezia	64	4
123	1589	Carminati, Benedetto	Venezia	64	10
124	1589	Manasi, Nicolò	Venezia	64	1
125	1589	Morosini, Bernardo	Venezia	64	1
126	1589	Farri, Domenico	Venezia	65	2
127	1589	Solarin, Sofia	Germania	65	10
128	1590	Polo, Girolamo	Venezia	65	2
129	1590	Agostini, Orazio	Venezia	66	10
130	1590	Sazilli, Mario	Roma	66	1
131	1591	Ricci, Giulio	Venezia	67	4
132	1591	Verdizzotti, Giovanni Maria	Venezia	67	3
133	1592	Bruno, Giordano	Nola	69	43
134	1592	Porta (dalla), Giovanni Battista	Napoli	69	2
135	1616	Marc' Antonio de Dominis	Spalato	71	20
136	1617	Vago, Giuseppe	Verona	72	4
137	1553	Donzelino, Girolamo	Brescia	11, 39, 75	116
138	1621	Meietti, Robert	Venezia	77	4
139	1621	Scaglia, Giacomo	Venezia	77	3

No.	Date.	Name.	Habitation.	Busta.	Number of Documents.
140	1622	Bilotto, Tadeo	Genova	78	4
141	1623	Barezzi, Barezzo	Venezia	78	2
142	1624	Cino, Orazio	Etruria	79	79
143	1624	Manzino, Gaspare	Toscana	79	
144	1625	Romano, Francesco	Venezia	80	3
145	1625	Agosti, Leonardo	Bergamo	81	2
146	1627	Peranda, Fra Stefano	Venezia	85	2
147	1628	Bonaventura, Fra	Vicenza	86	
148	1628	Negri (de), Salvatore	Apulia	86	44
149	1628	Pellegrini, Fra Giovani	Arbe	86	3
150	1630	Chiaramonte, Girolamo	Venezia	87	12
151	1631	Bonzi, Antonio	Bergamo	88	1
152	1633	Otavi (de'), Marcello	Venezia	89	1
153	1634	Corati, Francesco	Vicenza	90	3
154	1637	Bellovacco, Antonio	Francia	94	
155	1637	Modena, Leone	Venezia	94	20
156	1639	Compagni de Pietro	Pistoja	95	4
157	1646	Valmarana, Gasparo	Rovigo	101	66
158	1646	Balbi, Frà Antonio	Venezia	102	
159	1646	Verigola, Fra Ignazio	Venezia	102	
160	1646	Francesco, Fra	Pesaro	103	2
161	1647	Cabianca, Bonifacio	Venezia	103	4
162	1647	Donà Pellegrina	Venezia	103	2
163	1648	Batti, Giacomo	Belluno	103	17
164	1648	Combi Eredi	Venezia	103	5
165	1648	Valvasense, Francesco	Valvasone	103	100
166	1650	Francesco	Venezia	105	2
167	1650	Desiderio, Fra	Vicenza	105	2
168	1650	Ponte, Carlo	Bassano	105	4
169	1650	Torelli (de), Francesco	Roma	105	1
170	1651	Battocchio, Bartolomeo	Venezia	106	1
171	1653	Pedrini, Domenico	Bologna	107	5
172	1655	Scalvinoni, Giovanni Battista	Venezia	108	4

173	1656	Beltramelli, Mariano	Bergamo	108	5
174	1656	Gei, Bartolomeo	Venezia	108	5
175	1656	Gisberti, Domenico	Murano	108	2
176	1660	Ponte (da), Angela	Venezia	109	3
177	1661	Franchez, Donato	Salerno	110	2
178	1662	Comin, Pietro	Venezia	110	1
179	1662	Patrizii, Pietro	Trento	110	2
180	1664	Giuliani, Andrea	Venezia	111	6
181	1674	Crannebiter, Francesco	Venezia	117	3
182	1676	Zucco, Giovanni	Roma	119	1
183	1678	Lapi, Giovanni	Firenze	120	2
184	1686	Scocatti, Giovanni Battista	Feltre	124	
185	1686	Bontempo, Lelio	Brescia	124	
186	1686	Loredan, Francesco	Venezia	124	10
187	1687	Dace, Giovanni		124	1
188	1688	Moretti, Fra Paolo, Inquisitor		125	5
189	1689	Chiesa, Domenico	Venezia	125	1
190	1694	Mazoni, Natale	Reggio	127	9
191	1703	Capra, Lelio	Vicenza	130	3
192	1713	Mazarini, Ventura	Bergamo	136	12
193	1713	Pedrizzioli, Giovanni Battista	Venezia	136	
194	1730	Checozzi, Giovanni	Vicenza	141	390

The Index to all the Trials before the Holy Office in Venice has been compiled by Sigri. L. Pasini and G. Giomo.

DOCUMENTS.

VIII.

VIII.

DAY BOOK OF A VENETIAN BOOKSELLER. 1484.[1]

No. 1. *Extracts from the List of Sales.*

	D.	L.	S.
OPERE Sancti Augustini	0	2	0
Valturio	0	4	10
Missaletto d' Ottaviano	0	2	0
Sermon di fra michele	1	1	6
Rationale	0	2	10
Bibia del grisolare	1	1	10
Mischino	0	1	0
Inamoramento d' orlando	0	2	0
Facetie del Poggio	0	0	9
Burchiello	0	0	10
Columella ligato	1	0	10
Epistole pape pii	0	2	10
De contemptu mundi	0	0	10
Breviario de piero Veronese	0	3	0
Missaletto del bressan	0	3	0
Officietti del bressan	0	0	10
Manipulus curatorum	0	0	14
Filocolo	0	2	10
Peregrenatio Ierusalem	0	0	10
Vita e miraculi	0	1	0
Lucano	0	1	0
Tullio de officiis cum commento	0	2	0
Decreto picolo	1	0	0
Prisciano ligato	0	6	10
Tullio de oratore	0	1	10
Commentum Tullii de oratore	0	2	10

[1] Marciana, It. Cl. xi. Cod. xlv., leaves 114, paper. First date, 1484, *adi* 17 *Mazo*; last date, 1487, *adi* 23 *Zanar*. (m. v.).

		D.	L.	S.
Retorica cum commento		0	2	0
Cecho dascoli		0	0	16
Breviario de magistro nicolo de S. dominico		0	3	0
Catolicon		1	1	0
Sermon de ruberto		0	4	10
Dubii de magistro pollo		0	0	15
Canzonetti del Justiniano		0	0	8
Bibia con Nicolo de lira		0	9	0
Mamotretto		0	1	10
Prisciano		0	4	0
Junianus		0	3	0
Officietti in carta bona de la compagnia		0	3	0
Deche del biondo		0	4	10
Dante con commento		1	0	0
Petrarcha con commento		0	3	0
Bibia de magistro Silvestro (?)		0	4	0
Legendario		0	3	0
Regule guarini		0	0	8
Donato in carta bona		0	2	0
Summa orlandini		0	0	18
Valerio maximo cum commento		0	2	10
Vocabulista grecho grande		0	3	0
Polibius		0	3	10
Erotemata grecha		0	0	10
Platina, de honesta voluptate		0	0	14
Morgante		0	1	10
Bibia con Nicolo de lira ligata		5	0	0
Evangelii epistole volgare Fior de virtu Fioretti de la bibia Prediche de ruberto volgare Profetie de Merlino Cinquanta novelle Fatige d' ercules Petrarcha con commento Facetie de poggio Fiammetta Canzon del Justiniano Canzon di Cosmico Filomena Filostratto Burchiello Ovidio de arte amandi	in massa venduto a Misser Alvise Capello	2	1	0
Formularium instrumentorum		0	2	0
Psalmista grande		0	0	16
Supplementum cronicarum		0	3	14

	D.	L.	S.
Pratica raynaldi de villa nova	0	2	10
Messue ligato	1	1	16
Esopo istoriado	0	1	0
Summa Astesana	1	0	16
Arte del ben morire	0	0	6
Platina de vitis pontificum ligato	0	5	10
Cronica datto in baratto d' oglio.			
Meditation de la passion	0	0	8
Omelie de San Gregorio	0	2	10
Iginus de syderibus	0	1	0
Diodorus Siculus	0	1	8
Conciliator	1	0	6
Cinquanta novelle	0	1	0
Missale Silvestro ligato	1	3	6
Trionfi di Virtu	0	0	10
Inamoramento de orlando	0	2	0
Ninfale	0	0	10
Istorie de rodi	0	0	4
Oratio et terentio con commento ligato	0	3	10
Vita e miraculi della Madonna datti a lazaro ligadore.			
Regule sipontini	0	0	16
Fasciculus temporum	0	1	5
Cento novelle } Cinquanta novelle }	0	2	10
Fatige d' ercules	0	1	0
Euclides	0	2	10
Margarita decreti	0	1	0
Cornelio Celso	0	2	10
Epistole Cipriani	0	2	0
Consilia Montagnane	2	0	0
Cantica de S. Bernardo	0	2	10
Quintilian declamation	0	1	0
Arte de ciromantia	0	0	10
Magistro de le sententie	0	2	10
Laude de la madonna	0	0	10
Clipeus tomistarum	0	3	0
Petrarcha de viris illustribus	0	4	0
Juvenale volgare	0	1	0
Abade de la compagnia	6	0	0
Isidoro	0	1	10
Genealogia deorum	0	4	0
Deche di livio stampa del Grisolare	1	1	6
Fior de virtu ligato	0	0	16
Inamoramento de Carlo	0	2	0
Virgilio con servio	0	3	0
Spera mundi	0	0	15

	D.	L.	S.
Loyca de magistro pollo della pergola .	0	0	10
Catullus, Tibullus, etc.	0	2	0
Esiodus et theocritus	0	1	5
Tavole de Alfonso	0	1	12
Epistole Ovidii cum commento . .	0	1	0
Salustio	0	1	0
Opera Ovidii	0	4	10
Aulo gelio	0	2	10
Pomponio mella	0	0	10
Dionisio de situ orbis	0	0	10
Epistole plinii	0	1	0
Michel Scotto	0	0	10
Teofrasto	0	1	10
Cento novelle dato a magistro pezzi ligator.			
Quinto Curtio	0	2	10
[Dati ad uno todesco insieme con altri libri de magazeno.]			
Silio Italico con commento	0	2	10
Plutarchi, Vite, ligato	2	3	0
Altobello	0	0	15
[Mandati a roma.]			
Officietti istoriado	0	0	10
Duirno de la compagnia	0	1	0
[Summa hostiensis data a Andrea d' Asola et Bartolamio de lasandria.]			
Virgilio senza servio	0	1	15
Guidon in cirosia	0	3	2
Troiano	0	1	0
[Cento et cinquanta novelle dati in ligatore di libri.]			
Bibia picola } dati a magistro piero corretore.			
Mamotretti }			
Legendario literale }			
Angelo de Maleficiis . . .	0	3	5
Burleus super artem veterem . .	0	1	3
Josefo de antiquitate . . .	0	3	10
[Dati ad uno frate minore a credenza.]			
Pratica raynaldi datto a dionisio a conto di libri.			
Lucius Florus	0	0	13
Fior de Virtu dato a lazaro garbelador.			
Albertus de secretis mulierum	0	0	10
Orationes tullii dati in baratto di vino.			
Secunda secunde santi tome Officietti grandi ligati. Dati a bernardin da novara.			
Catena aurea	1	0	10
Virgilio con servio ligato barratatti in quarti 2 di vino Schiavone et s. 30 in denari.			
Coriolano	0	0	10
Ovidio de fastis con commento .	0	2	10

Libro d' abaco dato in miniatore.

Aristotle de animalibus
Dioscorides
Teofrastus
Euclides
Dottrinale con commento
Regule guarini. 2.
Donato
Breviarii de la compagnia. 2.
Posteriora pauli cum textu
Fisica sancti tome

} Dati a Ser Ostathio et a ser filipo in farina.

Opera sancti agustini 4 dati a don Cornelio da la Carita.

[Mandati a roma.]

Eusebio de preparatione Evangelica mandata a roma.

	D.	L.	S.
Lancroia	0	1	4
Oratio con commento	0	2	10
Pisanella de pagani	0	2	0
Abram de nativitatibus	0	0	10
Pisanella de magistro francesco	0	2	0
Novele de zohane andrea	0	5	0
Summa orlandina	0	0	16
Vita de Christo in rima	0	1	0
Esopus	0	0	7
Epistole Ieronimi da parma	2	1	0
Sermones d San Zuane Grisostomo	0	0	18
Digesto vechio	1	5	6
Esiodo theocrito in grecho	0	1	4
Suetonio pizolo	0	0	5
Sonetti di Petrarcha	0	1	5
Pirolarium pantaleonis	0	0	10
Libro de la beata Caterina da Bologna	0	0	12
Diogenes laertius	0	1	10
Consolatoria Filelfi	0	0	18
Flos testamenti	0	0	14
Statio achileados con commento. No. 3	0	1	7
Egidius de regimine principum	0	2	10
Papias Vocabulista	0	2	0
Aurispa	0	0	15
Blondo de Italia lustrata	0	1	15
Palmista in grecho	0	3	10
Erotemata grecha	0	0	7
Armando	0	1	0
Settanta novelle } Cinquanta novelle }	0	2	18
Vite Plutarchi	2	0	0
Finistrella	0	0	8

	D.	L.	S.
Dialogo de Santa Caterina de Sena } Libro de la beata Caterina da Bologna }	0	2	0
Tractatus de balneis	0	0	12
Savonarola } Conciliator } . .	1	3	10
Strabone	0	4	0
Lucretio	0	1	15
Orbello metafisica . . .	0	1	13
Tutidides	0	1	9
Desisiones rotæ de roma . .	0	5	0
Opera Platonis } Dante } Petrarcha } Digenis laertio }	2	1	0
Savonarola de febribus . .	0	2	10
Vegetio de re militari . .	0	0	10
Tolomeo con figure . .	3	4	18
Paulo Vengerio . . .	0	0	5
Suetonio pizoli . . .	0	0	4
Temistius de anima . .	0	2	0
Martiale pizoli . . .	0	0	15
Vitruvio	0	3	0
Quadratura de Magistro paulo .	0	2	0
Francesco Matarazo . .	0	0	5

No. 2. *The stock-in-trade, and additions thereto.*

yhs 1484. adi 17 mazo.

Quà si fara ricordo de' libri intrarano in bottega et prima.

	No.
Epistole tullij familiares	2
Comentum epistolarum tullii	2
Epistole tullii cum comento	4, 4
Tullius de Oratore	2, 1
Orationes tullii picole	4
Orationes. t. grande	2
Tullius de officiis cum comento	5
Questiones tusculane	3
Questiones tusculane cum comento	2, 2
Tullius de finibus	2
Retorica tullii	2
Retorica cum comento	4
Dionisius alicarnaseus	2
Junianus in forma magna	1
Juniano in forma picola	2
Catolicon	4
Justinus et emilius ligatus	1
Paulus orosius	4
Strabo	2
Dionisius de situ orbis	5
Pomponius mella	5

	No.
Nonius marcellus	2, 1
Coriolinus	5
Ovidio mazore	2
Epistole ovidii cum comento	5
Ovidius de fastis cum comento	4
Opera ovidii	2
Commentarii cesaris	4
Quintilianus	2
Declamationes quintiliani	4
Terentius	2
Terentius cum donato	4
Claudianus	4
Plautus	2
Juvenalis cum comento	10
Oratius	2
Oratius cum comento	4
Columella	1, 1
Elegantie Valle	4
Elegantiole Valle	2
Elegantiole augustini dati	10
Salustius	2
Persius cum comento	6
Suetonius	1
Lucius florus et solinus	1
Plinius de naturali istoria	4
Dechades livii grande	1
Valerius maximus	3
Valerius maximus cum comento	4
Virgilius	2
Virgilius cum servio	4
Martialis	2
Martialis cum comento	4
Opera senece ligatus	1
Josefo cumpito	1
Problemata plutarchi	5
Epistole falaris	5
Diomedes	2
Catullus tibullus propertius et silvius	2
Silve statii cum comento	2
Genealogia deorum	2
Diodorus siculus	4
Aulus gelius	2
Blondus de roma instaurata	4
Blondus de roma trionfante	2
Silius italicus	2

	No.
Silius italicus cum comento	4
Epistole plinii	4
Satira filelfi	1
Epistole pape pii	2
Vocabulista greco grande	4
Vocabulista greco picolo	2
Erotemata greco	10
Grammatica constantini	1
Esiodus et theocritus	4
psalmista in greco	2
fabule esopi in greco	2, 1
Retorica aristotelis	2
Vite plutarchi ligatus	1
Valturius de re militari literale	1
Aurispa	1
Lucanus	4, 1
Michel scoto	10
Theofrastus	7
Priscianus	1
Isidorus etimologiarum	10
Platina de honesta voluptate	3, 4
Supplementum cronicarum	4, 2
Eusebius de temporibus	4
Tucidides	4
Commentum persii	3
M. Antonius Sabellicus	3
Dechades blondi	2
Egidius de regimine principium	3
Erodotus	1
Polibius	1
Epitoma artis oratorie	4
Bibia de magistro francesco	4
Bibia de zuane grande	4
Nicolo de lira dott° ligado	1
Bibia con Nicolo de lira de la con ligato	1
Mamotretti	25, 1
Morali de Nicolo de lira	4
Nicolo de lira su li atti	2
Bibia con Nicolo de lira de magistro francesco	4
Istorie eclesiastice	1, 1
legende sanctorum literale	2, 1
Rationale	4
Epistole hyerò da parma	1
Epistole hyerò da Venetia	1

	No.
Augustinus de civitate dei	2
Quadragesimale leonardi	1
Sermones de sanctis eiusdem	2
Sermones fratris michaelis	3
Quadragesimale ambrosii	2
Catena aurea sancti tome	3
Prima pars sancti tome	1
Prima sententie sancti tome	2
Secunda sententie	2
Quartum sancti tome	2
Summa contra gentiles sancti tome	2
Tabula sancti tome	1
Prima antonini	2
Secunda antonini	6
Tertia antonini	2
Quarta antonini	4
Antonina defecerunt	3, 1
Manipulus curatorum	4
Pisanella stampa de gregorio	1
Pisanella cum supplemento	10
Pisanella senza supplemento	4, 1
Summa astesana	2, 1
Summa hostiensis	1
Reportation di scotto	4
Clipeus tomistarum	2
Atanasius contra gentiles	1
Breviarii de magistro silvestro	2, 1, 5
Breviarii dott°	2, 4
Breviarii de evangelista	10
Breviario de piero Veronese	10
Breviario de s do°° de magistro silvestro	1
Breviario de sancto domenico de magistro Nicolo	1
Breviario de sancto domenico de gregorio	2
Breviario de camera	4
Missale de silvestro	1
Missale dott° grande	1
Missaletti dott° secondo la corte	4
Missaletti del bressano	4
Missale de san domenico grande	2
Missaletti de san domenico	4
Diurnale	4
Diurno di San domenico magistro Nicolo et bressana	1, 1, 2

	No.
Psalmista picolo	4
Psalmista grande	5
Officioli istoriadi	4
Officietti del bressano	4
Officietti picoli	12
Moralia gregorii ligatus	1
lactantius	1
Epistole cipriani	4
Compendium theologie	4
Cantica sancti bernardi	2
Tractatus de annatis	2
Origenes	2
Psalmista cum comento	1
Sermones leonis pape	3
Magister sententiarum	2
Vita patrum literale	1, 1
Biblia pauperum	2
Cristoforus landinus	1
Questiones Scoti	4
Glosa ordinaria	1
De contemptu mundi	6
Opere de sancto Augustino	2
Regule sipontini grande	5
Regule sipontini picole	4
Regule guarini	6
Regule francisci nigri	1, 1
Regule gaspar	4
Grammatica pomponii	10
Doctrinale cum comento	5
Donato	12
Psalteriola	10
Regule sulpitii	1, 2
Donadi in carta bona	3
Donado in carta bona ligatus	1
Decreto grande	1
Decretale grande ligatus	1
Sexto e clementine grande	2
Decreto picolo	4
Decretale picola	4
Sexto e clementine picole	1
Geminianus sopra 2da parte Sexti	2
Mercuriales	4
Abbas	1
Cautelle cepolle	1
Tractatus de privilegiis dotalibus	2

	No.
Tractatus contra hereticam pravitatem	2
Vocabularium juris	4
Digestum vetus	2
Digestum novum	2
Codex	2
Infortiatum ligatum	1
Volumen	2
Instituta	5
Formulario ligatus	1
Paulus de castro sopra prima Infortiati	2
Baldus sopra prima sententiarum veteris	1
Bartolus	2
Consilia, questiones et tractatus bartoli	1
Baldus super Infortiato	1
Cinus super codice	4
Alexander super 2da sententiarum novi	1
Alexander super prima et secunda codicis	1
Alexander super 2da infortiati	1
Dictionarium Alberici	1
Singularia ludovici de roma cum additionibus	1
Repertorium bertachini	1
Repertorium speculi	1
Pratica papiensis	2
Summa orlandini	6
Angelus de maleficiis	2
Flos testamenti	2, 3
Consilia abbatis	1
Alverotus de usibus feudorum	2
De sententia excomunicationis	2
Bibia dott^{o}	2
Bibia del grisolaro	3
Bibia de misser leonardo	1, 2
Legendario de santi	1, 1, 1
Vita patrum volgare	4
Augustini de civitate dei volgare	2
Evangelii epistole volgare	10
Fioretti de la Bibia	5
Fior de virtu	6
Prediche de fra ruberto	4

	No.
Miraculi de la madona	5
Vita e miraculi de la madona	4
Arte de ben morire	3
Transito di San hyeronimo	1, 1
Psalmista con exposition	2
Dialogo di San gregorio	2
Omelie di San gregorio	2, 1
Profetie di Merlino	2, 2
Petrarcha de viris illustribus	1
Petrarcha senza comento	2
Petrarcha con comento	2, 6
Plinio volgare	4
Deche de livio del grisolaro	2
Calendario in astrologia	3
Retorica per volgare	2
Ceco dascoli	3
Juvenale per volgare	2
Cento novelle	10
Filocolo	2, 2
Ninfale	1, 1
Mischino	5
Regule d' abacho	2
Arte d' abaco	1
Inamoramento de Carlo	4
Inamoramento dorlando	6
Danese	4
Troiano	2
Lancroia	2
Spagna	1
Ranaldo	2
Altobello	5
Morgante	1, 1
Fiammetta	2
Canzonette del Justiniano	6
Canzonette de Cosmico	1, 1, 1
Valturio volgare	2
Filomena	5
Filostrato	2
Burchiello	7
Ovidio de arte	7
Fatige de ercule	1, 1
Esopo istoriado	2
Antonina volgare	8
Arte de ciromantia	1
Cronica de sancto isidoro	4
Facetie de poggio	5

	No.
Laude de la madona	4
Meditation de la passion	10
Istoria de san Josafat	5
Lamenti e pianti de la madona	3
Avicena grande ligatus	1
Avicena picolo	3
Jacobus de forlivio super primo	2
Gentilis super 3°	1
Gentilis de febribus	2
Ugo super 4[m] sententiarum	1
Dioscorides	2
Pandecte	4
Aggregator	2
Argillata	2, 1
Pratica arculani	1
Pratica gradi	1
Pratica guaynerii	1
Artesella	4
Sermo 2 Nicolai	2
Sermo 3	2
Sermo 4	2
Sermo 5	2
Sermo 6	4
Serapion con pit	1, 1
Tractatus de venenis et de peste	1
Mesue ligatus	1
Guido in cirugia	2
Silanus super nono (?)	1
Cornelius Celsus	2, 1
Jacobus de Forlivio super afforismos	1
Consiglia montagnane	1
Consiglia gradi	1
Almansor	1
Conciliator	2
Pratica raynaldi de villanova	2, 2
Consilia ugonis	2
Textus logice	1
Textus phisice	1
Antonius Andree super artem veterem	2
Burleus super artem veterem	4
Johannes canonicus super fisicam	2
Burleus super fisicam cum textu	2
Metafisica sancti tome	1, 2
Metafisica antonii andree	3
Posteriora sancti tome	1

	No.
Posteriora pauli cum textu	4
Burleus super eticam	2
Sanctus tomas super eticam	3
Paulus Venetus de anima	2
Sanctus tomas de anima	2, 1
Gaietanus de anima	2
Temistius	2
Albertus de celo et mundo	2
Ars chiromantie	5
Questiones Johannis magistri	3, 3
Problemata Aristotelis cum comento	2
Marsilius de generatione et corruptione	3
Logica pauli de la pergola	10
Albertus de secretis mulierum	4
Geraldus super eticam	2
Universalia scoti cum comento	4
Mengus super logicam	4
Gaietanus super regulam	4
Euclides	4
Iginus de syderibus	5
Calendarium literale	4
Tabule Alfonsii	2
Tacuini	4
Spera mundi	4
Bartoli compiti	2
Secunda de lantonina	22
Addition del Nicolo de lira	6, 3
Isidorus etimologiarum	80
Bibia con Nicolo de lira	7
Cino sul codice	1
Repertorium bertachini	1
Lancroia	3
Opere de sancto Augustino	6
Breviario de piero Veronese ligatus	1
Posteriora de san tomaso	2
Statii con comento	4
Dante con comento dott°	2
Cento novelle	4
Vita e miraculi de la madona grande	2
Scansiones guarini et perotti	5
Peregrinationes Ierusalem	13
Sermones ruberti	4
Margarita decreti	1
Breviario dott° ligatus	1
Defensio calderini	4

	No.
Dubii de magistro pollo, etc.	6
Operetta de sancto Agustino de vita clericorum	3
Breviario de magistro silvestro	1
Archidiacono sul decreto	2

Libri ligati cioe.

Summa astensis	1
Virgilio con servio	1
Missale de silvestro	1
Valturio literale	1
Quadragesimales leonardi	1
Blondo de roma trionfante	1
Columella	1
Priscianus	1
Secunda sermone San tome	1
Secunda pars antonini	1
Terentio et horatio con comento	1
Decreto grande	1
Sexto clementine grande	1

Libri ligadi.

Digesto vechio	1
Digesto novo	1
Codice	1
Volume con instituta	1
Epistole hyeronimi	1
Jandono de anima	1
Bibia con nicolo de lira in doy volumi	1
Ptolomeo con le figure	1
Mamotretti	4
Aristotele de animalibus	1
Quintiliano	1
Macrobio	1
Augustin de civitate dei	1
Scotus super 2° cum quolibetis	1
Deche de livio volgare	1
Platina de vitis ponteficum et de obsoniis	1
Epistole tullii cum comento	1
Virgilius sine servio	1
prima sermone s. tome	1
Officietti del bressan	4
Officietti di piero Veronese et de Andrea	4

	No.

Libri sciolti posti in bottega ala zornata et prima adi 31 mazo.

Officietti in carta bona stampa del bressan	2
Officietti in carta bona picolo de la compagnia	1, 1, 2
Bibia picola de magistro Silvestro	6
Pisanelle con suplemento	10
Officietti de lettera grossa	2
Donati in carta bona	2
Registrum gregorii ligatum	1
Juvenale con comento	1
Epistole pape pii	2
Infortiatum	3
Metaphisica gabrielis zerbi	2

A di 9 zugno.

Bartolus compitum	1
Priscianus	2
Formularium procuratorum	2
Formularium instrumentorum	2, 2
Breviarium decretorum	2
Valerio maximo con commento	4
Textus logice	1
Albertus de celo et mundo	3
Questiones tusculane cum commento	2
Psalmista in greco	2
Archidiaconus super decretum	1
Junianus	4
Peregrinationes Ierusalem	32
Cinquanta novelle	7

A di 21 zugno.

Consilia primi volumis (sic) Alexandri	1
Statuti de Venesia	1
Diurni in carta bona monastici	2
Breviario de San domenico in carta bona	2
Breviario de piero Veronese ligatus	2
Missaletto de stampa de magistro Nicolo	6, 4
Decretale grande	1
Geminiano su la prima del sexto	1

	No.
Quinto curtio	2
Algorismus	7
Anatomia mundini	7
De ente et essentia	5
Tractatus de pulsibus magistri Egidii cum commento gentilis de fulgineo	5
Tractatus de urinis magistri Egidii cum commento ejusdem	4
Scansiones sulpitii	1, 4

1484, a di 28 zugno.

Logica de piero da Mantua	5
Questiones Marliani	2
Cristoforus porcus super institutis	2
Jacobus de forlivio super tegni (?)	2
Geminianus super prima parte sexti	1
Margarita poetarum	2
Sibille	4
Regule de canti	2
Arbor retorice	3
Novella Johannis andree super 6°	2
Valturio literale	2
Invetive del Valla	2
Trionfo de Virtu	4
Tractatus de calendis	7
Preceptorium divini legis	2
Trionfi del petrarcha con commento	2
Diurnale ott°	2
Breviario de Andrea d' Asola	3
Antonina 4ta pars	3
Donati ligati	2

A di 30 luyo.

Officietto piccolo ligato	1
Officietto del bressan ligato	1

A di 3 de Agosto.

Alexandri prima infortiati	1
Alex super prima Sententiarum novi	1
Alex super prima sententiarum veteris	1
Alex super secunda sententiarum veteris	1

A di 4 de Agosto.

Officietti de bressano ligati	3
Officietti picholi ligato et indorato	2
Legenda santorum latino	2
Bibia volgare	2

A di 5 de Agosto.

Metafisicha cabrielis	1
Almansor rasis	1

A di 8 de Agosto.

Catolichon	2
Problemata ristotelis cum (?)	1
Esopii istoriati	3

A di 12 de Agosto.

Margarita decreti	4
Bortolus compito	1

A di 18 de Agosto.

Fasciculus temporum	5, 1
Cronicha suplementum	1
Albertus de secretis mulierum	3
Psalterioli in carta bona	2
Missali de bernardino	2
Petrarcha con commento	4

A di 25 Agosto.

Prima parte de S. Tomaso	1
Digesto novo	1
Diurni de la corte	2
Gaietan de celo et mundo	3
Codex	1
Guido	2
Officietti del bressan in carta bona	2
Formularium procuratorum	2

A di 30 Agosto.

Bibie picole	4
Missaletti del bressan	4
Opere de santo agustino	4
Missaletto stampa de Magistro Silvestro	1
Vocabulista greco grande	2

1484, a di 9 Settembrio.	No.
Missale grande dott°	1
Etica sancti tome	4
Margarita decreti	3, 1
Macrobius	2
Declamation de quintilian	5
Volumen	2
De contemptu mundi	8
Summa Astestana	2
Preceptorium divine legis	2
Vita de la madona	3
Prediche de fra ruberto volgare	8
A di 20 detto.	
Alexandro magno	1
Deche del biondo	2
Persio con commento	4
Decreta pizzoli	3
Decretale grande	2
Michele scotto	15
Breviarii picoli dott°	3
Genealogia deorum	2
Deche de livio per volgare stampa del grisolaro	2
Valerio maximo con commento	1
Elegantie valle	1
Epistole ovidii cum commento	3
Commentum tullii de oratore	1
Fasciculus temporum	2
Regule siponti grande	2
Virgilio senza servio	1
Esopo istoriado	1
Regule guarini	5
Prima 2da S. tome	2
Summa contra gentiles	1
Opere de s. agustino	6
A di 18 Settembrio.	
Vocabulista greco grande	2
Missaletti del bressano	4
Psalmista picolo	4
Ars metrica mataratii	8
Quadripartite de ptolomeo	4
Nicolo de lira de la compagnia	1
Morali de gregorio	1

	No.
Arbor actionum	3
Bortolo su li 3 libri del codice	3
Disputation de labate	2
Zabarella su le clementine	1
Archidiacono sul decreto	1
Commentadore in philosophia naturali	1
Commentadore in philosophia morali	1
Abadi compito della compagnia	2
Salicetti compiti sul codice	1
Innocentio su lo decretale	2
Apostille abatis	2
Repertorio brixiense	1
Scotto sul primo	2
" secondo	1
" terzo	1
" quarto	1
Formularium instrumentorum	2
Alexander de Ales super 3°	1
Cinquanta novelle	5
Prisciano	1
Deche de livio da Millano	1
Breviario dott°	1
Macrobio	1
Bibia con Nicolo de lira	3, 2
Margarita poetarum	4
Rationale	4
1484, a di 5 ottobrio.	
Sermones ruberti	2
Catolicon	2
Catullo tibullo propertio	2
Bibia picola	4
Opera di ovidio	2
Magister sententiarum	2
Opere de s. agustino	4
Mischini	3
Virgilio con servio	3
Epistole de tullio con commento	3
Missale dott°	1
Cantica de san bernardo	2
Transito de s. hyeronimo	5
Elegantie del valla	5
Questiones del Jandon	4
Angelo de maleficiis	3

	No.
Alexander de Ales sul 3°	1
Vita patrum de bona stampa	2
Repertorio del bertachin	1
Inamoramento de Carlo	4
Laude della madonna	4
Breviarium decretorum	3
Vita patrum litterale	2
Instituta picola	2
Fioretti de san francesco	5
Terentio con donado	3
Vita de la Madonna grande	2
Breviario dott°	6
Deche del biondo	3
Cinquanta novelle	5
Cento novelle	5
Catena aurea	1
Officietti in carta bona del bressan	2
Justini per volgare	4

Adi 19 ottobrio.

	No.
Missaletti di San domenico	2
Terza parte de lantonina	1
Dubii de magistro pollo	3
Posteriora pauli cum textu	3
Breviarii de piero Veronese	6
Supplementum cronicarum	2
Sermones de sanctis fratris leonardi	3
Terzo de scotto	1
Epistole hyeronimo da parma	1
Opere de sancto agustino	2, 6
Opere de ovidio	1
Cinquanta novelle	5
Breviarii de S. Domenico stampa de gregorio	1
Digesti novi	2
Legendario per volgare	8
Profetie de Merlino	3
Inamoramento dorlando	4
Epistole ovidii cum commento	5
Mengo	4
Tacuino	2
Decreto grande	1
Missaletti dott°	4
Breviario da camera dott°	1

	No.
Canzonetti de Justiniano	2
Arte de ben morire	2
Fiametta	3
Vita patrum volgare	6
Baldus super infortiato	1

A di 30 Ottobrio 1484.

	No.
Breviario secondo la corte de Magistro Nicolo	3

A di 2 Novembrio.

	No.
Regule Sipontini grande	1
Bibia volgar	4
Bibia volgar grisolar	1
Missale in carta bona	1
Digesto Vechio	1

A di 3 Novembrio.

	No.
Regule sipontini picholi	2
Breviarii ligati piero Verones	2
Salicetto compitto	1
Opera ovidii	4
Diurni della compagnia	8
Lactantio	1
Secunda sermone S. tome	3
Missaletti de S. Domenico	3
Mischini	4
Officietti istoriadi	4
Diurno de San domenico	2
Officietti del bressan	9
Petrarcha con commento	5
Pratica papiensis	4
Mercuriales Johannis andree	1
Missale de silvestro	2
Burleus su la fisica con testo	2
Summa Astesana	2
Decreti picoli	2
Dante con commento	2
Decretale grande	1
Croniche	3
Tullius de Officiis	5
Margarita poetarum	2
Antonina defecerunt	4
De contemptu mundi	5
Diomedes	2
Psalmista picolo	1

	No.
Psalteriolo da puti	11
Psalmista grande	6
Manipulus curatorum	6
Epistole tullii cum commento	4
Repertorium bertachini	1
Legendario leterale	2
Secondo de Scotto	1
3° de Scotto	1
4° de Scotto	1
Quolibetta de Scotto	2
Alverotto	1
Sermo 3 Nicoli	1
Sermo 4 Nicoli	1
Geminianus super prima et secunda parte sexti	1
Singularia ludovici de roma	1
Cautelle cepolle	1
Pratica raynaldi de villa nova	1
Merlino	1
Filocolo	1
Diurni stampa dottaviano	2
Psalmista picolo	2
Burchiello	1
Nicolo de lira con testo	4
Addition del Nicolo de lira	5
Retorica cum commento	7
Margarita decreti	8
Breviario de S. domenico Magistro Nicolo	4
Dante con commento	3
Petrarcha senza commento	3
Prima pars Antonini	4

1484 a di 29 Novembrio.

Bibia picola de magistro Silvestro	4
Vite plutarchi	2
Legende sanctorum leterale	1
Iginus de syderibus	1
Valerio Maximo con commento	2
Macrobio	2
Question de evangelii	1
Tortellii	4
Priscianus	3
Infortiato	2
Officietti ligati picoli	17
Guidon in cirusia	3

	No.
Alexander de ales super 3° sententiarum	2
Bibia per volgare	3
Fasciculus temporum	6
Regule sipontini picole	5
Prediche de ruberto per volgare	3
Fioretti de la bibia	6
Ranaldo	1
Donati ligati	8
Psalterioli ligati	3
Officietti picoli del bressan	4
Gaietanus de celo et mundo	3
Breviario da camera dottaviano	1
Breviario de San domenico stampa de la compagnia	3
Margarita poetarum	2
Epistole hyeronimo da Venetia	2
Breviarii monastici	2
Secunda secunde S. tome	2
De contemptu mundi	1

A di 14 Decembrio.

Angelus de maleficiis	3
Cento novelle	6
Cinquanta novelle	7

A di 15 detto.

Burleo su larte vechia	4
Mischin	1
Officietti del bressan ligati et de Antonio d' alasandra	6
Nicolo de lira	2
Euclides	3
Valerio Maximo con commento	6
Vita miraculi de la madonna	3
Sermones ruberti	2
Commentador compito	1

A di 29 Decembrio.

Mesue	2
Legendarii literali	3
Universale de Scotto	3
Questiones su la metaura	5
Pillularum pantaleonis	8
Quinto curtio	1

	No.
Angelo su li autentici	4
Retorica per volgare	1
Epistole de Tullio cum commento	3
Decreto picolo	3
Lattantio	2

A di 5 Zenaro.

Almansor	1
Dialogo volgar	3
Regule sulpitii	4
Formularium instrumentorum	5
Bonaventura super 2da sententiarum	2
Burchiello	5
Tacuini	2
Secunda 2^{a} S. tome ligato	1
Dante con commento	2
Decretale picola	3
Pratica di ranaldo villanova	3

A di 7 Zenaro 1484.

Burleo su larte vechia	3
Margarita poetarum	2
Missaletti dottaviano	4
Transito de S. hyeronimo	7
Fioretti de la bibia picoli	5
Missale del bressan grande	5
Loyca de magistro paulo da la pergola	10
Loyca de magistro pollo da Venesia	5
Breviarii de S. benedeto	2
Calendarii literali	6
Calendarii volgare	5
Tabule Alfonsii	3
Elegantiole augustini dati	5
Regule guarini	10
Epistole Evangelii volgare	6
Mamotretti	10
Bibia pauperum	3
Altobello	2
Esiodus et teocritus	2
Virgilii con servio	3
Deche del biondo	4
Biondo de italia illustrata	4
Pratica raynaldi de villanova	2

	No.
Digesto vechio	2
Missaletti del bressan	8
Cantica di avicenna	2
Margarita poetarum	2
Spera mundi	1
Salustio	2
Repertorio de speculo	1
Elegantiole valle	3
Instituta pizola	2
Erotemata greca	6
Terentio con donato	3
Legendario volgare	6
Platina de honesta voluptate	4
Primo de Scotto	1
Epistole hyeronimo da parma	2
Florianus super X^{o} digestorum	4
Baldus super feudis	3
Sermones ruberti	3, 4
Breviario secondo la corte de Magistro Nicolo	2
Sermones leonis pape	3
Serapion compito	1
Rationale	2
Vocabulista greco	3
Burleo su larte vechia con lo texto	1
Epitoma artis oratorie	1
Oration de tullio	5

A di 26 zenaro.

Plinio literale	2
Loyca de magistro paulo da Venesia	5
Cronacha	4
Esiodus et teocritus in greco	2
Regule sipontini grande	6
Genealogia deorum	1
psalmista in greco	1
Missaletti dottaviano	2
Prima decha di Livio	1
Missaletti de magistro Nicolo	2
Dubii de Magistro pollo	3
Suetonio	3

1484 a di 28 zenaro.

Breviario de magistro Nicolo	2

	No.
Regule sipontini picole de Silvestro	3
Zabarella su le clementine	2
Vita patrum literale	2
Inamoramento de carlo	2
Testi de loyca	4
Sexti clementine picole	3
Epistole tullii con commento	3
Missaletti de Magistro Nicolo	2
Nicolo de lira con testo	4
Decreto pizolo	1

A di 8 febraro.

Digesto novo	2
Digesto vechio	2
Infortiato	2
Volumen	2
Egidius de regimine principum	3
Archidiacono sul decreto	2
Decretale grande	1
Sexto clementine grande	1
Abade de la compagnia	1
Zabarella su le clementine	1
Epistole hyeronimo da parma	1
Cronica	1
Secunda secunde S. tome	1
Virgilio con servio	1
Epistole tullii cum commento	1, 4
Dottrinale cum commento	1
Nicolo de lira con texto	1
Bibia per volgare	1
Diurni de la compagnia	3
Euclides	3
Ovidio mazore	3
Breviario de Magistro Nicolo secondo la corte	6
Breviario de piero Veronese	4
Bibia per volgare	4
Pisanella con supplimento	12
Vita patrum volgare	4
Inamoramento dorlando	2
Laude de la madonna	5
Deche del biondo	4
Dotrinale con commento	4
Virgilio senza servio	2
Terentio senza donato	3

	No.
Cronica	4
Vocabularium juris	2, 2
Diomedes	1
Comentum acronis	1
Preceptorium divine legis	3
Bibia per volgare	4
Petrarcha con commento	3
Petrarcha senza commento	4
Canzonetti Justiniano	5
Miraculi de la madonna	4
Vergilio con servio	3, 1
Tortellio	2
Opera sancti augustini	4
Diurni de la compagnia	4
Quintiliano	4
Arte de ben morire literale	3
Burleo su letica	2
Missaletti dottaviano	2, 2, 4, 2
Valturio per volgare	2
Oratio con commento	4, 4, 4
Regule sipontini picole	5
Loyca de Polo da Venesia	10
Burleo su larte vechia	2
Bibia per volgare stampa del grisolaro	2
Regule guarini	10

1484 a di 21 febraro.

Missaletto de Magistro Nicolo	1, 8
Evangelii Epistole volgare	10
Missaletti del bressan	7
Augustin de civitate dei literale	4
Diurni dottaviano	2
Fiammetta	2
Compendium teologie	1
Scansiones peroti	7

A di primo marzo 1485.

Breviarii picoli de Andrea d' Asola	10
Digesto novo	1
Volume	2
Marsilio de generatione et corruptione	1
Alex super prima infortiati	1
Antonina per volgare	4

	No.
Burleo su letica	1
Alberto de celo et mundo	2
Officietti grandi del bressan	4
Virgilio con servio	1
Eusebio de temporibus	1
Rationale divinorum	2
Breviario de evangelista	1
Burleo su l' arte vechia	2
Breviario de piero Veronese	4
Inamoramento dorlando	2
Filocolo	1
Quintiliani	3
Commentum persii	3

A di 3 marzo.

Terentio con donado	4
Primo di Scotto	1
Fasciculus temporum	6
Mesue	4, 2
Augustin de civitate dei volgare	3
Quintiliano	4
Declamation	6
Primi sen (?) de febribus	5
Bonaventura super 2° sententiarum	2
Platina de vitis pontificum	4
Pandette	3
de contemptu mundi	6
Oration de tullio	3
Commentador in loyca	2
Pratica raynaldi de villanova	3
Epistole tullii cum commento	2
Sermoni de ruberto	6
Evangelii Epistole volgare	10
Officietti del bressan in carta bona	3
Opera de Sancto agustino	8
Bibia pizola dottaviano	1

A di 9 marzo.

Decreti pizoli	4
Decretale pizole	4
Epistole cipriani	2
Antonina defecerunt	10
Legendario literale	2
Breviarii de magistro Nicolo secondo la corte	10

	No.
Martiale con commento	4
Catolicon	2
Commentum alexandrini in juvenale	5
Ceco dascoli	6
Dante con commento	4
Breviarii monastici	4
Tibullo con commento	8
Libri de abaco	3
Igino	6
Sermones de S. leone papa	6
Statuti de Venesia	2
Juvenale con commento	6

1485, a di 16 marzo.

Mamotretti	10
Officietti picoli	10
Arbor Christi	4
Petrarca de viris illustribus	2
Breviarii de la compagnia	10
Psalterioli	15
Addition	4
Mesue	4
Dottrinale cum commento	3
Compendium theologie	3
Spera mundi	5
Tullio de oratore con commento	4
Josefo compito	1
Bibia de zuan grande	2
Epistole de tullio con commento	4
Missali del bressan grandi ligati	6
Ugo super 4^b sententiarum primi	8

Adi 28 marzo.

Commentadore in philosophia naturale	1
Epistole ovidii	10
Tacuini	2
Pratica papiensis	3
Psalmista grande	10
Junianus	1
Prima pars sancti tome	2
Terentio con donato	3
Quolibeti de Scotto	2
Scotto sul primo	1

Adi 7 Aprile.	No.
Breviario de San domenico de la compagnia	1
Arbor retorice	2
Marsilio de generatione	2
Ovidio de fastis con commento	2
Almansor	2
Missali del bressan grandi	4
Diurni de la compagnia	6

Adi 12 Aprile.	
Esopo istoriato	3
Sermo 4° Nicoli	1
Sermo 3° Nicoli	1
Sermo 7° Nicoli	1
Sermo primo Nicoli	2
Breviarii picoli dantonio dalexandria	7
Meditation de la passion	9
Missali dottaviano grandi	2
Vita e miraculi de la madonna	4
Opere de Sancto agustino	4
Fior de virtu	10
Asconio pediano	2
Fisica santi tome	2
Spechio della croce	4
Versorio in loyca	2
Transito de San Ieronimo	5
Donadi ligati	6
Psalterioli ligati	6
Bibia per volgare	4
Diurni monastici	3
Spechio della croce	4
Prediche de fra ruberto	4

A di 19 Aprille.	
Egidius de regimine principum	3
Missaletti del bressano	7
Epistole tullii senza commento	4
Commentadore compito	1

A di 19 Aprile 1485.	
Valerio maximo con commento	1
Oration de tullio	1
Tibullo catullo etc.	2
Propertio sollo	2

	No.
Rationale	4
Michele scotto	5
Dante con commento	2
Platina de vitis pontificum	2
Commentarii de cesare	2
Tractatus clausularum	1
Repetition de ludovigo da Roma	2
Vite plutarchi	1
Sexti clementine picole	4
Missale de Silvestro	2

A di 26 detto Aprille.	
De censuris	2
Gaietano de celo et mundo	5
Mesue	4
Pissanella con supplemento	10
Menghi	4
Virgilio con servio	4
Epistole de tullio con commento	4
Tortellii	4
Legendarii volgare	6
Juvenale con commento	6
Meditation della passion	10
Croniche	4
Oratio con commento	2
Terentio con donato	4
Commentadore compito in carta mezana	1
Valerio maximo con commento	6
Bibie volgar in carta mezana	2
Plinio literale	4
Martiale con commento	4
Prisciano	2
Altobello	2
Alexander super prima codicis	2
Virgilio senza servio	3
Epistole hyeronimo da parma	1
Seconda secunde S. tome	3
Vita patrum literale	1
Formularium instrumentorum	4
Bartolus super autenticis	1
Officietti de antonio dalexandria	5
Officietti picoli ligati	6
Salustii	8
De re militari litterale	2

	No.
Officietti grandi ligati	5
Aulo gelio	4
Oration de tullio	4
Alchibitio con commento	3
Quarto de Scotto	1

A di 10 Mazo.

Dottrinale con commento	6
Nonio marcello etc.	4
Tullio de officiis con commento	4
Breviarii de la compagnia	6
Arbor Christi	4
Missali de S. domenico grandi	3
Diurni de S. domenico	4
Pisanella de paganino	4
Petrarcha con commento	3
Donati	10
Psalterioli	25
Bovo dautoria (?)	7

1485 a di 16 mazo.

Dottrinale cum commento	14
Psalmista con commento da Millano	1
Vocabulista greco grande	4
Summa orlandini	6
Vita e miraculi de la madonna	5
Diurni de la compagnia	2
Persiani	4
Missali bressano	4
Vocabularium juris	4
Officietti pizoli ligati	2
Fasciculus temporum	6
Terza parte de lantonina	5
peregrinatio ad ierusalem	36
Margarita decreti	8
Missali in bona carta	1
De contemptu mundi	6

	No.
Paulo orosio	1
Missale in carta bona	1

A di 29 de mazo.

Breviario picholi de antonio d' alesandria	8
Platina de honesta volutate	6
Decreti picholi	4
Justino volgare	4
Mischini	5
Consilia lodoviso da Roma	2
Psalmista grande	6
De mutatione æris (?)	8
Felino Instituzione decretalium	2
Legende santorum latine	2

30 de mazo.

Breviarii de magistro Nicolo	2

31 detto.

Antonino prima pars	4
Regule sipontini picholi	5
Antonino de volgar	5

A di primo zugno.

Bibia volgare	4
Mercuriale de zovane andree	2
Vita patrum literale	1
Seconda secunde sancti thome	3
Antonina 3ra parte	4
Logicha pauli veneti	10
Summa astesana	2

A di 4 zugno.

Arcibizio cum commento	2
Breviario de andrea asola	8

1485 a di 11 de zugnio.
Qua si notarano li retrati de la botega in primis.

	D.	L.	S.
A di 11 de zugnio . . .	33	4	4
item a di 15 de zugnignio. .	17	4	12
item adi 25 de zugnio . .	25	2	11
item adi 30 de zugnio . .	18	5	9
item adi 9 de luglio . .	32	1	2
item adi 16 dito . . .	17	6	2
item adi 23 dito . . .	8	3	16
item adi 30 dito . . .	12	3	13
item adi 5 de Agosto . .	8	2	13
item adi 13 de Agosto . .	4	4	9
item adi 20 dito . . .	15	4	4
item adi 27 dito . . .	3	3	10
item adi 30 dito . . .	7	1	4
item adi 3 Settembrio . .	10	0	0
item adi 10 Settembrio . .	12	1	9
item adi 17 dito . . .	15	1	17
item adi 24 ditto . . .	4	1	15
item adi primo ottobrio . .	2	3	5

piazza (?)

Qua si notarano le feste ne le quale si tene serate le botege a rialto et prima et quelle harano signata la * se tene aperto a mezo et non si mete fora robe in la balcone.

Sancto vito adi 15 zugno.
*Sancto marco adi 26 zugno.
Sancto marsiliano adi primo luglio.
Sancta maria elisabet adi 2 luglio.
Santa Croce adi 14 Settembre.
*San magno adi 6 Ottobre.
*San marco adi 8 Ottobre.
*San sebastiano adi 20 zenaro.
*San marcho adi primo febraro.

Qua si notara lo rettrato de la bottega et prima.

	D.	L.	S.
Adi 7 Settembrio 1484 in bottega (?) per avanti . .	215	0	0
Adi 18 detto	17	2	0
Item adi 24 detto	30	4	14
Item adi primo ottobrio	27	2	15
Item adi 7 detto	23	2	5
Item adi 9 detto	36	2	10
Item adi 12 detto	6	0	18
Item adi 15 detto	9	5	14
Item adi 16 detto	1	2	0

	D.	L.	S.
Item adi 23 detto .	32	0	0
Item adi 27 detto .	8	1	5
Item adi 8 novembrio	14	0	0
Item adi 12 deto .	12	3	14
Item adi 22 detto .	20	4	4
Item adi 27 detto .	29	2	17
Item adi 4 decembrio	18	1	6
Item adi 11 detto .	6	3	16
Item adi 19 detto .	13	3	1
Item adi 24 detto .	7	4	16
Item adi 8 zenaro .	18	3	2
Item adi 15 detto .	13	3	1
Item adi 22 detto .	12	0	2
Item adi 29 detto .	32	0	0
Item adi 5 febraro .	19	6	0
Item adi 12 detto .	70	0	0
Item adi 19 detto .	29	0	0
Item adi 26 detto .	16	4	15
Item adi 5 marzo .	21	1	5
Item adi 12 detto .	32	5	0
Item adi 19 detto .	19	3	0
Item adi 26 detto .	9	3	0
Item adi 2 Aprile .	10	4	7
adi 15 detto .	47	0	0
adi 22 detto .	25	3	5
adi 30 detto .	20	3	4
adi 7 mazo .	22	0	0
adi 14 detto .	36	1	14
adi 27 detto .	15	3	4
adi 28 detto .	24	1	6

INDEX.

3 N

INDEX.

CORRECTIONS AND ADDITIONS.

Page 6, line 28, omit from "The document" to "Appendix."

Page 14. After these sheets were passed for press, I saw and transcribed the Will of Thomaso Giunti (Arch. d. Stato. Testamenti, Angelo de Canal, No. 527), from which it appears that, besides other bequests, Thomaso left four thousand ducats to his unmarried daughter in the event of her marriage, not one hundred thousand ducats to each of his daughters, as I have stated it, following Sig. Castellani.

Page 17, note 2, omit "I do not find" to "doing so."

Page 27. For another example of a contract see *Archivio Veneto*, xxxii. 190.

Page 36, line 9, *for* "19" *read* "23."

Page 53, line 23, *for* "five hundred" *read* "five."

Page 185, line 17, *for* "ninety-two" *read* "thirty-two."

Page 423, between No. 51 and No. 52, insert "1570, Giustinian, Marc' Antonio, Venezia, 28, 10."

CHISWICK PRESS:—C. WHITTINGHAM AND CO., TOOKS COURT,
CHANCERY LANE.

ΑἸΣΏΠΟΥ ΜΎΘΟΙ.

ἈΕΤῸΣ ΚΑῚ ἈΛΏΠΗΞ.

ἀ ετὸς καὶ ἀλώπηξ φιλιωθέντες, πλησίον ἀλλήλων οἰκεῖν ἔγνωσαν, βεβαίωσιν φιλίας ποιούμενοι τὴν συνήθειαν. ὁ μὲν οὖν ἐφ' ὑψηλοῦ δένδρου τὴν καλιὰν ἐπήξατο. ἡ δὲ ἀλώπηξ ἐν τοῖς ἔγγιστα θάμνοις ἐτεκνοποιήσατο. ἐπὶ νομὴν δὲ ποτε τῆς ἀλώπεκος προελθούσης, ὁ ἀετὸς τροφῆς ἀπορῶν, καταπτὰς εἰς τὸν θάμνον, καὶ τὰ τέκνα ταύτης ἀν-

Gabriel Braccio. Æsop, *Fabulæ*. 1498.

ἀνθρώποις γένμην θαυμαστὸν
ἐνμερόπων φύλαισι θεῖον ὅμηρον
ὡς θεὸν ὑμνῶν
θεὸν δοξάζειν
ὅν βούλονται
ὃν προσίψωται ὁ ποιητὴς ἐκάλει
ἀκολούθως
ἐπιτάγε,
φαινερὸν ἔργον
ἀλλὰ μαι φαμὶ δὸμοις παρέχειν
ὁ δόξασαι
ἡμίθεον δοξάσαντων
ὅντινα ὁ ὁ ἐγέμησεν
ὄνγε μὲ ὅλης καλίρους ἔθνη τὸ
ἀπὸ τῆς
μελπομένης·

LAONICO CRETESE. HOMER, *Batrachomyomachia*. 1486.
(With scholia interlined in rubric.)

Ἀ παρὰ τὸ στοιχεῖον, ὅπερ κά-
δμος ἐστὶν εὕρημα. ἢ κάπ-
πα ὄν, τὸ ἔχον ὀπὴν, ὅ ἐστι
φωνήν. τὰ γὰρ ψιλὰ, ὑπὸ
κάτω τῆς γλώττης ἔχει
τὴν προφορὰν τῆς φωνῆς.
καὶ κῆπος, χῆπος τις ὢν ὁ
ἔχων τὴν πόσιν διὰ τοῦ ὕδα-
τος τοῖς φυτοῖς.

Κατεχειροτόνησαν ἀλλήλου,

Κιάβαισος, ὁ ἄπληστος διὰ δὲ τοῦ προπαροξύνεται. παρὰ τὸ
κάβον, ὅ ἐστι μέτρον σιτικόν. κρατῖνος μαλθακοῖς. ἔστι δὲ κύ-
ριον ποιητικὸν παρὰ τὸ αἶσαι. ὧρος ὁ μιλήσιος.

Καβησός, πόλις θράκης. ἀπὸ καβήσου.

Κάβαξ, πανοῦργος.

Κάβειροι, οἱ ἐκ θεῶν πατέρων. ἀξίερος ἀξιόκερσα ἀξιόκερσος. ἀξίερος μὲν οὖν ἐστιν ἡ δημήτηρ. ἀξιόκερσα,
ἡ περσεφόνη. ἀξιόκερσος δὲ, ὁ ἅδης. κάβειροι δὲ δο-
κοῦσι προσαγορευθῆναι, ἀπὸ καβείρων ὀρέων φρυγίας.
ἐπεὶ ἐντεῦθεν μετηνέχθησαν. οἱ δὲ δύο εἶναι τοὺς κα-

CALLIERGI. SUIDAS, *Etymologicum.* 1499.

ἈΡΙΣΤΟΤΈΛΟΥΣ ΠΕΡῚ ἙΡΜΗΝΕΊΑΣ.

ΡΩ͂ΤΟΝ δεῖ θέσθαι τί ὄνομα καὶ τί ῥῆμα· ἔπειτα τί ἐστιν ἀπόφασις καὶ κατάφασις, καὶ ἀπόφανσις, καὶ λόγος. ἔστι μὲν οὖν τὰ ἐν τῇ φωνῇ, τῶν ἐν τῇ ψυχῇ παθημάτων, σύμβολα· καὶ τὰ γραφόμενα τῶν ἐν τῇ φωνῇ· καὶ ὥσπερ οὐδὲ γράμματα πᾶσι τὰ αὐτά· οὐδὲ φωναὶ αἱ αὐταί· ὧν μέντοι ταῦτα σημεῖα πρώτων, ταὐτὰ πᾶσι παθήματα τῆς ψυχῆς· καὶ ὧν ταῦτα ὁμοιώματα, πράγματα ἤδη ταὐτά· περὶ μὲν οὖν τούτων, εἴρηται ἐν τοῖς περὶ ψυχῆς· ἄλλης γὰρ ταῦτα πραγματείας. ἔστι δ᾽ ὥσπερ ἐν τῇ ψυχῇ ὁτὲ μὲν, νόημα ἄνευ τοῦ ἀληθεύειν ἢ ψεύδεσθαι, ὁτὲ δὲ, ἤδη ᾧ ἀνάγκη τούτων ὑπάρχειν θάτερον. οὕτω καὶ ἐν τῇ φωνῇ· περὶ γὰρ σύνθεσιν καὶ διαίρεσίν ἐστι τὸ ψεῦδός τε καὶ τὸ ἀληθές· τὰ μὲν οὖν ὀνόματα αὐτὰ καὶ τὰ ῥήματα, ἔοικε τῷ ἄνευ συνθέσεως καὶ διαιρέσεως νοήματι· οἷον τὸ, ἄνθρωπος ἢ τὸ λευκὸν, ὅταν μὴ προστεθῇ τι· οὔτε γὰρ ψεῦδος, οὔτε ἀληθές πω· σημεῖον δ᾽ ἐστὶ τοῦδε· καὶ γὰρ ὁ τραγέλαφος σημαίνει μέν τι· οὔπω δὲ ἀληθὲς ἢ ψεῦδος, ἂν μὴ, τὸ εἶναι, ἢ τὸ μὴ εἶναι προστεθῇ, ἢ ἁπλῶς ἢ κατὰ χρόνον.

ALDUS. ARISTOTLE, *Opera*. 1495.

www.ingramcontent.com/pod-product-compliance
Lightning Source LLC
Chambersburg PA
CBHW030728280326
41926CB00086B/513

* 9 7 8 3 7 4 2 8 3 7 6 2 2 *